Microeconomic Theory

THE IRWIN SERIES IN ECONOMICS

Consulting Editor
LLOYD G. REYNOLDS
Yale University

Microeconomic Theory

C. E. FERGUSON
Late Professor of Economics
Texas A&M University

1972   Third Edition
RICHARD D. IRWIN, INC., Homewood, Illinois   60430
IRWIN-DORSEY INTERNATIONAL, London, England   WC2H 9NJ
IRWIN-DORSEY LIMITED, Georgetown, Ontario   L7G 4B3

© RICHARD D. IRWIN, INC., 1966, 1969, and 1972

ALL RIGHTS RESERVED. No part of this publication may be
reproduced, stored in a retrieval system, or transmitted,
in any form or by any means, electronic, mechanical,
photocopying, recording, or otherwise, without prior
written permission of the publisher.

THIRD EDITION

First Printing, February, 1972
Second Printing, November, 1972
Third Printing, May, 1973
Fourth Printing, October, 1973
Fifth Printing, February, 1974

Library of Congress Catalog Card No. 71–168295
Printed in the United States of America

PREFACE TO THE THIRD EDITION

The Preface to the first edition of this book began as follows: "This is a textbook; its content is taken from the public domain of economic literature. Conventional topics are treated in conventional ways; and there is no real innovation." All of this held for the revised edition, and it holds for the third edition as well. This is a textbook in neoclassical price theory that is designed for, and intended primarily to be used by, undergraduate students. Indeed, it must be, for it would otherwise have no chance of passing the market test which, gratifyingly enough, the first two editions did.

Having undertaken this revision as *homo oeconomicus,* I have tried to do the work as *homo academicus.* In the former capacity, I hope I have further differentiated the product; in the latter, I hope I have improved it as well.

For the benefit of those who are acquainted with the revised edition, the principal changes contained in the third edition are detailed below. I would like to emphasize that these are only the *principal* changes; almost every page has been subject to some revision. *General:* (*a*) additional problems and especially analytical exercises have been added in many chapters; (*b*) there has been some expansion of the mathematical footnotes; and (*c*) many graphs have been enlarged and revised.

The Introduction has been expanded to include a discussion of statics and comparative statics. The chief revisions in Part I consist of the addition of substantial sections that analyze the trade-off between income and leisure and the trade-off between present and future goods (time preference). In Part II the concept of expenditure elasticity has been introduced so as (*a*) to classify factors of production as superior, normal, or inferior; and (*b*) to relate this classification to shifts in average and marginal cost incident to a change in factor price.

Part III of the revised edition has not been changed materially except for the addition of numerous analytical exercises. This is still a textbook in *theory;* indeed, the number of theoretical topics discussed has been expanded. However, if I were called upon to point out the *one* salient feature of the third edition, I would say that it is the increased emphasis on *analysis*.

The revision of Part IV has been chiefly directed toward factor demand functions. The number of explanatory graphs has been increased, and I have tried to give a clearer explanation of the so-called substitution, output, and profit-maximizing effects of a change in factor price. This, of course, utilizes the previously introduced concept of expenditure elasticity and factor classification. Finally, only minor changes have been made in Part V. The last sentence raises an additional point. Because of the time at which this revision was completed, I did not have the opportunity (*a*) to refer to Bent Hansen's excellent text (elementary math required) on general equilibrium theory, and (*b*) to give references to the revised edition of Henderson and Quandt (i.e., all references cited are to the first edition).

I stated above that the text is primarily designed for, and intended to be used by, undergraduate students. Nonetheless, I believe that graduate students may find the text quite helpful. Naturally, it can be used as a review guide. Beyond this, there are three features that should prove helpful. First, the mathematical footnotes, which are now more thorough, can be used by mathematically trained students. Second, at the end of each major part of the book, there is a bibliography especially selected for beginning graduate students. These bibliographies, which are classified by topic, contain the "required" and "first alternate" readings from my microeconomic theory courses as they have evolved at Duke, Michigan State, and Texas A&M.

So far as graduate student usefulness is concerned, I have saved the best for last, both in this discussion and in the text. As an appendix, the book contains a "Comprehensive Examination in Microeconomic Theory for Graduate Students." Emphasis should be placed upon the last two words because it is indeed a graduate-level examination. Even a student who knows the contents of this text perfectly is not adequately equipped for the examination.

I only wish I could claim to be the author of the appendix because any teacher would take great pride in having developed such a searching, demanding, and penetrating set of questions. Most economists who read the appendix could easily guess the author. Yet for the record, I will state that the questions were prepared by Professor Fritz Machlup to be used in conjunction with the two-semester course in microeconomic theory he taught while at Johns Hopkins. I wish to express my deep appreciation to Professor Machlup for his permission to use this set of questions in all three editions of this book.

During the first two editions I have received a number of letters concerning errors of substance, and obscure points. Such comments are very helpful. I urge readers of the third edition to correspond with me on any issue that arises. Space limitations preclude my listing all those with whom I have corresponded. However, I would like to record my gratification at the number of letters received from undergraduate students. This indicates not only that there are a lot of serious and intelligent students around the country, but also that they are being stimulated by some very good teachers. This is, of course, the most important consideration of all.

As I have said, many people have contributed helpful suggestions that have been incorporated in the successive editions of *Microeconomic Theory*. I cannot list them all, but I would be remiss if I did not recognize the continued help of Professor Lloyd Valentine of the University of Cincinnati. Without his invaluable aid, the first edition of this book would also have been the last. I also wish to acknowledge the very helpful comments and suggestions of my colleagues, Professors S. Charles Maurice and Paul W. Thompson, who have used this book at Texas A&M.

Finally, I bow to custom and reluctantly assume responsibility for the errors that will inevitably remain. I would suggest to the reader, however, that *perfection* is an unrealistic standard by which to appraise either real-world markets or textbooks.

January, 1972   C. E. F.

CONTENTS

for *Continuous Case. Production Isoquants. Fixed-Proportions Production Functions.* Input Substitution: *Marginal Rate of Technical Substitution. Diminishing Marginal Rate of Technical Substitution. Economic Region of Production.* Optimal Combination of Resources: *Input Prices and Isocosts. Maximizing Output for a Given Cost. Minimizing Cost Subject to a Given Output.* The Expansion Path: *Isoclines. Changing Output and the Expansion Path. Expenditure Elasticity.* Changes in Input Price: *The Substitution and Output Effects. "Inferior Factors" and the Output Effect.* Analogies Between Consumer and Producer Behavior. Conclusion.

Introduction: *Social Cost of Production. Private Cost of Production.* Short and Long Runs. Theory of Cost in the Short Run: *Total Short-Run Cost. Average and Marginal Cost. Geometry of Average and Marginal Cost Curves. Short-Run Cost Curves.* Long-Run Theory of Cost: *Short Run and the Long. Long-Run Average Cost Curve. Long-Run Marginal Cost.* Long-Run Cost and the Production Function: *The Expansion Path and the Envelope Curve. Relation between SAC and LAC. Relation between SMC and LMC. Cost Elasticity and the Function Coefficient.* Shape of LAC: *Economies of Scale. Diseconomies of Scale.* Long-Run Cost and Changes in Factor Price: *Changes in Long-Run Average Cost. Changes in Long-Run Marginal Cost and Minimum Average Total Cost.* Conclusion.

Introduction. Perfect Competition: *Small Size, Large Numbers. Homogeneous Product. Free Mobility of Resources. Perfect Knowledge.* Conclusion. Equilibrium in the Market Period: *Industry Equilibrium in the Market Period. Price as a Rationing Device.* Short-Run Equilibrium of a Firm in a Perfectly Competitive Market: *Short-Run Profit Maximization, Total Revenue—Total Cost Approach. Short-Run Profit Maximization, the Marginal Approach. Proof of the Short-Run Equilibrium. Profit or Loss? Short-Run Supply Curve of a Firm in a Perfectly Competitive Industry.* Short-Run Equilibrium in a Perfectly Competitive Industry: *Short-Run Industry Supply Curve. Short-Run Market Equilibrium, Profit and Loss. Demand-Supply Analysis.* Long-Run Equilibrium in a Perfectly Competitive Market: *Long-Run Adjustment of an Estab-*

lished Firm. Long-Run Adjustment of the Industry. Long-Run Equilibrium in a Perfectly Competitive Firm. Constant Cost Industries. Increasing Cost Industries. Conclusion.

man. Numerical Example. Linear Programming: A Graphical Analysis: *The Graphical Technique. The Cigarette Manufacturer. The Diet Problem.* Conclusion.

Introduction. Demand for a Productive Service: *Demand of a Firm for One Variable Productive Service. Individual Demand Curves When Several Variable Inputs Are Used. Determinants of the Demand for a Productive Service. Market Demand for a Variable Productive Service.* Supply of a Variable Productive Service: *General Considerations. Indifference Curve Analysis of Labor Supply. The Market Supply of Labor.* Marginal Productivity Theory of Input Returns: *Market Equilibrium and the Returns to Variable Productive Services. Short Run and Quasi Rents. Clark-Wicksteed Product Exhaustion Theorem.* Distribution and Relative Factor Shares: *Least-Cost Combination of Inputs and Linearly Homogeneous Production Functions. The Elasticity of Substitution. Elasticity of Substitution and Changes in Relative Factor Shares. Classification of Technological Progress. Biased Technological Progress and Relative Factor Shares.*

Introduction. Monopoly in the Commodity Market: *Marginal Revenue Product. Monopoly Demand for a Single Variable Service. Monopoly Demand for a Variable Productive Service When Several Variable Inputs Are Used. Market Demand for a Variable Productive Service. Equilibrium Price and Employment. Monopolistic Exploitation.* Monopsony: Monopoly in the Input Market: *Marginal Expense of Input. Price and Employment under Monopsony When One Variable Input Is Used. Price and Employment under Monopsony When Several Variable Inputs Are Used. Monopsonistic Exploitation. Monopsony and the Economic Effects of Labor Unions.*

Introduction: *Quesnay's "Tableau Economique." Walras, Pereto, and Leontief. Algebraic Statement of the Problem. Equilibrium of Ex-*

INTRODUCTION

Scope and Methodology
of Economics

I.1 SCOPE OF ECONOMICS

Over the past hundred years or more, economics has become a well-defined member of the social sciences. While several related disciplines are concerned with social action dominated by a means-end relation, the particular relation unique to economics can be stated with some precision. As most *Principles* texts avow, economics is a study of the proper method of allocating scarce physical and human means (resources) among competing ends—an allocation that achieves a stipulated *optimizing* or *maximizing* objective. The area of study is circumscribed by the stipulation that the means consist of human, man-made, and natural resources and that the ends be economic goods or economic objectives.

I.1.a Ends and Goals

It is helpful to distinguish between *ends* and *goals.* The combined process of production and exchange is one in which a collection of resources distributed among individuals is transformed into a collection of economic goods, the latter being distributed among the economic agents responsible for production. The two distributions are, of course, not necessarily the same. Let us define economic goods themselves as *ends.* Then the word *goal* may be used to describe the fundamental motivations of the various economic agents. For example, economists frequently assume that consumers attempt to maximize satisfaction and

1

that entrepreneurs attempt to maximize profit. So defined, the *goals* of economic agents provide the economist with a frame of reference that permits systematic analysis of individual economic behavior. The behavior of one agent vis-à-vis another is likely to be, in some sense, competitive. But in a broader view, it is the mutual cooperation of agents with conflicting goals that is ultimately responsible for the production of economic goods and services.

When the principles of microeconomic behavior have been discovered, our attention can be focused on a macroeconomic problem that has beset economics from its inception as a science. Indeed, one might say it was the attempt to resolve this problem that caused economics to become a science. The problem may be stated as a question: Will the independent maximizing behavior of each economic agent eventually result in a social organization that, in a normative sense, maximizes the well-being of society as a whole? Adam Smith suggested an answer to this when he presented his doctrine of the "invisible hand." According to Smith, each individual, bent on pursuing his own best interest, is inevitably led, as if by an unseen hand, to pursue a course of action that benefits society as a whole. This is a happy and optimistic doctrine. It has, however, been increasingly questioned as the social and industrial milieu has undergone great change. If all economic agents are atomistic in size relative to the total economic society, either Smith's "invisible hand" or an IBM machine will seek out an optimal organization of economic activity. But, on the contrary, if all agents are not atomistic, one is compelled to ask if this optimum will be reached. Or will the very large agents play an economic game in which they achieve gains, but only at the expense of counterbalancing losses on the part of smaller units? The answers to these questions are not at all clear. But they are very important, both from the standpoint of theory and from that of policy.

Although the course for which this text has been prepared is primarily concerned with the analysis of microeconomic behavior, we must not lose sight of the dominant *quaesitum,* i.e., social welfare. To this end, we shall assess each facet of individual behavior in terms of social welfare and finally conclude with a chapter devoted to welfare economics.

I.1.b Norms and Policy

The discussion of ends and goals, especially in the last paragraph above, leads to a further discussion of *welfare norms* and economic policy (*positive* economics). Economists, in their role as economists, cannot establish normative objectives for a society. For example, an economist cannot say that free public education is desirable or that some minimum level of income should be received by each family unit. Of course, as a citizen he can vote for school bond issues and for legislators who favor income redistribution; but an economist *as an economist* cannot determine social goals.

The business of an economist is a positive, not a normative, one. That is, given a social objective, the economist can analyze the problem and suggest the most efficient means by which to attain the desired end. This book is accordingly devoted to the positive aspects of economic analysis, not to the normative decisions that a society must make.

I.1.c Relation of Economics to Other Social Disciplines[1]

Broadly conceived, social science is the study of the totality of man's social behavior. However, this totality is so extensive in scope that no individual scholar could hope to gain meaningful knowledge of every aspect of social behavior. As Smith long ago pointed out, division of labor tends to augment total physical production; similarly, division of academic labor tends to enhance our total understanding of man's social action. But the division of a social totality into compartments is not so easily accomplished as the division of jobs along an assembly line; nor do the division lines tend to stay put once they are established. The various areas of study are interrelated, and it is only by somewhat arbitrary decisions that the subject matter of social science is divided among the various specialties.

In this light, Spengler wrote that ". . . since the several segments of social studies are mutually interrelated, a specialist's mastery of the behavior-forms allotted to his social science is governed by his understanding of related behavior-forms treated by other social sciences."[2] Yet this understanding is, to some extent, made more difficult by the very process of specialization itself. In the first place, ". . . important modes of collective behavior have escaped significant analysis because no unseen hand has been present to coordinate the activities of diverse specialists and insure analysis of *all* significant forms of interpersonal behavior." Second, ". . . developments within fields of specialization

---

[1] For a thorough discussion, see J. J. Spengler, "Generalists versus Specialists in Social Science: An Economist's View," *American Political Science Review,* Vol. XLIV (1950), pp. 358–79.

[2] *Ibid.,* p. 359.

frequently have weakened and sometimes have nearly destroyed inter-field communication. The comparatively homogeneous tongue of what passed for social science in the past seemingly has given place to a Babel of symbol-ridden jargons."[3]

Accordingly, to promote a wider general understanding of social be-havior, there is need for interdisciplinary cooperation in the study of certain problems that transcend any one special field and, furthermore, for the development of a comparatively uniform language base. Through foundation grants and certain university-sponsored interdisci-plinary projects, some advances have been made in the direction of greater cooperation among specialists. This, in turn, has been facilitated by the comparatively recent introduction of a new language that per-mits specialists to communicate with one another with precision and clarity. Specifically, the utilization of mathematics, its language and its logic, has stimulated, perhaps more than ever before, interdisciplinary understanding and cooperation.[4]

I.2 METHODOLOGY

A person observing the real world of economic phenomena is con-fronted with a mass of data that is, at least superficially, meaningless. To discover order in this morass of facts and to arrange them in a mean-ingful way, it is necessary to develop theories to explain various aspects of human behavior, and thus to explain the otherwise meaningless data. By abstracting from the real world, it is possible to achieve a level of simplicity at which human action may be analyzed. But in the process of abstraction, the analyst must be careful to preserve the essential fea-tures of the real world problem with which he is concerned. That is to say, simplification is necessary; but at the same time a theory must cap-ture the essence of the fundamental economic problem it is designed to solve.

I.2.a Model Analysis

Since this text is exclusively concerned with economic models and their use in analyzing real world economic problems, it is especially important to give attention to the use of model analysis in general be-

[3] *Ibid.*, p. 360.

[4] As examples, see Paul Lazerfeld (ed.), *Mathematical Thinking in the Social Sciences* (Glencoe, Ill.: The Free Press, 1954); and Herbert Simon, *Mathematical Models of Man* (New York: John Wiley & Sons, Inc., 1957).

fore undertaking a study of specific economic models. It is convenient to do this schematically with the aid of the following diagram:[5]

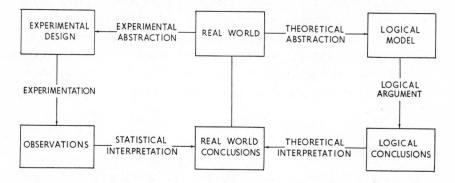

The real world is usually the starting point. A particular problem, or merely a desire to understand, motivates one to move from the complicated world of reality into the domain of logical simplicity. By means of theoretical abstraction, one hopefully reduces the complexities of the real world to manageable proportions. The result is a logical model presumably suited to explain the phenomena observed. By logical argument (i.e., deduction) one then arrives at logical or model conclusions. However, these must be transformed, by means of theoretical interpretation, into conclusions about the real world.

Let us summarize to this point. The economist, having begun with a portion of the real world, proceeds, through the use of completely theoretical means, to arrive at conclusions about the real world. His first step entails abstraction from the real world into a simplified logical model. His second step requires the use of logical argument to arrive at an abstract conclusion. His final step consists of a return to the real world by means of an interpretation that yields conclusions in terms of the concrete, sensible world of physical reality.

The same result may presumably be achieved by another method. Let us call it the *statistical method* to distinguish it from the *deductive method* previously discussed. Again starting from the real world, we may, by means of experimental abstraction, arrive at an experimental design. That is, we may, by a process of simplification, design a statistical model that is useful in analyzing the real world. In this instance, however, we obtain observations of real world data rather than theo-

[5] Adapted from a diagram appearing in C. H. Coombs, Howard Raiffa, and R. M. Thrall (eds.), "Mathematical Models and Measurement Theory," *Decision Processes* (New York: John Wiley & Sons, Inc., 1954), p. 22.

rems by logical deduction. These observations, given the proper statistical interpretation, yield conclusions concerning the real world.

Although there is some disagreement over the relative merit of the two methods, the tenor of present thinking is that they are complementary. That is to say, deductive and statistical methods are mutually reinforcing rather than alternative instruments of analysis. However, since professional opinion regarding methodology is still somewhat diverse, this chapter contains a brief discussion of three positions commonly held.[6]

I.2.b Extreme Apriorism

One group embraces theorists who feel that only the right-hand portion of our diagram is applicable. This group, prominent since the time of John Stuart Mill, has such modern advocates as Mises,[7] Robbins,[8] and Knight,[9] all of whom presumably believe that economic theory is not amenable to verification or refutation on purely empirical grounds. Instead, they think that ". . . economic science is a system of a priori truths, a product of pure reason . . . , a system of pure deduction from a series of postulates. . . ."[10]

One of the clearest explanations of the position held by these writers is found in Mises's definition of a praxeologist, or what Machlup calls an extreme apriorist. According to Mises, a praxeologist is one who believes (*a*) that the fundamental premises and axioms of economics are absolutely true; (*b*) that the theorems and conclusions deduced from these axioms by the laws of logic are, therefore, absolutely true; (*c*) that, consequently, there is no need for empirical testing of either the axioms or the theorems; and (*d*) that the deduced theorems could not be tested, even if it were desirable to do so. Thus the extreme apriorist relies upon introspection and logic to develop the whole body of economic principles.

---

[6] The remainder of this section is based on Fritz Machlup, "The Problem of Verification in Economics," *Southern Economic Journal,* Vol. XXII (1955), pp. 1–21.

[7] Ludwig von Mises, *Human Action* (New Haven, Conn.: Yale University Press, 1959).

[8] Lionel Robbins, *An Essay on the Nature and Significance of Economic Science* (2d ed.; London: Macmillan & Co., Ltd., 1935).

[9] Frank H. Knight, "The Limitations of Scientific Method in Economics," in R. G. Tugwell (ed.), *The Trend of Economics* (New York: Appleton-Century-Crofts Co., Inc., 1930). Reprinted in *The Ethics of Competition* (New York: Harper & Bros., 1935).

[10] Machlup, *op. cit.,* p. 5.

I.2.c Ultraempiricism

At the opposite pole is a group, led by T. W. Hutchinson,[11] whose members Machlup calls ultraempiricists. Fundamentally, this group ". . . refuses to recognize the legitimacy of employing at any level of analysis propositions not independently verifiable."[12] Instead of beginning with a system of axioms, the ultraempiricists presumably prefer to start with a body of what they call facts. Starting with facts of course entails sacrificing the simplicity that is sought. This approach involves all of the complexities of the real world; and the analyst is deprived of the use of the single tool—model analysis—that enables him to escape the morass of otherwise meaningless facts and to reach conclusions of some generality.

I.2.d Logical Positivism

The final methodological position is labeled "logical positivism." It has been clearly stated by Bridgman[13] and various "operational philosophers,"[14] and it finds wide acceptance among modern economists.[15] The positive economists agree that the basic axioms or assumptions of theory are not subject to independent empirical verification. At the same time, they consider it both possible and desirable to test the deduced hypotheses, and thereby to test indirectly the system of axioms underlying economic theory.

In sum, the apriorists believe that no aspect of economic theory is susceptible of empirical test, whereas the ultraempiricists think that

---

[11] T. W. Hutchinson, *The Significance and Basic Postulates of Economic Theory* (London: Macmillan & Co., Ltd., 1938).

[12] Machlup, *op. cit.,* p. 7. Professor Hutchison does not agree with Machlup and my probably hasty interpretation (methodology is not my cup of tea). In a recent letter, Professor Hutchison wrote: "I do not recognize myself in the description there given of me [i.e., in the sentence above]. I did not accept Machlup's account of my views in the article you mention. But you seem to go beyond Machlup in asserting that I reject any kind of abstract or model analysis. Nor do I think that I have ever 'led a group.' I think I agree with Samuelson, who does *not* agree with Friedman."

For expanded comment, see T. W. Hutchison, "Professor Machlup on Verification in Economics," *Southern Economic Journal,* Vol. XXII (1956), pp. 476–83.

[13] P. W. Bridgman, *The Logic of Modern Physics* (New York: The Macmillan Co., 1927).

[14] See, for example, Anatol Rapoport, *Operational Philosophy* (New York: Harper & Bros., 1954).

[15] For example, P. A. Samuelson, *Foundations of Economic Analysis* (Cambridge, Mass.: Harvard University Press, 1947); Milton Friedman, "The Methodology of Positive Economics," *Essays in Positive Economics* (Chicago: University of Chicago Press, 1953), pp. 3–43; and Machlup, *op. cit.*

every facet of theory can and must be proved empirically at each step in a chain of analysis. The positive economists take a middle position. They assert that the conclusions (or theorems) of a model should be tested. If these conclusions are found to be in sufficiently close correspondence with reality, the basic assumptions underlying the model are deemed acceptable. Accordingly, positive economics puts primary emphasis upon the predictive powers of a model: if the predictions derived from one model prove "better" than the corresponding predictions drawn from another model, the former is tentatively selected as preferable. If subsequently a theory is advanced that explains more of the relevant facts or, in a probabilistic sense, conforms more closely to reality, this new theory is deemed superior to the one previously accepted. In every case the test is a pragmatic one: that theory is preferred which best explains the observable phenomena of economic life.

I.3 EQUILIBRIUM AND COMPARATIVE STATICS

Methodologically, I side with the logical positivists. Theory comes first, and then an empirical or statistical investigation to determine whether the results of that theory correspond to the real world. In this course, however, we are concerned only with economic theory and economic analysis—the right-hand side of the diagram on page 5. Empirical testing is left to the specialized field called econometrics.

To reemphasize, this course is concerned first with developing well-established microeconomic theories and second with analyzing real world problems by means of these theories. To elucidate more, and perhaps to give some warning to the student, we quote what Donald Dewey said of one of his own books, but which applies equally well to this one: "this book employs the method of austere, sustained, and, I regret, largely humorless abstraction that has served economics so well in the past. Given the excruciating complexity of so many of the problems . . . , I cannot see that any other method will allow us to cut through to first principles and deal with these problems according to their importance. Either we simplify drastically . . . , or we wander forever in the wilderness. . . ."[16]

I.3.a Equilibrium

Most of economic theory can conveniently be divided into "equilibrium statics," "comparative statics," "equilibrium dynamics," and "com-

---

[16] Donald J. Dewey, *Modern Capital Theory* (New York: Columbia University Press, 1965), p. vii.

parative dynamics." This text concerns only the first two, which contain by far the larger part of economic theory. The word "statics" denotes that our attention is focused on one moment in time and, in particular, that we do not allow time to enter our analysis in such a way as to affect the results. Thus we cannot analyze speculation in commodity markets, nor can we decide when to cut a tree or to stop maturing wine; but we can analyze a very wide variety of economic problems.

"Equilibrium" means balance; more specific to our needs, it means *balancing of forces*. This is something that it will be well to remember, because throughout the rest of the book we determine equilibrium by balancing opposing forces. For example, in the theory of consumer behavior we balance what a consumer would *like* to do with what he is *able* to do with his limited money income. In the theory of the firm, we balance the demand for a producer's output with the technical and market forces that determine supply.

These examples could be multiplied many times over. In the remainder of this chapter we simply explain the meaning of equilibrium and comparative statics by means of the simplest and most important model in economic theory—the model of demand and supply. Most of the rest of the book is concerned with the determinants of demand and supply. At present, but not subsequently, we will assume that the student has only a rudimentary familiarity with the demand-supply model.

Consider Figure I.3.1. The negatively sloped *DD'* curve shows de-

FIGURE I.3.1

Demand and Supply

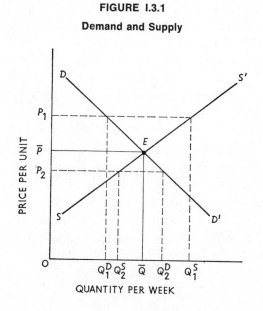

mand. The positively sloped SS' curve shows the supply. The negative and positive slopes simply indicate that buyers are willing to take more and sellers to offer less the lower is price. Our object is to prove that point E (with price $O\overline{P}$ and quantity $O\overline{Q}$) is the market equilibrium, the point where the two opposing forces are in balance. To get the proof, we show that at any price other than $O\overline{P}$, there will be forces that push the price in the direction of $O\overline{P}$.

First, suppose price is *anywhere* above $O\overline{P}$, say OP_1. At this price suppliers wish to sell OQ_1^S. They place their orders or produce accordingly. But at the price OP_1, buyers are only willing to purchase OQ_1^D. As a result, sellers accumulate costly and unwanted inventories. The sellers have a clear incentive to reduce price so as to get rid of their undesired inventories.

Further, this is not only true of the price OP_1 but of *any* price above $O\overline{P}$. At any price above $O\overline{P}$, the quantity sellers wish to offer exceeds the quantity buyers are willing to purchase. Thus at any point above $O\overline{P}$, price must be reduced in the direction of $O\overline{P}$ to clear out undesired accumulations of stock.

Let us now look at the other side. When price is "too low," buyers take the initiative. Suppose price is anywhere below $O\overline{P}$, say OP_2. Buyers wish to purchase OQ_2^D; but at this price sellers are only willing to supply OQ_2^S per week. All who wish to buy at the price OP_2 cannot do so. Some of the dissatisfied buyers therefore bid slightly more in the hope of getting the commodity in question away from others. In part they are successful because some people are only willing to buy at the price OP_2 or less. But others are willing to pay more than OP_2; and until the price is bid up to $O\overline{P}$, there will be dissatisfied buyers in the market who will offer more for the product.

Here we have two opposing forces: buyers who are willing to purchase larger quantities at lower prices, and sellers who are only willing to offer larger quantities at higher prices. The two opposing forces are in balance at E, the point of equilibrium where both buyers and sellers are satisfied.

The above account may seem to be somewhat unrealistic in that consumers seldom make price bids (except in the stock market). Prices are set by sellers and are not changed *immediately* to establish an equilibrium. However, sellers are sensitive to sales and will not hesitate to raise price in order to ration existing quantities. If they do not, a second market—called a black market—will develop; and in this market, consumers truly make price bids.

I.3.b Comparative Statics

When our equilibrium position is determined, as in Figure I.3.1, we can say that price will be $O\overline{P}$ and that $O\overline{Q}$ will be sold. This analysis is based upon the *given* demand and supply curves. But demand and/or supply can change; and we should like to be able to say what will happen to equilibrium price and quantity. This is the object of comparative statics.

Briefly, comparative statics involves the comparison of two static equilibria for the purpose of determining what happens to the variables when there is a shift from one equilibrium to another. Now consider Figure I.3.2. D_1D_1' and SS' are again demand and supply. Our equi-

FIGURE I.3.2

Comparative Statics

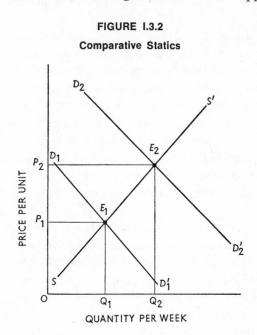

librium analysis shows us that market price is OP_1 and quantity demanded and supplied is OQ_1.

Demand depends upon several things, especially taste, money income, and the prices of related commodities. Let us suppose that demand increases from D_1D_1' to D_2D_2'. Our equilibrium moves from E_1 to E_2; price rises from OP_1 to OP_2, and quantity increases from OQ_1 to OQ_2. This is the method of comparative statics. We postulate a basic change in one of the functional relations in the model and then inquire how this affects the equilibrium values of the variables. From this example we can say that an increase in demand, supply remaining constant, will cause an increase in both equilibrium price and quantity.

I.4 EQUILIBRIUM: PARTIAL AND GENERAL

As we have seen, our study of microeconomic theory is to be the analysis of equilibrium and the comparative static analysis of changes between equilibria. But even then there are two fundamental approaches to static and comparative static analysis—called the "general equilibrium method" and the "partial equilibrium method." Curiously enough, both methods had their basic development at about the same time, in the late 19th century.

There is no doubt that all facets of an economy are interrelated. If pressed far enough, the price of beef depends not only on the price of pork but upon the prices of buttons, color television sets, and tickets to the Masters golf tournament. The wages of unskilled labor depend not only on the wages of semiskilled labor but on the charges of neurosurgeons as well. Everything is related to everything else; and a *complete* treatment of economic theory must take this into account. This was the approach of Walras in his pathbreaking *Elements of Pure Economics*. He analyzed—mathematically, to be sure—the *general equilibrium* of the entire economic system when all interdependencies are recognized.

The resulting system of equations, theorems, and proofs—and it should be emphasized that general equilibrium theory is *essentially* mathematical—is a delight to mathematicians and mathematical economists alike. Indeed, the work of John von Neumann and others on general equilibrium theory has contributed significantly to the development of pure mathematics.

But if the equilibrium system of general equilibrium economics is beautiful, the comparative static system is indescribably messy. Except for very restrictive and specialized cases, one simply cannot say what will happen when there is some change in the economy. Yet surely economists and intelligent laymen must be able to do so. What will happen if minimum prices are set for agricultural products or labor? when an excise tax is imposed on beer, color television sets, and perfume? when there is a freeze in Florida?

There are thousands of questions of this type that are important both to individuals and to governments; and they can be given answers that are *approximately* correct. To get these comparative static answers we must sacrifice the beauty of general equilibrium models for the practicality of partial equilibrium models.

The development of partial equilibrium theory is the most significant contribution Marshall made in his *Principles of Economics*. Everything depends upon everything else; but most things depend in an essential way upon only a *few other things*. Basically, Marshall suggested that we ignore the general interdependence of everything and concentrate only upon the *close interdependence* of a few variables.

The demand for beef obviously depends upon the prices of other meats and fowl. On the other hand, as a first approximation we can ignore the price of automobiles, airplane fares, and so forth. According to Marshall and his many followers, we can temporarily hold *other things constant*—impound them in a *ceteris paribus* assumption, in the jargon of economics—and concentrate our attention on a few closely related variables. Thus in the previous section we were able to say that when the demand for a certain commodity increased, its price and quantity sold increased. We could not have done this—and certainly we could not have done it graphically—if we had to consider the remote and tedious relations that run through thousands of markets.

In this text—as, for that matter, in all intermediate theory texts—we adopt the approach of Marshall. We assume that *most,* but not *all,* of the economic interrelations can be ignored. We analyze our problems and realize that our answers are first approximations. But now return to the diagram on page 5. We build our model on the basis of real world conditions, and then we go through purely logical analysis. Before we make any definite statements or predictions about the real world, we must go through the "interpretation" stage. Here it is necessary to realize that we have held many "other things" constant. Thus we conclude that an increase in demand will cause an increase in price and quantity supplied. If our partial equilibrium theory is sound, as it is in this example, our answers—even though first approximations—will be qualitatively correct. This is about all one can demand of economic theory. Quantitative results are up to the econometricians.

SUGGESTED READINGS

Friedman, Milton. "The Methodology of Positive Economics," *Essays in Positive Economics,* pp. 1–43. Chicago: University of Chicago Press, 1953.

Machlup, Fritz. "The Problem of Verification in Economics," *Southern Economic Journal,* Vol. XXII (1955), pp. 1–21.

Advanced Reading

Buchanan, James M. *"Ceteris Paribus:* Some Notes on Methodology," *Southern Economic Journal,* Vol. XXIV (1958), pp. 259–70.

Harrod, R. F. "Scope and Method of Economics," *Economic Journal,* Vol. XLVIII (1938), pp. 383–412.

Hurwicz, Leonid. "Mathematics in Economics: Language and Instrument," in *Mathematics and the Social Sciences* (ed. **James C. Charlesworth**), pp. 1–11. Philadelphia: The American Academy of Political and Social Science, 1963.

Knight, Frank H. "What Is Truth in Economics?" *Journal of Political Economy,* Vol. XLVIII (1940), pp. 1–32.

Koopmans, T. C. "Measurement without Theory," *Review of Economics and Statistics,* Vol. XXIX (1947), pp. 161–72.

Krupp, Sherman Roy. "Equilibrium Theory in Economics and in Functional Analysis as Types of Explanation," in *Functionalism in the Social Sciences* (ed. **Don Martindale**), pp. 65–83. Philadelphia: The American Academy of Political and Social Science, 1965.

Morgenstern, Oskar. "Limits to the Uses of Mathematics in Economics," in *Mathematics and the Social Sciences* (ed. **James C. Charlesworth**), pp. 12–29. Philadelphia: The American Academy of Political and Social Science, 1963.

PART I

Theory of Consumer
Behavior and Demand

There are three sets of economic agents: consumers, entrepreneurs, and resource owners. Resource owners furnish the inputs used to produce whatever bill of goods is dictated by market forces. In return for the use of their resources, the resource owners receive money income. This money income, in turn, enables them to function as consumers.

Entrepreneurs organize production and, ultimately, determine the supply of goods and services in free markets. Those entrepreneurs who organize production efficiently and are successful in anticipating consumer desires are rewarded with money income in the form of profit. They are thereby also able to enter the market as consumers.

Some people earn money income by selling resources or the use of resources. Others earn income by using their special resource (entrepreneurial skill) to organize production. All people who earn money income belong to the set of economic agents called consumers. There are, of course, other members of this group. Family members who are dependent upon the income earner participate in the household budget decisions and are, therefore, consumers. People who are not able to earn money income receive money by some type of transfer payment and are also in the consumer category.

For our present purpose, the *source* of money income is not material. Only the fact that money is received by households and spent on consumer goods is of importance. Each household determines how to allocate its money income among the vast array of consumer goods available. In other words, each household decides upon its demand for every item (even though the quantity demanded at any price may be zero for many items). The aggregate of these demand decisions constitutes market demand, an expression of how society wants its resources allocated.

The fundamental purpose of Part I is to analyze the process by which market demand is formed—to find, in other words, the basic determinants of market demand. Part II is devoted to an analysis of physical production and how it establishes the cost conditions an entrepreneur faces. Demand and cost are brought together in Part III; the behavior of different classes of producers is analyzed and the formation of market prices is studied. In Part IV we go behind the demand for and supply of commodities to determine the prices received by resource owners for the use of their resources in the production process. Finally, the general welfare of an economic society is analyzed in Part V. We begin with various data: the wishes of consumers as expressed by market demand, the pool of resources available to a society, and the technological conditions of production. Given this information, we want to determine the conditions that must exist—the type of economic organization a society must have—if its pool of resources is to be allocated so as to maximize the economic well-being of its members.

THEORY OF UTILITY AND PREFERENCE: HISTORICAL APPROACH

1.1 INTRODUCTION

Each individual or household has a fairly accurate notion of what its money income will be for a reasonable planning period, say a year. It also has some notion—perhaps not too well defined—of the goods and services it wants to buy. The task confronting every household is to spend its limited money income so as to maximize its economic well-being. No individual or household, of course, actually succeeds in this task. To some extent this failure is attributable to the lack of accurate information; but there are other reasons as well, such as impulse buying. Yet in any event, the more or less conscious effort to attain maximum satisfaction from a limited money income determines individual demand for goods and services.

To analyze the formation of consumer demand more accurately, we use some simplifying assumptions that do not distort the crucial aspects of economic reality.

1.1.a Full Knowledge

First, we assume that each consumer or family unit has complete information on all matters pertaining to its consumption decisions. A consumer knows the full range of goods and services available in the market; he knows precisely the technical capacity of each good or service to satisfy a want. Furthermore, he knows the exact price of each good and service, and he knows these prices will not be changed by his actions in the market. Finally, the consumer knows precisely what his money income will be during the planning period.

In point of fact, the assumptions introduced above are unnecessarily restrictive so far as demand theory is concerned. In order to derive demand functions and indifference curves (see below), it is only neces-

17

sary to assume that (*a*) the consumer is aware of the existence of some goods and services; (*b*) he has some reactions to them, i.e., he prefers some goods to others; and (*c*) he has some money income so as to make these reactions significant in the market. Actually, the more rigid set of assumptions contained in the previous paragraph are necessary only when we come to the theory of welfare economics (at the end of the book). But since an assessment of economic welfare resulting from competitive markets is the central task of microeconomic theory, the more restrictive assumptions are introduced at this time.

1.1.b The Preference Function

A consuming unit—either an individual or a household—derives *satisfaction* or *utility* from each good or service consumed during a given time period. In order to attain its objective—maximization of satisfaction or utility for a given level of money income—the consuming unit must be able to rank different bundles of commodities. That is, the consumer must be able to compare alternative *budgets* or bundles of commodities and to determine his order of preference among them.

To this end we assume that each consuming unit has a *preference function* defined by and possessing the following characteristics:

i) The preference function establishes a *rank ordering* for every conceivable budget (or bundle of commodities).[1]

ii) For every two budgets *A* and *B*, the preference function indicates that *A* is preferred to *B*, that *B* is preferred to *A*, or that the consumer is *indifferent* between these two alternatives. Furthermore, if *A* is preferred to *B*, *B* cannot be preferred to *A*; and if *A* is indifferent or equivalent to *B*, *B* is indifferent to *A*.

iii) Consider any three budgets *A*, *B*, and *C*. If *A* is preferred to *B* and *B* is preferred to *C*, *A* must be preferred to *C*. Similarly, if *A* is indifferent to *B* and *B* is indifferent to *C*, *A* must be indifferent to *C*.

iv) A greater budget is always preferred to a smaller one. One budget is greater than another if it contains as many units of every commodity and more units of at least one commodity.

In summary, the preference function is characterized by two relations: *preference* and *indifference*. When two or more budgets are

---

[1] By *rank ordering* we mean that a consumer can rank alternative budgets ordinally, i.e., first, second, third, etc. Thus, for example, a consumer may say that he prefers budget *A* to budget *B*. We do *not* require, for example, that he be able to say that *A* is twice as preferable as *B*. Only *rankings* are required.

compared, the preference function indicates the rank order of preference (two bundles that are indifferent are tied in rank).[2] The greater the budget, the higher its rank in the ordering. An example will help to explain.

Suppose there are only two goods, X and Y. A portion of a preference function is shown in Table 1.1.1 and illustrated in Figure 1.1.1. Budget A is clearly preferred to all other budgets (by iv) since it con-

TABLE 1.1.1

Rank Ordering of Commodity Bundles or Budgets

Budget	Amount of X	Amount of Y	Rank Order
A..................5	5	1
B..................3	5	2
C..................4	3	2
D..................5	2	2
E..................3	4	3
F..................1	4	4
G..................2	2	4
H..................3	1	4

tains more of both commodities. Budget B is also clearly inferior to A because it contains the same amount of Y and less X. Budgets C and D are, by assumption, indifferent to B. The consumer is willing to take less Y if he gets some more X in return. Budget B, however, must be preferred to E because the latter has less Y and the same quantity of X. Similarly, E must be preferred to F because the latter has less X and the same quantity of Y. Finally, G and H are indifferent to F, the consumer being willing to substitute X for Y in his consumption pattern.

---

[2] Mathematically, one may write the preference function as $\Phi = \Phi$ $(x_1, x_2, \ldots, x_n)$, where x_i indicates the quantity of the i-th commodity. Any, and therefore every, set of quantities defines a budget and a value of Φ. For example, the set of quantities x_i^a defines

$$\Phi^a = \Phi(x_1^a, x_2^a, \ldots, x_n^a),$$

or the budget A. The characteristics stated above require that Φ establish a *complete rank ordering* of the budgets in commodity space. The preference function indicates two types of relations: preference and indifference. The indifference relation (I) is reflexive, symmetric, and transitive. Thus for any three bundles A, B, and C, the following must hold: AIA; if AIB, then BIA; if AIB and BIC, then AIC. The preference relation (P) is antisymmetric and transitive. For any three bundles, APB implies B not PA; APB and BPC implies APC. Finally, condition (iv) is a nonsatiety assumption. This implies that Φ does not possess a maximum point.

The assumptions necessary to analyze consumer behavior can be set out in the following compact form:

Assumptions: (a) Each consumer has exact and full knowledge of all information relevant to his consumption decisions—knowledge of the goods and services available and of their technical capacity to satisfy his wants, of market prices, and of his money income.

(b) Each consumer has a preference function that (i) establishes a rank ordering among all budgets; (ii) for pairwise comparisons, indicates that A is preferred to B, B preferred to A, or that they are indifferent; (iii) for three-or-more-way comparisons, indicates that if A is preferred (indifferent) to B and B is preferred (indifferent) to C, A must be preferred (indifferent) to C; (iv) states that a greater budget is always preferred to a smaller one.

Note: Do the problem at the end of the chapter now.

FIGURE 1.1.1

Ordering of Budgets in Table 1.1.1

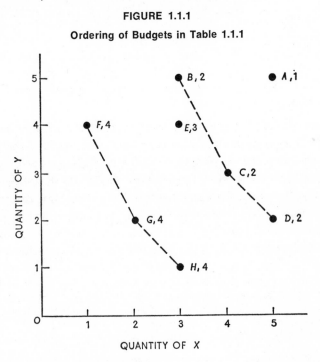

1.2 UTILITY AND PREFERENCE

Economists define "utility" as that quality which makes a commodity desired. This is, of course, a highly subjective phenomenon because each person's physiological and psychological makeup is different from another's. Yet if one sought a single criterion to distinguish modern microeconomic theory from its classical antecedents, he would probably decide it is to be found in the introduction of *subjective value theory* into economics.

Historically, the process was a long one. Our discussion will build up to the modern theory of consumer behavior by outlining some of its intellectual precursors.

1.2.a The Original Approach

The modern theory of demand is based upon a psychological approach to the analysis of economic behavior. The first steps in this direction were hedonistic, based upon the notion of subjective utility. In the original approach—attributable to Gossen (1854), Jevons (1871), and Walras (1874)—utility was regarded as a *measurable* quality of any commodity and was further assumed to be an *additive* quality.[3]

Any good or service deliberately consumed by a household provides utility; and the greater the rate of consumption, the greater the total utility associated with that good. These early writers merely assumed that utility is *cardinally* measurable and that the utility obtained from one good is *not affected* by the rate of consumption of another. For example, one slice of bread per day might yield a measurable five "utils" of utility. Two slices per day might yield 9 utils; three slices, 11 utils; etc. Furthermore, the utility gained from cheese was assumed to be independent of the quantity of bread consumed. Thus one slice of cheese might yield 20 utils; two slices, 37 utils; three slices, 50 utils; etc. Total utility associated with consuming two slices of bread and two of cheese would therefore be 46 utils.[4]

This approach is illustrated in Figure 1.2.1. We assume that there are two commodities, X and Y. Panels a and b show hypothetical utility functions for an individual. The curve OU_X in panel a shows the level of utility associated with each rate of consumption of X. Thus if OX_1 units of X are consumed per period of time, the utility obtained is OU_1 utils. Similarly, OU_Y is the function relating utility to the consumption

---

[3] Alfred Marshall (1890) is also usually placed in the group of originators. In his *Principles* Marshall did indeed assume that utilities are independent and additive. However, it is not clear whether Marshall intended to be taken at his word or whether he regarded this as an approximation for small movements.

[4] Let U represent utility and let goods 1, 2, . . . , n be consumed in the amounts $x_1, x_2, . . . , x_n$. $U_i(x_i)$ is the utility yielded by the i-th good, and total utility, according to this early approach, was simply given by

$$U = U_1(x_1) + U_2(x_2) + \cdots + U_n(x_n) .$$

FIGURE 1.2.1

Utility Functions When Utilities Are Independent

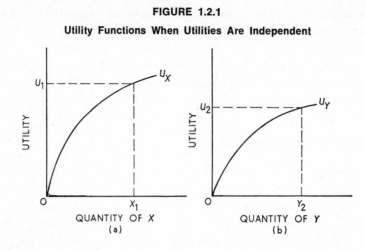

QUANTITY OF X
(a)

QUANTITY OF Y
(b)

of Y. If OY_2 units are consumed per period, utility is OU_2. Therefore, total utility is the measurable magnitude

$$U = OU_1 + OU_2 .$$

There are two fundamental objections to this approach to the theory of consumer behavior. First, it is doubtful that the intensity of satisfaction (utility) can be measured *cardinally*—that is, measured by numbers such as 25, 56.5, and so on. Second, even if measurable, *independent* and *additive* utility is clearly an untenable assumption. The utility or satisfaction a person obtains from steak is related to his consumption of roast; the utility of tennis balls must be partially dependent upon the quantity of tennis rackets.

1.2.b The Second Phase

The second objection to the earliest subjective value theory was soon removed. Edgeworth (1881), Antonelli (1886), and Irving Fisher (1892), among others, realized that utility theory in no way depended upon the additivity assumption. Hence these writers assumed that utility is a *measurable quality* that is generally nonadditive. Total utility depends upon the quantities of each good consumed per period of time, but it is not simply the *sum* of the independent utilities obtained separately from each good.[5]

Rather than constructing a utility function for *each* good, one must

---

[5] In the notation of footnote 4,

$$U = U(x_1, x_2, \ldots , x_n) .$$

now construct a utility surface relating the level of utility to the rates of consumption of all goods simultaneously. Assuming there are two goods, X and Y, a utility surface is illustrated in Figure 1.2.2. The utility surface is $OXZY$. Thus if OX_1 units of X and OY_1 units of Y are consumed per period of time, utility is the measurable magnitude PP'. Similarly, if OX_2 and OY_2 are consumed per period of time, total utility is QQ'.

FIGURE 1.2.2

Utility Surface

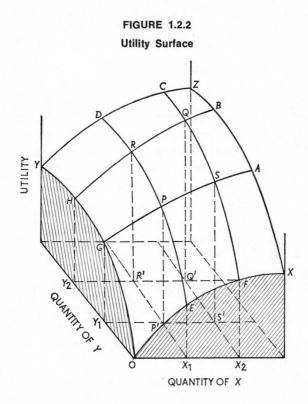

Suppose the rate of consumption of X is fixed at OX_1. The curve $EPRD$ then shows the total utility associated with OX_1 units of X and variable amounts of Y. If consumption is OY_1, utility is PP'; if consumption is OY_2 ($>OY_1$), utility is RR' ($>PP'$), etc. In like manner, if the consumption of X is held fixed at OX_2 units per period of time, the curve $FSQC$ relates total utility to the rate of consumption of Y. The same analysis can be applied to a fixed rate of consumption of Y and a variable rate for X. If the consumption of Y is fixed at OY_1, total utility is PP' if OX_1 units of X are consumed per period of time, SS' ($>PP'$) if the rate of consumption is OX_2 ($>OX_1$), etc. Thus the curve *GPSA* shows the level of total utility associated with OY_1 units of *Y* and various rates of consumption of *X*. Similarly, *HRQB* shows the same thing when the rate of consumption of *Y* is fixed at OY_2 units per period of time.

The Edgeworth-Antonelli-Fisher approach removed one serious objection to the original form of subjective value theory, namely the assumption that utilities are independent and additive. Nonetheless, in this somewhat newer form the theory of consumer behavior rested upon the questionable assumption of cardinally measurable utility.

1.2.c Pareto: The Final Step

The work of Vilfredo Pareto (1906) laid the foundation for removing this last objection, although Pareto himself did not exploit his discovery. Pareto's basic approach is formally the same as that of Edgeworth, Antonelli, and Fisher, as illustrated in Figure 1.2.2. There is only a change in interpretation; but this is very important because it enabled later writers to develop the theory of consumer behavior without resort to the assumption that utility is cardinally measurable.[6]

Pareto's contribution may be explained by means of Figure 1.2.3. There are two goods, *X* and *Y,* and the total utility surface is *OXZY,* just as in Figure 1.2.2. If OX_1 units of *X* and OY_3 units of *Y* are consumed per period of time, total utility is *RR'*. If the consumption of *X* is greater—at the rate OX_2, for instance—the consumption of *Y* remaining unchanged, the level of utility is greater. But an essential feature of utility theory is that one commodity may be *substituted* for another in consumption in such a way as to leave the level of total utility unchanged. For example, X_1X_2 units of *X* may be substituted for Y_3Y_2 units of *Y* without changing total utility. If the rates of consumption are OX_1 of *X* and OY_3 of *Y,* total utility is *RR'*. If the rates are OX_2 of *X* and OY_2 of *Y,* total utility is $PP' = RR'$. Similarly, OX_3 of *X* and OY_1 of *Y* yield total utility of $SS' = PP' = RR'$.

In other words, one may "slice" or intersect the utility surface at the level $RR' = PP' = SS'$ and determine all combinations of *X* and *Y* that will yield this constant level of utility. These combinations are

---

[6] This statement does not mean that utility is *not* cardinally measurable. Whether it is or not is a question that has never been answered satisfactorily. However, utilizing Pareto's results, it is no longer necessary to *assume* cardinal measurability. By the Law of Parsimony—often called Occam's Razor—if two theories have equal predictive power, the one with the fewer assumptions is preferred. We thus dispense with the assumption of cardinally measurable utility and study the *ordinal* theory of consumer behavior.

FIGURE 1.2.3

Utility Surface with Constant Utility Contours

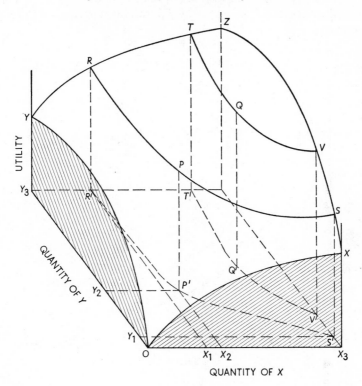

shown by the dashed curve $R'P'S'$ in the X–Y plane. Since each combination of X and Y on $R'P'S'$ yields the same level of utility, a consumer would be indifferent to the particular combination he consumed. In like manner, all combinations of X and Y on the dashed curve $T'Q'V'$ yield the same total utility ($TT' = QQ' = VV'$). A consumer would thus be indifferent as to the particular combination consumed. But a consumer would *not* be indifferent between a combination of X and Y lying on $R'P'S'$ and a combination lying on $T'Q'V'$. Each combination on $T'Q'V'$ is preferred to any combination on $R'P'S'$ because the former yields a higher level of total utility (for example, $TT' > RR'$).

Curves such as $R'P'S'$ and $T'Q'V'$ are called *indifference curves.*

Definition: An indifference curve is a locus of points—or particular budgets or combinations of goods—each of which yields the same level of total utility, or to which the consumer is indifferent.

A partial set of indifference curves is shown in Figure 1.2.4.[7] Graphs such as this are called *indifference maps*.

The curve labeled *I* in Figure 1.2.4 might represent all combina-

FIGURE 1.2.4

Indifference Curves

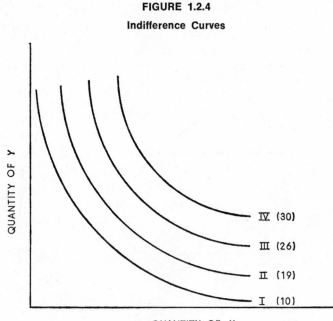

QUANTITY OF Y

IV (30)

III (26)

II (19)

I (10)

QUANTITY OF **X**

tions of *X* and *Y* that yield 10 utils of utility to a certain person. Similarly *II, III,* and *IV* represent all combinations yielding 19, 26, and 30 utils respectively. Now, the important contribution of Pareto lay in recognizing that the specific utility numbers attached to *I, II, III* and *IV* are immaterial—the numbers could be 10, 19, 26, and 30, or 100, 190, 270, and 340, or any other set of numbers that *increase.* The salient point is that for the theory of consumer behavior, only the shape of the *indifference map* matters—the underlying *utility surface* is immaterial. The indifference map can be defined on a psychological-behavioristic basis without making use of the concept of measurable utility. The indifference curves and the concept of preference are all that are required

---

[7] Using the utility function in footnote 5, an indifference curve is given by the equation

$$U(x_1, x_2, \ldots, x_n) = c ,$$

where c is a constant. An indifference map is generated by allowing c to assume every possible value.

—all budgets situated on the same indifference curve are equivalent; all budgets lying on a higher curve are preferred.

Relations: A consumer regards all budgets yielding the same level of utility as equivalent. The locus of such budgets is called an indifference curve because the consumer is indifferent as to the particular budget he consumes. The higher, or further to the right, an indifference curve, the greater is the underlying level of utility (compare *R'P'S'* and *T'Q'V'* in Figure 1.2.3). Therefore, the higher the indifference curve, the more preferred is each budget situated on the curve.

1.2.d Summary

We have now passed from the original concept of measurable, additive utility and the associated utility surface to the concept of preference and indifference as defined by the indifference map. The essential difference between the two concepts lies in the nature of the measurement scale involved. In the older approaches, utility was assumed to be *cardinally measurable* in some units such as utils. The contribution of Pareto was to show that only *ordinal* measurement is required.

The cardinal measure of utility associated with each indifference curve is immaterial. The only requirement is that indifference curves rank budgets according to preference. Thus in Figure 1.2.4, all combinations on *IV* are most preferred; all budgets on *III* are preferred to those on *II* and *I* and are less desirable than those on *IV*, and so on. To repeat, cardinal measurement is not required. Ordinal measurement —ranking budgets first, second, third, etc.—is sufficient.

1.3 CHARACTERISTICS OF INDIFFERENCE CURVES

Indifference curves have four characteristics that are important in our discussion of the modern theory of consumer behavior in Chapter 2. The first property is attributable to the substitutability of goods in consumption. The second property is actually an assumed one; the third is a logical necessity; and the fourth is required by the condition (discussed in Chapter 2) that a consumer behave so as to maximize the satisfaction obtainable from a given money income.

For simplicity, assume that there are only two goods, X and Y. The X–Y plane is called *commodity space.* The first characteristic is that indifference curves are *negatively sloped.* The negative slope reflects the fact (or assumption) that one commodity may be substituted for another in such a way as to leave the consumer with the same level of satisfaction. The second property results from the following assumption: an indifference curve passes through *each* point in commodity space. In the language of mathematics, indifference curves are "everywhere dense." For example, draw any two indifference curves. An infinite number of indifference curves lie between the two you have drawn. This property is very similar to a property possessed by · rational numbers: there are an infinite number of rational numbers lying between 1/99 and 1/100 (or any other pair of rational numbers).

Third, indifference curves cannot intersect. This property is a logical necessity, as illustrated in Figure 1.3.1. In this graph *I* and *II* are indifference curves, and the points *P, Q,* and *R* represent three different budgets (or combinations of *X* and *Y*). *R* must clearly be preferred to *Q* because it contains more of both goods (characteristic *iv* in subsection 1.1.b). *R* and *P* are equivalent because they are situated on the same indifference curve. In like manner, *P* and *Q* are indifferent. By characteristic *iii,* subsection 1.1.b, indifference is a "transitive" relation— that is, if *A* is indifferent to *B* and *B* is indifferent to *C, A* must be indifferent to *C.* In our present case, *R* is indifferent to *P* and *P* is indifferent to *Q;* hence *R* must be indifferent to *Q.* But as previously shown, *R* is preferred to *Q* because it contains more of both goods. Hence intersecting indifference curves, such as those shown in Figure 1.3.1, are logically impossible given the "rationality" assumption.

The fourth property of indifference curves is required in order for

FIGURE 1.3.1

Indifference Curves Cannot Intersect

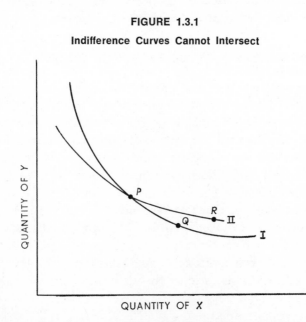

QUANTITY OF *X*

a consumer to maximize satisfaction for a given expenditure of money income.[8] The property is that indifference curves are *concave from above*—that is, an indifference curve must lie above its tangent at each point, as illustrated by panel b, Figure 1.3.2. This implies that indifference curves cannot look like the curve constructed in panel a of that figure.

Properties: Indifference curves possess the following characteristics: (a) indifference curves are negatively sloped; (b) an indifference curve passes through each point in commodity space; (c) indifference curves cannot intersect; and (d) indifference curves are concave from above.

FIGURE 1.3.2

Indifference Curves Are Concave from Above

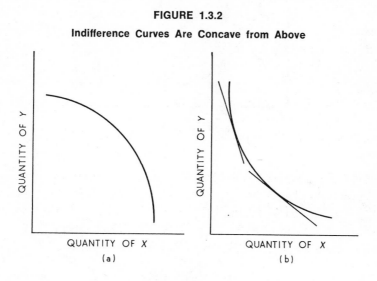

QUANTITY OF Y

QUANTITY OF X
(a)

QUANTITY OF Y

QUANTITY OF X
(b)

1.4 MARGINAL RATE OF SUBSTITUTION

As previously stressed, an essential feature of the subjective theory of value is that different combinations of commodities can yield the same level of utility.[9] In other words, the consumer is indifferent as to the particular combination he obtains. Therefore, as market prices might dictate, one commodity can be substituted for another in the right amount so the consumer remains just as well off as before. He will, in other words, remain on the same indifference curve. It is of

---

[8] This proposition is proved in footnote 4, Chapter 2.

[9] Some writers have questioned the existence of indifference loci on the grounds of the so-called psychological perception threshold. Notable among these is Professor Georgescu-Roegen. For references to some of his works, see the Advanced Readings at the end of this Part.

considerable interest to know the *rate* at which a consumer is *willing* to substitute one commodity for another in his consumption pattern.

Consider Figure 1.4.1. An indifference curve is given by the curve

FIGURE 1.4.1

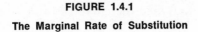

The Marginal Rate of Substitution

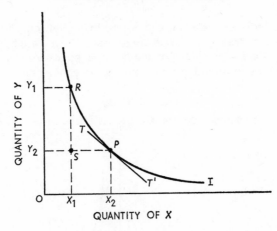

labeled *I*. The consumer is indifferent between the budget *R*, containing OX_1 units of *X* and OY_1 units of *Y*, and the budget *P* containing $OX_2 > OX_1$ units of *X* and $OY_2 < OY_1$ units of *Y*. The consumer is willing to substitute X_1X_2 units of *X* for Y_1Y_2 units of *Y*. The rate at which he is willing to substitute *X* for *Y*, therefore, is

$$\frac{OY_1 - OY_2}{OX_2 - OX_1} = \frac{RS}{SP}.$$

This ratio measures the average number of units of *Y* the consumer is willing to forego in order to obtain one additional unit of *X* (over the range of consumption pairs under consideration). Stated alternatively, the ratio measures the amount of *Y* that must be sacrificed per unit of *X* gained if the consumer is to remain at precisely the same level of satisfaction.

The rate of substitution is given by the ratio stated above. But as the point *R* moves along *I* toward *P*, the ratio *RS/SP* approaches closer and closer to the slope of the tangent *TT'* at point *P*. In the limit, for very small movements in the neighborhood of *P*, the slope of *I* or of its tangent at *P* is called the *marginal rate of substitution* of *X* for *Y*.

Definition: The marginal rate of substitution of *X* for *Y* measures the number of units of *Y* that must be sacrificed per unit of *X* gained so as to maintain a constant level of satisfaction. The marginal rate of substitution is given by the negative of the slope of an indifference curve at a point. It is defined only for movements along an indifference curve, never for movements among curves.[10]

The requirement that indifference curves be concave from above implies that the marginal rate of substitution of X for Y diminishes as X is substituted for Y along an indifference curve. This is illustrated in Figure 1.4.2.

FIGURE 1.4.2

The Diminishing Marginal Rate of Substitution

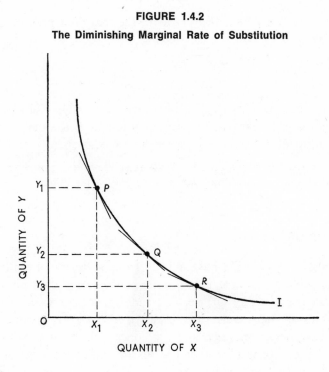

QUANTITY OF X

---

[10] Let the utility function be $U(x, y)$, so an indifference curve is given by $U(x, y) = c$, where c is a constant. Taking the total derivative, one obtains

$$\frac{\partial U}{\partial x} dx + \frac{\partial U}{\partial y} dy = 0 .$$

Solving for dy/dx, the slope of the indifference curve, we find that

$$-\frac{dy}{dx} = MRS_{x \text{ for } y} = \frac{\dfrac{\partial U}{\partial x}}{\dfrac{\partial U}{\partial y}}.$$

In older terminology, $\partial U/\partial x$ was called the marginal utility of x, $\partial U/\partial y$ the marginal utility of y. Thus the marginal rate of substitution of x for y is the ratio of the marginal utilities of x and y.

I is an indifference curve; and *P, Q,* and *R* are three budgets situated on this curve. The horizontal axis is measured so that $OX_1 = X_1X_2 = X_2X_3$. Consider first the movement from *P* to *Q*. If *P* is very close to *Q*, or the amount X_1X_2 is very small, the marginal rate of substitution of *X* for *Y* at *Q* is

$$\frac{OY_1 - OY_2}{OX_2 - OX_1} = \frac{Y_1Y_2}{X_1X_2}.$$

Similarly, for a movement from *Q* to *R*, the marginal rate of substitution at *R* is

$$\frac{OY_2 - OY_3}{OX_3 - OX_2} = \frac{Y_2Y_3}{X_2X_3}.$$

By construction $X_1X_2 = X_2X_3$; but very obviously, $Y_1Y_2 > Y_2Y_3$. Hence the marginal rate of substitution is less at *R* than at *Q*. This is also shown by the decreasing slopes of the tangents at *P, Q,* and *R*.

Principle: As *X* is substituted for *Y* so as to leave the consumer on the same indifference curve, the marginal rate of substitution of *X* for *Y* diminishes.[11]

1.5 CONCLUSION

Historically, economists have turned from a theory of utility to a theory of preference to explain consumer behavior and demand. Instead of using the entire utility surface, only indifference curves are required. These curves are negatively sloped, pass through every point in commodity space, never intersect, and are concave from above. The last-mentioned property implies that the marginal rate of substitution of *X* for *Y* diminishes as *X* is substituted for *Y* so as to maintain the same level of satisfaction.

These concepts and relations are used in Chapter 2 to develop the

---

[11] A diminishing marginal rate of substitution does *not* require, of necessity, diminishing marginal utilities of the goods involved in the utility function. Diminishing marginal utility is neither a necessary nor a sufficient condition for diminishing marginal rates of substitution unless the preference function is homogeneous of degree one. There is, to my knowledge, no satisfactory literary explanation of this well-established fact. Essentially, it depends not only on the *independent* changes in marginal utilities but also upon the *interdependent* changes. Even such a renowned expositor as Hicks in *Value and Capital* could not give an explanation. Mathematically, the relation is shown in footnote 4, Chapter 2, equation (2.4.10).

modern theory of consumer behavior and to determine the shape of individual demand curves.[12]

PROBLEM

There are three commodities *X, Y,* and *Z.* The table contains a list of budgets composed of different combinations of these three goods. Determine the rank order of the budgets (in this problem, there are no budgets among which the consumer is indifferent) and list them on a separate sheet.

	Amount of		
Budget	X	Y	Z
A..........................	86	88	77
B..........................	86	87	76
C..........................	100	90	80
D..........................	79	80	69
E..........................	85	87	76
F..........................	79	79	68
G..........................	95	89	79
H..........................	80	80	70
I..........................	79	79	69
J..........................	86	87	77

---

[12] One special class of preference functions, often used by theorists because of mathematical simplicity, is the class of functions homogeneous of degree one. Because of their special characteristics, these functions deserve brief treatment.

Let the preference function be given by

$$U = U(x_1, x_2, \ldots, x_n), \qquad (1.12.1)$$

where x_i is the quantity of the *i*-th commodity consumed. Let all commodities consumed be increased (or decreased) in the same proportion λ. If (1.12.1) is homogeneous of degree one, we have

$$U(\lambda x_1, \lambda x_2, \ldots, \lambda x_n) \equiv \lambda U(x_1, x_2, \ldots, x_n). \qquad (1.12.2)$$

Consequently, if all commodities are increased (or decreased) in the same proportion, utility increases (or decreases) in the same proportion. Each commodity separately has diminishing marginal utility; but proportional increases in *all* items consumed leads to constant (not declining) increases in utility.

Second, the partial derivatives of a function homogeneous of degree one are themselves homogeneous of degree zero. That is,

$$\frac{\partial U(x_1, x_2, \ldots, x_n)}{\partial x_i} = U_i\left(\frac{x_1}{x_i}, \frac{x_2}{x_i}, \ldots, \frac{x_n}{x_i}\right) \qquad (i = 1, 2, \ldots, n). \quad (1.12.3)$$

Thus marginal utilities are *independent* of the absolute level of consumption of each

QUESTIONS

1. What role do indifference curves play in economic theory and what economic principles do they illustrate? In what sense does this tool of analysis indicate the meaning of the basic economic problem of relating scarce resources to alternative goals?

2. Explain the following statement: the distance between two indifference curves is immaterial; the only relevant issue is which is higher and which is lower.

3. Suppose there are two goods, each of which causes a reduction in total utility beyond a certain rate of consumption (i.e., marginal utility for each becomes negative beyond some point). What would be the shape of a typical indifference curve and how would the utility surface look?

SUGGESTED READINGS

Henderson, James M., and Quandt, Richard E. *Microeconomic Theory: A Mathematical Approach,* chap. 2, pp. 6–12. New York: McGraw-Hill Book Co., Inc., 1958. [Elementary math necessary.]

Hicks, John R. *Value and Capital,* pp. 1–25. 2d ed. Oxford: Oxford University Press, 1946.

Marshall, Alfred. *Principles of Economics,* Book III, chaps. 5–6, pp. 117–37. 8th ed. London: Macmillan & Co., Ltd., 1920.

Samuelson, Paul A. *Foundations of Economic Analysis,* chap. V, pp. 90–96. Cambridge, Mass.: Harvard University Press, 1947. [Advanced math necessary.]

Stigler, George J. "The Development of Utility Theory, I," *Journal of Political Economy,* Vol. LVIII (August, 1950), pp. 307–24.

---

good; they depend only upon the *ratio* in which all goods are consumed. For example, the marginal utility of each good is unchanged if the consumption of all goods is doubled or halved.

Finally, since the marginal rate of substitution between two goods is the ratio of their marginal utilities, the marginal rate of substitution is itself homogeneous of degree zero and thus possesses the same characteristics as the marginal utility functions. Thus, for example, if relative prices remain constant, the ratio in which all commodities are consumed does not change if income is doubled or halved (this point can only be understood after Chapter 2 has been studied).

The interested student should figure out the very special properties of the following two-commodity preference functions:

$$U = Ax_1^\alpha x_2^{1-\alpha} \quad (0 < \alpha < 1), \tag{1.12.4}$$

$$U = a[bx_1^{-c} + (1-b)x_2^{-c}]^{-\frac{1}{c}} \quad (c > -1), \tag{1.12.5}$$

where A, α, a, b, and c are constants.

Chapter 2 | MODERN THEORY OF CONSUMER BEHAVIOR

2.1 INTRODUCTION

Pareto failed to exploit his substantial discoveries, as already indicated. The task of developing the modern theory of consumer behavior remained for Slutsky (1915), Hicks and Allen (1934), Hotelling (1935), and Hicks (1939).

2.1.a Maximization of Satisfaction

The principal assumption upon which the theory of consumer behavior and demand is built is: a consumer attempts to allocate his limited money income among available goods and services so as to maximize his satisfaction. In short, a consumer arranges his purchases so as to maximize satisfaction subject to his limited money income. Given this assumption and the properties of indifference curves (developed in Chapter 1), individual demand curves can easily be determined. It is to this task that the present chapter is devoted.

2.1.b Limited Money Income

If each consumer had an unlimited money income—in other words, if there were an unlimited pool of resources—there would be no problems of "economizing," nor would there be "economics." But since this utopian state does not exist, even for the richest members of our society, people are compelled to determine their behavior in light of limited financial resources. For the theory of consumer behavior, this means that each consumer has a maximum amount he can spend per period of time. The consumer's problem is to spend this amount in the way that yields him maximum satisfaction.

Continue to assume that there are only two goods, X and Y, bought in quantities x and y. Each individual consumer is confronted with market-determined prices p_x and p_y of X and Y, respectively. Finally, the consumer in question has a known and fixed money income (M) for the period under consideration. Thus the maximum amount he can spend per period is M, and this amount can be spent only upon goods X and Y.[1] Thus the amount spent on X (xp_x) plus the amount spent on Y (yp_y) must not exceed the stipulated money income M. Algebraically,

$$M \geqq xp_x + yp_y. \tag{2.1.1}$$

Expression 2.1.1 is an inequality that can be graphed in commodity space since it involves only the two variables X and Y. First consider the equality form of this expression:

$$M = xp_x + yp_y. \tag{2.1.2}$$

This is the equation of a straight line. Solving for y—since y is plotted on the vertical axis—one obtains

$$y = \frac{1}{p_y} M - \frac{p_x}{p_y} x. \tag{2.1.3}$$

Equation 2.1.3 is plotted in Figure 2.1.1. The first term on the right-hand side of equation (2.1.3), $\frac{1}{p_y} M$, shows the amount of Y that can be purchased if X is not bought at all. This is represented by the distance OA in Figure 2.1.1; thus $\frac{1}{p_y} M$ is the *ordinate intercept* of the equation.

The second term on the right-hand side of equation (2.1.3), i.e., $-\frac{p_x}{p_y}$, is the *slope* of the line. Consequently, the slope of the line is the negative of the price ratio. To see this, consider the quantity of X that can be purchased if Y is not bought. This amount is $\frac{1}{p_x} M$, shown by the

---

[1] In more advanced cases, *saving* may be considered as one of the many goods and services available to the consumer. Graphical treatment limits us to two dimensions; thus we ignore saving. This does *not* mean that the theory of consumer behavior precludes saving—depending upon his preference ordering, a consumer may save much, little, or nothing. Similarly, spending may in fact exceed income in any given period as a result of borrowing or from assets acquired in the past. The "M" in question for any period is the total amount of money to be spent during the period. For a more sophisticated treatment of this problem, see Ralph W. Pfouts, "Hours of Work, Savings and the Utility Function," in Pfouts (ed.), *Essays in Economics and Econometrics in Honor of Harold Hotelling* (Chapel Hill: University of North Carolina Press, 1960), pp. 113–32.

distance OB in Figure 2.1.1. Since the line obviously has a negative slope, its slope is given by[2]

$$-\frac{OA}{OB} = -\frac{\dfrac{1}{p_y}M}{\dfrac{1}{p_x}M} = -\frac{p_x}{p_y}.$$

FIGURE 2.1.1

The Budget Line

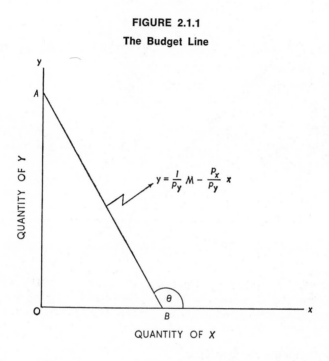

QUANTITY OF X

The line in Figure 2.1.1 is called the *budget line.*

Definition: The budget line is the locus of budgets (or combinations of goods) that can be purchased if the entire money income is spent. Its slope is the negative of the price ratio.

The budget line is the graphical counterpart of equation (2.1.3), but it is not the graph of the inequality in expression (2.1.1). The latter includes the budget line, but it also includes all budgets whose total cost is not as great as M. Inequality (2.1.1) is shown graphically in

[2] The slope is tan $\theta = -\tan(180 - \theta) = -OA/OB$, etc.

Figure 2.1.2 by the triangular shaded area—it is the entire area enclosed by the budget line and the two axes. This area is called the *budget space.*[3]

FIGURE 2.1.2

Budget Space

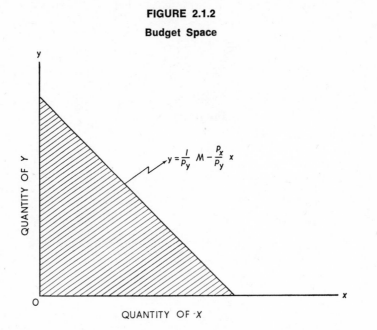

QUANTITY OF Y

$$y = \frac{I}{p_y} M - \frac{p_x}{p_y} x$$

O

QUANTITY OF ·X

Definition: The budget space is the set of all budgets that may be purchased by spending some or all of a given money income. The budget space comprises only a part of (or is a subset of) commodity space.

2.1.c Shifting the Budget Line

In much of the analysis that follows, we are interested in *comparative static* changes in quantities purchased resulting from changes in price or money income. The latter changes are graphically represented by shifts in the budget line.

First consider an increase in money income from M to $M^* > M$, commodity prices remaining unchanged. The consumer can now purchase *more*—more of Y, more of X, or more of both. The maximum

---

[3] Mathematically, it is more correct to say that the budget space is defined by the following three inequalities:

$$M \geqq x p_x + y p_y \, ,$$
$$x \geqq 0 \, ,$$
$$y \geqq 0 \, .$$

purchase of Y increases from $\dfrac{1}{p_y} M$ to $\dfrac{1}{p_y} M^*$, or from OA to OA' in Figure 2.1.3. Similarly, the maximum purchase of X increases from

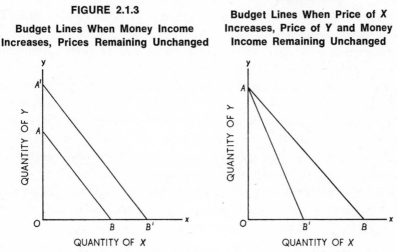

FIGURE 2.1.3

Budget Lines When Money Income Increases, Prices Remaining Unchanged

FIGURE 2.1.4

Budget Lines When Price of X Increases, Price of Y and Money Income Remaining Unchanged

$\dfrac{1}{p_x} M$ to $\dfrac{1}{p_x} M^*$, or from OB to OB'. Since prices remain constant, the *slope* of the budget line does not change. Thus an increase in money income, prices remaining constant, is shown graphically by shifting the budget line upward and to the right. Since the slope does not change, the movement might be called a "parallel" shift. It readily follows that a decrease in money income is shown by a parallel shift of the budget line in the direction of the origin.

Figure 2.1.4 shows what happens to the budget line when the price of X increases, the money price of Y and money income remaining constant. Let the price of X increase from p_x to $p_x{}^*$. Since p_y and M are unchanged, the ordinate intercept does not change—it is OA in each case. But the slope of the line, the negative of the price ratio, changes from $-\dfrac{p_x}{p_y}$ to $-\dfrac{p_x{}^*}{p_y}$. Since $p_x{}^* > p_x$, $-\dfrac{p_x{}^*}{p_y} < -\dfrac{p_x}{p_y}$. In other words, the slope of the budget line becomes *steeper*.

Alternatively, the price change can be explained as follows. At the original price p_x, the maximum purchase of X is $\dfrac{1}{p_x} M$, or the distance OB. When the price changes to $p_x{}^*$, the maximum purchase of X is

$\dfrac{1}{p_x{}^*}$ M, or the distance OB'. Thus an increase in the price of X is shown by rotating the budget line *clockwise* around the ordinate intercept. A decrease in the price of X is represented by a *counterclockwise* movement.

Before summarizing these relations, it may be helpful to state the obvious and emphasize that *relative* prices are crucial. If money income remains constant and the nominal prices of both commodities change proportionately, there is no change in relative price; the change in this case is tantamount to an increase in income (if prices decline) or a decrease in income (if prices rise). Similarly, let money income and the nominal price of Y remain constant. An increase in the nominal price of X is equivalent to a decrease in the relative price of Y, and vice versa. As we shall subsequently see, given money income, only relative prices are relevant to a consumer's decision-making process. Hence the student should pay particular heed to the connections among nominal money income, real money income, nominal prices, and relative prices.

Relations: (*i*) An increase in money income, prices unchanged, is shown by a parallel shift of the budget line—outward and to the right for an increase in money income, and in the direction of the origin for a decrease in money income. (*ii*) A change in the price of X, the price of Y and money income constant, is shown by rotating the budget line around the ordinate intercept—to the left for a price increase, and to the right for a decrease in price.

2.2 CONSUMER EQUILIBRIUM

All bundles of goods in commodity space are available to the consumer in the sense that he *may* purchase them if he *can*. The consumer's indifference map establishes a rank ordering of all these bundles. The consumer's budget space is established by his fixed money income and relative commodity prices; it shows the bundles he *can* purchase. Our fundamental assumption that each consumer attempts to maximize satisfaction from a given money income simply means the following: that the consumer must select the most preferred bundle of goods in his budget space.

2.2.a The Relevant Part of Commodity Space

Graphically, the consumer's problem is depicted in Figure 2.2.1. The entire $x–y$ plane is commodity space; his indifference map, represented by the five indifference curves drawn in that figure, indicates his preferences among all budgets in this space. Similarly, the consumer's budget space—the line LM and the shaded area enclosed by LM and the two axes—shows the feasible budgets, those the consumer can buy. Clearly, the consumer cannot purchase any budget lying above and

FIGURE 2.2.1

Budget Space and the Indifference Map

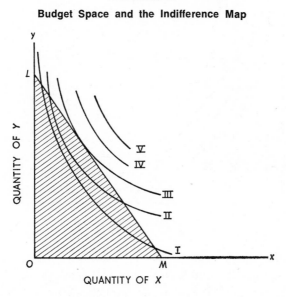

to the right of the budget line LM. He would prefer such a budget if it were attainable; but his income is not sufficient to pay for it.

Thus his choice is limited to those bundles lying in the budget space. But again, we can eliminate most of these. In particular, no point in the interior of the budget space—below the budget line LM—can yield maximum satisfaction because a higher indifference curve can be reached by moving out to the budget line. Hence the only portion of commodity space relevant to the consumer's decision is the budget line.

2.2.b Maximizing Satisfaction Subject to a Limited Money Income

The way in which a consumer maximizes satisfaction subject to a limited money income is illustrated in Figure 2.2.2. The budget line is LM, and the curves labeled I, II, III, and IV are a portion of an individual's indifference map. As already observed, the consumer cannot attain a position on any indifference curve, such as IV, that lies entirely beyond the budget line.

FIGURE 2.2.2

Consumer Equilibrium

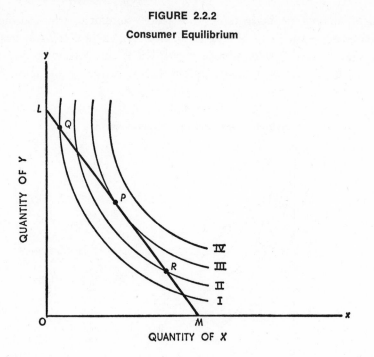

Three of the infinite number of attainable budgets on *LM* are represented by the points *Q, P,* and *R.* Each of these, and every other point on the budget line *LM,* is attainable with the consumer's limited money income.

Suppose the consumer were located at *Q.* Without experimenting, he cannot know for certain whether *Q* represents a maximum position for him. Thus let him experimentally move to budgets just to the left and right of *Q.* Moving to the left from *Q* lowers his level of satisfaction to some indifference curve below *I.* But moving to the right brings him to a higher indifference curve; and continued experimentation will lead him to move at least as far as *P,* because each successive movement to the right brings the consumer to a higher indifference curve. If he continued to experiment, however, by moving to the right of *P,* the consumer would find himself upon a lower indifference curve with its lower level of satisfaction. He would accordingly return to the point *P.*

Similarly, if a consumer were situated at a point such as *R,* experimentation would lead him to substitute *Y* for *X,* thereby moving in the direction of *P.* He would not stop short of *P* because each successive substitution of *Y* for *X* brings the consumer to a higher indifference curve. Hence the position of maximum satisfaction—or the point of consumer equilibrium—is attained at *P,* where an indifference curve is just tangent to the budget line.

As you will recall, the slope of the budget line is (the negative of) the price ratio, the ratio of the price of *X* to the price of *Y.* As you will also recall, the slope of an indifference curve at any point is called the marginal rate of substitution of *X* for *Y.* Hence the point of consumer equilibrium is defined by the condition that the marginal rate of substitution equals the price ratio.

The interpretation of this proposition is very straightforward. The marginal rate of substitution shows the rate at which the consumer *is willing to substitute* X for Y. The price ratio shows the rate at which he *can substitute* X for Y. Unless these two are equal, it is possible to change the combination of *X* and *Y* purchased so as to attain a higher level of satisfaction. For example, suppose the marginal rate of substitution is two—meaning the consumer is willing to give up two units of *Y* in order to obtain one unit of *X.* Let the price ratio be unity, meaning one unit of *Y* can be exchanged for one unit of *X.* Clearly, the consumer will benefit by trading *Y* for *X,* since he is willing to give two *Y*'s for one *X* but only has to give one *Y* for one *X* in the market. Generalizing, unless the marginal rate of substitution and the price ratio are equal, some exchange can be made so as to push the consumer to a higher level of satisfaction.

Principle: The point of consumer equilibrium—or the maximization of satisfaction subject to a limited money income—is defined by the condition that the marginal rate of substitution of *X* for *Y* equals the ratio of the price of *X* to the price of *Y.*[4]

---

[4] This statement obviously holds if, and only if, each consumer consumes a positive amount of each good. Suppose that in a two-good world a consumer in fact consumes some amount of each good. Let there be two goods *X* and *Y* with given market prices p_x and p_y. The consumer has a given money income (M) and consumes the two goods in quantities x and y. His preference function is given by

$$U = U(x,y) . \tag{2.4.1}$$

His budget constraint is

$$M = xp_x + yp_y . \tag{2.4.2}$$

To maximize (2.4.1) subject to the constraint (2.4.2) is a simple Lagrangean extremum problem. Construct the function

$$L = U(x,y) - \lambda(xp_x + yp_y - M) , \tag{2.4.3}$$

where λ is a Lagrangean multiplier. The first-order conditions require that both partial derivatives equal zero:

2.3 CHANGES IN MONEY INCOME

Changes in money income, prices remaining constant, usually result in corresponding changes in the quantities of commodities bought. In

---

$$\frac{\partial L}{\partial x} = \frac{\partial U}{\partial x} - \lambda p_x = 0 \, ,$$

$$\frac{\partial L}{\partial y} = \frac{\partial U}{\partial y} - \lambda p_y = 0 \, .$$

(2.4.4)

Transferring the second term to the right-hand side in each equation and dividing the first equation by the second, one obtains

$$\frac{\dfrac{\partial U}{\partial x}}{\dfrac{\partial U}{\partial y}} = \frac{p_x}{p_y} .$$

(2.4.5)

As shown in footnote 10, Chapter 1, the expression on the left-hand side of (2.4.5) is the marginal rate of substitution. Thus one obtains the condition stated in the text.

The second-order conditions for a maximum require that

$$\frac{d^2U}{dx^2} = \frac{\partial^2 U}{\partial x^2} + 2 \frac{\partial^2 U}{\partial x \partial y}\left(-\frac{p_x}{p_y}\right) + \frac{\partial^2 U}{\partial y^2}\left(-\frac{p_x}{p_y}\right)^2 < 0 \, .$$

(2.4.6)

Multiplying (2.4.6) by $p_y{}^2$, a positive number, one obtains

$$\frac{\partial^2 U}{\partial x^2} p_y{}^2 - 2 \frac{\partial^2 U}{\partial x \partial y} p_x p_y + \frac{\partial^2 U}{\partial y^2} p_x{}^2 < 0 \, .$$

(2.4.7)

A true maximum is obtained if (2.4.7) holds in addition to (2.4.4).

The slope of an indifference curve at a point, as shown in footnote 10, Chapter 1, is dy/dx. Taking its derivative, one obtains

$$\frac{d^2y}{dx^2} = -\frac{1}{\left(\dfrac{\partial U}{\partial y}\right)^3}\left[\frac{\partial^2 U}{\partial x^2}\left(\frac{\partial U}{\partial y}\right)^2 - 2 \frac{\partial^2 U}{\partial x \partial y}\left(\frac{\partial U}{\partial x}\right)\left(\frac{\partial U}{\partial y}\right) + \frac{\partial^2 U}{\partial y^2}\left(\frac{\partial U}{\partial x}\right)^2\right] .$$

(2.4.8)

Substituting

$$\frac{\partial U}{\partial x} = \frac{p_x}{p_y}\frac{\partial U}{\partial y} \qquad \text{[from (2.4.5)]}$$

(2.4.9)

in (2.4.8), one obtains

$$\frac{d^2y}{dx^2} = -\frac{1}{\dfrac{\partial U}{\partial y} p_y{}^2}\left[\frac{\partial^2 U}{\partial x^2} p_y{}^2 - 2 \frac{\partial^2 U}{\partial x \partial y} p_x p_y + \frac{\partial^2 U}{\partial y^2} p_x{}^2\right] .$$

(2.4.10)

Inequality (2.4.7) ensures that the bracketed term on the right-hand side of (2.4.10) is negative. Hence d^2y/dx^2 is positive, implying that indifference curves must be concave from above to ensure a stable constrained maximum. To reinforce this point, the student should do the following

Exercise: Prove graphically that a stable equilibrium cannot exist unless indifference curves are everywhere concave from above.

particular, for so-called "normal" or "superior" goods an increase in money income leads to an increase in consumption and a decrease in money income to a decrease in consumption. It is of considerable interest to analyze the effects upon consumption of changes in income. To do so, we will hold nominal prices constant so as to observe the effects of income changes alone.[5]

2.3.a The Income-Consumption Curve

As explained in subsection 2.1.c, an increase in money income shifts the budget line upward and to the right, and the movement is a parallel

FIGURE 2.3.1

The Income-Consumption Curve

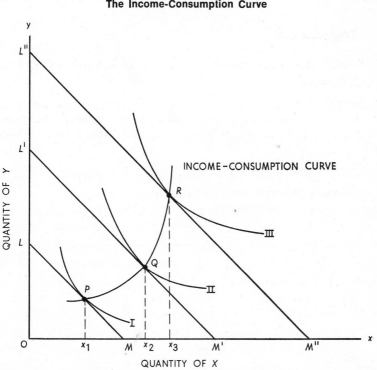

shift because nominal prices are assumed to be constant. In Figure 2.3.1, the price ratio is given by the slope of LM, the original budget line, and remains constant throughout.

With money income represented by LM, the consumer comes to equilibrium at point P on indifference curve I, consuming Ox_1 units of X. Now let money income rise to the level represented by $L'M'$. The

---

[5] We assume throughout the discussion that the good is a "normal" or "superior" good. "Inferior" goods are treated in Chapter 3.

consumer shifts to a new equilibrium at point Q on indifference curve *II*. He has clearly gained. He also gains when money income shifts to the level corresponding to $L''M''$. The new equilibrium is at point R on indifference curve *III*.

As income shifts, the point of consumer equilibrium shifts as well. The line connecting the successive equilibria is called the income-consumption curve. This curve shows the *equilibrium combinations* of X and Y purchased at various levels of money income, nominal prices remaining constant throughout.

Definition: The income-consumption curve is the locus of equilibrium budgets resulting from various levels of money income and constant money prices. The income-consumption curve is positively sloped throughout its entire range when both goods are "normal" or "superior."

2.3.b   Engel Curves

The income-consumption curve may be used to derive Engel curves for each commodity.

Definition: An Engel curve is a function relating the equilibrium quantity purchased of a commodity to the level of money income. The name is taken from Christian Lorenz Ernst Engel, a 19th-century German statistician.

Engel curves are important for applied studies of economic welfare and for the analysis of family expenditure patterns.

Engel curves relating the consumption of commodity X to income are constructed in Figure 2.3.2. Neither panel a nor panel b is directly based upon the particular income-consumption curve in Figure 2.3.1; but the process of deriving an Engel curve from an income-consumption curve should be clear.

At the original equilibrium point P in Figure 2.3.1, money income is $p_x \cdot OM$ (or $p_y \cdot OL$). At the income $p_x \cdot OM$, Ox_1 units of X are purchased. This income-consumption point can be plotted on a graph such as panel a, Figure 2.3.2. When the budget line shifts from LM to $L'M'$ (Figure 2.3.1), money income increases to $p_x \cdot OM'$ and consumption to Ox_2 units. This income-consumption pair constitutes another point on the Engel curve graph. Repeating this process for all levels of money income generates a series of points on a graph such as panel a, Figure 2.3.2. The Engel curve is formed by connecting these points by a line.

Two basically different types of Engel curves are shown in panels a and b, Figure 2.3.2. In panel a, the Engel curve slopes upward rather gently, implying that changes in money income do not have a substantial effect upon consumption. An Engel curve with this property indi-

FIGURE 2.3.2

Engel Curves

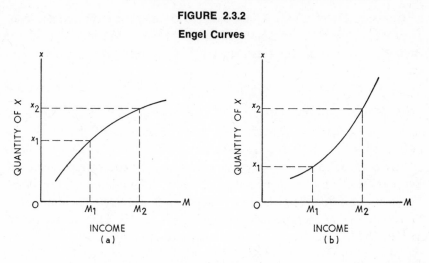

cates that the good is bought when income is low, but the quantity purchased does not expand rapidly as income increases. If "food" is treated as a single commodity, its Engel curve would look something like the curve in panel a, even though the curve for "steak" as a separate commodity probably would not.

On the other hand, steak and many other types of goods give rise to Engel curves more nearly represented by the curve in panel b. The relatively steep upward slope indicates that the quantity bought changes markedly with income.[6]

2.3.c Engel Curves and the Income Elasticity of Demand

The income elasticity of demand, which is discussed much more thoroughly in Chapter 4, has the following

Definition: The income elasticity of demand is the proportional change in the consumption of a commodity divided by the proportional change in income.

Income elasticity may be related to the slope or curvature of an Engel curve and, in part, to the classification of commodities as superior, normal, or inferior.[7]

---

[6] If he likes, the student may associate "necessities" and "luxuries" with commodities whose Engel curves look like those in panels a and b respectively. One should be warned, however, that such associations are very rough and highly sensitive to the particular definitions of the commodities in question.

[7] The relation between the curvature of an Engel function and the income elasticity of demand may easily be shown mathematically when the Engel curve is homogeneous. By definition, income elasticity is

Consider Figure 2.3.3. Our object is to determine the income elasticity of demand at any point on an Engel curve. As indicated in the definition above, income elasticity (η_m) is given by the formula

$$\eta_m = \frac{dx}{dM} \frac{M}{x}.$$ (2.3.1)

Suppose a consumer of good X is situated at point B on the Engel curve. The tangent at B is given by the straight line *EF*. By the definition and formula (2.3.1), income elasticity is the reciprocal of the slope of the tangent to the Engel curve multiplied by the reciprocal of the proportion of income spent on commodity X. The slope of the Engel curve at point B is *HB/EH*, so its reciprocal is *EH/HB*. The amount of X bought is *OH* and the income spent on X is *HB*. Thus its reciprocal is *HB/OH*. Therefore, the income elasticity at point B is

$$\eta_m = \frac{EH}{HB} \cdot \frac{HB}{OH} = \frac{EH}{OH} < 1.$$ (2.3.2)

It should thus be clear that if the tangent line to the Engel curve intersects the horizontal axis to the *right* of the origin, the income elas-

---

$$\eta_m = \frac{dx}{dM} \frac{M}{x}.$$ (2.7.1)

Set this expression equal to some constant b, obtaining

$$\frac{dx}{dM} \frac{M}{x} = b,$$ (2.7.2)

or

$$\frac{dx}{x} = b \frac{dM}{M}.$$ (2.7.3)

Integrating this first-order differential equation yields

$$\ln x = b \ln M + \ln c,$$ (2.7.4)

where c is an arbitrary constant and $\ln$ denotes logarithms to the base e. Thus from (2.7.4), the Engel curve is

$$x = cM^b,$$ (2.7.5)

whose slope is

$$\frac{dx}{dM} = cbM^{b-1},$$ (2.7.6)

and whose curvature is given by

$$\frac{d^2x}{dM^2} = cb(b-1)M^{b-2}.$$ (2.7.7)

In the special case of unitary income elasticity ($b = 1$), the Engel curve is a straight line emanating from the origin.

FIGURE 2.3.3

Engel Curves and Income Elasticity of Demand

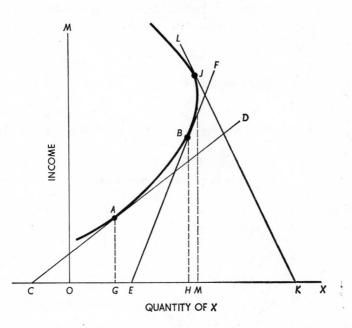

QUANTITY OF **X**

ticity of demand is less than unity. Similarly, if the tangent line intersects the horizontal axis to the *left* of the origin, the income elasticity of demand is greater than unity. Finally, consider point *J*. If the tangent to *J* intersects the horizontal axis to the right of *M,* the income elasticity is negative.

Definition: A good is said to be superior, normal, or inferior according as its income elasticity exceeds unity, is less than unity but positive, or negative. At a point on an Engel curve, a good is said to be superior, normal, or inferior according as the tangent to that point intersects the horizontal axis to the left of the origin, to the right of the origin but short of the corresponding point on the horizontal axis, or to the right of the origin *and* the corresponding point on the horizontal axis.

Exercise: Prove the conditions stated above for superior goods and inferior goods using the point *A* for a superior good and the point *J* for an inferior good.

2.4 CHANGES IN PRICE

The reaction of quantity purchased to changes in price is perhaps even more important than the reaction to changes in money income.

In this section we will assume that nominal money income and the nominal price of Y remain constant while the nominal price of X falls. We are thus able to analyze the effect of price upon quantity purchased without simultaneously considering the effect of changes in nominal money income.[8]

2.4.a The Price-Consumption Curve

In Figure 2.4.1 the relative price of X falls from the amount indicated by the slope of the original budget line *LM* to the amount indi-

FIGURE 2.4.1

The Price-Consumption Curve

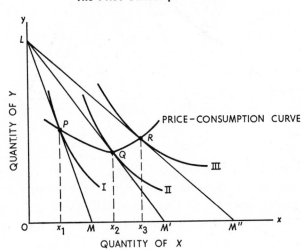

cated by the slope of *LM'* and then to the amount represented by the slope of *LM"*.

With the original budget line *LM*, the consumer reaches equilibrium at point *P* on indifference curve *I*. When the price of X falls, the budget line becomes *LM'* and the new equilibrium is attained at *Q* on indifference curve *II*. Finally, when the price falls again, the new equilibrium is point *R* on indifference curve *III* and budget line *LM"*. The line connecting these successive equilibrium points is called the price-consumption curve.

---

[8] The student should realize that if the nominal price of *y* and nominal money income remain constant while the nominal price of *x* declines, the real price of *y* increases, the real price of *x* decreases, and real money income increases. Our discussion refers almost exclusively to nominal prices and income.

Definition: The price-consumption curve is the locus of equilibrium budgets resulting from variations in the price ratio, nominal money income remaining constant. Nothing can be said a priori about the slope of the price-consumption curve.

2.4.b The Demand Curve

The individual consumer demand curve for a commodity can be derived from the price-consumption curve, just as an Engel curve is derivable from an income-consumption curve.

Definition: The demand curve for a specific commodity relates equilibrium quantities bought to the market price of the commodity, nominal money income and the nominal prices of other commodities held constant.

When the price of X is given by the slope of LM in Figure 2.4.1, Ox_1 units of X are purchased. This price-consumption pair constitutes one point on the graph in Figure 2.4.2. Similarly, when the price of X falls to the level indicated by the slope of LM', quantity purchased increases to Ox_2. This price-consumption pair is another point that can be plotted on Figure 2.4.2. Plotting all points so obtained and connecting them with a line generates the consumer demand curve, as shown in Figure 2.4.2. Its shape indicates an important principle, called the Law of Demand.

FIGURE 2.4.2

The Demand Curve

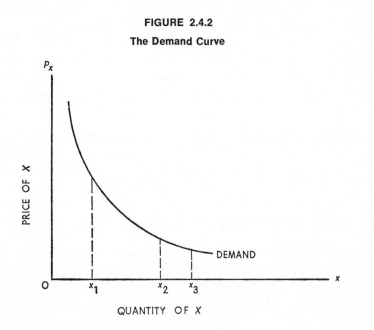

QUANTITY OF X

Principle: Quantity demanded varies inversely with price, nominal money income and nominal prices of other commodities remaining constant.

(In the next chapter a minor exception to this principle is discussed.)

2.4.c The Elasticity of Demand

The elasticity of demand is an important concept and one known to you already.

Definition: Elasticity of demand is the relative responsiveness of quantity demanded to changes in price. It may also be determined from the changes in price and in the money income spent upon a good.

At this point it may be helpful briefly to review the relation between price elasticity of demand and changes in the total expenditure upon the good in question. First, suppose the nominal price of good X declines by 1 percent. The demand for X is said to be price elastic, of unitary price elasticity, or price inelastic according as the quantity of X demanded expands by more than 1 percent, by exactly 1 percent, or by less than 1 percent.

Next, recall that the total expenditure upon a good is the product of price per unit and the number of units purchased. Given an initial price and quantity bought, a unique initial total expenditure is determined. Now let price fall by 1 percent. If demand is price elastic, quantity demanded expands by more than 1 percent. Thus total expenditure must expand when price falls and demand is price elastic. By the same argument, one finds (a) that total expenditure remains constant when price falls and demand has unitary price elasticity, and (b) that total expenditure declines when price falls and demand is price inelastic.

Exercise: Suppose the price of X increases rather than falls as in the explanation above. By an analogous argument, show that demand is price elastic, has unitary price elasticity, or is price inelastic according as total expenditure declines, remains constant, or increases.

2.4.d Elasticity of Demand and the Price-Consumption Curve

The elasticity of demand can be determined immediately from the slope of the price-consumption curve. Consider panel a, Figure 2.4.3. Let Y represent "all other goods," or what is frequently called "Hicks-Marshall" money. This is plotted on the vertical axis and labeled

FIGURE 2.4.3

Price-Consumption Curves and the Elasticity of Demand

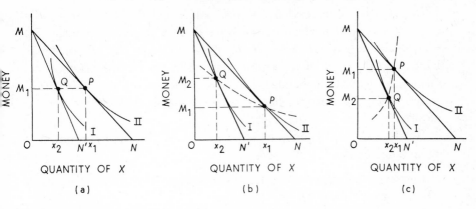

(a)   (b)   (c)

"money," whose price is unity. Thus money income is fixed at OM, and its price is fixed at one. The original budget line is MN, and its slope is the price of $X \left(\dfrac{p_x}{1} = p_x \right)$.[9]

The original equilibrium is at point P on the indifference curve II. At this point $Ox_1 = M_1P$ units of X and OM_1 units of "money" are bought. The slope of MN is (the negative of) $\dfrac{MM_1}{M_1P}$, so the price of X is $\dfrac{MM_1}{M_1P}$. The total amount spent on X is accordingly $M_1P \left(\dfrac{MM_1}{M_1P} \right) = MM_1$. When the price of X increases to the level given by the slope of MN', the quantity of X purchased drops to Ox_2, the amount of "money" bought remains constant at OM_1, and the amount spent on X remains unchanged. Price increases to $\dfrac{MM_1}{M_1Q}$, quantity purchased declines to M_1Q, and total expenditure on X is $M_1Q \left(\dfrac{MM_1}{M_1Q} \right) = MM_1$. The proportionate increase in the price of X is exactly offset by the proportionate decrease in the quantity of X bought. Consequently, demand has unitary elasticity over this range. And notice: the price-consumption curve

[9] In microeconomic theory, a *price level* is not determined. That chore is left to macroeconomic theory. Thus we can take the "price" of Hicks-Marshall money to be whatever we wish it to be. Setting its price at unity is both logical and helpful. The determinants of the price level are determined and explained in courses in macroeconomic theory and monetary theory. Here we concentrate exclusively upon relative prices.

is QP. Thus when the price-consumption curve is horizontal, price elasticity of demand for X is unitary.

In panel b, an increase in the price of X (from that given by the slope of MN to that given by the slope of MN') is accompanied by a decrease in expenditure on X from MM_1 to MM_2. The proportionate increase in the price of X is more than offset by the proportionate reduction in quantity demanded. Demand is therefore elastic. The price-consumption curve is $QP;$ hence when the price-consumption curve is negatively sloped, demand is elastic.

By the same reasoning, panel c illustrates the price-consumption curve when demand is inelastic.

Exercise: The student should prove this proposition for himself on the basis of panel c, Figure 2.4.3.

Thus we have the following

Relations: Demand has unitary price elasticity, is price elastic, or is price inelastic according as the price-consumption curve is horizontal, negatively sloped, or positively sloped. Thus the price-consumption curve in Figure 2.4.1 reflects commodity demand that is first (at higher prices) elastic, becomes unitary at a point, and is inelastic thereafter.

2.5 CONCLUSION

The basic principles of consumer behavior and of individual demand have now been developed. In the following chapter various important, but subsidiary, topics are analyzed using the tools introduced in Chapters 1 and 2. The fundamental conclusion of this chapter is explained more fully and one special exception is noted, but this conclusion remains as fundamental as ever: if individual consumers behave so as to maximize satisfaction from a limited money income, individual quantities demanded will vary inversely with price.[10]

---

[10] The discussion of one important characteristic of consumer demand functions must be relegated to a footnote because the explanation is necessarily mathematical. The features are first summarized for the reader who is not trained in mathematics.

Relations: (i) Quantity demanded is invariant under proportional changes in all prices *and* income; *(ii)* the sum of all price cross-elasticities of demand and of income elasticity equals the direct price elasticity of demand.

In its most general form, consumer demand may be written as a function of all prices and money income. Without loss of generality, we may consider commodity 1 in an n-commodity world; its demand function may thus be written

$$q_1 = f(p_1, p_2, \ldots, p_n, M) . \qquad (2.10.1)$$

QUESTIONS

1. One of the basic assumptions underlying the theory of consumer be-
    havior states that increases in utility tend to diminish as the consump-
    tion of a good increases. (*a*) If you think this is true, show what role
    the assumption plays in the development of the theory and in its con-
    clusions. (*b*) If you think it is false, demonstrate that the main results
    of the theory of consumer behavior can be obtained anyway.

2. Both the marginal utility approach and the indifference curve approach
    yield the same equilibrium position for a rational consumer. Compare

---

To eliminate the possibility of a "money illusion" or "money veil," one requires that
quantity demanded be invariant under proportional changes in all prices and money
income. Thus, for example, a doubling or a halving of all prices and income does
not affect quantity demanded.

Let the factor of proportional change be λ. Mathematically, our invariance
property requires that

$$f(p_1, p_2, \ldots, p_n, M) = f(\lambda p_1, \lambda p_2, \ldots, \lambda p_n, \lambda M) = \lambda^0 q_1 = q_1 . \quad (2.10.2)$$

By mathematical definition, a function satisfying (2.10.2) is homogeneous of degree zero. Therefore, demand functions are homogeneous of degree zero in all prices
and money income.

By Euler's theorem, homogeneity of degree zero implies that

$$\sum_{i=1}^{n} \frac{\partial q_1}{\partial p_i} p_i + \frac{\partial q_1}{\partial M} M \equiv 0 . \quad (2.10.3)$$

We can, without affecting the identity in (2.10.3), divide each term by q_1, obtaining

$$\sum_{i=1}^{n} \frac{\partial q_1}{\partial p_i} \frac{p_i}{q_1} + \frac{\partial q_1}{\partial M} \frac{M}{q_1} = 0 . \quad (2.10.4)$$

Now introduce the following conventional definitions:

$$-\eta_{11} = \frac{\partial q_1}{\partial p_1} \frac{p_1}{q_1} = \text{direct price elasticity,}$$

$$\eta_{1i} = \frac{\partial q_1}{\partial p_i} \frac{p_i}{q_1} \quad \text{for} \quad i \neq 1 = \text{price cross-elasticity,} \quad (2.10.5)$$

$$\eta_{1M} = \frac{\partial q_1}{\partial M} \frac{M}{q_1} = \text{income elasticity.}$$

Substituting (2.10.5) in (2.10.4) yields

$$\sum_{i=2}^{n} \eta_{1i} + \eta_{1M} = \eta_{11} . \quad (2.10.6)$$

Thus the direct price elasticity of demand is equal to the sum of all price cross-
elasticities and of income elasticity.

these explanations of equilibrium and discuss the relative advantage of the two approaches.

3. Comment on the following pair of statements: (*a*) consumer preferences are measured by relative prices; (*b*) consumer preferences are independent of relative prices.

4. A certain college student who is cramming for final exams has only six hours study time remaining. His goal is to get as high an *average* grade as possible in three subjects: economics, mathematics, and statistics. He must decide how to allocate his time among the subjects. According to the best estimates he can make, his grade in each subject will depend upon the time allocated to it according to the following schedule:

Economics		Mathematics		Statistics	
Hours of Study	Grade	Hours of Study	Grade	Hours of Study	Grade
0	20	0	40	0	80
1	45	1	52	1	90
2	65	2	62	2	95
3	75	3	71	3	97
4	83	4	78	4	98
5	90	5	83	5	99
6	92	6	86	6	99

How should the student allocate his time? How did you get the answer?

5. Consider a consumer in a two-commodity world whose indifference map is such that the slope of the indifference curves is everywhere equal to $-\left(\dfrac{y}{x}\right)$, where y is the quantity of good Y (measured along the vertical axis) and x is the quantity of good X (measured along the horizontal axis).

   a) Show that the demand for X is independent of the price of Y and that the price elasticity of demand for X is unitary. (Hint: Setting the marginal rate of substitution equal to the price ratio gives $\left(\dfrac{p_x}{p_y}\right) = \left(\dfrac{y}{x}\right)$, or $xp_x = yp_y$. Since $xp_x + yp_y = M$, where M is the given constant money income, one has $xp_x = (\frac{1}{2})\ M$. Thus the demand function is $x = \left(\dfrac{1}{2\,p_x}\right)M$. Go on from here).

   b) Explain precisely the meaning of the term "marginal rate of substitution." What is the value of the equilibrium *MRS* for this consumer, given that the price of X is \$1, the price of Y is \$3, and the consumer's income is \$120?

SUGGESTED READINGS

Henderson, James M., and Quandt, Richard E. *Microeconomic Theory: A Mathematical Approach,* pp. 12–24. New York: McGraw-Hill Book Co., Inc., 1958. [Elementary math necessary.]

Hicks, John R. *Value and Capital,* pp. 26–30. 2d ed. Oxford: Oxford University Press, 1946.

Samuelson, Paul A. *Foundations of Economic Analysis,* pp. 96–100. Cambridge, Mass.: Harvard University Press, 1947. [Advanced math necessary.]

Chapter 3

TOPICS IN CONSUMER DEMAND

3.1 INTRODUCTION

The theory of consumer behavior was developed in Chapter 2, and it was shown that an individual consumer demand curve normally slopes downward to the right—that quantity demanded varies inversely with price. This chapter presents a closer analysis of consumer demand and of market demand for related commodities.

3.2 SUBSTITUTION AND INCOME EFFECTS

A change in the nominal price of a commodity actually exerts two influences on quantity demanded. In the first place, there is a change in *relative* price—a change in the terms at which a consumer *can* exchange one good for another. The change in relative price alone leads to a *substitution effect*. Second, a change in the nominal price of a good (nominal income remaining constant) causes a change in *real* income, or in the size of the bundle of goods and services a consumer can buy. If the nominal price of one good falls, all other nominal prices remaining constant, the consumer's real income rises because he can now buy more, either of the good whose price declined or of other goods. In other words, his level of satisfaction must increase. The change in the level of real income may or may not—depending upon the consumer's preference map—cause a significant change in his pattern of consumption. In any event, the change in real income leads to an *income effect* upon quantity demanded.

3.2.a The Substitution Effect in the Case of a Normal or Superior Good

When the price of one good changes, the prices of other goods and money income remaining constant, the consumer moves from one equilibrium point to another. In normal circumstances, if the price of a good diminishes, more of it is bought; if its price increases, fewer units are taken. The overall change in quantity demanded from one equilibrium position to another is referred to as the *total effect.*

Definition: The total effect of a price change is the total change in quantity demanded as the consumer moves from one equilibrium to another.

The total effect of a price change is illustrated in Figure 3.2.1. The original price ratio is indicated by the slope of the budget line LM. The

FIGURE 3.2.1

Substitution and Income Effects for a Normal or Superior Good in Case of a Price Rise

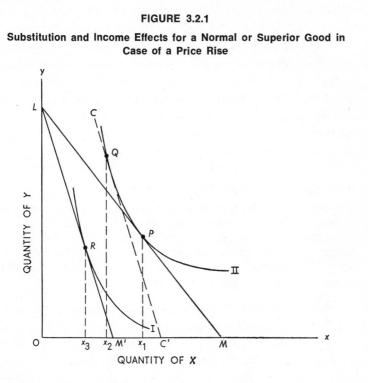

consumer attains equilibrium at point P on indifference curve II, purchasing Ox_1 units of X. When the price of X rises, as indicated by shifting the budget line from LM to LM', the consumer moves to a new equilibrium position at R on indifference curve I. At this point he purchases Ox_3 units of X. The total effect of the price change is indicated by the movement from P to R, or by the reduction in quantity demanded from Ox_1 to Ox_3. In other words, the total effect is $Ox_1 - Ox_3 = x_1x_3$. This is called a negative total effect because quantity demanded is reduced by x_1x_3 units.

The total effect of a price change, however, can be decomposed into two effects, the *substitution effect* and the *income effect*. Let us first examine the substitution effect. Consider Figure 3.2.1. When the price of X increases, the consumer suffers a decline in real income, as indicated by the movement from indifference curve *II* to indifference curve *I*. Suppose that coincident with the price rise the consumer were given an amount of (additional) money income just sufficient to compensate him for the loss in real income he would otherwise sustain. That is, he is given a compensatory payment just sufficient to enable him to remain on indifference curve *II* under the *new* price regime.

Graphically, this compensation is shown by constructing a fictitious budget line tangent to the *original* indifference curve, but whose slope corresponds to the *new* price ratio. The dashed line CC' in Figure 3.2.1 is the fictitious budget line for this example—it is tangent to the original indifference curve *II* at point Q; but it is parallel to the new budget line LM', thereby reflecting the new price ratio.

The substitution effect is represented by the movement from the original equilibrium position at P to the imaginary equilibrium position at Q, both points being situated on the original indifference curve. In terms of quantity, the substitution effect is the reduction in quantity demanded from Ox_1 to Ox_2, or by x_1x_2 units.

Definition: The substitution effect is the change in quantity demanded resulting from a change in relative price after compensating the consumer for his change in real income. In other words, the substitution effect is the change in quantity demanded resulting from a change in price when the change is restricted to a movement along the original indifference curve, thus holding real income constant.

The substitution effect in the case of a price decline is illustrated in Figure 3.2.2. The original equilibrium is point P on indifference curve *I*, the price ratio being indicated by the original budget line LM. The price of X now declines to that indicated by the slope of LM'. In the absence of a compensatory payment, the consumer would enjoy an increase in real income, moving to equilibrium on indifference curve *II*. In this case, we compensate by imagining a decrease in money income by an amount just sufficient to maintain real income constant at the new price ratio. Graphically, this is illustrated by the dashed line CC'.

As a result of the price change alone, real income held constant, the consumer moves from the original equilibrium at P to the imaginary equilibrium at Q. The movement from P to Q along the original indifference curve represents the substitution effect. In quantity units, it is the expansion of quantity demanded from Ox_1 to Ox_2.

Comparing the cases in Figures 3.2.1 and 3.2.2, one readily sees that the substitution effect is *always negative*—an increase in the price of X, real income constant, leads to a substitution of Y for X, while a fall in the price of X under the same circumstances induces a substitution of X for Y. Expressed somewhat differently, quantity demanded

FIGURE 3.2.2

Substitution and Income Effects for a Normal or Superior Good in Case of a Price Decrease

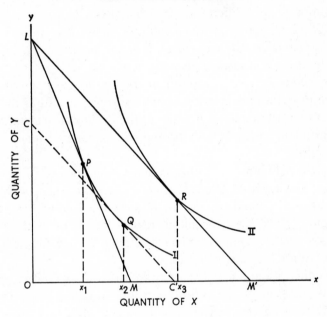

always varies inversely with price for movements along an indifference curve.

3.2.b The Income Effect in the Case of a Normal Good

In determining the substitution effect, one is constrained to movements along the original indifference curve. However, the total effect of a price change, money income and the prices of other commodities held constant, always entails a shift from one indifference curve to another, or a change in real income.

Definition: The income effect of a change in the price of one commodity is the change in quantity demanded resulting exclusively from a change in real income, all other prices and nominal money income held constant.

Consider Figure 3.2.1. When the price of X rises, as indicated by the shift of the budget line from LM to LM', the consumer attains his new equilibrium on indifference curve I. The movement from P to Q along indifference curve II represents the substitution effect. Now let the consumer's real income fall from the level represented by the fictitious budget line CC'. The movement from the imaginary equilibrium position Q on indifference curve II to the actual new equilibrium position R on indifference curve I indicates the income effect. Since CC' and LM' are parallel, the movement does not involve a change in relative prices. It is a real income phenomenon.

Real income declines as a result of the rise in the price of X. The reduction in quantity demanded from Ox_2 to Ox_3 measures the change in purchases attributable exclusively to the decline in real income, the change in relative price already having been accounted for by the substitution effect.

Similarly, in Figure 3.2.2, the decline in the price of X leads to an increase in real income. The substitution effect accounts for the movement from P to Q, and the income effect is represented by the movement from Q to R. Real income increases as a result of the price decrease, and quantity demanded increases from Ox_2 to Ox_3, *exclusively* as a result of the increase in real income.

From either graph one may readily see that the total effect of a price change is the sum of the substitution and income effects. In Figure 3.2.1, the total effect of the rise in the price of X is a reduction in quantity demanded from Ox_1 to Ox_3. The movement from Ox_1 to Ox_2 is attributable to the substitution effect and the movement from Ox_2 to Ox_3 is the income effect. The same reasoning applies, *mutatis mutandis,* for the total effect shown in Figure 3.2.2.

3.2.c Normal or Superior Goods

As indicated by the subheadings above, our analysis has so far been restricted to the case of "normal" or "superior" goods, but a "normal" or "superior" good has not yet been defined except in terms of income elasticity of demand. We now have the tools necessary for a more refined definition.

Note from Figure 3.2.1 that when the price of a commodity rises, real income declines and the income effect causes a decrease in quantity demanded. On the other hand, a price decline (Figure 3.2.2) leads to an increase in real income and to an increase in quantity purchased attributable to the income effect. In both these cases, the income effect is *positive:* an increase in real income leads to an increase in quantity demanded and vice versa.

Definition: A normal or superior good is one for which the income effect is positive.

Principle: A positive income effect reinforces the negative substitution effect. Thus for a normal or superior good, quantity demanded always varies inversely with price. The law of demand applies to all normal or superior goods.

The result of this section may be summarized as follows.[1]

---

[1] Mathematically, the substitution and income effects can be explained succinctly. Consider a consumer who may select the quantities $x_1, x_2, \ldots, x_n$ of n goods at fixed prices $p_1, p_2, \ldots, p_n$. Let his money income be

$$M = \sum_{j=1}^{n} p_j x_j , \qquad (3.1.1)$$

and let

$$u = u(x_1, x_2, \ldots, x_n) \qquad (3.1.2)$$

be an ordinal index of preference for this consumer.

Maximizing (3.1.2) subject to the linear constraint (3.1.1) yields the n equations

$$u_i = \lambda p_i \qquad (i = 1, 2, \ldots, n) , \qquad (3.1.3)$$

where $u_i = \partial u / \partial x_i$ and λ is the Lagrangean multiplier. Equations (3.1.3) and (3.1.1) together provide $n + 1$ equations to solve for the $n + 1$ unknowns $x_1, x_2, \ldots x_n$, and λ.

For the stability of equilibrium it is necessary and sufficient that the elements of

$$[U] = \begin{bmatrix} 0 & u_i \\ \hline u_j & u_{ij} \end{bmatrix} \qquad (i, j = 1, 2, \ldots, n) \qquad (3.1.4)$$

be associated with a quadratic form that is negative definite under constraint. This, in turn, requires the successive bordered principal minors to alternate in sign.

The effect of a change in money income upon quantities demanded may be determined by taking the partial derivatives of (3.1.3) and (3.1.1) with respect to M (holding all prices constant) and solving the resulting system of equations by Cramer's rule. A typical solution term is

$$\frac{\partial x_i}{\partial M} = \frac{\lambda U_i}{U} \qquad (i = 1, 2, \ldots, n) , \qquad (3.1.5)$$

where U_i is the cofactor of u_i in $[U]$ and U is the determinant of $[U]$.

The effect of a price change on quantities demanded is found by taking the partial derivatives with respect to p_i and solving by Cramer's rule. A typical term is

Relations: The total effect of a price change may be decomposed into a substitution effect and an income effect. The substitution effect is the change in quantity demanded attributable exclusively to a change in the price ratio. The substitution effect is always negative. The income effect is the change in quantity demanded attributable exclusively to a change in real income. For normal or superior goods, the income effect is positive. A positive income effect reinforces the negative substitution effect. Thus for normal or superior goods, the demand curve always slopes downward to the right.

3.3 INFERIOR GOODS

"Normal" or "superior" goods are given this name because in almost all cases the income effect is positive—this is the "normal" situation. In certain unusual cases, however, the income effect may cause a switch from margarine to butter, from dried to fresh vegetables. Thus an increase in real income may result in a decrease in the consumption of certain commodities. These commodities are called inferior goods.

Definition: An inferior good is one for which the income effect is negative.

$$\frac{\partial x_i}{\partial p_i} = \frac{-\lambda x_i U_i + \lambda U_{ii}}{U} \quad (i = 1, 2, \ldots, n), \tag{3.1.6}$$

where U_{ii} is the cofactor of u_{ii} in $[U]$. Substituting (3.1.5) into (3.1.6), one obtains what is sometimes called the fundamental equation of value theory:

$$\frac{\partial x_i}{\partial p_i} = -x_i \frac{\partial x_i}{\partial M} + \frac{\lambda U_{ii}}{U}. \tag{3.1.7}$$

(Total effect) = (Income effect) + (Substitution effect).

For normal or superior goods, $\partial x_i/\partial M > 0$. Further, since the successive bordered principal minors of $[U]$ must alternate in sign, $U_{ii}/U < 0$. Hence

$$\frac{\partial x_i}{\partial p_i} = -x_i \frac{\partial x_i}{\partial M} + \frac{\lambda U_{ii}}{U} < 0 \tag{3.1.8}$$

necessarily for normal or superior goods. The total effect, $\dfrac{\partial x_i}{\partial p_i}$ can only be positive when $\dfrac{\partial x_i}{\partial M} < 0$ and

$$\left| x_i \frac{\partial x_i}{\partial M} \right| > \left| \frac{\lambda U_{ii}}{U} \right|. \tag{3.1.9}$$

If condition (3.1.9) holds, one obtains the case of Giffen's Paradox, discussed in section 3.3.

3.3.a Inferior Goods and Giffen's Paradox

An increase in real income may be attributable to an increase in money income, commodity prices remaining constant, or to a decline in prices, money income remaining constant. Figure 3.3.1 shows an increase in income from the level given by the budget line *LM* to that given by *L'M'*. The two budget lines are parallel, so no change in rela-

FIGURE 3.3.1

Illustration of an Inferior Good

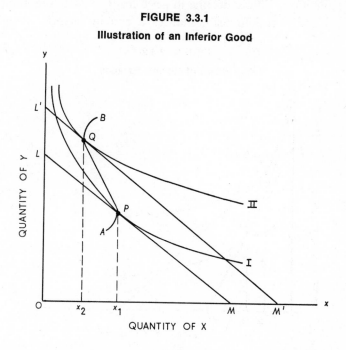

tive price has occurred. Real income increases from *LM* to *L'M'* either by an increase in money income, prices constant, or by uniform percentage reduction in both prices.

In the change, the position of consumer equilibrium shifts from point *P* on indifference curve *I* to point *Q* on indifference curve *II*. As a result of the *increase* in real income at the constant *relative* prices, the quantity demanded of good X falls from Ox_1 to Ox_2. The income-consumption curve, over this range of real income values, rises backward from *P* to *Q;* and the entire income-consumption curve might resemble the curve *APQB*.

Figure 3.3.1 illustrates an indifference map involving one inferior good (X). The income effect is negative, a rise in real income at a constant price ratio leading to a decline in quantity demanded. Similarly, if $L'M'$ is regarded as the original income level, LM represents a lower real income. In this case, a decline in real income would be accompanied by an increase in the quantity of X demanded.

Generally, the negative substitution effect of a price change is great enough to offset a negative income effect. But in one case, called Giffen's Paradox, the income effect is so strong that it more than offsets the substitution effect. Thus a decline in price leads to a decline in quantity demanded and a rise in price induces a rise in quantity demanded.

FIGURE 3.3.2

Illustration of Giffen's Paradox

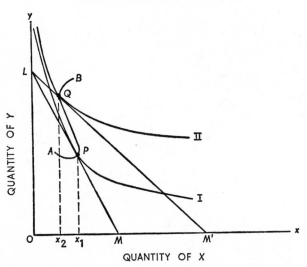

Figure 3.3.2 is an illustration of Giffen's Paradox. The original price of X is given by the slope of LM. With given money income and a constant price of Y, the price of X falls to the level indicated by the slope of LM'. The position of consumer equilibrium shifts from point P on indifference curve I to point Q on indifference curve II. Over this range, the price-consumption curve is PQ, and throughout the entire range it might look like the curve $APQB$. In the case of Giffen's Paradox, the price-consumption curve is *backward rising* over a certain range.

Definition: Giffen's Paradox refers to a good whose quantity demanded varies directly with price. A good must be an inferior good to belong in this category; but not all inferior goods conform to the conditions of Giffen's Paradox. The class of goods for which Giffen's Paradox holds constitutes the only exception to the law of demand.

3.3.b   Income and Substitution Effects for an Inferior Good

The relations described in subsection 3.3.a are shown more clearly by separating the total effect into its component parts. Figure 3.3.3 is an illustration of the income and substitution effects for an inferior good not subject to the conditions of Giffen's Paradox.

FIGURE 3.3.3

**Income and Substitution Effects for an Inferior Good Not
Subject to Giffen's Paradox**

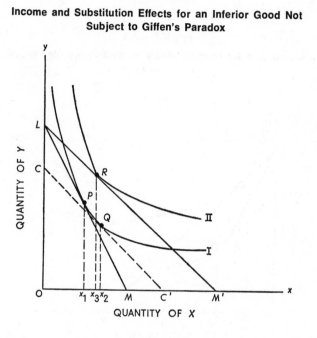

In Figure 3.3.3, *LM* is the original budget line. The price of *X* falls so that the budget line is shifted to *LM'*. Equilibrium shifts from point *P* on indifference curve *I* to point *R* on indifference curve *II*. In the process, the quantity of *X* demanded *increases* from Ox_1 to Ox_3. This case, even though it involves an inferior good, does not violate the law of demand—the negative substitution effect more than counterbalances the negative income effect.

To see this, construct the fictitious budget line *CC'* showing the old level of real income and the new price ratio. The movement from *P* to *Q*—or the increase in quantity demanded from Ox_1 to Ox_2—is the substitution effect. It is strongly negative, for the decrease in price results in a significant increase in quantity demanded, real income held constant. The income effect is also negative in this case, as is shown by the movement from Q to R or by the decrease in quantity demanded from Ox_2 to Ox_3.

Here we have a case in which the negative substitution effect is partially offset by a negative income effect. But the negative income effect is not strong enough to cause quantity demanded to vary directly with price. The law of demand holds, but demand is very inelastic over this range (as indicated by the steep upward slope of the price-consumption curve from P to R).

FIGURE 3.3.4

Income and Substitution Effects for Giffen's Paradox When Price Declines

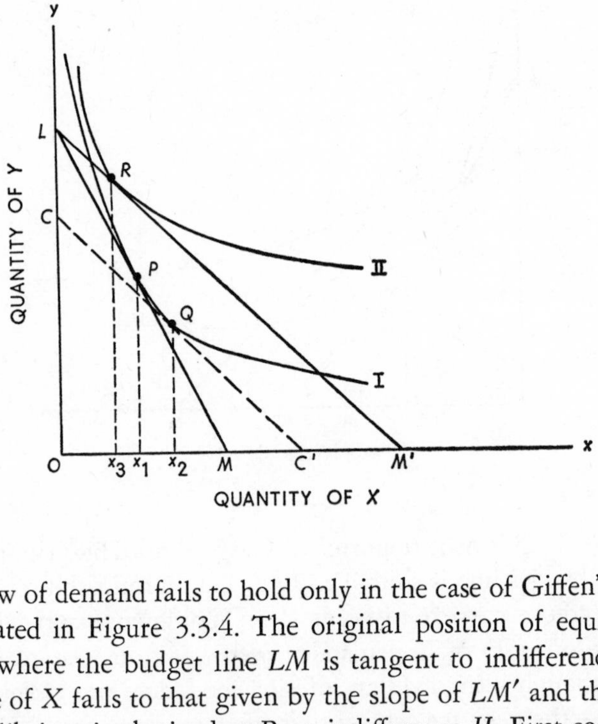

The law of demand fails to hold only in the case of Giffen's Paradox, as illustrated in Figure 3.3.4. The original position of equilibrium is point P, where the budget line LM is tangent to indifference curve I. The price of X falls to that given by the slope of LM' and the ultimate new equilibrium is obtained at R on indifference II. First construct the fictitious budget line CC' showing the old level of real income and the new price ratio. The substitution effect is represented by the movement from P to Q along indifference curve I, or by the *increase* in quantity demanded from Ox_1 to Ox_2.

The income effect is represented by the movement from Q on I to R on II, or by the decrease in quantity demanded from Ox_2 to Ox_3. Adding the negative substitution and income effects together, the total effect of the price decline is the *decrease* in quantity demanded from Ox_1 to Ox_3. For a commodity such as this, the law of demand is not valid.[2]

3.3.c The Nature of Inferior Goods

Whether a commodity is an inferior good or not has nothing to do with the total effect of a price change. It is strictly an income phenomenon. Giffen's Paradox, on the other hand, relates only to certain inferior goods that violate the law of demand.

As an example, oleomargarine may be an inferior good, but it certainly does not belong to the Giffen's Paradox category. As we have definitely seen in the past, a reduction in the price of oleomargarine leads to a substitution of margarine for butter. However, an increase in the real income of a family may cause that consumption unit to switch from margarine to butter. But in this case the income effect is not great enough to offset the substitution effect.

In all probability there are very few households in the United States or other advanced nations for which Giffen's Paradox obtains. A negative income effect is not all that is required for this case—the good must also be very important in the entire family budget. The classic example is potatoes in 19-century Ireland. The typical Irish peasant was so poor, it was said, that he spent almost all his cash income for the least expensive means of subsistence, potatoes.

Now suppose the price of potatoes falls. The same number of calories can now be bought for less expenditure on potatoes, so some money is available for green vegetables and perhaps meat. But these items also contain calories, so the consumption of potatoes can actually be reduced. Thus Giffen's Paradox is obtained—a reduction in price leads to a reduction in quantity demanded.

Giffen's Paradox is a bona fide exception to the law of demand. However, in the type of society with which we are presently concerned,

---

[2] In this text, and in almost all other usages, demand and the law of demand are defined in terms of constant nominal money income. Thus real income changes as one moves along a demand curve; Giffen's Paradox can occur; and the law of demand is not universally valid. For certain uses, however, it is convenient to construct a demand curve based on constant real income (and, therefore, varying nominal money income). Such demand curves are called income-compensated demand curves. The "income effect" is, in effect, subtracted, leaving only the substitution effect. Such demand curves always slope downward to the right, irrespective of the type of good. For a thorough discussion of income-compensated demand curves, see Milton Friedman, "The Marshallian Demand Curve," *Journal of Political Economy,* Vol. LVII (1949), pp. 463–95.

Giffen's Paradox is a rare phenomenon. It occurs in few consumer units and, within these units, for very few commodities. Thus when all individual demand curves are aggregated to obtain market demand curves, it is safe to assume that market quantity demanded varies inversely with price for every commodity.

3.4 SUBSTITUTION AND COMPLEMENTARITY

When an individual's demand schedule is constructed, his preference pattern, his nominal money income, and the nominal prices of related commodities are held constant. Thus a demand schedule shows the relation between the nominal price of a commodity and the quantity of it demanded, all other demand influences held constant (or impounded in a *ceteris paribus* assumption). This partial equilibrium demand function is quite useful for some purposes, but much less useful for others. In some situations a general equilibrium view of the problem is required. So far as demand analysis is concerned, this means that one or more of the *ceteris paribus* assumptions must be relaxed.

More particularly, if the nominal prices of related commodities are allowed to vary, there will be definite repercussions on the quantity demanded of the commodity in question. By observing these repercussions, one is able to classify pairs of commodities as substitute or complementary goods. Historically, the first method of classification was based upon the *total effect* upon quantity demanded of good X resulting from a change in the price of good Y. After the appearance of Hicks' *Value and Capital* it was realized that a more accurate classification can be obtained by analyzing the *substitution effect* alone. But while the latter method is more accurate, it is also more difficult to utilize on an empirical level. Thus in actual problems the older and less precise method must usually be used. For that reason both classificatory schemes are presented in this section.

3.4.a Classification by Cross-Elasticities

If all prices are allowed to vary, the quantity of good X demanded depends not only upon its own price but upon the prices of related goods as well. Instead of a demand *curve* there is a demand *surface* such as shown in Figures 3.4.1 and 3.4.2.

For illustrative purposes suppose good X is related to only one other commodity, good Y. Schematically, the demand function can no longer be written as $q = h(p)$. Instead, one must write $q_x = f(p_x, p_y)$, where

q and p represent quantity and price and the subscripts indicate the commodity in question.

The price elasticity of demand, or "own" elasticity, is

$$\eta_{xx} = -\left(\frac{\Delta q_x}{q_x} \div \frac{\Delta p_x}{p_x}\right),$$

where Δ means "the change in." The direct price elasticity, in other words, is the proportional change in quantity demanded of good X resulting from a given proportional change in the price of good X. The elasticity formula is applicable whether the demand function has the form shown in the first or second equation. When the price of a related good enters the demand function, however, it is possible to define the price cross-elasticity of demand:

$$\eta_{xy} = \frac{\Delta q_x}{q_x} \div \frac{\Delta p_y}{p_y}.$$

The price cross-elasticity of demand is the proportional change in the quantity of X demanded resulting from a given relative change in the price of the related good Y.

According to the cross-elasticity classification, goods X and Y are substitutes or complements according as the price cross-elasticity of demand is positive or negative. As trivial examples, consider the following. An increase in the price of pork, the price of beef remaining constant, will tend to augment the quantity of beef demanded; η_{xy} is positive and beef and pork are said to be substitute goods. On the other hand, an increase in the price of gin will tend to reduce the quantity of vermouth demanded (the price of vermouth remaining constant); in this case η_{xy} is negative and gin and vermouth are said to be complementary goods.

Linear demand surfaces for the two-good case are shown in Figures 3.4.1 and 3.4.2. In each graph, the quantity of X demanded is plotted on the vertical or "height" axis, while the prices of X and Y are plotted on the "width" and "length" axes. In each case, the plane $ABCD$ is the demand surface.

Figure 3.4.1 shows a linear demand surface in the case where goods X and Y are substitutes over the range of prices considered. First, notice that the law of demand holds: as the price of X increases, its quantity demanded falls. Thus if the price of Y is held fixed at Op_{y1}, an increase in the price of X from Op_{x1} to Op_{x2} causes a decline in quantity demanded from RR' to TT'. Now hold the price of X constant at Op_{x1}. As the price of Y increases from Op_{y1} to Op_{y2}, the quantity of X de-

FIGURE 3.4.1

Demand Surface for Good *X* When
X and *Y* Are Substitutes

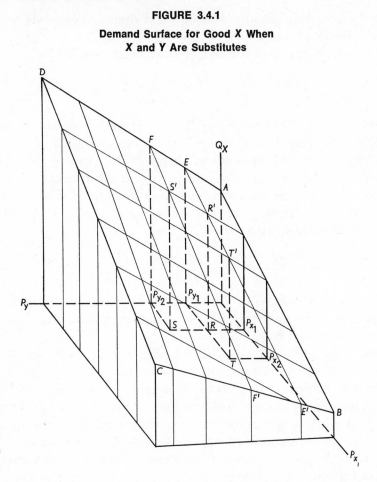

manded rises from *RR′* to *SS′*—an increase in the price of good *Y* causes an increase in the quantity of *X* demanded. To put it differently, an increase in the price of *Y* causes the demand curve in the $Q_x - P_x$ plane to *shift* from *EE′* to *FF′*. Thus the coefficient η_{xy} is positive, and the goods are said to be substitutes.

Figure 3.4.2 shows the opposite relation over the range of prices considered. Again, first note that the law of demand obtains. For a fixed price of *Y*, Op_{y1}, an increase in the price of *X* from Op_{x1} to Op_{x2} causes a reduction in quantity demanded from *RR′* to *TT′*. But now hold the price of *X* constant at Op_{x1}. An increase in the price of *Y* from Op_{y1} to Op_{y2} also causes a decline in the quantity of *X* demanded, from *RR′* to *SS′* in this case. Alternatively, one may say that the demand *curve* for *X* shifts from *EE′* to *FF′*. Accordingly, the coefficient of price

FIGURE 3.4.2

**Demand Surface for Good *X* When
X and *Y* Are Complementary**

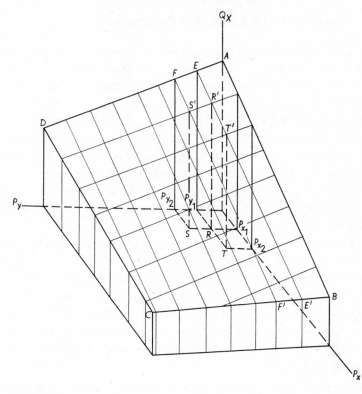

cross-elasticity is negative and the commodities are said to be complementary goods.

The cross-elasticity approach to commodity classification directs attention to the change in quantity demanded resulting from a change
in the price of a related good *without* compensating for the change in
the level of real income. The *total effect* of a price change is thus the
criterion used in this classification scheme. On an empirical level, this
is the only feasible method of commodity classification because market
demand functions can be computed while individual preference functions cannot (from readily available data).

Furthermore, in applied problems, one is usually interested in the
market relation among commodities rather than the commodity relation
as viewed by an individual consumer. Thus the cross-elasticity classification of commodity relations is the one most frequently encountered

in applied studies. Indeed, reference to market cross-elasticities has even appeared in Supreme Court antitrust decisions.

3.4.b Classification by Preference Functions

So far as one individual is concerned, however, commodities can be classified as substitute or complementary goods more accurately by reference to the preference function. For example, a very significant decrease in the price of beef might lead to an observed increase in the consumption of both beef and pork. The income effect of the price change, in this case, might more than offset the normally adverse substitution effect of an increase in the relative price of pork. The observed cross-elasticity would be negative, and one might be tempted to classify beef and pork as complementary goods. This temptation, however, should be resisted, for the result is attributable to an important change in real income.

As seen in section 3.2, when there are only two goods the substitution effect is always negative. In other words, if there were only two goods they would necessarily be substitute goods. Complementarity can enter only through third markets. Let there be three commodities, good X, good Y, and what is often called "Hicks-Marshall" money (the amount spent on all other goods taken together or the value sum of other expenditures). Hicks defines substitute and complementary relations in the following way:

Definitions: Y is a substitute for X if the marginal rate of substitution of Y for money is diminished when X is substituted for money in such a way as to leave the consumer no better off than before.

Y is complementary with X if the marginal rate of substitution of Y for money is increased when X is substituted for money in such a way as to leave the consumer no better off than before.

The qualifying phrase in this definition restricts one to movements along the same *indifference surface*—since the definition requires three goods, it is not possible to illustrate the relation by using two-dimensional indifference *curves*. Indifference surfaces illustrating substitute and complementary goods are shown in Figures 3.4.3 and 3.4.4 respectively.

First consider Figure 3.4.3. One indifference surface is ABC. The individual is indifferent among all combinations of X, Y, and (Hicks-Marshall) money represented by a point on the surface. For example, he is indifferent between OX_1 units of X, OY_1 units of Y, and RP units of money and the combination of OX_2 units of X, OY_1 units of Y, and SQ units of money. Let the consumer be situated at point P on the sur-

FIGURE 3.4.3

Indifference Surface When X and Y Are Substitute Goods

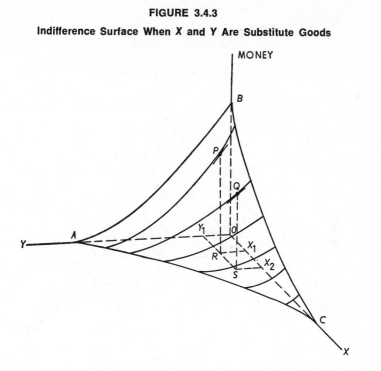

face. The slope of the tangent drawn at that point is the marginal rate of substitution of Y for money. Now let the consumer substitute X for money so as to remain on the surface—he increases his consumption of X from OX_1 to OX_2 and diminishes money from RP to SQ. The marginal rate of substitution of Y for money at point Q is given by the slope of the tangent drawn at that point. Since the slope at Q is less than the slope at P, commodities X and Y are substitute goods—when X is substituted for money so as to keep real income constant, the marginal rate of substitution of Y for money diminishes.

The meaning of Hicks' definition can be explained in two stages. The original equilibrium is at point P on the indifference surface ABC. Now let the price of X in terms of money fall (the price of money is unity), and let the consumer's real income be reduced so that he is restricted to the original indifference surface. The consumer substitutes X for money when its price falls, moving to a *temporary* equilibrium at point Q. But at point Q, the marginal rate of substitution of Y for money has decreased. The price of Y has not changed, so Q does not represent an ultimate equilibrium point because the marginal rate of substitution of Y for money does not equal the ratio of the price of Y to the price of money. To attain a final equilibrium, the consumer must curtail his con-

FIGURE 3.4.4

Indifference Surface When X and Y Are Complementary Goods

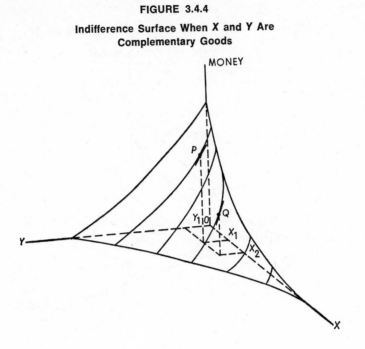

sumption of Y (substitute X or money for Y) until the marginal rate of substitution of Y for money rises to the level of the unchanged price ratio.

An entirely analogous explanation applies to Figure 3.4.4. When X is substituted for money, moving from point P to point Q, the marginal rate of substitution of Y for money increases. The two goods are complementary. Since the nominal price of Y has not changed (the Y-money price ratio is constant), and since the marginal rate of substitution of Y for money has increased, the consumer must increase his consumption of Y in order to attain a final equilibrium position. He must substitute Y for money until the marginal rate of substitution falls to the level of the unchanged price ratio.

Generalizing and simplifying somewhat, goods X and Y are substitutes if after compensating for the change in real income incident to a change in the nominal price of X, a decrease in the price of X leads to a decrease in the quantity of Y consumed. Similarly, the two goods are complementary if an income-compensated decrease in the price of X leads to an increase in the quantity of Y consumed.

Note: The student should be alerted to the fact that this definition is "unusual" in the "usual" context of economic theory. Most of our definitions refer to equilibrium positions. Hicks' definition of substitute and complementary goods refers to a disequilibrium situation. If full equilibrium adjustments were allowed, the marginal rates of substitution would equal the respective price ratios for all pairs of commodities. Hicks' definition is a *disequilibrium* definition in the sense that commodities cannot be classified as substitutes or complements if a consumer is in equilibrium. It is only when an instantaneous change moves the consumer out of equilibrium that we can classify commodities according to Hicks' definition.

Author's Note: It is for this reason that I still prefer the older, less rigorous, classification based on cross-elasticities. It has its shortcomings, but so does Hicks' definition as well.

3.5 SUBSTITUTION, COMPLEMENTARITY, AND THE EFFECTS OF A CHANGE IN RELATIVE PRICE

Using the definitions of substitution and complementarity introduced above, we can now summarize the entire market effects of a change in relative price. Let us do this from the standpoint of a single commodity X. Specifically, let the price of X fall, nominal money income and all other prices remaining constant.[3] This price change affects the demand for X and the demand for other commodities by means of an income effect and a substitution effect.

First consider the X market. The substitution effect must augment quantity demanded; the income effect will too unless X is an inferior good. But only in the case of Giffen's Paradox will quantity demanded vary directly with price.

Next consider the market for Hicks-Marshall money, or the expenditure on all other goods taken together. The substitution effect will always cause a decrease in demand (i.e., when all goods are divided into two groups, the groups must be substitutes). The income effect, prac-

---

[3] The object of a textbook, of course, is to illuminate, not confuse. Yet at the expense of some possible confusion, it might be well to pose a murky question: if the preference patterns and nominal incomes of all consumers are held constant, how can the price of *only one* good rise or fall? The change in price must come about through a change in commodity supply which, in its turn, must come about through a change in resource supplies. Now resources may be classified broadly as general resources—those used in the production of two or more goods—and commodity-specific resources—those used exclusively in the production of one good. Without arguing in detail, it is possible for only one price to change if, and only if, the commodity in question is produced exclusively by means of commodity-specific resources. Otherwise, a change in the supply of a resource used to produce X must ultimately have repercussions on the supply of some other good(s) and, accordingly, on its price(s). For more detailed discussion of this point, see Leland Yeager, *"Methodenstreit* over Demand Curves," *Journal of Political Economy,* Vol. LXVIII (1960), pp. 53–64.

tically speaking, will almost always increase demand. Thus the demand for all other goods taken together may either increase or decrease as the result of a decrease in the price of X.

The change in the demand for Hicks-Marshall money in fact depends upon the elasticity of the demand for X (see Figure 2.4.3). Recall that by assumption, money income and all prices other than X are constant. If the demand for X is inelastic, a decrease in the price of X will cause a proportionately smaller increase in the quantity of X purchased. A smaller amount is spent on X and, consequently, a greater amount is spent on Hicks-Marshall money. At constant prices, this implies that the demand for all other goods increases. The same type of analysis applies in the cases of unitary and elastic demand in the X market. Hence if the price of X falls, the demand for Hicks-Marshall money increases or decreases according as the demand for X is inelastic or elastic. On the other hand, if the price of X increases, the demand for Hicks-Marshall money decreases or increases according as the demand for X is inelastic or elastic.

Finally consider the market for a specific commodity Y. If the price of X falls, the substitution effect will cause a decrease in the demand for Y unless X and Y are complementary goods. The income effect on the other hand, will cause an increase in the demand for Y unless Y is an inferior good. The total change may go either way.

Four cases may be isolated: (*i*) If Y is strongly complementary with X, the substitution effect will likely be great enough to offset the income effect if Y is an inferior good. In this case, the demand for Y will almost surely increase. (*ii*) If X and Y are mildly complementary, the demand for Y will definitely increase if Y is a normal good. If Y is an inferior good, however, the income effect may dominate. If so, the demand for Y will decline. (*iii*) If X and Y are mildly substitutable, the income and substitution effects generally work in opposite directions. In this case nothing can be said conclusively. However, if Y is an inferior good, its demand will definitely decline. (*iv*) If X and Y are strong substitutes, the substitution effect will dominate. The demand for Y will decline, and it will decline all the more if Y is an inferior good.

Exercise: Do the entire analysis of this section under the assumption that the price of X rises.

3.6 APPLICATION OF INDIFFERENCE CURVE ANALYSIS: THE ECONOMIC THEORY OF INDEX NUMBERS

An interesting application of indifference curve analysis can be made in the field of index numbers. For simplicity, let us restrict our attention to a consumer who buys two commodities, X_1 and X_2, in two different time periods, 0 and 1. In time period 0 he buys x_1^0 units of X_1 at price p_1^0 and x_2^0 units of X_2 at price p_2^0. Similarly, in period 1 he purchases x_1^1 and x_2^1 units of X_1 and X_2 at prices p_1^1 and p_2^1 respectively. The essential problem of index numbers is as follows: has the individual's standard of living increased or decreased in period 1 as compared with period 0?

To make the comparison of standards of living at all meaningful, it is necessary to assume that the consumer's taste (preference map) does not change over the time period under consideration. Given this assumption, some information can be gained from indifference curve analysis.

An indifference map for a consumer is partially represented by curves *I, II,* and *III* in Figure 3.6.1. In the original period (called the *base* pe-

FIGURE 3.6.1

Theory of Index Numbers

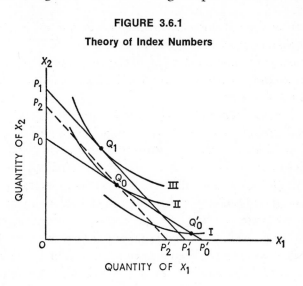

riod), the consumer's money income and the prices p_1^0 and p_2^0 give rise to the budget line P_0P_0'. The consumer comes to equilibrium at point Q_0 on *II*. In period 1 prices change so that the budget line becomes P_1P_1' (the price of X_2 falls relative to the price of X_1). The consumer attains a new equilibrium at point Q_1 on indifference curve *III*. If the indifference-curve map is actually known, one also immediately knows that the consumer has enjoyed a gain in real income because he has shifted to a higher indifference curve.

In the usual case, however, the indifference curves are not known. Rather than the full graph in Figure 3.6.1, one can usually observe only the price lines and the consumption points Q_0 and Q_1. Thus suppose that the curves *I, II,* and *III* are erased. Without specific knowledge of the indifference curves,[4] what can be said about the consumer's change in real income? In the absence of specific knowledge, we can proceed as follows.

3.6.a Information from the Budget Map

First, point Q_0 is preferred to any other point lying on or below the budget line P_0P_0' because all budgets in the space OP_0P_0' were attainable and Q_0 was the budget actually chosen. Similarly, Q_1 must be preferred to any combination lying on or below the budget line P_1P_1'.

Second, in this specific case we can say that the consumer definitely enjoyed an increase in his standard of living because Q_0 lies below the budget line P_1P_1'.

However, in general this kind of inference is not possible. For example, the consumer might have purchased the combination represented by Q_0' in period 0.[5] The budget Q_0' lies to the right of the budget line P_1P_1'; thus no inference would be possible. Some additional knowledge can be gained, nevertheless.

The total expenditure in period 1 was $p_1^1x_1^1 + p_2^1x_2^1$, while the total cost of goods in period 0 was $p_1^0x_1^0 + p_2^0x_2^0$. Now the budget Q_0 was purchased in period 0 at the prices ruling in that period, and the budget Q_1 was bought in period 1 at the period 1 prices. If Q_0 were actually preferred to Q_1 (remember that Q_1 was actually purchased in period 1), it must have been impossible for the individual to purchase the combination represented by Q_0 at the prices prevailing in period 1. In other words, if Q_0 were preferred to Q_1 and if Q_0 were attainable at period 1 prices, it would have been purchased instead of Q_1. Thus the total cost of budget Q_0 at period 1 prices, in this case, must have exceeded the cost of Q_1 at period 1 prices. That is, if Q_0 were preferred to Q_1, the following would have had to hold:

$$p_1^1x_1^0 + p_2^1x_2^0 > p_1^1x_1^1 + p_2^1x_2^1 .$$

Turning the argument to focus on time period 1 (the given year), Q_1 could only have been preferred to Q_0 if it had been possible to purchase the base-year quantities at the given-year prices (Q_1 was actually purchased, so the consumer *elected* not to purchase Q_0). In other words,

---

[4] Except for the knowledge that if the consumer does attain equilibrium, Q_0 and Q_1 each lie on *some* indifference curve.

[5] Knowing the indifference map, this would not be an equilibrium or optimal budget.

the cost of the Q_0 budget in period 1 prices must have been less than the cost of the Q_1 budget at the period 1 prices. Thus Q_1 could have been preferred to Q_0 if, and only if,

$$p_1^1 x_1^1 + p_2^1 x_2^1 > p_1^1 x_1^0 + p_2^1 x_2^0 .$$

Writing this expression as a sum and suppressing the subscripts, the individual can be better off in period 1 only if

$$\Sigma p^1 x^1 > \Sigma p^1 x^0 . \qquad (3.6.1)$$

By the same line of reasoning, Q_0 could have been preferred to Q_1 only if it had been possible to buy the given-year quantities at the base-year prices. That is, the consumer bought the budget Q_0 in period 0. If he could have bought the Q_1 budget at the base-period prices but did not do so, he must have preferred Q_0 to Q_1. Thus the individual can be better off in period 0 as compared with period 1 only if

$$\Sigma p^0 x^0 > \Sigma p^0 x^1 . \qquad (3.6.2)$$

These two inequalities can be shown graphically, although only the first [expression (3.6.1)] is shown here. The slope of the budget line $P_1 P_1'$ indicates the prices in period 1. The cost of the base-year quantities at the given-year prices is less than the actual expenditure in the given year if Q_0 lies on a line parallel to and beneath $P_1 P_1'$. Since in Figure 3.6.1, Q_0 lies on the line $P_2 P_2'$, which is parallel to $P_1 P_1'$ but closer to the origin, the inequality (3.6.1) is satisfied. As stated before, in this illustration Q_1 is clearly preferred to Q_0. In other cases, it is not so easy to determine.

3.6.b   Index Numbers as Indicators of Individual Welfare Changes

The analysis can be pushed somewhat further by introducing three index numbers. The first of these index numbers measures the change in the consumer's income from the base year to the given year. Since it is assumed that income equals expenditure, the incomes of the base year and the given year are $\Sigma p^0 x^0$ and $\Sigma p^1 x^1$ respectively. Consequently, the index of income change is

$$E = \frac{\Sigma p^1 x^1}{\Sigma p^0 x^0} . \qquad (3.6.3)$$

The next index number to be introduced is called the Laspeyre index. This index number measures the cost, relative to the base period, of purchasing the base-year quantities at the given-year prices. Since the cost of the base-year quantities at given-year prices is $\Sigma p^1 x^0$, the Laspeyre index is

$$L = \frac{\Sigma p^1 x^0}{\Sigma p^0 x^0}. \tag{3.6.4}$$

Finally, the Paasche index measures the cost of purchasing the given-year quantities at given-year prices relative to their cost at base-year prices. Since the cost of given-year quantities at base-year prices is $\Sigma p^0 x^1$, the Paasche index is

$$P = \frac{\Sigma p^1 x^1}{\Sigma p^0 x^1}. \tag{3.6.5}$$

Now from expression (3.6.1), the individual is better off in period 1 if $\Sigma p^1 x^1 > \Sigma p^1 x^0$. Dividing both sides of this inequality by $\Sigma p^0 x^0$, we have

$$\frac{\Sigma p^1 x^1}{\Sigma p^0 x^0} > \frac{\Sigma p^1 x^0}{\Sigma p^0 x^0}, \tag{3.6.6}$$

or

$$E > L. \tag{3.6.7}$$

Similarly, from expression (3.6.2), the individual is better off in the base period if $\Sigma p^0 x^0 > \Sigma p^0 x^1$. Dividing both sides of this inequality by $\Sigma p^1 x^1$, we have

$$\frac{\Sigma p^0 x^0}{\Sigma p^1 x^1} > \frac{\Sigma p^0 x^1}{\Sigma p^1 x^1}, \tag{3.6.8}$$

or

$$\frac{1}{E} > \frac{1}{P}, \tag{3.6.9}$$

or

$$E < P. \tag{3.6.10}$$

From this analysis, especially expressions (3.6.7) and (3.6.10), four cases are possible.

1. E is greater than either P or L. By expression (3.6.7), the individual's standard of living increases from period 0 to period 1. By (3.6.10) his standard of living does not fall. Hence the individual is definitely better off in period 1.

2. E is less than either P or L. By expression (3.6.10), the individual was better off in the base period. By (3.6.7) he was not better off in the

given period. An unequivocal answer is again obtained: the individual's standard of living falls from period 0 to period 1.

3. $L > E > P$. In this case neither expression (3.6.7) nor (3.6.10) is satisfied. $L > E$ implies that the consumer is not better off in period 1. But $E > P$ implies that he was not better off in period 0 either. Consequently, no conclusion can be drawn.

4. $P > E > L$. This situation, though possible, is totally inconsistent. By expression (3.6.10), $P > E$ implies that the individual was better off in the base period. But $E > L$ implies, by (3.6.7), that he was better off in period 1. The individual's standard of living has both risen and fallen! Such a contradiction may be attributable to a change in the individual's preference pattern. In any event, it precludes an inference concerning the change in the individual's welfare.

In summary, it is sometimes possible to determine whether an individual's standard of living has increased or decreased by means of index number comparisons. In other situations, however, the results are inconclusive or contradictory. Therefore, in these cases the theory of index numbers has nothing to contribute to the analysis of individual welfare changes.

3.7 APPLICATIONS OF INDIFFERENCE CURVE ANALYSIS: THE CHOICE BETWEEN LEISURE AND INCOME

The theory of consumer behavior as formulated above is quite general, and it leads to many interesting and important propositions concerning demand and consumer choice. However, it is useful to simplify the theory and to introduce *leisure* into the preference function. To that end, let us aggregate expenditures on all goods and services into the simple term *income*.[6] Since by our assumptions all income is spent on goods and services (which includes saving), this *income* is simply our familiar budget constraint.

At the same time, the amount of income received by a consumer depends upon the amount of time allocated to work. The more one works, the greater is his income. Yet the more one works, the less is the leisure time remaining to him. Leisure also has utility to most people; therefore, each consumer is confronted with a fundamental tradeoff between

---

[6] This is not the same as Hicks-Marshall money. It is our conventional budget equation,

$$M = \sum_{i=1}^{n} p_i x_i .$$

the consumption of goods and services and the consumption of leisure. The object of this section is to analyze this tradeoff in some very simple cases.

3.7.a The Income-Leisure Graph

Consider Figure 3.7.1. Income is plotted on the vertical axis, and leisure on the horizontal axis in the rightward direction. The unit of time

FIGURE 3.7.1

Income Constraint

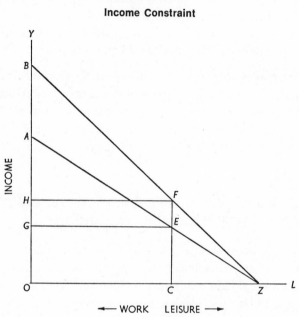

in which leisure is measured is not relevant—it may be hours per day, weeks per year, or any other measurement unit. The essential point is that the total amount of time is fixed (say, 24 hours per day); and the sum of work time and leisure time must equal this fixed total time. Thus work time may be measured in a leftward direction along the horizontal axis. In Figure 3.7.1, OZ is the total time available. If OC hours per day are taken as leisure, then CZ hours are spent at work.

Let us now make two simplifying assumptions. First, the individual may work as many hours per day as he desires.[7,8] Second, the income per

---

[7] Recall that the unit of measurement of time is irrelevant. For the sake of brevity, we speak of hours per day. Any other time measurement may be substituted.

[8] We shall later discuss the case in which work time is restricted, say, to eight hours per day or 50 weeks per year, etc.

hour is the same irrespective of the number of hours worked. Thus if the individual works CZ hours per day and receives income of $CE = OG$, his hourly wage is $\dfrac{CE}{CZ}$. But since CEZ and OZA are similar triangles, $\dfrac{CE}{CZ} = \dfrac{OA}{OZ}$. Thus the slope of the straight line ZA represents the hourly wage rate.[9]

Exercise: Suppose an individual works CZ hours per day and receives income CF. Show that the slope of ZB represents the hourly wage rate.

3.7.b Equilibrium between Income and Leisure

Since income (or consumption) and leisure are competitive sources of utility, the consumer's preference pattern between them may be represented by an indifference map such as that shown in Figure 3.7.2.[10]

FIGURE 3.7.2

Tradeoff between Income and Leisure

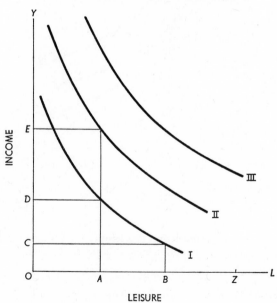

LEISURE

---

[9] ZA is a straight line because we have assumed that the hourly wage rate is constant.

[10] Note that this is exactly the same as saying that goods X and Y are alternative sources of utility and that there must be a tradeoff between them.

The indifference curves have all the properties of the usual indifference curves (see Chapter 1.3). Thus the consumer is indifferent between OA hours of leisure and income OD and OB hours of leisure and income OC. Of course, the higher the indifference curve, the greater is utility. For example, suppose that OA hours of leisure are taken. Then the consumer gains greater utility if his income is OE than if it is OD.

Let us now put Figures 3.7.1 and 3.7.2 together, as shown in Figure 3.7.3. In the customary manner, we may determine the point of utility maximization (consumer equilibrium).[11] The marginal rate of substitu-

FIGURE 3.7.3

Consumer-Worker Equilibrium

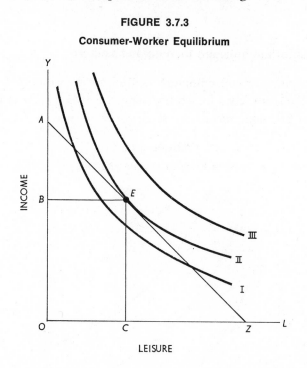

LEISURE

---

[11] Let Y, L, W, and T represent income, leisure, work time, and total available time respectively. From our assumption concerning time distribution, it follows that

$$T = W + L .$$ (3 11.1)

Utility is a function of income and leisure. Thus a typical utility function may be written as

$$u = u(Y, L) .$$ (3.11.2)

Since the more hours worked, the greater the income received, the income function is

$$Y = f(W) = f(T - L) .$$ (3.11.3)

tion is given by the (negative of the) slope of the indifference curve. The "price ratio" is given by the (negative of the) slope of ZA. Equilibrium is attained point E on II, with CZ hours of work and income OB. Indifference curve III cannot be attained at the given wage rate. Any curve lower than II will result in less utility since there is a possible tradeoff that will make the consumer-worker better off.

3.7.c Overtime Rates

It is now customary that union-management contracts require extra pay for "overtime" work. In the situation represented by Figure 3.7.4, "overtime" is any work in excess of CZ hours per day. Further assume that the "overtime" wage is half again as great as the "straight-time" wage. Thus the slope of ZA represents the regular wage and the slope of ZFB represents the straight-time and overtime wage (where CZ hours of work is straight time). Finally, assume that the worker can work overtime or not according to his choice.

It is clear from Figure 3.7.4 that the result of overtime pay for any individual is uncertain. A person with an indifference map represented by I will clearly choose to work overtime, while an individual with an indifference map represented by I'' will never voluntarily work overtime. An intermediate case is illustrated by the indifference curve I'.

Under our present assumptions, equation (3.11.3) is linearly homogeneous. Thus f_W is the constant wage rate and $-f_W$ is the price of leisure (the income foregone to receive more leisure).

Our problem is to maximize equation (3.11.2) subject to equation (3.11.3). Construct the Lagrange function

$$u(Y, L) - \lambda[Y - f(T - L)] , \qquad (3.11.4)$$

where λ is the Lagrange multiplier. The first-order conditions give

$$\frac{\partial u}{\partial Y} = u_Y - \lambda = 0 ,$$

$$\frac{\partial u}{\partial L} = u_L - \lambda f_L = u_L + \lambda f_W = 0 . \qquad (3.11.5)$$

Eliminating the Lagrange multiplier yields

$$\frac{u_Y}{u_L} = -\frac{1}{f_W} . \qquad (3.11.6)$$

Equation (3.11.6) provides the usual, and expected, interpretation. The marginal rate of substitution between leisure and income must equal the price of leisure in terms of income. In light of equation (3.11.1), the price of leisure must be the negative of the hourly wage rate. From our assumption of linear homogeneity [equation (3.11.3)], f_W is the wage rate.

FIGURE 3.7.4

Overtime Rates

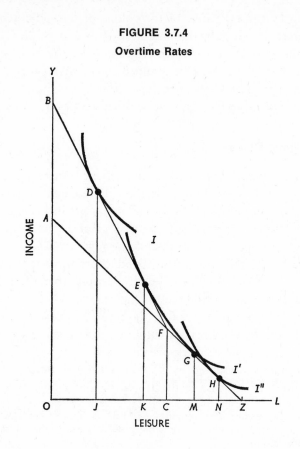

Such an individual is indifferent between working *KZ* hours for *KE* income or working *MZ* hours for *MG* income.

In the absence of auxiliary side agreements between union or individual worker and management, it is impossible to predict the effect of overtime wages.

3.7.d Effect of Work Restrictions

Let us now ignore the possibilities of overtime work but recognize a predominate characteristic of employment; namely, a worker cannot choose the number of hours per day that he works. Assume that except for illness or injury, he must work eight hours per day or not work at all. One representation of this example is illustrated in Figure 3.7.5.

As above, assume that the worker must take 16 hours of leisure and work $24 - 16 = 8$ hours per day. Further assume that the individual has attained an equilibrium at point *C* on indifference curve *I*, where the

FIGURE 3.7.5

Effect of Work Restrictions

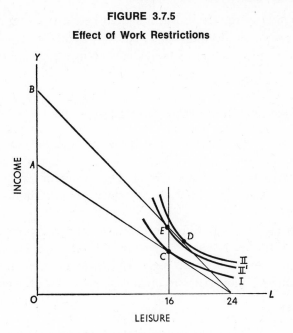

LEISURE

marginal rate of substitution equals the price ratio. Now suppose the wage rate increases, as represented by the slope of $24 - B$. If allowed optimal adjustment, in this construction the worker would move to point D, reducing the number of hours worked. He would therefore attain indifference curve *II.*

However, by the rules of this game, he must work eight hours. He therefore must move to the *disequilibrium* point E on indifference curve $II' < II$. The restriction on work time precludes the individual from attaining a point of utility-maximizing equilibrium. Of course, the set of indifference curves can be constructed so that there is a tangency at point E. In this case the worker would not be made worse off by the restriction; but he would also not be made better off.

Principle: Restrictions of any kind placed upon an individual can never increase his utility. That is, a person with freedom of choice is always at least as well off as a person whose choice is restricted.

Exercise: Try to construct a graph, similar to Figure 3.7.5, in which a restriction benefits the individual restricted. Convince yourself that it is impossible to do so.

In summary, imposed restrictions always reduce the utility or welfare of the individual upon whom they are imposed. It does not necessarily mean that total *social* welfare is reduced. This question is deferred until the last chapter in the book. But it should be clear that any restriction imposed upon a single individual reduces *his* utility. This holds true irrespective of the number of individuals upon whom the restriction is imposed.

3.7.e Demand for General Assistance Payments[12]

Among many of the social welfare programs that have been proposed for adoption by the federal government is one that would provide a minimum annual income per family. This program has not yet been adopted; nonetheless we may analyze some potential economic consequences of it.

Refer to Figure 3.7.6. Suppose the wage rate is represented by the slope of *ZA*. In the absence of a guaranteed minimum income, an individual whose indifference map is given by *I, II* would attain equilibrium at *B*, working *CZ* hours and receiving income OY_o. If a minimum in-

FIGURE 3.7.6

Demand for General Assistance Payments

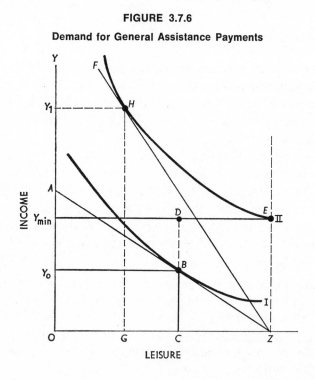

come of OY_{min} is guaranteed by the government, this individual might still work CZ hours, earn income of OY_o, and receive supplementary payment from the government of $BD = Y_o - Y_{min}$. In this case, however, the individual can attain a greater level of satisfaction by doing no work at all—by moving to point E on indifference curve II and receiving the minimum guaranteed income from the government.

From the point E the individual can be induced to work. In terms of Figure 3.7.6, if the wage rate should rise to ZF (or higher), he would forego his government payment, work GZ hours, and receive income of OY_1. From this example it is clear that a guaranteed minimum income can never lead to an increase in labor time. When all individuals in the society are considered, it will also surely lead to a reduction in labor time (and, consequently, in national output). The exact result, however, depends upon the leisure-income preferences of individuals, the level of the minimum income, and the wage rate available to each individual in question.

Exercise: Suppose an individual does not like to receive welfare payments. More specifically, assume that he regards $1 in welfare payments as equivalent to $0.50 of earned income. Analyze the effects of a guaranteed minimum income under these circumstances.

Exercise: There has recently been some policy discussion of a negative income tax. Under this scheme, a *base income* would be stipulated. A person earning more than the base income would pay a positive tax; one earning less than the base income would receive a subsidy proportional to the difference between the base income and his earned income. Suppose the factor of proportionality is 50 percent. (a) Analyze this welfare program by means of a graph such as Figure 3.7.6, and (b) compare the results of a negative income tax with the results of a guaranteed minimum income.

3.8 TIME PREFERENCE

In the previous section we investigated how a person might allocate his time between work (earning income) and leisure. A closely related question concerns how an individual might decide between present and future consumption. To introduce this, let us suppose that you have $100 and the bank rate of interest is 5 percent per year. You have two alternatives: (1) spend the $100 now on consumption, or (2) place the $100 in a bank saving account and spend $105 one year from now. How do you make your decision?

The decision, obviously, depends upon how much you want *now* and how much you want in the future. If you want *more now,* you will spend the money. If you want more in the future, you will obviously invest it. There is a tradeoff between present and future consumption (possibly the consumption of your heirs). The possibility of this tradeoff is faced directly or indirectly by every income recipient.

Let us return to a variant of our initial example. Suppose that at your current and expected future income per month you have the option of loaning $100 per month at 5 percent interest or borrowing $100 per month at 5 percent interest. If you loan this month, one year from now you receive $105, which permits you to consume more one year from now. If you borrow $100 you can consume more now, but one year from now you must repay $105, which reduces your consumption by that amount. There is a definite choice that must be made.

Definition: The rate of time preference is the rate of discount of future income or consumption. That is, if a person prefers $100 now to $105 one year from now, his rate of time preference is greater than 5 percent. If a person is *indifferent* between $100 now and $106 a year from now, his rate of time preference is 6 percent.

By the marginal calculations we have repeatedly used above, the following proposition should be clear:

Proposition: Each individual will borrow or loan (consume or save) until the point is reached at which his rate of time preference is equal to the rate of interest he can confidently expect to receive on saved and invested income.

Of course, all of this is subject to *expectations,* with which we shall not deal. A person does not know with certainty exactly how long he will live; he does not know with certainty whether his investment will be wiped out by the economic conditions that prevail in the future. But like it or not, expectations must be determined and some sort of tradeoff between present and expected future consumption made.

Exercise: Suppose that upon graduation from college a person has the option of taking a job paying $10,000 per year or borrowing money to go through a medical school. Why would anyone become a medical doctor?

Exercise: Why would an attractive young girl just out of high school become a call girl or a prostitute?

Exercise: Why do more unmarried women lose their virginity in wartime than in peacetime?

QUESTIONS

1. Using an indifference map, construct a consumer's demand curve for a normal good and an inferior good.

2. Explain the income effect of a price change and relate it precisely to the income elasticity of demand.

3. Answer "true," "false," or "uncertain," and give a defense of your answer:

    a) If two goods are substitutes in consumption, a fall in the price of one will lead to a fall in the price of the other. Does it matter whether the initial decline in price is demand-led or supply-led?

    b) If two goods are complementary in consumption, a fall in the price of one will lead immediately to a rise in the price of the other. Does it matter whether the initial price decline is demand-led or supply-led?

    c) A shift in the demand for kerosene will not affect the price of gasoline.

    d) In year 1, your income is $2,000; in year 2, it is $4,000. The goods you bought in year 1 for $2,000 cost exactly $4,000 in year 2. (i) You are better off in year 2. (ii) You cannot be worse off in year 2. Select the proper answer.

    e) It is not possible for all goods consumed to be inferior goods.

SUGGESTED READINGS

Ferguson, C. E. "Substitution Effect in Value Theory: A Pedagogical Note," *Southern Economic Journal,* Vol. XXVI (1960), pp. 310–14.

Georgescu-Roegen, Nicholas. "A Diagrammatic Analysis of Complementarity," *Southern Economic Journal,* Vol. XIX (1952), pp. 1–20.

Henderson, James M., and Quandt, Richard E. *Microeconomic Theory,* pp. 24–30. New York: McGraw-Hill Book Co., Inc., 1958. [Elementary math necessary.]

Hicks, J. R. *Value and Capital,* pp. 42–52. 2d ed. Oxford: Oxford University Press, 1946.

Samuelson, Paul A. *Foundations of Economic Analysis,* pp. 100–107. Cambridge, Mass.: Harvard University Press, 1947. [Advanced math necessary.]

Staehle, Hans. "A Development of the Economic Theory of Price Index Numbers," *Review of Economic Studies,* Vol. II (1935), pp. 163–88. [Elementary math necessary.]

Chapter	CHARACTERISTICS OF
4	MARKET DEMAND

4.1 INTRODUCTION

The analysis of Part I has firmly established the proposition that individual demand curves slope downward to the right—that quantity demanded varies inversely with price. The only exception is a truly insignificant one, Giffen's Paradox. But even if a few individuals are in a situation such that Giffen's Paradox applies, it is doubtful that the *market* demand curve would show the same properties.

This last chapter of Part I makes the transition from individual to market demand—from the demand of one individual for a particular commodity to the demand of all consumers taken together for that commodity. Having derived the market demand function, we can go on to describe many of its characteristics by means of such concepts as marginal revenue, direct price elasticity, price cross-elasticity, and income elasticity.

4.2 FROM INDIVIDUAL TO MARKET DEMAND

The demand function of one individual for a particular commodity is obtained by the process of maximizing satisfaction for a given level of money income. The process has been described in Chapter 2. From this discussion it is evident that the individual's preference function has an important role to play in determining his demand for each specific commodity. But it is not the only force. Indeed, there are four important determinants of quantity demanded.

4.2.a The Determinants of Demand

One of the four determinants of individual demand establishes quantity demanded given the *level* of the demand curve, while the others determine the level of demand itself.

The first and, in most cases, the most important determinant is the *price of the commodity* under consideration. According to the law of demand, quantity demanded varies inversely with price. Another way of expressing this principle is to say that the demand curve is negatively sloped; expressed in yet a different way, changes in nominal price cause movements *along* a given demand function, the movements representing the opposite changes in quantities demanded.

This familiar proposition is illustrated in panel a, Figure 4.2.1. As is *always* the case, price is plotted along the vertical axis and quantity demanded along the horizontal axis.[1] When price decreases from OP_1 to OP_2, quantity demanded increases from OQ_1 to OQ_2. This change represents a movement along the given demand curve DD' from E_1 to

FIGURE 4.2.1

Shifting the Determinants of Demand

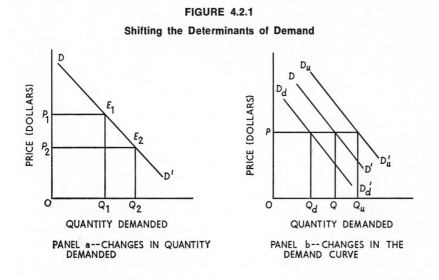

PANEL a--CHANGES IN QUANTITY
DEMANDED

PANEL b--CHANGES IN THE
DEMAND CURVE

E_2. To reemphasize, changes in the price of a commodity lead to changes in *quantity demanded,* the demand curve remaining unchanged.

The remaining determinants establish the level or position of the entire demand curve. *Money income* is one of the important determinants. For almost all individuals and for almost all commodities, the greater the money income the greater the demand (meaning, the higher and further to the right the demand curve lies).[2] Consider panel b, Figure 4.2.1. DD' is the original demand curve. Let money income increase. Demand will also increase, shifting the demand curve outward to the right, to a position such as D_uD_u'. If money income should fall

---

[1] This manner of plotting is just the reverse of the accepted mathematical procedure of plotting the independent variable on the horizontal axis.

[2] Certain exceptions are discussed in subsection 4.3.

from its original level, on the other hand, demand would fall, or move downward and to the left. $D_d D_d'$ represents such a shift.

Note that when demand increases, price remaining unchanged, quantity demanded increases as well. If price is OP and demand increases from DD' to $D_u D_u'$, quantity demanded increases from OQ to OQ_u. However, the important force in this situation is the change in money income that leads to the shift in demand.

The third determinant of demand is *taste*. The tastes or preference patterns of most individuals change from time to time. An increase in the intensity of one's desire for a commodity naturally leads to an increase in his demand for the commodity. The opposite occurs, of course, if a person's taste for a commodity lessens.

Finally, the *prices of related commodities* condition the level of demand for the commodity in question. In Chapter 3 the concepts of substitution and complementarity were discussed. Using the demand-function approach, two goods are said to be substitutes if an increase in the price of one leads to an increase in the consumption of the other. Let panel b, Figure 4.2.1, refer to the demand for beef. For a given price of pork, the original demand is DD'. If the price of pork increases, the *demand* for beef increases to $D_u D_u'$. If the price of beef remains unchanged (at OP), the quantity of beef demanded increases from OQ to OQ_u. Similarly, if the price of pork falls, the demand for beef would fall to $D_d D_d'$ and the quantity demanded would decline to OQ_d.

The opposite relation holds for complementary goods. Let panel b now represent the demand for golf clubs. A complementary good is a golf course. If the price of country club membership rises, fewer people will join the club and fewer will play golf. Thus the demand for golf clubs will decline. On the other hand, if the cost of playing golf declines, the demand for golf clubs is likely to expand.

These four factors—price, income, taste, and prices of related commodities—jointly determine the level of demand and the quantity demanded of every good by every individual. The next step is to aggregate individual demands to obtain a market demand for each commodity.

4.2.b Determining Market Demand

The market demand for a specific commodity is nothing more than the *horizontal summation* of the individual demands of each consumer. In other words, the market quantity demanded at each price is the sum of all individual quantities demanded at that price.

Table 4.2.1 and its accompanying diagram, Figure 4.2.2, provide an illustration when three consumers are in the market. Furthermore, it shows that even though Giffen's Paradox holds for individual C's demand, the derived market demand curve obeys the law of demand.

In the ordinary case a vast number of consumers are in each market;

TABLE 4.2.1

Individual and Aggregate Demand in a Three-Consumer Market

Price	Quantity Demanded by A	Quantity Demanded by B	Quantity Demanded by C	Market Quantity Demanded
10	2	0	0	2
9	5	1	0	6
8	8	5	0	13
7	12	10	5	27
6	16	14	12	42
5	21	18	14	53
4	27	22	12	61
3	35	25	11	71
2	45	27	14	86
1	60	29	16	105

FIGURE 4.2.2

From Individual to Market Demand

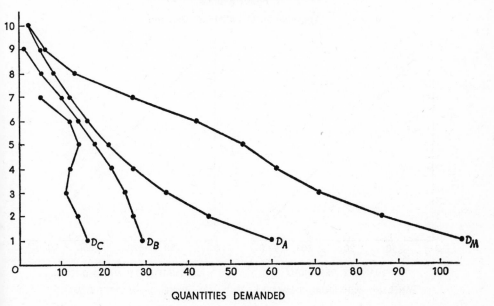

QUANTITIES DEMANDED

and they are not likely to have individual demands that differ as widely as those in Figure 4.2.2. Thus to depict the more usual situation, assume a market in which there are 75,000 consumers, each with identical

TABLE 4.2.2

Individual and Market Demand in a Large Market

Price	Quantity Demanded by a Typical Individual	Market Quantity Demanded
8....................	3	225,000
7....................	8	600,000
6....................	13	975,000
5....................	18	1,350,000
4....................	23	1,725,000
3....................	28	2,100,000
2....................	33	2,475,000
1....................	38	2,850,000

individual demands. Table 4.2.2 shows the demand of one individual and the aggregate market demand. Similarly, panel a, Figure 4.2.3, shows a plot of the individual demand curve; panel b shows the corresponding market demand.

FIGURE 4.2.3

Aggregation of Individual Demand

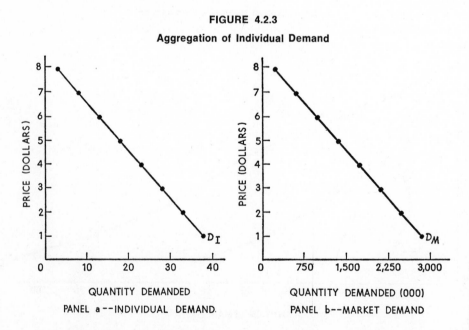

PANEL a --INDIVIDUAL DEMAND.   PANEL b--MARKET DEMAND

The results of this section may be summarized as follows:

Relation: Market demand is the horizontal sum of the individual demands of all consumers in the market. Thus at each price, market quantity demanded is the sum of all individual quantities demanded at the same price. Although some individuals may have demands subject to Giffen's Paradox for a few commodities, the normal demands of other individuals will usually outweigh the Giffen effect. Thus market demand curves will ordinarily slope downward to the right.

4.3 ELASTICITIES OF DEMAND

The concept and computation of demand elasticities are familiar already; indeed, the measure of price cross-elasticity has been discussed in some detail in Chapter 3. However, the various demand elasticities are so important—on both the theoretical and the empirical level—that they are all discussed in this section.

4.3.a Price Elasticity of Demand

As noted above, the quantity of a commodity demanded depends upon its price. It is of interest to measure the relative change in quantity demanded ensuing upon a given proportional change in price. This measure is called the price elasticity of demand, which is given by the following

Definition: The price elasticity of demand is the relative responsiveness of quantity demanded to changes in commodity price; in other words, price elasticity is the proportional change in quantity demanded divided by the proportional change in price.

The coefficient of price elasticity is usually denoted by the lowercase Greek eta (η); when there is any danger of misinterpreting the elasticity under consideration, direct price elasticity is denoted by η_{xx}.

Since quantity demanded and price vary inversely, a positive change in price will be accompanied by a negative change in quantity demanded. Thus, in order to make the coefficient of price elasticity positive, a "minus" sign is introduced into the formula:[3]

$$\eta_{xx} = -\frac{\Delta q}{q} \div \frac{\Delta p}{p} = -\frac{\Delta q}{\Delta p}\frac{p}{q}. \qquad (4.3.1)$$

---

[3] Let the demand function for commodity i be

$$q_i = f(p_1, p_2, \ldots, p_n, M), \qquad (4.3.1)$$

where q_i is quantity demanded, p_i is the price of the i-th commodity, M is income,

Equation (4.3.1) gives the formula for what is called "point" price elasticity of demand. This means that the coefficient computed is valid for very small movements only.

As an example, suppose we have the following information:

Price	Quantity Demanded
$29.001 ($p_1$)	2,999 (q_1)
29.000 (p_2)	3,000 (q_2)

Obviously, $\Delta p = -\$0.001$ and $\Delta q = +1$. In the formula for point elasticity, one must also use p and q; but a question could arise: should one use p_1 and q_1 or p_2 and q_2? For very small changes such as these, it is immaterial—either may be used, so the point elasticity formula is applicable. This may readily be seen from the following calculations:

$$\eta = -\frac{\Delta q}{\Delta p}\frac{p_1}{q_1} = -\frac{+1}{-.001}\frac{29.001}{2,999} = +9.70357,$$

$$\eta = -\frac{\Delta q}{\Delta p}\frac{p_2}{q_2} = -\frac{+1}{-.001}\frac{29.000}{3,000} = +9.66667.$$

The difference in the two computed elasticities is very small, only 0.03690 in a magnitude exceeding 9. For such cases, point elasticity is the appropriate calculation.

In many cases, however, observed changes in price and quantity are much larger. For example, one might have the following data:

Price	Quantity Demanded
$0.60 ($p_1$)	400,000 (q_1)
0.50 (p_2)	800,000 (q_2)

Again, the "changes" are not questionable: $\Delta p = -0.10$ and $\Delta q = +400,000$. Now let us compute the coefficient of price elasticity. Using original price and quantity figures, one finds

$$\eta = -\frac{\Delta q}{\Delta p}\frac{p_1}{q_1} = -\frac{400,000}{-.10}\frac{.60}{400,000} = +6.0.$$

When the new price-quantity figures are used, however, the coefficient is vastly different:

$$\eta = -\frac{\Delta q}{\Delta p}\frac{p_2}{q_2} = -\frac{400,000}{-.10}\frac{.50}{800,000} = +2.5.$$

---

and where we have assumed that there are n commodities in the system. Definitionally, then, the direct price elasticity of demand is

$$\eta_{ii} = -\frac{\partial q_i}{\partial p_i}\frac{p_i}{q_i} = -\frac{\partial \ln q_i}{\partial \ln p_i}, \tag{4.3.2}$$

where ln denotes logarithms to the base e.

In this case the two calculations do not yield sufficiently similar results. Elasticity must therefore be measured over an *arc of the demand curve* rather than at a specific *point* on the curve. To do this, one normally uses the *average* of the two price figures and the *average* of the two quantity figures. Thus the formula for *arc* price elasticity of demand is

$$\eta = -\frac{\Delta q}{\Delta p} \cdot \frac{\left(\frac{p_2 + p_1}{2}\right)}{\left(\frac{q_2 + q_1}{2}\right)} = -\frac{\Delta q}{\Delta p} \frac{(p_2 + p_1)}{(q_2 + q_1)}. \qquad (4.3.2)$$

Applying formula (4.3.2) to the calculation above, one obtains an average price elasticity over the arc of the demand curve covered by these observations:

$$\eta = -\frac{400,000}{-.10} \frac{1.10}{1,200,000} = +3.6667.$$

The coefficient thus obtained is a much more accurate estimate of the price elasticity relevant to this problem.[4]

4.3.b Coefficient of Price Elasticity

Demand is classified as price elastic, of unitary price elasticity, or as price inelastic depending upon the value of η. If $\eta > 1$, demand is said to be *elastic*—a given percentage change in price will result in a greater percentage change in quantity demanded. Thus small price changes will result in much more significant changes in quantity demanded.

When $\eta = 1$, demand has unit elasticity, meaning that the percentage changes in price and quantity demanded are precisely the same.

---

[4] The term "arc elasticity," while conventional, may be somewhat misleading. Suppose the demand curve is represented by DD' in the footnote figure. One wishes to compute the price elasticity associated with a movement from point A to point B, or over the true arc AB. The arc-elasticity formula given by equation (4.3.2) actually measures arc elasticity over a very special arc connecting A and B, namely the dashed line AB. Ideally, one should like to measure elasticity along the true arc (the demand curve from A to B). However, the demand curve is usually not known, only the two points A and B; but even if known, the proper weighting of the two price-quantity combinations might be very difficult. Therefore, one approximates the true arc elasticity from A to B by the arc elasticity over a straight line from A to B. Obviously, the greater the concavity of the demand curve from A to B the poorer the linear approximation represented by formula (4.3.2.)

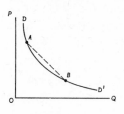

Finally, if $\eta < 1$, demand is inelastic. A given percentage change in price results in a smaller percentage change in quantity demanded.

These relations may be summarized in the following

Definition: Commodity demand is elastic or inelastic according as the coefficient of price elasticity is greater than or less than unity. If the coefficient is exactly one, demand is said to have unitary price elasticity.

4.3.c Graphical Measurement of Point Elasticity

For relatively precise measurement, the formula for arc elasticity is frequently necessary. However, an approximate knowledge of elasticity can be obtained merely by a visual inspection of the demand curve. If the demand curve is known, the coefficient of elasticity can be computed graphically or mathematically. Understanding the method of graphical computation permits one to estimate elasticity by inspection.

Consider Figure 4.3.1. The demand curve is DD', and the problem

FIGURE 4.3.1

Computation of Point Elasticity

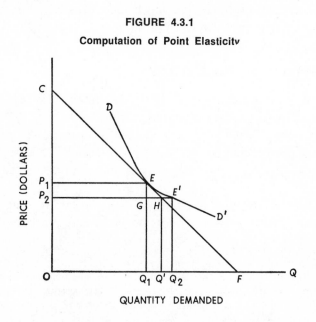

QUANTITY DEMANDED

is to measure the price elasticity of demand at the point E (where price is OP_1 and quantity demanded is OQ_1). First, construct the line CEF tangent to DD' at the point E. Let price fall from OP_1 to OP_2, so that quantity demanded increases from OQ_1 to OQ_2. As a linear approximation, however, if OP_2 is very near OP_1, OQ' is close to OQ_2. That is, for a small change for which point elasticity is a suitable measurement, Q' will be *very* near Q_2, and it can be used in lieu of Q_2 in the calculation. Next, consider the formula for point elasticity:

$$\eta = -\frac{\Delta q}{q} \div \frac{\Delta p}{p}.$$

From the figure, $\Delta q = Q_1Q'$ and $q = OQ_1$. Similarly $\Delta p = P_1P_2$ and $p = OP_1$. Thus

$$\eta = \frac{Q_1Q'}{OQ_1} \div \frac{P_1P_2}{OP_1} = \frac{Q_1Q'}{P_1P_2} \cdot \frac{OP_1}{OQ_1}.$$

From the figure one may readily see that

$$\frac{Q_1Q'}{P_1P_2} = \frac{GH}{EG}.$$

Furthermore, EGH and EQ_1F are similar right triangles inasmuch as each corresponding angle is equal. Thus

$$\frac{GH}{EG} = \frac{Q_1F}{EQ_1} = \frac{Q_1F}{OP_1}.$$

Hence

$$\eta = \frac{Q_1F}{OP_1} \cdot \frac{OP_1}{OQ_1} = \frac{Q_1F}{OQ_1}.$$

But $\dfrac{Q_1F}{OQ_1} = \dfrac{EF}{EC}$, so graphically the coefficient of price elasticity at the point E is approximately

$$\eta = \frac{EF}{EC}. \tag{4.3.3}$$

The measure of point elasticity in formula (4.3.3) is an exact measure if demand is linear and a close approximation when demand is nonlinear and the price change is small.

Utilizing formula (4.3.3), it is easy to determine the ranges of demand elasticity for a linear demand curve. In Figure 4.3.2, DD' is a linear demand curve. Notice first from formula (4.3.3) that demand has unitary elasticity when $EF = EC$. Thus locate a point P on DD' such that $DP = PD'$. At this point, demand has unitary price elasticity, or $\eta = 1$. Next, consider *any* point to the left of P, such as P_1. At P_1, $\eta = \left(\dfrac{P_1D'}{DP_1}\right) > 1$. Thus for a linear demand curve, the coefficient of

FIGURE 4.3.2

Ranges of Demand Elasticity for Linear Demand Curve

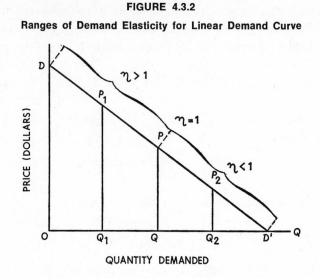

QUANTITY DEMANDED

price elasticity is greater than unity at any point to the left of the mid-point on the demand curve. Demand is elastic in this region. Finally, at any point to the right of *P*, say P_2, the coefficient of price elasticity is

$$\eta = \left(\frac{P_2 D'}{DP_2}\right) < 1.$$ Over this range, demand is inelastic.

These results may be summarized as follows:

Relations: Given any point *E* on a demand curve, construct the straight-line tangent to the curve at *E*. Call this line *CEF*. The coefficient of price elasticity is approximately *EF/CE*. If the demand curve is linear, this measure is precise. Furthermore, for a linear demand function: (*a*) demand is elastic at higher prices, (*b*) has unit elasticity at the midpoint of the demand curve, and (*c*) is inelastic at lower prices. Thus in case of linear demand, elasticity declines as one moves downward along the curve.[5]

4.3.d Factors Affecting Price Elasticity

Whether demand is elastic or inelastic is an important consideration, especially for government policy in individual commodity markets. For example, suppose the demand for wheat were highly price elastic. An increase in the price of wheat would accordingly result in a propor-

---

[5] The last proposition holds for almost all demand curves, though there can be exceptions. For a treatment of the unusual case, see C. E. Ferguson, "A Note on Elasticity," *Southern Economic Journal,* Vol. XXVI (1960), pp. 239–40.

tionately greater reduction in quantity demanded. The farmer would thus obtain a smaller total revenue from the sale of his wheat. Now suppose the government establishes a minimum wheat price above the market-equilibrium price. Wheat sales would be reduced, and so too would farmers' incomes, unless the price support were accompanied by a minimum-sales guarantee.

This is but one example; a large book could be filled with similar ones. The policy importance of price elasticity has led to many statistical studies designed to estimate numerical values of price elasticity. Table 4.3.1 reproduces some of these estimates.

As you see from the table, price elasticities range quite widely. Two basic factors determine elasticity: availability of substitute goods and the number of uses to which a good may be put. These factors go a long way toward explaining the variations observed in Table 4.3.1.

The more and better the substitutes for a specific good the greater its price elasticity will tend to be. Goods with few and poor substitutes

TABLE 4.3.1

Estimated Price Elasticity of Demand of Selected Commodities

Commodity	Elasticity Coefficient	Authority
Agricultural products at the farm level:		
Corn	0.77	Schultz
Cotton	0.51	"
Hay	0.78	"
Wheat	0.03	"
Potatoes	0.69	"
Oats	0.54	"
Barley	0.17	"
Buckwheat	1.50	"
Food:		
Beef	0.50	Wold
Pork	0.45	"
Butter	0.70	"
Milk	0.31	"
Goods other than food:		
Raw apparel wool	1.32	Ferguson
Furniture	3.04	Stone
Air transportation	1.10	Frisch

SOURCES: Henry Schultz, *The Theory and Measurement of Demand* (Chicago: University of Chicago Press, 1938); Herman Wold, *Demand Analysis* (New York: John Wiley & Sons, Inc., 1953); C. E. Ferguson and Metodey Polasek, "The Elasticity of Import Demand for Raw Apparel Wool in the United States," *Econometrica*, Vol. XXX (1962), pp. 670–99; Richard Stone and D. A. Rowe, "The Durability of Consumers' Durable Goods," *Econometrica*, Vol. XXVIII (1960), pp. 407–16; Ragnar Frisch, "A Complete Scheme for Computing All Direct Cross Demand Elasticities in a Model with Many Sectors," *Econometrica*, Vol. XXVII (1959), pp. 177–96.

—wheat and salt, for example—will always tend to have low price elasticities. Goods with many substitutes—wool, for which cotton and man-made fibers may be substituted, for instance—will have higher elasticities.

Similarly, the greater the number of possible uses of a commodity the greater its price elasticity will be. Thus a commodity such as wool— which can be used in producing clothing, carpeting, upholstery, draperies and tapestries, and so on—will tend to have a higher price elasticity than a commodity with only one or a very few uses—butter, for example.

4.3.e Price Cross-Elasticity of Demand

The measurement of price cross-elasticity of demand has been discussed in connection with the definition of substitute and complementary goods (Chapter 3, subsection 3.4.a). The discussion is repeated briefly at this point.

The demand curve, as previously stated, shows the relation between price and quantity demanded under the assumption that money income, tastes, and nominal prices of related goods remain unchanged. In certain cases related goods are so important, however, that one should consider a demand *surface* rather than a demand curve—that is, one's analysis should be generalized to include changes in the nominal prices of related goods.

As an example, consider the situation in which commodity X is related to only one other good, commodity Y. The quantity of X demanded is accordingly a function of the prices of both X and Y:

$$q_x = f(p_x, p_y). \tag{4.3.4}$$

Definition: The price cross-elasticity of demand measures the relative responsiveness of quantity demanded of a given commodity to changes in the price of a related commodity. In other words, it is the proportional change in the quantity demanded of good X divided by the proportional change in the price of good Y.

Using the demand function in equation (4.3.4), the coefficient of price cross-elasticity of demand is defined as[6]

$$\eta_{xy} = \frac{\Delta q_x}{q_x} \div \frac{\Delta p_y}{p_y} = \frac{\Delta q_x}{\Delta p_y} \frac{p_y}{q_x}. \tag{4.3.5}$$

As you will recall, goods may be classified as substitutes or complements

---

[6] As in footnote 3, let the demand function be

$$q_i = f(p_1, p_2, \ldots, p_n, M). \tag{4.6.1}$$

according as $\eta_{xy} \gtrless 0$. Linear demand surfaces illustrating these two cases, over certain price ranges, are shown in Figures 4.3.3 and 4.3.4.

FIGURE 4.3.3

Linear Demand Surface When X and Y Are Substitutes ($\eta_{xy} > 0$)

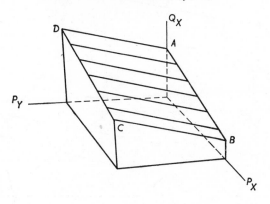

The interrelations of demand have been investigated in some statistical studies. Schultz tested cross-elasticity for many agricultural commodities and found both substitute and complementary relations.[7] Unfortunately, he did not express his results in terms of price cross-

TABLE 4.3.2

Coefficients of Price Cross-Elasticity of Demand

Commodity	Cross-Elasticity with Respect to Price of—	Coefficient of Price Cross-Elasticity
Beef........................	Pork	+0.28
Pork........................	Beef	+0.14
Butter......................	Margarine	+0.67
Margarine..................	Butter	+0.81
Flour.......................	All animal foods	+0.56

SOURCE: Herman Wold, *Demand Analysis* (New York, John Wiley & Sons, Inc., 1953).

elasticities. Various writers have provided estimates of price cross-elasticity, however. A few illustrative coefficients, taken from Wold, are presented in Table 4.3.2.

Then the price cross-elasticity of demand between goods i and j is

$$\eta_{ij} = \frac{\partial q_i}{\partial p_j} \frac{p_j}{q_i} \qquad (i \neq j; i, j = 1, 2, \ldots, n). \qquad (4.6.2)$$

[7] Henry Schultz, *The Theory and Measurement of Demand* (Chicago: University of Chicago Press, 1938).

FIGURE 4.3.4

Linear Demand Surface When X and Y Are Complementary ($\eta_{xy} < 0$)

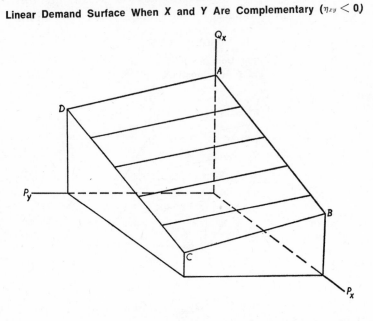

All the measured relations in Table 4.3.2 show the commodities to be substitute goods. In some cases the commodities are quite competitive (butter and margarine), while in other cases the relation is relatively weak.

4.3.f Income Elasticity of Demand

The purchases of certain commodities are very sensitive to changes in nominal and real money income. Thus it is sometimes desirable to relax the assumption that money income is held constant. In a simple case, the demand function can then be written as

$$q = f(p, M), \tag{4.3.6}$$

where M is money income. Following the concepts of elasticity already developed, the income elasticity of demand is given by the following

Definition: The income elasticity of demand is the relative responsiveness of quantity demanded to changes in income. In other words, it is the proportional change in quantity demanded divided by the proportional change in nominal income.

Symbolically,[8]

$$\eta_M = \frac{\Delta q}{q} \div \frac{\Delta M}{M} = \frac{\Delta q}{\Delta M} \frac{M}{q} .$$ (4.3.7)

Equation (4.3.6) generates a demand surface from which the elasticity formula (4.3.7) can be computed. Typical linear demand surfaces corresponding to positive and negative income elasticities are illustrated in Figures 4.3.5 and 4.3.6 respectively for certain ranges of money income.

Certain writers have suggested that commodities can be classified as "necessities" and "luxuries" on the basis of income elasticity. If income elasticity is very low (certainly less than one), quantity demanded is not very responsive to changes in income. Consumption remains

FIGURE 4.3.5

Linear Demand Surface for Good with Positive Income Elasticity of Demand

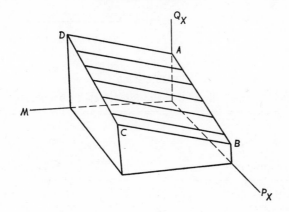

about the same irrespective of income level. This suggests that the commodity in question is a "necessity." On the other hand, an income elasticity greater than one indicates that the commodity is more or less a luxury. Indeed, certain empirical "laws of consumption" were developed in the 19th century by the German statistician Christian Lorenz

---

[8] As in footnote 3, let the demand function be

$$q_i = f(p_1, p_2, \ldots , p_n, M) .$$ (4.8.1)

Then the income elasticity of demand for the i-th commodity is

$$\eta_{iM} = \frac{\partial q_i}{\partial M} \frac{M}{q_i} \qquad (i = 1, 2, \ldots , n) .$$ (4.8.2)

FIGURE 4.3.6

Linear Demand Surface for Good with Negative Income Elasticity of Demand

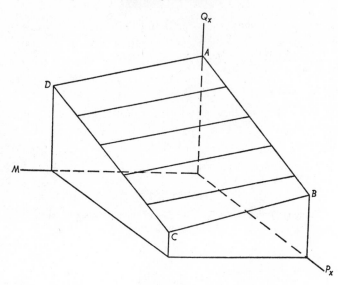

TABLE 4.3.3

Income Elasticity of Demand for Selected Commodities

Commodity	Estimated Income Elasticity of Demand	Authority
Milk and cream	0.07	Wold
Cream only	0.56	"
Butter	0.42	"
Margarine	−0.20	"
Cheese	0.34	"
Eggs	0.37	"
Meat	0.35	"
Flour	−0.36	"
Fruits and berries	0.70	"
Liquors	1.00	"
Tobacco	1.02	"
Restaurant consumption	1.48	"
Housing	0.38	Leser
Clothing	2.01	"
Durable goods (consumer)	2.90	"
Household goods	1.54	"

SOURCE: Herman Wold, *Demand Analysis* (New York: John Wiley & Sons, Inc., 1953); C. E. V. Leser, "Commodity Group Expenditure Functions for the United Kingdom, 1948–1957," *Econometrica*, Vol. XXIX (1961), pp. 24–32.

Ernst Engel. According to Engel, the income elasticity of demand for food is very low; those for clothing and shelter are about unity; while recreation, medical care, and other "luxury" goods have income elasticities in excess of unity. Therefore, according to Engel, the percentage of income spent on food by a family or a nation is a very good index of welfare—the poorer a family or a nation, the larger the percentage of expenditure that must go for food.

The latter generalization is somewhat crude; nonetheless, it does provide a rough measure of welfare. Some of Engel's specific statements regarding income elasticity, however, presumably no longer hold, as may be seen from the selected estimates of income elasticity presented in Table 4.3.3. Margarine and wheat flour have negative income elasticities, indicating that the consumption of these goods declines as family income increases. This implies that they are inferior goods, because the latter is indicated by a negative income effect ensuing upon a price change.

4.4 MARGINAL REVENUE

Having developed the concept of market demand and of its price, cross, and income elasticities, our attention can be directed to a closely related concept: marginal revenue.

The market demand curve shows for each specific price the quantity of the commodity that buyers will take. For example, consider Figure 4.4.1. At the price OP per unit, OQ units are demanded and sold. From the standpoint of sellers, $OP \times OQ$, or price times sales, is the *total revenue* obtainable when a price of OP per unit is charged. Thus total revenue is the area of the rectangle $OPRQ$ in Figure 4.4.1.

Of perhaps greater importance than total revenue is the variation in total revenue incident to an expansion or contraction of sales. In the now familiar terminology of economics, this is called *marginal revenue.*

Definition: Marginal revenue is the change in total revenue attributable to a one-unit change in output.[9]

---

[9] Let the demand function, in inverse form, be $p = F(q)$. Total revenue is pq, and marginal revenue (MR) is

$$MR = \frac{d(pq)}{dq} = \frac{d[qF(q)]}{dq} = F(q) + qF'(q) = p + q\frac{dp}{dq}.$$

Naturally, so long as the law of demand holds, $F'(q) = (dp/dq) < 0$. Hence $p > MR$ when the demand curve is negatively sloped. If the demand curve is a horizontal line $dp/dq = 0$ and $p = MR$.

FIGURE 4.4.1

The Measurement of Total Revenue

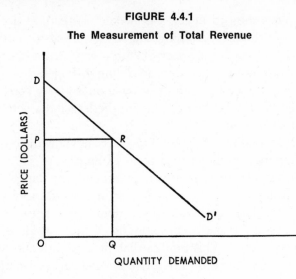

QUANTITY DEMANDED

4.4.a Calculation of Marginal Revenue

Consider carefully the definition of marginal revenue (MR)—the change in total revenue (TR) attributable to a one-unit change in output. For the first unit sold, total, average, and marginal revenue are identical; for a quantity sold of one, each is precisely equal to price. To expand sales to the rate of two units per period of time, price must be reduced. The marginal revenue of the second unit is equal to total revenue from the sale of two units *minus* total revenue from the sale of one unit. It follows, therefore, since $MR = TR$ for one unit, that TR for two units $= MR$ for one unit $+ MR$ for two units. Generalizing, total revenue is the sum of all marginal revenue figures.[10] This point is illustrated by the hypothetical data presented in Table 4.4.1 and graphed in Figure 4.4.2.[11]

[10] Since $MR = \dfrac{d(TR)}{dq}$, it follows that for sales of (say) q units,

$$TR_q = \int_0^q (MR)dq \ .$$

[11] The graph in Figure 4.4.2 contains a slight inaccuracy that may trouble the mathematically trained student. The example upon which the graph is based contains discrete data. The TR curve is obtained by plotting the points and connecting them by straight-line segments. The D and MR curves are obtained in the same manner. But here is where the inconsistency enters. Over any range of values for which total revenue is linear, marginal revenue is constant; and when marginal revenue is constant, so too is the demand function. To be exactly correct, the D and MR curves should be drawn as step-decreasing functions rather than as continuous functions with continuous first derivatives. However, the example is *merely illustrative;* and it seems better to illustrate a more general situation.

TABLE 4.4.1

Demand, Total Revenue and Marginal Revenue

Price	Quantity	Total Revenue	Marginal Revenue	Sum of MR Entries
11....................	0	0	—	—
10....................	1	10	10	10
9....................	2	18	8	18
8....................	3	24	6	24
7....................	4	28	4	28
6....................	5	30	2	30
5....................	6	30	0	30
4....................	7	28	−2	28
3.............../......	8	24	−4	24
2....................	9	18	−6	18
1....................	10	10	−8	10

The first two columns of this table contain price and quantity figures —the ingredients determining the demand curve (D) in Figure 4.4.2. The third column shows, total revenue, the product of the corresponding entries in columns 1 and 2. The data in this column give rise to the TR curve in the figure. Column 4 contains the figures for marginal revenue calculated, according to the definition, as

$$MR_1 = \Delta TR_1 = TR_1 - TR_0,$$
$$MR_2 = \Delta TR_2 = TR_2 - TR_1,$$
$$\cdot \quad \cdot \quad \cdot \quad \cdot \quad \cdot \quad \cdot \quad \cdot \quad \cdot$$
$$MR_{10} = \Delta TR_{10} = TR_{10} - TR_9.$$

The final column is a check calculation to show that the sum of marginal revenue figures equals the associated total revenue. Using the notation employed above:

$$TR_1 = MR_1$$
$$TR_2 = MR_1 + MR_2$$
$$\cdot \quad \cdot \quad \cdot \quad \cdot \quad \cdot \quad \cdot \quad \cdot \quad \cdot$$
$$TR_{10} = MR_1 + MR_2 + \cdots + MR_{10}.$$

This relation enters in an important way in the following subsection.

The data for marginal revenue are plotted in Figure 4.4.2 as the curve labeled MR. This curve has two crucial features. First, at the "outset" marginal revenue equals demand or average revenue. In this discrete example, $D = MR$ at quantity one and price \$10. In a continuous case, the two are equal infinitesimally close to the vertical axis. Second, $MR = 0$ when total revenue is at its maximum. When marginal revenue is *positive,* total revenue increases; and when marginal

FIGURE 4.4.2

Graph of Hypothetical Data in Table 4.4.1

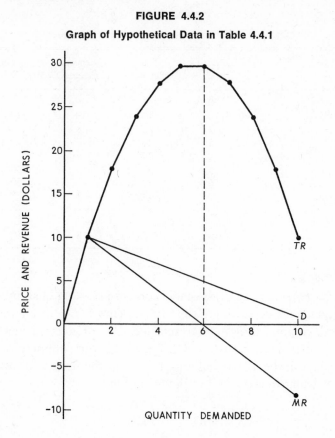

revenue is *negative,* total revenue declines. Naturally enough, when the *addition* to total revenue is zero, it (TR) must be at its maximum point.

4.4.b   Determination of Marginal Revenue at a Point on a Linear Demand Curve[12]

When the demand function is given in tabular form, as in Table 4.4.1, the calculation of marginal revenue is easy. Suppose, however, that you are given only a linear demand curve such as curve DD' in

---

[12] The method of determining marginal revenue at a point as used in this section is actually based upon the fact that the marginal revenue function is linear when the demand function itself is linear. To see this relation, let the demand function in inverse form be

$$p = a - bq , \tag{4.12.1}$$

where a and b are positive constants. Total revenue is accordingly

FIGURE 4.4.3

Finding a Point on the Marginal Revenue Curve with Linear Demand

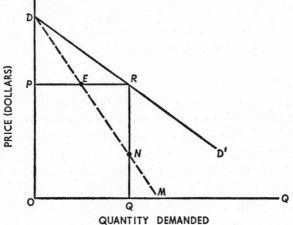

QUANTITY DEMANDED

Figure 4.4.3. The problem is to find the marginal revenue associated with any (and hence every) point on the curve.

Suppose price is *OP,* so quantity demanded is *OQ* and total revenue is equal to the area of the rectangle *OPRQ.* Furthermore, from subsection 4.4.a you know that the total revenue corresponding to any quantity is the sum of all marginal revenue figures up to and including the marginal revenue for the quantity under consideration. Graphically, this means that total revenue is equal to the area under the marginal revenue curve.

If we already *knew* the marginal revenue curve *DM* in Figure 4.4.3, total revenue would also equal the area *ODNQ.* At the moment this curve is not known; indeed, our problem is to determine the marginal revenue (*QN*) associated with quantity *OQ* and price *OP = QR.* The only thing we know right now is that there must be an area *ODNQ*

$$TR = pq = aq - bq^2 \text{ ,} \tag{4.12.2}$$

thus marginal revenue is

$$MR = \frac{d(pq)}{dq} = a - 2bq \text{ .} \tag{4.12.3}$$

Equation (4.12.3) is obviously a linear function. Further, comparing equations (4.12.1) and (4.12.3), it is seen that when the demand function is linear, the marginal revenue function (*a*) is linear, (*b*) has the same ordinate intercept, and (*c*) has a slope twice as great as the slope of the demand function.

which is equal to total revenue, or the area $OPRQ$. Our problem is to locate the point N. When the proper N is found, we know that the area $ODNQ$ equals the area $OPRQ$.

These two geometrical shapes have a substantial area in common, namely $OPENQ$. The triangle ERN is unique to $OPRQ$, and the triangle EPD is unique to $ODNQ$. Since $OPENQ$ is common, the area of $ODNQ$ will equal the area $OPRQ$ if, and only if, the area of EDP equals the area of ERN.

At this point, we have three pieces of information. First, since the opposite angles formed by two intersecting straight lines are equal, angle DEP equals angle REN. Second, both triangles are right triangles (that is, angles DPE and ERN are right angles). Since two angles are equal, the third must be as well. The two triangles are, accordingly, similar triangles. Finally, we know that if properly constructed, the two triangles have equal area. But similar triangles of equal area are congruent, so the corresponding sides must be equal. Hence $PE = ER$ and $DP = RN$.

We have thus obtained a method for finding marginal revenue corresponding to any point on a linear demand curve. Suppose the point in question is R. From R, drop a perpendicular RQ to the quantity axis and a perpendicular RP to the price axis. On the perpendicular RQ mark off a distance RN that is equal to DP. When this is done, the distance NQ is the marginal revenue associated with the output of OQ units.

Another method that is equally valid but does not directly follow the logic of locating the point N is: from the point R, drop perpendiculars RP and RQ to both axes. Find the midpoint E of the line RP. Draw a straight line from D to E and extend this line until it intersects RQ. The point of intersection is N, the point in question.

4.4.c Derivation of the Marginal Revenue Curve When Demand Is Linear

The method of subsection 4.4.b can be applied to many points (two are enough) on a linear demand curve to generate the corresponding marginal revenue curve. The process is shown in Figure 4.4.4.

Let the given demand curve be DD'. Select a point R_1 and drop perpendiculars (R_1P_1 and R_1Q_1) to the axes. On the line R_1Q_1 mark off a distance $R_1N_1 = DP_1$. The distance N_1Q_1 is marginal revenue, and N_1 is a point on the marginal revenue curve. Next, select another point

FIGURE 4.4.4

**Derivation of the Marginal Revenue Curve
When Demand Is Linear**

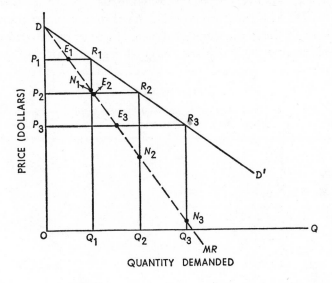

QUANTITY DEMANDED

R_2 and repeat the process, finding a point N_2 such that $R_2N_2 = DP_2$. N_2 is also a point on the marginal revenue curve.

Exercise: Carry out the same argument for the point R_3.

Alternatively, the marginal revenue curve can be determined as follows. Find the midpoint E_1 of the line R_1P_1. Draw a straight line from D to E_1 and extend this line until it intersects R_1Q_1. The point of intersection is N_1. Next, find the midpoint E_2 on R_2P_2. A straight line from D through E_2 to the line R_2Q_2 determines N_2. Connecting D, N_1, N_2, etc., forms the marginal revenue curve.

Exercise: Carry out the same argument for the point R_3.

4.4.d Derivation of the Marginal Revenue Curve Associated with a Nonlinear Demand Curve

The basic process used in subsection 4.4.c can be used, with a slight modification, to derive the marginal revenue curve associated with a nonlinear demand curve. The mechanics are explained by means of Figure 4.4.5.

DD' is the demand curve. The problem is to find marginal revenue corresponding to such points as R_1, R_2, and R_3 on DD' so that the marginal revenue curve can be constructed. From point R_1 first drop perpendiculars (R_1P_1 and R_1Q_1) to both axes. Next, construct the tangent to DD' at R_1 and extend the tangent so that it cuts the vertical axis at point S_1. Since the slope of the curve and its tangent are the same at the point of tangency, the marginal quantities are also the same.

FIGURE 4.4.5

**Derivation of Marginal Revenue from
Nonlinear Demand Curve**

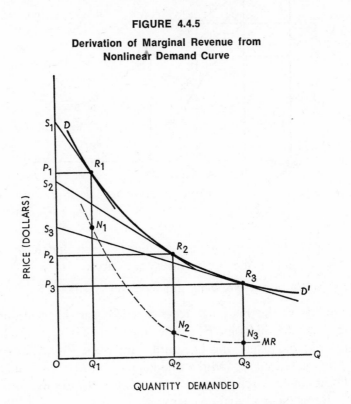

QUANTITY DEMANDED

Thus to find marginal revenue at point R_1, mark off a distance $R_1N_1 = S_1P_1$. Then N_1Q_1 is marginal revenue and N_1 is a point on the marginal revenue curve.

Proceeding in the same fashion, select another point R_2 on DD' and drop perpendiculars (R_2P_2 and R_2Q_2) to the axes. Next, construct the tangent to DD' at R_2 and extend the tangent line to cut the vertical axis at S_2. Finally, mark off the distance $R_2N_2 = S_2P_2$. Marginal revenue is N_2Q_2 and N_2 is another point on the marginal revenue curve.

Exercise: Carry out the same argument for the point R_3.

Connecting all points thus generated—and for accuracy, there must be many of them—establishes the marginal revenue curve corresponding to the given nonlinear demand curve.

4.5 DEMAND, REVENUE, AND ELASTICITY

After studying sections 4.3 and 4.4, you should be aware of a close relation between price elasticity of demand and the revenue function. Two types of relations are developed in this section.

4.5.a Elasticity and Total Revenue

If demand is elastic over an arc of the demand curve—that is, the coefficient of price elasticity exceeds unity—a decline in price will result in a proportionately greater expansion of quantity demanded and a rise in price will result in a proportionately greater decline in quantity demanded. Now, since "price times quantity" gives total revenue, it is readily seen that if demand is elastic a decline in price will increase total revenue because quantity demanded increases proportionately more than price declines, and a rise in price will decrease total revenue because quantity demanded falls proportionately more than price increases.

This is illustrated in panel c, Figure 4.5.1. DD' is the demand curve;

FIGURE 4.5.1

Demand, Total Revenue, and Elasticity

PANEL a --UNIT ELAS-   PANEL b--INELASTIC   PANEL c --ELASTIC
TICITY OF DEMAND   DEMAND   DEMAND

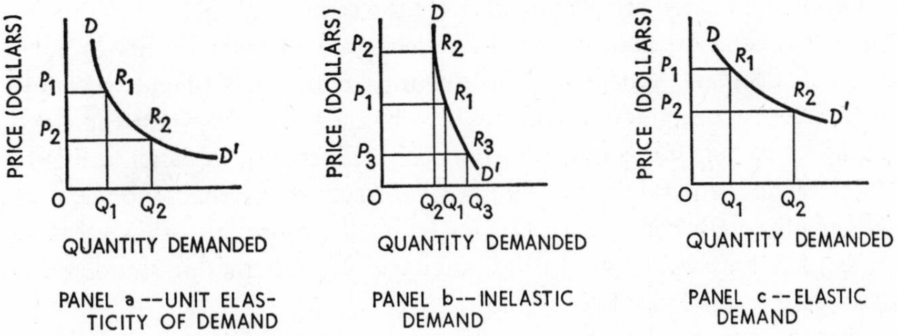

OP_1, OQ_1 is the initial position. Let price fall to OP_2 so that quantity demanded increases to OQ_2. It is easily seen that demand is elastic because

$$\frac{P_1 P_2}{OP_1} < \frac{Q_1 Q_2}{OQ_1}.$$

Furthermore, total revenue just as obviously increases, from the area of $OP_1 R_1 Q_1$ to the area of $OP_2 R_2 Q_2$. Working this in reverse, for a price increase from OP_2 to OP_1, total revenue diminishes as price increases.

If demand is inelastic, on the other hand, the results are just the opposite. An increase in price causes a proportionately smaller decline in quantity demanded, and a decrease in price results in proportionately smaller expansion of quantity demanded. Thus if demand is inelastic over an arc of the demand curve, an increase in price will lead to an increase in total revenue because quantity demanded declines proportionately less than price increases; a decrease in price will cause a decrease in total revenue because quantity demanded will expand proportionately less than price decreases.

These results are illustrated in panel b, Figure 4.5.1. DD' is the demand curve, and the initial position is OP_1, OQ_1. From this position let price increase to OP_2. Demand is clearly inelastic because

$$\frac{P_1 P_2}{OP_1} > \frac{Q_1 Q_2}{OQ_1}.$$

Similarly, total revenue expands because the area of $OP_2 R_2 Q_2$ exceeds the area of $OP_1 R_1 Q_1$.

Exercise: Show the results when price declines from OP_1 to OP_3.

Finally, when demand has unit elasticity, the changes in price and quantity demanded are proportionately the same in absolute amount. In other words, a 10 percent increase (decrease) in price results in a 10 percent decrease (increase) in quantity demanded. Total revenue, therefore, is completely unaffected by changes in price when the price elasticity of demand is unity. Such a case is illustrated in panel a, Figure 4.5.1. The demand curve DD' is constructed so that the area of $OP_1 R_1 Q_1$ equals the area of $OP_2 R_2 Q_2$. Furthermore, all other areas so constructed are the same. In the language of mathematics, the demand curve is a *rectangular hyperbola*.

Briefly, the results of this section may be summarized as follows.

Relations: When demand has unit elasticity, total revenue is not affected by changes in price. If demand is elastic, total revenue varies inversely with price; if demand is inelastic, total revenue varies directly with price.

These relations are given more explicitly in Table 4.5.1.

TABLE 4.5.1

Relations between Price Elasticity and Total Revenue

	Elastic Demand	*Unitary Elasticity*	*Inelastic Demand*
Price rises.................	TR falls	No change	TR rises
Price falls.................	TR rises	No change	TR falls

4.5.b Elasticity and Marginal Revenue

Since elasticity is related to total revenue it is necessarily related to marginal revenue as well. The precise relation follows from a comparison of Figure 4.4.2 and Table 4.5.1.

To review the important content of Figure 4.4.2, when total revenue rises, marginal revenue is positive; when total revenue declines, marginal revenue is negative; when total revenue is constant, marginal revenue is zero. Notice that marginal revenue is zero when total revenue is at its maximum point. On the basis of these relations, we can construct Table 4.5.2, which is very similar to Table 4.5.1.

TABLE 4.5.2

Relation between Marginal Revenue and Price Elasticity of Demand

Marginal Revenue Positive	*Marginal Revenue Zero*	*Marginal Revenue Negative*
Elastic demand	Unitary elasticity	Inelastic demand

An even more precise relation among price, marginal revenue, and the coefficient of price elasticity can be derived from Figure 4.5.2. Let DD' be a linear demand curve. This is used merely for convenience because the formula to be developed holds for nonlinear demand curves as well. Consider the point R on DD', corresponding to a price of $OP = QR$ and quantity demanded of $OQ = PR$. NQ is the marginal revenue associated with point R because, by construction, $RN = DP$. Furthermore, by the method developed in section 4.3, at point R the coefficient of price elasticity (η) is RD'/DR.

First note that

$$NQ = RQ - RN. \tag{4.5.1}$$

FIGURE 4.5.2

Relation among Price, Marginal Revenue and Price Elasticity of Demand

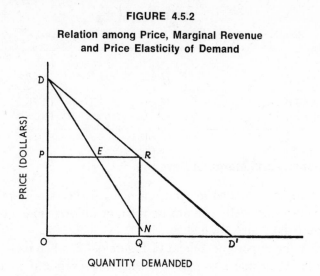

QUANTITY DEMANDED

Now since $\dfrac{DP}{PR} = \dfrac{RQ}{QD'}$ and $RN = DP$, it follows that

$$RN = PR\left(\frac{RQ}{QD'}\right) = RQ\left(\frac{PR}{QD'}\right). \qquad (4.5.2)$$

Substituting equation (4.5.2) in equation (4.5.1),

$$\begin{aligned}
NQ &= RQ - RN \\
&= RQ - RQ\left(\frac{PR}{QD'}\right) \qquad (4.5.3) \\
&= RQ\left[1 - \frac{PR}{QD'}\right].
\end{aligned}$$

Next, observe that

$$\frac{PR}{QD'} = \frac{OQ}{QD'} = \frac{DR}{RD'} = \frac{1}{\eta}. \qquad (4.5.4)$$

Finally, substituting equation (4.5.4) in equation (4.5.3), one obtains

$$NQ = RQ\left[1 - \frac{1}{\eta}\right]. \qquad (4.5.5)$$

Since NQ is marginal revenue (MR) and RQ is price (p), equation (4.5.5.) can be written to express the relation among marginal revenue, price, and the coefficient of price elasticity:[13]

$$MR = p\left(1 - \frac{1}{\eta}\right). \qquad (4.5.6)$$

---

[13] Let the demand function in inverse form be

$$p = F(q), \qquad F'(q) = \frac{dp}{dq} < 0. \qquad (4.13.1)$$

4.5.c Demand Curve for a Firm in Perfect Competition

All the relations thus far developed can be used to describe the demand curve facing an individual producer in a perfectly competitive market.

Suppose that panel a, Figure 4.5.3, depicts the equilibrium of a market in which there are a large number of sellers, each of approximately the same size. DD' and SS' are the market demand and market supply curves. Their intersection determines the equilibrium price $O\overline{P}$ and quantity demanded $O\overline{Q}$.

Let us now be more specific and stipulate that there are 25,000 sellers (say, wheat farmers) of approximately the same size in the market. If any one seller increases his output and sales by 100 percent, the total market sales will increase by only $\frac{1}{250}$ of 1 percent. Such a change is both graphically and *economically* so small as to have an imperceptible influence on price. Thus each individual seller may assume with confidence that variations in his *own* output and sales will have a negligible effect upon market price. Concerted action by a large number of sellers can influence market price; but one seller acting alone cannot. The individual seller may therefore assume that the demand curve facing *him* is a horizontal line at the level of price established by demand-and-supply equilibrium in the market.

The demand curve for a perfectly competitive producer is shown in panel b, Figure 4.5.3. The shape of the curve shows that the producer believes changes in his volume of output will have no perceptible effect

---

Total revenue is, therefore,

$$TR = pq = qF(q) , \qquad (4.13.2)$$

and marginal revenue is

$$MR = \frac{d[qF(q)]}{dq} = F(q) + qF'(q) = p + q\frac{dp}{dq} . \qquad (4.13.3)$$

Next, factor p from the right-hand side of equation (4.13.3):

$$MR = p\left(1 + \frac{q}{p}\frac{dp}{dq}\right) . \qquad (4.13.4)$$

By definition

$$\eta = -\frac{dq}{dp}\frac{p}{q} . \qquad (4.13.5)$$

Substituting equation (4.13.5) in equation (4.13.4) yields the expression for marginal revenue shown in equation (4.5.6) in the text.

upon market price. And if the producer is in fact in a perfectly competitive market, his belief is well founded. A change in his rate of sales per period of time will change his total revenue, but it will not affect market price.

The producer in a perfectly competitive market, therefore, does not have to reduce his price in order to expand his rate of sales. Any number of units per period of time can be sold at the market equilibrium price. If he were to charge a higher price, he could sell nothing. A lower price would result in a needless loss of revenue. He thus charges the market price for whatever quantity he wishes to produce and sell.

FIGURE 4.5.3

Derivation of Demand for a Perfectly Competitive Firm

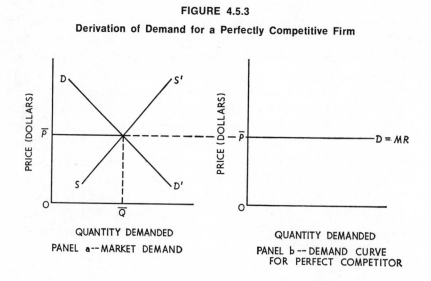

QUANTITY DEMANDED

PANEL a -- MARKET DEMAND

QUANTITY DEMANDED

PANEL b -- DEMAND CURVE
FOR PERFECT COMPETITOR

Since price remains constant, each additional unit sold increases total revenue by its (constant) price. In this special case, therefore, price and marginal revenue are equal at every level of sales. Therefore, the demand curve and the marginal revenue curve are identical for a producer in a perfectly competitive market. For this reason, the curve in panel b is labeled $D = MR$.

When the demand curve is horizontal, demand is said to be perfectly elastic, meaning that the coefficient of price elasticity increases without bound as the percentage change in price becomes smaller and smaller. Take a numerical example. Suppose the market equilibrium price is $5 and a particular producer is selling 1,000 units at that price. If he increased his price to $5.01, his sales would fall to zero. Thus

$$\frac{\Delta q}{q} = \frac{-1000}{1000} \quad \text{and} \quad \frac{\Delta p}{p} = \frac{1}{500}.$$

The coefficient of price elasticity would be

$$\eta = - \frac{\Delta q}{q} \div \frac{\Delta p}{p} = 1 \div \frac{1}{500} = 500 \ .$$

If he increased the price to only $5.001, his sales would also fall to zero and η would be 5,000. Thus one generalizes by saying that for infinitesimally small price changes the coefficient of price elasticity approaches infinity under condition of perfect competition.

The results of this section may be summarized as follows:

Relations: The demand for a producer in a perfectly competitive market is a horizontal line at the level of the market equilibrium price. The output decisions of the seller do not affect market price. In this case, the demand and marginal revenue curves are identical; demand is perfectly elastic and the coefficient of price elasticity approaches infinity.

PROBLEMS

1. The following table gives hypothetical data for a consumer. Compute all meaningful elasticity coefficients (price, cross, and income). Remember that income must be constant when price elasticities are computed, and prices must be constant when income elasticity is computed.

Year	Price of X	Quantity Purchased	Income	Price of Y
1.	$1.00	100	$5000	$0.50
2.	1.01	95	5000	.50
3.	1.01	100	5500	.51
4.	1.01	105	5500	.52
5.	1.00	100	5500	.50
6.	1.00	105	5500	.51
7.	1.00	100	5000	.51
8.	1.02	105	5500	.51
9.	1.02	95	5500	.50
10.	1.03	90	5500	.50
11.	1.03	100	6500	.51
12.	1.03	105	7000	.51

2. The following table gives hypothetical data for market demand. Compute total revenue, marginal revenue, and the price elasticity of demand on a separate sheet. Plot the demand, total revenue, and marginal revenue curves.

Price	Quantity Demanded	Price	Quantity Demanded
$70.00	1	$23.33	7
50.00	2	20.00	8
40.00	3	17.50	9
35.00	4	15.00	10
30.00	5	12.50	11
26.67	6	10.00	12

QUESTIONS

1. Answer "true," "false," or "uncertain," and give a defense of your answer:

   a) If the income elasticity of demand for a commodity exceeds one, the relative price of that commodity will rise as real per capita income increases, i.e., will rise relative to the goods whose income elasticity is less than one.

   b) If the utility of each good is independent of the quantities of all other goods consumed, then all goods must have positive income elasticities (i.e., all goods are normal goods).

   c) If total consumer expenditures are the same before and after a tax, then an excise tax on a consumer good with elastic demand will lead to an increase in consumption spending on other consumer goods, while an excise tax on a good whose demand is inelastic will lead to a decrease in consumption spending on other goods.

2. The following statement is taken from the *Wall Street Journal,* March 30, 1966: "A retired Atlanta railroad conductor complains that he can no longer visit his neighborhood tavern six times a week. Since the price of his favorite beer went up to 30 cents a glass from 25 cents, he has been dropping in only five times a week." Assuming the man in question consumed the same amount of beer *per visit* before and after the price change, calculate the elasticity of his demand for tavern-dispensed beer.

3. "The experience with rail passenger transport indicates that traffic is negatively related to income—the richer one gets, the less he wants of the rails. For the trains that have survived, a mixture of the aged and low-income groups is the ideal combination; not surprisingly, the patronage on East Coast–Florida trains holds up better than on almost any others. The Illinois Central's *City of New Orleans,* running the length of Mississippi, is typically one of the strongest trains in the country, and passenger service in prosperous California is sick unto death." (G. W. Hilton, "What Went Wrong," *Trains,* Vol. XXVII [January, 1967], p. 39.)

   a) From this statement, what can you say about the income elasticity of demand for rail passenger service? What type of good is rail passenger service?

b) If (say) the Grand Trunk Western lowers its passenger fares, can you say anything about the income and substitution effects?

c) Suppose a person gets a salary increase and accordingly uses the trains less. Using his indifference curves, show this response to his increased income.

SUGGESTED READINGS

Marshall, Alfred. *Principles of Economics,* pp. 92–113. 8th ed. New York: The Macmillan Co., 1920.

Robinson, Joan. *The Economics of Imperfect Competition,* pp. 29–40. London: Macmillan & Co., Ltd., 1933.

Advanced Reading, Part I

I. THEORY OF CONSUMER BEHAVIOR, GENERAL

Georgescu-Roegen, Nicholas. "The Pure Theory of Consumer Behavior," *Quarterly Journal of Economics,* Vol. L (1935–36), pp. 545–93.

Hicks, John R. *Value and Capital,* pp. 11–41, 305–11. 2d ed.; Oxford: Clarendon Press, 1946.

Hotelling, Harold. "Edgeworth's Taxation Paradox and the Nature of Demand and Supply Functions," *Journal of Political Economy,* Vol. XL (1932), pp. 577–616.

————. "Demand Functions with Limited Budgets," *Econometrica,* Vol. III (1935), pp. 66–78.

Samuelson, Paul A. *Foundations of Economic Analysis,* pp. 90–117. Cambridge, Mass.: Harvard University Press, 1947.

Schultz, Henry. *The Theory and Measurement of Demand,* pp. 5–58. Chicago: University of Chicago Press, 1938.

Wold, Herman O. A., with Jureen, Lars. *Demand Analysis,* pp. 81–139. New York: John Wiley & Sons, Inc., 1953.

II. COMPLEMENTARITY AND RELATED GOODS

Ferguson, C. E. "Substitution Effect in Value Theory: A Pedagogical Note," *Southern Economic Journal,* Vol. XXVI (1960), pp. 310–14.

Georgescu-Roegen, Nicholas. "A Diagrammatic Analysis of Complementarity," *Southern Economic Journal,* Vol. XIV (1952), pp. 1–20.

Hicks, John R. *Value and Capital,* pp. 42–52, 311–14. 2d ed.; Oxford: Clarendon Press, 1946.

Ichimura, S. "A Critical Note on the Definition of Related Goods," *Review of Economic Studies,* Vol. XVIII (1950–51), pp. 179–83.

Morishima, M. "A Note on Definitions of Related Goods," *Review of Economic Studies,* Vol. XXIII (1955–56), pp. 132–34.

Samuelson, Paul A. *Foundations of Economic Analysis,* pp. 183–89. Cambridge, Mass.: Harvard University Press, 1947.

Schultz, Henry. *The Theory and Measurement of Demand,* pp. 569–85, 607–28. Chicago: University of Chicago Press, 1938.

III. SPECIAL TOPICS IN DEMAND THEORY

A. Income-Compensated Demand Curves

Bailey, Martin J. "The Marshallian Demand Curve," *Journal of Political Economy,* Vol. XLII (1954), pp. 255–61.

Friedman, Milton. "The Marshallian Demand Curve," *Journal of Political Economy,* Vol. LVII (1949), pp. 463–95.

Knight, Frank H. "Realism and Relevance in the Theory of Demand," *Journal of Political Economy,* Vol. LII (1944), pp. 289–318.

Yeager, Leland B. *"Methodenstreit* over Demand Curves," *Journal of Political Economy,* Vol. LXVIII (1960), pp. 53–64.

B. Revealed Preference and Index Numbers

Frisch, Ragnar. "Annual Survey of General Economic Theory: The Problem of Index Numbers," *Econometrica,* Vol. IV (1936), pp. 1–38.

Georgescu-Roegen, Nicholas. "Choice and Revealed Preference," *Southern Economic Journal,* Vol. XXI (1954), pp. 119–30.

Hicks, John R. *A Revision of Demand Theory.* Oxford: Clarendon Press, 1956.

Houthakker, H. S. "Revealed Preference and the Utility Function," *Economica,* N.S. Vol. XVII (1950), pp. 159–74.

Samuelson, Paul A. "A Note on the Pure Theory of Consumer Behavior," *Economica,* N.S. Vol. V (1938), pp. 61–71.

———. *Foundations of Economic Analysis,* pp. 144–63. Cambridge, Mass.: Harvard University Press, 1947.

Staehle, Hans. "A Development of the Economic Theory of Price Index Numbers," *Review of Economic Studies,* Vol. II (1935), pp. 163–88.

C. Cardinal Utility of Analysis of Choice under Risk

Alchian, A. A. "The Meaning of Utility Measurement," *American Economic Review,* Vol. XLII (1953), pp. 26–50.

Baumol, W. J. "The Neumann-Morgenstern Utility Index—An Ordinalist View," *Journal of Political Economy,* Vol. LIX (1951), pp. 61–66.

————. "The Cardinal Utility which Is Ordinal," *Economic Journal,* Vol. LXVII (1958), pp. 665–72.

Ferguson, C. E. "An Essay on Cardinal Utility," *Southern Economic Journal,* Vol. XXV (1958), pp. 11–23.

Friedman, Milton, and Savage, L. J. "The Utility Analysis of Choices Involving Risk," *Journal of Political Economy,* Vol. LVI (1948), pp. 279–304.

————, and Savage, L. J. "The Expected-Utility Hypothesis and the Measurability of Utility," *Journal of Political Economy,* Vol. LX (1952), pp. 463–74.

Georgescu-Roegen, Nicholas. "Choice, Expectations and Measurability," *Quarterly Journal of Economics,* Vol. LXVIII (1954), pp. 503–34.

Markowitz, Harry. "The Utility of Wealth," *Journal of Political Economy,* Vol. LX (1952), pp. 151–58.

Ozga, S. A. "Measurable Utility and Probability—A Simplified Rendering," *Economic Journal,* Vol. LXVI (1956), pp. 419–30.

Strotz, Robert H. "Cardinal Utility," *American Economic Review, Papers and Proceedings,* Vol. XLII (1953), pp. 384–97.

Von Neumann, John, and Morgenstern, Oskar. *Theory of Games and Economic Behavior,* pp. 15–31, 617–32. Princeton, N.J.: Princeton University Press, 1944.

IV. MARKET STABILITY

Henderson, James M., and Quandt, Richard E. *Microeconomic Theory: A Mathematical Approach,* pp. 109–113, 146–53. New York: McGraw-Hill Book Co., Inc., 1958.

Hicks, John R. *Value and Capital,* pp. 62–77, 245–82, 315–19, 333–37. 2d ed.; Oxford: Clarendon Press, 1946.

Kuenne, Robert E. "Hicks's Concept of Perfect Stability in Multiple Exchange," *Quarterly Journal of Economics,* Vol. LXXIII (1959), pp. 309–15.

Metzler, Lloyd A. "Stability of Multiple Markets: The Hicks Conditions," *Econometrica,* Vol. XIII (1945), pp. 277–92.

Samuelson, Paul A. *Foundations of Economic Analysis,* pp. 17–19, 260–65, 269–76. Cambridge, Mass.: Harvard University Press, 1947.

PART II

Theory of Production and Cost

In older textbooks it was conventional to define production as "the creation of utility" where utility meant "the ability of a good or service to satisfy a human want." In one respect this definition is too broad to have much specific content. On the other hand, it definitely points out that "production" embraces a wide range of activities and not *only* the fabrication of material goods. Rendering legal advice, writing a book, showing a motion picture, and servicing a bank account are all examples of "production." It is rather difficult to specify the inputs used in producing the outputs of these illustrative cases. Nevertheless, most people would probably agree that some kinds of technical and intellectual skills are required to perform the services.

Thus while "production" in a general sense refers to the creation of any *good or service* people will buy, the concept of production is much clearer when we speak only of *goods*. In this case it is simpler to specify the precise inputs and to identify the quantity and quality of output. Producing a bushel of wheat requires, in addition to suitable temperature and rainfall, a certain amount of arable land, seed, fertilizer, the services of agricultural equipment such as plows and combines, and human labor.

Even in our presently advanced state of automation, every act of production requires the input of human resources. Other inputs are usually required as well. In particular, production normally requires various types of capital equipment (machines, tools, conveyors, buildings) and raw or processed materials. The theory of production consists of an analysis of *how* the businessman—given the "state of the art" or technology—combines various inputs to produce a stipulated output in an economically efficient manner.

Since the concept of production is clearer when applied to goods rather than services, our discussion will be restricted to production in agricultural and manufacturing industries. The student should be aware, nevertheless, that problems of resource allocation in service trades and government are not less serious because they are less discussed in this text. Indeed, as the population becomes more and more concentrated in the under 20 and over 65 age groups, the importance of of services relative to goods increases. The principles of production studied here are as applicable to the output of services as to the output of goods, even though the application may be more difficult in the former case.

The same statement applies to the theory of cost. It is simpler to study a manufacturing business engaged in producing a specific good. Even then both costing and pricing are difficult matters—but not nearly so difficult as in service trades and government. Thus our discussion is restricted to producers of goods.

The theory of cost consists of an analysis of the costs of production —how costs are determined from a knowledge of the production function, the effects of diminishing returns, cost in the short and long runs, the "four cost curves," and so on. But more importantly, it establishes the basis for studying the pricing practices of business firms, which occupies Part III.

Chapter 5 | PRODUCTION WITH ONE VARIABLE INPUT

5.1 INTRODUCTION

Production processes typically require a wide variety of inputs. These are not as simple as "labor," "capital," and "materials"; many qualitatively different types of each input are normally used to produce an output. To clarify the analysis, this chapter introduces some simplifying assumptions whose purpose is to cut through the complexities of dealing with hundreds of different inputs. Thus our attention can be focused upon the essential principles of production.

More specifically, we assume that there is only one *variable input*. In subsequent discussion, this variable input is usually called "labor," although any other input could just as well be used. Second, we assume that this variable input can be combined in different proportions with one *fixed input* to produce various quantities of output. The fixed input is called "land"; our discussion is thus principally concerned with one specific example of production: agricultural output.

Finally, note that three assumptions are actually embodied in the two propositions stated above: (*a*) there is only one variable input; (*b*) there is only one fixed input; and (*c*) inputs may be combined in *various* proportions to produce the commodity in question.

5.1.a Fixed and Variable Inputs, the Short and Long Runs

In analyzing the process of physical production and the closely related costs of production, it is convenient to introduce an analytical fiction: the classification of inputs as fixed and variable. Accordingly, a *fixed input* is defined as one whose quantity cannot readily be changed when market conditions indicate that an immediate change in output is desirable. To be sure, no input is ever *absolutely* fixed, no matter how short the period of time under consideration. But frequently, for the sake of analytical simplicity, we hold some inputs fixed, reasoning perhaps that while these inputs are in fact variable, the cost of immediate variation is so great as to take them out of the range of relevance for the particular decision at hand. Buildings, major pieces of machinery, and managerial personnel are examples of inputs that cannot be rapidly augmented or diminished. A *variable input,* on the other hand, is one whose quantity may be changed almost instantaneously in response to desired changes in output. Many types of labor services and the inputs of raw and processed materials fall in this category.

Corresponding to the fiction of fixed and variable inputs, economists introduce another fiction, the short and long runs. The *short run* refers to that period of time in which the input of one or more productive agents is fixed. Therefore, changes in output must be accomplished exclusively by changes in the usage of variable inputs. Thus if a producer wishes to expand output in the short run, he must usually do so by using more hours of labor service with the existing plant and equipment. Similarly, if he wishes to reduce output in the short run, he may discharge certain types of workers; but he cannot immediately "discharge" a building or a diesel locomotive, even though its usage may fall to zero.

In the long run, however, even this is possible, for the *long run* is defined as that period of time (or planning horizon) in which all inputs are variable. The long run, in other words, refers to that time in the future when output changes can be achieved in the manner most advantageous to the businessman. For example, in the short run a producer may be able to expand output only by operating his existing plant for more hours per day. This, of course, entails paying overtime rates to workers. In the long run, it may be more economical for him to install additional productive facilities and return to the normal work day.

In this chapter we are mostly concerned with the short-run theory of production, combining different quantities of variable inputs with a specific quantity of fixed input to produce various quantities of output. The long-run organization of production is largely determined by the relative cost of producing a desired output by different input combinations. Discussion of the long run is thus postponed until Chapters 6 and 7.

5.1.b Fixed or Variable Proportions

As already indicated, our discussion focuses largely upon the use of a *fixed* amount of one input and a *variable* amount of another to produce *variable* quantities of output. This means our attention is restricted mainly to production under conditions of *variable proportions*. The *ratio of input quantities* may vary; the businessman, therefore, must determine not only the level of output he wishes to produce but also the optimal proportion in which to combine inputs (in the long run).

There are two different ways of stating the principle of variable proportions. First, variable-proportions production implies that output can be changed in the short run by changing the amount of variable inputs used in cooperation with the fixed inputs. Naturally, as the amount of one input is changed, the other remaining constant, the *ratio* of inputs changes. Second, when production is subject to variable proportions, the *same* output can be produced by various combinations of inputs—that is, by different input ratios. This may apply only to the long run, but it is relevant to the short run when there is more than one variable input.

Most economists regard production under conditions of variable proportions as typical of both the short and long run. There is certainly no doubt that proportions are variable in the long run. When making an investment decision a businessman may choose among a wide variety of different production processes. As polar opposites, an automobile can be almost handmade or it can be made by assembly-line techniques. In the short run, however, there may be some cases in which output is subject to fixed proportions.

Fixed-proportions production means there is one, and only one, ratio of inputs that can be used to produce a good. If output is expanded or contracted, all inputs must be expanded or contracted so as to maintain the fixed input ratio. At first glance this might seem the usual condition: one man and one shovel produce a ditch, two parts hydrogen and one part oxygen produce water. Adding a second shovel or a second part of oxygen will not augment the rate of production.

But in actuality examples of fixed-proportions production are hard to come by. Even the production of most chemical compounds is subject to variable proportions. It is true, for example, that hydrogen and nitrogen must be used in the fixed ratio $3:1$ to produce ammonia gas. But if three volumes of hydrogen and one volume of nitrogen are mixed in a glass tube and heated to $400°$ C., only minute traces of ammonia will be found (and that only after heating for a very long time). However, if finely divided iron is introduced into the tube under the same conditions, almost the entire amount of hydrogen and nitrogen are converted to ammonia gas within minutes. That is to say, the *yield* of ammonia for any given amount of hydrogen and nitrogen depends upon the amount of the catalyst (finely divided iron) used. Proportions are indeed variable from the standpoint of the catalyst, not only in this instance but in the production of almost every chemical compound.

The hydrogen-nitrogen-ammonia illustration serves as a convenient introduction to a general view of production processes. One might say that in the short run there are three classes of productive inputs. First, there are certain fixed inputs whose quantity cannot be varied in the short run. Second, there are variable inputs whose usage may be changed. Finally, there are "ingredient" inputs whose quantities may be readily changed but must bear fixed proportions to one another and to output.

It is not difficult to find examples of "ingredient" inputs. Each brand of cigarettes contains its own special blend of tobaccos. That is, various tobaccos are blended in fixed proportions. And a fixed amount of tobacco blend must be used in each cigarette produced. But the production of cigarettes requires more than the fixed-proportions ingredient inputs. Certain capital equipment—rolling machines, packaging machines, and the like—must be used and human labor services are necessary. In the short run, the building and capital equipment are fixed inputs and most labor services are variable.

In the discussion of production the fixed and variable inputs are stressed. Ingredient inputs are necessary; and they must be used in fixed or relatively fixed proportions or else the quality or character of the output will change. The businessman has little or no choice in this regard. Hence our attention is directed to those aspects of production over which a businessman can exert control.

5.2 THE PRODUCTION FUNCTION

The discussion so far, especially in subsection 5.1.b, has emphasized that the quantity of output depends upon, or is a function of, the quantities of the various inputs used. This relation is more formally described by a *production function* associating physical output with input.

Definition: A production function is a schedule (or table, or mathematical equation) showing the maximum amount of output that can be produced from any specified set of inputs, given the existing technology or "state of the art." In short, the production function is a catalogue of output possibilities.

5.2.a Total Output or Product

The production function may be shown as a table or, alternatively, as a mathematical equation. In either case the short-run production function gives the total (maximum) output obtainable from different amounts of the variable input, given a specified amount of the fixed input and the required amounts of the ingredient inputs.[1]

As an example, consider an experiment in the production of wheat on 10 acres of land. The fixed input is land, the ingredient input is seed, the variable input is man-years of labor time, and the output is bushels of wheat. An agricultural experiment station blocks off 8 tracts of land, each containing 10 acres. The first tract is worked for a producing season by one man; the second tract is worked by two men; and so on until the eighth tract is worked by eight men. Total output on the various tracts of land might be as shown in Table 5.2.1.

TABLE 5.2.1

**Output of Wheat in Bushels on
10-Acre Tracts of Land**

Tract No.	Number of Workers	Total Output
1	1	10
2	2	24
3	3	39
4	4	52
5	5	61
6	6	64
7	7	65
8	8	64

The hypothetical data in Table 5.2.1 are graphed in Figure 5.2.1. Since output is a function of input, the former—output or total product—is plotted on the vertical axis. The independent variable—number of workers—is plotted on the horizontal axis. Joining the successive points by straight-line segments, one obtains the total product curve. It is important to note that the curve first rises slowly, then more rapidly, and then more slowly again until it finally reaches a maximum and

---

[1] Let q represent the quantity of output. Suppose there is one variable input x and one fixed input y. Mathematically, the short-run production function could be written as $q = f(x|y)$, where the vertical bar means "given."

The two most popular forms of production functions ever to appear in economic literature are called the Cobb-Douglas function and the constant elasticity of substitution (CES) function. In their linearly homogeneous form, these two functions are given, respectively, by

$$q = Ax^{\alpha}y^{1-\alpha} \qquad (0 < \alpha < 1), \tag{5.1.1}$$
$$q = \gamma[\delta x^{-\rho} + (1-\delta)y^{-\rho}]^{-\frac{1}{\rho}} \qquad (\rho > -1). \tag{5.1.2}$$

In the equations above, A, a, γ, δ, and ρ are constants.

begins to decrease. The reasons for this curvature lie in the familiar principle of diminishing marginal physical returns.

FIGURE 5.2.1

Total Product Curve Obtained from Hypothetical Data in Table 5.2.1

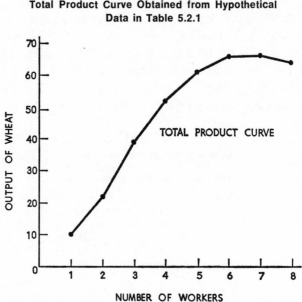

5.2.b Average and Marginal Products

Two important relations between inputs affect the level of output and the relation between output and input. The first of these is the *ratio* in which the inputs are used (in the present illustration, the land-labor ratio). Second, for any given input ratio the *scale* of inputs, or the absolute magnitude of input quantities, is important. To analyze scale effects there must be two or more variable inputs; so our attention in this chapter is confined to the effects incident to changes in the input ratio.

Table 5.2.2 is an expanded version of Table 5.2.1, with some change in the *Total Output* column. The first two columns still indicate the tract number and the number of workers on each tract. The third column shows the input ratio for each tract, or the average number of acres of land per worker. The fourth column reports the total output for each tract of land, while the fifth column shows the average output per worker, or the output-labor ratio. Finally, the sixth column contains the entries for marginal product.

TABLE 5.2.2

**Average and Marginal Products and the Input Ratio
for 10-Acre Tracts**

Tract Number	Number of Workers	Land-Labor Ratio	Total Output	Average Product of Labor	Marginal Product of Labor
1..................	1	10.0	10	10	—
2..................	2	5.0	24	12	14
3..................	3	3.33	39	13	15
4..................	4	2.50	52	13	13
5..................	5	2.00	61	12.2	9
6..................	6	1.67	66	11.0	5
7..................	7	1.43	66	9.4	0
8..................	8	1.25	64	8.0	−2

Definition: The average product of an input is total product divided by the amount of the input used to produce this output. Thus average product is the output-input ratio for each level of output and the corresponding volume of input.

Definition: The marginal product of an input is the addition to total product attributable to the addition of one unit of the variable input to the production process, the fixed input remaining unchanged. (*Note:* Marginal product refers only to comparisons of the results of simultaneous experiments and not to the successive addition of units of the variable input in one experiment.[2])

---

[2] Consider the production function in footnote 1: $q = f(x|y)$. The average product of the variable input x is

$$\frac{q}{x} = \frac{f(x|y)}{x},$$ (5.2.1)

and the marginal product is

$$\frac{dq}{dx} = \frac{df(x|y)}{dx}.$$ (5.2.2)

The average and marginal products derived from the Cobb-Douglas function are

$$\frac{q}{x} = A\left(\frac{x}{y}\right)^{-(1-\alpha)}, \quad \frac{\partial q}{\partial x} = \alpha A\left(\frac{x}{y}\right)^{-(1-\alpha)} = \frac{\alpha q}{x}.$$ (5.2.3)

For the CES function, since it is homogeneous of degree one, we have

$$q = \gamma x\left[\delta + (1-\delta)\left(\frac{x}{y}\right)^{\rho}\right]^{-\frac{1}{\rho}}.$$ (5.2.4)

Hence

$$\frac{q}{x} = \gamma\left[\delta + (1-\delta)\left(\frac{x}{y}\right)^{\rho}\right]^{-\frac{1}{\rho}}.$$ (5.2.5)

Table 5.2.2 and its accompanying graph, Figure 5.2.2, illustrate several important features of a typical production process. First, both average and marginal products initially rise, reach a maximum, and then decline. In the limit, average product could decline to zero because total product itself could conceivably decline to this point. Marginal product, on the other hand, may actually become negative—indeed,

FIGURE 5.2.2

Average and Marginal Products Obtained from Data in Table 5.2.2

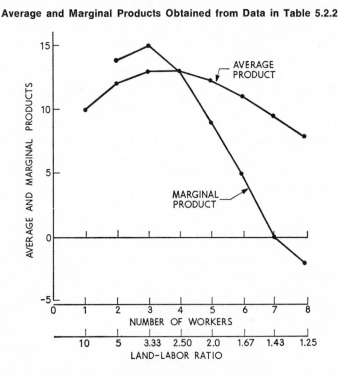

many economists suggest that the marginal product of agricultural workers in some underdeveloped countries is in fact negative. In the present example, the marginal product of labor becomes negative because the variable input is used too intensively with the fixed input (land).

A second feature of significance is that marginal product exceeds average product when the latter is rising, equals average product when

Further

$$\frac{\partial q}{\partial x} = \delta x^{-(1+\rho)} q [\delta x^{-\rho} + (1-\delta) y^{-\rho}]^{-1} \qquad (5.2.6)$$

$$= \delta \gamma^{-\rho} \left(\frac{q}{x}\right)^{1+\rho}.$$

the latter is a maximum, and lies below average product when the latter is falling. This proposition follows readily from the definitions of marginal and average product. So long as the *addition* to a total is greater than the previous average, the average must increase. If the *addition* to the total is less than the previous average, the newly computed average must be less. Thus, since the *additions* first rise and then decline so also must the averages; and the two curves must intersect at the point where the average curve reaches its maximum.[3]

The third feature to note is that as the input (land-labor) ratio declines, the output-labor ratio first rises and then declines indefinitely. The marginal product of labor behaves in a similar manner, as will be explained below.

These results may be summarized in the following

Relations: Both average and marginal products first rise, reach a maximum, and decline thereafter. When average product attains its maximum, average and marginal products are equal. These relations apply only to variable-proportions production functions. Further, within this class of functions, the Cobb-Douglas and CES functions are special cases in that average and marginal products decrease monotonically.

5.2.c Law of Diminishing Marginal Physical Returns

The shape of the marginal product curve in Figure 5.2.2 graphically illustrates an important principle that is already familiar to you: the "law" of diminishing marginal physical returns.

When the outputs of tracts 1 and 2 are compared (Table 5.2.2), one sees that using two workers rather than one increases output by 14 bushels, the marginal product of labor when there are two workers. Similarly, comparing tracts 2 and 3, the use of a third worker augments

---

[3] For simplicity, ignore the fixed input and write the production function as $q = f(x)$. Thus average product is q/x and marginal product is dq/dx. Average product is a maximum when

$$\frac{d\left(\frac{q}{x}\right)}{dx} = \frac{1}{x}\left[\frac{dq}{dx} - \frac{q}{x}\right] = 0.$$

Since $x > 0$, $\frac{1}{x}\left[\frac{dq}{dx} - \frac{q}{x}\right]$ can equal zero only when $\frac{q}{x} = \frac{dq}{dx}$.

Thus marginal product equals average product when the latter is at its maximum value.

Note that marginal and average products in the Cobb-Douglas and CES cases do not have maxima. Both MP and AP are monotonically decreasing functions in both cases.

output by 15 bushels. The marginal physical product of labor increases as the number of workers increases. This may well happen when the land-labor ratio is very high.

Ultimately, however, as the input ratio declines so also must the marginal product of the variable input. When the number of units of the variable input increases, each unit, so to speak, has on the average fewer units of the fixed input with which to work. At first, when the fixed input is relatively plentiful, more intensive utilization of fixed inputs by variable inputs may increase the marginal output of the variable input. Nonetheless, a point is quickly reached beyond which an increase in the intensity of use of the fixed input yields progressively less and less additional returns. Psychologists have even found that this holds true for consecutive study time.

Principle (the law of diminishing marginal physical returns): As the amount of a variable input is increased, the amount of other (fixed) inputs held constant, a point is reached beyond which marginal product declines.[4]

5.2.d Product Curves for Different Amounts of the Fixed Input

The fixed input is a parameter that causes the whole set of product curves to shift. Generally, the greater the amount of fixed input available the greater the input ratio and the greater also the total, average, and marginal products. Increasing the land-labor ratio increases the amount of fixed input available per unit of variable input. This normally results in an increase in the marginal, average, and total product of the variable input.

This proposition is illustrated in Table 5.2.3 and shown graphically in Figures 5.2.3 and 5.2.4.[5] The first row in each part of the table shows data from an hypothetical agricultural experiment on 1-acre tracts of land. The second row shows the corresponding data for experiments on 2-acre tracts. Comparing each set of rows, the table shows that for each amount of variable input, the total, average, and marginal

---

[4] It might be well at this point to emphasize that the "law of diminishing returns" is actually an *empirical assertion about reality*. It is not a theorem derived from an axiom system; it is not a logical proposition that is susceptible of mathematical proof or refutation. It is a simple statement concerning physical relations that have been observed in the real economic world. It is of some worth to note that a contrary observation has never been recorded.

[5] As you will see in section 5.3, when the average product of the variable input is increasing the marginal product of the fixed input is negative. Hence the results of this subsection *hold only for the range of production from maximum average product to zero marginal product of the variable input.*

TABLE 5.2.3

Total, Average, and Marginal Products on 1- and 2-Acre Tracts of Land

Product	Size of Tract	Number of Workers					
		1	*2*	*3*	*4*	*5*	*6*
Total...............	1 acre	20	30	37.5	44	50	55.5
....	2 acres	25	40	52.5	64	75	85.5
Average.............	1 acre	20	15	12.5	11	10	9.25
....	2 acres	25	20	17.5	16	15	14.25
Marginal............	1 acre	—	10	7.5	6.5	6	5.5
....	2 acres	—	15	12.5	11.5	11	10.5

FIGURE 5.2.3

Total Product Curves for 1- and 2-Acre Tracts of Land

FIGURE 5.2.4

Average and Marginal Product Curves for 1- and 2-Acre Tracts of Land

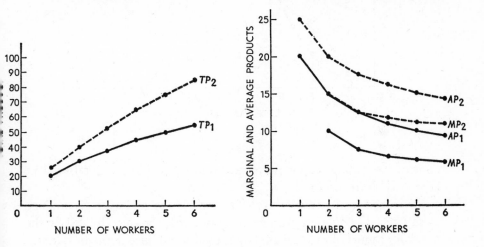

products are greater on the 2-acre tracts of land. The table, together with the associated figures, clearly shows that over the relevant range of production (see section 5.3) augmenting the fixed input augments the productivity of the variable input.

5.3 THE STAGES OF PRODUCTION

This study of production has so far focused attention upon one specific, discrete production function given in tabular form. We turn now to a more general formulation in which both discrete and continuous production functions are used.

5.3.a   Geometry of Average Product Curves

A typical form of the (continuous) total product curve is shown in Figure 5.3.1. In this, as in all other one-variable-input product graphs,

FIGURE 5.3.1

Geometry of Marginal and Average Product Curves

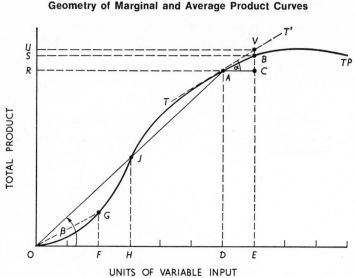

units of the variable input are plotted on the abscissa and total product is plotted on the ordinate.

Given the total product curve *TP,* we wish to find average product. First, from its definition average product is total product divided by the number of units of the variable input used to produce it, or the output–variable input ratio. Producing total output $OR = DA$ requires OD units of the variable input. Thus the average product of OD units of variable input is DA/OD. Similarly, the average product of *OF* units of variable input is FG/OF and of OH units is HJ/OH. In each case, to obtain the average product corresponding to a given point on the total product curve, we found the slope of the line joining the origin with the point in question. In other words, we found the tangent of the angle formed by the abscissa and the line from the origin to the given point on the total product curve.

As we have seen, the average product corresponding to point *A* is DA/OD, but this is precisely the slope of the line *OA,* or the tangent of the angle β. Notice also that average product must be the same for *OH* as for OD units of the variable input because the slopes of OJ and of OA are identical (in each case, average product is the tangent of angle β). Since average product is rising for movements along TP from the origin to point J, and since it is obviously falling for movements from A to B, there is reason to suspect that average product reaches its maximum at a point between J and A on the total product curve.

Average product does, in fact, attain its maximum at an intermediate point, as may be seen more clearly in Figure 5.3.2. Points Q and R in Figure 5.3.2 correspond to points J and A, respectively, in Figure 5.3.1, in that each pair of points lies on a common ray from the origin. Thus the average product at point Q is equal to the average product at point R. Since average product is the slope of a ray from the origin to a point

FIGURE 5.3.2

Maxima of Average and Marginal Products

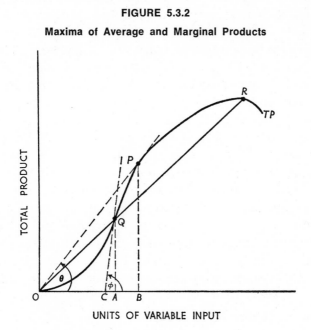

on the curve, average product is a maximum when the slope of the line is steepest. This occurs, of course, when the line from the origin is just tangent to the total product curve, at point P with angle θ in Figure 5.3.2.

As one moves from the origin through point Q toward point P, the line from the origin to the curve becomes steeper. Similarly, as one moves from point P toward point R, the line moves downward, becoming less steep. Thus we have proved the following important points:

Relations: Average product corresponding to any point on the total product curve is given by the slope of a ray from the origin to the point in question. Average product attains its maximum value when this line is tangent to the total product curve.

5.3.b Geometry of Marginal Product Curves

Using Figures 5.3.1 and 5.3.2 again, similar qualitative and quantitative relations may be found for the marginal product curve.

Turn first to Figure 5.3.1. By definition, marginal product is the addition to total product attributable to the addition of one unit (or a small amount) of the variable input to a given amount of the fixed input. Let the amount of variable input increase from *OD* to *OE,* or by the amount *DE = AC.* Output consequently increases from *OR* to *OS,* or by the amount *RS = BC.* Marginal product is, therefore, *BC/AC.* In this discrete case, there is no convenient slope measurement because the arc *AB* is not linear. That is, a unique slope measure cannot be obtained because the slope of the angle formed by arc *AB* and line *AC* changes over the interval *DE = AC.*

But let us suppose for a minute that the total product curve were linear from *A* to the point *V.* Then an increment of amount *DE* in the variable input would cause output to increase from *OR* to *OU,* or by *RU = CV.* In this case, marginal product would be *CV/AC,* or the tangent of angle *a.* The measure *CV/AC* overstates the true magnitude of marginal product, *BC/AC.* However, as the increment of variable input becomes smaller and smaller the approximation becomes better and better. In the limit, for a very tiny increase in variable input the slope of the tangent to point *A,* labeled *TT',* approaches the true slope of the total product curve. Hence for sufficiently small changes in the variable input, the slope of the total product curve at any point is a good approximation of marginal product.[6]

---

[6] Let $q = f(x)$ be the production function. If the increment of variable input is denoted Δx, the new output is $f(x + \Delta x)$. Thus, by definition, marginal product is

$$MP = \frac{f(x + \Delta x) - f(x)}{\Delta x}.$$

But also by definition, the derivative of $f(x)$ is

$$\frac{dq}{dx} = \lim_{\Delta x \to 0} \frac{f(x + \Delta x) - f(x)}{\Delta x}.$$

Hence in the limit, marginal product *is* the slope (dq/dx) of the total product curve. For finite changes, the slope is an approximation of marginal product.

The slope of a curve at any point is given by the slope of its tangent at that point. Thus the marginal product corresponding to point Q in Figure 5.3.2 is the slope of the line CQ, or the tangent of angle $\phi = AQ/CA$. As Figure 5.3.2 is constructed, marginal product is a maximum when OA units of variable input are used. This is true because the slope of the tangent to the total product curve is steeper at point Q than at any other point.

Other interesting relations can be determined from Figure 5.3.2. First, recall that maximum average product is associated with OB units of variable input and corresponds to point P. Hence marginal product attains its maximum at a lower level of variable input usage than does average product. Second, notice that the tangent to the total product curve at point P—the line whose slope gives marginal product corresponding to point P—is the line OP. We have already seen in subsection 5.3.a that the slope of OP also gives average product associated with point P and that average product attains its maximum value at that point. Hence, as we have seen previously, marginal product equals average product when the latter is at its maximum.

The principal information contained in this subsection can be summarized as follows:

Relations: Marginal product corresponding to any point on the total product curve is given by the slope of the tangent to the curve at that point. Marginal product attains its maximum value when the slope of the tangent is steepest. The point of maximum marginal product occurs at a smaller level of variable input usage than does maximum average product; and marginal product equals average product when the latter attains its maximum value.

5.3.c Total, Average, and Marginal Products

The relations discussed in the two preceding subsections are illustrated in Figure 5.3.3.[7] In this graph one can see not only the relation

---

[7] This graph is constructed under the assumption that output is zero if the input of the variable factor is zero. Thus if the production function is $q = f(x|y)$, we assume that $f(0|y) = f(x|0) = f(0|0) = 0$. For an alternative approach, see Frank Knight, *Risk, Uncertainty, and Profit*, Reprints of Economic Classics (New York: Augustus M. Kelley, 1964), p. 100.

It might be well to point out that not all production functions give rise to product curves such as those shown in Figures 5.3.3 and 5.3.4. For example, the Cobb-Douglas and CES functions do not have regions in which marginal and average products increase, nor do they have a region in which marginal product is negative. Further, the CES function with $y > 0$ has a positive ordinate intercept.

One form of a linearly homogeneous function that would give rise to the curves in Figures 5.3.3 and 5.3.4 is

FIGURE 5.3.3

Total, Average, and Marginal Products

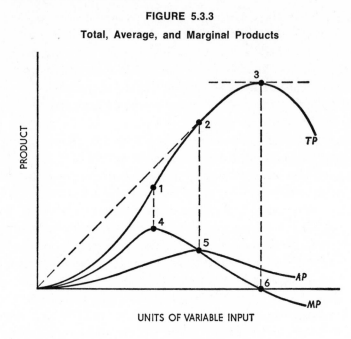

between marginal and average products but also the relation of these two curves to total product.

Consider first the total product curve. For very small amounts of the variable input, total product rises gradually. But even at a low level of input it begins to rise quite rapidly, reaching its maximum slope (or rate of increase) at point 1. Since the slope of the total product curve equals marginal product, the maximum slope (point 1) must correspond to the maximum point on the marginal product curve (point 4).[8]

$$q = a \left[\frac{bx^3y^2 + cx^2y^3}{ex^4 + gy^4} \right] , \qquad (5.7.1)$$

where a, b, c, e, and g are positive constants. For a more detailed treatment of the general case and a numerical example of equation (5.7.1), see C. E. Ferguson, *The Neoclassical Theory of Production and Distribution* (London and New York: Cambridge University Press, 1969), pp. 122–24.

[8] This point may easily be shown mathematically. Let the production function be $q = f(x|y)$. Since y is held fixed, we may use straight derivative notation rather than partial derivative notation. Let f', f'', and f''' denote the first, second, and third derivatives with respect to x.

Marginal product is, by definition, $f'(x|y)$. For the marginal product to be a maximum, it is necessary for $f''(x|y)$ to be zero and for $f'''(x|y)$ to be negative. That is,

After attaining its maximum slope at point 1, the total product curve continues to rise. But output increases at a decreasing rate, so the slope is less steep. Moving outward along the curve from point 1, soon the point is reached at which a ray from the origin is just tangent to the curve (point 2). Since tangency of the ray to the curve defines the condition for maximum average product, point 2 lies directly above point 5.

As the quantity of variable input is expanded from its value at point 2, total product continues to increase. But its rate of increase is progressively slower until point 3 is finally reached. At this position total product is at a maximum; thereafter it declines until it (conceivably) reaches zero again. Over a tiny range around point 3, additional input does not change total output. The slope of the total product curve is zero. Thus marginal product must also be zero. This is shown by the fact that points 3 and 6 occur at precisely the same input value. And since total product declines beyond point 3, marginal product becomes negative.

Most of the important relations have so far been discussed with reference to the total product curve. To emphasize certain relations, however, consider the marginal and average product curves in Figure 5.3.3. Marginal product at first increases, reaches a maximum at point 4 (the point of diminishing marginal physical returns), and declines thereafter. It eventually becomes negative beyond point 6, at which total product is at its maximum.

Average product also rises at first until it reaches its maximum at point 5, where marginal and average products are equal. It subse-

---

$$f'(x|y) = \text{maximum implies} \qquad (5.8.1)$$
$$f''(x|y) = 0 \text{ and } f'''(x|y) < 0 .$$

Now consider the production function $f(x|y)$. Any function whose second derivative is zero for some input value has a point of inflection at that input value. Further, if the third derivative is negative, the concavity of the function changes from concave from above to concave from below at that point. One may easily see this change in concavity in Figures 5.3.3 and 5.3.4.

Here, as elsewhere, I depart from the conventional mathematical language of "convex-concave." In my usage, a curve is concave from above or concave from below at a point according as the tangent to the curve at that point lies otherwise below or above the curve. For the convenience of the mathematically trained reader, the following is added:

Definition: Consider any function $\eta = \phi(\xi)$. The function is said to have a point of inflection at $\xi = x$ if $\phi_{xx} = 0$. If $\phi_{xxx} < 0$, the function changes from concave from above to concave from below; if $\phi_{xxx} > 0$, concavity changes in the opposite direction.

quently declines, conceivably becoming zero when total product itself becomes zero. Finally, one may observe that marginal product exceeds average product when the latter is increasing and is less than average product when the latter is decreasing.

5.3.d Three Stages of Production

The relations among total, average, and marginal products are used to define three stages of production, as illustrated in Figure 5.3.4.

FIGURE 5.3.4

Stages of Production

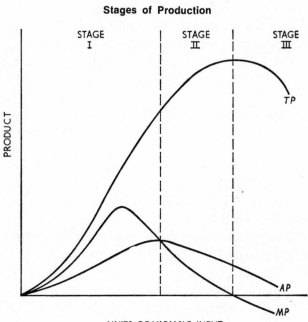

STAGE I   STAGE II   STAGE III

TP

AP

MP

PRODUCT

UNITS OF VARIABLE INPUT

Stage I covers that range of variable input usage over which average product is rising. In other words, stage I corresponds to increasing *average* returns to the variable input. But, as explained in the next subsection, increasing average returns to the variable input are associated with negative marginal returns to the fixed input. The fixed input is present in uneconomically large proportion relative to the variable input in stage I. A rational producer would never operate in this range of production. If market conditions dictated such a small level of total output, the output would be produced by using fewer units of the fixed input—the entire set of product curves would be *shifted* from the position shown in Figure 5.3.4.

Production would also never occur in stage III, as is more or less obvious from the graph. Stage III is defined as the range of negative marginal product or declining total product. Additional units of variable input during this stage of production actually cause a decrease in total output. Even if units of the variable input were *free,* a rational producer would not employ them beyond the point of zero marginal product because their use entails a reduction in total output. If market conditions dictate an expansion of output, additional units of the fixed input must be used, shifting the entire set of product curves upward (as illustrated in Figures 5.2.3 and 5.2.4).

In stage III the variable input is combined with the fixed input in uneconomically large proportions. In terms of agriculture, land is cultivated too intensively. Indeed, the point of zero marginal product of the variable input is called the *intensive margin.* Similarly, in suggestive terminology, at the point of maximum average product of the variable input the cultivation of land is extensive; and the point of maximum average product of the variable input is called the *extensive margin.*[9]

We have now eliminated stages I and III. Production must occur in stage II—between the extensive margin and the intensive margin, or over the range of variable input usage from maximum average product to zero marginal product. If output must be produced in quantities not covered by production in stage II, there must be some change in the quantity of fixed input. If a smaller output is desired, the units of fixed input must be reduced; if a larger output is required, it can be achieved only by augmenting fixed input.

5.3.e Symmetry of the Stages of Production

The purpose of this concluding subsection is to demonstrate that the stages of production are symmetrical when viewed from the standpoints of the variable and of the fixed input. This, in turn, will explain the so-far ambiguous statement that rising average returns to the variable input correspond to negative marginal returns to the fixed input.[10]

---

[9] As shown in subsection 5.3.e, when the production function is homogeneous of degree one, the point of maximum average product of the variable input corresponds to the point of zero marginal product of the fixed input. Hence the extensive margin, from the standpoint of the variable input, is the intensive margin in terms of the fixed input, and vice versa.

[10] The results presented in this section are *strictly* true if, and only if, production is subject to constant returns to scale. "Constant returns to scale" means that if the

TABLE 5.3.1

**Total, Average, and Marginal Products of Labor in Cultivating
1-Acre Tracts of Land**

Acres of Land	Number of Workers	Land-Labor Ratio	Total Product (Labor)	Average Product (Labor)	Marginal Product (Labor)
1	1	1	5	5	5
1	2	$\frac{1}{2}$	13	$6\frac{1}{2}$	8
1	3	$\frac{1}{3}$	23	$7\frac{2}{3}$	10
1	4	$\frac{1}{4}$	38	$9\frac{1}{2}$	15
1	5	$\frac{1}{5}$	50	10	12
1	6	$\frac{1}{6}$	60	10	10
1	7	$\frac{1}{7}$	68	$9\frac{5}{7}$	8
1	8	$\frac{1}{8}$	75	$9\frac{3}{8}$	7
1	9	$\frac{1}{9}$	81	9	6
1	10	$\frac{1}{10}$	86	$8\frac{3}{5}$	5

Table 5.3.1 contains an example similar to that discussed in section 5.2. Ten 1-acre tracts of land are simultaneously cultivated. One worker is on the first tract; two workers are on the second; and so on until 10 workers cultivate the 10th tract. Table 5.3.1 shows the total, average, and marginal products of labor (the variable input) determined from this experiment.

We can now use Table 5.3.1 to derive the implicit total, average, and marginal products of land, the fixed input. From the last row of Table 5.3.1 it is seen that 1 acre of land cultivated by 10 workers produces 86 units of output. In this experiment, each worker on the average cultivates $\frac{1}{10}$ acre of land. Hence if one worker were to cultivate $\frac{1}{10}$ acre of land, total product would be $\frac{1}{10}$ as great as when 10 workers cultivate 1 acre.[11] Therefore, total product with $\frac{1}{10}$ acre of land and one worker is $\frac{1}{10}$ of 86, or $8\frac{3}{5}$. This is shown in the first entry in column 4 of Table 5.3.2 as the Total Product of Land.

Similarly, from the next-to-last row of Table 5.3.1, 1 acre of land

input of each productive agent is multiplied by a number *m* (however large or small), output is also multiplied by *m*. In other words, constant returns to scale implies that two workers, each cultivating 1 acre of land, can in total produce exactly the same output as two workers jointly cultivating two acres of land.

Mathematically, constant returns to scale implies that the production function is homogeneous of degree one. By definition of first-degree homogeneity, if $q = f(x, y)$, then $f(mx, my) = mq$. This is precisely what is meant by constant returns to scale.

[11] This statement is strictly true if, and only if, the production function is homogeneous of degree one.

worked by 9 units of labor produces 81 units of output. Therefore, 1/9 acre of land cultivated by one worker will produce one ninth this much, or nine units of output. This is shown as the second entry in the

TABLE 5.3.2

Total, Average, and Marginal Products of Land When Various Tracts Are Cultivated by One Worker

Acres of Land	Number of Workers	Land-Labor Ratio	Total Product (Land)	Average Product per Acre	Marginal Product per Acre
1/10	1	1/10	8⅗	86	—
1/9	1	1/9	9	81	36
1/8	1	1/8	9⅜	75	27
1/7	1	1/7	9⁵/₇	68	19
1/6	1	1/6	10	60	12
1/5	1	1/5	10	50	0
1/4	1	1/4	9½	38	−10
1/3	1	1/3	7⅔	23	−22
1/2	1	1/2	6½	13	−20
1	1	1	5	5	−3

Total Product column in Table 5.3.2. Proceeding in this manner from the bottom to the top of Table 5.3.1, we may determine the total product of land (column 4, Table 5.3.2). One should notice that the method of computation necessarily implies that for each land-labor ratio, the total product of land is precisely the same as the average product of labor.[12]

Next we need to determine the marginal product per acre of land. In Table 5.3.2, when the amount of land changes from 1/10 acre to 1/9 acre, the total product of land increases from 8⅗ to 9, or by ⅖ units. The fixed input has increased by $1/9 - 1/10 = 1/90$ acre. Hence the marginal product of an additional *acre* is ⅖ × 90 = 36 units of output. Similarly, when the units of fixed input increase from 1/9 acre to 1/8 acre, total product increases from 9 to 9⅜, or by ⅜ units of output. Accordingly, at this point marginal product is ⅜ × 72 = 27. Proceeding in this manner, the marginal product of land (the fixed factor) can be

---

[12] The reverse relation—that the total product of the variable factor equals the average product of the fixed factor—holds in this example and in all examples in which the measure of the fixed factor is standardized on unity. The reverse relation, however, does not necessarily hold. For a contrary example, see the revised edition of C. E. Ferguson, *Microeconomic Theory* (Homewood, Ill.: Richard D. Irwin, Inc., 1969), pp. 132–34.

determined for the various acreages in the experiment. These figures are shown in the last column of Table 5.3.2.

Finally, the average product per acre of land can be derived in an analogous fashion. In combination with one worker, $\frac{1}{10}$ acre of land can produce $8\frac{3}{5}$ units of output. Hence 1 acre of land has an average product of $10 \times 8\frac{3}{5} = 86$ units of output. Similarly, $\frac{1}{9}$ acre of land and one worker produce nine units of output. Hence at this input point, the average product per acre of land is $9 \times 9 = 81$ units of output. By employing this method for each value of land input, the average product per acre of land is obtained (next-to-last column, Table 5.3.2).

The hypothetical data in Tables 5.3.1 and 5.3.2 are plotted in Figure 5.3.5. Notice carefully that the horizontal axis represents the

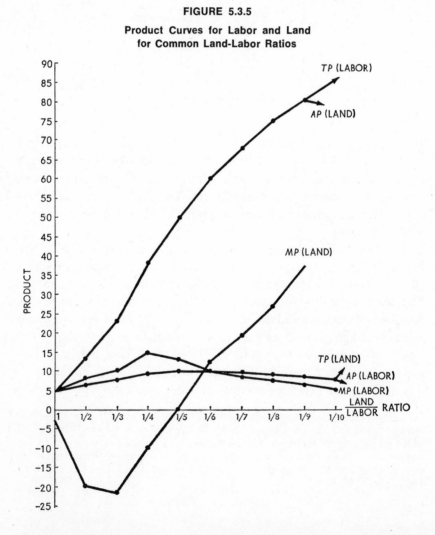

FIGURE 5.3.5

**Product Curves for Labor and Land
for Common Land-Labor Ratios**

land-labor ratio and that it *declines* in value as one moves to the right along the axis. The origin of coordinates is 1, 0 rather than the customary 0, 0. Furthermore there is another important difference in the measurement scale on the horizontal axis. Normally, a unit distance measures a unit change in the variable. Thus the distance from 1 to 2 is the same as the distance from 9 to 10. In this graph, however, unit distance along the axis measures a unit change in the denominator of a fraction whose numerator remains constant. Thus the distance from 1 to ½ is the same as the distance from ⅑ to ⅒.

First observe that the total, average, and marginal product curves for labor are exactly the same as in Figures 5.2.1 and 5.2.2. Stage I for labor ends at the point where the average product of labor attains its maximum value. Similarly, stage III for labor begins at the point where the marginal product of labor is zero (total product is a maximum). For greater clarity this is also illustrated in panel a, Figure 5.3.6, which represents a more general, continuous case.[13]

Figure 5.3.5 shows the average and marginal products of land (the total product of land is the same as the average product of labor). The

FIGURE 5.3.6

Symmetry of the Stages of Production

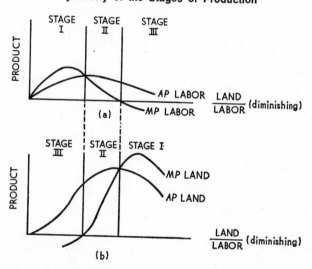

---

[13] In the discrete case shown in Figure 5.3.5, stage I ends when average labor product attains its maximum value of 10. At this point, due to discontinuous data, marginal product exceeds average product—but it is equal at the next input point, where marginal product equals maximum average product equals 10. In the continuous case shown in Figure 5.3.6, average product has a *unique* maximum associated with a *unique* land-labor ratio. In this situation, as in Figure 5.3.4, stage I ends where the marginal and average products of labor are equal.

graph clearly illustrates—and Figure 5.3.6 reemphasizes—the symmetry of the three stages of production. The marginal product of land is first negative and reaches zero when the total product of land (the average product of labor) is a maximum. Hence large land-labor ratios define stage III, the area in which the marginal product of land is negative. Similarly, the average product of land attains its maximum at the same land-labor ratio as that which reduces the marginal product of labor to zero. Hence this point defines stage I for land and stage III for labor.[14]

---

[14] The essential feature is that the marginal product of the fixed factor is negative when the average product of the variable factor is rising, positive when it is falling. Because of this relation, the marginal product of the fixed factor is zero when the average product of the variable factor attains its maximum.

These relations are easily proved. Let the production function be

$$q = f(x, y) , \qquad (5.14.1)$$

where f is homogeneous of degree one in x and y. By Euler's mathematical theorem on homogeneous functions, we have

$$q = xf_x + yf_y , \qquad (5.14.2)$$

where subscripts denote partial derivatives. Further, by the homogeneity of f, we know that

$$xf_{xx} = -yf_{xy} . \qquad (5.14.3)$$

(For a discussion of the properties of functions homogeneous of degree one, see R. G. D. Allen, *Mathematical Analysis for Economists* [New York: St. Martin's Press, 1938], pp. 315–19.)

From equation (5.14.2), the average product of x, the variable factor, may be written as

$$\frac{q}{x} = f_x + \frac{y}{x} f_y . \qquad (5.14.4)$$

For the average product of the variable factor to be a maximum, it is necessary that

$$\frac{\partial \left(\frac{q}{x} \right)}{\partial x} = f_{xx} - \frac{y}{x^2} f_y + \frac{y}{x} f_{xy} = 0 . \qquad (5.14.5)$$

Using equation (5.14.3) in equation (5.14.5), one obtains

$$\frac{\partial \left(\frac{q}{x} \right)}{\partial x} = - \frac{y}{x^2} f_y = 0 . \qquad (5.14.6)$$

Since the inputs are positive, equation (5.14.6) implies that $f_y = 0$. Next, for a proper maximum equation (5.14.6) must be positive when the input ratio is less than the critical one, negative when the input ratio is larger. Since the sign of f_y is the opposite, the relation stated at the beginning of this footnote is proved.

At this point it seems worthwhile to give a brief mathematical explanation of why standardizing on unity makes (*i*) the average product of the variable factor

Stage II is the same from either point of view—and it is the only stage in which production will take place. From the standpoint of the variable input, stage II lies between the extensive and the intensive margins. But what is extensive for the variable input is intensive for the fixed input, and vice versa. Thus stage II, from the standpoint of the fixed input, lies between the intensive and extensive margins.

The many points discussed in this subsection may be summarized as follows.

Relations: (1) There is a symmetry of the three stages of production for the variable and for the fixed input. In particular, stage I (or III) for the variable input and stage III (or I) for the fixed input cover precisely the same range of values of the fixed-to-variable-input ratio. Stage II is the

---

equal to the total product of the fixed factor, and (ii) the total product of the variable factor equal to the average product of the fixed factor.

Assume that the production function is $q = f(x, y)$, where x and y are the variable and fixed factors respectively. When $f(x, y)$ is homogeneous of degree one, we know from Euler's theorem that we can write

$$q = f(x, y) = yf\left(\frac{x}{y}, 1\right) = xf\left(1, \frac{y}{x}\right). \tag{5.14.7}$$

Thus the average product of x is

$$\frac{q}{x} = f\left(1, \frac{y}{x}\right) = \frac{y}{x}f\left(\frac{x}{y}, 1\right). \tag{5.14.8}$$

When calculating the product functions for x, y (acres of land) is held fixed at unity. Therefore, equations (5.14.7) and (5.14.8) become

$$q = f(x, y) = f(x, 1), \tag{5.14.9}$$

and

$$\frac{q}{x} = \frac{1}{x}f(x, 1). \tag{5.14.10}$$

From equation (5.14.7) it follows that

$$\frac{q}{x} = \frac{y}{x}f\left(\frac{x}{y}, 1\right) = \frac{1}{x}f(x, 1) \tag{5.14.11}$$

when $y \equiv 1$.

Equation (5.14.11) is the expression for the average product of x. Now turn it around to calculate the total product of y. In this case, x is held fixed at unity. Thus equation (5.14.11) becomes

$$q = f(x, 1), \tag{5.14.12}$$

which is identical to equation (5.14.9), *q.e.d.*

Similar procedures may be used to prove the reverse relation.

For a more detailed analysis of production functions homogeneous of degree one, see C. E. Ferguson, *The Neoclassical Theory of Production and Distribution* (London and New York: Cambridge University Press, 1969), chap. 5.

same for both. (2) Over the range of rising average returns (product) to the variable input, the marginal returns of the fixed input are negative. Similarly, the range of rising average product of the fixed input corresponds to the range of negative marginal product of the variable input. (3) Stated differently, the extensive margin with respect to the variable input corresponds to the intensive margin for the fixed input, and vice versa. (4) Over the range of input ratio values for which the average product of the variable input is rising, production will not occur because the fixed input is present in uneconomically large proportion—it is used beyond its intensive margin. Over the range for which the marginal product of the variable input is negative, production will not occur because the variable input is present in uneconomically large proportion— it is used beyond its intensive margin. Thus production will occur only in stage II, the range of input ratio values lying between the intensive margins of the fixed and variable inputs respectively.

5.4 LINEARLY HOMOGENEOUS PRODUCTION FUNCTIONS

Whether production functions typically reflect constant returns to scale is at best an empirical question and at worst a moot one. Nonetheless, the mathematical simplicity of functions homogeneous of degree one frequently causes economists to assume constant returns to scale. That is, many of the more advanced economic models are simply not soluble unless linear homogeneity of the production function is assumed. Since constant-returns-to-scale production functions are so prevalent in the literature, some of their chief characteristics are discussed here and in Chapter 6.

5.4.a The Meaning of Linear Homogeneity

"Linear homogeneity" and "constant returns to scale" are interchangeable terms when used to describe a production function. Both get at the essential concept: if all inputs are expanded in the same proportion, output is expanded in that proportion. Consider the simple Cobb-Douglas function:

$$q = f(x, y) = Ax^{\alpha}y^{1-\alpha}, \qquad (5.4.1)$$

where A and α are positive constants and $0 < \alpha < 1$. Now let both x and y be increased in the proportion λ. One then has

$$\begin{aligned} f(\lambda x, \lambda y) &= A(\lambda x)^{\alpha}(\lambda y)^{1-\alpha} = A\lambda^{\alpha}\lambda^{1-\alpha}x^{\alpha}y^{1-\alpha} \\ &= A\lambda x^{\alpha}y^{1-\alpha} = \lambda(Ax^{\alpha}y^{1-\alpha}) = \lambda f(x, y) = \lambda q . \end{aligned} \qquad (5.4.2)$$

Thus if the usage of all inputs is expanded in the same proportion, output expands in that proportion. This is precisely what is meant by "constant returns to scale."

The other essential feature of linearly homogeneous production functions is as follows: the average and marginal products depend upon the *ratio* in which the inputs are combined, but their values are *independent* of the absolute magnitudes of the inputs. Again consider the Cobb-Douglas function. Divide both sides of equation (5.4.1) by x to obtain the average product of X:

$$AP_x = \frac{q}{x} = Ax^{\alpha-1}y^{1-\alpha} = A\left(\frac{y}{x}\right)^{1-\alpha}. \qquad (5.4.3)$$

This clearly shows that the average product of x depends only upon the factor input ratio or factor proportions. For example, suppose $A = 100$ and $\alpha = \frac{1}{2}$. If $y = 4$ and $x = 1$, the average product of X is 200. If $y = 400$ and $x = 100$, the ratio is the same and so is the magnitude of the average product.

The same relation may be shown for the marginal product. Let y be constant and let the input of X increase from x to $x + \Delta x$. The difference in output is

$$\Delta q = A(x + \Delta x)^\alpha y^{1-\alpha} - Ax^\alpha y^{1-\alpha} = Ay^{1-\alpha}[(x + \Delta x)^\alpha - x^\alpha]. \quad (5.4.4)$$

Using the binomial theorem, we can expand the term $(x + \Delta x)^\alpha$ as follows:

$$(x + \Delta x)^\alpha = x^\alpha + \alpha x^{\alpha-1} \Delta x + \frac{\alpha(\alpha - 1)x^{\alpha-2}(\Delta x)^2}{2!} + \cdots. \quad (5.4.5)$$

Now for small values of Δx, we may ignore the terms that involve higher powers of Δx, i.e., $(\Delta x)^2$, $(\Delta x)^3$, etc. Thus $(x + \Delta x)^\alpha$ is approximately equal to $x^\alpha + \alpha x^{\alpha-1} \Delta x$. Substituting this in equation (5.4.4), we obtain

$$\Delta q = Ay^{1-\alpha}[x^\alpha + \alpha x^{\alpha-1}\Delta x - x^\alpha] = \alpha Ay^{1-\alpha}x^{\alpha-1}\Delta x. \quad (5.4.6)$$

Hence the marginal product of X can be written as

$$\frac{\Delta q}{\Delta x} = \alpha A\left(\frac{y}{x}\right)^{1-\alpha}, \qquad (5.4.7)$$

which shows that the marginal product depends upon the input ratio only.

The essential features of linearly homogeneous production functions may be summarized as follows:

Relations: If the production function is homogeneous of degree one, (*i*) there are constant returns to scale, i.e., to proportional expansions of all inputs; and (*ii*) the marginal and average product functions depend only upon the ratio in which the inputs are combined and, in particular, they are independent of the absolute amounts of the inputs employed.

5.4.b The Product Curves

The fact that the marginal and average products depend exclusively upon the input ratio has some special implications for the product curve graphs. Suppose X is the variable factor and Y is held constant at the level $y = y_0$. The marginal and average product curves are shown in Figure 5.4.1. The marginal product curve reaches its maximum

FIGURE 5.4.1

Marginal and Average Product Curves for a Production Function Homogeneous of Degree One

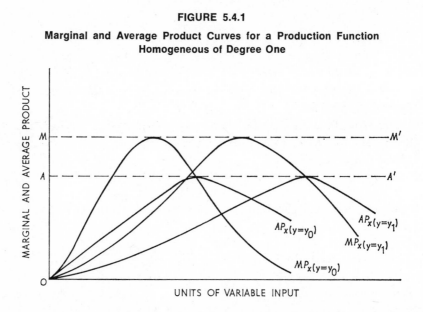

of OM, then declines and intersects the average product curve at its maximum OA. Now suppose the fixed input Y is increased to $y_1 > y_0$. The product curves shift, and both attain new maxima at a greater level of X usage. But since the maxima of both functions depend only on the input ratio, the maxima must be the same when $y = y_0$, when $y = y_1$, and when y has any other value. Hence the marginal and average product curves shift as shown in Figure 5.4.1, marginal product always having the same maximum OM and average product the same maximum OA.

These relations may also be illustrated by shifting total product curves, as in Figure 5.4.2. As you will recall, the slope of a ray from the origin to a point on the total product curve is average product; and, in particular, average product is a maximum when the ray is just tangent to the total product curve. Given $y = y_0$, a ray from the origin is tangent to $f(x|y = y_0)$ at A. But since the maximum value of average product

FIGURE 5.4.2

**Total Product Curves for a Production Function
Homogeneous of Degree One**

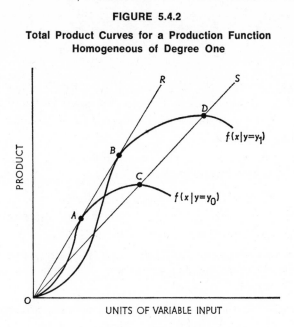

is the same irrespective of the value of y, $f(x|y = y_1)$ and all other total product curves must be tangent to the ray OR. For similar reasons, the maxima of the total product curves must all lie on a ray such as OS in Figure 5.4.2.

Exercise: Demonstrate the last relation for yourself.

5.4.c Output Elasticities and the Function Coefficient

You have seen in your study of demand that an elasticity coefficient always measures the proportional change in a dependent variable (e.g., quantity bought) induced by a given proportional change in an independent variable (e.g., price). This applies to production as well as demand. Let us begin, therefore, with the following

Definition: Given the production function $q = f(x, y)$, the *output elasticity* of X is the proportional change in output resulting from a given proportional change in X, the input of Y held constant. Similarly, the *output elasticity* of Y is the proportional change in output resulting from a given proportional change in Y, the input of X held constant.

As in the case of demand elasticities, output elasticities may be expressed as formulas. Let ϵ_X and ϵ_Y denote the output elasticities of X and Y respectively. Then

$$\epsilon_X = \frac{\Delta q}{q} \div \frac{\Delta x}{x} = \frac{\Delta q}{\Delta x}\frac{x}{q} = \frac{\Delta q}{\Delta x} \div \frac{q}{x}, \tag{5.4.8}$$

$$\epsilon_Y = \frac{\Delta q}{q} \div \frac{\Delta y}{y} = \frac{\Delta q}{\Delta y}\frac{y}{q} = \frac{\Delta q}{\Delta y} \div \frac{q}{y}. \tag{5.4.9}$$

Now focus attention on the right-most terms in the two equations above. $\Delta q / \Delta x$ and $\Delta q / \Delta y$ are, by definition, the marginal products of X and Y. Similarly, q/x and q/y are the average products of X and Y. Hence we may state the following

Relation: The output elasticity of an input is equal to its marginal product divided by its average product.

Now turn back to Figure 5.3.6 and consider panel a. In the general case, marginal and average products vary as the input ratios change. Hence the output elasticity varies as well.

Exercise: Use equations (5.4.3) and (5.4.7) to prove that in the very special case of Cobb-Douglas production functions, the output elasticities are constant.

In particular, at the point of maximum average product, marginal and average products are equal, and the output elasticity is unity. Similarly, when marginal product is zero, average product is positive, and the output elasticity is zero.

The above paragraph applies to the variable factor in Figure 5.3.6. Now consider panel b, which pertains to the fixed factor. When the average product of the variable factor is a maximum ($\epsilon_X = 1$), the marginal product and the output elasticity of the fixed factor is zero ($\epsilon_Y = 0$). Further, by the symmetry of the stages of production, when the marginal product of the variable factor is zero ($\epsilon_X = 0$), the average product of the fixed factor attains its maximum. It is, of course, equal to the corresponding marginal product at this point, so the output elasticity of the fixed factor is unity ($\epsilon_Y = 1$).

Now let us file this definition away for the moment and introduce another one.

Definition: The *function coefficient* (ϵ) shows the proportional change in output that results when all inputs are expanded in the same proportion.

The function coefficient may also be expressed as a formula. The proportional change in output is, of course, $\Delta q / q$. Let all inputs be expanded in the proportion $\Delta\lambda / \lambda$. Then by definition

$$\epsilon = \frac{\Delta q}{q} \div \frac{\Delta\lambda}{\lambda} = \frac{\Delta q}{\Delta\lambda}\frac{\lambda}{q}. \tag{5.4.10}$$

In general, the function coefficient is a variable that depends upon the scale of operation. However, in the special case of constant returns to scale, we know that output expands in the same proportion as the inputs. Hence if a production function is homogeneous of degree one, the function coefficient is *identically one.*

By some very simple algebra, let us now relate the function coefficient to the output elasticities. Let the production function be $q = f(x, y)$. Then the increase in output resulting from an increase in the inputs is the increase attributable to X plus the increase attributable to Y. The added input of X expands output by its marginal product per unit change ($\Delta q / \Delta x$) multiplied by the number of units by which its usage changes (Δx). A similar statement applies to Y. Hence an increase in output may always be written as

$$\Delta q = \frac{\Delta q}{\Delta x} \cdot \Delta x + \frac{\Delta q}{\Delta y} \cdot \Delta y . \tag{5.4.11}$$

We now need to juggle this equation around a bit. On the right-hand side, multiply and divide the first term by x, the second by y:

$$\Delta q = x \cdot \frac{\Delta q}{\Delta x} \cdot \frac{\Delta x}{x} + y \cdot \frac{\Delta q}{\Delta y} \cdot \frac{\Delta y}{y} . \tag{5.4.12}$$

Next, divide every term in the equation by q:

$$\frac{\Delta q}{q} = \frac{x}{q} \cdot \frac{\Delta q}{\Delta x} \cdot \frac{\Delta x}{x} + \frac{y}{q} \cdot \frac{\Delta q}{\Delta y} \cdot \frac{\Delta y}{y} . \tag{5.4.13}$$

Now let both inputs increase in the same proportion; letting the common proportional increase be $\Delta\lambda/\lambda$ (i.e., $\Delta x/x = \Delta y/y = \Delta\lambda/\lambda$), we have

$$\frac{\Delta q}{q} = \left[\frac{\Delta q}{\Delta x} \frac{x}{q} + \frac{\Delta q}{\Delta y} \frac{y}{q} \right] \frac{\Delta\lambda}{\lambda} . \tag{5.4.14}$$

Transferring terms, we get

$$\frac{\Delta q}{q} \div \frac{\Delta\lambda}{\lambda} = \frac{\Delta q}{\Delta x} \frac{x}{q} + \frac{\Delta q}{\Delta y} \frac{y}{q} . \tag{5.4.15}$$

Finally, using the definition of output elasticity [equations (5.4.8) and (5.4.9)] and the definition of the function coefficient [equation (5.4.10)], we may write equation (5.4.15) as

$$\epsilon = \epsilon_X + \epsilon_Y . \tag{5.4.16}$$

To summarize, we have the following

Relations: The function coefficient shows the proportional change in output resulting from a given proportional change in all inputs. In the case of constant returns to scale, the function coefficient is unity. In all cases, the function coefficient is the *sum of the output elasticities* of all inputs.

The concepts we have just discussed are mentioned in the next chapter, but they enter importantly in Chapter 7 on cost.[15]

5.5 CONCLUSION

The principles of physical production have now been analyzed for a simple case: one variable and one fixed input. But the discussion in subsection 5.3.e and section 5.4 bring us close to a more realistic case:

---

[15] The results of this section may be generalized and summarized mathematically. Assume that a production function homogeneous of degree one in n inputs is given by

$$q = f(x_1, x_2, \ldots, x_n) . \tag{5.15.1}$$

Because of its homogeneity property, this function may always be written as

$$q = x_i f\left(\frac{x_1}{x_i}, \frac{x_2}{x_i}, \ldots, \frac{x_{i-1}}{x_i}, 1, \frac{x_{i+1}}{x_i}, \ldots, \frac{x_n}{x_i}\right) . \tag{5.15.2}$$

Thus the average product of the i-th input is

$$\frac{q}{x_i} = f\left(\frac{x_1}{x_i}, \ldots, \frac{x_n}{x_i}\right) \qquad (i = 1, 2, \ldots, n) . \tag{5.15.3}$$

and it is homogeneous of degree zero. Further, the marginal products are the first derivatives of the functions; and the first derivatives of functions homogeneous of degree one are themselves homogeneous of degree zero. Hence the marginal and average product functions are dependent only upon the *ratio* in which the inputs are combined.

Next, the output elasticity of the i-th input is, by definition,

$$\epsilon_i = f_i \frac{x_i}{q} \qquad (i = 1, 2, \ldots, n) , \tag{5.15.4}$$

where $f_i = \partial q / \partial x_i$. The total differential of the production function is

$$dq = \sum_{i=1}^{n} f_i dx_i = \sum_{i=1}^{n} x_i f_i \frac{dx_i}{x_i} , \tag{5.15.5}$$

or

$$\frac{dq}{q} = \sum_{i=1}^{n} f_i \frac{x_i}{q} \frac{dx_i}{x_i} . \tag{5.15.6}$$

Let $dx_i / x_i = d\lambda / \lambda$ for all i's. Then equation (5.15.6) may be written as

$$\frac{dq}{q} \div \frac{d\lambda}{\lambda} = \sum_{i=1}^{n} f_i \frac{x_i}{q} . \tag{5.15.7}$$

Using the definitions of ϵ and ϵ_i immediately gives

$$\epsilon = \sum_{i=1}^{n} \epsilon_i .$$

production in situations requiring more than one variable input. The basic illustration used in this chapter, for example, could easily be constructed to allow both land and labor to be variable inputs, while (say) x pounds of fertilizer per acre is the fixed input. Alternatively, all inputs may be allowed to vary. The next chapter is concerned with the theory of production in the multi-input case.

PROBLEM

Below are hypothetical data for a manufacturer possessing a fixed plant who produces a commodity that requires only one variable input. Total product is given. Compute and graph the average and marginal product curves. Make your basic calculations and set them up in tabular form using the following information for the stub and column (1) entries and your calculations for Average Product in column (2) and Marginal Product in column (3). Save them as they form the basis for a subsequent problem in Chapter 7.

Units of Variable Input	Total Product (1)
1.	100
2.	250
3.	410
4.	560
5.	700
6.	830
7.	945
8.	1050
9.	1146
10.	1234
11.	1314
12.	1384
13.	1444
14.	1494
15.	1534
16.	1564
17.	1584
18.	1594

After completing the table and graph, answer the following questions:

1. When marginal product is increasing, what is happening to average product?

2. Does average product begin to fall as soon as marginal product does? That is, which occurs first, the point of diminishing marginal or average returns?

3. When average product is at its maximum, is marginal product less than, equal to, or greater than average product?

4. Does total product increase at a decreasing rate: (*a*) When average product is rising? (*b*) When marginal product is rising? (*c*) When average product begins to fall? (*d*) When marginal product passes its maximum value?

5. When average product equals zero, what is total product?

6. (*a*) If average product is to the left of its maximum, which type of input is present in too large proportion? (*b*) Which is in too small proportion? (*c*) What are two ways of changing the proportion so as to increase average product? (*d*) If either of these were done, what would happen to total product? (*e*) In view of these facts, is it desirable or undesirable, from a social point of view, for a producer to operate with average product below its maximum (to the left)? With marginal product at its maximum? Why is your answer true in each case?

QUESTIONS

1. What is the precise relation between a two-factor production function and the marginal product curve for one factor?

2. Beginning with a production function or schedule involving two inputs, explain how one derives the total, average, and marginal products for a single factor.

3. Comment on the following statement: if the production of wheat requires only land and labor, if there are constant returns to scale, and if labor has an increasing average product, then the world's wheat supply could be grown in a flower pot, provided the pot were small enough.

SUGGESTED READINGS

Clark, J. M. "Diminishing Returns," *Encyclopaedia of the Social Sciences,* Vol. V, pp. 144–46. New York: The Macmillan Co., 1931.

Ferguson, C. E. *The Neoclassical Theory of Production and Distribution,* chaps. 1–6. London and New York: Cambridge University Press, 1969. [Advanced math necessary.]

Henderson, James M. and Quandt, Richard E. *Microeconomic Theory: A Mathematical Approach,* pp. 43–47. New York: McGraw-Hill Book Co., Inc., 1958. [Elementary math necessary.]

Knight, Frank H. *Risk, Uncertainty, and Profit,* pp. 94–104. Boston: Houghton Mifflin Co., 1921.

Machlup, Fritz. "On the Meaning of the Marginal Product," *Explorations in Economics,* pp. 250–63. New York: McGraw-Hill Book Co., Inc., 1936. Reprinted in AEA, *Readings in the Theory of Income Distribution,* pp. 158–74. Philadelphia: Blakiston Co., 1951.

PRODUCTION AND OPTIMAL INPUT PROPORTIONS: TWO VARIABLE INPUTS

6.1 INTRODUCTION

The fundamental physical relations of production were discussed in Chapter 5 under the assumption that there is only one variable input. The analysis is continued in this chapter for a more general case. Graphically, production is studied under the assumption that there are two variable inputs. One may regard these inputs either as cooperating with one or more fixed inputs or as the only two inputs. The latter situation, of course, is relevant only for the long run. In either case, however, the results of the two-input model are easily extended to cover multiple inputs.

6.1.a Production Table

The land-labor example used in Chapter 5 may be expanded to introduce the theory of production with two variable inputs. In the illustration we considered an agricultural experiment in which 10-acre tracts of land comprised the fixed input. Labor was the variable input, and we obtained eight sample observations corresponding to the cultivation of the 10-acre tracts by one worker, two workers, and so on. In the present example the agricultural experiment is pushed further so as to obtain 64 sample observations. Land is, in a sense, still the fixed input; but now we suppose there are eight 1-acre tracts, eight 2-acre tracts, and so on up to eight 8-acre tracts. Each of the sets of 8 constant-acre tracts is cultivated by one worker, two workers, etc., up to eight workers. Thus we have samples ranging from one worker on 1 acre to eight workers on 8 acres. The hypothetical data are listed in Table 6.1.1.

The entries in the row corresponding to 3-acre tracts of land are exactly the same as the entries in Table 5.2.2. Indeed, in every respect this table is just a "larger" example of the hypothetical experiment in Chapter 5.

TABLE 6.1.1

Data from Hypothetical Agricultural Experiment*

		Output in Bushels							
	8	9	46	69	92	109	124	136	144
	7	13	46	69	91	108	123	134	140
	6	16	42	66	88	106	120	128	132
Acres of Land per Tract	5	15	37	60	80	100	113	120	121
	4	13	30	54	72	85	93	95	95
	3	10	24	39	52	61	66	66	64
	2	6	12	17	21	24	26	25½	24½
	1	3	6	8	9	10	10	9	7
		1	2	3	4	5	6	7	8

Workers per Tract of Land

* Notice that this production schedule does not represent a production function homogeneous of degree one.

In the spirit of Chapter 5, consider land as the fixed input. The entries in each row show the total outputs produced on the stipulated acreage when different numbers of workers cultivate the land. By successive subtractions along each row, the marginal product of labor is obtained. Next, by going to successively higher rows one sees that the total, average, and marginal products of labor increase as larger and larger tracts of land are used—that is, as the fixed input is expanded relative to the variable input.

Up to a point! But just as too many workers per acre of land make cultivation too intensive, too many acres of land per worker make cultivation too extensive. Instead of viewing acres per tract as the fixed input, we can regard workers per tract as fixed and the number of acres per tract as variable. We then read up the columns rather than across the rows; but the same fundamental physical relations are exhibited.

With one worker per tract, output increases as the size of the tract increases until 6 acres per tract is reached. Thereafter total output declines and the marginal product of land is negative. As the number of workers per tract is expanded, thus diminishing the land-labor ratio for each given acreage, total product expands continuously beyond 3-acre tracts. Total product in these cases does not reach a maximum in the range shown in this example. But in each case the point of diminishing marginal returns is reached; thereafter output expands at a decreasing rate.

6.1.b Input Substitution

Table 6.1.1 shows that the basic principles of physical production hold whether workers per tract are varied with acres per tract constant or whether acres per tract are varied with workers per tract constant. It also illustates another very important physical relation between inputs: the same amount of total output may be produced by different input combinations. For example, an output of 66 bushels can be produced by using six workers on 3 acres of land or by using three workers on 6 acres. Similarly, 120 bushels can be produced either by seven workers on 5 acres or by six workers on 6 acres.

In this example no more than two different input combinations can be used to produce the same output. In a more general, continuous case, however, a given level of output can be produced by a wide variety of different input combinations. In other words, one input may be *substituted* for another in producing a specified volume of output. One of the important tasks of a businessman is to select the particular input combination that minimizes the cost of producing any given level of output. The chief purpose of this chapter is to show how this is done.

6.2 PRODUCTION SURFACE

Selection of the least-cost input combination requires knowledge of substitution possibilities and of relative input prices. For an individual producer, we assume that the input prices are given by market forces of supply and demand. Input substitution is the center of our interest. To get at an explanation requires the use of a device much like the one used in Part I to describe a consumer's preference surface. In the theory of consumer behavior we used equal-satisfaction contour lines, or indifference curves. Here we use equal-output contours, or *isoquants*.

6.2.a Production Surface for Discrete Case

As an introduction, first look at the total production surface. Figure 6.2.1 is a graph of the discrete production function given in Table 6.1.1. The height of the rectangular blocks indicates the volume of output. By

FIGURE 6.2.1

Physical Production Surface for Example in Table 6.1.1

following the heights visually in either "horizontal" direction, one may see how the total product curve is shaped for a fixed amount of one input and variable amounts of the other. But as we have already observed in this example, substitution possibilities are very limited. In certain cases two different input combinations yield the same output. However this example is *too* discrete to illustrate a wide range of production possibilities.

6.2.b Production Surface for Continuous Case

For this purpose a *continuous* production function is required. Let us imagine a manufacturing process that requires two inputs—labor and capital—to produce a specific commodity. The production function for this good is continuous; it cannot, therefore, be shown conveniently in tabular form. However, either a mathematical or a graphical representation is suitable.[1] The production function for this particular exam-

---

[1] Let Q, K, and L represent the quantities of output, capital, and labor, respectively. The production function may be written $Q = f(K, L)$, where $\partial Q / \partial K$ and $\partial Q / \partial L$ are the marginal products of capital and labor respectively.

ple is shown in Figure 6.2.2., a three-dimensional diagram in which height measures quantity of output and the two "flat" or "horizontal" dimensions measure quantities of the two inputs.[2]

FIGURE 6.2.2

Physical Production Surface for a Continuous Production Function

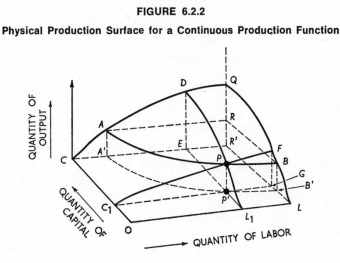

The production surface is $OCQL$. Any point on this surface represents a particular quantity of output. Dropping perpendiculars from the point to the axes shows the quantities of inputs required. For example, P is a point on the surface, and PP' is the associated volume of output. Drawing perpendiculars to the axes, $OL_1 (=C_1P')$ units of labor and $OC_1 (=L_1P')$ units of capital are required to produce the amount PP' at this particular point.

The production surface may be viewed in a different manner. Hold the capital input constant at the amount OC_1. The total product curve for OC_1 units of capital and variable inputs of labor is C_1PF. At labor input OL_1, total output is PP'; and at labor input OL, total output is FG. The total product curve C_1PF rises rapidly for small quantities of labor input, reaches a point of maximum slope (the point of diminishing marginal physical returns to labor for the given capital input OC_1), and thereafter increases at a decreasing rate.

The same statement applies to a typical total product curve for a fixed labor input and variable capital usage. Hold the input of labor constant at OL_1 units. L_1PD is the curve of total output resulting from

---

[2] In constructing Figure 6.2.2 we have assumed that $f(K, 0) = f(0, L) = f(0, 0) = 0$.

variable inputs of capital. For example, when OC_1 units of capital are used output is PP'; when OC units are employed output is DE.

6.2.c Production Isoquants

Still using Figure 6.2.2, let us determine all the different input combinations capable of producing PP' units of output. To do this, we slice (or "intersect") the production surface $OCQL$ at the height $PP' = AA' = BB'$. This slicing process generates the curve APB, a locus of points equidistant $(AA' = PP' = BB')$ from the C–L plane. By dropping perpendiculars from each point on the APB curve to the C–L plane, one obtains the input combinations associated with each point. In other words, the curve APB is projected onto the C–L plane, generating the curve $A'P'B'$. The latter is a locus of points each of which represents a combination of inputs capable of producing the stipulated quantity of output $PP' = AA' = BB' = RR'$. For examples, the following three combinations of capital and labor are points on the curve $A'P'B'$: OC, CA'; OC_1, OL_1; LB', OL.

The curve $A'P'B'$ is called an *isoquant*.[3]

-----

[3] Let the production function be $Q = f(K, L)$ as in footnote 1. The different input combinations that can produce Q units of output can be found by solving $f(K, L) = \bar{Q}$ for K and L. This expression is the equation for the isoquant associated with $\bar{Q}$ units of output. The isoquant map is generated by allowing Q to vary over all possible output values.

Alternatively, the isoquant map may be determined from the following differential equation:

$$dQ = \frac{\partial Q}{\partial K} dK + \frac{\partial Q}{\partial L} dL = 0 . \tag{6.3.1}$$

To illustrate, suppose $f(K, L)$ takes the Cobb-Douglas form:

$$Q = AK^\alpha L^{1-\alpha} , \tag{6.3.2}$$

where A and α are positive constants and $0 < \alpha < 1$. Then

$$dQ = \alpha AK^{\alpha-1}L^{1-\alpha}dK + (1 - \alpha)AK^\alpha L^{-\alpha}dL = 0 . \tag{6.3.3}$$

Equation (6.3.3) may be solved to obtain

$$-\frac{dK}{dL} = \frac{(1 - \alpha)K^\alpha L^{-\alpha}}{\alpha K^{\alpha-1}L^{1-\alpha}} = \frac{1 - \alpha}{\alpha} \frac{K}{L} . \tag{6.3.4}$$

Next, write the differential equation (6.3.4) in the readily integrable form

$$-\alpha \frac{dK}{K} = (1 - \alpha) \frac{dL}{L} . \tag{6.3.5}$$

A simple quadrature yields

$$-\alpha \log K = (1 - \alpha) \log L + \log B , \tag{6.3.6}$$

Definition: An isoquant is a curve in input space showing all possible combinations of inputs physically capable of producing a given level of output. The entire three-dimensional production surface can be exactly depicted by a two-dimensional isoquant map, the quantity of output being represented by the distance of the isoquant from the origin.

A portion of an isoquant map, derived from a production surface such as $OCQL$ in Figure 6.2.2, is shown in Figure 6.2.3.[4] The two axes

FIGURE 6.2.3

Typical Set of Isoquants

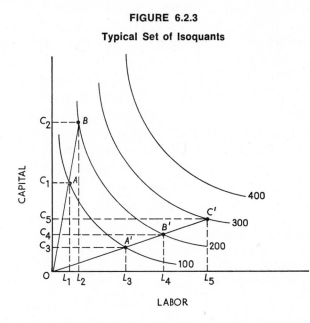

measure the quantities of inputs and the curves show the different input combinations that can be used to produce 100, 200, 300, and 400 units of output respectively. As is obvious, the further northeast a curve lies the greater is the output associated with it.

Consider first the isoquant for 100 units of output. Each point on this curve shows a capital-labor combination that can produce 100 units

where B is a positive constant of integration and "log" denotes logarithm to the base e. Transforming (6.3.6) yields

$$K^{-\alpha} = BL^{1-\alpha}, \qquad (6.3.7)$$

or

$$BK^\alpha L^{1-\alpha} = 1, \qquad (6.3.8)$$

which is the desired equation for the isoquant. By equation (6.3.2), the constant of integration (B) is $A/\overline{Q}$.

[4] The excluded portion of the isoquant map is discussed in subsection 6.3.d.

of output. For example, OC_1 units of capital and OL_1 units of labor may be used, or OC_3 units of capital and OL_3 units of labor, or any other input combination found by dropping perpendiculars to the axes from a point on the curve.

A ray from the origin, such as OAB or $OA'B'C'$, defines a constant capital-labor input ratio. In particular, the slope of the ray is the input ratio. For example, at points A and B, 100 and 200 units of output, respectively, are produced at the capital-labor ratio $OC_1/OL_1 = OC_2/OL_2$. Similarly, at points A', B', and C', 100, 200, and 300 units of output, respectively, are produced at the capital-labor ratio $OC_3/OL_3 = OC_4/OL_4 = OC_5/OL_5$.

Along the ray OAB, various levels of output are producible by the same input ratio; the magnitude of the inputs increases as one moves out the ray but the capital-labor ratio remains unchanged. This contrasts clearly with movements along an isoquant. In this case the level of output remains unchanged and the capital-labor ratio changes continuously.

These points may be summarized as follows.

Relations: An isoquant represents different input combinations, or input ratios, that may be used to produce a specified level of output. For movements *along an isoquant,* the level of output remains constant and the input ratio changes continuously. A ray from the origin defines a specific, constant input ratio. For movements *along a ray,* the level of output changes continuously and the input ratio remains constant.

6.2.d Fixed-Proportions Production Functions

Using the isoquant device, it is easy to illustrate the case of fixed-proportions production functions, briefly mentioned in Chapter 5. As you will recall, production is subject to fixed proportions when one, and only one, combination of inputs can produce a specified output.[5] For example, consider the hypothetical production process illustrated in Figure 6.2.4. Two inputs, capital and labor, must be used in the fixed ratio 2:3. That is, 2 units of capital and 3 units of labor are required to

---

[5] A fixed-proportions production function, which is frequently called a Leontief function, may be represented by

$$Q = \text{minimum}\left(\frac{K}{\alpha}, \frac{L}{\beta}\right),$$

where α and β are constants and "minimum" means that Q equals the smaller of the two ratios. For a detailed treatment of the fixed-proportions case, see C. E. Ferguson, *The Neoclassical Theory of Production and Distributions* (London and New York: Cambridge University Press, 1969), chaps. ii–iii.

FIGURE 6.2.4

Isoquant Map for Fixed-Proportions Production Function

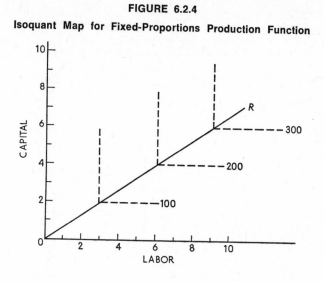

produce 100 units of output. Thus 4 units of capital and 6 units of labor can produce 200 units of output; 6 units of capital and 9 units of labor can produce 300 units, and so on.

The required capital-labor ratio is shown by the slope of the ray OR in Figure 6.2.4. Isoquants are constructed for 100, 200, and 300 units of output. Rather than taking the more conventional shape shown in Figure 6.2.3, the isoquants for fixed-proportions processes are L-shaped curves. This illustrates, for example, that if 3 units of labor and 2 units of capital are employed, 100 units of output are obtainable. However, if the quantity of capital is expanded, labor input held constant, no additional output can be obtained. Similarly, if capital input is held constant and labor expanded, output is unchanged. In other words, the marginal product of either labor or capital is zero if its usage is expanded while the other input is held constant. On the other hand, doubling inputs at the required ratio doubles output; trebling inputs at the required ratio trebles output, etc.[6]

A rather realistic case is that in which many, but not an infinite number of, different fixed-proportions processes are available. For example, Table 6.2.1 contains hypothetical data regarding the production of a commodity for which five different fixed-proportions processes are

---

[6] It is readily seen from the Leontief function in footnote 5 that fixed-proportions production functions are homogeneous of degree one, i.e., such functions reflect constant returns to scale.

TABLE 6.2.1

Production When Several Fixed-Proportion Processes Are Available

Ray	Capital-Labor Ratio	Capital Input	Labor Input	Total Output
OA	11:1	11	1	100
		22	2	200
OB	8:2	8	2	100
		16	4	200
OC	5:4	5	4	100
		10	8	200
OD	3:7	3	7	100
		6	14	200
OE	1:10	1	10	100
		2	20	200

FIGURE 6.2.5

Isoquant Map When Five Fixed-Proportions Processes Are Available

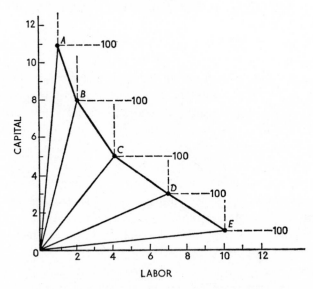

available. The 100-output isoquants, together with the capital-labor ratio rays, are plotted in Figure 6.2.5.

Heavily shaded straight lines have been drawn to connect the different possible input combinations. Each of the points on this kinked line represents an input combination capable of producing 100 units of output. The kinked line *ABCDE* looks very much like the "normal" isoquant shown in Figure 6.2.3. It is different, however, in that no input combination lying on the arc between *A* and *B, B* and *C,* etc., is itself *directly* a feasible input combination. For example, it is not possible to produce 100 units of output by *one* process using 7.25 units of capital and 2.5 units of labor.

On the other hand, if input units are sufficiently divisible, any particular input ratio—represented by a point on the kinked line—can be achieved. All that is required is the proper combination of the two fixed-proportions processes with which it is most closely associated. For example, suppose a producer wished to obtain 100 units of output by using 7.25 units of capital and 2.5 units of labor. He could do so by producing 75 units of output by the process represented by the ray *OB* and 25 units by the process *OC*. To produce 75 units at the 8:2 ratio requires 6 units of capital and 1.5 units of labor. Producing 25 units at the 5:4 ratio requires 1.25 units of capital and 1 unit of labor. Thus 100 units of output can be produced at the desired ratio 7.25:2.5 by combining the two processes represented by the rays *OB* and *OC*.

Finally, suppose there are many fixed-proportions processes by which a given level of output can be produced. Instead of the five points in Figure 6.2.5 there would be many points. Similarly, there would be many straight-line facets of the type *AB, BC,* etc. As the number of processes increases, the kinked line looks more and more like a typical isoquant. Indeed, an isoquant depicting a variable-proportions production function is just the limiting case of fixed-proportions processes as the number of processes increases without bound.

This argument, in fact, constitutes one rationale for the use of smooth isoquants and variable-proportions production functions in economic theory. Many manufacturing processes may be characterized by fixed, or almost fixed, proportions; however, usually many different fixed-proportions processes are available. Constructing smooth isoquants rather than multiple facet lines simplifies analysis while leading to relatively unimportant departures from real world conditions. The chief difference is that with smoothly continuous isoquants, any desired capital-labor ratio can be attained (if it is feasible) by using one process, whereas when there are many fixed-proportions processes, a desired combination may require the proper mixture of two processes.

6.3 INPUT SUBSTITUTION

One of the chief features of production under conditions of variable proportions—or a large number of alternative fixed-proportions processes—is that different combinations of inputs can produce a given level of output. In other words, one input can be *substituted* for another in such a way as to maintain a constant level of output. Great theoretical and practical importance attaches to the *rate* at which one input must be substituted for another in order to keep output constant and to the proportionate change in the input ratio induced by a given proportionate change in the rate of substitution.

6.3.a   Marginal Rate of Technical Substitution

Consider the representative isoquant I_1 in Figure 6.3.1. P and R are two of the many different input combinations that may be used to

FIGURE 6.3.1

Marginal Rate of Technical Substitution

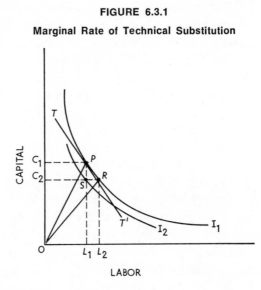

produce the I_1-level of output. If production occurs at P, OC_1 units of capital and OL_1 units of labor are required. OC_2 units of capital and OL_2 units of labor are required for production at R. Thus P is associated with the capital-labor ratio given by the slope of $OP = OC_1/OL_1$ and R with the capital-labor ratio given by the slope of $OR = OC_2/OL_2$.

If there is a change from P to R, the same level of output is produced by using *more* labor and less capital—labor can be substituted for capital by moving from P to R, and *vice versa*. The rate at which labor can be substituted for capital over the arc PR is given by

$$-\frac{OC_1 - OC_2}{OL_1 - OL_2} = \frac{PS}{SR},$$

where the minus sign is affixed so as to yield a positive number. Stated alternatively, the rate of substitution is the change in capital usage divided by the change in labor usage, or the slope of the curvilinear angle PRS.

As the distance from P to R diminishes the slope of the curvilinear segment PR approaches the slope of the tangent TT' at point P. In the limit, for a very tiny movement in the neighborhood of P the slope of the tangent at P measures the rate of substitution. In this case—for small movements along I_1—it is called the *marginal rate of technical substitution*, just as the slope of a consumer's indifference curve is called the marginal rate of substitution in consumption.

Next, suppose labor input is held constant at the OL_1 level while the input of capital is increased from OC_2 to OC_1. Output would increase from the I_2 level (say, Q_2) to the I_1 level (say Q_1). The marginal product of capital is, of course, the increase in output per unit increase in input, or

$$\frac{Q_1 - Q_2}{OC_1 - OC_2}.$$

Since $OC_1 - OC_2 = PS$, the marginal product of capital is

$$\frac{Q_1 - Q_2}{PS}.$$

Now return to the I_2 level and hold capital input constant at OC_2 while increasing labor input from OL_1 to OL_2, or by the amount SR. The marginal product of labor for this change is

$$\frac{Q_1 - Q_2}{SR}.$$

The ratio of the marginal product of labor to that of capital is

$$\frac{Q_1 - Q_2}{SR} \div \frac{Q_1 - Q_2}{PS} = \frac{PS}{SR},$$

the rate of substitution of capital for labor.[7] Thus in the limit, as the distance from P to R becomes very small, the marginal rate of technical substitution of capital for labor is equal to the ratio of the marginal product of labor to the marginal product of capital.

These results may be summarized as follows:

---

[7] The standard terminology in the theory of production differs slightly from that in the theory of consumer behavior. Let X and Y be commodities and I an indifference curve. In keeping with standard terminology, we defined the marginal rate of substitution of X for Y as the number of units by which Y-consumption must be decreased when X-consumption is increased by one unit while maintaining the same level of satisfaction. In symbols:

Relations: The marginal rate of technical substitution measures the reduction in one input per unit increase in the other that is just sufficient to maintain a constant level of output. The marginal rate of technical substitution of input *X* for input *Y* at a point on an isoquant is equal to the negative of the slope of the isoquant at that point. It is also equal to the ratio of the marginal product of input *Y* to the marginal product of input *X*.[8]

$$MRS_{X \text{ for } Y} = -\left. \frac{\Delta Y}{\Delta X} \right]_{\text{utility constant}} = -\left. \frac{dY}{dX} \right]_{du=0} .$$

In the theory of production, the concept of the marginal rate of technical substitution is entirely analogous to the marginal rate of substitution in the theory of consumer behavior. However, there is a change in terminology. Let *K* and *L* be inputs and *I* an isoquant. The marginal rate of technical substitution, just as the marginal rate of substitution in consumption, is defined as (the negative of) the slope of the isoquant. But it is called the marginal rate of technical substitution of *K* for *L*. That is,

$$MRTS_{K \text{ for } L} = -\left. \frac{\Delta K}{\Delta L} \right]_{\text{output constant}} = -\left. \frac{dK}{dL} \right]_{dq=0} .$$

To emphasize: the concepts are analogous, the terminology reversed.

Note: To preserve terminological consistency, in the first edition of this text I wrote "marginal rate of technical substitution of *L* for *K*." However, at a later stage this raised some problems. So in this edition I bow to common usage and write "marginal rate of technical substitution of *K* for *L*." The essential point is that the student realize that the concepts are the same, only terminology has been changed.

[8] These relations can easily be expressed mathematically. The production function is that of footnote 1:

$$Q = f(K, L) , \tag{6.8.1}$$

where

$$\frac{\partial Q}{\partial K}, \quad \frac{\partial Q}{\partial L} \tag{6.8.2}$$

are the marginal products of capital and labor respectively.

Consider the total differential of the production function in equation (6.8.1):

$$dQ = \frac{\partial f}{\partial K} dK + \frac{\partial f}{\partial L} dL . \tag{6.8.3}$$

For movements along an isoquant, output is constant, so $dQ = 0$. Substituting in equation (6.8.3) gives

$$\frac{\partial f}{\partial K} dK + \frac{\partial f}{\partial L} dL = 0 , \tag{6.8.4}$$

the equation for an isoquant. The marginal rate of technical substitution, by definition, is $-dK/dL$. From equation (6.8.4), therefore,

$$MRTS_{K \text{ for } L} = -\frac{dK}{dL} = \frac{\frac{\partial f}{\partial L}}{\frac{\partial f}{\partial K}} = \frac{MP_L}{MP_K} , \tag{6.8.5}$$

6.3.b Diminishing Marginal Rate of Technical Substitution

The marginal rate of technical substitution of capital for labor diminishes as more and more labor is substituted for capital. This proposition sounds plausible; and it is not difficult to explain. Of course, the opposite applies as capital is substituted for labor.

As additional units of labor are added to a fixed amount of capital the marginal product of labor diminishes. Furthermore, as shown in Figure 5.2.4, if the amount of the "fixed" input is diminished the marginal product of labor diminishes. Thus two forces are working to diminish the marginal product of labor: (*a*) less of the "fixed" input causes a downward *shift* of the marginal product of labor curve; (*b*) more units of the "variable" input (labor) causes a downward movement *along* the marginal product of labor curve. Thus as labor is substituted for capital the marginal product of labor must decline.

For analogous reasons, the marginal product of capital rises. As shown in Figure 5.3.6, over stage II—the relevant range of production—the marginal product of capital rises as the marginal product of labor falls. A decrease in the capital-labor ratio is the cause of both. With the quantity of labor fixed, the marginal product of capital rises as fewer units of capital are used. But simultaneously there is an increase in labor input thereby shifting the marginal product of capital curve upward. The same two forces are present in this case: a movement along a marginal product curve and a shift in the location of the curve. In this situation, however, both forces work to increase the marginal product of capital. Thus as labor is substituted for capital the marginal product of capital increases.

---

by expression (6.8.2).

To illustrate, suppose the production function takes the CES form:

$$Q = \gamma[\delta K^{-\rho} + (1 - \delta)L^{-\rho}]^{-\frac{1}{\rho}}, \tag{6.8.6}$$

where γ, δ, and ρ are constants and $\gamma > 0$, $\delta > 0$. Setting $dQ = 0$, one obtains

$$dQ = \gamma\delta K^{-\rho-1}[\delta K^{-\rho} + (1 - \delta)L^{-\rho}]^{-\frac{1}{\rho}-1}dK$$

$$+ (1 - \delta)\gamma L^{-\rho-1}[\delta K^{-\rho} + (1 - \delta)L^{-\rho}]^{-\frac{1}{\rho}-1}dL = 0, \tag{6.8.7}$$

or

$$-\frac{dK}{dL} = MRTS_{K \text{ for } L} = \frac{\gamma(1 - \delta)L^{-\rho-1}}{\gamma\delta K^{-\rho-1}} = \left(\frac{1 - \delta}{\delta}\right)\left(\frac{K}{L}\right)^{1+\rho}. \tag{6.8.8}$$

Equation (6.8.8) is the expression for the marginal rate of technical substitution of capital for labor for the CES function.

Exercise: Carry out the same mathematical analysis for the Cobb-Douglas production function.

As already defined, the marginal rate of technical substitution is the ratio of the marginal product of labor to the marginal product of capital. As labor is substituted for capital, the marginal product of labor declines and the marginal product of capital increases. Hence the marginal rate of technical substitution of capital for labor declines as labor is substituted for capital so as to maintain a constant level of output. This may be summarized as follows:

Relation: As labor is substituted for capital along an isoquant (so that output is unchanged), the marginal rate of technical substitution declines.

The fact that the marginal rate of technical substitution falls as labor is substituted for capital means that isoquants must be concave from above (that is, in the neighborhood of a point of tangency, the isoquant must lie above the tangent line). This is illustrated in Figure 6.3.2.

FIGURE 6.3.2

Diminishing Marginal Rate of Technical Substitution

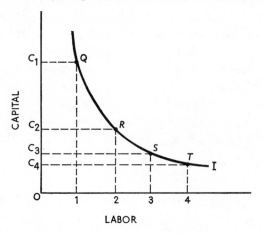

Q, R, S, and T are four input combinations lying on the isoquant I. Q has the combination OC_1 units of capital and one unit of labor; R has OC_2 units of capital and two units of labor; and so on. For the movement from Q to R, the marginal rate of technical substitution of capital for labor is, by formula,

$$-\frac{OC_1 - OC_2}{1 - 2} = OC_1 - OC_2 .$$

Similarly, for the movements from R to S and S to T, the marginal rates of technical substitution are $OC_2 - OC_3$ and $OC_3 - OC_4$, respectively.

Since the marginal rate of technical substitution of capital for labor diminishes as labor is substituted for capital, it is necessary that $OC_1 - OC_2 > OC_2 - OC_3 > OC_3 - OC_4$. Visually, the amount of capital replaced by successive units of labor will decline if, and only if, the isoquant is concave from above. Since the amount *must* decline, the isoquant must be concave from above.[9]

Relation: Isoquants must be concave from above at every point in order to satisfy the principle of diminishing marginal rate of technical substitution.

6.3.c Economic Region of Production

Many production functions lead to initial isoquant maps such as shown in Figure 6.2.3. Others, however, generate an isoquant map such as that shown in Figure 6.3.3. It is like the map in Figure 6.2.3 in that the isoquants do not intersect; the higher the isoquants the greater the level of output; and over a range of input values they are negatively sloped. The only difference lies in the fact that the isoquants in Figure 6.3.3 "bend back upon themselves," or have positively sloped segments.

FIGURE 6.3.3

Full Isoquant Map and the Relevant Range of Production

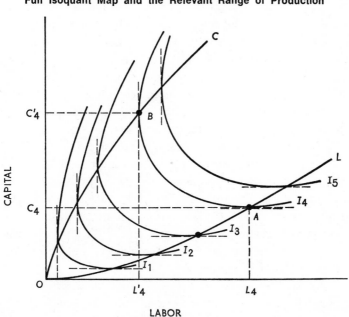

---

[9] This proposition is proved in footnote 12.

The parallel dashed lines in Figure 6.3.3 indicate the points at which the isoquants bend back upon themselves. The lines OC and OL join these points and form, as we will see, the boundaries for the economic region of production (or the stage II region).

Suppose the quantity represented by isoquant I_4 is to be produced. Producing this amount requires a *minimum* of OC_4 units of capital, inasmuch as any smaller amount would not permit one to attain the I_4 level of output. With OC_4 units of capital, OL_4 units of labor must be used. Beyond this level of input, additional units of labor in combination with OC_4 units of capital would yield a smaller level of output. To maintain the I_4 level of output with a greater labor input would require a greater input of capital as well—a palpably uneconomic use of resources.

Since an expansion of labor input beyond OL_4, in the face of the constant capital input OC_4, reduces total output, point A on I_4 represents the intensive margin for labor. Its marginal product is zero, and hence the marginal rate of technical substitution of capital for labor is zero. This is shown by the horizontal tangent at point A. At this point labor has been substituted for capital to the maximum extent consistent with the level of output I_4.

Similarly, producing at the I_4 level requires a certain minimum input of labor, OL'_4 in Figure 6.3.3. The I_4 level cannot be attained without at least this much labor; and with this minimum amount additions to capital input beyond OC'_4 would reduce rather than augment output. Thus the marginal product of capital is zero at point B and negative for quantities in excess of OC'_4 units (in combination with OL'_4 units of labor). Since the marginal product of capital is zero, the marginal rate of technical substitution of capital for labor is infinite or undefined at this point; capital is used to its intensive margin.

Now as we saw in subsection 5.3.e, the intensive margin with respect to one input is the extensive margin with respect to the other. Hence with OL_4 units of labor in use the average product of capital rises until OC_4 units are in use. Point A, therefore, separates stages I and II for capital and stages II and III for labor. In like manner, with OC'_4 units of capital the average product of labor rises until OL'_4 units are employed. Point B represents the boundary between stages I and II for labor and between stages II and III for capital.

By connecting the points of zero marginal labor product, the line OL is formed. Similarly, OC is the locus of points for which the marginal product of capital is zero. Production must take place within this range.

Hence the "ridge" lines *OL* and *OC* separate the economic from the uneconomic regions of production. To summarize:

Relations: If the production function is such that intensive and extensive margins for each input exist, the total isoquant map is like the one in Figure 6.3.3. Only those portions of the isoquants lying between the ridge lines (the loci of zero marginal products) are relevant to production. These economic portions of the isoquants are uniquely associated with stage II production of each input.

Stage I production for any input conforms to the region of rising average product; and if average product rises, marginal product must exceed average product. Since a stage I area must be present to generate the isoquant map shown in Figure 6.3.3, the "normal" set of product curves—as shown in Figure 5.3.3—must be associated with the production function giving rise to this isoquant map. This "normal" set of product curves is reproduced in panel a, Figure 6.3.4.

FIGURE 6.3.4

Product Curves for Different Types of Isoquant Maps

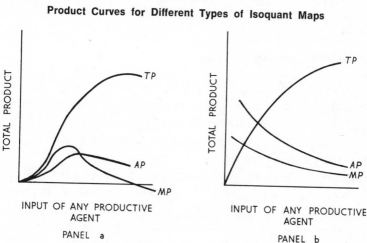

Some production functions, however, generate isoquant maps such as that in Figure 6.2.3. There is neither a stage I nor a stage III range for either input. The entire production function represents stage II, or the economic region. Marginal and average products decline continuously, but neither reaches zero because there is not a maximum point on the total product curve. Such a production function is shown in panel b, Figure 6.3.4. The average and marginal product curves begin some distance from the origin. This is a mere convenience. They are both defined for infinitesimally small amounts of input; but at input levels less than unity, average and marginal products exceed total product.

The importance of production functions giving rise to the product curves of panel b is an empirical question. For expository purposes, production functions of the type shown in panel a are generally used. In empirical, statistical, and econometric applications, however, a broad class of production functions such as shown in panel b are most often used. The distinction, in fact, is relevant only in theory because observed production relations are always those of stage II.[10]

6.4 OPTIMAL COMBINATION OF RESOURCES

So far the theory of production has been analyzed from the standpoint of an individual entrepreneur. However, nothing has been said regarding the *optimal* way in which he should combine resources. Any desired level of output can normally be produced by a number of different combinations of inputs. Our task now is to determine the specific combination a producer should select.

6.4.a Input Prices and Isocosts

Inputs, just as outputs, bear specific market prices. In determining his *operating* input combination a producer must pay heed to relative input prices if he is to minimize the cost of producing a given output or maximize output for a given level of cost. In the long run the producer must do this to obtain the *maximum* attainable profit.

Input prices are determined, just as the prices of goods, by supply and demand in the market. For producers who are not monopsonists or

---

[10] *Exercise:* Prove that if the production function is homogeneous of degree one and takes either the Cobb-Douglas (CD) or CES form, both marginal and average products of both factors are always positive and decrease monotonically.

Having proved this, you have proved that the linearly homogeneous CD and CES functions give rise to product graphs such as that shown in panel b, Figure 6.3.4. Now a word of caution is in order. The CD and CES functions do not give rise to an "uneconomic region of production" (however, a CES function homogeneous of degree $m \neq 1$ may do so; the CD function, irrespective of the degree of homogeneity, never does). But one should not conclude that functions homogeneous of degree one *cannot* display uneconomic regions. The isoquant map associated with such functions does not "look" exactly like the map in Figure 6.3.3. At the point of zero marginal product there is a point of inflection, the isoquant thereafter bending back to the left (rather than reaching a maximum and continuing to the right). For an excellent discussion that does not require mathematics, see George Borts and E. J. Mishan, "Exploring the 'Uneconomic Region' of the Production Function," *Review of Economic Studies,* Vol. XXIX (1962), pp. 300–312.

oligopsonists, input prices are given by the market and his rates of purchase do not change them. Let us now concentrate upon a producer who is a perfect competitor in the input market, even though he may be a monopolist or an oligopolist in his output market. (Consideration of monopsony and oligopsony is deferred to Chapter 14.)

Let us continue to assume that the two inputs are labor and capital, although the analysis applies equally well to any two productive agents. Denote the quantity of capital and labor by K and L, respectively, and their unit prices by r and w. The total cost C of using any volume of K and L is $C = rK + wL$, the sum of the cost of K units of capital at r per unit and of L units of labor at w per unit.[11]

To take a more specific example, suppose capital costs $1,000 per unit ($r = \$1,000$) and labor receives a wage of $2,500 per man-year ($w = \$2,500$). If a total of $15,000 is to be spent for inputs, the following combinations are possible: $\$15,000 = \$1,000\,K + \$2,500\,L$, or $K = 15 - 2.5\,L$. Similarly, if $20,000 is to be spent on inputs, one can purchase the following combinations: $K = 20 - 2.5\,L$. More generally, if the fixed amount $\overline{C}$ is to be spent, the producer can choose among the combinations given by

$$K = \frac{\overline{C}}{r} - \frac{w}{r}L.$$

This is illustrated in Figure 6.4.1. If 15,000 is spent for inputs and no labor is purchased, 15 units of capital may be bought. More generally, if C is to be spent and r is the unit cost, $\overline{C}/r$ units of capital may be purchased. This is the vertical-axis *intercept* of the line. If one unit of labor is purchased at $2,500, two and five-tenths units of capital must be sacrificed; if two units of labor are bought, five units of capital must be sacrificed; and so on. Thus as the purchase of labor is increased, the purchase of capital must be diminished. For each additional unit of labor, w/r units of capital must be foregone. In Figure 6.4.1, $w/r = 2.5$. Attaching a negative sign, this is the *slope* of the straight lines constructed in this graph.

The solid lines in Figure 6.4.1 are called *isocost curves* because they show the various combinations of inputs that may be purchased for a stipulated amount of expenditure. In summary:

---

[11] The $w - L$ measurement should be clear. L is the number of man-hours and w is the wage per hour. The $r - K$ measurement may not be so clear. Various interpretations may be used. For simplicity, suppose that K is the dollar value of capital invested. Then r is the market rate of interest that the entrepreneur must "charge" himself because he could receive rK by investing his money otherwise. In competitive markets, of course, r must also be the rate of profit.

FIGURE 6.4.1

Isocost Curves for $r = \$1,000$ and $w = \$2,500$

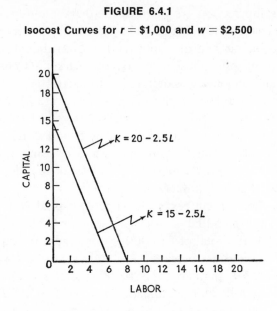

Relation: At fixed input prices r and w for capital and labor, respectively, a fixed outlay $\overline{C}$ will purchase any combination of capital and labor given by the following linear equation:

$$K = \frac{\overline{C}}{r} - \frac{w}{r} L.$$

This is the equation for an isocost curve, whose intercept $(\overline{C}/r)$ is the amount of capital that may be purchased if no labor is bought and whose slope is the negative of the input-price ratio (w/r).

6.4.b Maximizing Output for a Given Cost

Suppose at given input prices r and w, a producer can spend only $\overline{C}$ on production. Subject to this input cost, he only operates efficiently if he maximizes the output attainable. To do this he must select the proper input combination. That is, among all input combinations he can purchase for the fixed amount $\overline{C}$, he must select the one that results in the greatest level of output.

Let the given level of cost $\overline{C}$ be represented by the isocost curve KL in Figure 6.4.2. The slope of KL is therefore equal to the (negative) ratio of the price per unit of labor to the price per unit of capital. I_1, I_2, and I_3 are isoquants representing various levels of output. First, observe that the I_3-level of output is not obtainable because the *avail-*

FIGURE 6.4.2

**Optimal Input Combination to Maximize Output
Subject to a Given Cost**

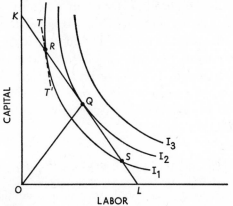

able input combinations are limited to those lying on or beneath the isocost curve *KL*.

Next, the producer could operate at points such as *R* and *S*. At these two points, the input combinations *required* to produce the I_1-level of output are *available* for the given cost represented by the isocost *KL*. In this case, however, output can be increased without incurring additional cost by the selection of a more appropriate input combination. Indeed, output can be expanded until the I_2-level is reached—the level at which an isoquant is just tangent to the specified isocost curve. A greater output is not obtainable for the given level of expenditure; a lesser output is inefficient because production can be expanded at no additional cost. Hence the input combination represented by the slope of the ray *OQ* is optimal because it is the combination that maximizes output for the given level of cost.

After studying the theory of consumer behavior, this proposition should be more or less obvious. However, a sound reason lies behind it. For a moment suppose the entrepreneur contemplated producing at point *R*. The marginal rate of technical substitution of capital for labor —given by the slope of the tangent TT'—is relatively high. Suppose it is $3:1$, meaning that one unit of labor can replace three units of capital at that point. The relative input price, given by the slope of *KL,* is much less, say $1:1$. In this case, one unit of labor costs the same as one unit of capital but it can replace three units of capital in production. The producer would obviously be better off if he substituted labor for capital. The opposite argument holds for point S, where the marginal rate of technical substitution is less than the input-price ratio.

Following this argument, the producer reaches equilibrium (maximizes output for a given level of cost) only when the marginal rate of technical substitution of capital for labor is equal to the ratio of the price of labor to the price of capital. The market input-price ratio tells the producer the rate at which he *can substitute* one input for another *in purchasing*. The marginal rate of technical substitution tells him the rate at which he *can substitute in production*. So long as the two are not equal, a producer can achieve either a greater output or a lower cost by moving in the direction of equality.[12]

---

[12] Let the production function be $Q = f(K, L)$. Total cost is $C = rK + wL$. Maximizing output subject to a *given* cost and given input prices is a simple exercise in the Lagrange technique for constrained extrema. Introduce the multiplier λ and construct the Lagrange function

$$f(K, L) - \lambda(rK + wL - \bar{C}) . \tag{6.12.1}$$

Taking the first partial derivatives, one obtains

$$\frac{\partial f}{\partial L} - \lambda w = 0 .$$

$$\frac{\partial f}{\partial K} - \lambda r = 0 . \tag{6.12.2}$$

Transferring the second term to the right-hand side, one obtains

$$\frac{\partial f}{\partial L} = \lambda w ,$$

$$\frac{\partial f}{\partial K} = \lambda r , \tag{6.12.3}$$

or

$$\frac{\frac{\partial f}{\partial L}}{w} = \frac{\frac{\partial f}{\partial K}}{r} = \lambda . \tag{6.12.4}$$

This is one way in which the principle may be stated: in equilibrium, the marginal product per dollar's worth of input must be the same for each input.

Rearranging equation (6.12.4):

$$\frac{\frac{\partial f}{\partial L}}{\frac{\partial f}{\partial K}} = MRTS_{K \text{ for } L} = \frac{w}{r} , \tag{6.12.5}$$

the principle as stated in the text.

The second-order conditions for a constrained maximum require that the quadratic form associated with the bordered determinant

Principle: To maximize output subject to a given total cost and given input prices, the producer must purchase inputs in quantities such that the marginal rate of technical substitution of capital for labor is equal to the input-price ratio (the price of labor to the price of capital). Thus

$$MRTS_{K \text{ for } L} = \frac{MP_L}{MP_K} = \frac{w}{r}.$$

6.4.c Minimizing Cost Subject to a Given Output

As an alternative to maximizing output for a given cost, an entrepreneur may seek to minimize the cost of producing a stipulated level of output. The problem is solved graphically in Figure 6.4.3. The

FIGURE 6.4.3

Optimal Input Combination to Minimize Cost Subject to a Given Level of Output

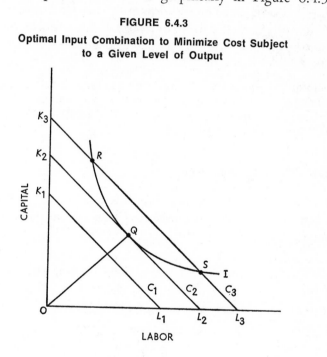

$$\begin{vmatrix} 0 & f_K & f_L \\ f_K & f_{KK} & f_{KL} \\ f_L & f_{KL} & f_{LL} \end{vmatrix} \tag{6.12.6}$$

be negative definite, where

$$f_K = \frac{\partial f}{\partial K}, f_{KL} = \frac{\partial^2 f}{\partial K \partial L}, \quad \text{etc.}$$

Expanding, this requires that

$$f_L^2 f_{KK} - 2f_K f_L f_{KL} + f_K^2 f_{LL} < 0. \tag{6.12.7}$$

Condition (6.12.7) means that the isoquants *must* be concave from above, as previously indicated.

isoquant I represents the stipulated level of output, while C_1, C_2, and C_3 are isocost curves with the same slope (input-price ratio).

First notice that the level of cost represented by C_1 is not feasible because the I-level of output is not physically producible by any input combination available for this outlay. Next, the I-level could be produced, for example, by the input combinations represented by the points R and S, both at the cost level C_3. But by moving either from R to Q or from S to Q, the entrepreneur can obtain the same output at lower cost.

By the very same arguments used in subsection 6.4.b, a position of equilibrium is attained only at point Q where the isoquant is just tangent to an isocost curve. Thus in equilibrium the marginal rate of technical substitution of capital for labor must equal the ratio of the price of labor to the price of capital. The previous principle may thus be elaborated.[13]

Principle: In order either to maximize output subject to a given cost or to minimize cost subject to a given output, the entrepreneur must employ inputs in such amounts as to equate the marginal rate of technical substitution and the input-price ratio.

6.5 THE EXPANSION PATH

The object of an entrepreneur, or so it is assumed, is to maximize profit. But to do this, he must organize production in the most efficient or economical way. This involves, as we have now seen, adjusting factor

---

[13] Using the notation of footnote 12, we now wish to minimize $rK + wL$ subject to producing $\overline{Q} = f(K, L)$ units of output. Again, introduce a Lagrange multiplier λ^* and construct the function

$$rK + wL - \lambda^*[f(K,L) - \overline{Q}] .$$ (6.13.1)

Setting the first partial derivatives equal to zero, one obtains

$$w - \lambda^* \frac{\partial f}{\partial L} = 0 ,$$ (6.13.2)

$$r - \lambda^* \frac{\partial f}{\partial K} = 0 .$$

Transferring the second term on the left-hand side of each equation to the right-hand side and dividing the first equation by the second to eliminate λ^*, one obtains

$$\frac{w}{r} = \frac{\dfrac{\partial f}{\partial L}}{\dfrac{\partial f}{\partial K}} = MRTS_{K \text{ for } L} ,$$ (6.13.3)

precisely the result obtained in the text and in footnote equation (6.12.5).

proportions until the marginal rate of technical substitution equals the factor-price ratio—or what is the same, adjusting factor proportions until the marginal product of a dollar's worth of each input is the same. When this task is accomplished, equilibrium is attained at a point such as Q in Figures 6.4.2 and 6.4.3.

Now let us digress for a moment to recall the procedure we used when studying the theory of consumer behavior. First, the position of consumer equilibrium was established. Then we posed and answered the following question: how will the combination of goods be changed when price or income changes? We must now pose the same type of question from the standpoint of a producer: how will factor proportions change when output or the factor-price ratio changes?

6.5.a Isoclines

Consider panel a, Figure 6.5.1. The curves *I, II,* and *III* are isoquants depicting a representative production function. T_1, T_2, and T_3 are tan-

FIGURE 6.5.1

Isoclines

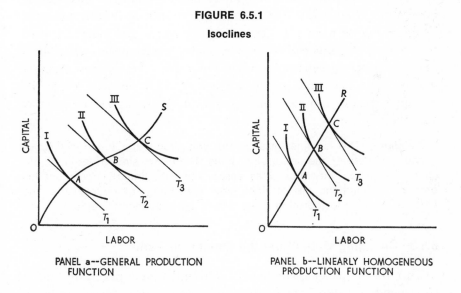

PANEL a--GENERAL PRODUCTION
FUNCTION

PANEL b--LINEARLY HOMOGENEOUS
PRODUCTION FUNCTION

gents to *I, II,* and *III,* respectively; and the tangents have been constructed so that they are parallel to one another. That is, the marginal rate of technical substitution of capital for labor is the same at points *A, B,* and *C.* These points have been connected by a smooth curve labeled *OS,* which is called an *isocline.*

Definition: An isocline is a locus of points along which the marginal rate of technical substitution is constant.

In general, isoclines may have almost any shape. The one in panel a has been constructed so as to ramble through the isoquant map. The *special* isoclines in Figure 6.3.3 have a very regular shape. We may now pause to point out the following

Relation: The "ridge lines" defining the economic region of production are isoclines inasmuch as the marginal rate of technical substitution is constant along the lines. In particular (see Figure 6.3.3), *OC* is the isocline along which the marginal rate of technical substitution of capital for labor is infinite, *OL* is the isocline along which it is zero.

Now turn to panel b, Figure 6.5.1, in which the labeling corresponds to that of panel a—with one important exception: the *curve OS* has become the *ray OR*. This is always true when the production function is homogeneous of degree one. In that case, all marginal products are functions of the input ratio only. Thus the marginal rate of technical substitution, which is the ratio of the marginal products, is itself a function of the input ratio and of nothing else. Therefore, whenever the input ratio is constant—for example, 200:100, 400:200, etc.—the marginal rate of technical substitution is constant and independent of the absolute magnitude of the inputs. Since a ray from the origin (such as *OR* in panel b) defines a constant input ratio, the ray must intersect the successive isoquants at points (such as *A, B,* and *C*) where the marginal rates of technical substitution are the same. Hence we may state the following

Relations: The isoclines associated with production functions homogeneous of degree one are straight lines. Therefore, since ridge lines are special isoclines, the ridge lines associated with linearly homogeneous production functions are straight lines (providing, of course, that the function under consideration gives rise to an uneconomic region).

6.5.b Changing Output and the Expansion Path

Turn now to panel a, Figure 6.5.2. Given the input prices, the output corresponding to isoquant *I* can be produced at least cost at point *A,* where the isoquant is tangent to the isocost curve *KL*. This is the position of producer equilibrium. With input prices remaining constant, suppose the entrepreneur wishes to expand output to the level corresponding to the isoquant *II*. The new equilibrium is found by shifting the isocost curve until it is tangent to *II*. Since factor prices remain constant, the slope of the isocost curve does not change. Hence it shifts

FIGURE 6.5.2

Expansion Paths

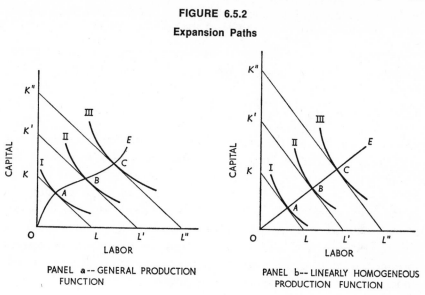

PANEL a-- GENERAL PRODUCTION
FUNCTION

PANEL b-- LINEARLY HOMOGENEOUS
PRODUCTION FUNCTION

from KL to $K'L'$. Similarly, if the entrepreneur wished to expand output to the amount corresponding to the isoquant III, he would produce at point C on III and $K''L''$.

Connecting all points such as A, B, and C generates the curve OE. Now let us assemble some facts. First, factor prices have remained constant. Second, each equilibrium point is defined by equality between the marginal rate of technical substitution and the factor-price ratio. Since the latter has remained constant, so has the former. Therefore, OE is an isocline, a locus of points along which the marginal rate of technical substitution is constant. But it is an isocline with a special feature. Specifically, it is the isocline along which output will expand when factor prices are constant. We may accordingly formulate this result as a

Definition: The *expansion path* is the particular isocline along which output will expand when factor prices remain constant. The expansion path thus shows how factor proportions change when output or expenditure changes, input prices remaining constant throughout.

Turn now to panel b. Since the isoclines of a linearly homogeneous production function are straight lines, the expansion path is also. Let us state this as the following

Relation: The expansion path corresponding to a production function homogeneous of degree one is a straight line. This reflects the fact that under constant returns to scale, factor proportions depend only upon the factor-price ratio (the slope of the isocost curve); and in particular, factor proportions are independent of the level of output.

As we shall see in Chapter 7, the expansion path is crucial in determining the long-run cost of production.

6.5.c Expenditure Elasticity[14]

In Chapters 2 and 4 the income elasticity of commodity demand was discussed. In particular, income elasticity was related to the income-consumption curve; and commodities were classified as superior, normal, or inferior according as income elasticity exceeds unity, lies in the unit interval, or is negative. The expenditure elasticity of a factor of production is an analogous concept: its measurement is restricted to the expansion path; and factors are classified as superior, normal, or inferior according as the corresponding expenditure elasticity exceeds unity, lies in the unit interval, or is negative.

Let us begin with the following

Definition: Consider a well-defined factor *X*. The expenditure elasticity of *X* is the relative responsiveness of the usage of *X* to changes in total expenditure. In other words, the expenditure elasticity of *X* is the proportional change in the usage of *X* divided by the proportional change in total expenditure. In this definition changes in total expenditure *are restricted to movements along the expansion path.*

Symbolically, the formula for the expenditure elasticity is

$$\eta_x = \frac{dx}{x} \div \frac{dc}{c} = \frac{dx}{dc}\frac{c}{x},$$

where x is the usage of factor X and c is total expenditure on factors of production.

Next we introduce another

Definition: A factor of production is said to be superior, normal, or inferior according as its expenditure elasticity exceeds unity, lies in the unit interval, or is negative.

This definition is illustrated schematically in Figure 6.5.3. Consider the expansion path and concentrate on factor X. Along ray OR both inputs expand proportionally. At points such as A the usage of factor X expands proportionally more than total expenditure along the expansion path. At all such points the factor is superior. At points such as B factor

[14] For a mathematical elaboration of this subsection, see C. E. Ferguson and Thomas R. Saving, "Long-Run Scale Adjustments of a Perfectly Competitive Firm and Industry," *American Economic Review*, Vol. LIX (1969), pp. 774–83.

FIGURE 6.5.3

Expenditure Elasticity and Factor Classification

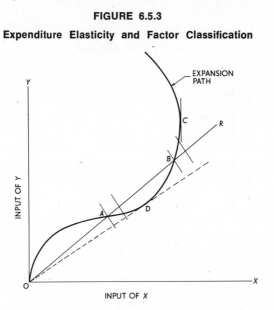

usage expands proportionally less than total expenditure. Expenditure elasticity lies in the unit interval, and the factor is said to be normal. At D the change in usage of both inputs is proportional and the expenditure elasticity is unity. Analysis is the same along any ray from the origin.

In certain—presumably unusual—cases, the usage of a factor may decline when output and resource expenditure are increased. At point C in Figure 6.5.3 the expenditure elasticity of X is instantaneously zero. Beyond point C, the expansion path "bends back" on itself. The usage of X diminishes as expenditure is increased beyond point C. Over this range of expenditure and output, X is an inferior factor. There is a further discussion of inferior factors in section 6.6, and the concept of expenditure elasticity is used in Chapter 7 to analyze the changes in cost curves that result from changes in factor price.

6.6 CHANGES IN INPUT PRICE

From Part I you know a change in the price of a good has two theoretically discernible effects: the substitution effect and the income effect. The substitution effect is always negative; and the income effect is normally positive and reinforces it. Much the same type of effects may be isolated for changes in input price.

First consider Figure 6.6.1. This graph illustrates increases in the price of labor inputs, the price of the capital input remaining constant.

FIGURE 6.6.1

**Shifting Isocost Curves to Show an Increase
in the Price of Labor**

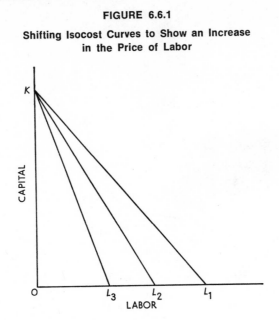

The original factor-price ratio is given by the slope of the isocost curve KL_1. As this isocost curve shifts leftward to KL_2 and KL_3, the price of labor increases because the same total expenditure on labor will at first purchase OL_1 units, then OL_2 units, and finally only OL_3 units.

6.6.a The Substitution and Output Effects

The substitution and output effects are shown in Figure 6.6.2. The original point of equilibrium is Q. The level of output is indicated by the isoquant I_1, and the input-price ratio by the slope of the isocost curve KL_1; and Ok_1 units of capital and Ol_1 units of labor are used. Now let the price of labor increase, the price of capital remaining unchanged. This shifts the isocost curve to KL_2. If the producer maximizes the output attainable for this given cost, the equilibrium point changes from Q to S, the level of output falling to that indicated by the isoquant I_2. In the ultimate equilibrium position, Ok_3 units of capital and Ol_3 units of labor are used. The total effect of the wage rate change on labor usage is, therefore, a decrease from Ol_1 to Ol_3, or a reduction of l_1l_3 units of labor.

The total effect may be decomposed into two components. The change in labor usage attributable *exclusively* to the change in the relative input price is called the *substitution effect*. To determine this effect

FIGURE 6.6.2

Output and Substitution Effects of a Rise in the Price of Labor

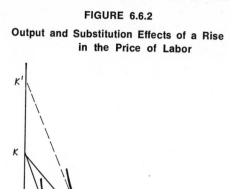

graphically, construct the fictitious isocost line $K'L'$. This line is constructed so there is a fictitious equilibrium at the *old* output level and the *new* input prices. In other words, the rise in input prices has been compensated by an increase in expenditure sufficient to maintain the old level of output. A fictitious equilibrium is reached at point R, and the movement from Q to R represents the substitution effect, the change in input usage attributable only to the change in relative input prices, the level of output remaining constant. In input units, the substitution effect reduces labor input from Ol_1 to Ol_2, or by the amount l_1l_2. Capital is substituted for labor, increasing capital usage from Ok_1 to Ok_2, or by k_1k_2.

When an input price increases, however, there must be a decrease in output if the level of expenditure does not increase. The *output* effect is represented by the shift from the fictitious equilibrium point R on I_1 to the ultimate equilibrium point S on I_2. The output effect leads to a reduction in labor input from Ol_2 to Ol_3, or by the amount l_2l_3. Capital usage is also reduced by the output effect, from Ok_2 to Ok_3, or by k_2k_3.

The effect upon labor usage attributable to the rise in the price of labor is simply the sum of the two effects:

$$l_1l_3 \quad = \quad l_1l_2 \quad + \quad l_2l_3$$
$$(Effect) \quad (Substitution\ effect) \quad (Output\ effect)$$

Summarizing, we have the following

Relation: The effect of a change in the price of an input upon the usage of this input may be decomposed into two components. The substitution effect shows the change in input usage attributable exclusively to the change in relative input prices, output held constant. This effect is always negative in that a rise in input price leads to a reduction, and a fall in input price to an increase, in the usage of the input. The output effect shows the change in input usage attributable exclusively to a change in the level of output, input prices remaining constant. It should be emphasized that these adjustments are for a fixed total expenditure. They do not allow for adjustment to a point of profit maximization.

6.6.b "Inferior Factors" and the Output Effect[15]

Just as there may be inferior goods, there may be inferior factors of production; and just as the former is associated with a negative income effect, the latter is associated with a negative output effect. The case of factor inferiority is illustrated in Figure 6.6.3, which is, for all practical purposes, the same as Figure 6.5.3.

The initial equilibrium is at Q on I_1, where the slope of the isocost KL_1 indicates the factor-price ratio and Ol_1 units of labor are employed. Now let the wage rate rise so as to rotate the isocost curve to KL_2. The point of equilibrium shifts to S on I_2, and the usage of labor *expands* to Ol_3. To see the components of the change, construct the fictitious isocost curve $K'L'$ so that it is tangent to the original isoquant but has a slope reflecting the new price ratio. The tangency occurs at R, and it shows the combination of inputs that would be used if the *old* level of output were produced at the *new* input-price ratio. The movement from Q to R, or the decrease from Ol_1 to Ol_2, is the substitution effect; and, as in all cases, it is negative. That is, the quantity of an input demanded varies inversely with its price for movements along an isoquant.

The movement from the fictitious equilibrium at R to the proper equilibrium at S, or the increase from Ol_2 to Ol_3, represents the output effect of the wage rate change. In this case it is negative: the *reduction* in output from the I_1 level to the I_2 level causes an *increase* in the usage of the factor. Whenever this relation occurs, the factor under consideration is said to be an inferior factor.

---

[15] For a detailed treatment of factor inferiority, upon which this section is based, see C. E. Ferguson, *The Neoclassical Theory of Production and Distribution* (London and New York: Cambridge University Press, 1969), chap. ix.

FIGURE 6.6.3

Optimal Input Combination to Maximize Output

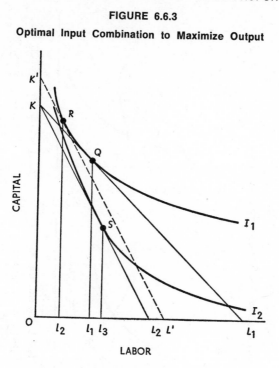

LABOR

Definition: An inferior factor of production is one that has a negative output effect or a negative expenditure elasticity.[16]

We are now treading dangerously close to drawing a mistaken
analogy between consumers and producers. It might be well to recount
the analogies that can and cannot be drawn between the theories of
consumer and producer behavior.

6.7 ANALOGIES BETWEEN CONSUMER AND PRODUCER BEHAVIOR

We have already seen that there are many analogies between the
theories of consumer and producer behavior. The valid ones may be
summarized graphically by using Figure 6.7.1. First consider panel a.
The curve labeled I may either be an indifference curve or an isoquant
(over the economic region of production). Both are negatively sloped

---

[16] Professor Hicks calls this a "regression relation" and suggests that an inferior
factor is one that is particularly suited for small-scale production of the product in
question. See John R. Hicks, *Value and Capital* (2d ed. Oxford: Clarendon Press,
1946), pp. 93–96, especially p. 96.

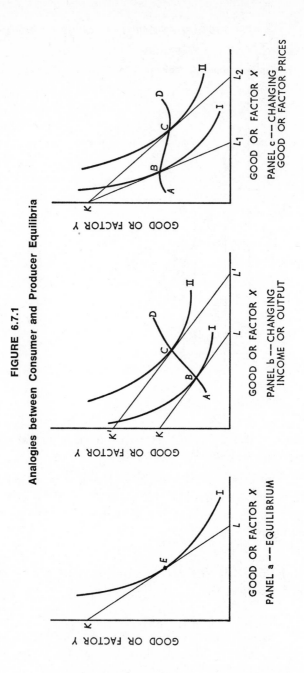

FIGURE 6.7.1

Analogies between Consumer and Producer Equilibria

PANEL a — EQUILIBRIUM

GOOD OR FACTOR X

GOOD OR FACTOR Y

PANEL b — CHANGING
INCOME OR OUTPUT

GOOD OR FACTOR X

GOOD OR FACTOR Y

PANEL c — CHANGING
GOOD OR FACTOR PRICES

GOOD OR FACTOR X

GOOD OR FACTOR Y

and concave from above, and the intersection of two indifference curves or two isoquants is impossible. Isoquants will not be "everywhere dense" unless the product is perfectly divisible, but this is a negligible difference. The only difference of any significance whatsoever is that an indifference map provides an *ordinal* ranking of utility levels whereas an isoquant map provides a *cardinal* ranking of output levels.

Next, the line labeled *KL* may either be the budget line or an isocost curve. In either case its slope indicates the price ratio (commodity or factor). Finally, equilibrium is attained at *E*, where the marginal rate of substitution (of goods in consumption or inputs in production) equals the price ratio. Further comment on the exact nature of this equilibrium is deferred for the moment.

Now turn to panel b. Let the original budget line or isocost curve be *KL*, so that *K'L'* represents an increase in money income or an increase in expenditure on input, with the associated increase in utility or output (price held constant). The locus *ABCD* is thus the income-consumption curve or the expansion path.

Finally, consider panel c. Using similar graphs (Figures 6.6.2 and 6.6.3), we have already shown that (*a*) there are substitution and output effects in production that correspond to the substitution and income effects in consumption; and (*b*) there may exist "inferior factors" of production just as there may exist "inferior goods" in consumption. Now in panel c, let the initial budget line or isocost be KL_1; KL_2 thus represents a decline in the price of good or factor *X*. If we are talking about consumption, the locus *ABCD* is the price-consumption curve; and the consumer demand function for *X* can be determined immediately from the price-consumption curve. But here the analogy stops. The locus *ABCD* is absolutely meaningless in the theory of production.

To get at the implications of this, return to panel a and consider the equilibrium at *E*. To the consumer, the equilibrium corresponds to utility maximization (subject to his limited money income). It is the point, in other words, where he attains *his objective*. To the producer, the equilibrium at *E* is an equilibrium only in the sense that the input combination at *E* is the one appropriate to the level of expenditure represented by *KL*. It says nothing whatsoever about *maximizing profit*,[17] which is the objective of the entrepreneur.

Now consider panel c again. The movement from *B* to *C* shows how the optimal input ratio would change as a result of the decrease in the

---

[17] This statement is strictly correct only in the short run, as you will see in Chapter 7. In the long run, the entrepreneur will achieve maximum profit only by operating at points such as *B* or *C* in panel b.

price of factor X *if the same amount were to be spent on inputs before and after the input price change.* In fact, the same amount would never be spent by a profit-maximizing entrepreneur. In a way that will be perfectly clear after the next two chapters, a fall in an input price will cause a reduction in the long-run average cost of producing the good in question; the supply function will shift to the right, commodity price will fall, and quantities demanded and supplied will increase. Thus while there are substitution and output effects to be considered, there is a "profit maximizing" effect as well (coming from the commodity demand function). The total effect of a change in resource price is the sum of all three.

The paragraph just above may seem murky indeed; but this is simply because we have gotten a bit ahead of ourselves. But while the explanation may be unclear, the central point should be apparent. A consumer demand function may be derived from a graph such as panel c, Figure 6.7.1, because the successive equilibria such as B and C represent points at which the consumer attains his objective. The demand for a factor of production *cannot be derived from such a graph* because the points such as B and C do not correspond to profit-maximizing equilibria. Let us summarize this as a

False Analogy Theorem: Using the tools of analysis illustrated in Figure 6.7.1, many analogies can be drawn between the theories of consumer and producer behavior. However, while a consumer demand function may be derived from a graph such as panel c, a producer's input demand function cannot because the "equilibrium" points obtained by rotating the isocost curve are not profit-maximizing equilibria.

6.8 CONCLUSION

Chapters 5 and 6 contain an explanation of the theory of production and of the optimal combination of inputs when input prices are constant. We turn next to the theory of cost, which relies upon the physical laws of production and upon the prices an entrepreneur must pay for his inputs.

PROBLEM

Suppose that Transport Service must produce a certain output of cargo and passenger service per year. The Service is confronted with the following combinations of HC100 aircraft and mechanics which can be used to yield this required output over its route pattern and meet schedule requirements.

Combination	Number of Aircraft	Number of Mechanics
No. 1......................	60	1000
2......................	61	920
3......................	62	850
4......................	63	800
5......................	64	760
6......................	65	730
7......................	66	710

1. If Transport Service is using 60 aircraft and 1,000 mechanics, how many men can it dispense with and still maintain its output if it acquires an additional HC100? _____

2. Your answer in (1) is called the _____ _____ of _____ in economic theory.

3. If the additional annual cost resulting from the operation of another HC100 is $250,000, and if mechanics cost Transport Service $6,000 each annually should the Service acquire a 61st HC100? _____

4. Which combination of aircraft and mechanics should Transport system use to minimize its costs? No. _____

5. Suppose the *annual* cost of an HC100 drops to $200,000 and the cost of mechanics rises to $7,000 per year. What combination should now be employed to minimize annual costs? No. _____

6. Can the data presented above be used to illustrate the law of variable proportions? _____ Why or why not?

QUESTIONS

1. Suppose that a product requires two inputs for its production. Then is it correct to say that if the prices of the inputs are equal, optimal behavior on the part of producers will dictate that these inputs be used in equal amounts?

2. What role do isoquants play in economic theory and what economic principles do they explain? In what sense does this tool of analysis indicate the meaning of the basic economic problem of relating scarce resources to alternative ends?

3. The Norfolk and Western Railway did not change from steam to diesel locomotives until nearly all other railroads had done so. This was probably because: (*a*) the N & W wanted to conserve national oil reserves for future generations; (*b*) since the railroad ran through the heart of the Appalachians, coal was cheap relative to diesel fuel; (*c*) N & W management—like some economics professors—couldn't bear to part with the "Iron Horse"; (*d*) all of the above.

4. A railroad would be most likely to substitute expensive signaling systems for multiple track operation if (a) second and third tracks were heavily taxed by the counties through which they passed, (b) signaling equipment was produced by a monopolist, (c) all railroad officers took Principles of Economics, (d) none of the above.

SUGGESTED READINGS

Borts, George H., and Mishan, E. J. "Exploring the 'Uneconomic Region' of the Production Function," *Review of Economic Studies,* Vol. XXIX (1962), pp. 300–12.

Cassels, John M. "On the Law of Variable Proportions," *Explorations in Economics,* pp. 223–36. New York: McGraw-Hill Book Co., Inc., 1936.

Ferguson, C. E. *The Neoclassical Theory of Production and Distribution,* chaps. 1–6. London and New York: Cambridge University Press, 1969. [Advanced math necessary.]

———, and Saving, Thomas R. "Long-Run Scale Adjustments of a Perfectly Competitive Firm and Industry," *American Economic Review,* Vol. LIX (1969), pp. 774–83. [Advanced math necessary.]

Henderson, James M., and Quandt, Richard E. *Microeconomic Theory: A Mathematical Approach,* pp. 47–53. New York: McGraw-Hill Book Co., Inc., 1958. [Elementary math necessary.]

Hicks, John R. *Value and Capital,* pp. 78–98. 2d ed. Oxford: Oxford University Press, 1946.

Samuelson, Paul A. *Foundations of Economic Analysis,* pp. 57–76. Cambridge, Mass.: Harvard University Press, 1947. [Advanced math necessary.]

Chapter 7

THEORY OF COST

7.1 INTRODUCTION

The physical conditions of production, the price of resources, and the economically efficient conduct of an entrepreneur jointly determine the cost of production of a business firm. The production function furnishes the information necessary to trace out the isoquant map. Resource prices establish the isocost curves. Finally, efficient entrepreneurial behavior dictates the production of any level of output by that combination of inputs which equates the marginal rate of technical substitution and the input-price ratio. Each position of tangency therefore determines a level of *output* and its associated *total cost*. From this information, one may construct a table, a schedule, or a mathematical function relating total cost to the level of output. This is the cost schedule or cost function that is one of the subjects of this chapter.

It is not the only subject, however, because in the short run, by definition, all inputs are not variable. Some are fixed, and the entrepreneur cannot instantaneously achieve the input combination that corresponds to economic efficiency (i.e., the one that equates the marginal rate of technical substitution with the input-price ratio). He will operate as efficiently as possible; but in the short run, a point on the expansion path will generally not be attained. We must thus analyze not only long-run cost but short-run cost as well.

Before turning to the mechanics of cost analysis, however, we need to pause for a somewhat broader view and to pose the question, "Just *what* constitutes the legitimate costs of production?" There are two answers to this question which, under ideal circumstances, happen to become one and the same. At present we must be content with the two; but in Chapter 16 we set out the conditions under which the answers are the same.

7.1.a Social Cost of Production

Economists are principally interested in the social cost of production, the cost a society incurs when its resources are used to produce a given commodity. At any point in time a society possesses a pool of resources either individually or collectively owned, depending upon the political organization of the society in question. From a social point of view the object of economic activity is to get as much as possible from this existing pool of resources. What is "possible," of course, depends not only upon the efficient and full utilization of resources but upon the specific list of commodities produced. A society could obviously have a greater output of automobiles if only small compact cars were produced. Larger, more luxurious cars require more of almost every input. But in their private evaluation schemes some members of the society may attach much greater significance to luxury cars than to compact cars.

Balancing the relative resource cost of a commodity with its relative social desirability entails a knowledge of both social valuations and social cost. This broad problem is deferred to Chapter 16 so that our attention can now be directed exclusively to social cost.

The social cost of using a bundle of resources to produce a unit of commodity X is the number of units of commodity Y that must be sacrificed in the process. Resources are used to produce both X and Y (and all other commodities). Those resources used in X production cannot be used to produce Y or any other commodity. To use a popular wartime example, devoting more resources to the production of guns means using fewer resources to produce butter. The social cost of guns is the amount of butter foregone.

Economists speak of this as the *alternative* or *opportunity cost* of production.

Definition: The *alternative* or *opportunity cost* of producing one unit of commodity X is the amount of commodity Y that must be sacrificed in order to use resources to produce X rather than Y. This is the social cost of producing X.

7.1.b Private Cost of Production

There is a close relation between the opportunity cost of producing commodity X and a calculation the producer of X must make. The use of resources to produce X rather than Y entails a social cost; there is a private cost as well because the entrepreneur must pay a price to get the resources he uses.

Suppose he does. The entrepreneur pays a certain amount to purchase resources, uses them to produce a commodity, and sells the commodity. He can compare the receipts from sales with the cost of resources and, roughly speaking, determine whether he has made an accounting profit or not. But an accountant would be quick to tell the entrepreneur he should make some further calculations. He has invested his time and money in producing commodity X. If he had not undertaken this line of business, he could have invested his time and money elsewhere—in another line of business, perhaps, or by purchasing securities with his money and using his time as an employee of another entrepreneur.

The producer of X incurs certain *explicit costs* by purchasing resources. He incurs some *implicit costs* also, and a full accounting of profit or loss must take these implicit costs into consideration. The pure economic profit an entrepreneur earns by producing commodity X may be thought of as his accounting profit minus what could be earned in the best alternative use of his time and money. These two elements are called the implicit cost of production.

Definition: The implicit costs incurred by an entrepreneur in producing a specific commodity consist of the amounts he could earn in the best alternative use of his time and money. He earns a pure economic profit from producing X if, and only if, his total receipts exceed the sum of his explicit and implicit cost.

Implicit costs are thus a fixed amount (in the short run) that must be added to explicit costs in a reckoning of pure economic profit.

7.2 SHORT AND LONG RUNS

In Chapter 5 a convenient analytical fiction was introduced, namely the *short run,* defined as a period of time in which certain types of inputs cannot be increased or decreased. That is, in the short run there are certain inputs whose usage cannot be changed regardless of the level of output. Similarly, there are other inputs, variable inputs, whose usage can be changed. In the long run, on the other hand, all inputs are variable—the quantity of all inputs can be varied so as to obtain the most efficient input combination.

Corresponding to fixed inputs are short-run fixed costs. The various fixed inputs have unit prices; the fixed explicit cost is simply the sum of unit prices multiplied by the fixed number of units used. In the short run, implicit costs are also fixed; thus it is an element of fixed cost.

Definition: Total fixed cost is the sum of the short-run explicit fixed cost and the implicit cost incurred by an entrepreneur.

Inputs that are variable in the short run give rise to short-run variable cost. Since input usage can be varied in accordance with the level of output, variable costs also vary with input. If there is zero output, no units of variable input need be employed. Variable cost is accordingly zero and total cost is the same as total fixed cost. When there is a positive level of output, however, variable inputs must be used. This gives rise to variable costs, and total cost is then the sum of total variable and total fixed cost.

Definition: Total variable cost is the sum of the amounts spent for each of the variable inputs used.

Definition: Total cost in the short run is the sum of total variable and total fixed cost.

7.3 THEORY OF COST IN THE SHORT RUN

Our analysis of cost begins with the theory of short-run cost; we then move to the "planning horizon" in which all inputs are variable and study the theory of cost in the long run, when the optimal input combination can be obtained.

7.3.a Total Short-Run Cost

Analysis of total short-run cost depends upon two propositions already discussed in this chapter: (*a*) the physical conditions of production and the unit prices of inputs determine the cost of production associated with each possible level of output; and (*b*) total cost may be divided into two components, fixed cost and variable cost.

Suppose an entrepreneur has a fixed *plant* that can be used to produce a certain commodity. Further suppose this plant costs $100. Total fixed cost is, therefore, $100—it does not change in magnitude irrespective of the level of output. This is reflected in Table 7.3.1 by the column of $100 entries labeled "Total Fixed Cost." It is furthermore shown by the horizontal line labeled *TFC* in Figure 7.3.1. Both table and graph emphasize that fixed cost is indeed fixed.

Variable inputs must also be used if production exceeds zero. In the spirit of Chapter 5, you might suppose there is only one variable input; alternatively, the multiple-input approach of Chapter 6 may be adopted. The choice is really not material, because an increase in the level of output requires an increase in the usage of inputs—whether this be one variable input or many variable inputs used in the optimal combi-

TABLE 7.3.1

Fixed, Variable, and Total Cost

Quantity of Output	Total Fixed Cost	Total Variable Cost	Total Cost
1.	$100	$ 10.00	$ 110.00
2.	100	16.00	116.00
3.	100	21.00	121.00
4.	100	26.00	126.00
5.	100	30.00	130.00
6.	100	36.00	136.00
7.	100	45.50	145.50
8.	100	56.00	156.00
9.	100	72.00	172.00
10.	100	90.00	190.00
11.	100	109.00	209.00
12.	100	130.40	230.40
13.	100	160.00	260.00
14.	100	198.20	298.20
15.	100	249.50	349.50
16.	100	324.00	424.00
17.	100	418.50	518.50
18.	100	539.00	639.00
19.	100	698.00	798.00
20.	100	900.00	1000.00

nation. In either case, the greater the level of variable input the greater the variable cost of production. This is shown in column 3 of Table 7.3.1 and by the curve labeled *TVC* in Figure 7.3.1.

Summing total fixed and total variable cost gives total cost, the entries in the last column of Table 7.3.1 and the curve labeled *TC* in Figure 7.3.1. From the figure, one may see that *TC* and *TVC* move together and are, in a sense, parallel. That is to say, the slopes of the two curves are the same at every output point; and at each point, the two curves are separated by a vertical distance of $100, the total fixed cost.

7.3.b Average and Marginal Cost

The total cost of production, including implicit cost, is very important to an entrepreneur. However, one may obtain a deeper understanding of total cost by analyzing the behavior of various average costs and of marginal cost.

The illustration of Table 7.3.1 is continued in Table 7.3.2. Indeed

FIGURE 7.3.1

Fixed, Variable, and Total Cost Curves

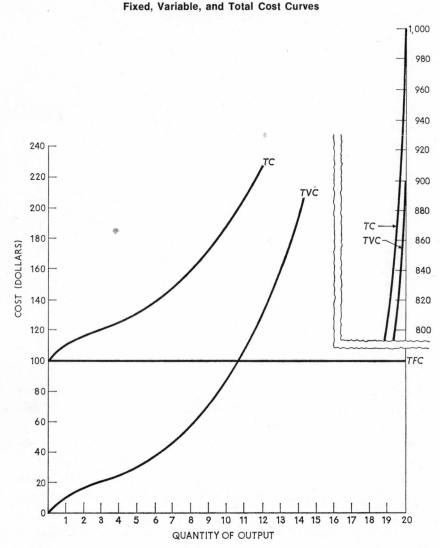

the first four columns of the latter exactly reproduce Table 7.3.1. The remaining four columns show the new concepts to be introduced.

First consider the column labeled "Average Fixed Cost."

Definition: Average fixed cost is total fixed cost divided by output.

The calculation is very simple. When one unit of output is produced, AFC is $100/1 = $100. When two units are produced, $AFC = $100/2 = $50; and so on. Graphically, average fixed cost is shown

TABLE 7.3.2

Average and Marginal Cost Calculations

Quantity of Output	Total Fixed Cost	Total Variable Cost	Total Cost	Average Fixed Cost	Average Variable Cost	Average Total Cost	Marginal Cost
1...........	$100	$ 10.00	$ 110.00	$100.00	$10.00	$110.00	$———
2...........	100	16.00	116.00	50.00	8.00	58.00	6.00
3...........	100	21.00	121.00	33.33	7.00	40.33	5.00
4...........	100	26.00	126.00	25.00	6.50	31.50	5.00
5...........	100	30.00	130.00	20.00	6.00	26.00	4.00
6...........	100	36.00	136.00	16.67	6.00	22.67	6.00
7...........	100	45.50	145.50	14.29	6.50	20.78	9.50
8...........	100	56.00	156.00	12.50	7.00	19.50	10.50
9...........	100	72.00	172.00	11.11	8.00	19.10	16.00
10...........	100	90.00	190.00	10.00	9.00	19.00	18.00
11...........	100	109.00	209.00	9.09	9.90	19.00	19.00
12...........	100	130.40	230.40	8.33	10.87	19.20	21.40
13...........	100	160.00	260.00	7.69	12.30	20.00	29.60
14...........	100	198.20	298.20	7.14	14.16	21.30	38.20
15...........	100	249.50	349.50	6.67	16.63	23.30	51.30
16...........	100	324.00	424.00	6.25	20.25	26.50	74.50
17...........	100	418.50	518.50	5.88	24.38	30.50	94.50
18...........	100	539.00	639.00	5.55	29.94	35.50	120.50
19...........	100	698.00	798.00	5.26	36.74	42.00	159.00
20...........	100	900.00	1000.00	5.00	45.00	50.00	202.00

by the curve designated *AFC* in Figure 7.3.2. Cost in dollars is plotted on the vertical axis and output on the horizontal axis. The *AFC* curve is negatively sloped throughout because as output increases the ratio of fixed cost to output must decline.[1] Mathematically, the *AFC* curve is a rectangular hyperbola.

Next move to column 6, Table 7.3.2. This column is labeled "Average Variable Cost," a concept that is entirely analogous to average fixed cost.

Definition: Average variable cost is total variable cost divided by output.

Again the calculation is simple and gives rise to the curve labeled *AVC* in Figure 7.3.2.[2] But now there is a great difference between *AVC* and

---

[1] Let the cost function be $C = A + g(q)$, where A is total fixed cost and $g(q)$ gives the total variable cost associated with each level of output. Thus average fixed cost is A/q and its slope is $-A/q^2$.

[2] Using footnote 1, average variable cost is $g(q)/q$ and its slope is

$$\frac{qg'(q) - g(q)}{q^2} = \frac{1}{q}\left[g'(q) - \frac{g(q)}{q}\right].$$

FIGURE 7.3.2

Average and Marginal Cost Curves

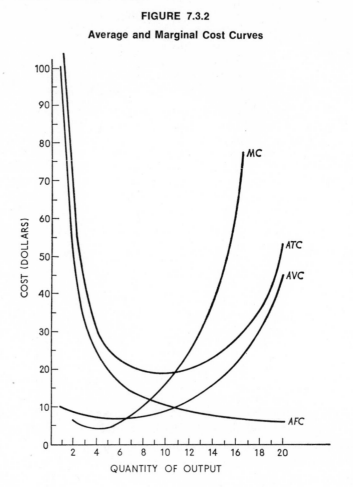

AFC: the former does not have a negative slope throughout its entire range. Indeed, in this illustration *AVC* first declines, reaches a minimum, and rises thereafter.

The reason for this curvature lies in the theory of production. Total variable cost equals the number of units of variable input used (*V*) multiplied by the unit price of the input (*P*). Thus in the one-variable-input case, $TVC = PV$.

Average variable cost is *TVC* divided by output *O,* or

$$AVC = \frac{TVC}{O} = P\frac{V}{O}.$$

Consider the term V/O, the number of units of input divided by the number of units of output. In Chapter 5, average product (*AP*) was defined as total output (O) divided by the number of units of input (V). Thus

$$AVC = P\left(\frac{1}{AP}\right),$$

or price per unit of input multiplied by the reciprocal of average product. Since average product normally rises, reaches a maximum, and then declines, average variable cost normally falls, reaches a minimum, and rises thereafter.

Relation: A production function such as that shown in Figure 5.2.1 gives rise to the average product curve shown in Figure 5.2.2. This type of production function also determines a total variable cost curve such as that in Figure 7.3.1 and the average variable cost curve shown in Figure 7.3.2.

Column 7, Table 7.3.2, contains the entries for average total cost, which may also be called average cost or unit cost.

Definition: Average total cost is total cost divided by output.

In light of this definition, ATC may be computed by dividing the entries in column 4 by the corresponding entries in column 1.[3]
However, since

$$TC = TFC + TVC,$$
$$ATC = \frac{TC}{O} = \frac{TFC}{O} + \frac{TVC}{O} = AFC + AVC.$$

Thus one may calculate average cost as the sum of average fixed and average variable cost.

This method of calculation also explains the shape of the average total cost curve in Figure 7.3.2. Over the range of values for which both AFC and AVC decline, ATC must obviously decline as well. But even after AVC turns up, the marked decline in AFC causes ATC to continue to decline. Finally, however, the increase in AVC more than offsets the decline in AFC; ATC therefore reaches its minimum and increases thereafter.

Finally, column 8 of Table 7.3.2 contains the entries for marginal cost.

---

[3] In the notations of the previous footnotes,

$$ATC = \frac{C}{q} = \frac{A}{q} + \frac{g(q)}{q}$$

and its slope is

$$-\frac{A}{q^2} + \frac{qg'(q) - g(q)}{q^2} = \frac{qg'(q) - A - g(q)}{q^2} = \frac{qg'(q) - C}{q^2} = \frac{1}{q}\left[g'(q) - \frac{C}{q}\right].$$

Definition: Marginal cost is the addition to total cost attributable to the addition of one unit to output.

Marginal cost is thus calculated by subtracting successively the entries in the Total Cost column.[4] For example, the marginal cost of the second unit produced is $MC_2 = TC_2 - TC_1$. Since only variable cost changes in the short run, however, marginal cost may be computed by successive subtraction of the entries in the Total Variable Cost column. Thus the marginal cost of the second unit is also $MC_2 = TVC_2 - TVC_1$.

As shown in Figure 7.3.2, MC—just as AVC—first declines, reaches a minimum, and rises thereafter. The explanation for this curvature also lies in the theory of production. Let Δ denote "the change in." As shown just above, $MC = \Delta (TVC)$ for a unit change in output. More generally, if output does not change by precisely one unit, $MC = \Delta(TVC)/\Delta O$. In our previous notation, $TVC = PV$. Thus $\Delta TVC = P(\Delta V)$ for an entrepreneur who is a perfect competitor in the input market (input price is given by market demand and supply and changes in his purchases do not affect the price).

Using the two relations,

$$MC = P\frac{\Delta V}{\Delta O}.$$

In Chapter 5, marginal product (MP) was defined as the change in output attributable to a change in input, or $MP = \Delta O/\Delta V$. Thus

$$MC = P\left(\frac{1}{MP}\right).$$

Since marginal product normally rises, reaches a maximum, and declines, marginal cost normally declines, reaches a minimum, and rises thereafter.

Relation: A production function such as that shown in Figure 5.2.1 gives rise to the marginal product curve shown in Figure 5.2.2. This type of production function also determines a total cost curve such as that in Figure 7.3.1 and the marginal cost curve shown in Figure 7.3.2.

7.3.c Geometry of Average and Marginal Cost Curves

In Chapter 5, the average and marginal product curves were derived geometrically from the total product curve. In like manner, the average and marginal cost curves may be derived from the corresponding total cost curve.

---

[4] For infinitesimally small changes in output, $MC = dC/dq = g'(q)$ and its slope is $g''(q)$.

Figure 7.3.3 illustrates the derivation of average fixed cost. (Note: vertical axes of panels a and b have different scales.) In panel a, total fixed cost is plotted and the outputs Oq_1, Oq_2, and Oq_3 are measured so that $Oq_1 = q_1q_2 = q_2q_3$. Since $AFC = TFC/O$, average fixed cost is

FIGURE 7.3.3

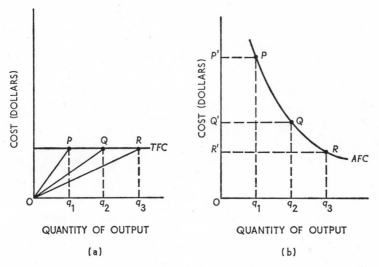

Derivation of the Average Fixed Cost Curve

given by the slope of a ray from the origin to a point on the TFC curve. For output Oq_1, AFC is the slope of the ray OP, or q_1P/Oq_1. Similarly, for output Oq_2, AFC is q_2Q/Oq_2, and so on. Since TFC is always the same, $q_1P = q_2Q = q_3R$. By construction, $Oq_2 = 2Oq_1$, and $Oq_3 = 3Oq_1$. Thus AFC for output Oq_2 is $q_2Q/Oq_2 = q_1P/2Oq_1 = 1/2$ $(q_1P/Oq_1) = 1/2$ AFC for output Oq_1. This is shown in panel b by the difference in OP' and OQ'—more specifically, $OQ' = 1/2$ OP'. Similarly, as you can demonstrate for yourself, $OR' = 1/3$ OP'. The remaining points on AFC are determined in the same way.

Figure 7.3.4 shows how AVC is derived from TVC. As is true of all "average" curves, the average variable cost associated with any level of output is given by the slope of a ray from the origin to the corresponding point on the TVC curve. As may easily be seen from panel a, the slope of a ray from the origin to the curve steadily diminishes as one passes through points such as P; and it diminishes until the ray is just tangent to the TVC curve at point Q, associated with output Oq_2. Thereafter the slope increases as one moves from Q toward points

FIGURE 7.3.4

Derivation of the Average Variable Cost Curve

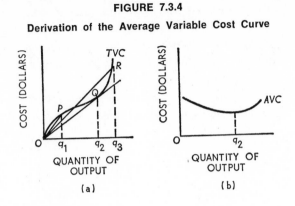

(a)

(b)

such as R. This is reflected in panel b by constructing AVC with a negative slope until output Oq_2 is attained. After that point, the slope becomes positive and remains positive thereafter.

Exactly the same argument holds for panels a and b of Figure 7.3.5,

FIGURE 7.3.5

Derivation of the Average Total Cost or Unit Cost Curve

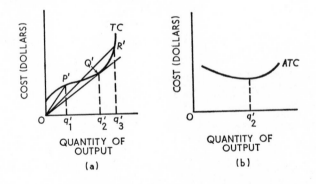

(a)

(b)

which show the derivation of ATC from TC. The slope of the ray diminishes as one moves along TC until the point Q' is reached. At Q' the slope of the ray is least, so minimum ATC is attained at the output level Oq'_2. Thereafter the slope of the ray increases continuously, and the ATC curve has a positive slope. (Note: The output level Oq_2 does not represent the same quantity in Figures 7.3.3–7.3.6.)

Finally, the derivation of marginal cost is illustrated in Figure 7.3.6. Panel a contains the total cost curve TC. As output increases from Oq_1 to Oq_2, one moves from point P to point Q, and total cost increases from TC_1 to TC_2. Marginal cost is thus

$$MC = \frac{TC_2 - TC_1}{Oq_2 - Oq_1} = \frac{QR}{PR}.$$

Now let the point P move along TC toward point Q. As the distance between P and Q becomes smaller and smaller the slope of the tangent T at point Q becomes a progressively better estimate of QR/PR. And in the limit, for movements in a tiny neighborhood around point Q the slope of the tangent is marginal cost.

FIGURE 7.3.6

Derivation of the Marginal Cost Curve

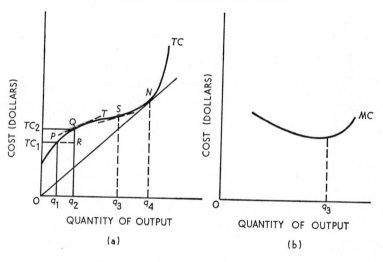

As one moves along TC through points such as P and Q the slope of TC diminishes. The slope continues to diminish until point S is reached at output Oq_3. Thereafter the slope increases. Therefore, the MC curve is constructed in panel b so that it decreases until output Oq_3 is attained and increases thereafter.[5]

---

[5] Recall from Chapter 5 that marginal product attains its maximum when there is a point of inflection on the total product curve. Indeed it was shown that since marginal product was a maximum at this point, the total product curve changed from concave from above to concave from below. Since marginal cost and marginal product are inversely related, marginal cost is a minimum when there is a point of inflection on the total cost curve; and at that point, the total cost curve changes from concave from below to concave from above. This is easy to prove. Given the cost function

$$C = A + g(q),\qquad (7.5.1)$$

marginal cost is

$$MC = \frac{dC}{dq} = g'(q).\qquad (7.5.2)$$

One final point should be noted about Figures 7.3.4 and 7.3.6. As already shown, TC and TVC have the same slope at each output point; TC is simply TVC displaced upward by the constant amount TFC. Since the slopes are the same, MC is given by the slope of either curve. In panel a, Figure 7.3.4, the slope of the ray OQ gives minimum AVC. But at this point the ray OQ is just tangent to TVC; hence it also gives MC at this point. Thus $MC = AVC$ when the latter attains its minimum value.[6] Similarly, in panel a, Figure 7.3.6, the slope of the ray ON gives minimum ATC. But at this point the ray is tangent to TC; thus its slope also gives MC. Consequently $MC = ATC$ when the latter attains its minimum value.[7]

7.3.d Short-Run Cost Curves

The properties of the average and marginal cost curves, as derived in subsection 7.3.c, are illustrated by the "typical" set of short-run cost curves shown in Figure 7.3.7. The properties may be summarized as follows.

Relations: (i) AFC declines continuously, approaching both axes asymptotically, as shown by points 1 and 2 in the figure. AFC is a rectangular hyperbola. (ii) AVC first declines, reaches a minimum at point 4, and rises thereafter. When AVC attains its minimum at point 4, MC equals AVC. As AFC approaches asymptotically close to the horizontal axis, AVC

Marginal cost attains its *minimum* when $g''(q) = 0$ and $g'''(q) > 0$. But $g''(q) = 0$ implies that there is a point of inflection on the total cost curve; and $g'''(q) > 0$ implies the change of concavity stated above, *q.e.d.*

[6] The equality of MC and AVC when the latter is a minimum follows from the relation of MC and MP, AVC and AP. *Explain why.*

[7] Using the notation of the previous footnotes, these two points can easily be proved mathematically. $AVC = g(q)/q$; hence AVC reaches its minimum when $d(AVC)/dq = 0$. Performing this operation, we have

$$\frac{d\left(\frac{g(q)}{q}\right)}{dq} = \frac{qg'(q) - g(q)}{q^2} = \frac{1}{q}\left(g'(q) - \frac{g(q)}{q}\right) = 0 \ .$$

Since $q > 0$, the expression in parentheses must be zero, or $g'(q) = g(q)/q$ at the point of minimum AVC.

Similarly, $ATC = A/q + g(q)/q$. Equating its first derivative with zero, one obtains

$$\frac{d\left(\frac{A}{q} + \frac{g(q)}{q}\right)}{dq} = -\frac{A}{q^2} + \frac{qg'(q) - g(q)}{q^2} = 0 \ .$$

Thus $qg'(q) = A + g(q)$, or $g'(q) = A/q + g(q)/q$ at the point of minimum ATC.

FIGURE 7.3.7

Typical Set of Cost Curves

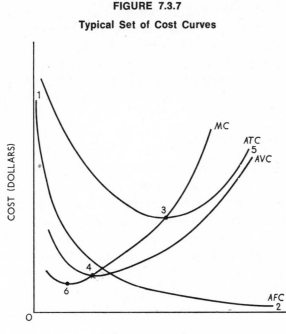

approaches *ATC* asymptotically, as shown by point 5. (*iii*) *ATC* first declines, reaches a minimum at point 3, and rises thereafter. When *ATC*
attains its minimum at point 3, *MC* equals *ATC*. (*iv*) *MC* first declines,
reaches a minimum at point 6, and rises thereafter. *MC* equals both *AVC*
and *ATC* when these curves attain their minimum values. Furthermore, *MC*
lies below both *AVC* and *ATC* over the range in which the curves decline;
it lies above them when they are rising.

7.4 LONG-RUN THEORY OF COST

The conventional definition of the long run given in Chapter 5 and
elsewhere is "a period of time of such length that all inputs are variable." Another aspect of the long run has also been stressed—an aspect
that is, perhaps, the most important of all. The long run is a *planning
horizon*. All production, indeed all economic activity, takes place in
the short run. The "long run" refers to the fact that economic agents—
consumers and entrepreneurs—can plan ahead and choose many aspects
of the "short run" in which they will operate in the future. Thus in a
sense, the long run consists of all possible short-run situations among
which an economic agent may choose.

As an example, *before* an investment is made an entrepreneur is in a long-run situation. He may select any one of a wide variety of different investments. After the investment decision is made and funds are congealed in fixed capital equipment, the entrepreneur operates under short-run conditions. Thus perhaps the best distinction is to say that an economic agent *operates* in the short run and *plans* in the long run.

7.4.a Short Run and the Long

To begin with a highly simplified situation, suppose technology is such that plants in a certain industry can have only three different sizes. That is, the fixed capital equipment comprising the "plant" is available in only three sizes—small, medium, and large.

The plant of smallest size gives rise to the short-run average cost curve labeled SAC_1 in Figure 7.4.1; the medium-size plant has short-

FIGURE 7.4.1

Short-Run Average Cost Curves for Plants of Different Size

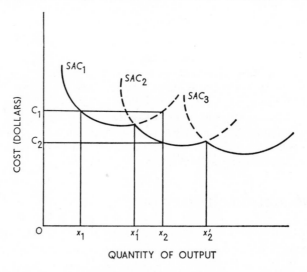

QUANTITY OF OUTPUT

run average cost given by SAC_2; and the large plant has an average cost given by SAC_3. In the long run, an entrepreneur has to choose among the three investment alternatives represented by the three short-run average cost curves. If he expects his most profitable output to be Ox_1, he will select the smallest plant. If he expects Ox_2 to be most profitable, he will select the medium plant; and so forth. Such decisions would be made because the entrepreneur chooses the plant capable of producing the expected output at the lowest unit cost.

If he expected to produce either Ox_1' or Ox_2', his decision would be more difficult. At each of these points, two plants give rise to the same average cost. An entrepreneur might choose the smaller plant because it requires a smaller investment. On the other hand, he might select the larger plant in order to meet a possible expansion of demand. In these two examples the entrepreneur's decision would be based upon considerations other than least cost output.

In all other cases his decision is determined by unit cost. Suppose he expects to produce output Ox_1. He accordingly builds the plant represented by SAC_1. Now suppose he actually finds it desirable to produce Ox_2 units. He can do this with his plant, at an average cost of Oc_1 per unit. In the short run this is all he can do; he has no option. But he can plan for the future. Once his old plant has "worn out" he can replace it with a new one—and it will be a medium-size plant because the output Ox_2 can be produced for an average cost of Oc_2 per unit, substantially less than with the small plant.

In the short run, an entrepreneur must operate with SAC_1, SAC_2, or SAC_3. But in the long run, he can plan to build the plant whose size leads to the least average cost for any given output. Thus as a planning device he regards the heavily shaded curve as his long-run average cost curve because this curve shows the least unit cost of producing each possible output. This curve is frequently called the "envelope curve."

7.4.b Long-Run Average Cost Curve

The illustration above is, as we said, highly simplified. An entrepreneur is normally faced with a choice among quite a wide variety of plants. In Figure 7.4.2, six short-run average cost curves are shown; but this is really far from enough. Many curves could be drawn between each of those shown. These six plants are only representative of the wide variety that could be constructed.

These many curves, just as the three in subsection 7.4.a, generate LAC as a planning device. Suppose an entrepreneur thinks the output associated with point A will be most profitable. He will build the plant represented by SAC_1 because it will enable him to produce this output at the least possible cost per unit. With the plant whose short-run average cost is given by SAC_1, unit cost could be reduced by expanding output to the amount associated with point B, the minimum point on SAC_1. If demand conditions were suddenly changed so this larger out-

FIGURE 7.4.2

Long-Run Average Cost Curve

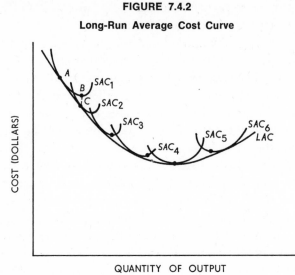

QUANTITY OF OUTPUT

put were desirable, the entrepreneur could easily expand—and he would add to his profitability by reducing unit cost. Nevertheless, when setting his future plans the entrepreneur would decide to construct the plant represented by SAC_2 because he could reduce unit costs even more. He would operate at point C, thereby lowering his unit cost from the level at point B on SAC_1.

The long-run planning curve, *LAC,* is a locus of points representing the least unit cost of producing the corresponding output. The entrepreneur determines the size of plant by reference to this curve. He selects that short-run plant which yields the least unit cost of producing the volume of output he anticipates.

7.4.c Long-Run Marginal Cost

A marginal cost curve may be constructed for the planning curve or the long-run average cost curve. This is illustrated in Figure 7.4.3. Consider the plant represented by the short-run average cost curve SAC_1 with the associated short-run marginal cost curve SMC_1. At point A, corresponding to output Ox_1, SAC and LAC are equal. Hence short-run and long-run total cost are also equal.

For smaller outputs, such as Ox_1', SAC_1 exceeds *LAC,* so short-run total cost is greater than long-run total cost. Thus for an expansion of output toward Ox_1, long-run marginal cost—whatever it may be—must exceed the known short-run marginal cost. That is, we have moved

FIGURE 7.4.3

Long-Run and Short-Run Marginal Cost

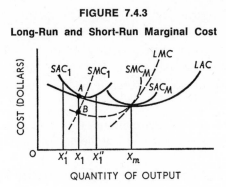

QUANTITY OF OUTPUT

from a point where short-run total cost exceeds long-run total cost to a point where they are equal. The addition to total cost, or marginal cost, must consequently be smaller for the short-run curve than for the long-run curve. Therefore LMC is greater than SMC to the left of point A.[8]

For an expansion of output from Ox_1 to Ox_1'', the opposite situation holds. SAC_1 is greater than LAC at Ox_1'', so short-run total cost exceeds long-run total cost at this point. Now we have moved from a point where short-run and long-run total cost are equal (Ox_1) to a point where short-run total cost exceeds long-run total cost (Ox_1''). Therefore, the addition to total cost, or marginal cost, must be greater for the short-run curve than for the long-run curve. Whatever LMC might be, it must be less than SMC_1 to the right of Ox_1.

Now we have the information to find one point on the LMC curve. LMC must exceed SMC_1 to the left of Ox_1 and it must be less than SMC_1 to the right of Ox_1. Therefore, LMC must equal SMC_1 at output Ox_1. This gives us point B on the LMC curve. To find all the other points, this process is repeated. Take the next short-run average cost curve, together with its known short-run marginal cost. LMC must equal this SMC for the output at which the SAC curve is tangent to LAC. Performing this process for all plant sizes generates the LMC curve.

There is one important point to notice. LMC intersects LAC when the latter is at its minimum point. There will be one, and only one, short-run plant size whose minimum short-run average cost coincides

---

[8] It might be well to emphasize this point by means of a simple numerical example. Refer to Figure 7.4.3. At output Ox_1', since $SAC > LAC$, let short-run total cost be \$100 and long-run total cost be \$90. At output Ox_1, they are equal, say \$110. Thus over the range Ox_1' to Ox_1, short-run marginal cost is \$10 while long-run marginal cost is \$20.

with minimum long-run average cost. This plant is represented by SAC_M and SMC_M in Figure 7.4.3. SMC_M equals SAC_M at the minimum point on the latter curve. SAC_M is tangent to LAC at their common minimum; and as we have shown, LMC equals SMC at the point where SAC and LAC are tangent. Therefore, LMC must pass through the minimum point on LAC.

Exercise: Explain the relation between LMC and SMC in terms of optimal adjustment (also see question 1 at the end of this chapter).

7.5 LONG-RUN COST AND THE PRODUCTION FUNCTION[9]

To this point our approach has been to develop the long-run average cost curve as the "envelope" of a set of short-run curves. This is of

---

[9] The long-run cost function may be derived directly from the production function if the latter is known. As will be obvious, a direct derivation can become a messy business even for very simple production functions.

Suppose the production function takes the Cobb-Douglas form:

$$q = ax_1{}^b x_2{}^c , \qquad (7.9.1)$$

where q represents physical output; x_1 and x_2 are the physical quantities of two inputs; and a, b, and c are technologically given, positive constants. Further, let w and r represent the given constant unit prices of the inputs x_1 and x_2 respectively. From equation (7.9.1) equality between the marginal rate of technical substitution and the input-price ratio requires that

$$\frac{w}{r} = \frac{bx_2}{cx_1} . \qquad (7.9.2)$$

Take the logarithms of equations (7.9.1) and (7.9.2) and write them as a pair of simultaneous equations:

$$b \log x_1 + c \log x_2 = \log q - \log a ,$$
$$-\log x_1 + \log x_2 = \log c - \log b + \log w - \log r . \qquad (7.9.3)$$

Solving equations (7.9.3) simultaneously yields the following expressions:

$$x_1{}^* = [a^{-1}qc^{-c}b^c w^{-c}r^c]^{\frac{1}{b+c}} , \qquad (7.9.4)$$
$$x_2{}^* = [a^{-1}qc^b b^{-b} w^b r^{-b}]^{\frac{1}{b+c}} ,$$

where $x_1{}^*$ and $x_2{}^*$ are the quantities of the inputs required to produce q units of output at the cost-minimizing input ratio given by equation (7.9.2). That is, for each q, the associated $x_2{}^*/x_1{}^*$ is a point on the expansion path.

The cost C of producing q units most efficiently is

$$C = wx_1{}^* + rx_2{}^* . \qquad (7.9.5)$$

Substituting equations (7.9.4) in (7.9.5) yields

$$C = r \left[\left(\frac{cw}{br} \right)^b \frac{q}{a} \right]^{\frac{1}{b+c}} + w \left[\left(\frac{cw}{br} \right)^{-c} \frac{q}{a} \right]^{\frac{1}{b+c}} . \qquad (7.9.6)$$

course legitimate, and it has a certain intuitive appeal. But the theory of long-run cost may be established much more precisely by relating cost directly to the production function.

7.5.a The Expansion Path and the Envelope Curve

Figure 7.5.1 shows the expansion path OE as it was developed in Chapter 6. Curves I, II, and III are isoquants; and CF, $C'F'$, and $C''F''$ are isocost curves representing successively greater expenditures at constant input prices. The successive equilibria are P, Q, R; and the expansion path is $OPQRE$. It should be clear that the long-run total

---

Now consider the following expansion of the right-most term above:

$$w\left[\left(\frac{cw}{br}\right)^{-c}\frac{q}{a}\right]^{\frac{1}{b+c}} = \frac{w\left[\left(\frac{cw}{br}\right)^{-c}\left(\frac{cw}{br}\right)^{b+c}\frac{q}{a}\right]^{\frac{1}{b+c}}}{\left[\left(\frac{cw}{br}\right)^{b+c}\right]^{\frac{1}{b+c}}}$$

(7.9.7)

$$= \frac{w\left[\left(\frac{cw}{br}\right)^{b}\frac{q}{a}\right]^{\frac{1}{b+c}}}{\left(\frac{cw}{br}\right)} = \frac{br}{c}\left[\left(\frac{cw}{br}\right)^{b}\frac{q}{a}\right]^{\frac{1}{b+c}}.$$

Substituting the final expression above in equation (7.9.6.), one obtains

$$C = r\left[\left(\frac{cw}{br}\right)^{b}\frac{q}{a}\right]^{\frac{1}{b+c}} + \frac{br}{c}\left[\left(\frac{cw}{br}\right)^{b}\frac{q}{a}\right]^{\frac{1}{b+c}},$$

(7.9.8)

or

$$C = r\left(\frac{b+c}{c}\right)\left[\left(\frac{cw}{br}\right)^{b}\left(\frac{q}{a}\right)\right]^{\frac{1}{b+c}}.$$

(7.9.9)

Since the technological parameters (a, b and c) and the market parameters (w and r) are given, equation (7.9.9) shows cost as a function of the level of output only. And notice: there is no "additive" constant representing fixed cost. In the long run optimal adjustment is achieved because all inputs are variable.

Exercise: Derive the average and marginal cost curves from equation (7.9.9) and compare them.

Exercise: Derive the cost function associated with the CES production function.

$$q = \gamma[\delta x_1^{-\rho} + (1-\delta)x_2^{-\rho}]^{-\frac{1}{\rho}}.$$

Then determine average and marginal cost and compare them. For this exercise, see C. E. Ferguson, *The Neoclassical Theory of Production and Distribution* (London and New York: Cambridge University Press, 1969), pp. 166–68.

FIGURE 7.5.1

**The Expansion Path and Suboptimal
Adjustment**

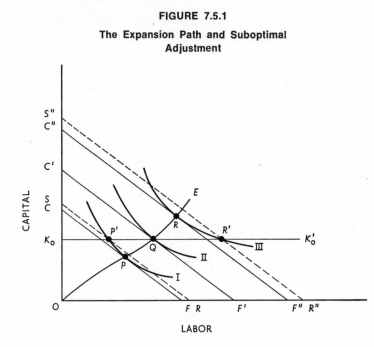

cost curve can be "read off" directly from the expansion path. Consider point *P*. *I* is the level of output and the total cost of producing *I* is the particular expenditure associated with the isocost curve *CF*. A similar statement applies to all other points on the expansion path. Hence the long-run total cost curve is just the cost-output space equivalent of the expansion path.

So, too, is the envelope curve. Again consider point *P*. Total cost is the expenditure represented by the isocost curve *CF*. Output is given by the isoquant *I*. Dividing the former by the latter gives long-run average cost. Hence the long-run average cost curve, or the envelope curve, is also the cost-output space equivalent of the expansion path in input space. Let us summarize these points as the following

Relation: The long-run total and average cost curves are directly derivable from the expansion path; indeed, both curves are simply the cost-output space equivalent of the expansion path.

7.5.b Relation between SAC and LAC

The point tangency relation between *LAC* and the set of *SAC*'s of which it is the envelope emerges clearly from Figure 7.5.1. Suppose an entrepreneur has attained the point *Q* on his expansion path; he thus produces the *II* level of output and has a plant (capital) of size OK_0. Now suppose this plant is fixed in the short run; only labor is instantaneously variable. The line K_0K_0' represents the fixed plant.

At point Q, total and average cost are the same whether one considers a short- or long-run situation. Input proportions are optimally adjusted, and the least feasible total cost is the expenditure associated with the isocost curve $C'F'$. Hence $SAC = LAC$ at point Q. Now suppose the entrepreneur wishes to expand output to the *III* level. In the long run (a period of time in which he can achieve optimal adjustment) he will move to point R, with the associated total cost represented by the isocost curve $C''F''$. But in the short run he cannot do this. Capital is fixed at the K_0K_0' level. The best he can do is move to the point R' on *III*. At that point he attains his desired level of output; but it is achieved at a total cost greater than that associated with $C''F''$. The cost at R' is represented by $S''R''$. Since short-run total cost is greater than long-run total costs, the corresponding average costs have the same relation. This explains why SAC lies above LAC to the right of their tangency.

Exercise: Use the same reasoning to explain why a contraction of output to the *I* level in the short run involves $SAC > LAC$.

These relations may be given an easy graphical representation. Consider Figure 7.5.2. In panel a, LTC is the long-run total cost curve derived from the expansion path. In panel b, LAC is the corresponding long-run average cost curve. Now suppose, as in Figure 7.5.1, that the producer has a fixed short-run investment of OK_0. There is one point—

FIGURE 7.5.2

Long-Run Cost as the Envelope Curve

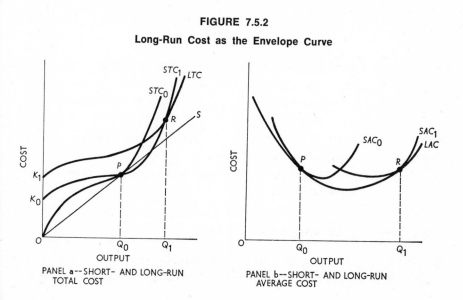

PANEL a--SHORT- AND LONG-RUN
TOTAL COST

PANEL b--SHORT- AND LONG-RUN
AVERAGE COST

such as Q in Figure 7.5.1 or P in Figure 7.5.2—at which OK_0 is the optimal adjustment amount of capital. At this point, short- and long-run total cost are identical. Otherwise, short-run total cost exceeds long-run total cost. In Figure 7.5.2 this is illustrated by constructing STC_0 above LTC except for their tangency at the optimal adjustment point P.

As we have previously seen, the slope of a ray from the origin gives average cost. Since STC_0 and LTC are tangent at point P, the ray OS has a common slope at this point. Thus in panel b, SAC_0 is tangent to LAC at the point P, corresponding to output OQ_0. The same reasoning applies to point R in both panels of Figure 7.5.2.

Exercise: Why does LTC begin at the origin while STC_0 and STC_1 have positive ordinate intercepts?

Exercise: Explain, by means of Figure 7.5.2, why LTC and LAC are loci of optimal adjustment points.

The reason *why* $SAC > LAC$ except at their point of tangency may also be explained by means of Figure 7.5.1. Consider the expansion of output *II* to *III*. In the long run the producer moves to R, where the marginal rate of technical substitution equals the input-price ratio. In the short run he is restricted to movements along $K_0K_0{}'$; hence he must move to R'. At that point the marginal rate of technical substitution is *less* than the factor-price ratio. That is, letting w and r denote the prices of labor and capital respectively, we have

$$MRTS = \frac{MP_L}{MP_K} < \frac{w}{r}, \tag{7.5.1}$$

or

$$\frac{MP_L}{w} < \frac{MP_K}{r}. \tag{7.5.2}$$

Since the capital input cannot be expanded, output can be increased only by using an uneconomically large amount of labor. The *reason* why it is uneconomical follows from (7.5.2): the marginal product of a dollar's worth of labor is less than that of capital. The *III* level of output could be produced more cheaply by using more capital and less labor; but in the short run this cannot be done.

Exercise: Carry out the same reasoning for a contraction of output to the *I* level in Figure 7.5.1.

7.5.c Relation between SMC and LMC

Finally, Figure 7.5.1 may be used to explain why LMC is less than SMC for an expansion of output beyond point Q and greater for contractions. At point Q, $SAC = LAC$ so $SMC = LMC$. This time suppose the entrepreneur wishes to reduce output to the I level. In the long run he will move to point P, in short run to point P'. The total cost at P', represented by the isocost curve SR, exceeds the total cost at P, given by CF. In the long run costs may be reduced by a greater amount because inputs are optimally adjusted. Hence the change in long-run total cost is greater than the change in short-run total cost and, therefore, long-run marginal cost exceeds its short-run counterpart.

Exercise: Explain the relation for an expansion to the *III* level of output.

At the risk of belaboring the obvious, let us emphasize that *optimal* adjustment is always preferable to *suboptimal* adjustment. This leads to a slightly different view of LAC and LMC. This is stated as a

Definition: The long-run average cost curve shows the *minimum unit cost* of producing every feasible level of output; the long-run marginal cost curve shows the *minimum amount* by which cost is increased when output is expanded and the *maximum amount* that can be saved when output is reduced.

7.5.d   Cost Elasticity and the Function Coefficient

A final and very important relation between the production function and the long-run total cost curve may now be established. To do so requires some manipulation of symbols. It is *not mathematical;* but it is "busy work" that is relegated to a footnote,[10] which all students should

---

[10] Let the production function be

$$q = f(x, y) . \tag{7.10.1}$$

We found in Chapter 5 that the function coefficient could be written as

$$\epsilon = \frac{\Delta q}{\Delta x}\frac{x}{q} + \frac{\Delta q}{\Delta y}\frac{y}{q} = MP_x\frac{x}{q} + MP_y\frac{y}{q} . \tag{7.10.2}$$

Now let the prices of the two inputs be p_x and p_y. Multiply and divide the first term on the right-hand side of equation (7.10.2) by p_x, the second term by p_y. One thus obtains

$$\epsilon = \frac{MP_x\,xp_x}{p_x}\frac{}{q} + \frac{MP_y\,yp_y}{p_y}\frac{}{q} . \tag{7.10.3}$$

In Chapter 6 we found that the expansion path is defined by equality between the marginal rate of technical substitution and the input-price ratio. Further, we saw that this may always be expressed by saying that the marginal product of a dollar's worth of each input must be the same. Symbolically,

$$\frac{MP_x}{p_x} = \frac{MP_y}{p_y} . \tag{7.10.4}$$

read. Recall that in Chapter 5 we defined the *function coefficient* as the proportional change in output resulting from a uniform proportional change in all inputs. We may now state the results of our "busy work" as the following

Relation: The function coefficient is equal to the ratio of long-run average cost to long-run marginal cost; in symbols,

$$\epsilon = \frac{LAC}{LMC}. \tag{7.5.3}$$

File this result for the moment and consider the elasticity of total cost. By definition, it is the proportional change in cost resulting from a given proportional change in output. In symbols, the formula is

$$\kappa = \frac{\Delta C}{C} \div \frac{\Delta q}{q} = \frac{\Delta C}{\Delta q} \frac{q}{C} = \frac{LMC}{LAC}. \tag{7.5.4}$$

As with all elasticities, it is the ratio of the marginal to the average. Let us emphasize this

---

Substituting equation (7.10.4) in (7.10.3), write

$$\epsilon = \frac{MP_x}{p_x}\left(\frac{xp_x}{q} + \frac{yp_y}{q}\right) = \frac{MP_x}{p_x}\left(\frac{xp_x + yp_y}{q}\right). \tag{7.10.5}$$

Finally, we need some information from this chapter. First, by definition, total cost (C) is the sum of the payments to all inputs, i.e., the price of each input multiplied by the number of units employed and summed over all inputs. Thus

$$C = xp_x + yp_y. \tag{7.10.6}$$

Further, we defined average cost as $AC = C/q$. Substitution in equation (7.10.5) gives

$$\epsilon = \frac{MP_x}{p_x}(AC). \tag{7.10.7}$$

The other bit of information we need from this chapter is that marginal cost (LMC) is equal to the input price divided by its marginal product:

$$LMC = \frac{p_x}{MP_x}. \tag{7.10.8}$$

Substituting in equation (7.10.7) completes our "busy work":

$$\epsilon = \frac{LAC}{LMC}, \tag{7.10.9}$$

the relation stated in the text.

It is worthwhile to emphasize one point. When we substituted equation (7.10.4) in (7.10.3), we eliminated MP_y/p_y. We could just as easily have eliminated MP_x/p_x. The results would be the same because marginal cost is equal to the input price divided by its marginal product. The result to emphasize is as follows: for movements along the expansion path, marginal cost is the same irrespective of the input for which it is calculated. This is just another way of stating the familiar proposition that "at the *margin*, all things are equally dear."

Relation: The elasticity of total cost equals the ratio of marginal cost to average cost.

Comparing equations (7.5.3) and (7.5.4), we find that

$$\kappa = \frac{1}{\epsilon},\tag{7.5.5}$$

which is the important relation we set out to find.

Relation: The elasticity of total cost is equal to the reciprocal of the function coefficient; specifically, the elasticity of total cost is less than, equal to, or greater than unity according as the function coefficient is greater than, equal to, or less than unity.

The implications of this relation are worth exploring in some detail. First, recall that there are increasing, constant, or decreasing returns to scale according as the function coefficient exceeds, equals, or is less than one. For example, suppose $\epsilon > 1$. This implies that a proportional expansion of inputs causes output to expand in greater proportion. Now if $\epsilon > 1$, $\kappa < 1$. This implies that a proportional increase in output causes cost to expand in smaller proportion. The reason is clear: since there are increasing returns to scale, the given proportional expansion of output can be achieved by a smaller proportional increase in input usage. At constant input prices, cost therefore increases by proportionately less than output.

Exercise: Carry out this type of argument for the case in which $\epsilon < 1$.

Now continue to assume that $\epsilon > 1$ and $\kappa < 1$. If total cost increases in smaller proportion than output, average cost declines. Thus over the range in which the production function exhibits increasing returns to scale, the long-run average cost curve declines (see Figure 7.5.3). On the other hand, when there are decreasing returns to scale ($\epsilon < 1$), the total cost function is elastic ($\kappa > 1$). This means that cost increases by proportionately more than output, so that average cost rises. Again the reason is clear: when $\epsilon < 1$, a given proportional increase in output requires inputs to be increased in greater proportion. At constant factor prices, total cost expands by proportionately more than output and average cost increases.

These results may be summarized as the following[11]

[11] Mathematically, this may be explained concisely. Let the cost function (long run, so there is no constant representing fixed cost) be $C = g(q)$. Thus the elasticity of total cost is

$$\kappa = \frac{dC}{dq}\frac{q}{C} = \frac{C'}{\overline{C}},\tag{7.11.1}$$

FIGURE 7.5.3

Long-Run Average Cost and the Function Coefficient

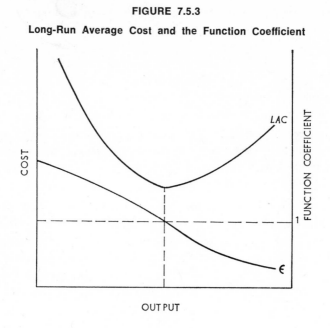

Relation: Long-run average cost decreases or increases according as there are increasing or decreasing returns to scale; this relation holds if, and only if, factor prices are constant throughout.

---

where $\bar{C}$ is average cost. Next consider the elasticity of average cost (γ):

$$\gamma = \frac{d\left(\frac{C}{q}\right)}{dq} \frac{q^2}{C} = \frac{qC' - C}{q^2} \frac{q^2}{C} = \frac{C'}{\bar{C}} - 1 = \kappa - 1 . \qquad (7.11.2)$$

Now introduce the relation $\kappa = 1/\epsilon$. Thus one may write equation (7.11.2) as

$$\gamma = \frac{1}{\epsilon} - 1 . \qquad (7.11.3)$$

Hence $\gamma \lesseqgtr 0$ according as $\epsilon \gtreqless 1$.

At this point we should note that when the production function is homogeneous of degree one, $\epsilon \equiv 1$. In this case the elasticity of total cost is unity and the elasticity of average cost is zero. That is, total cost expands in the same proportion as output (factor prices constant). The long-run average cost curve is consequently a horizontal line. Nonetheless, it is still the envelope of the U-shaped short-run average cost curves.

Exercise: Demonstrate this last point for yourself. That is, show that if the production function is homogeneous of degree one and factor prices are constant,

7.6 SHAPE OF *LAC*

The short- and long-run average cost curves are alike in that each has been drawn with a U shape. The reasons for this shape, however, are quite different. *SAC* is U-shaped because the decline in average fixed cost is ultimately more than offset by the rise in average variable cost—the latter occurring because average product reaches a maximum and declines. But this has nothing at all to do with the curvature of *LAC*. Increasing or decreasing returns to scale in the production function and certain financial economies and diseconomies of scale are the factors governing the shape of *LAC*.

7.6.a Economies of Scale

As the size of plant and the scale of operation become larger, considering expansion from the smallest possible plant, certain economies of scale are usually realized. That is, after adjusting *all* inputs optimally the unit cost of production can be reduced by increasing the size of plant.

Adam Smith gave one of the outstanding reasons for this: specialization and division of labor. When the number of workers is expanded, fixed inputs remaining fixed, the opportunities for specialization and division of labor are rapidly exhausted. The marginal product curve rises, to be sure; but not for long. It very quickly reaches its maximum and declines thereafter. When workers and equipment are expanded together, however, very substantial gains may be reaped by division of jobs and the specialization of workers in one job or another.

Proficiency is gained by concentration of effort. If a plant is very small and employs only a small number of workers, each worker will usually have to perform several different jobs in the production process. In doing so he is likely to have to move about the plant, change tools, and so on. Not only are workers not highly specialized but a part of

the long-run average cost envelope of short-run average cost curves resembles the figure below:

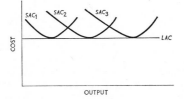

their work time is consumed in moving about and changing tools. Thus important savings may be realized by expanding the scale of operation. A larger plant with a larger work force may permit each worker to specialize in one job, gaining proficiency and obviating time-consuming interchanges of location and equipment. There naturally will be corresponding reductions in the unit cost of production.

Technological factors constitute a second force contributing to economies of scale. If several different machines, each with a different rate of output, are required in a production process, the operation may have to be quite sizable to permit proper "meshing" of equipment. Suppose only two types of machines are required, one that produces and one that packages the product. If the first machine can produce 30,000 units per day and the second can package 45,000, output will have to be 90,000 units per day in order fully to utilize the capacity of each machine.

Another technological element is the fact that the cost of purchasing and installing larger machines is usually proportionately less than the cost of smaller machines. For example, a printing press that can run 200,000 papers per day does not cost 10 times as much as one that can run 20,000 per day—nor does it require 10 times as much building space, 10 times as many men to work it, and so forth. Again, expanding size tends to reduce the unit cost of production.

A final technological element is perhaps the most important of all: as the scale of operation expands there is usually a *qualitative,* as well as a quantitative, change in equipment. Consider ditchdigging. The smallest scale of operation is one man and one shovel. But as the scale expands beyond a certain point one does not simply continue to add men and shovels. Shovels and most workers are replaced by a modern ditchdigging machine. In like manner, expansion of scale normally permits the introduction of various types of automation devices, all of which tend to reduce the unit cost of production.[12]

Thus two broad forces—specialization and division of labor and technological factors—enable producers to reduce unit cost by expand-

---

[12] This passage is murky indeed, and it might be struck from the book. It may seem to imply *technological progress.* It does not. Let us suppose that we are considering a continuum of fixed-proportions production processes. The *LAC* curve is simply the least-cost curve for the proper fixed-proportions process.

Suppose you are digging a ditch. If it is to be 2 feet long, the man-shovel method would probably be most economical. If it is to be 100 feet long, it may well be more economical to employ ditchdigging machinery.

ing the scale of operation.[13] These forces give rise to the negatively sloped portion of the long-run average cost curve.

But why should it ever rise? After all possible economies of scale have been realized, why does the curve not become horizontal?

7.6.b Diseconomies of Scale

The rising portion of *LAC* is usually attributed to "diseconomies of scale," which essentially means limitations to efficient management. Managing any business entails controlling and coordinating a wide variety of activities—production, transportation, finance, sales, etc. To perform these managerial functions efficiently the manager must have accurate information; otherwise the essential decision making is done in ignorance.

As the scale of plant expands beyond a certain point, top management necessarily has to delegate responsibility and authority to lower echelon employees. Contact with the daily routine of operation tends to be lost and efficiency of operation to decline. Red tape and paper work expand; management is generally not as efficient. This increases the cost of performing the managerial function and, of course, the unit cost of production.

It is very difficult to determine just when diseconomies of scale set in and when they become strong enough to outweigh the economies of scale. In businesses where economies of scale are negligible, diseconomies may soon become of paramount importance, causing *LAC* to turn up at a relatively small volume of output. Panel a, Figure 7.6.1, shows a long-run average cost curve for a firm of this type. In other cases, economies of scale are extremely important. Even after the efficiency of management begins to decline technological economies of scale may offset the diseconomies over a wide range of output. Thus the *LAC* curve may not turn upward until a very large volume of out-

---

[13] This discussion of economies of scale has concentrated upon physical and technological forces. There are financial reasons for economies of scale as well. Large-scale purchasing of raw and processed materials may enable the buyer to obtain more favorable prices (quantity discounts). The same is frequently true of advertising. As another example, financing of large-scale business is normally easier and less expensive; a nationally known business has access to organized security markets, so it may place its bonds and stocks on a more favorable basis. Bank loans also usually come easier and at lower interest rates to large, well-known corporations.

These are but examples of many potential economies of scale attributable to financial considerations. For a more detailed discussion, see William G. Husband and James C. Dockeray, *Modern Corporation Finance* (7th ed.; Homewood, Ill.: Richard D. Irwin, Inc., 1972).

put is attained. This case, typified by the so-called natural monopolies, is illustrated in panel b, Figure 7.6.1.

In many actual situations, however, neither of these extremes describes the behavior of *LAC*. A very modest scale of operation may enable a firm to capture all of the economies of scale; however, diseconomies may not be incurred until the volume of output is very great.

FIGURE 7.6.1

Various Shapes of LAC

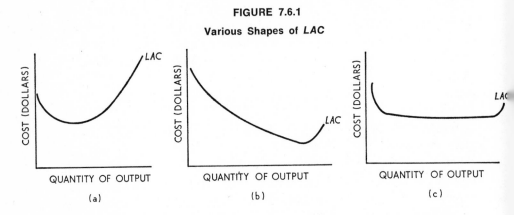

In this case, *LAC* would have a long horizontal section, as shown in panel c. Many economists and businessmen feel that this type of *LAC* curve describes most production processes in the American economy.

7.7 LONG-RUN COST AND CHANGES IN FACTOR PRICE[14,15]

Given the production function, costs change when factor prices change. In particular, total and average cost increase when a factor price increases, fall when a factor price declines. For simplicity, in this section we assume that only *one* factor price changes, and this change is represented by an increase in factor price.

7.7.a Changes in Long-Run Average Cost

Long-run average cost *obviously* increases when the price of any factor of production increases. Otherwise, increases in factor price would ultimately drive average cost to zero—a world of free goods with posi-

---

[14] This section contains a verbal summary of the mathematical and economic results presented in C. E. Ferguson and Thomas R. Saving, "Long-Run Scale Adjustments of a Perfectly Competitive Firm and Industry," *American Economic Review*, Vol. LIX (1969), pp. 774–83.

[15] This section may be omitted without loss in continuity. It is based upon mathematical results contained in Ferguson and Saving, *op. cit.* Unfortunately, these results do not have a simple verbal or graphical interpretation.

tive resource cost. This is a violation of the basic premise of economics, namely that *goods* have a positive price because the *resources* used to produce them are scarce and also have a positive price. This is illustrated in Figure 7.7.1 and explained more logically in the following paragraph.

To establish the proposition that an increase in a factor price leads to an increase in long-run average cost, consider *any* point on the curve, say average cost AC^0 corresponding to output q^0. Now let one factor price increase, all other factor prices remaining constant. At the same output q^0, the corresponding point on the *new* long-run average cost curve is AC^1. Clearly, the cost of the new set of inputs at the new factor prices is higher than the same set purchased at the old prices (for otherwise, the new set of inputs would have been purchased at the old factor prices). But at the old factor prices, the firm chose a different set of inputs, indicating that the cost of purchasing the old set was less than the cost of the new set at the old prices. Thus the cost of the new set of inputs at the new prices exceeds the cost of the new set at the old prices, which in turn exceeds the cost of the old set at the old prices.

Therefore, average cost must have increased, i.e., $AC^1 > AC^0$ at output q^0. But since the choice of q^0 was arbitrary, long-run average cost must be higher at every output. Now if output q^0 corresponded to the minimum point on the original long-run average cost curve, then every point on the long-run average cost curve associated with the new set of factor prices must be greater than AC^0. Hence the new level of minimum average cost must be higher so that the level of minimum average cost varies directly with factor price irrespective of factor classification.

FIGURE 7.7.1

**Schematic Illustration of Shifts in *AC* and *MC*
When Factor Price Increases**

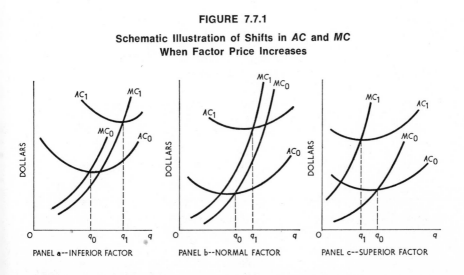

PANEL a--INFERIOR FACTOR   PANEL b--NORMAL FACTOR   PANEL c--SUPERIOR FACTOR

7.7.b   Changes in Long-Run Marginal Cost and Minimum Average Total Cost

As explained in footnotes 14 and 15, the results of this section are based upon mathematical analysis that is not readily susceptible of verbal explanation. For that reason the following relations are stated without proof (but see Figure 7.7.1).

Relation: When the price of a factor of production increases, long-run average cost increases. The new point of minimum long-run average cost corresponds to a greater output if the factor under consideration is normal or inferior. It corresponds to a smaller output if the factor is superior. The opposite relation holds if the price of the factor decreases.

Relation: If the price of a factor of production increases, long-run marginal cost decreases if the factor under consideration is inferior. Otherwise, long-run marginal cost increases. The opposite relation holds for a decrease in factor price.

7.8   CONCLUSION

The physical conditions of production and resource prices jointly establish the cost of production. This is very important to individual business firms and to the economy as a whole. But it is only half the story. Cost gives one aspect of economic activity: to the individual businessman it comprises his obligations to pay out funds; to the society as a whole it represents the resources that must be sacrificed to obtain a given commodity. The other aspect is revenue or demand. To the individual businessman revenue constitutes the flow of funds from which his obligations may be met. To society, demand represents the social valuation placed on a commodity.

Thus both demand and cost must be taken into consideration. It is to the demand side that we turn in Part III.

Exercise: Suppose that the employees of a certain firm establish a labor union and are able to negotiate an *effective* featherbedding contract (i.e., the firm must employ more workers than dictated by the conditions of optimal resource utilization). Determine how this featherbedding contract changes the short-run cost curves of the firm. Hold your answer to this exercise for a related exercise in Chapter 9.

PROBLEM

Return to the problem at the end of Chapter 5. Total product column (1) is given; and you have computed average product column (2) and marginal product column (3). You are also given the following information:

1. Total fixed cost (total price of fixed inputs) is $220 per period.

2. Units of the variable input cost $100 per unit per period. Using this information, add to your table entries for the new categories shown below in columns 4 through 10.

Units of Variable Input (1)	Total Product (2)	Average Product (2)	Marginal Product (3)	Total Fixed Cost (4)	Total Variable Cost (5)	Total Cost (6)	Average Fixed Cost (7)	Average Variable Cost (8)	Average Total Cost (9)	Marginal Cost (10)

I.   Graph the total cost curves on one sheet and the average and marginal curves on another

II. By reference to table and graph, answer the following questions.

1. When marginal product is increasing, what is happening to—
    a) Marginal cost?
    b) Average variable cost?

2. When marginal cost first begins to fall, does average variable cost begin to rise?

3. What is the relation between marginal cost and average variable cost when marginal and average products are equal?

4. What is happening to average variable cost while average product is increasing?

5. Where is average variable cost when average product is at its maximum? What happens to average variable cost after this point?

6. What happens to marginal cost after the point where it equals average variable cost?
    a) How does it compare with average variable cost thereafter?
    b) What is happening to marginal product thereafter?
    c) How does marginal product compare with average product thereafter?

7. What happens to total fixed cost as output is increased?

8. What happens to average fixed cost as:
    a) Marginal product increases?
    b) Marginal cost decreases?
    c) Marginal product decreases?
    d) Marginal cost increases?
    e) Average variable cost increases?

9. How long does average fixed cost decrease?

10. What happens to average total cost as:
    a) Marginal product increases?

  b) Marginal cost decreases?
  c) Average product increases?
  d) Average variable cost decreases?
  11. Does average cost increase:
  a) As soon as the point of diminishing marginal returns is passed?
  b) As soon as the point of diminishing average returns is passed?
  12. When does average cost increase? Answer this in terms of—
  a) The relation of average cost to marginal cost.
  b) The relation between the increase in average variable cost and the decrease in average fixed cost.

QUESTIONS

1. Consider the point where $SAC = LAC$. Explain precisely why LMC exceeds SMC for a decrease in output. (Hint: Both MC's show the reduction in cost attributable to the reduction in output.)

2. Comment on the following statement: long-run average cost is a meaningless concept since in this period most conditions underlying the cost function will probably change in unpredictable ways.

3. Beginning with a production function or schedule involving two variable inputs, explain how one derives both the short- and long-run average cost curves and the short-run marginal cost curve.

4. Given constant input prices and completely divisible and adaptable inputs, are the customary U-shaped short-run marginal and average variable cost curves consistent with a constant-returns-to-scale production function? Answer the same question for long-run average cost.

5. What are the relations between increasing returns to scale and decreasing long-run average cost? More generally, what relations, if any, exist between "returns to scale" and the shape of the long-run average cost curve?

6. The Southern Railway's lines from East St. Louis (Ill.) and Evansville (Ind.) to grain-consuming destinations in Georgia had substantial excess capacity. In deciding whether to invest in a sizable fleet of giant cars for carrying grain to these destinations and in settling rates for this traffic, Southern would rationally consider (*a*) fully allocated costs of the trackage, crew and fuel costs; (*b*) fully allocated cost of the trackage, extra equipment costs, crew and fuel costs; (*c*) cost of the new equipment, crew and fuel costs; (*d*) none of the above.

7. In the late 1950's, the development of trilevel "rack" cars for carrying new automobiles substantially lowered the costs of hauling such traffic. This represented (*a*) a change in demand for railroad services, (*b*) a

change in supply of railroad services, (*c*) a change in supply of trucking services for new automobiles, (*d*) all of the above.

8. Forty years ago, several trains used the Monon Railroad Station in Lafayette, Indiana, each day; eight years ago (and today), the station was used by one train per day in each direction. In deciding whether to tear down its older large station and to replace it with a smaller building, the Monon probably considered whether (*a*) the total cost of the old building was greater than the total cost of the new building, (*b*) the variable cost of operating the old building was greater than the total cost of the new building, (*c*) the variable cost of the old building was greater than the variable cost of the new building, (*d*) the total cost of the old building was greater than the variable cost of the new building.

SUGGESTED READING

Clark, J. M. *The Economics of Overhead Cost,* chaps. 4–6. Chicago: University of Chicago Press, 1923.

Ferguson, C. E. *The Neoclassical Theory of Production and Distribution,* chap. 7. London and New York: Cambridge University Press, 1969. [Advanced math required.]

————, and **Saving, Thomas R.** "Long-Run Scale Adjustments of a Perfectly Competitive Firm and Industry," *American Economic Review,* Vol. LIX (1969), pp. 774–83.

Henderson, James M., and Quandt, Richard E. *Microeconomic Theory: A Mathematical Approach,* pp. 55–62. New York: McGraw-Hill Book Co., Inc., 1958. [Elementary math required.]

Viner, Jacob. "Cost Curves and Supply Curves," *Zeitschrift für Nationalökonomie,* Vol. III (1931), pp. 23–46. Reprinted in AEA, *Readings in Price Theory,* pp. 198–232. Homewood, Ill.: Richard D. Irwin, Inc., 1952.

Advanced Reading, PART II

I. THE THEORY OF PRODUCTION

Arrow, Kenneth J.; Chenery, Hollis B.; Minhas, Bagicha; and Solow, Robert M. "Capital-Labor Substitution and Economic Efficiency," *Review of Economics and Statistics,* Vol. XLIII (1961), pp. 225–50.

Borts, George H., and Mishan, E. J. "Exploring the 'Uneconomic Region' of the Production Function," *Review of Economic Studies,* Vol. XXIX (1962), pp. 300–12.

Carlson, Sune. *A Study on the Pure Theory of Production,* Stockholm Economic Studies, No. 9. London: P. S. King & Sons, Ltd., 1939.

Cassels, John M. "On the Law of Variable Proportions," *Explorations in Economics,* pp. 223–36. New York: McGraw-Hill Book Co., Inc., 1936.

Ferguson, C. E. "Transformation Curve in Production Theory: A Pedagogical Note," *Southern Economic Journal,* Vol. XXIX (1962), pp. 96–102.

————. *The Neoclassical Theory of Production and Distribution,* chaps. 2–6. London and New York: Cambridge University Press, 1969.

————, and Saving, Thomas R. "Long-Run Scale Adjustments of a Perfectly Competitive Firm and Industry," *American Economic Review,* Vol. LIX (1969), pp. 774–83.

Machlup, Fritz. "On the Meaning of the Marginal Product," *Explorations in Economics,* pp. 250–63. New York: McGraw-Hill Book Co., Inc., 1936.

Samuelson, Paul A. *Foundations of Economic Analysis,* pp. 57–89. Cambridge, Mass.: Harvard University Press, 1947.

Shephard, Ronald W. *Cost and Production Functions.* Princeton, N.J.: Princeton University Press, 1953.

Stigler, George J. *Production and Distribution Theories.* New York: The Macmillan Co., 1946.

Walters, A. A. "Production and Cost Functions: An Econometric Survey," *Econometrica,* Vol. XXXI (1963), pp. 1–66, with extensive bibliography.

II. THE THEORY OF COST

Viner, Jacob. "Cost Curves and Supply Curves," *Zeitschrift für National-ökonomie und Statistik,* Vol. III (1931), pp. 23–46. This is the classic reference in the field. In addition, see Ferguson, *The Neoclassical Theory of Production and Distribution* (chaps. 7 and 8); Samuelson, *Foundations of Economic Analysis;* Shephard, *Cost and Production Functions;* and Walters, "Production and Cost Functions: An Econometric Survey," as listed above.

PART III

Theory of the Firm and Market Organization

The theory of business operation within an organized but uncontrolled market brings together the topics covered in Parts I and II. Demand, the broad topic of Part I, establishes the *revenue side* of business operation. Product demand determines either the quantity a firm can sell at any price it selects or the price a firm can obtain for any quantity it wishes to market. Market demand also helps to determine the type of industry structure that is likely to emerge in response to market conditions—whether the industry is likely to be competitive, monopolistic, or what have you.

The technical conditions of production and their reflection in business operating costs, the subject of Part II, establish the *cost side* of business operation and the *supply conditions* of the industry. Brought together, revenue and cost for the individual business concern and demand and supply for the entire market determine the market price and output of the firm and the industry. These forces accordingly determine the allocation of resources among industries as well.

The general purpose of Part III is to discover how the price-output decisions of individual entrepreneurs and the structure of the market jointly determine the allocation of resources. This inquiry inevitably entails an appraisal of the *efficiency* with which resources are allocated.

Given the conditions of demand and supply, or of revenue and cost, our analysis is based upon two fundamental assumptions.

Free Market. First, we assume that each market is free and operates freely in the sense that there is no external control of market forces. One form of external control is government intervention. The federal government (and upon occasion state and local governments as well) imposes various types of regulations that condition the economic milieu in which firms operate and to which they must ultimately adjust. The regulation of so-called public utilities by both federal and state governments is one example—perhaps the most well-known example, but still only one. Parity-price programs and acreage controls are examples of regulations applied largely to agricultural markets. Tariffs and certain antitrust regulations are examples of controls principally applicable to industrial markets.

Another type of government control, at times more subtle than the explicit regulations mentioned above, is "moral suasion." By "moral suasion" one generally means the more or less effective control of business (and sometimes labor union) activity by means of appeal to "social consciousness," "social responsibility," or "regard for public welfare." Incidences of moral suasion have run the gamut from President Dwight D. Eisenhower's rather weak appeal to all businessmen to resist price increases to President John F. Kennedy's forceful threat to steel producers, and President Nixon's freeze of wages and prices.

Irrespective of their nature, all these controls establish artificial market conditions to which business firms must adjust—they help to establish the economic environment in which business decisions are made. So also does another type of external control somewhat more amorphous than government regulation. To set the stage for explanation, let us quote Adam Smith: "People of the same trade seldom meet together, even for merriment and diversion, but the conversation ends in a conspiracy against the public, or in some contrivance to raise prices."[1] Simply, when only a small number of producers are in a certain field there is a strong incentive for them to act collusively to fix a monopoly or near monopoly price.

Such collusive behavior imposes an external control upon the market and thereby limits the free exercise of market forces. It is perhaps for this reason that the Sherman Antitrust Act was passed in 1890, declaring it illegal to (*a*) enter into a contract, combination, or conspiracy in restraint of trade (sec. 1); and (*b*) to monopolize, attempt to monopolize, or combine or conspire to monopolize trade (sec. 2).

While many markets are not "free" in the sense used here, a vast

---

[1] Adam Smith, *Wealth of Nations* (Cannan ed.; London: Methuen, 1904), Vol. 1, p. 130.

number are. The object is to analyze the efficiency of resource allocation in free markets. In case a market is not free, one may be able to draw inferences concerning the relative efficiency of free as against controlled markets.

Profit Maximization. The second fundamental assumption underlying Part III is that entrepreneurs try to maximize profit.[2] Without doubt, not all producers try to maximize profit at all times. Entrepreneurs may indeed be seekers after multiple goals. Nonetheless, a business cannot long remain viable unless profits are earned; and it is a very unusual businessman who treats profits in a cavalier fashion.

Whether profit maximization is a reasonable assumption is a question long debated in economics. Several important criticisms have been brought to bear. However, these criticisms do not overcome the supremely important fact that the assumption of profit maximization is the only one providing a general theory of firms, markets, and resource allocation that is successful both in explaining and predicting business behavior.

---

[2] For the purpose of *explaining* business behavior it is sufficient to assume that entrepreneurs act *as if* they tried to maximize profit. For the purpose of predicting business behavior the *as if* assumption is the only justifiable one.

Chapter	THEORY OF PRICE IN
8	PERFECTLY COMPETITIVE MARKETS

8.1 INTRODUCTION

"Perfect competition" is an exacting concept forming the basis of the most important model of business behavior. The essence of the concept, to be defined more fully below, is that the market is entirely *impersonal*. There is no "rivalry" among suppliers in the market and buyers do not recognize their competitiveness vis-à-vis one another. Thus in a sense perfect competition describes a market in which there is a complete absence of direct competition among economic agents. As a theoretical concept of economics it is the diametrical opposite of the businessman's concept of competition.

In ordinary conversation the market for automobiles, say, or for razor blades would be described as highly competitive; each firm competes vigorously with its rivals, who are few in number. The principal area of competition is in advertising. The advertisement of one firm will state that its product is superior to those of its rivals, which it will virtually name. Firms also strive to attract customers by means of style features, method of packaging, claims of durability, and such. More generally, there is active, if sometimes spurious, quality competition. In fact, firms compete in almost every conceivable way except by means of price reduction.

The type of market just described, however, is far from what the economist means when he speaks of perfect competition. When this austere concept is used, no traces of personal rivalry can appear. All relevant economic magnitudes are determined by impersonal market forces.

8.2 PERFECT COMPETITION

Four important conditions define perfect competition. Taken together, these conditions guarantee a free, impersonal market in which the forces of demand and supply—or of revenue and cost—determine the allocation of resources and the distribution of income.

8.2.a Small Size, Large Numbers

First, perfect competition requires every economic agent in the market to be so small, relative to the market as a whole, that it cannot exert a perceptible influence on price. From the standpoint of buyers this means that each consumer taken individually must be so unimportant that he cannot obtain special considerations from the sellers. Perhaps the most familiar special consideration is the rebate, especially in the area of transportation services. But there can be many others, such as special credit terms to large buyers, or rendering free additional services. None of these can prevail if the market is perfectly competitive.

From the seller's standpoint perfect competition requires each producer to be so small that he cannot perceptibly affect market price by changes in his output. As you have seen in Chapter 4, this provision means that each perfectly competitive producer believes his demand curve is a horizontal line. If all producers act in the same way at the same time, changes in quantity will definitely affect market price. But if perfect competition prevails, each producer is so small that individual changes will be unnoticed.

8.2.b Homogeneous Product

A closely related provision is that the product of any one seller in a perfectly competitive market must be identical to the product of any other seller. This ensures that buyers are indifferent as to the firm from which they purchase.

In this context the word "product" has a much more detailed meaning than it does in ordinary conversation, where one might regard an automobile or a haircut as a product. For us, this is not an adequate description: every changeable feature of the good must be included. When this is done it is possible to determine whether the market is characterized by a homogeneous, or perfectly standardized, commodity. If it is not, the producer who has a slightly differentiated product has a degree of control over the market and, therefore, over the price of his specific variety; he can thereby affect market price by changes in his output. This condition, as you have seen, is incompatible with perfect competition.[1]

---

[1] The classification of products and product differentiation is treated in greater detail in Chapter 10.

8.2.c Free Mobility of Resources

A third precondition for perfect competition is that *all* resources are perfectly mobile—that each resource can move in and out of the market very readily in response to pecuniary signals.

The condition of perfect mobility is an exacting one. First, it means that labor must be mobile, not only geographically but among jobs. The latter, in turn, implies that the requisite labor skills are few, simple, and easily learned. Next, free mobility means that the ingredient inputs are not monopolized by an owner or producer. Finally, free mobility means that new firms (or new capital) can enter and leave an industry without extraordinary difficulty. If patents or copyrights are required, entry is not free. Similarly, if vast investment outlays are required, entry certainly is not easy. If average cost declines over an appreciable range of output, established producers will have cost advantages that make entry difficult. In short, free mobility of resources requires free and easy entry and exit of new firms into and out of an industry—a condition very difficult to realize in practice.

8.2.d Perfect Knowledge

Consumers, producers, and resource owners must possess perfect knowledge if a market is to be perfectly competitive. If consumers are not fully cognizant of prices, they might buy at higher prices when lower ones are available. There will then not be a uniform price in the market. Similarly, if laborers are not aware of the wage rates offered, they may not sell their labor services to the highest bidder. Finally, producers must know their costs as well as price in order to attain the most profitable rate of output.

But this is only the beginning. In its fullest sense, perfect knowledge requires complete knowledge of the future as well as the present. In the absence of this omniscience, perfect competition cannot prevail.

The discussion to this point can be summarized by the following

Definition: Perfect competition is an economic model of a market possessing the following characteristics: each economic agent is so small relative to the market that it can exert no perceptible influence on price; the product is homogeneous; there is free mobility of all resources, including free and easy entry and exit of business firms; and all economic agents in the market possess complete and perfect knowledge.

8.2.e Conclusion

Glancing at the four requirements above should immediately convince one that no market has been or can be perfectly competitive.

Even in basic agricultural markets, where the first three requirements are frequently satisfied, the fourth is obviated by vagaries of weather conditions. One might therefore reasonably ask why such a palpably unrealistic model should be considered at all.

The answer can be given in as much or as little detail as desired. For our present purposes, it is brief. First, generality can be achieved only by means of abstraction. Hence no theory can be perfectly descriptive of real world phenomena. Further, the more accurately a theory describes one specific real world case the less accurately it describes all others. In any area of thought a theoretician does not select his assumptions on the basis of their realism; the conclusions, not the assumptions, are tested against reality.

This leads to a second point of great, if pragmatic, importance. The conclusions derived from the model of perfect competition have, by and large, permitted accurate explanation and prediction of real world phenomena. That is, perfect competition frequently *works* as a theoretical model of economic processes. The most persuasive evidence supporting this assertion is the fact that despite the proliferation of more "sophisticated" models of economic behavior, economists today probably use the model of perfect competition in their research more than ever before.

8.3 EQUILIBRIUM IN THE MARKET PERIOD

The short run and the long run were defined in Chapter 5. In the short run, some inputs are fixed—they are not instantaneously augmentable. Changes in the quantity of output per unit of time can be achieved only by changes in the usage of the instantaneously variable inputs. In the long run, on the other hand, all inputs are variable. Changes in the volume of output can be achieved by changes in the usage of any input.

These two "runs," however, do not cover all cases. In certain instances the quantity of a commodity available for sale is absolutely fixed for a short period of time. For example, after the harvest of an agricultural crop the quantity of the commodity cannot be increased until the next harvest. As another example, merchants hold inventories of goods. The quantity available for sale cannot be increased instantly because the order and delivery process inevitably entails some delay. Finally, in some cases quantity can be increased virtually instantaneously; but the cost of rapid production is so great as to preclude very quick changes. In all these cases, the short period of time in which supply is absolutely fixed is called the *market period*.

8.3.a   Industry Equilibrium in the Market Period

Definition: An industry is a collection of firms producing a homogeneous product.

In both the short run and long run each individual firm can adjust its output. Thus one must analyze equilibrium adjustments for the firm as well as the industry. In the market period, however, the individual business concerns cannot adjust at all. By definition, output cannot be changed in the market period. Hence the behavior of individual firms need not be studied—each firm has a fixed supply that it sells for the market-established price.

Since the supply of each firm is absolutely fixed in the market period, the market supply curve is simply the horizontal sum of all firms' supply curves. And again, since supply is fixed, the market supply curve is a straight line parallel to the vertical axis, as shown in Figure 8.3.1.

FIGURE 8.3.1

Equilibrium in the Market Period

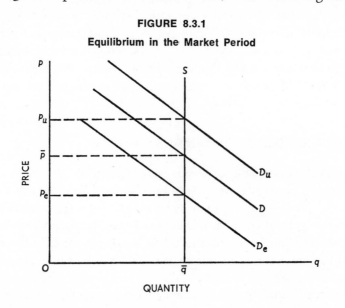

QUANTITY

The fixed quantity available for sale is $O\bar{q}$, and the market supply curve is the straight line labeled S.

Market equilibrium is attained, of course, at that price which exactly clears the market. If market demand is given by the curve labeled D in Figure 8.3.1, the market equilibrium price is $O\bar{p}$. If demand were greater, say D_u, the equilibrium price would also be greater, Op_u. But the market equilibrium quantity would be the same as before because supply is absolutely fixed. Similarly, if demand were less, D_e, the equilibrium price would be lower, Op_e. Thus in the market period demand *alone* determines the market equilibrium price, given the fixed supply, while supply *alone* determines the market equilibrium quantity. This result differs markedly from the corresponding result for the short and long runs in which demand and supply *jointly* determine *both* the equilibrium price and quantity.

8.3.b Price as a Rationing Device

The price a commodity bears may play various roles. It may be a signal to producers to expand or contract their rate of production. It may reflect the marginal social value of the commodity. And, among other things, it is always a rationing device.

In the market period, rationing the existing supply among prospective buyers is the chief function performed by market price. Since supply is not related to the cost of production when the former is fixed, price is exclusively a demand phenomenon. When the market equilibrium price is established, it rations the fixed supply of goods among those individuals who are willing and able to pay a unit price equal to or greater than the market equilibrium price. While this is true of an equilibrium price in any market in any "run," it is dramatically true in the market period.

8.4 SHORT-RUN EQUILIBRIUM OF A FIRM IN A PERFECTLY COMPETITIVE MARKET

In the short run, the rate of output per period of time can be increased or decreased by increasing or decreasing the use of variable inputs. The individual firm can adjust its rate of output over a wide range subject only to the limitations imposed by its fixed inputs (generally, plant and equipment). Since each firm adjusts until it reaches a profit-maximizing rate of output, the market or industry also adjusts until it reaches a point of short-run equilibrium.

8.4.a Short-Run Profit Maximization, Total Revenue—Total Cost Approach

As already noted, we assume that each firm adjusts its rate of output so as to maximize the profit obtainable from its business operation.

Since profit is the difference between the total revenue from sales and the total cost of operation, profit is a maximum for the rate of output that maximizes the excess of revenue over cost (or minimizes the excess of cost over revenue).

Consider the example contained in Table 8.4.1 and shown graphically in Figure 8.4.1. The first two columns of the table give the de-

TABLE 8.4.1
Revenue, Cost, and Profit for a Hypothetical Firm

Market Price	Rate of Output and Sales	Total Revenue	Total Fixed Cost	Total Variable Cost	Total Cost	Profit
$5.00	1	$ 5.00	$15.00	$ 2.00	$17.00	−$12.00
5.00	2	10.00	15.00	3.50	18.50	− 8.50
5.00	3	15.00	15.00	4.50	19.50	− 4.50
5.00	4	20.00	15.00	5.75	20.75	− 0.75
5.00	5	25.00	15.00	7.25	22.25	+ 2.75
5.00	6	30.00	15.00	9.25	24.25	+ 5.75
5.00	7	35.00	15.00	12.50	27.50	+ 7.50
5.00	8	40.00	15.00	17.50	32.50	+ 7.50
5.00	9	45.00	15.00	25.50	40.50	+ 4.50
5.00	10	50.00	15.00	37.50	52.50	− 2.50

mand curve for the perfectly competitive producer. Market price is $5 per unit; the producer can sell as many units as he chooses at this price. The product of columns 1 and 2 gives total revenue, the entries appearing in column 3. The straight line in Figure 8.4.1 is a graphical representation. Notice that the total revenue curve is always a straight line in the case of perfect competition because unit price does not change when quantity sold changes.

Columns 4, 5, and 6 give total fixed, total variable, and total cost respectively. Total cost is graphed as the curved line in Figure 8.4.1. Profit—the difference between total revenue and total cost—is shown in the last column of Table 8.4.1, and it is represented by the positive or negative distance between the total revenue and total cost curves in Figure 8.4.1. Profit is first negative, becomes positive, and is ultimately negative again. In Figure 8.4.1, the shaded areas denote the range of output over which profit is negative (a loss is incurred).

It is clear from either the table or the figure that maximum profit is $7.50, achieved with an output of either seven or eight units. The

FIGURE 8.4.1

Profit Maximization by the Total Revenue–Total Cost Approach

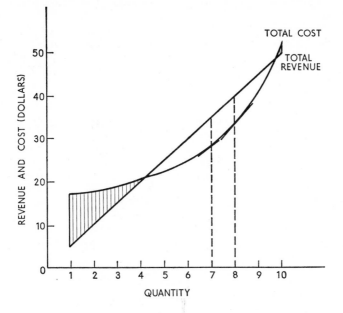

seeming indeterminacy of the rate of output is attributable to the discrete data used in this hypothetical example. If continuous data were used, it would be obvious that the profit-maximizing output is eight units per period of time. This is because the maximum distance separating the two curves occurs at the point where the tangents to the curves have the same slope. From the two tangents constructed in Figure 8.4.1, it is easily seen that the slopes are equal only at the output of eight units per period of time.

The total revenue–total cost approach is a useful one from some standpoints; however, it does not lead to an analytical interpretation of business behavior. To get at this, the familiar marginal approach must be adopted.

8.4.b Short-Run Profit Maximization, the Marginal Approach

The definitions of marginal revenue and marginal cost are familiar from Chapters 4 and 7 respectively. Similarly, the method of calculating each has been learned. Applying these methods to the data in Table 8.4.1, we obtain the information in Table 8.4.2.

TABLE 8.4.2

Marginal Revenue, Marginal Cost, and Profit

Output and Sales	Marginal Revenue or Price	Marginal Cost	Average Total Cost	Unit Profit	Total Profit
1.................	$5.00	$ 2.00	$17.00	−$12.00	−$12.00
2.................	5.00	1.50	9.25	− 4.25	− 8.50
3.................	5.00	1.00	6.50	− 1.50	− 4.50
4.................	5.00	1.25	5.19	− 0.19	− 0.75
5.................	5.00	1.50	4.45	+ 0.55	+ 2.75
6.................	5.00	2.00	4.04	+ 0.96	+ 5.75
7.................	5.00	3.25	3.93	+ 1.07	+ 7.50
8.................	5.00	5.00	4.06	+ 0.94	+ 7.50
9.................	5.00	8.00	4.50	+ 0.50	+ 4.50
10................	5.00	12.00	5.25	− 0.25	− 2.50

Columns 1 and 2 show the demand or marginal revenue curve, identical for the firm in a perfectly competitive market (as explained in Chapter 4). Column 3 contains the marginal cost figures, while average total or unit cost has been computed from column 6, Table 8.4.1, and entered in column 4. Unit profit, the difference between price and average total cost, is shown in column 5. Finally, total profit, the difference between total revenue and total cost, is contained in column 6.

As in the previous case, maximum profit corresponds to either seven

FIGURE 8.4.2

Profit Maximization by the Marginal Approach

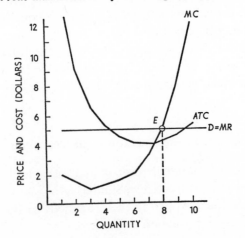

or eight units of output and sales per period of time. Unit profit is a maximum at seven units of output, but this is immaterial inasmuch as the entrepreneur is concerned with total profit.

The data in Table 8.4.2 are plotted in Figure 8.4.2. The short-run equilibrium of the firm is clearly attained at point *E*, where marginal cost equals marginal revenue. Alternatively stated, since marginal revenue equals price for a perfectly competitive producer, short-run equilibrium occurs at the output point for which marginal cost equals price.

8.4.c Proof of the Short-Run Equilibrium

To prove the proposition that a firm in perfect competition attains its profit-maximizing equilibrium at the rate of output for which marginal cost equals price, the hypothetical example of Figure 8.4.2 has been converted to the general representation in Figure 8.4.3. The theorem follows immediately from the definitions of marginal revenue and marginal cost.[2]

Marginal revenue is the addition to total revenue attributable to the addition of one unit to sales, while marginal cost is the addition to total cost resulting from the addition of one unit to output. Thus it should be evident that profit increases when marginal revenue exceeds marginal cost and diminishes when marginal cost exceeds marginal revenue. Profit must, therefore, attain its maximum when marginal revenue and marginal cost are equal.

---

[2] Let $p = f(q)$ represent the inverse demand function. Hence $qf(q)$ is total revenue. Further, let $C = A + g(q)$ be the total cost function. Profit (π) is thus $\pi = qf(q) - A - g(q)$. Profit is a maximum when $d\pi/dq = 0$ and $d^2\pi/dq^2 < 0$. Taking the first derivative and equating with zero,

$$\frac{d\pi}{dq} = f(q) - g'(q) = 0 \qquad (8.2.1)$$

or

$$f(q) = g'(q), \qquad (8.2.2)$$

because $p = f(q)$ is a given constant. Marginal cost is $g'(q)$; see Chapter 7. Marginal revenue and price are both given by $f(q)$. Hence equation (8.2.2) states that marginal revenue or price must equal marginal cost. This is the necessary condition for profit maximization. From equation (8.2.1) the second-order condition is that $d^2\pi/dq^2 = -g''(q) < 0$ or

$$g''(q) > 0. \qquad (8.2.3)$$

Hence stability of equilibrium, by inequality (8.2.3), requires a *positively sloped* marginal cost curve.

FIGURE 8.4.3

**Short-Run Equilibrium at Point Where
Marginal Cost Equals Price**

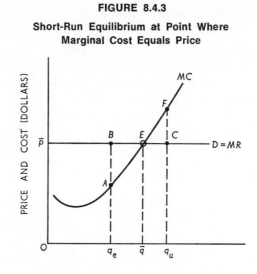

Consider Figure 8.4.3. The fundamental proposition is that at market price $O\bar{p}$, the firm attains a profit-maximizing equilibrium at point E, corresponding to the output of $O\bar{q}$ units per period of time. If the rate of output were less than $O\bar{q}$, say Oq_e, marginal revenue q_eB would exceed marginal cost q_eA. Adding a unit to output and sales would increase total revenue by more than total cost. Profit would accordingly increase, and it would continue to increase so long as marginal revenue exceeds marginal cost.

On the other hand, suppose the rate of output exceeded $O\bar{q}$—say Oq_u. At this point, marginal cost q_uF exceeds marginal revenue q_uC. This unit of output causes total cost to increase by more than total revenue, thereby reducing profit (or increasing loss). As is evident from the graph, profit must be reduced by adding a unit to output and sales whenever marginal cost exceeds marginal revenue.

Therefore, since profit increases when marginal revenue exceeds marginal cost and declines when marginal revenue is less than marginal cost, it must be a maximum when the two are equal. Furthermore, since price equals marginal revenue for a firm in perfect competition, the following theorem has been proved.

Proposition: A firm in a perfectly competitive industry attains its short-run, profit-maximizing equilibrium by producing the rate of output for which marginal cost equals the given, fixed market price of the commodity.

8.4.d Profit or Loss?

The equality of price and marginal cost guarantees either that profit is a maximum or that loss is a minimum. Whether a profit is made or a loss incurred can be determined only by comparing price and average total cost corresponding to the equilibrium rate of output. If price exceeds unit cost the entrepreneur will enjoy a profit in the short run. On the other hand, if unit cost exceeds price a loss must be incurred.

Figure 8.4.4 illustrates this. MC and ATC represent marginal cost and average total cost respectively. First, suppose short-run market equilibrium establishes the price Op_1 per unit. The demand and marginal revenue curves for the firm are, therefore, given by the horizontal line labeled $D_1 = MR_1$. Short-run equilibrium is attained when output is Oq_1 units per period of time. At this rate of output, total revenue (price times quantity) is given by the area of the rectangle Oq_1Cp_1. Similarly, total cost (unit cost times quantity) is the area Oq_1EF. Total revenue exceeds total cost, and profit is represented by the area of the rectangle $CEFp_1$.

FIGURE 8.4.4

Profit or Loss in the Short Run

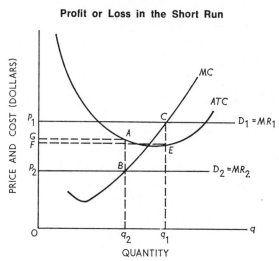

QUANTITY

On the other hand, suppose the market price-quantity equilibrium established the price Op_2. In that case the optimum rate of output would be Oq_2 units per period of time. Total revenue is the area of Oq_2Bp_2, while total cost is Oq_2AG. Since total cost exceeds total revenue, a loss is incurred in the amount represented by the area of p_2BAG.

When demand is $D_2 = MR_2$, there is no way the firm can earn a profit. If output were either smaller or greater than Oq_2 units per period of time the loss would simply be greater. One might therefore ask why the firm does not go out of business since a loss is incurred at any rate of output.

8.4.e Short-Run Supply Curve of a Firm in a Perfectly Competitive Industry

The basic answer to this question is that an entrepreneur incurring a loss will continue to produce in the short run if, and only if, he loses less by producing than by closing the plant entirely. As you will recall from Chapter 7, there are two types of costs in the short run: fixed costs and variable costs. The fixed costs cannot be changed and are incurred whether the plant is operated or not. Fixed costs, that is, are the same at zero output as at any other.

Therefore, so long as total revenue exceeds the total variable cost of producing the equilibrium output, a smaller loss is suffered when production takes place. Figure 8.4.5 is a graphical demonstration of this.

As previously explained, the business decision regarding production in the short run is not affected by fixed costs. Therefore, only the average total cost, average variable cost, and marginal cost curves are shown in Figure 8.4.5. Since our discussion involves only a loss situation, the price lines are constructed so as to lie entirely beneath the average total cost curve. First, suppose market price is Op_1, so the firm's demand–marginal revenue curve is given by $D_1 = MR_1$. Profit maximization (or loss minimization) leads to producing the output for which marginal cost equals price—production occurs at point B, or at the rate of Oq_1 units per period of time. At this rate of output the firm loses AB dollars per unit produced. However, at the price Op_1 average variable cost is not only covered but there is an excess of BC dollars per unit. The average cost of the variable inputs is q_1C dollars per unit of output. The price obtained per unit is q_1B. The excess of price over average variable cost, BC, can be applied to the fixed costs. Thus not all of the fixed costs are lost, as would be the case if production were discontinued. Although a loss is sustained, it is smaller than the loss associated with zero output.

This is not always the case, however. Suppose market price were as low as Op_2, so that demand is given by $D_2 = MR_2$. If the firm produced at all, its equilibrium output would be Oq_2 units per period of time.

Here, however, the average variable cost of production exceeds price. The firm producing at this point would not only lose its fixed costs, it would lose EF dollars per unit on its variable costs as well. Thus when price is below average variable cost, the short-run equilibrium output is zero.

FIGURE 8.4.5

Ceasing Production in the Short Run

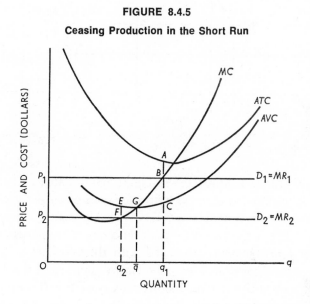

As shown in Chapter 7, average variable cost reaches its minimum at the point where marginal cost and average variable cost intersect—point G in Figure 8.4.5. If price is less than $\bar{q}G$ dollars per unit, equilibrium output is zero. For a price equal to or greater than $\bar{q}G$ dollars per unit, equilibrium output is determined by the intersection of marginal cost and the price line.

Using the proposition just discussed, it is possible to derive the short-run supply curve of an individual firm in a perfectly competitive

FIGURE 8.4.6

**Derivation of the Short-Run Supply Curve of an Individual
Producer in Perfect Competition**

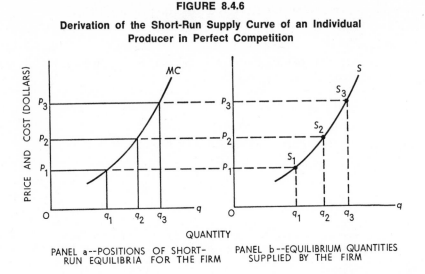

PANEL a--POSITIONS OF SHORT-   PANEL b--EQUILIBRIUM QUANTITIES
RUN EQUILIBRIA FOR THE FIRM   SUPPLIED BY THE FIRM

market. The process is illustrated in Figure 8.4.6. Panel a of the figure
shows the marginal cost curve of a firm for rates of output greater than
that associated with minimum average variable cost. Suppose market
price is Op_1. The corresponding equilibrium rate of output is Oq_1. Now
on panel b find the point associated with the coordinates Op_1, Oq_1.
Label this point S_1; it represents the quantity supplied at the price Op_1.

Next, suppose price is Op_2. In this case, equilibrium output is Oq_2.
Plot the point associated with the coordinates Op_2, Oq_2 on panel b—it
is labeled S_2. Similarly, other equilibrium quantities supplied can be
determined by postulating other market prices (for example, price
Op_3 leads to output Oq_3 and point S_3 on panel b). Connecting all of
the S-points so generated one obtains the short-run supply curve of the
firm, the curve labeled S in panel b. But by construction, the S-curve
is precisely the same as the MC curve. The following is therefore established:

Proposition: The short-run supply curve of a firm in perfect competition is precisely its marginal cost curve for all rates of output equal to or
greater than the rate of output associated with minimum average variable
cost. For market prices lower than minimum average variable cost, equilibrium quantity supplied is zero.

8.5 SHORT-RUN EQUILIBRIUM IN A PERFECTLY COMPETITIVE INDUSTRY

In Part I it was shown that market demand is simply the horizontal
sum of individual demand curves. Deriving the short-run industry

supply curve may not be such an easy matter as deriving the market demand.

8.5.a Short-Run Industry Supply Curve

As you will recall from Chapter 7, the short-run marginal cost curve of a firm is derived from its marginal product curve under the assumption that the unit price of the variable input is fixed. For most firms and inputs this is a reasonable assumption because one firm is usually so small, relative to all users of the resource taken together, that variations in its rate of purchase will not affect the market price of the resource. In other words, many resource markets are more or less perfectly competitive, at least on the *buying* side. Thus production and resource use can frequently be expanded in any one firm without affecting the market price of the resource.

But when *all* producers in an industry simultaneously expand output there may be a marked effect upon the resource market. As an example, consider farming as an industry. One single farmer can doubtless double his output, and therefore materially increase his inputs, without affecting the market price of fertilizer, tractors, etc. But if all farmers double output there will inevitably be a marked upward pressure on the prices of these inputs.

As a consequence, the industry supply curve usually cannot be obtained by summing horizontally the marginal cost curves of each producer. As industry output expands, input prices normally increase, thereby shifting each marginal cost curve upward.[3] A great deal of information would be required to obtain the exact supply curve. However, one may generally presume that the industry supply curve is somewhat more steeply sloped and somewhat less elastic when input prices increase in response to an increase in output. In this case, the concept of a competitive industry supply curve is less precise. Nonetheless, doubt is not cast upon the basic fact that in the short run, quantity supplied varies directly with price. The latter is all one needs to draw a positively sloped market supply curve.

The explanation above may be summarized in the following

Relation: If factor prices change in response to a change in *industry* factor usage, the industry supply curve is not the horizontal summation of

---

[3] If the only input whose price increases is an inferior input, each firm's marginal cost curve will shift downward to the right. This does not affect the argument in the text—the horizontal sum of all firms' marginal cost curves would still not yield the industry supply curve.

all firms' marginal cost curves. Each firm's marginal cost curve shifts when factor prices change. However, the industry supply curve is perfectly determinate—it is the sum of the quantities supplied by all firms, which is determined from the marginal cost curve corresponding to the prevailing set of factor prices.

8.5.b Short-Run Market Equilibrium, Profit and Loss

Given the market demand and supply curves, a short-run market price-quantity equilibrium is attained when quantity demanded and quantity supplied are equal. This proposition is so familiar that a proof is not given here, although the equilibrium is illustrated in panel a, Figure 8.5.1. DD' is market demand and SS' is market supply. The price-quantity equilibrium is attained at point G, with equilibrium price $O\overline{P}$ and equilibrium quantities demanded and supplied $O\overline{Q}$.

FIGURE 8.5.1

Short-Run Market Equilibrium and Profit or Loss in the Firm

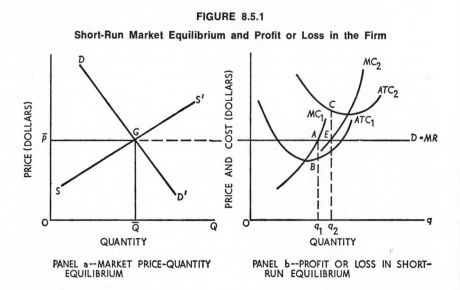

PANEL a--MARKET PRICE-QUANTITY
EQUILIBRIUM

PANEL b--PROFIT OR LOSS IN SHORT-
RUN EQUILIBRIUM

The market equilibrium price $O\overline{P}$, which establishes the horizontal demand or marginal revenue curve $D = MR$ for a typical firm in the industry, is shown in panel b. First, suppose the firm has cost represented by ATC_1 and MC_1. It then attains its profit-maximizing equilibrium at point A, producing Oq_1 units per period of time and earning a pure economic profit of AB dollars per unit. On the other hand, if cost is given by ATC_2 and MC_2, equilibrium is reached at point E. The firm produces Oq_2 units and incurs a pure loss of CE dollars per unit.

A perfectly competitive firm is merely a *quantity adjuster*. Price is given by the market; the firm produces the rate of output that maximizes profit or minimizes loss for its established plant. In the short run, no other alternative is available. In the long run, however, there is.

8.5.c Demand-Supply Analysis

Examples of demand-supply analysis and comparative statics were given in the Introduction. The analysis of market equilibrium is simple, but it is not simple-minded. Indeed, this type of analysis offers significant qualitative, if not quantitative, insight into the functioning of real world markets. Let us consider an example.

Suppose that the demand for coal at the retail level is elastic over the relevant price range. Further, suppose the government feels that the price of coal is too high. It therefore places a price ceiling or maximum on coal at the mine. What will happen to the price of coal at the retail level? Will total receipts of retailers increase or decrease?

As a first step let us consider what happens at the mine (or mining area). Assume for analytical purposes that coal mining is a perfectly competitive, increasing cost industry. Assume also that before the imposition of the ceiling price, the industry was in equilibrium; each firm produced the quantity at which $P = LAC$ and therefore enjoyed no pure profit. Figure 8.5.2 shows the market demand and supply for coal at the mine. Demand ($D_m D_m{}'$) is the demand curve of retailers for coal at the mine. It is derived holding the demand for coal from retailers

FIGURE 8.5.2

Supply and Demand at the Mine

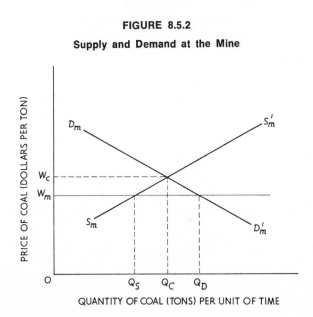

QUANTITY OF COAL (TONS) PER UNIT OF TIME

and other factors constant (we assume that individual consumers cannot purchase coal directly from the mine).

The long-run industry supply curve is $S_m S_m'$. It is the locus of long-run equilibria for the mining industry. Since we assume an increasing cost industry, $S_m S_m'$ is upward sloping. The equilibrium price at the mine is OW_c and equilibrium quantity is OQ_c.

Figure 8.5.3 shows demand and supply conditions at retail. $D_r D_r'$ is the consumers' demand for coal. $S_r S_r'$, based upon a given cost of coal at the mines to retailers (OW_c), is the retailers' supply curve. Since coal is an input for the retailers, the supply curve for coal at retail should shift when the price of coal at the mines changes, just as a change in the price of any factor of production changes the supply of the product produced. Specifically, when the price at the mine falls, other things remaining the same, the retail supply curve should shift to the right. That is, if retailers can buy coal cheaper, they would be willing and able to supply more retail coal at every retail price. Equilibrium in the retail market occurs at a price of OP_r (given a price at the mine of OW_c) and a quantity sold of OQ_c, obviously the same as OQ_c in Figure 8.5.2 because the retailers sell all that they buy.

Returning to Figure 8.5.2, assume that the government sets the ceiling price OW_m. Quantity demanded by retailers at the new price is OQ_D. The new price is below OW_c (the price at which neither profit nor loss occurs); thus firms begin to make losses and some leave the in-

FIGURE 8.5.3

Demand and Supply at Retail

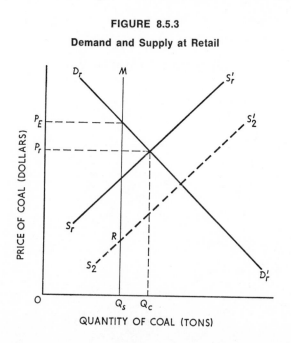

QUANTITY OF COAL (TONS)

dustry. Since we assume that mining is an increasing cost industry, the exit of firms and the decrease in quantity produced lowers factor prices and hence lowers the long-run average and marginal cost curves of the remaining firms in the industry. Figure 8.5.4 shows the process. Long-run average and marginal costs fall from LAC_1 and LMC_1 to LAC_2 and LMC_2. The minimum point on LAC_2 equals the ceiling price OW_m. Each remaining firm now produces Oq_m (the new equilibrium output) rather than Oq_c, but there are fewer firms, none of which makes pure profit. The new quantity supplied by the industry, indicated in Figure 8.5.2, is OQ_S. Thus a shortage (excess demand) of Q_SQ_D occurs at the mines since retailers now wish to purchase OQ_D but the mines are only willing to sell OQ_S. The mining industry must find some method of allocation (rationing, first come first served, favoritism, and so on) in order to determine which retailers get the available supply. In any case only OQ_S is available to the retailers.

Now according to our analysis the lower price of coal at the mine should cause supply at retail to shift to S_2S_2' (Figure 8.5.3). Retail price should fall and the quantity of coal sold should increase as determined by the intersection of D_rD_r' and S_2S_2'. But remember that only OQ_S is produced, so only OQ_S can be sold. The curve S_2S_2' specifies the quantities that retailers are *willing* to sell at the mine price of OW_m; the vertical line MQ_S indicates the maximum amount retailers are *able* to sell at that price. Therefore, the curve S_2RM shows the quantities that re-

FIGURE 8.5.4

Cost Curves of an Individual Firm

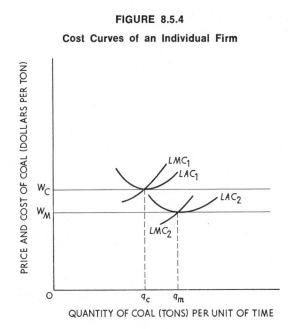

tailers are *willing and able* to sell at each retail price when the mine price is fixed at OW_m.

The intersection of supply and demand now occurs at the price OP_E, clearly higher than the old price. The quantity sold is OQ_S. After the ceiling price at the mine is imposed, consumers pay a higher price for less coal. Since demand was assumed to be elastic, retailers receive less total revenue.

8.6 LONG-RUN EQUILIBRIUM IN A PERFECTLY COMPETITIVE MARKET

Since all inputs are variable in the long run, an entrepreneur has the option of adjusting his plant size, as well as his output, to achieve maximum profit. In the limit, he can liquidate his business entirely and transfer his resources and his command over resources into a more profitable investment alternative. But just as established firms may leave the industry, new firms may enter the industry if profit prospects are brighter there than elsewhere. Indeed, adjustment of the number of firms in the industry in response to profit motivation is the key element in establishing long-run equilibrium.

8.6.a Long-Run Adjustment of an Established Firm

In the long run, an entrepreneur adjusts his plant size, and therefore his rate of output, in order to attain maximum profit. The adjustment process is illustrated in Figure 8.6.1.

Let market price be $O\bar{P}$ and suppose the firm has a plant whose costs are represented by SAC_1 and SMC_1 (short-run average total and marginal cost, respectively). With this plant, short-run equilibrium is reached at point A, corresponding to output of Oq_1 units per period of time. At this point the firm sustains a small loss on each unit of output produced and sold.

In looking to the long run, or the planning horizon, the entrepreneur has two options: he can go out of business or he can construct a plant of more suitable size. For example, he could decide upon the plant size represented by SAC_2 and SMC_2. At price $O\bar{P}$, he would produce Oq_2 units per period of time and make a pure profit of BC dollars per unit. However, with perfect knowledge, the plant represented by SAC_4 and SMC_4 would be constructed.

With this plant, operated so as to produce Oq_4 units per period of time, the maximum attainable profit is realized. The logical basis of this

FIGURE 8.6.1

Long-Run Adjustment of Plant Size

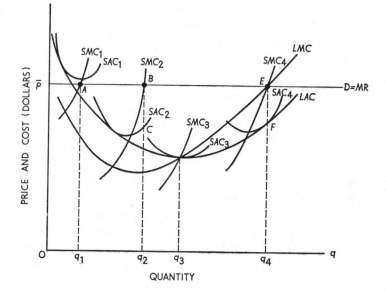

proposition is the same as in the case of short-run profit maximization. Long-run marginal cost shows the addition to total cost attributable to the addition of one unit to output, *after plant size has been adjusted so as to produce that rate of output at minimum achievable unit cost.* Marginal revenue, or demand, shows the increase in revenue attributable to the addition of one unit to sales. By the familiar argument, therefore, maximum profit is obtained by producing that rate of output in the plant of such size that long-run marginal cost equals price at the point where the relevant short-run marginal cost equals price.

In Figure 8.6.1, the optimum-size plant is larger than the plant for which unit cost reaches its minimum—the plant given by SAC_3. However, at the optimum rate of output, Oq_4, unit cost is smaller in the plant represented by SAC_4 than in a plant of any other size. So long as price is $O\bar{P}$, long-run equilibrium adjustment dictates building the plant SAC_4 and operating it so as to produce Oq_4 units per period of time.

8.6.b   Long-Run Adjustment of the Industry

If all firms in the industry originally had plants of size represented by SAC_1, the simultaneous expansion of plant size by all firms would shift the industry supply curve materially to the right. Market price would be reduced, and each firm would then possess a plant that is too large. Further adjustment of plant size by established firms would be necessary before long-run equilibrium could be attained.

On the other hand, if all firms except one originally possessed plants of optimum size, the expansion by one plant would not have a perceptible effect upon market price. All firms would be in a temporarily optimal situation, earning a pure economic profit of *EF* dollars per unit. (Figure 8.6.1).

As you will recall from Chapter 7, economic cost and economic profit are somewhat different from the corresponding accounting concepts. In particular, economic cost includes the returns that could be obtained from the most profitable alternative use of the invested resources. Hence a *pure economic profit* represents a return on investment in excess of that obtainable elsewhere. The appearance of such profit naturally attracts new firms into the industry, expanding industry supply and reducing market price. When this occurs, all firms—both old and new—must adjust; and the adjustment process must continue until a position of long-run equilibrium is attained.

The process of long-run equilibrium adjustment is illustrated by Figure 8.6.2. Suppose each firm in the industry is identical. The original size is represented by SAC_1 and SMC_1 in panel b. The market demand curve is given by DD' in panel a, and the market supply is S_1S_1'. Market equilibrium establishes the price of OP_1 dollars per unit and total output and sales of OQ_1 units per period of time. At price OP_1, each firm attains a point of short-run equilibrium where SMC_1 equals price. Each firm produces Oq_1 units per period of time and reaps a pure economic profit of *AB* dollars per unit. As panel b is constructed, this position could be one of long-run equilibrium inasmuch as *LMC* equals price at this point.

From the standpoint of the market as a whole, however, the present situation is not stable. Each firm in the industry enjoys a pure economic profit—a rate of return on invested resources greater than could be earned in any alternative employment. Therefore, in the long run some firms in less profitable industries will switch to the industry in question because a greater profit can be earned there.

The process of new entry might be very slow, or it might be very fast; this depends primarily upon the liquid assets in other industries. In any event, as time elapses new firms will enter the industry, thereby shifting the industry supply curve to the right. Suppose, indeed, the profit attraction is so strong that a substantial number of new firms

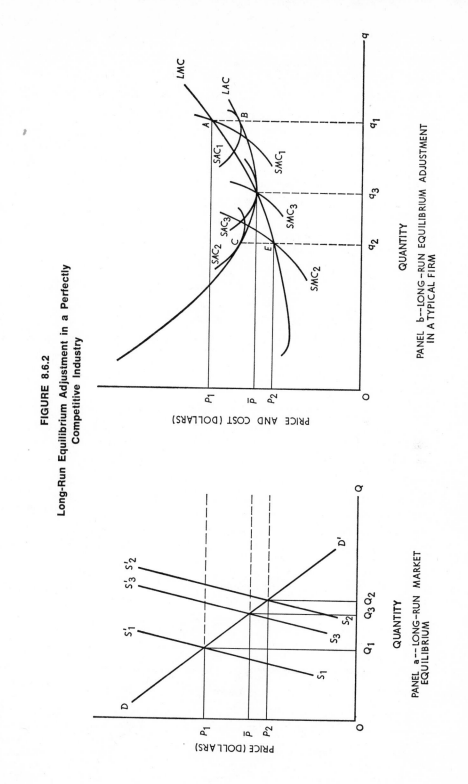

FIGURE 8.6.2

Long-Run Equilibrium Adjustment in a Perfectly Competitive Industry

PANEL b—LONG-RUN EQUILIBRIUM ADJUSTMENT IN A TYPICAL FIRM

PANEL a—LONG-RUN MARKET EQUILIBRIUM

enters the industry, shifting the industry supply curve to S_2S_2' in panel a. In this situation equilibrium quantity will expand to OQ_2.

When each firm adjusts optimally to the new market price, however, the output of each will be smaller. The larger number of firms accounts for the overall increase in output. When market price falls some firms will be ready to build new plants, so they can adjust their plant size quite rapidly. Others will have relatively new plants of size represented by SAC_1. These firms will be quite slow in making the optimal size adjustment. But even the firms that quickly adjust to optimal plant size—given by SAC_2 and SMC_2 in panel b—lose money at the rate of CE dollars per unit. Those whose size is not quickly adapted lose even more.

As in the previous case, short-run and long-run marginal cost both equal price. Each firm has adjusted as best it can; but the situation is still not consistent with long-run equilibrium. In the present case each firm incurs a pure economic loss, even though it may earn an accounting profit. In any event, profit is less than in alternative investments. Hence firms will tend to leave the industry as their plants and equipment wear out. Investment in some other industry is more attractive because the profit outlook is better.

As a consequence industry supply shifts to the left, raising the market equilibrium price. As shown in the next subsection, industry supply must shift until it is represented by S_3S_3'. With the given demand curve, market price is $O\overline{P}$. Each firm, after adjustment, has a plant represented by SAC_3 and SMC_3. Price is just equal to short-run marginal and average total cost and to long-run marginal and average total cost as well. Neither pure profit nor pure loss is present.

The adjustment process described above may be summarized by the following

Proposition: In perfect competition there is a tendency for firms to enter or exit until each existing firm earns neither pure profit nor pure loss.

8.6.c Long-Run Equilibrium in a Perfectly Competitive Firm

The proposition of long-run equilibrium is inevitable from and is embodied in the assumptions of profit maximization and free entry. Each firm strives to achieve the maximum possible profit. In the short run a firm in perfect competition can do nothing more than adjust its output so that marginal cost equals price. In the long run it can adjust the size of its plant and it can select the industry in which it operates—both with an eye to profit.

The long-run equilibrium of a firm in a perfectly competitive industry is explained by means of Figure 8.6.3. If price is above the level $O\overline{P}$, each established firm in the industry earns a pure profit. New firms are attracted into the industry, shifting the market supply curve to the right. Market equilibrium price declines, and the horizontal demand curve confronting each firm falls to a lower level. On the other hand, if price is below $O\overline{P}$, each firm in the industry incurs a pure economic loss. As their plants and equipment depreciate, some firms will leave the industry, thereby causing the market supply curve to shift to the left. Market price and, accordingly, the horizontal individual demand curves rise.

The only conceivable point of long-run equilibrium occurs at point E in Figure 8.6.3. Here firms in the industry receive neither pure profit nor pure loss. There is no incentive for further entrance because the rate of return in this industry is the same as in the best alternative. But for the same reason there is no incentive for a firm to leave the industry. The number of firms stabilizes, each firm with a short-run plant represented by SAC and SMC.

The position of long-run equilibrium is actually determined by the horizontal demand curve confronting each firm. Since the industry is perfectly competitive by assumption, firms will enter or leave the industry if there is either pure profit or pure loss. Therefore, since the position of long-run equilibrium must be consistent with *zero* profit (and zero loss), it is necessary that price equal average total cost. For a

FIGURE 8.6.3

Long-Run Equilibrium of a Firm in a Perfectly Competitive Industry

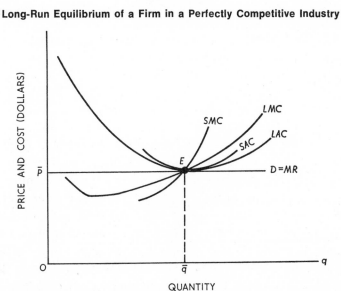

QUANTITY

firm to attain its individual equilibrium, price must be equal to marginal cost. Therefore, price must equal both marginal and average total cost. This can only occur at the point where average total and marginal cost are equal, or at the point of minimum average total cost.

The statement, so far, could conceivably apply to any SAC and SMC. However, unless it applies *only* to the short-run plant that coincides with minimum long-run average cost, a change in plant size would lead to the appearance of pure profit, and the wheels of adjustment would be set in motion again. These arguments establish the following

Proposition: Long-run equilibrium for a firm in perfect competition occurs at the point where price equals minimum long-run average cost. At this point minimum short-run average total cost equals minimum long-run average total cost, and the short- and long-run marginal costs are equal. The position of long-run equilibrium is characterized by a "no profit" situation—the firms have neither a pure profit nor a pure loss, only an accounting profit equal to the rate of return obtainable in other perfectly competitive industries.

8.6.d Constant Cost Industries

The analysis of subsections 8.6.b and 8.6.c was based upon the tacit assumption of "constant cost," in the sense that expanded resource usage does not entail an increase in resource prices. To carry the analysis further, and to make it more explicit, both constant and increasing cost industries are examined in this subsection. The phenomenon of decreasing cost is not examined inasmuch as it is not consistent with all the requirements of perfect competition.

Long-run equilibrium and long-run supply price under conditions of constant cost are explained by means of Figure 8.6.4. Panel a shows the long- and short-run conditions of a typical firm in the industry, while panel b depicts the market as a whole. D_1D_1' and S_1S_1' are the original market demand and supply curves, establishing a market equilibrium price of $O\overline{P}$ dollars per unit. Assume that the industry has attained a position of long-run equilibrium, so the position of each firm in the industry is depicted by panel a—the price line is tangent to the long- and short-run average total cost curves at their minimum points.

Now suppose demand increases to D_2D_2'. Instantaneously, with the number of firms fixed, the price will rise to OP' and each firm will move to equilibrium at point A. However, at point A each firm earns a pure economic profit, thereby attracting new entrants into the industry and shifting the industry supply curve to the right. In this case we assume that all resources used in the industry are *unspecialized;* so in-

FIGURE 8.6.4

Long-Run Equilibrium and Supply Price in a Perfectly Competitive Industry Subject to Constant Cost

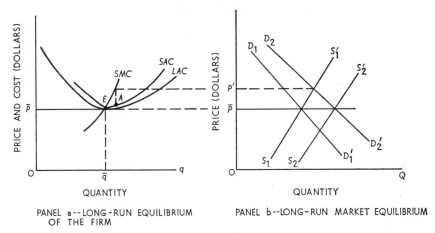

PANEL a—LONG-RUN EQUILIBRIUM OF THE FIRM

PANEL b—LONG-RUN MARKET EQUILIBRIUM

creased usage does not affect the market price of the resources. As a consequence, the entrance of new firms does not increase the costs of existing firms; the *LAC* curve of established firms does not shift and new firms can operate with an identical *LAC* curve. Long-run equilibrium adjustment to the shift in demand is accomplished when the number of firms expands to the point at which S_2S_2' is the industry supply curve.

In other words, since output can be expanded by *expanding the number of firms* producing $O\overline{q}$ units per period of time at average cost $O\overline{P}$, the industry has a *constant long-run supply price* equal to $O\overline{P}$ dollars per unit. If price were above this level, firms of size represented by *SAC* would continue to enter the industry in order to reap the pure profit obtainable. If price were less than $O\overline{P}$, some firms would ultimately leave the industry to avoid the pure economic loss. Hence in the special case in which an expansion of resource usage does not lead to an increase in resource price, the long-run industry supply price is constant. This is precisely the meaning of a "constant-cost" industry.

Let us now summarize and emphasize. First, we need the following

Definition: The long-run industry supply price shows for each level of output the *minimum* price required to induce this industry output after (a) each firm in the industry has made the optimal internal adjustment and (b) the number of firms in the industry has, by entry or exit, been optimally adjusted.

Exercise: What are the precise relations and analogies between long-run supply price for a perfectly competitive industry and long-run average cost for a perfectly competitive firm?

Long-run industry supply price will be constant if, and only if, the industry output can be expanded or contracted by expanding or contracting the number of firms without affecting minimum long-run average cost. This condition, in turn, will exist if, and only if, all resources used by the industry are unspecialized—which means that the prices the firms must pay for all resources do not change with the level of resource use. To put it another way, the supply curve of each resource used in the industry must be perfectly elastic so far as the firms in *that* industry are concerned. This means that the industry *as a whole* must be a perfect competitor in each resource market—the industry must have a position vis-à-vis each resource market that is exactly like the position of a consumer vis-à-vis each commodity market.

In Chapters 5 and 6 there was a discussion of "returns to scale," and in Chapter 7 this was related to the shape of a firm's long-run average cost curve. The relations merit further comment. First, suppose all resource prices are constant. If the firm's production function first shows increasing and then decreasing returns to scale, its long-run average cost curve will have a U shape; *but* the long-run industry supply price will be constant because resource prices are constant (the number of firms producing at minimum *LAC* can be changed without affecting the *LAC* of any firm.). On the other hand, if the production function exhibits constant returns to scale, the long-run average cost curve will rise if resource prices vary directly with resource usage. As we will now see, industry supply price also rises in this case. Before reading further, however, think through the *important* exercise that follows.

Exercise: Suppose all resource prices are constant and that the production function of each firm in an industry exhibits constant returns to scale. Samuelson (*Foundations,* pp. 78–80) refers to this as the "indeterminacy of purest competition." Explain the meaning of this phrase.

8.6.e Increasing Cost Industries

Increasing cost or increasing industry supply price is depicted by Figure 8.6.5. The original situation is the same as in Figure 8.6.4. The industry is in a position of long-run equilibrium. D_1D_1' and S_1S_1' are the market demand and supply curves respectively. Equilibrium price is OP_1. Each firm operates at point E_1, where price equals minimum average cost, both long- and short-run cost. Thus each firm is also in a position of long-run equilibrium.

FIGURE 8.6.5

**Long-Run Equilibrium and Supply Price in a Perfectly Competitive Industry
Subject to Increasing Cost**

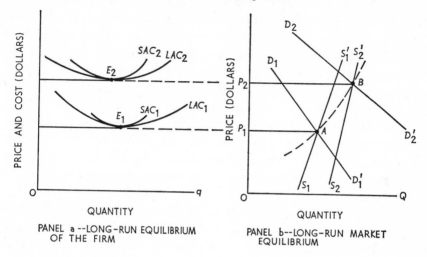

PANEL a --LONG-RUN EQUILIBRIUM
OF THE FIRM

PANEL b--LONG-RUN MARKET
EQUILIBRIUM

Let demand shift to D_2D_2', so price instantaneously rises to a much
higher level. The higher price is accompanied by pure economic profit;
new firms are consequently attracted into the industry. The usage of
resources expands and now, we assume, resource prices expand with
resource usage. The cost of inputs therefore increases for the established
firms as well as for the new entrants. As a result the entire set of cost
curves shifts upward, say to a position represented by LAC_2 in panel a.

Naturally, the process of equilibrium adjustment is not instantaneous. The LAC curve gradually shifts upward as new entrants gradually join the industry. The marginal cost curve of each firm shifts to the
left, thereby tending to shift the industry supply curve to the left. However, more firms are producing and this tends to shift industry supply
to the right. The latter tendency must dominate, for otherwise new
firms would have obtained resources *only* by bidding them away from
established firms in the industry. Total output could not expand as
dictated by the increase in market price. New resource units must have
entered the industry, so the supply curve shifts to the right, though not
by as much as it would in a constant-cost industry.

The process of adjustment must continue until a position of full
long-run equilibrium is attained. In Figure 8.6.5, this is depicted by the
intersection of D_2D_2' and S_2S_2', establishing an equilibrium price of
OP_2 dollars per unit. Each firm produces at point E_2, where price equals

minimum average total cost. The important point to emphasize is that in constant-cost industries new firms enter until price returns to the unchanged level of minimum, long-run average cost. For industries subject to increasing long-run supply price, new firms enter until minimum long-run average cost shifts upward to equal the new price. The number of firms and the industry output increase. However there is no way to predict what will happen to the equilibrium output per firm. It may decrease, as shown in Figure 8.6.5, or it may remain constant or increase. But these items are certain: industry output, the number of firms, and long-run supply price will all increase.

In the transition from one long-run equilibrium to the other, the long-run supply price increases from OP_1 to OP_2. This is precisely what is meant by an "increasing-cost industry" or increasing long-run industry supply price. In keeping with this, the long-run industry supply curve is given by a line joining such points as A and B in panel b. Thus an increasing-cost industry is one with a positively sloped long-run supply curve. Alternatively stated, after all long-run equilibrium adjustments are made, an increasing-cost industry is one in which an increase in output requires an increase in the long-run supply price.[4]

The result of this section can be summarized as follows:

Relations: Constant or increasing cost in an industry depends entirely upon the way in which resource prices respond to expanded resource usage. If resource prices remain constant the industry is subject to constant cost; if resource prices increase the industry is one of increasing cost.

The long-run supply curve for a constant-cost industry is a horizontal line at the level of the constant long-run supply price. The long-run industry supply curve under conditions of increasing cost is positively sloped, and the long-run supply price increases as long-run equilibrium quantity supplied expands.

8.7   CONCLUSION

Up to this point the salient feature of perfect competition is that in long-run market equilibrium, market price equals minimum average total cost. This means that each unit of output is produced at the lowest

---

[4] Notice that in the short run an increase in output will be induced only by an increase in price, regardless of the nature of the industry. In the special case of constant cost an increase in output can be achieved at a constant price after *all* long-run equilibrium adjustments have been made.

possible cost, either from the standpoint of money cost or of resource usage. The product sells for its average (long-run) cost of production; each firm accordingly earns the "going" rate of return in competitive industries, nothing more or less.

But so far we have seen only one side of perfect competition—the operation of firms within a perfectly competitive industry. The pricing of productive services under conditions of perfect competition is also an important feature, as is the question of general economic welfare in a perfectly competitive economy. While all of these studies are based upon a highly stylized set of assumptions, they ultimately provide criteria by which to evaluate actual market operation and practice.

PROBLEM

Use the output-cost data computed for the problem in Chapter 7.

1. Suppose the price of the commodity is $1.75 per unit.
   a) What would net profit be at each of the following outputs? (i) 1,314; (ii) 1,384; (iii) 1,444; (iv) 1,494; and (v) 1,534.
   b) What is the greatest profit output?
   c) Is there any output that will yield a greater profit at any price?
   d) How much more revenue is obtained by selling this number of units than by selling one fewer? What is the relation between marginal revenue and selling price?
   e) If you are given selling price, how can you determine the optimum output by reference to marginal cost?

2. Suppose price is 70 cents.
   a) What would net profit be at each of the following outputs: (i) 410; (ii) 560; (iii) 700; (iv) 830; (v) 945; (vi) 1,234; (vii) 1,444.
   b) Is there any output that will earn a net profit at this price?
   c) When price is 70 cents, what is the crucial relation between price and average variable cost?
   d) Consider any price for which the corresponding marginal cost is equal to or less than 70 cents. At such a price, what is the relation between marginal cost and average variable cost?
   e) When the relation in (d) exists, what is the relation between average and marginal product?
   f) What will the producer do if faced with a permanent price of 70 cents?
   g) Why is it not socially desirable to have a producer operating when price is 70 cents?

3. Suppose price is 80 cents.
   a) What will the optimum output be?
   b) Can a profit be made at this price?
   c) Will the producer operate at all at this price?
   d) How long?

4. Determine the supply schedule of this individual producer listing the quantity supplied at the following prices: $.60, .70, .80, .90, 1.00, 1.10, 1.20, 1.30, 1.40, 1.50, 1.60, 1.70, 1.80, 1.90, and 2.00.

QUESTIONS

1. The following report appeared in the *Wall Street Journal:* "The world's first plant for the manufacture of gasoline from natural gas will be shut down as uneconomical, it was announced today by the Amoco Chemical Corp.
   "The plant, at Brownsville, Texas, will be closed within the next few months, with a reduction of the work force to begin Oct. 1.
   "J. A. Forrester, president of Amoco, a subsidiary of the Standard Oil Co. (Indiana) said: 'We have determined that the Brownsville plant cannot make gasoline and chemicals from natural gas at present market prices as cheaply as they can be made by other processes . . .'
   "Mr. Forrester declared: 'We have proved the technical soundness of the process. However, results indicate that the units are more costly to operate and maintain than we had anticipated.' "
   Consider whether it was wasteful to close down the plant (*a*) from the point of view of the firm, and (*b*) from the point of view of society.

2. New York City licenses taxicabs in two classes: for operation by companies with fleets and for operation by independent driver-owners each having only one cab. The city also fixes the rates the taxis may charge. For many years now, no new licenses have been issued in either class. There is an unofficial market for the "medallions" that signify the possession of a license. A medallion for an independent cab sold, in 1959, for about $17,000.
   a) Discuss the factors determining the price of a medallion.
   b) What factors would determine whether a change in the fare fixed by the city would raise or lower the price of a medallion?
   c) Cab drivers, whether hired by companies or owners of their own cabs, seem unanimous in opposing any increase in the number of cabs licensed. They argue that an increase in the number of cabs, by increasing competition for customers, would drive down what they consider as an already unduly low return to drivers. Is their economics correct? Who would benefit and who would lose from an expansion in the number of licenses issued at a nominal fee?

3. Comment on the following quotation: "The orthodox tools of supply

and demand assume that sellers and buyers are free to buy or sell any quantity they wish at the prices determined by the market. This assumption cannot validly be made when price controls or rationing are imposed by the government. It follows that these tools are useless in analyzing the effects of such governmental action. Economists should free themselves from slavish adherence to outmoded concepts and fashion new tools of analysis for the new problems raised by the modern Leviathan."

4. Assume that the demand for shoes at the retail level is elastic. Further assume that a ceiling price below the current market price is placed on shoes at the factory (i.e., a maximum price the shoe manufacturer can charge the retail dealer). The total revenue received from the sale of shoes at the retail level will increase because of the imposition of the ceiling price at the factory level. *Problem:* Decide whether the conclusion above is true, false, or uncertain and defend your answer.

5. Suppose a frost kills a large portion of the orange crop, with a resulting higher price of oranges. It has been said that such an increase in the price benefits no one since it cannot elicit a supply response; the higher price, it is said, simply "lines the pockets of profiteers." Analyze this position (*hint:* be sure to focus on the rationing function of market price).

6. Assume that crab packing is a perfectly competitive industry on a national scale, or at least along the Eastern seaboard and Gulf Coast. The North Carolina crab packers have insisted that if the minimum wage is increased to $1.60 an hour, they will have to close their plants. Assume that they are correct. State the assumptions that must (implicitly) underlie their analysis and explain the situation graphically.

SUGGESTED READINGS

Henderson, James M., and Quandt, Richard E. *Microeconomic Theory: A Mathematical Approach,* pp. 85–98. New York: McGraw-Hill Book Co., Inc., 1958. [Elementary math required.]

Knight, Frank H. *Risk, Uncertainty and Profit,* chaps. 1, 5, 6. London School Reprints of Scarce Works, No. 16, 1933.

Machlup, Fritz. *Economics of Sellers' Competition,* pp. 79–125, esp. pp. 79–85 and pp. 116–25. Baltimore: The Johns Hopkins Press, 1952.

Stigler, George J. "Perfect Competition, Historically Contemplated," *Journal of Political Economy,* Vol. LXV (1957), pp. 1–17.

Chapter 9 | THEORY OF PRICE UNDER PURE MONOPOLY

9.1 INTRODUCTION

"Perfect competition" provides the economist with a very useful analytical model, even though the exacting conditions of the model never exist in the real world. The same statement almost applies to the model of pure monopoly, to which we now turn. The conditions of the model are exacting; and it is difficult, if not impossible, to pinpoint a pure monopolist in real world markets. On the other hand, many markets closely approximate monopoly organization, and monopoly analysis often explains observed business behavior quite well.

9.1.a Definition

A pure monopoly is said to exist if there is one, and only one, seller in a well-defined market. Thus from the sales or revenue side pure monopoly and perfect competition are polar opposites. The perfectly competitive firm has so many "rivals" in the market that competition becomes impersonal and rivalry, or "competition" in the popular sense, does not exist at all. Rivalry does not exist in the case of pure monopoly either, for the simple reason that there are no rivals. There is no "competition" in the popular sense; and there is no competition in the technical sense either.

Yet this may overstate the case somewhat, for two types of *indirect competition* and one source of *potential competition* tend to moderate the price-output policies of pure or near-pure monopolies. The first source of indirect competition is the general struggle for the consumer's dollar. *All* commodities compete for a place in the consumer's budget—the products of monopolists as well as the products of perfectly competitive firms. Unless a monopolist can secure a market for his product, his monopoly position is worthless. For example, the files of the U.S.

284

Patent Office would reveal many patents (and therefore output monopoly) for products that were never produced or were produced for only a short period of time. Monopoly does not guarantee success; it only guarantees that the monopolist can make the most of whatever demand conditions exist.

A second source of indirect competition lies in the existence of substitute goods. Needless to say, there are no *perfect* substitutes for a monopoly product; otherwise a monopoly would not exist. However, imperfect substitutes exist; and the true market power of a monopolist depends upon the extent to which other commodities may be used as substitutes in consumption. For example, whale oil lamps and gaslights, candles and Coleman Lanterns are very poor substitutes for electricity in residential and commercial lighting. Therefore, electricity for lighting purposes closely approximates pure monopoly. On the other hand, there are quite good substitutes for electrical heating. Fuel oil and natural gas are strong competitors in the residential heating market; coal-fired steam heat, in addition to oil and gas, competes in the commercial market. As a consequence, the "monopoly" position of electrical power companies is very weak in these markets.

As has been said, the presence of indirect competition tends to moderate the price-output policies of monopolists. The threat of potential competition does so as well. Various reasons explain the establishment of a monopoly position (see subsection 9.1.b). An entrepreneur can sometimes maintain his monopoly position, however, only if he does not fully exploit it. In many cases potential competitors will be attracted into the market if profit prospects are bright. This is particularly true when the price-output policy of the existing monopolist is such that potential competitors feel they can readily capture a substantial portion of the market. While this situation is especially applicable to local or regional markets served by only one firm, it applies in broader situations as well. Whenever entry is possible, the position of an existing monopoly is perilous. To protect it the monopolist must serve his market well; otherwise new entrants will be attracted and the monopoly broken.

To summarize:

Definition: A pure monopoly exists when there is only one producer in a market. There are no direct competitors or rivals in either the popular or technical sense. However, the policies of a monopolist may be constrained by the indirect competition of all commodities for the consumer's dollar and of reasonably adequate substitute goods, and by the threat of potential competition if market entry is possible.

9.1.b Bases of Monopoly

Since the business of businessmen is profit, one might wonder why a monopoly ever arises, i.e., why other firms do not enter the industry in an attempt to capture a part of the monopoly profit. Many different factors may lead to the establishment of a monopoly or near monopoly. Thus, on a local level the personal characteristics of the owner-monopolist may bring all the trade to his door. Other seemingly trivial reasons may explain monopoly; but monopolies so established are destined for a short life. Permanent monopoly must rest on firmer ground.

One of the most important bases for monopoly lies in the control of raw material supplies. Suppose input x is required to produce output y. If one person has exclusive control over or ownership of x, he can easily establish a monopoly over y by refusing to sell x to any potential competitors. An interesting example of input-control monopoly can be taken from the economic history of the United States. Bauxite is a necessary ingredient in the production of aluminum. For many years the Aluminum Company of America (Alcoa) owned almost every source of bauxite in the United States. The control of resource supply, coupled with certain patent rights, provided Alcoa with an absolute monopoly in aluminum. Indeed, it was only after World War II that the federal courts effectively broke Alcoa's monopoly of the aluminum market.

The discussion of Alcoa brings to light another important source of monopoly. The patent laws of the United States make it possible for a person to apply for and obtain the exclusive right to produce a certain commodity or to produce a commodity by means of a specified process. The patent lasts for 17 years, and may not be renewed after that time. Obviously, such exclusive rights can easily lead to monopoly. Alcoa is an example of a monopoly based upon both resource control and patent rights. E. I. du Pont de Nemours & Co. has enjoyed patent monopolies over many commodities, cellophane being perhaps the most notable. The Eastman Kodak Company enjoyed a similar position (by lease from a German company); the Minnesota Mining and Manufacturing Company ("Three M") has enjoyed patent monopoly or near monopoly with products such as their Scotch Tape and Thermofax Copier.

Despite these notable examples, patent monopoly may not be quite what it seems in many instances. A patent gives one the exclusive right to produce a particular, meticulously specified commodity or to use a particular, meticulously specified process to produce a commodity others can produce. But a patent does not preclude the development of closely related substitute goods or closely allied production processes. International Business Machines has the exclusive right to produce IBM machines; but other millisecond digital computers are available and there is keen competition in the computer market. The same is true of production processes. Thus while patents may sometimes establish pure monopolies, at other times they are merely permits to enter highly— but not perfectly—competitive markets.

A third source of monopoly lies in the cost of establishing an efficient production plant, especially in relation to the size of the market. The situation we are now discussing is frequently called "natural" monopoly. It comes into existence when the minimum average cost of production occurs at a rate of output sufficient, almost sufficient, or more than sufficient to supply the entire market at a price covering full cost.

Suppose a situation such as this exists but two firms are in the market. If the market is split between the two, each must necessarily produce at a relatively high average cost. Each has an incentive to lower price and increase output because average cost will also decline. But if both act in this fashion, price will surely fall more rapidly than average cost. Economic warfare ensues, and the ultimate result is likely to be the emergence of only one firm in a monopoly position.[1] The term "natural" monopoly simply implies that the "natural" result of market forces is the development of a monopoly organization.

Examples of natural monopoly are not hard to come by. Virtually all public utilities are natural monopolies and vice versa. Municipal waterworks, electrical power companies, sewage disposal systems, telephone companies, and many transportation services are examples of natural monopolies on both local and national levels.

The final source of monopoly to be discussed here is the market franchise. Use of a market franchise is frequently associated with natural monopolies and public utilities, but it need not be. A market franchise is actually a contract entered into by some governmental body (for instance, a city government) and a business concern. The governmental unit gives a business firm the exclusive right to market a good or service within its jurisdiction. The business firm, in turn, agrees to permit the governmental unit to control certain aspects of its market conduct. For example, the governmental unit may limit, or attempt to limit, the firm to a "fair return on fair market value of assets." In other cases the governmental unit may establish the price and permit the firm to earn whatever it can at that price. There are many other ways in which the governmental unit can exercise control over the firm. The essential feature, however, is that a governmental unit establishes the firm as a

---

[1] For the classical treatment of this situation, see F. Zeuthen, *Problems of Monopoly and Economic Warfare* (London: Routledge, 1930).

monopoly in return for various types of control over the price and output policies of the business.

9.2 DEMAND UNDER MONOPOLY

The most important object of Part I was to show that market demand curves are negatively sloped (except for the truly insignificant case of Giffen's Paradox). Now, since a monopoly constitutes a one-firm market, the market demand curve *is* the monopoly demand curve. As explained in Chapter 4.4, when demand is negatively sloped average and marginal revenue are different, and for marginal profit calculations the latter is the relevant concept.[2]

Consider an hypothetical situation given by the data in Table 9.2.1. Market demand is indicated by the first two columns and is plotted graphically in Figure 9.2.1. Total revenue, the product of price and quantity, is given in column 3 and depicted graphically in Figure 9.2.1. (*Note:* The right-hand ordinate refers to total revenue while the customary left-hand ordinate refers to price and marginal revenue.) Finally, marginal revenue is shown in column 4.

As you will recall, marginal revenue is the addition to total revenue attributable to the addition of one unit to output (or sales). In this example, quantity does not increase by single units. Thus marginal revenue must be calculated as the *average* marginal revenue over the corresponding quantity range. Thus[3]

---

[2] The remainder of this section is a brief review of section 4.4 in Chapter 4. Students thoroughly familiar with the content of this section may proceed immediately to section 9.3.

[3] For continuous cases, the demand function in inverse form may be written

$$p = f(q), \quad f'(q) < 0, \tag{9.3.1}$$

where p and q denote price and quantity respectively. Thus total revenue is

$$pq = qf(q), \tag{9.3.2}$$

and marginal revenue is

$$MR = \frac{d(pq)}{dq} = f(q) + qf'(q). \tag{9.3.3}$$

As you will recall from section 4.4 in Chapter 4, price elasticity of demand is

$$\eta = -\frac{dq}{dp}\frac{p}{q} = -\frac{1}{f'(q)}\frac{p}{q} = -\frac{p}{qf'(q)}. \tag{9.3.4}$$

Now, factor $p = f(q)$ from the right-hand side of expression (9.3.3), obtaining

$$MR = p\left(1 + \frac{qf'(q)}{p}\right). \tag{9.3.5}$$

TABLE 9.2.1   Demand and Marginal Revenue under Monopoly

Quantity	Price	Total Revenue	Marginal Revenue
5	$2.00	$10.00	—
13	1.10	14.30	$0.54
23	.85	19.55	.52
38	.69	25.92	.42
50	.615	30.75	.35
60	.55	33.00	.23
68	.50	34.00	.13
75	.45	33.75	−.03
81	.40	32.40	−.23
86	.35	30.10	−.46

FIGURE 9.2.1   Demand and Revenue under Monopoly

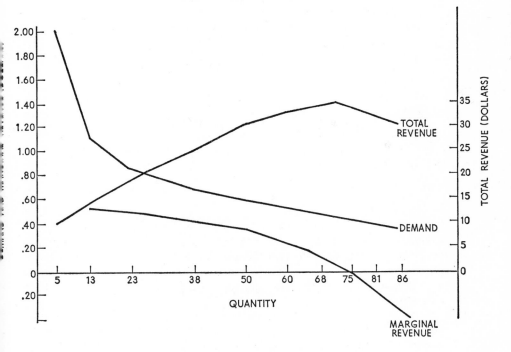

$$MR = \frac{\Delta TR}{\Delta Q} = \text{(for example)} \ \frac{\$14.30 - \$10.00}{13 - 5} = \$0.54 \ .$$

The corresponding plot is shown in Figure 9.2.1.

Thus from expression (9.3.4),

$$MR = p\left(1 - \frac{1}{\eta}\right). \tag{9.3.6}$$

The highly discrete case in Figure 9.2.1 is generalized in Figure 9.2.2. The important relations, already discussed, are immediately apparent from the figure.

FIGURE 9.2.2

Relations among Demand, Total Revenue, and Marginal Revenue

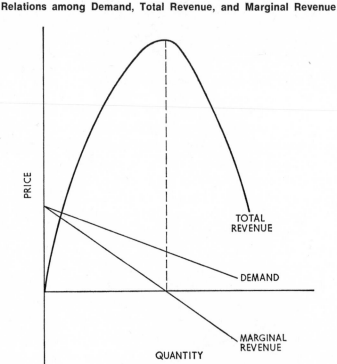

Relations: When demand is negatively sloped, marginal revenue is negatively sloped as well. Furthermore, marginal revenue is less than price at all relevant points. The difference between marginal revenue and price depends upon the price elasticity of demand, as shown by the formula $MR = p(1 - 1/\eta)$.

Total revenue at first increases, reaches a maximum, and declines thereafter. The maximum point on the total revenue curve is attained at precisely that rate of output and sales (quantity) for which marginal revenue is zero.

9.3 COST AND SUPPLY UNDER MONOPOLY

The short-run cost conditions confronting a monopolist may be, for all practical purposes, identical to those faced by a perfectly competitive firm. In particular, an entrepreneur who is a monopolist in the commodity market may indeed be a perfect (buying) competitor in the market for productive inputs. This would tend to be true if the monopolist required only unspecialized inputs, such as unskilled labor. In this event, the analysis of Chapter 7 would apply straightforwardly to cost under monopoly. In many instances, however, the monopolist requires certain *specialized* inputs for which there is no broad general market. There are only a few buyers of the specialized input (in the limit, only one). Thus the commodity-market monopolist may be a monopolist or near monopolist in various input markets as well.[4]

9.3.a Cost with Monopoly in the Input Market

The analysis in Part I was based on the assumption that each consumer is a perfect competitor in the *buying* market. That is, each consumer is such a small purchaser, relative to the entire market, that he may buy any quantity he wishes without affecting market price. The same type of assumption was used in Chapter 7: each producer employs such a small quantity of each input, relative to the entire market for that input, that he may employ any amount he desires without affecting input price. But if a producer is a monopolist or near monopolist in an input market, the price of that input will depend in part upon the purchases of the producer in question.

This is a simple matter of demand and supply analysis. If the commodity-market monopolist is a monopolist in the input market, his individual input demand curve is the *market* input demand curve as well. Given a (positively sloped) input supply curve, input price is determined and is, among other things, a function of input demand.

To get at this another way, consider Table 9.3.1 and the associated Figure 9.3.1. Assume that only one variable input is required in the production process, as shown in columns 1 and 2. The remaining columns contain cost data. Total fixed cost is $10, given in column 3. Under present assumptions, the commodity monopolist is a monopolist in the input market as well. He thus faces a rising supply curve for the input. Columns 1 and 4 give the supply of input curve, which is shown graphically in Figure 9.3.1. Given the supply of input curve, total variable cost (column 5) is obtained by multiplying the number of units of the variable input used by the supply price of that number of units.

Column 6 introduces a new concept. When a producer is a perfect competitor in the input market he can purchase any quantity of the in-

---

[4] In this case the monopolist is called a monopsonist or an oligopsonist. The use of this terminology is deferred until Chapter 14, where the present case is analyzed more intensely.

TABLE 9.3.1   Cost under Monopoly in the Input Market

Units of Variable Input	Total Product	Fixed Cost	Price of Variable Input	Total Variable Cost	Marginal Expense of Input	Total Cost	Average Variable Cost	Average Total Cost	Marginal Cost
0........	0	$10	$2.00	0	—	$10.00	—	—	—
1........	5	10	2.25	$ 2.25	—	12.25	$0.45	$2.45	$0.45
2........	13	10	2.50	5.00	$2.75	15.00	.39	1.15	.34
3........	23	10	2.75	8.25	3.25	18.25	.36	.80	.33
4........	38	10	3.00	12.00	3.75	22.00	.32	.58	.25
5........	50	10	3.25	16.25	4.25	26.25	.33	.53	.35
6........	60	10	3.50	21.00	4.75	31.00	.35	.52	.48
7........	68	10	3.75	26.25	5.25	36.25	.39	.53	.66
8........	75	10	4.00	32.00	5.75	42.00	.43	.56	.82
9........	81	10	4.25	38.25	6.25	48.25	.47	.60	1.04
10........	86	10	4.50	45.00	6.75	55.00	.52	.64	1.35

put he desires without affecting market price. Thus the price of the input is equal to the marginal expense of the input, just as price of output equals marginal revenue in a perfectly competitive selling market. Implicit in the above statement is the following

Definition: The marginal expense of a variable input is the addition to total variable cost attributable to the addition of one unit of the variable input to the production process.

The marginal expense of the variable input is computed in the same manner as any other "marginal" quantity: the difference in total variable cost is divided by the difference in the number of units of the variable input. Thus the first entry in column 6 is

$$\frac{\$5.00 - \$2.25}{2 - 1} = \$2.75 \,.$$

The marginal expense of input is shown graphically in Figure 9.3.1. Using this figure, provide a nonmathematical, but logical, answer to the following

Exercise: Given a positively sloped supply of variable input curve, prove that the marginal expense of input curve lies above, and rises more rapidly than, the associated supply curve (the latter will not hold if the supply curve is concave from below). Also, compare and contrast the relations between demand and marginal revenue and supply and the marginal expense of input.[5]

---

[5] A mathematical answer is as follows:

The supply of input curve in inverse form is given by

$$p = g(q), \qquad g'(q) > 0, \qquad (9.5.1)$$

FIGURE 9.3.1 Supply and Marginal Expense of Input

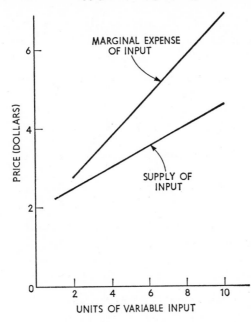

The last four columns of Table 9.3.1 follow by the calculations developed in Chapter 7. Two important elements are to be gleaned from this analysis. First, a rising supply price of a variable input causes an input-market monopolist to be confronted with a higher and also rising marginal expense of input curve. The significance of this relation will become quite clear in Chapter 14.

Second, the rising supply price of the variable input causes the cost curves to rise more rapidly than if the supply price of input were constant. Thus, for example, marginal cost of output rises not only because of diminishing marginal physical productivity of the input but also because the price of the input rises as its use expands.

---

where p and q represent price and quantity supplied of the variable input respectively. The condition $g'(q) > 0$ implies that the supply curve is positively sloped. Total variable cost is

$$TVC = pq = qg(q),\qquad(9.5.2)$$

so the marginal expense of input is

$$\frac{d[qg(q)]}{dq} = g(q) + qg'(q).\qquad(9.5.3)$$

In light of expression (9.5.1), $g(q) + qg'(q) > g(q)$. Hence the marginal expense of input curve must lie above the supply of input curve. Further, from expression (9.5.1) the slope of the supply curve is $g'(q)$, while from expression (9.5.3) the slope of the marginal expense curve is $2g'(q) + qg''(q)$. For linear curves,

9.3.b A Word on Monopoly Supply

Short-run monopoly supply is discussed in some detail in subsection 9.4.d. However, since cost conditions have been introduced, a word of caution is in order. The marginal cost curve is *not* the monopolist's supply curve. In fact, as you will see below, "supply" generally has a much less-precise meaning in monopoly than in perfect competition.

9.4 SHORT-RUN EQUILIBRIUM UNDER MONOPOLY

The analysis of perfect competition was based upon two important assumptions: each entrepreneur attempts (or acts as though he attempts) to maximize profit; and the firm operates in an environment not subject to outside control. Monopoly analysis rests upon the same two assumptions; accordingly, the results must be modified when applied to franchise monopoly or to monopolies subject to some form of government regulation and control.

9.4.a Total Revenue—Total Cost Approach

The monopolist, just as the perfect competitor, attains maximum profit by producing and selling at that rate of output for which the positive difference between total revenue and total cost is greatest. (Or, he minimizes loss when the negative difference is least.) To illustrate the total revenue-total cost approach, the hypothetical revenue and cost data from Tables 9.2.1 and 9.3.1 are reproduced in Table 9.4.1. These data are illustrated graphically in Figure 9.4.1.

$g''(q) = 0$; so the marginal expense curve has a steeper slope than the supply curve. If the supply curve is concave from above, $g''(q) > 0$, and the conclusion holds *a fortiori*. However, if the supply curve is positively sloped but concave from below, $g''(q) < 0$. In this case the marginal expense curve lies above the supply curve but approaches it asymptotically as q increases without bound.

Next, the elasticity of supply is the relative responsiveness of quantity supplied to a change in supply price. In the present notation, this may be written

$$\theta = \frac{p}{q}\frac{dq}{dp} = \frac{p}{q}\frac{1}{\frac{dp}{dq}} = \frac{p}{q}\frac{1}{g'(q)}. \tag{9.5.4}$$

Equation (9.5.3) may be written

$$MEI = p\left(1 + \frac{q}{p}g'(q)\right), \tag{9.5.5}$$

since $p = g(q)$. Substituting expression (9.5.4) in expression (9.5.5), one obtains

$$MEI = p\left(1 + \frac{1}{\theta}\right). \tag{9.5.6}$$

The analogy with demand-marginal revenue is obtained from this last expression.

TABLE 9.4.1

Profit Maximization by the Total Revenue–Total Cost Approach

Output and Sales	Price	Total Revenue	Total Cost	Profit
5....	$2.00	$10.00	$12.25	$ −2.25
13..................	1.10	14.30	15.00	−.70
23..................	.85	19.55	18.25	+1.30
38..................	.69	25.92	22.00	+3.92
50..................	.615	30.75	26.25	+4.50
60..................	.55	33.00	31.00	+2.00
68..................	.50	34.00	36.25	−2.25
75..................	.45	33.75	42.00	−8.25
81..................	.40	32.40	48.25	−15.85
86..................	.35	30.10	55.00	−25.10

FIGURE 9.4.1

Profit Maximization by the Total Revenue–Total Cost Approach

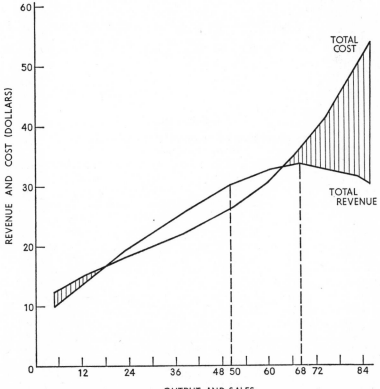

The table and graph are almost self-explanatory. One should note that maximum profit ($4.50) is attained at 50 units of output and sales. By reference to Table 9.3.1, this rate of output is less than that associated with minimum unit cost. Similarly, it is less than the maximum revenue output; and it is also less than the rate of output (somewhat greater than 60) for which price equals marginal cost. The latter condition is the "rule" for profit maximization under perfect competition. But it does not hold for monopoly, as the *marginal* approach makes clear.

9.4.b Marginal Revenue–Marginal Cost Approach

Since all underlying concepts have been introduced, this section begins with a continuation of the example previously used. Table 9.4.2 provides the relevant data, shown graphically in Figure 9.4.2.

Under monopoly, maximum profit is attained at that rate of output and sales for which marginal cost equals marginal revenue. The hypothetical data in Table 9.4.2 clearly illustrate this proposition. For a proof, however, the continuous case represented by Figure 9.4.3 is used.

Marginal cost and marginal revenue are given by curves of customary shape, intersecting at point E. We wish to prove that producing output $O\overline{q}$ associated with this intersection leads to maximum profit or minimum loss. The method of attack is "proof by contradiction." Suppose $O\overline{q}$ were not the profit-maximizing output. First, assume that it is less than $O\overline{q}$—say, Oq_l. At that point marginal cost is OA and

TABLE 9.4.2

**Marginal Revenue–Marginal Cost Approach to
Profit Maximization**

Output and Sales	Price	Total Revenue	Total Cost	Marginal Revenue	Marginal Cost	Profit
5	$2.00	$10.00	$12.25	—	$0.45	$-2.25
13	1.10	14.30	15.00	$0.54	.34	−.70
23	.85	19.55	18.25	.52	.33	+1.30
38	.69	25.92	22.00	.42	.25	+3.92
50	.615	30.75	26.25	.35	.35	+4.50
60	.55	33.00	31.00	.23	.48	+2.00
68	.50	34.00	36.25	.13	.66	−2.25
75	.45	33.75	42.00	−.03	.82	−8.25
81	.40	32.40	48.25	−.23	1.04	−15.85
86	.35	30.10	55.00	−.46	1.35	−25.10

FIGURE 9.4.2

Profit Maximization by the Marginal Revenue–Marginal Cost Approach

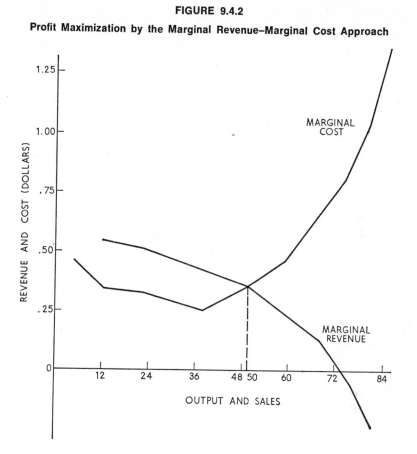

marginal revenue is $OB > OA$. Hence adding a unit to output and sales will increase total revenue by more than it increases total cost. Therefore profit can be expanded, or loss reduced, by expanding output from the rate Oq_l. And this statement must hold for *any* output less than $O\overline{q}$ since $MR > MC$ over the entire range from O to $O\overline{q}$.

Next, suppose the profit-maximizing output were greater than $O\overline{q}$ —say, Oq_h. At this point marginal revenue is OC and marginal cost is $OD > OC$. At this rate of output an additional unit of output and sales adds more to total cost than to total revenue. Profit is accordingly diminished or loss augmented. Further, this must hold for *any* output greater than $O\overline{q}$ because $MC > MR$ over that entire range of output.

Since the profit-maximizing output can neither exceed nor be less than $O\overline{q}$, the following proposition is established:[6]

---

[6] Let the monopolist's demand function in inverse form be $p = f(q)$ and let his cost be $C = C(q)$. Thus profit (π) is

FIGURE 9.4.3

Proof of *MC* = *MR* Theorem for Profit Maximization

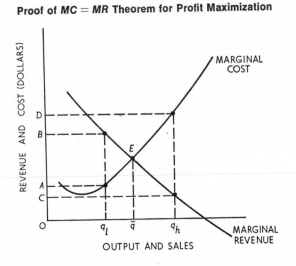

Proposition: A monopolist, or any other producer, will maximize profit or minimize loss by producing and marketing that output for which marginal cost equals marginal revenue. Whether a profit or loss is made depends upon the relation between price and average total cost.

$$\pi = qf(q) - C(q).$$ (9.6.1)

The first-order condition for profit maximization requires that the first derivative of expression (9.6.1) equal zero, or

$$d\pi/dq = f(q) + qf'(q) - C'(q) = 0.$$ (9.6.2)

Marginal revenue is $d[qf(q)]/dq = f(q) + qf'(q)$. Similarly, marginal cost is $dC/dq = C'(q)$. Hence expression (9.6.2) gives the profit-maximization rule stated in the text.

For a true local maximum, the second derivative of expression (9.6.1) must be less than zero. That is, the second-order condition requires that

$$d^2\pi/dq^2 = 2f'(q) + qf''(q) - C''(q) < 0.$$ (9.6.3)

The first two terms give the slope of the marginal revenue curve while $C''(q)$ is the slope of the marginal cost curve. The second-order condition requires that the slope of the marginal revenue curve be less than the slope of the marginal cost curve (with respect to the quantity axis). Given a negatively sloped marginal revenue curve the condition is obviously satisfied when marginal cost is positively sloped. However, monopoly differs from perfect competition in that the marginal cost curve may be negatively sloped at the profit-maximizing point provided its slope is less steep (absolute value of slope is less) than that of marginal revenue.

Note: While very rare, certain segments of commodity demand curves may give rise to positively sloped marginal revenue curves. The student may verify, for example, that the demand curve $p = q + \dfrac{a}{q}$ ($a > q^2$) gives rise to a positively sloped marginal revenue curve.

9.4.c Short-Run Equilibrium

Using the proposition just established, the position of short-run equilibrium under monopoly is easily described. Figure 9.4.4 is a graphical representation. The revenue side is given by the demand and marginal revenue curves, D and MR respectively. Costs are depicted by the average total cost and marginal cost curves, ATC and MC respectively.

The profit-maximization "rule" states that short-run equilibrium occurs at point E where marginal cost equals marginal revenue. The associated price and output are $O\overline{P}$ and $O\overline{Q}$. At the rate of output $O\overline{Q}$, average total or unit cost is $O\overline{C}$ ($= \overline{Q}B$). Profit per unit is $O\overline{P} - O\overline{C}$ $= \overline{PC}$. Thus short run monopoly profit is $\overline{PC} \times O\overline{Q} = \overline{P}AB\overline{C}$. It is thus represented by the area of the shaded rectangle in Figure 9.4.4.

In the example of Figure 9.4.4, the monopolist earns a pure profit in the short run, just as a perfect competitor may. If demand is sufficiently low relative to cost he may also incur a loss, just as a perfect competitor may. In the short run the primary difference between monopoly and perfect competition lies in the slope of the demand curve. Either may earn a pure economic profit; either may incur a loss. Other comparisons are difficult. If it happened that Figure 9.4.4 also exactly represented a perfect competitor with horizontal demand curve intersecting MC at point F, one could say that price would be lower and the output greater under perfect competition than under monopoly.

This type of comparison is very risky, however, because it involves

FIGURE 9.4.4   Short-Run Equilibrium under Monopoly

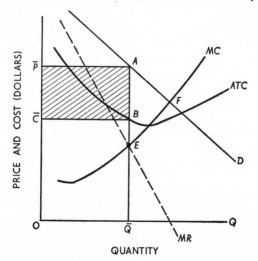

all sorts of assumptions concerning the behavior of cost as plant size expands or contracts. In particular, one must assume that *MC* somehow represents competitive supply. But as we have already seen, the competitive supply curve usually cannot be taken as the sum of individual marginal cost or supply curves. As a consequence, short-run comparisons are fraught with danger. About the best that can be said is that a monopolist is more likely to earn a pure profit in the short run because he can effectively exercise some market control.

9.4.d Monopoly Supply in the Short Run

We previously indicated that "monopoly supply" has a much less precise meaning than "competitive supply." The analysis of this section will make the reasons clear.

Suppose the market demand curve for a monopolist is fixed and gives rise to the marginal revenue curve constructed in Figure 9.4.5. Given the marginal cost curve *MC*, equilibrium output is $O\overline{Q}$, corresponding to the intersection of *MC* and *MR*. Further, suppose the demand curve is such as to establish the equilibrium market price $O\overline{P}$. One can definitely say that point *S* is one point on the monopoly supply curve. But that is about all that can be said. The monopoly supply curve is certainly not $\overline{Q}S$, because the monopolist would produce and market $O\overline{Q}$ units only at the price $O\overline{P}$. One might regard $\overline{P}S$ as the monopoly supply curve because the monopolist would supply any amount up to $O\overline{Q}$ units at the price $O\overline{P}$. However, this is also fictitious because the level $O\overline{P}$ is established prior to the line $\overline{P}S$ by the $MC = MR$ rule. For stationary demand and cost conditions, monopoly supply is best regarded as the single point *S*.

FIGURE 9.4.5 Short-Run Monopoly Supply with Fixed Demand

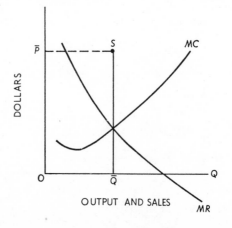

If demand shifts while the cost curves remain unchanged one can construct a monopoly supply curve. But note that it does not have the meaning of a competitive supply curve, which is based entirely on prevailing cost conditions. In perfect competition one can define a unique "supply price" for each quantity: q units will be supplied for \$$x$ per unit (or more). In monopoly, supply price is not unique. A given quantity would be supplied at different prices, depending upon market demand and marginal revenue.

This point will become clearer after a discussion of Figure 9.4.6. In panel a, there is one stationary marginal cost curve MC. Suppose demand is D_1, with the associated marginal revenue curve MR_1. Equilibrium is attained at point e_1, with output OQ_1 at price OP_1. This price-output pair is plotted in panel b as the point E_1. Next, suppose demand shifts to D_2 with marginal revenue MR_2. Equilibrium now shifts to e_2 with output OQ_2 and price OP_2. The latter price-output pair is plotted in panel b as point E_2. Connecting all points such as E_1 and E_2 generated by a particular pattern of demand shifts, one obtains the curve labeled SS in panel b.

SS may be regarded as a monopoly supply curve for the *particular set of demand shifts*. But if demand had shifted differently there would have been a different set of supply prices and a correspondingly different supply curve. For example, if demand had shifted to D_2' instead of D_2, quantity supplied would nonetheless be OQ_2, because MR_2' inter-

FIGURE 9.4.6 Monopoly Supply with Shifting Demand

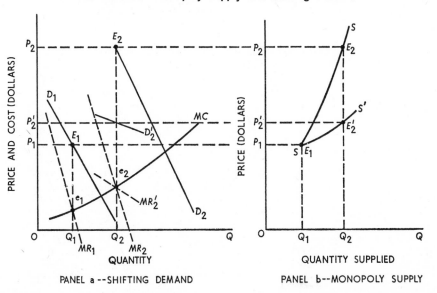

PANEL a --SHIFTING DEMAND   PANEL b--MONOPOLY SUPPLY

sects *MC* at that rate of output. Price, however, would be $OP_2' < OP_2$; and the associated point on panel b would be E_2'. The supply curve based on this set of demand shifts would be SS', which is significantly different from *SS*.

In summary:

Relations: For stationary demand and cost conditions short-run monopoly supply is best regarded as a single point in the *P–Q* plane. If demand shifts while cost conditions remain stationary, a monopoly supply curve can be constructed. But the curve depends upon the precise set of demand shifts. In neither case does monopoly supply have the clear and exact meaning that competitive supply has; and the concept of supply price is entirely meaningless in monopoly.

9.4.e Multiplant Monopoly in the Short Run

The discussion has so far been based upon the implicit assumption that a monopolist owns and produces by means of only one plant. This, however, is not necessarily the case. The monopolist may operate more than one plant, and cost conditions may differ from one plant to another. A hypothetical two-plant example is given in Table 9.4.3 and illustrated graphically in Figure 9.4.7.

The first three columns of Table 9.4.3 provide the revenue data, while the last three contain the relevant cost data. The marginal costs of plants 1 and 2 are shown in columns 4 and 5, and they are plotted in panel a, Figure 9.4.7. Similarly, demand and marginal revenue are plotted in panel b. The final column, "Monopoly Marginal Cost," is derived from the marginal cost curves of the individual plants.

TABLE 9.4.3

Profit Maximization in a Multiplant Monopoly

Output and Sales	Price	Marginal Revenue	Marginal Cost Plant #1	Marginal Cost Plant #2	Monopoly Marginal Cost
1............	$5.00	$ —	$1.92	$2.04	$1.92
2............	4.50	4.00	2.00	2.14	2.00
3............	4.10	3.30	2.08	2.24	2.04
4............	3.80	2.90	2.16	2.34	2.08
5............	3.55	2.55	2.24	2.44	2.14
6............	3.35	2.35	2.32	2.54	2.16
7............	3.20	2.30	2.40	2.64	2.24
8............	3.08	2.24	2.48	2.74	2.24
9............	2.98	2.18	2.56	2.84	2.32
10............	2.89	2.08	2.64	2.94	2.34

If output is expanded from zero to one, the one unit should clearly be produced in plant 1, whose marginal cost is \$1.92 ($<$\$2.04 in plant 2). Hence marginal cost for the multiplant monopoly is \$1.92. If output is to be two units, both should be produced in plant 1 because its marginal cost for the second unit (\$2) is less than the marginal cost of producing one unit in plant 2. Hence monopoly marginal cost for two units is \$2. If three units of output are to be produced, however, plant 2 should enter production because its marginal cost for the first unit (\$2.04) is less than the marginal cost of the third unit in plant 1. By producing two units in plant 1 and one unit in plant 2, the multiplant monopoly has a marginal cost of \$2.04 for the third unit. Column 6, "Monopoly Marginal Cost," is derived by continuing this line of reasoning for each successive unit of output.

Monopoly marginal cost is plotted in panel b, Figure 9.4.7. It intersects marginal revenue at point E, corresponding to eight units of output and market price of \$3.08. By the $MC = MR$ rule, this price-output combination is the one for which monopoly profit is a maximum. The problem faced by the monopolist is the allocation of production between plants 1 and 2.

First, observe that $MC = MR = \$2.24$ at the equilibrium point. A horizontal dashed line at the \$2.24 level has been extended from panel

FIGURE 9.4.7

Short-Run Profit Maximization for a Multiplant Monopoly

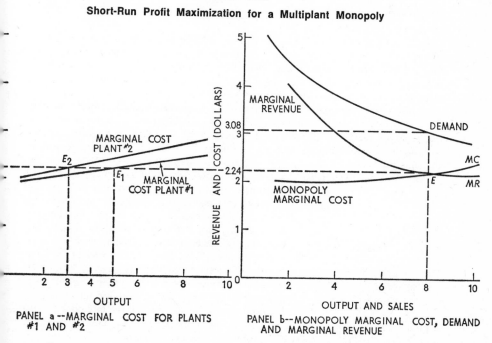

PANEL a --MARGINAL COST FOR PLANTS #1 AND #2

PANEL b--MONOPOLY MARGINAL COST, DEMAND AND MARGINAL REVENUE b to panel a. The line intersects the plant marginal cost curves at E_1 and E_2, the points at which $MC_1 = MC_2 = MC = MR$. The associated outputs are five units for plant 1 and three units for plant 2; their combined quantity is precisely eight units, the profit-maximizing output. Thus the monopolist allocates production to his plants by equating plant marginal cost with the common value of monopoly marginal cost and marginal revenue at the equilibrium output.

Generalizing, we obtain the following

Proposition: A multiplant monopolist maximizes profit by producing that output for which monopoly marginal cost equals marginal revenue. Optimal allocation of production among the various plants requires each plant to produce that rate of output for which the plant marginal cost is equal to the common value of monopoly marginal cost and marginal revenue at the monopoly equilibrium output.

9.5 LONG-RUN EQUILIBRIUM UNDER MONOPOLY

A monopoly exists if, and only if, there is only one firm in the market. Among other things this statement implies that *entrance* into the market is not possible. Thus whether or not a monopolist earns a pure profit in the short run, no other producer can enter the market in the hope of sharing whatever pure profit exists. Therefore, pure economic profit is not eliminated in the long run, as it is in the case of perfect competition.[7]

---

[7] Certain economists prefer to say that in the long run pure profit does not exist irrespective of the type of market organization (whether perfectly competitive, monopolistic, etc.). They contend that the monopoly position or the monopoly-causing "ingredient" should be capitalized, thereby increasing total cost by the amount of the pure profit that would otherwise exist (in the absence of capitalization). This is a perfectly defensible argument; however, the interpretation used in the text is retained to facilitate comparisons among long-run equilibria under various types of market organization. If the no-profit approach is preferred by the student, he should compare long-run equilibria in terms of differential returns to the same inputs.

The way in which LAC changes when monopoly profit is capitalized may be illustrated graphically. In the figure, LAC is the "regular" envelope curve. Suppose revenue conditions are such that the monopolist earns only the competitive rate of profit at OQ_1 and OQ_2. For outputs less than OQ_1 or greater than OQ_2, the monopolist incurs a pure economic loss. Then LAC' indicates the "monopoly profit capitalized" long-run average cost curve. Note that it must lie *below* the usual long-run average cost curve when the monopolist incurs a pure loss, and it must lie above when the monopolist reaps a pure long-run profit. Thus it must equal the usual LAC at the points where the monopolist earns the going rate of profit that prevails in competitive industries.

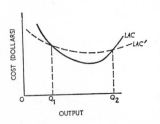

9.5.a Long-Run Equilibrium in a Single-Plant Monopoly

Long-run equilibrium adjustment in a single-plant monopoly must take one of two possible courses. First, if the monopolist incurs a short-run loss and if there is no plant size that will result in pure profit (or at least, no loss), the monopolist goes out of business. Second, if he earns a short-run profit with his original plant, he must determine whether a plant of different size (and thus a different price and output) will enable him to earn a larger profit.

The first situation requires no comment. The second is illustrated by Figure 9.5.1. DD' and MR show the market demand and marginal revenue confronting a monopolist. LAC is his long-run envelope cost curve (see Chapter 7), and LMC is the associated long-run marginal cost curve. Suppose in the initial period the monopolist builds the plant represented by SAC_1 and SMC_1. Equality of short-run marginal cost and marginal revenue leads to the sale of $O\overline{Q}_{SR}$ units at the price OA. At this rate of output unit cost is $OD = \overline{Q}_{SR}C$; short-run monopoly profit is represented by the area of the shaded rectangle $ABCD$.

Since a pure economic profit can be reaped, the monopolist would

FIGURE 9.5.1

Long-Run Equilibrium for a Single-plant Monopolist

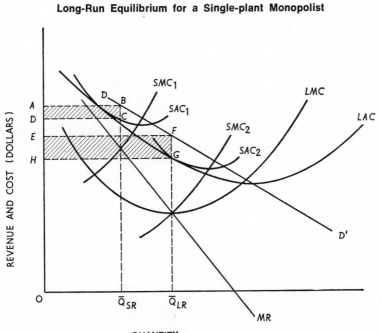

not consider going out of business. However he would search for a more profitable long-run organization. To this end, long-run marginal cost becomes the relevant consideration. By an argument analogous to the one used in subsection 9.4.b to establish the $MC = MR$ rule, the profit-maximum *maximorum* is attained when long-run marginal cost equals marginal revenue. The associated rate of output is $O\overline{Q}_{LR}$, and price is OE.

By reference to LAC, the plant capable of producing $O\overline{Q}_{LR}$ units per period at the least unit cost is the one represented by SAC_2 and SMC_2. Unit cost is accordingly OH, and long-run maximum monopoly profit is given by the area of the shaded rectangle $EFGH$. This profit is obviously (visually) greater than the profit obtainable from the original plant.

Generalizing, we have the following

Proposition: A monopolist maximizes profit in the long run by producing and marketing that rate of output for which long-run marginal cost equals marginal revenue. The optimal plant is the one whose short-run average total cost curve is tangent to the long-run average cost curve at the point corresponding to long-run equilibrium output. At this point short-run marginal cost equals marginal revenue.

The organization described by the proposition above is the best the monopolist can attain; and he *can* attain it because in the long run his plant size is variable and the market is effectively closed to entry.

9.5.b Comparison with Perfect Competition

The long-run equilibrium positions of a monopolist and a perfect competitor are somewhat more comparable than their short-run equilibria. The comparison is based upon the graphical illustrations of long-run equilibrium in Figures 8.6.3 and 9.5.1.

First, under perfect competition production occurs at the point of minimum long- and short-run average cost. While the monopolist utilizes the plant capable of producing his long-run equilibrium output at the least unit cost, this plant is not the one associated with absolute minimum unit cost (for any output).[8] Thus in a sense to be described more fully in Chapter 16, society's limited resources are used relatively more efficiently in perfectly competitive markets than in monopoly markets.[9]

Second, the perfect competitor produces at the point where marginal cost and price are equal. For the monopolist, price exceeds marginal cost by a substantial amount. Under certain conditions,[10] demand represents the marginal *social* valuation of a commodity by the members of the society. Similarly, long-run marginal cost usually represents the marginal *social* cost of production. Under monopoly, the marginal *value* of a commodity to society exceeds the marginal cost of its production to society. The society as a whole would therefore benefit by having more of its resources used in producing the commodity in question. The profit-maximizing monopolist will not do so, however, for producing at the point where price equals marginal cost would eliminate all, or almost all, of his profit. Indeed, he might incur a loss. Therefore, all other things equal, social welfare tends to be promoted more by competitive than by monopolistic market organization.

---

[8] Of course, the demand curve *could* be such that marginal revenue intersects long-run marginal cost at the point where the latter intersects the long-run average cost curve. In this instance the single-plant monopolist would produce at minimum long-run unit cost. Such a case would indeed be rare, and the slightest change in demand would upset it.

[9] This statement is concerned with relative economic efficiency and ignores the fact that cost comparisons between monopoly and perfect competition are *generally impossible*. Comparison is possible if the industry in question is truly a constant-cost industry, for minimum long-run average cost is attained at the same level irrespective of the scale of operation. On the other hand, comparisons are not valid for long-run decreasing- or increasing-cost industries.

[10] The exceptions are noted in Chapter 16.

9.5.c Long-Run Equilibrium in a Multiplant Monopoly

In the long run a multiplant monopolist adjusts the number of plants to attain equilibrium. The process is illustrated in Figure 9.5.2.

FIGURE 9.5.2

Long-Run Equilibrium in a Multiplant Monopoly

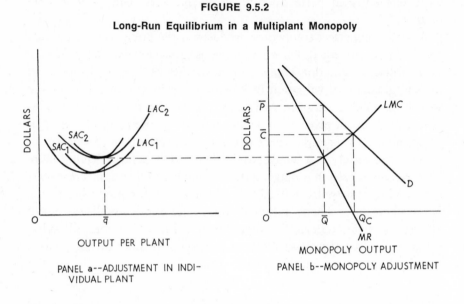

OUTPUT PER PLANT

PANEL a--ADJUSTMENT IN INDI-
VIDUAL PLANT

MONOPOLY OUTPUT

PANEL b--MONOPOLY ADJUSTMENT

The adjustment of each individual plant is shown in panel a. Irrespective of original plant size, in the long run the monopolist can construct *each* plant of such size that short-run average cost coincides with long-run average cost at the minimum point on the latter curve. In other words, he can construct each plant of such size that the desired rate of output per plant can be produced at the irreducible minimum unit cost. But as he expands output by expanding the number of plants operating at minimum long-run average cost, the cost curves for each plant shift upward. This must be true because input prices increase with input usage (that is, one must presume that if *all* resources used were unspecialized, there would be a competitive market organization).

In Chapter 8 this type of situation was discussed. In that case we said the competitive industry was an increasing cost industry, and we showed how to construct the long-run supply curve (or curve showing the long-run supply price). A similar curve can be constructed for the multiplant monopolist; but it does *not* relate to long-run supply or long-run run supply price (long-run supply, as well as short-run supply, is not well defined in the case of monopoly). To the monopolist this curve is his long-run marginal cost curve because it shows the *minimum increase in cost* attributable to an expansion of output by expanding the number of optimally adjusted plants (i.e., plants operating at minimum long-run average cost).

The long-run marginal cost curve thus derived is labeled *LMC* in panel b. The revenue conditions are shown by *D* and *MR*. Invoking the *LMC = MR* rule, long-run profit maximizing equilibrium is attained at an output of $O\overline{Q}$ units per period and a price of $O\overline{P}$. The optimum output per plant is $O\overline{q}$. The number of plants n_m the monopolist constructs and utilizes is $n_m = O\overline{Q}/O\overline{q}$.

9.5.d Comparison with Perfect Competition

In the long run both perfectly competitive firms and multiplant monopolists operate their plants at minimum long- and short-run unit cost. In this respect they are alike. Their differences will become clear by considering an hypothetical case.

Suppose each firm in a perfectly competitive industry is represented by panel a, Figure 9.5.2. Then long-run industry equilibrium would occur at OQ_c in panel b, where demand equals long-run supply. The associated market price is $O\overline{C}$, and the equilibrium number of firms n_c is presumably greater than n_m, the number of plants operated by the multiplant monopolist.

Next, suppose all firms are bought by the same individual, who creates an effective monopoly. As shown before, the monopolist will produce $O\overline{Q}$ units and sell them at $O\overline{P}$ each. He would require only $n_m < n_c$ plants; he would accordingly scrap the superfluous plants (in number, $n_c - n_m$). Thus while either organization would be characterized by minimum-cost production, in comparison with the perfectly competitive industry, the multiplant monopolist would sell fewer units, charge a higher price, and operate fewer plants. In this case, as in the case of a single-plant monopoly, social welfare tends to be promoted to a greater extent by competition than by monopoly.

9.6 SPECIAL TOPICS IN MONOPOLY THEORY

Sections 9.1 through 9.5 comprise the theory of price under conditions of monopoly. In this concluding section two special types of monopoly organization are discussed.

9.6.a Price Discrimination

Certain commodities are purchased by two or more distinct types of buyers. For example, commercial and residential purchasers of electric power can usually be sharply divided on the basis of demand elasticity. Similarly, tourists and traveling salesmen constitute two different types of markets for motel accommodations. If a monopolist possesses a market divisible in this manner and if he can effectively separate it, he may practice *discriminatory pricing* to augment his monopoly profit.

Price discrimination occurs when different prices are charged for the same commodity in different markets. The analysis of discriminatory pricing is a straightforward application of the $MR = MC$ rule; but in a sense it is diametrically opposite to the application of the rule to multiplant monopoly. In the latter, plant marginal cost curves are aggregated to obtain the monopoly marginal cost, which is equated to marginal revenue. In price discrimination, submarket marginal revenue curves are aggregated to obtain the monopoly marginal revenue, to which marginal cost is equated.

For simplicity, consider the case in which a general market can be separated into two distinct submarkets. Panel a, Figure 9.6.1, shows de-

FIGURE 9.6.1

Market Conditions Leading to Price Discrimination

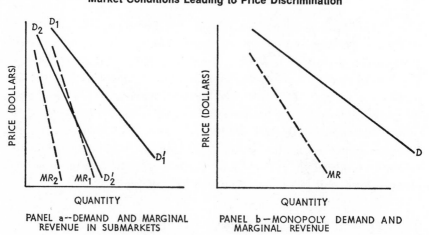

PANEL a--DEMAND AND MARGINAL REVENUE IN SUBMARKETS

PANEL b—MONOPOLY DEMAND AND MARGINAL REVENUE

mand ($D_1 D_1'$, $D_2 D_2'$) and marginal revenue (MR_1, MR_2) for submarkets one and two respectively. Aggregating the demand and marginal revenue curves horizontally yields the market demand and marginal revenue curves shown in panel b. The allocation of sales between the two markets is the basic problem encountered by the price-discriminating monopolist.

Suppose, for the moment, that the monopolist has somehow correctly allocated the sale of q units. Next, suppose he decides to expand output and sales to $q + 1$ units. In which market should the additional unit be sold? The answer should be obvious: the additional unit should be sold so as to increase total revenue by the greatest possible amount. This will occur, of course, if the unit is sold in the market with the higher marginal revenue corresponding to the prior allocation of the q units.

Generalizing, the total output to be sold should be allocated between the two markets in such a way that marginal revenue is the same in both markets. If marginal revenue were higher in market 1 than in market 2, for example, the monopolist could augment his profit by shifting some units from market 2 to market 1. Maximum profit is obtained only when marginal revenue is the same in both markets.

This argument establishes the basis of allocating a given volume of sales between two markets. It also permits an easy explanation of the fundamental market condition required for profitable and meaningful price discrimination. Recall that marginal revenue may be expressed in the following way:

$$MR = p\left(1 - \frac{1}{\eta}\right),$$

where p is price and η is the elasticity of demand. As just shown, MR must be the same in each market. If η were also the same in each market, p would necessarily be the same. In this case the two sub-markets would be indistinguishable since all revenue-connected magnitudes are the same. Consequently, profitable price discrimination requires that the elasticity of demand differ between the two markets.

As has been said, the first problem confronting a price-discriminating monopolist is the allocation of a given level of sales between his markets. The second problem is determining the optimal level of sales and, therefore, the level of price in each of the submarkets. For this calculation cost data are required.

In Figure 9.6.2, AC and MC represent the (aggregate) unit and marginal cost of producing the monopolized output. D_1D_1' and D_2D_2' are the submarket demand curves; MR_1 and MR_2 are the corresponding marginal revenue curves. Aggregating the two marginal revenue curves, just as we previously aggregated plant marginal costs, the monopoly

FIGURE 9.6.2

Profit Maximization with Price Discrimination

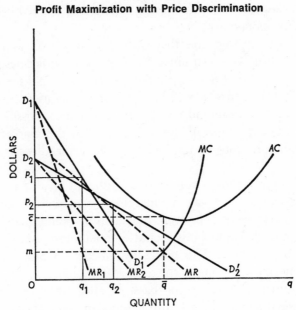

marginal revenue curve MR is obtained. Next, invoking the $MC = MR$ rule, the profit-maximizing output is $O\bar{q}$ units. The marginal revenue associated with this output is Om.

The market allocation rule, previously determined, requires that marginal revenue be the same in each submarket. Thus Oq_1 units are sold in market 1 and Oq_2 units in market 2 $(Oq_1 + Oq_2 = O\bar{q})$. Furthermore, given the submarket demand curves, the price in each submarket is determined. A price of Op_1 per unit is charged in market 1, and Op_2 per unit is charged in market 2.

At any given output it is visually apparent that demand is more elastic in market 2 than in market 1. Using this information in conjunction with the results above brings out an interesting, albeit rather obvious, point: the more elastic the submarket demand the lower the equilibrium price in the submarket.[11] Among other things, this principle

---

[11] This proposition is easily proved. First, recall that marginal revenue may always be written as

$$MR = p\left(1 - \frac{1}{\eta}\right).$$
(9.11.1)

Next, since marginal revenue must be equal in both markets, we have

$$MR_1 = MR_2,$$
(9.11.2)

accounts for the price differential favoring commercial, as against residential, users of electrical power.

Summarizing these results:

Proposition: If the aggregate market for a monopolist's product can be divided into submarkets with different price elasticities, the monopolist can profitably practice price discrimination. Total output is determined by equating marginal cost with aggregate monopoly marginal revenue. The output is allocated among the submarkets so as to equate marginal revenue in each submarket with aggregate marginal revenue at the $MR = MC$ point. Finally, price in each submarket is determined directly from the submarket demand curve, given the submarket allocaton of sales.

9.6.b Bilateral Monopoly

The final special topic, bilateral monopoly, is analyzed chiefly to explain the meaning of *indeterminacy* in economics. Our general conclusion is that price and quantity is *indeterminate* in cases of bilateral monopoly. This does not mean that the market collapses or that the parties fail to reach a definite agreement on price and quantity. Rather it means the information the economist has is not sufficient to determine the precise market solution. The solution, in other words, is based not only upon conditions of demand and cost, with which the economist can deal, but also upon bargaining skills and other personal characteristics anterior to the realm of economic analysis.

A bilateral monopoly is said to exist when one producer has an output monopoly and there is only one buyer for the product (a purchase monopoly). Thus a bilateral monopoly would exist if there were only one copper-mining firm and one brass manufacturer in the world. This example is somewhat fanciful; however, the situation is sometimes approximated quite closely in the real world. A "one-mill" town with

---

where subscripts denote the market. Using expression (9.11.1) in expression (9.11.2), we obtain

$$p_1\left(1 - \frac{1}{\eta_1}\right) = p_2\left(1 - \frac{1}{\eta_2}\right). \tag{9.11.3}$$

Let market one be characterized by the higher price elasticity of demand. Hence,

$$\eta_1 > \eta_2,$$

and thus

$$\left(1 - \frac{1}{\eta_1}\right) > \left(1 - \frac{1}{\eta_2}\right).$$

Using the latter inequality in expression (9.11.3), equality between the left- and right-hand sides requires $p_2 > p_1$.

an effective labor union, while not exactly a bilateral monopoly situation, is very close to being one.

Bilateral monopoly is analyzed by means of Figure 9.6.3. D is the

FIGURE 9.6.3

Bilateral Monopoly

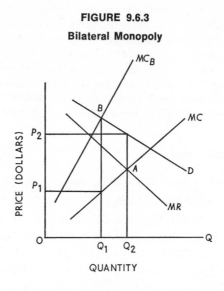

demand curve of the single buyer in the market; hence D and MR are the demand and marginal revenue curves confronting the monopolistic seller. Similarly, MC is the marginal cost curve of the single producer. MC and MR intersect at point A; hence the output monopolist wishes to sell OQ_2 units at a price of OP_2 per unit. If he could do so, his profit from operation would be maximized.

If the output monopolist could force the single buyer to behave as though he were a buyer in a large and impersonal market, he could do so. But in this situation the single buyer realizes his potential power as a buying monopolist. In the limit, if the single buyer could control the market completely he could make the output monopolist behave as if he were a perfect competitor. Then MC would be the supply curve as well as the marginal cost curve. If it were, the curve marginal to MC, labeled MC_B, would be the *marginal cost of buying* an additional unit.[12]

Optimally, the single buyer would like to equate his marginal valuation of the product (given by his demand curve) with the marginal cost of purchasing. He would strive to attain point B with the purchase

---

[12] With necessary verbal changes to allow for the difference between buying products and hiring inputs, MC_B in Figure 9.6.3 is entirely analogous to the marginal expense of input curve in Figure 9.3.1.

of OQ_1 units at a price of OP_1 (determined by the MC equals potential supply curve) per unit. If a large number of producers were in the market, or if he could get the monopolist to act as if he were a perfect competitor, he could do so.

However, the single buyer can no more induce the output monopolist to act as a perfectly competitive producer than the single seller can induce the purchase monopolist to act as a perfectly competitive buyer. Each realizes the situation that exists and tries to do his best. The economist cannot determine the solution. He can say the "best" the output monopolist can do is to sell OQ_2 units at OP_2 per unit. Similarly, the "best" the purchase monopolist can do is to buy OQ_1 units at OP_1 per unit. Neither extreme is likely to materialize. Output will lie somewhere between OQ_1 and OQ_2 and price somewhere between OP_1 and OP_2. The precise result is determined by factors beyond the purview of economic analysis.

Exercise: In Chapter 7 there was an exercise concerning the short-run effect of featherbedding on the cost curves of a firm. Now suppose a monopolist is suddenly confronted with a featherbedding contract and, merely for simplicity, assume that there is no change in the wage rate (only in the number of union workers employed). (*i*) Assuming profit maximization by the monopolist, what will be the direction of change in his price and output? (*ii*) Assume that the monopolist expects the featherbedding contract to be permanent. What type of long-run changes is he likely to make?

QUESTIONS

1. Federal Milk Marketing Orders, covering most metropolitan areas, impose a specified price to be paid dairy farmers for milk used for industrial purposes (e.g., in making cheese, ice cream, etc.) and a higher price for milk used for direct consumption (i.e., drinking).

    a)   Does such an arrangement affect the returns to the dairy farming industry?

    b)   How do the Marketing Orders affect the allocation of resources and economic welfare of the community?

2. In a Consent Decree signed in the mid-1950's, IBM agreed to sell, as well as rent, various business machines. IBM also agreed to dispose of the facilities used to produce punch cards that were required to operate the machines and agreed further that IBM would no longer sell punch cards. Firms renting IBM machines formerly had to buy their punch cards from IBM. At this time IBM owned 90 percent of all machines in its field. What effect would prohibiting the producing and selling of punch cards have on IBM's pricing policy for machines?

3. In a number of university towns, college professors receive discounts

from the local bookstores, usually about 10 percent. Students are generally not given similar discounts. Assuming that this practice constitutes price discrimination, what conditions make it feasible and desirable for the stores?

4. Some time ago, most of the major airlines issued student travel cards at a nominal price. These cards permit college students to fly "space available" (i.e., no reservations allowed) at substantial discounts. All but one of these lines are now wondering whether this strategy has really paid off; older non-students have been found using the cards, and some students have been insuring themselves available space by reserving seats for fictitious passengers who then do not show up for the flight.

a) Do the discounts represent price discrimination?

b) Do the conditions necessary for successful discrimination exist?

5. From 1923 to 1946, Du Pont was virtually the sole American producer of "moistureproof Cellophane," a product for which it held the key patents. In its opinion, which exonerated Du Pont of possessing any economically meaningful monopoly, the Supreme Court held "an appraisal of the 'cross-elasticity' of demand in the trade" to be of considerable importance to the decision. Why?

SUGGESTED READINGS

Allen, R. G. D. *Mathematical Analysis for Economists,* chap. 18. London: Macmillan & Co., Ltd., 1956. [Elementary math required.]

Hicks, J. R. "Annual Survey of Economic Theory: The Theory of Monopoly," *Econometrica,* Vol. III (1936), pp. 1–20. [Elementary math required.]

Machlup, Fritz. *The Political Economy of Monopoly.* Baltimore: Johns Hopkins Press, 1952.

——. *The Economics of Sellers' Competition,* pp. 543–66. Baltimore: Johns Hopkins Press, 1952.

Robinson, Joan. *The Economics of Imperfect Competition,* pp. 47–82. London: Macmillan & Co., Ltd., 1933.

Samuelson, Paul A. *Foundations of Economic Analysis,* pp. 57–89. Cambridge, Mass.: Harvard University Press, 1947. [Advanced math required.]

Simkin, C. G. F. "Some Aspects and Generalizations of the Theory of Discrimination," *Review of Economic Studies,* Vol. XV (1948–49), pp. 1–13. [Advanced math required.]

THEORY OF PRICE UNDER MONOPOLISTIC COMPETITION

10.1 INTRODUCTION

Chapters 8 and 9 dealt with the "pure" and "extreme" cases of perfect competition and monopoly. The two models are pure in that the analytical results are completely independent of personal influences, especially entrepreneurial expectations and speculation concerning the behavior of rivals. Indeed, there are no *rivals* in either perfect competition or monopoly. They are "extremes" from the standpoint of numbers and profit. In perfect competition the number of firms in an industry is indefinitely large, while at the opposite end of the "numbers" spectrum, monopoly is a one-firm industry. Similarly, zero economic profit per firm is the central characteristic of long-run equilibrium in perfect competition. In contrast, monopolization of a market guarantees the single firm a greater long-run pure profit than it could earn under any other organization of the market (that is, than if there were one or more rival firms in the market).

10.1.a Historical Perspective

With the exception of a few "naïve" duopoly theories, discussed in Chapter 11, the theories of perfect competition and monopoly constituted "classical" microeconomic theory from Marshall to Knight. In point of fact, the theory of perfect competition was not perfectly developed until the publication of Knight's *Risk, Uncertainty, and Profit.*[1] Stigler even argued that Knight's meticulous discussion of perfect competition, clearly pointing out the austere nature of the rigorously defined concept, caused a widespread reaction against the use of perfect competition as a model of economic behavior.[2] This is probably true; but

---

[1] London School Reprints of Scarce Works, No. 16 (1933).

[2] George J. Stigler, "Perfect Competition, Historically Contemplated," *Journal of Political Economy,* Vol. LXV (1957), pp. 1–17.

whatever the cause, in the late 1920's and early 1930's there was definitely a reaction against the use both of perfect competition and of pure monopoly as analytical models of business firms and market behavior.

A Cambridge economist, Piero Sraffa, was among the first to point out the limitations of "competition-or-monopoly" analysis;[3] he was soon followed by others. Hotelling emphasized that "the difference between the Standard Oil Company in its prime and the little corner grocery is quantitative rather than qualitative. Between the perfect competition and monopoly of theory lie the actual cases."[4] Similarly, Zeuthen urged that "neither monopoly nor competition are ever absolute, and the theories about them deal only with the outer margins of reality, which is always to be sought between them."[5]

In the late 1920's and early 1930's economists began turning their attention to the middle ground between monopoly and perfect competition. Two of the most notable achievements were attributable to an English economist, Joan Robinson,[6] and to an American, Edward Chamberlin.[7] Our attention in this chapter is directed toward Chamberlin's unique achievement.

10.1.b Product Differentiation

Chamberlin based his theory of "monopolistic competition" on a solid, empirical fact: there are very few monopolists because there are very few commodities for which close substitutes do not exist; similarly, there are very few commodities that are entirely homogeneous among producers. Instead, there is a wide range of commodities, some of which have relatively few good substitutes and some of which have many good, but not perfect, substitutes.

Let us begin with an example. The American Tobacco Company has an absolute monopoly in the manufacture and sale of Lucky Strike cigarettes. To be sure, another concern could manufacture identically

---

[3] Piero Sraffa, "The Laws of Returns under Competitive Conditions," *Economic Journal*, Vol. XXXVI (1926), pp. 535–50.

[4] Harold Hotelling, "Stability in Competition," *Economic Journal*, Vol. XXIX (1929), pp. 41–57; citation from p. 44.

[5] F. Zeuthen, *Problems of Monopoly and Economic Warfare* (London: Routledge, 1930), p. 62.

[6] Joan Robinson, *The Economics of Imperfect Competition* (London: Macmillan & Co., Ltd., 1933).

[7] E. H. Chamberlin, *The Theory of Monopolistic Competition* (6th ed.; Cambridge, Mass.: Harvard University Press, 1950).

the same cigarette; but it could *not* label the cigarette Lucky Strike. However, other concerns can manufacture cigarettes and call them Chesterfield, Camel, etc. Just as American Tobacco has an absolute monopoly of Lucky Strikes, Liggett and Myers has an absolute monopoly of Chesterfields, and Reynolds Tobacco has an absolute monopoly of Camel. Each concern has a monopoly over its own product; but the various brands are closely related goods and there is intense, *personal,* competition among the firms.

Two important points are to be gleaned from the example. First, the products are *heterogeneous* rather than homogeneous; hence perfect, and *impersonal,* competition cannot exist. Second, although heterogeneous, the products are only slightly differentiated. Each is a very close substitute for the other; hence competition exists but it is a *personal* competition among rivals who are well aware of each other.

This general type of market is characterized by product differentiation; and product differentiation, in turn, characterizes most American markets. There is not one homogeneous type of automobile; nor, for that matter, are there homogeneous types of soap, men's suits, television sets, grocery stores, magazines, or motels. Each producer tries to differentiate his product so as to make it unique; yet to be in the market at all his particular product must be closely related to the general product in question.

There are many ways of differentiating products, some quite real and others very spurious. In case of real product differentiation one can usually catalog the differences in terms of chemical composition, services offered by the sellers, horsepower, cost of inputs, and so on. In other cases—which many regard as spurious—product differentiation is based upon advertising outlays, difference in packaging material or design, brand name only (consider the aspirin market), and others.

In any event, when products are differentiated each product is unique and its producer has some degree of monopoly power he can exploit. But usually it is very little, because other producers can market a closely related commodity. It is not by chance that the selling price of cigarettes is almost uniform from brand to brand.

10.1.c Industries and Product Groups

In Chapter 8, an industry was defined as a collection of firms producing a homogeneous good. For example, by specifying clip, denier, and other characteristics of raw apparel wool, we can define the "raw apparel wool" industry. But when products are differentiated one cannot define an industry in this narrow sense. There is no "automobile" industry or "furniture" industry. Each firm having a distinct product is, in a sense, an industry in itself, exactly as a monopoly was described in Chapter 9. Nonetheless, one can usefully lump together firms producing very closely related commodities and refer to them as a *product group*. Thus hand soap, ready-to-eat cereal, or automobiles, for example, comprise instantly recognizable product groups, even though in our terminology they cannot be called industries.

Naturally enough, combining firms to make product groups is somewhat arbitrary. It is not possible to state precisely how "good" the substitutes must be. Chewing gum is a substitute for cigarettes, at least to people who are trying to quit smoking. But it is doubtful that anyone would place the Wrigley Company in the "cigarette" product group. "On the other hand, decaffeinated coffee is not a substitute for regular coffee for many people. Yet few would not place Sanka in the "coffee" product group.

Fortunately, at our level of abstraction precise distinction is not material. When "industry" is used perfect competition or monopoly is implied. When product differentiation is an important feature of the market, "product group" is used to denote the collection of firms, however combined, that produce some variety of the "product."

10.2 SHORT-RUN EQUILIBRIUM: MONOPOLY ASPECT OF MONOPOLISTIC COMPETITON

The theory of monopolistic competition is essentially a "long-run" theory. In the short run there is virtually no difference between the analysis of monopoly and of monopolistic competition. Each producer of a differentiated product behaves so as to maximize profit. If he knows his demand and marginal revenue curves, as in Figure 10.2.1, he equates marginal cost with marginal revenue. In the specific example of the figure, this lead to an output of $O\overline{Q}$ units per period and a price of $O\overline{P}$ per unit. In the resulting short-run equilibrium, pure profit is represented by the area of the shaded rectangle $\overline{P}AB\overline{C}$.

So far as the short run is concerned there appears to be very little *competition* in monopolistic competition. But when a longer view is taken one essential element of monopoly is missing. In particular, a monopoly cannot be maintained if there is free entry into the industry. Other firms will enter and produce the homogeneous product; and they

FIGURE 10.2.1

**Short-Run Equilibrium of the Firm
under Monopolistic Competition**

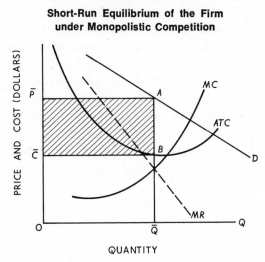

will continue to enter until all pure profit is eliminated or until the competitive solution is reached.

In the present case the product is differentiated, not homogeneous, so there is no "industry" to enter. But other firms are free to produce a closely related product; "entrance" into the product group is not closed.[8] If one or a few firms are obviously enjoying a highly prosperous situation, other firms will begin to produce a closely related product. They will "enter" the product group, as it were, and their entrance will have market repercussions not greatly different from the entrance of perfectly competitive firms into an industry.

10.3 LONG-RUN EQUILIBRIUM: COMPETITIVE ASPECTS OF MONOPOLISTIC COMPETITION

To follow Chamberlin's development of the theory of monopolistic competition it is necessary to distinguish between two types of demand curves. This is developed in the following subsection, after which we turn to the theory of long-run equilibrium under price and nonprice competition.

---

[8] Otherwise, we would classify the situation as oligopoly rather than monopolistic competition.

10.3.a Two Demand Curves

In the analysis of perfect competition two demand curves were used: the negatively sloped industry demand curve and the horizontal demand curve confronting each seller. As you will recall, the latter is horizontal because each producer of the *homogeneous product* must accept the going price or sell nothing at all. If he were to raise his price he would forfeit all sales. If he were to lower it he would needlessly forfeit some revenue.

The two curves required for the theory of monopolistic competition, shown in Figure 10.3.1, are very similar. Suppose the firm in question is

FIGURE 10.3.1

Two Demand Curves

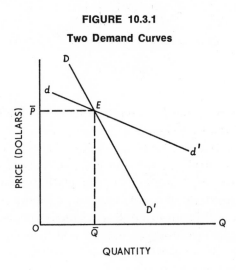

instantaneously situated at the point E, with output $O\overline{Q}$ and price $O\overline{P}$ per unit. Suppose further that the entrepreneur contemplates price maneuvering in order to obtain greater profit.

One of Chamberlin's fundamental assumptions is that there is a large number of monopolistic competitors in each product group.[9] Another is that all firms in the group produce closely related and readily substitutable goods. Hence if the entrepreneur contemplates a price reduction from $O\overline{P}$, he will *expect* a substantial expansion in sales. First, sales to his existing clientele will expand. Second, and more important, if other

---

[9] Chamberlin also discusses the "small-group" equilibrium case, *op. cit.*, pp. 100–104; this is deferred at present since it is properly a part of oligopoly analysis.

entrepreneurs do not reduce price he will capture a part of their markets. Thus he can expect an appreciable expansion of sales.

On the other hand, he can expect a substantial loss in sales if he increases his price. Not only will sales to existing customers decline but some of his customers will switch to other producers who have not raised their prices. Consequently, assuming such a large number of sellers in the market that *each expects his actions to go unnoticed by his rivals,* every entrepreneur will expect his demand curve to be very elastic. The entrepreneur's expected or anticipated demand curve is shown by the relatively elastic curve *dd'* in Figure 10.3.1.

Anticipating highly elastic demand, each entrepreneur has an incentive to reduce price; and thus *all* entrepreneurs have this incentive. But if all prices are reduced simultaneously, each entrepreneur will gain only that increment in sales attributable to the general price reduction. He will not capture portions of his rivals' markets. Thus if the actions of one entrepreneur are matched by all other entrepreneurs in the product group, demand will be far less elastic, such as the curve *DD'* in Figure 10.3.1. In other words, *DD'* is the curve showing the quantity demanded from any one seller at various prices under the assumption that his competitors' prices are always identical with his.

Relations: The curve *dd'* shows the increased sales any entrepreneur can expect to enjoy by lowering his price, providing all other entrepreneurs maintain their original prices. *DD'*, on the other hand, shows the actual sales to be gained or lost when all firms change price simultaneously.[10]

10.3.b Summary of Assumptions

All of Chamberlin's specializing assumptions have been discussed or inferred; it may be well to recount them now. First, a large number of firms is producing a differentiated product. Each commodity within the product group is a fairly close substitute for every other commodity; and such a large number of sellers is in the product group that each expects his competitive maneuvering to go unnoticed by his rivals. Second, for the present, price is the variable entrepreneurs manipulate in an effort to increase profit. Finally, as Chamberlin puts it, there is the ". . . heroic assumption that both demand and cost curves for all the 'products'

---

[10] *Exercise:* Read Chamberlin's discussion of the *DD'* and *dd'* curves in *op. cit.,* pp. 90–92. See if you can discover a small error in his argument on p. 91.

[11] Chamberlin, *op. cit.,* pp. 82–83.

are uniform throughout the group. . . . [This only requires] that consumers' preferences be evenly distributed among the different varieties,
and that differences between them [the products] be not such as to give
rise to differences in cost."[11]

The last assumption merits further comment. In perfect competition
all products are homogeneous. Thus it is not unreasonable to assume
identical production cost for all entrepreneurs in the industry—an assumption that greatly facilitates analysis because it permits long-run
industry equilibrium to be explained by means of a graph pertaining to
only one firm. This is precisely the purpose of the assumption under discussion; but it is clearly more restrictive in this case. Basically one assumes that product differences are not so great as to entail cost differences. Different scents for toilet soaps, slightly different tobacco blends,
differences in the color of packaging material, and differences in the
collar style of men's shirts are but a few examples of product differences
that would give rise to little, if any, differences in cost. Yet the assumption is quite restrictive since *marked* quality differences (Chevrolet
vis-à-vis Cadillac) are generally precluded.

10.3.c Large-Group, Long-Run Equilibrium with Price Competition

With these assumptions and analytical tools in hand we can proceed
immediately to the analysis of long-run equilibrium in the large-group
case with price competition. The analysis is accomplished in two stages.
The first, illustrated in Figure 10.3.2, pertains to the situation in which
the "proper" or "optimal" number of firms is already in the product
group.

DD' and dd' (solid) give the two demand curves discussed in subsection 10.3.a; LAC is the long-run average cost curve for the "typical"
firm in question. We assume that an initial (short-run) equilibrium is
attained at point A, with output OQ_1 and price OP_1; short-run pure
profit is represented by the area of the shaded rectangle P_1ABC. Each
entrepreneur, regarding dd' as his demand curve, believes he can increase profit by reducing price and expanding output (according to the
elastic dd'). Hence each reduces price. But instead of expanding along
dd', each in fact moves along DD'. In Chamberlin's terms, dd' slides
downward along DD'.

Despite the frustration of their initial plans, entrepreneurs hold firm
in their belief that dd' represents their demand curve. Hence they con-

FIGURE 10.3.2

**Long-Run Equilibrium When Optimal Number
of Firms Already Exists**

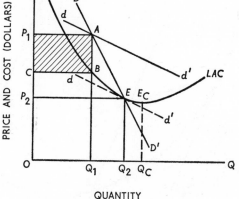

QUANTITY

tinue to reduce price in an effort to augment profit; and dd' continues to slide downward along DD'. Indeed, it must continue its downward movement until it comes to point E, where it is shown as the dashed curve. Of course, dd' might fall below the dashed-line position; all entrepreneurs would then incur a pure loss and price would be raised, shifting dd' upward.

The position of long-run equilibrium is E, where dd' is tangent to LAC. Each firm, while having a monopoly of its own "product," is forced to a zero profit position by the competition of rivals producing readily substitutable goods. The reasoning process is as follows:

Proposition: Large-group, long-run equilibrium under price competition in a monopolistically competitive product group is attained when the anticipated demand curve (dd') is tangent to the long-run unit cost curve. If dd' lies above LAC, each entrepreneur believes he can increase profit by reducing price; if dd' is below LAC, price must be increased to eliminate the pure loss incurred.

Certain questions concerning this equilibrium solution should have been raised in the reader's mind. In particular, one might ask what happens if the anticipated demand curve dd' does not have precisely the right slope so as to be tangent to LAC at the point where DD' cuts LAC. Explaining the long-run equilibrium adjustment where there is entry of new firms helps to provide an answer.

FIGURE 10.3.3

Long-Run Equilibrium with Entry of Firms

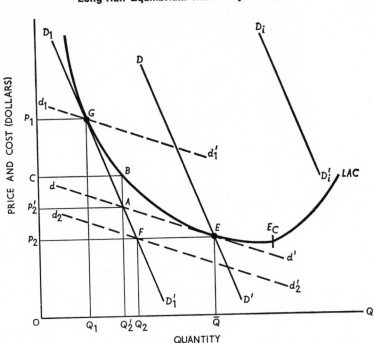

Consider Figure 10.3.3, in which $D_i D_i'$ is the initial demand curve and LAC is the long-run unit cost curve. The firm in question, and any other in the product group, reaps a substantial pure profit. Since entry into the product group is open, new firms selling slightly differentiated products are attracted. The greater variety of available products causes the demand for each seller's product to contract. In the process, DD' shifts to the left and probably becomes somewhat more elastic. Simultaneously, if entrepreneurs experiment with price policy, dd' slides down the instantaneously existing DD' and also probably becomes somewhat more elastic.

The transition from the initial $D_i D_i'$ curve to the ultimate long-run equilibrium at point E could come about in a number of ways. One method is illustrated in Figure 10.3.3, where it is assumed that new firms enter the product group until the proportional demand curve shifts from $D_i D_i'$ to $D_1 D_1'$. It might seem that equilibrium is attained at G, with output of OQ_1 and price OP_1 per unit, inasmuch as pure profit is zero at that point. However, each entrepreneur thinks $d_1 d_1'$ is his demand curve. A reduction in price would, in his belief, cause an expansion along $d_1 d_1'$; profit would accordingly be expanded. But each entrepreneur has the same incentive; so as price is reduced by all, dd' slides down D_1D_1' for each.

Suppose now that price has fallen to OP_2', with output OQ_2'. Each firm incurs a pure loss represented by the area of the rectangle $CBAP_2'$. It might seem that each firm could eliminate its pure loss by reducing price to OP_2 and moving to point E. Yet with the number of firms giving rise to D_1D_1', a reduction in price to OP_2 would shift the subjective demand curve further down D_1D_1', to the position d_2d_2'. Temporary equilibrium would be attained at F, with sales of OQ_2 rather than $O\overline{Q}$ per firm. The situation is necessarily transitory, however, since each firm incurs a pure loss at F. Ultimately some firms must leave the product group; and there is an incentive to do so. As firms leave the group the proportional demand curve shifts to the right, together with the anticipated demand curve; and both probably become somewhat less elastic. The exit of firms must continue until the proportional curve becomes DD' and the anticipated curve dd'. Long-run equilibrium is attained at E, with the identical long-run conditions detailed above.[12]

10.3.d "Ideal Output" and Excess Capacity

The concept of ideal output and the associated concept of excess capacity refer only to the long run. In the short run, under any type of market organization, there can be all sorts of departures from the ideal, reflecting incomplete adjustment to existing market conditions.

From Marshall to such later writers as Kahn, Harrod, and Cassels,[13] the ideal output of a firm was generally regarded as that output associated with minimum long-run average cost, the outputs corresponding to the points labeled E_c in Figures 10.3.2 and 10.3.3. Consequently, the ideal plant size is the one giving rise to the short-run average cost curve that is tangent to the long-run average cost curve at the latter's minimum point. Excess capacity, therefore, is the difference between ideal output and the output actually attained in long-run equilibrium. In Figure 10.3.2, excess capacity is measured by the difference between OQ_c and OQ_2, or Q_2Q_c units of output; in this case, excess capacity is "deficient capacity" or "negative" excess capacity.

---

[12] At this point of long-run equilibrium, as before, dd' must be tangent to LAC; otherwise each entrepreneur would believe that a change in his price-output policy could augment profit, thus an equilibrium would not exist, contrary to hypothesis.

[13] R. F. Kahn, "Some Notes on Ideal Output," *Economic Journal,* Vol. XLV (1935), pp. 1–35; R. F. Harrod, "Doctrines of Imperfect Competition," *Quarterly Journal of Economics,* Vol. XLIX (1934–35), pp. 442–70; and J. M. Cassels, "Excess Capacity and Monopolistic Competition," *Quarterly Journal of Economics,* Vol. LI (1936–37), pp. 426–43.

FIGURE 10.3.4

Ideal Output and Excess

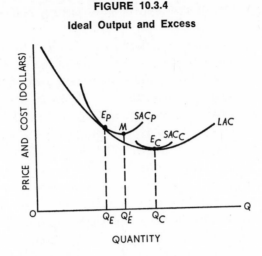

Following Cassels, excess capacity is composed of two parts, as illustrated in Figure 10.3.4. Suppose in a monopolistically competitive market a typical firm attains long-run equilibrium at the point E_p, with output OQ_E. From the standpoint of the *firm*, long-run optimal plant size is given by SAC_p. According to the present view of ideal output, the socially optimal plant size is represented by SAC_c, and excess capacity (negative, notice) is measured as Q_EQ_C units of output.

The measure of excess capacity may be divided in two parts. First, given the plant SAC_p, the firm operates at point E_p rather than at the point of minimum unit cost M. From a social point of view, the resources used by the firm would be more efficiently utilized if OQ_E', rather than OQ_E, units were produced. Thus a portion of excess capacity, represented by Q_EQ_E', is attributable to socially inefficient utilization of the resources actually used. The second portion of excess capacity, $Q_E'Q_C$, arises because socially and individually optimal sizes differ. The monopolistically competitive firm does not employ enough of society's resources to attain minimum unit (dollar and resource) cost.

The view of ideal output just expounded rests, fundamentally, upon the horizontal demand curve faced by a perfect competitor. But if individual demand curves are negatively sloped, if active price competition characterizes the market, and if entry is free into the product group, Chamberlin argues that E_c does not correspond to ideal output. Product heterogeneity is desired per se; and it inevitably gives rise to negatively sloped individual demand curves.

"Differentness" is considered a quality of the product and entails a cost just as any other quality. The cost of differentness is represented by production to the left of minimum average cost. The difference between actual (long-run equilibrium) output and output at minimum cost is, then, a measure of the "cost" of producing "differentness" rather than a measure of excess capacity. But this is true only so long as there is effective price competition in the market. The presence of price competition guarantees that buyers can select the "amount" of differentness they wish to purchase. In the case of price competition, Chamberlin regards E_p as a "sort of ideal" for a market in which there is product differentiation.[14]

10.3.e Nonprice Competition and Excess Capacity

According to Chamberlin, long-run equilibrium under monopolistic competition does not give rise to excess capacity so long as the market is characterized by active price competition. In his view, excess capacity arises when free entry is coupled with the absence of price competition. This brand of excess capacity is illustrated by Figure 10.3.5.

FIGURE 10.3.5

Long-Run Equilibrium with Nonprice Competition and Excess Capacity

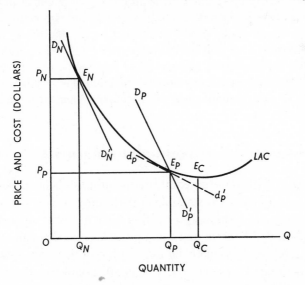

LAC, as usual, represents long-run average cost. If there is free entry and price competition, long-run equilibrium is attained at E_p, where the anticipated demand curve $d_p d_p'$ is tangent to *LAC.* As noted, E_p must lie

---

[14] Chamberlin, *op. cit.,* p. 94.

to the left of the competitive equilibrium E_o; but with active price competition it will tend to lie rather close to the competitive point.

For many reasons, active price competition may not characterize certain markets. A "live and let live" outlook on the part of sellers, tacit agreements, open price associations, price maintenance, customary prices, and professional ethics are a few causes of nonaggressive price policies. If price competition is, in fact, lacking, individual entrepreneurs will have no regard for the existence of curves such as dd'. They will be concerned only with the effects of a general price rise or decline, or with the DD' curve.

With free entry in the absence of price competition, long-run equilibrium is attained (pure profit eliminated) only when enough firms have entered the industry to push the demand curve to $D_N D_N'$. Equilibrium is attained at E_N, with output OQ_N and price OP_N per unit. In Chamberlin's opinion, $Q_N Q_P$ represents excess capacity: it is the difference in output attributable to the absence of effective price competition. If the latter prevails, the firm attains a "sort of ideal" output.

Chamberlin then concludes that by nonaggressive price policies sellers

". . . protect, over short periods, their profits, but over longer periods, their numbers, since when prices do not fall costs rise, the two being equated by the development of excess productive capacity . . . for which there is no automatic corrective. . . . It may develop over long periods with impunity, prices always covering costs, and may . . . become permanent and normal through a failure of price competition to function. The result is high prices and waste . . . [attributable to] the monopoly element in monopolistic competition."[15]

10.4 COMPARISONS OF LONG-RUN EQUILIBRIA

A comparison of long-run equilibria is rather difficult inasmuch as it must rest essentially upon statements pertaining to cost curves. Conditions giving rise to monopoly probably lead to noncomparable differences between competitive and monopolistic costs; for similar reasons, noncomparability is also likely between either of these two and monopolistic competition. However, a few generalizations are possible if one bears in mind that the statements are relative, not absolute. The relevant points follow immediately from a comparison of Figures 8.6.3, 9.5.1, and 10.3.2.

[15] *Ibid.,* pp. 107, 109.

10.4.a   Equilibrium in the Firm

For emphasis, it may be well to recount the "competitive" and "monopolistic" aspects of monopolistic competition. A monopolistically competitive firm is like a monopoly in that it faces negatively sloped demand and marginal revenue curves; it therefore determines its price-output policy by equating marginal cost with marginal revenue rather than with price as in perfect competition. At the same time, the monopolistically competitive firm is like a perfectly competitive one in that it faces direct market competition. The long-run result is the absence of pure profit, just as in the competitive case. While all three types may enjoy economic profit in the short run—freedom of entry eliminates it in the long run, except under conditions of pure monopoly. The qualitative nature of rivalry is also different. In perfect competition rivalry is completely impersonal. At the opposite extreme, there is no direct (only indirect and potential) rivalry under monopoly. The case of monopolistic competition is somewhat different, but it lies closer to perfect competition. The monopolistic competitor, at least in abstract, is aware of the slightly differentiated, highly substitutable products of other firms. There would be personal rivalry except for the condition of large numbers—so large that each entrepreneur believes his actions will go unnoticed by his competitors (because they are so numerous that his actions will not have a readily perceptible effect upon any *one* of them).

10.4.b   Long-Run Equilibria in Industries and Product Groups

In long-run competitive equilibrium, total industry output is produced in a group of plants each of which operates at (long-run) minimum average cost. The product is sold at a price equal to minimum average cost, and it is significant to note that long-run marginal cost equals both price and average cost at this point.

Under monopoly the long-run equilibrium situation is substantially different. The industry output is produced by one firm which may operate one or more plants. If the monopolist operates one plant, it is very unlikely to be of such size as to produce at (long-run) minimum average cost; if multiple plants are used, however, each will operate at minimum cost. In neither case will price equal minimum average cost or marginal cost. Indeed, price will exceed both so that in long-run equilibrium, the marginal social valuation of the commodity exceeds the marginal cost of its production.

In the competitive case, each firm operates a plant of ideal size and the industry produces the ideal output. Thus, according to the Marshall-

Kahn-Cassels version, there is no excess capacity in long-run competitive equilibrium. In a multiplant monopoly each plant is of ideal size; however, there are not enough plants to produce the ideal industry output. As a consequence there is long-run (negative) excess capacity under monopoly market organization.

Monopolistic competition is somewhat more difficult to analyze in these terms. In large-group equilibrium with active price competition, price is above marginal cost, although it equals average cost. The latter is not minimum average cost; but Chamberlin argues that the difference between cost at E_p and E_c is itself the "cost" of product differentiation. Since product heterogeneity is apparently desired per se, the cost of differentiation is a valid social cost. Hence, according to Chamberlin's argument, E_p actually represents the minimum attainable average cost when *all* relevant social costs are included. Each firm, and the product group as a whole, produces the "sort of ideal" output, and excess productive capacity does not appear in long-run equilibrium.

If Chamberlin's argument is accepted (and it is *not,* universally), one difficulty remains. Suppose E_p does represent minimum attainable unit cost, including the "cost" attributable to the "ideal" amount of product differentiation. Even then long-run price exceeds short-run marginal cost for the plant in question. The marginal social valuation of the product exceeds its marginal cost for the established level of differentiation. Socially, output should be expanded and price reduced until $P = MC$. Given the plant size, plant MC intersects $D_p D_p'$ somewhere below both SAC and LAC. Hence the socially desirable output would cause each firm to sustain a long-run pure loss, a situation incompatible with private enterprise.

In short, the social welfare aspects of monopolistic competition are ambiguous. From a very microscopic standpoint, each firm produces less than the socially optimal output. On the other hand, if each firm were somehow forced to produce this seemingly desirable level of output at marginal-cost price, private enterprise would no longer represent a viable economic system. Finally, the abolition of private enterprise would violate a macroscopic welfare criterion that apparently transcends microscopic considerations, at least in the United States and most industrially advanced Western nations. Thus while the theoretical analysis of monopolistic competition is quite clear, the welfare implications of this analysis are not. Micro- and macroeconomic welfare criteria are not consistent and/or reconcilable. The economist *qua* economist can only indicate the dilemma; establishing definitive social goals and welfare standards is beyond his professional capacity.

QUESTIONS

1. In most large cities, taxicab fares are fixed by the municipality. Suppose anyone who wishes to operate a cab at the established rates is automatically granted a license to do so. Analyze the equilibrium position corresponding to any given fare. Contrast the characteristics of the equilibrium positions when the fare set by the city is relatively "high" and relatively "low," in terms of the number of cabs, income of cab owners and drivers, and any other relevant characteristic.

2. Comment on the following statement: "Monopolistic competition leads to waste through the unnecessary proliferation of real or imagined differences among varieties of a commodity."

3. The National Association of Retail Druggists reports that individual drug store operators must receive an average markup of 40 percent of retail price in order to cover minimum cost of store operation.

    a) What is the relation, if any, between the $MC = MR$ pricing of economic theory and the cost-plus-markup pricing used by firms such as drugstores?

    b) What is the relation, if any, between the structure of the retail drug market and the minimum markup necessary for long-run survival of individual drugstores?

SUGGESTED READINGS

Chamberlin, E. H. *The Theory of Monopolistic Competition,* esp. chap. 5, pp. 71–116. 6th ed. Cambridge, Mass.: Harvard University Press, 1950.

Ferguson, C. E. "A Social Concept of Excess Capacity," *Metroeconomica,* Vol. VIII (1956), pp. 84–93.

Machlup, Fritz. *The Economics of Sellers' Competition,* pp. 135–241. Baltimore: Johns Hopkins Press, 1952.

Robinson, Joan. *The Economics of Imperfect Competition,* pp. 133–76. London: Macmillan & Co., Ltd., 1933.

Smithies, Arthur. "Equilibrium in Monopolistic Competition," *Quarterly Journal of Economics,* Vol. LV (1940), pp. 95 ff. [Advanced math required.]

Triffin, Robert. *Monopolistic Competition and General Equilibrium Theory,* pp. 17–96. Cambridge, Mass.: Harvard University Press, 1949.

Chapter 11

THEORIES OF PRICE IN OLIGOPOLY MARKETS

11.1 INTRODUCTION

Oligopoly, or its limiting form duopoly, is a market situation intermediate between the cases previously studied. In monopoly only one seller is in the market; competition, in either the technical or the popular sense, does not exist. Perfect competition and large-group monopolistic competition represent the opposite. So many firms are in the market that the actions of each is expected to be imperceptible to the others. There is competition in the technical sense, but little or none in the popular sense. The reverse tends to be true in oligopoly; technically competition is lacking but sometimes there is intense rivalry or competition in the popular sense.

Oligopoly is said to exist when more than one seller is in the market, but when the number is not so large as to render negligible the contribution of each. If only two sellers are in the market, the special case of duopoly exists. For simplicity the duopoly market organization will be discussed rather than the more general oligopoly; since the fundamental problem is the same, generality is not sacrificed.

11.1.a The Oligopoly Problem

The discussion so far may seem to indicate that there is primarily a quantitative difference among the various types of market organizations. In monopoly there is one seller; in duopoly two; and so on. To be sure, a quantitative difference does exist; and it is convenient to classify markets according to this difference. Yet there is a qualitative difference of transcending importance. Briefly, when numbers are few each seller must be acutely conscious of the actions of his rivals and of their reactions to changes in his policies.

Consider a duopoly market. Each seller must almost surely recognize that his actions affect his rival; and the latter will almost surely react to any measures that affect him adversely. Since the market is divided between the two, most courses of action benefiting one firm will be harmful to the other; hence action by one rival will have its counterpart in a maneuver by the other. Thus many different courses of action may result.

The rivals may spend their lives trying to "second guess" each other; they may tacitly agree to compete by advertising but not by price changes; or, recognizing their monopoly potential, they may form a coalition and cooperate rather than compete. In fact, there are just about as many different results as there are oligopolies; to examine each would carry taxonomy too far. Thus we concentrate our attention on two sets of oligopoly theories. First, a few "classical" solutions to the duopoly problem are analyzed. Next, some theoretical "market" solutions are examined. But our investigation cannot be complete, for that would require one or more volumes in itself. Nonetheless, the principal feature of oligopoly markets should be clear. The firms are interdependent; the policies of one directly and perceptibly affect the others. Hence competition cannot be impersonal.

11.1.b Some Concepts and Assumptions

First, for analytical convenience we assume that the products within an oligopoly market are homogeneous. As a practical matter, most oligopolies are characterized by product differentiation; yet the distinction is not of paramount importance because the firms are interdependent whether they produce identical commodities or not. Second, we assume that oligopolistic firms purchase inputs in perfectly competitive markets. This may or may not be true; it may hold for some inputs but not for others. However, when the assumption does great violence to reality, a small modification of the cost curves is all that is required. Finally, for the present we assume that the firms behave independently even though they are interdependent in the market. That is, the case of collusive oligopoly is ruled out even though to the firms concerned it is a highly desirable and sometimes realized solution. Since the Sherman Act, this is more a legal than an economic matter.

11.2 SOME "CLASSICAL" SOLUTIONS TO THE DUOPOLY PROBLEM

Formal speculation about the duopoly problem is sometimes dated from the work of a French economist, A. A. Cournot. Beginning with his famous "mineral springs" case, some of the outstanding theories of oligopoly behavior will be analyzed. Except for game-theory models and the Hotelling case, little credence is today accorded these solutions. However, as Machlup put it, "Familiarity with the classical models has become a kind of hallmark of the education of an economic theorist, even if it helps him more in the comprehension of the traditional lingo than in the analysis of current economic problems."[1]

11.2.a Cournot Case[2]

Assume, with Cournot, that two mineral springs, furnishing identical mineral water, are situated side by side. One is owned by **A**, the other by **B**. The springs are actually artesian wells to which purchasers must

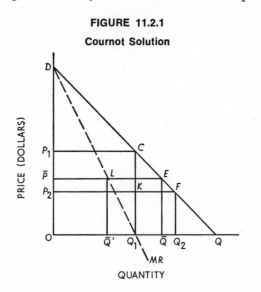

FIGURE 11.2.1

Cournot Solution

bring their own containers. Consequently the only costs are the fixed costs of sinking the wells; in particular, marginal cost is zero for each producer. The duopoly market so constructed is illustrated in Figure 11.2.1. DQ is the market demand for mineral water, and MR is the marginal revenue curve.

Suppose **A** is initially the only seller in the market. To maximize his

---

[1] Fritz Machlup, *The Economics of Sellers' Competition* (Baltimore: Johns Hopkins Press, 1952), p. 369.

[2] Augustin Cournot, *Recherches sur les principes mathématiques de la théorie des richesses* (Paris, 1838). English translation by Nathaniel T. Bacon entitled *Researchers into the Mathematical Principles of the Theory of Wealth* (New York: Macmillan & Company, 1897; reprinted 1927).

profit he sells OQ_1 units of mineral water, so that marginal revenue equals the zero marginal cost. Price is OP_1 per unit, and profit is OQ_1CP_1. Now **B** enters the market and Cournot's crucial assumption comes into the picture.

To get at an analytical solution of a duopoly situation one must make a behavioral assumption concerning each entrepreneur's expectations of his rival's policies. Cournot's assumption is that each entrepreneur expects his rival *never* to change his output. Thus when **B** enters the market, he expects **A** always to market OQ_1 units of mineral water. He accordingly views the segment CQ as that portion of total demand from which his demand curve is derived—that portion of the market remaining after **A** sells OQ_1 units. To maximize his profit, **B** decides to sell Q_1Q_2 units at price OP_2.[3] His anticipated profit is Q_1Q_2FK, and **A**'s anticipated profit falls to OQ_1KP_2.[4]

Now **A**, in his turn, expects **B** always to market $Q_1Q_2 = Q_2Q$ units of mineral water. Hence, according to his belief OQ_2 represents the total market available to him. With straight-line demand and marginal revenue curves, the best he can do is to market $1/2\ OQ_2$ units. Thus he reduces his output somewhat and market price rises accordingly. **B** views the situation anew and sees more of the market now available, specifically $OQ - 1/2\ OQ_2$. Consequently, **B** increases his output to $1/2\ (OQ - 1/2\ OQ_2)$, price falls somewhat, and **A** must reappraise the situation.

Believing **B** will forevermore sell $1/2\ (OQ - 1/2\ OQ_2)$ units, the available market for **A** appears to be $OQ - 1/2\ (OQ - 1/2\ OQ_2)$. His profit-maximizing output is thus $1/2[OQ - 1/2\ (OQ - 1/2\ OQ_2]$, somewhat less than previously. And so the process continues, **A** gradually decreasing his sales and **B** increasing his. But there is a limit; the adjustment mechanism converges.

---

[3] Recall the method of deriving marginal revenue from demand and the fact that marginal cost equals zero.

[4] The dynamics of transition from an initial monopoly position to an ultimate duopoly equilibrium can be explained in various ways, none of which is particularly satisfactory. The presentation in the text is adopted because it is the one most frequently found in the literature and because if one ignores certain minor points, it is the most easily understood. But the "minor points" may cause the serious student some concern. For example, when **B** enters the market, he charges a price of OP_2 per unit. Price for both **A** and **B** is accordingly OP_2 and total sales are OQ_2. But since the products of **A** and **B** are homogeneous, OQ_2 would be evenly divided between **A** and **B**, not divided two thirds for **A** and one third for **B**, as the analysis in the text assumes. With some considerable graphical difficulty, the analysis can be revised to allow for market sharing subsequent to price changes. The same conclusion, however, ultimately emerges. Mathematical treatment of the Cournot case is not encumbered by this difficulty.

To see the ultimate result, concentrate first on **B**. He initially sells $Q_1Q_2 = Q_2Q = 1/4\ OQ$ units. In other words, he has one fourth of the market. Then he increases his output to $1/2(OQ - 1/2\ OQ_2) = 1/2$ $(OQ - 3/8\ OQ) = OQ(1/2 - 3/16) = 5/16\ OQ$. He thus expands by $5/16 - 1/4 = 1/16$. His next expansion is by $1/64$; the next by $1/256$; and so on. His final output is $OQ(1/4 + 1/16 + 1/64 + \ldots) = 1/3\ OQ$.

A, on the other hand, initially had one half of the market, $OQ_1 = \frac{1}{2}\ OQ$. His output first falls to $\frac{1}{2}OQ_2 = \frac{1}{2}(\frac{3}{4}\ OQ) = \frac{3}{8}\ OQ$. Hence he loses $\frac{1}{8}$ of the market in the first round. Next, his output falls to $\frac{1}{2}[OQ - \frac{1}{2}(OQ - \frac{3}{8}\ OQ)] = \frac{11}{32}\ OQ$. In this round he loses $\frac{1}{32}$ of the market; in the next he loses $\frac{1}{128}$, and so on. His final output is $OQ(\frac{1}{2} - \frac{1}{8} - \frac{1}{32} - \frac{1}{128} - \ldots) = \frac{1}{3}\ OQ$.

Graphically, **A** produces $O\overline{Q}'$ units, **B** produces $\overline{Q}'Q$ units, and market price is $O\overline{P}$. A's profit is $O\overline{Q}'L\overline{P}$. B's is $\overline{Q}'\overline{Q}EL$, and the total profit is $O\overline{Q}E\overline{P}$. If price were set equal to (zero) marginal cost, OQ units would be sold, and profit would be zero. This is the perfectly competitive solution. Under monopoly, output would be $1/2\ OQ$ and profit would be OQ_1CP_1. Thus duopoly output ($2/3\ OQ$) is smaller than the competitive output but somewhat larger than monopoly output. The duopoly price ($O\overline{P}$) is two thirds of the monopoly price; total duopoly profit is two thirds of potential monopoly profit.

The Cournot case is one possible solution to the duopoly problem. However, it is based upon an extraordinarily naïve assumption: each entrepreneur believes his rival will never change his volume of sales, even though he repeatedly observes such changes. The next duopoly model is based upon a similarly naïve assumption.[5]

---

[5] The Cournot model has an easy mathematical solution. Let there be two producers, 1 and 2, who have only fixed cost F_1 and F_2. Their products are homogeneous, so the demand function may be written as

$$p = f(Q_1 + Q_2) = f(Q), \tag{11.5.1}$$

where Q_i is the output of the i-th entrepreneur, and

$$\frac{\partial f}{\partial Q_i} = \frac{df(Q)}{dQ}\frac{\partial Q}{\partial Q_i} = f'(Q) \qquad (i = 1, 2). \tag{11.5.2}$$

The profit function is

$$\pi_i = Q_i f(Q) - F_i \qquad (i = 1, 2). \tag{11.5.3}$$

Assume that each entrepreneur attempts to maximize profit under the assumption that his rival will never change his quantity supplied. The latter, of course, implies that

$$\frac{\partial Q_2}{\partial Q_1} = \frac{\partial Q_1}{\partial Q_2} = 0. \tag{11.5.4}$$

11.2.b Edgeworth Case

Although written in 1838, Cournot's work received little attention until a much later date. Indeed, it was 1883 before a review of his book appeared. This review was written by a French mathematician, Joseph Bertrand, who criticized Cournot for having his entrepreneurs assume that quantity is held constant. Instead, said Bertrand, a solution should be based on the assumption that entrepreneurs believe their rivals will maintain a constant price.[6] This suggestion was developed by Edge-

---

The first-order maximizing conditions are, from equations (11.5.3),

$$\frac{\partial \pi_1}{\partial Q_1} = f(Q) + Q_1 f'(Q) = 0 \,, \tag{11.5.5}$$

$$\frac{\partial \pi_2}{\partial Q_2} = f(Q) + Q_2 f'(Q) = 0 \,. \tag{11.5.6}$$

Now subtract equation (11.5.6) from (11.5.5), obtaining

$$(Q_1 - Q_2) f'(Q) = 0 \,. \tag{11.5.7}$$

Now since $f'(Q) \neq 0$ by assumption (see below), one has

$$Q_1 = Q_2 \,, \tag{11.5.8}$$

the Cournot result that the duopolists will produce identical amounts.

Cournot explicity assumed a linear demand function, which we may write as

$$p = a - bQ \,, \tag{11.5.9}$$

where a and b are positive constants. Under perfect competition $p = MC = 0$. Thus from equation (11.5.9) the competitive output (Q_c) is

$$Q_c = \frac{a}{b} \,. \tag{11.5.10}$$

A monopolist produces at the point where $MR = MC = 0$. Marginal revenue is, from equation (11.5.9),

$$\frac{d(pQ)}{dQ} = a - 2bQ \,. \tag{11.5.11}$$

Setting this equal to zero gives the monopoly output (Q_M):

$$Q_M = \frac{a}{2b} \,, \tag{11.5.12}$$

the result given in the text above.

Finally, to find duopoly output, add equations (11.5.5) and (11.5.6):

$$2f(Q) + Qf'(Q) = 0 \,. \tag{11.5.13}$$

Substituting equation (11.5.9) and its derivative yields

$$Q_D = \frac{2a}{3b} \,, \tag{11.5.14}$$

the result given in the text. That is, monopoly output is one half and duopoly output two thirds of the competitive output.

[6] Joseph Bertrand, "Theorie Mathématique de la Richesse Sociale," *Journal des Savants* (Paris, 1883), pp. 499–508.

worth into the duopoly solution that bears his name.[7] This classical case is illustrated by Figure 11.2.2.

FIGURE 11.2.2

Edgeworth Solution

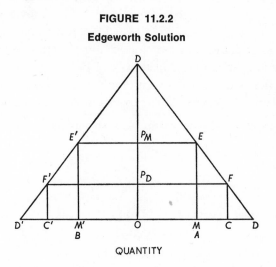

QUANTITY

As in the Cournot situation, suppose two firms are situated side by side, selling a homogeneous product produced at zero marginal cost. The entire market is pictured as being divided equally between entrepreneurs **A** and **B**. DD is the demand facing A, DD' is B's demand curve. Each entrepreneur has a maximum achievable rate of output and, hence, rate of sale.[8] These maxima are represented by OC units for **A** and OC' units for **B**. Finally, the ordinate OD is the price axis.

---

[7] F. Y. Edgeworth, "La teoria pura del monopolio," *Giornale degli Economisti,* Vol. XV (1897), pp. 13–31. The article was reprinted in English as "The Pure Theory of Monopoly," in Edgeworth, *Papers Relating to Political Economy* (London: Macmillan & Co., Ltd., 1925), Vol. I, pp. 111–42.

[8] Graphical treatment of the Edgeworth case suffers from difficulties and vagueness, much as the graphical analysis of Cournot's problem. For example, to set DD and DD' as the demand curves for **A** and **B** respectively, one must assume that the market is segregated between the two sellers (a person who buys from **A** is not a potential customer of **B**, and vice versa). Yet when price falls to OP_D one must assume that the markets merge, for **A** (or **B**) behaves as he does because he believes his rival's quantity is limited so that he can attract some of his rival's potential clientele. Next, when price rises to OP_M one must again assume that the markets diverge. Similarly, the assumption that each producer has a maximum attainable rate of output and sales is very questionable in studies of long-run equilibrium. This assumption does more than violate reality for the sake of analytical convenience; it violates one of the fundamental conditions of long-run analysis—that output is always augmentable in the long run, especially if higher unit cost is economically feasible. Thus the long-run conclusions that emerge from Edgeworth's case are based upon an assumption that is contradictory to long-run equilibrium analysis; a slight change

By construction, $OM = MD$ and $OM' = M'D'$. If **A** enters the market first, he will produce and market OM units, selling each for the monopoly price OP_M. He reaps the maximum monopoly profit $OMEP_M$. Now **B** enters the market and assumes that **A** will never change his price. Thus **B** sets his price very slightly below OP_M and sells his maximum producible output OC'. In other words, **B**'s price being lower than **A**'s and their products being identical, **B** sells as much as he can produce, capturing a substantial portion of **A**'s market.

Now it is **A**'s turn to appraise the situation. Assuming (as he does) that **B** will never change his price, **A** can lower his price slightly below **B**'s and sell his maximum producible output OC. In the process, he captures most of **B**'s market. Then **B**, still assuming that **A** will not change his price, reduces his price below **A**'s; and so forth. Thus, according to Edgeworth, price will be successively lowered by **B** and **A** until the level OP_D is reached. OP_D is the total disposal price; both **A** and **B** sell their maximum outputs.

But once the price OP_D is attained, one of the entrepreneurs (say **A**) will notice an interesting fact. At price OP_D, **B** sells his entire output. Thus if **B** retains that price, **A** can raise his price to OP_M, sell OM units, and again reap the monopoly profit $OMEP_M$. Consequently, **A** raises his price to OP_M. Then **B** observes that if he raises his price from OP_D to an amount slightly below OP_M, while **A** maintains the price OP_M, he can sell his entire output and reap a greater profit. So he raises price accordingly. Then **A** recognizes that if he lowers his price slightly below **B**, he can sell his entire output. . . .

And so it goes, price continually moving between OP_D and OP_M. The duopoly situation, according to Edgeworth, is unstable and indeterminate (in the same sense that the solution to the bilateral monopoly problem is indeterminate). The Edgeworth case, just as the Cournot case, requires no comment because it is based upon a naïve hypothesis that is itself continually shown to be wrong by market results.[9]

---

in the assumption leads to entirely different results. It is very undesirable to have one's conclusions so sensitive to one assumption, especially when the assumption is questionable on grounds of theory as well as reality.

[9] The above explanation rests upon the fact that $OC' < EE'$, for otherwise **B** could not sell his entire output at a price slightly less than OP_M (with **A** holding price at OP_M). This inequality follows immediately, however, from our analysis of marginal revenue. By assumption, demand is linear and marginal cost is zero. Therefore, marginal revenue must intersect the horizontal axis (and result in profit maximization) at the point M or M'. Further, since $MM' = EE'$ and $OM = OM' = \frac{1}{2}OD = \frac{1}{2}OD'$, EE' must equal $OD' > OC'$. Thus $OC' < EE'$. The rest of the analysis follows immediately.

11.2.c Stability in Oligopoly Markets: Hotelling Solution

While being entirely unacceptable, the Edgeworth solution improves upon Cournot's analysis in one way. Specifically, *price* rather than *output* is the relevant decision variable for the entrepreneur.[10] Yet in Edgeworth's model, the result of using price as the decision variable is to introduce indeterminacy. Empirically, duopoly and oligopoly markets tend to be very stable. To be sure, occasional price wars occur; but typically prices fluctuate very seldom in these markets. To explain stability in duopoly and oligopoly markets, Hotelling constructed a model that has become famous for its far-reaching significance.[11] The operation of Hotelling's model is partially illustrated by Figure 11.2.3.

FIGURE 11.2.3

Hotelling Solution

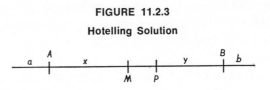

A and B are two entreprenurs who produce a physically identical product at zero marginal cost. However, the products of the duopolists are differentiated in the eyes of the buyers because of the locations of A and B. As Hotelling points out, markets are commonly subdivided into regions within each of which one seller enjoys a quasimonopolistic position. He accordingly assumes that buyers are uniformly distributed along a line of length *L,* which may be Main Street or a transcontinental railroad. Entrepreneurs A and B are located at points *A* and *B* in this market.

Each buyer must go to the vending point and transport his purchases home at a cost of *c* per unit bought per unit distance carried. Thus a buyer located *x* units distance from A must pay a transportation cost of *cx* for each unit of product he buys. Next, Hotelling assumes that demand is completely inelastic and is given by the following specifications. The market is *L* units in length; one buyer resides in each unit of length; and in each unit of time, each buyer purchases one unit of the com-

---

[10] Within this simple context, at least. In more sophisticated cases, advertising, location, and other nonprice variables are frequently the more important decision variables.

[11] Harold Hotelling, "Stability in Competition," *Economic Journal,* Vol. XXXIX (1929), pp. 41–57.

modity. There are a buyers situated to the left of **A**, b buyers situated to the right of **B**, and $x + y$ buyers between them. Thus total sales in each unit of time is $L = a + x + y + b$.

A and **B** have some leeway in setting their price, although, for example, **B** would never set his price so high that the b buyers to his right find it less expensive to purchase from **A** and transport the goods home. This gives a hint as to how a determinate and stable price is set. Since the products differ only in transportation cost, delivered price must be equal. Let **A**'s price be p_A and **B**'s be p_B. Each has his "sheltered" market of a and b respectively. For any particular pair of prices the $x + y$ buyers located between **A** and **B** will be divided by a point such as P in Figure 11.2.3. The condition is that delivered price must be equal, or $p_A + cx = p_B + cy$. **A**'s profit will be $p_A (a + x)$ and **B**'s will be $p_B (b + y)$. Maximizing these two profit expressions always yields unique, stable, and determinate prices.[12]

----

[12] Mathematical demonstration of this point is simple. We have, from the text, two equations:

$$a + x + y + b = L, \tag{11.12.1}$$
$$p_A + cx = p_B + cy. \tag{11.12.2}$$

Solving expressions (11.12.1) and (11.12.2) simultaneously, we have

$$x = \frac{1}{2}\left(L - a - b + \frac{p_B - p_A}{c} \right), \tag{11.12.3}$$

and

$$y = \frac{1}{2}\left(L - a - b + \frac{p_A - p_B}{c} \right). \tag{11.12.4}$$

Thus profits are

$$\Pi_A = p_A(a + x) = \frac{1}{2}(L + a - b)p_A - \frac{p_A^2}{2c} + \frac{p_A p_B}{2c}, \tag{11.12.5}$$

and

$$\Pi_B = p_B(b + y) = \frac{1}{2}(L - a + b)p_B - \frac{p_B^2}{2c} + \frac{p_A p_B}{2c}. \tag{11.12.6}$$

Edgeworth's assumption is retained: each entrepreneur believes his rival will not change his price. Thus profit maximization leads to

$$\frac{\partial \Pi_A}{\partial p_A} = \frac{1}{2}(L + a - b) - \frac{p_A}{c} + \frac{p_B}{2c} = 0, \tag{11.12.7}$$

and

$$\frac{\partial \Pi_B}{\partial p_B} = \frac{1}{2}(L + a - b) - \frac{p_A}{2c} - \frac{p_B}{c} = 0. \tag{11.12.8}$$

There is a determinate, short-run equilibrium; and the long-run results are equally clear. When the plants of **A** and **B** deteriorate they must be replaced. **A** has an incentive to move as far toward **B** as possible, thereby expanding the "sheltered" market to his left. **B** has a similar incentive. As a consequence, they will both locate in the center of the market, *M* in Figure 11.2.3. If **A** located to the right of *M*, **B** could locate just left of *A* and obtain the larger sheltered market. Similarly, if **B** located to the left of *M*, **A** could locate just to his right and obtain the larger "sheltered" market. Hence both **A** and **B** must ultimately situate at *M*.

Price is determinate and stable, and so is the location of the sellers. But Hotelling reads yet another interesting meaning into his solution. From the standpoint of social welfare, **A** and **B** should locate at the quartile points of the linear market in order to minimize transportation cost and, therefore, delivered prices. Instead they locate at the median point, maximizing transportation cost; thus a duopoly market organization, according to Hotelling, militates against social welfare. Generalizing the argument, it militates against ideal product differentiation as well. Location of seller is only one of the many ways in which products are differentiated. However, drawing on the median as against quartile solutions, Hotelling suggests that the platforms of the Republican and Democratic parties are too similar, and to cite his colorful expression, "Our cities become uneconomically large and the business districts within them are too concentrated. Methodist and Presbyterian churches are too much alike; cider is too homogeneous."[13]

Equations (11.12.7) and (11.12.8) can be solved simultaneously to yield

$$p_A = c\left(L + \frac{a-b}{3}\right), \tag{11.12.9}$$

and

$$p_B = c\left(L - \frac{a-b}{3}\right). \tag{11.12.10}$$

Substituting equations (11.12.9) and (11.12.10) into (11.12.3) and (11.12.4), and adding *a* and *b* respectively, one obtains

$$q_A = a + x = \frac{1}{2}\left(L + \frac{a-b}{3}\right), \tag{11.12.11}$$

and

$$q_B = b + y = \frac{1}{2}\left(L - \frac{a-b}{3}\right). \tag{11.12.12}$$

Hence both equilibrium prices and quantities sold are uniquely determinable.

[13] Hotelling, *op. cit.*, p. 57.

11.2.d Stability in Oligopoly Markets: Chamberlin Solution

Somewhat after the appearance of Hotelling's seminal paper, Chamberlin proposed a stable duopoly solution that depends upon mutual recognition of market interdependence.[14] Chamberlin's case is exactly that of Cournot except for the final result (see Figure 11.2.4). DQ is

FIGURE 11.2.4

Chamberlin Solution

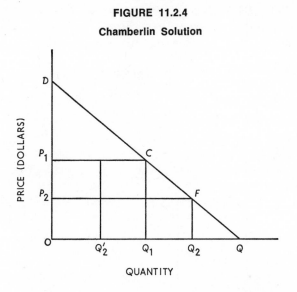

the linear demand for mineral water. **A** first enters the market and sells OQ_1 units at price OP_1, thereby reaping monopoly profit. **B** next enters the market. Seeing that **A** produces OQ_1 units, **B** regards CQ as his demand function. The best he can do is to market Q_1Q_2 units. Price falls to OP_2, and total profit for both entrepreneurs is OQ_2FP_2.

The difference between Cournot and Chamberlin now arises. According to the latter, **A** will survey the market situation after **B**'s entry, recognize their mutual interdependence, and recognize also that sharing monopoly profit OQ_1CP_1 is the best either he or **B** can do. **A** consequently reduces his output to $OQ_2' = \frac{1}{2} OQ_1$. **B** also recognizes the best solution; he therefore maintains his output at $Q_1Q_2 = Q_2'Q_1 = \frac{1}{2} OQ_1$. Hence total output is OQ_1, price is OP_1, and **A** and **B** share equally the monopoly profit OQ_1CP_1.

Chamberlin's solution has much to recommend it. Most important, his entrepreneurs behave in a sophisticated way in that they understand

---

[14] E. H. Chamberlin, *The Theory of Monopolistic Competition* (Cambridge, Mass.: Harvard University Press, 1933), pp. 46–51.

reality and act accordingly. This alone is a great improvement; but in addition he obtains a stable solution that is not too far from reality in situations of homogeneous oligopoly.

11.2.e   Stability in Oligopoly Markets: Sweezy Solution

Another model of stable oligopoly price that was at one time popular is the "kinked demand-curve hypothesis" of Sweezy,[15] illustrated in Figure 11.2.5. Suppose the demand curve confronting an oligopolist

FIGURE 11.2.5

Sweezy Solution

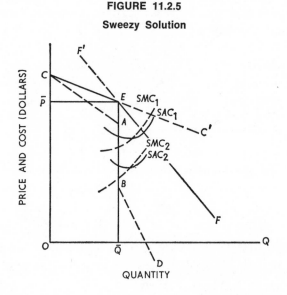

QUANTITY

is given by the "kinked" curve *CEF.* The slope of the curve changes drastically at the point *E,* corresponding to price $O\overline{P}$. The kink in the demand curve causes a finite discontinuity in the marginal revenue curve, which is given by the dashed line *CABD. CA* is the segment corresponding to the *CE* portion of the demand curve; *BD* corresponds to the less elastic *EF* segment. At point *E,* however, there is a finite discontinuity represented by the segment *AB.*

The principal feature is the absolutely vertical section *AB.* Marginal cost can intersect marginal revenue at any point from *A* to *B* and nonetheless result in the same market price $O\overline{P}$ and sales $O\overline{Q}$. For example, suppose initial cost conditions give rise to the plant represented by SAC_2 and SMC_2. SMC_2 intersects marginal revenue in the vertical seg-

[15] Paul Sweezy, "Demand under Conditions of Oligopoly," *Journal of Political Economy,* Vol. XLVII (1939), pp. 568–73.

ment *AB,* so price is $\overline{OP}$. If costs rise appreciably, so that SAC_1 and SMC_1 now represent the plant operating costs, price does not change. Or going the other way around, cost could fall from SMC_1 to SMC_2 without affecting market equilibrium price and quantity. Thus, according to Sweezy, oligopoly price tends to be very sticky, changing only infrequently and as the result of very significant changes in cost.[16]

The question on which the Sweezy thesis falls is *why* the kink occurs at a specific point *E* and remains there. One approach is to regard *CC'* as Chamberlin's *dd'* curve, *F'F* as his *DD'* curve. This would set a temporary price at *E.* Then one must assume that each entrepreneur believes (*a*) his competitors will not match a price increase, so *CE* is relevant for price increases, but (*b*) they will match any price decreases, so the proportional market demand curve *EF* is relevant for price declines. This analysis explains *how* a kink occurs but it does not explain *where.* If one knows the equilibrium price ($\overline{OP}$) he can rationalize it by means of the Sweezy hypothesis. But the purpose of price theory is to explain how the interaction of demand and cost establishes a unique price-quantity equilibrium. The kinked demand theory does not do this because market equilibrium is consistent with a wide variety of cost situations. The Sweezy thesis, accordingly, must be regarded as an ex-post rationalization rather than as an ex-ante explanation of market equilibrium.

11.2.f Theory of Games and Oligopoly Behavior

For a time one of the most exciting new developments in economic theory was John von Neumann and Oskar Morgenstern's *Theory of Games and Economic Behavior.*[17] After 10 or 15 years' experience with game theory models, the consensus seems to be that game theory is more relevant to the study of specific business problems than to general theory. Nonetheless, it represents a unique approach to the analysis of business decisions; and these decisions comprise the ultimate raw material with which economic theorists must work.

The general object of game theory is to determine standards of

---

[16] For a variety of recent views concerning oligopoly price, consult the papers by Ackley, Alderson, Bailey, Baumol, Lanzillotti, Lerner, and Weston, in *The Relationship of Prices to Economic Stability and Growth, Compendium of Papers Submitted by Panelists appearing before the Joint Economic Committee* (Washington, D.C.: U.S. Government Printing Office, 1958).

[17] John von Neumann and Oskar Morgenstern, *Theory of Games and Economic Behavior* (Princeton, N.J.: Princeton Universtiy Press, 1953). Even the nonmathematical student can read with profit pp. 1–45. The mathematical reader should first try the Shubik volume cited at the end of this chapter.

rational behavior in situations in which the outcomes depend upon the actions of interdependent "players." Indeed, Von Neumann and Morgenstern had, as their purpose, ". . . to find the mathematically complete principles which define 'rational behavior' for the participants in a social economy, and to derive from them the general characteristics of that behavior. . . . The immediate concept of a solution is plausibly a set of rules for each participant which tell him how to behave in every situation which may conceivably arise."[18]

Initially, it will be helpful not to restrict ourselves to an economic context. A "game" is any situation in which two or more people compete. Tennis and poker are good examples, but so also are Russian roulette and duopoly markets. For simplicity, we restrict our discussion to games in which there are two participants, called "players." Whatever data are initially available comprise the "rules of the game," such as the dimensions of a tennis court, the ranking of poker hands, exact specification of commodities, and so forth. In a game one assumes that all possible courses of action for each player are known. Each particular course of action is called a "strategy" which, by definition, is a complete specification of the action to be taken by a player under every possible contingency in the playing of the game. Obviously, this information requirement is satisfied in few, if any, real world situations because each player must know the full set of strategies available not only to him but to his opponent as well.

In certain cases the information required is even greater. In a wide variety of games (games of chance), the outcome is not known with certainty; it depends upon a chance variable. When chance enters the picture one must assume perfect knowledge of the probability of each possible outcome corresponding to every possible combination of strategies by the players. The necessary information is readily available for the game of matching pennies; but in more interesting games such as bridge or duopoly the probability that the probabilities are known is negligible.

The simplest class of games, and the only class to be discussed here, are "strictly adversary" games in which the possible outcomes are ranked in opposite order by the players. Among the games of this class the most prevalent are "constant-sum" games, which means that the sum of the winnings of the players is the same regardless of its distribution among participants. A market in which demand is completely inelastic is illustrative of constant-sum games. For example, in the Hotelling linear market case, total sales are $L = a + x + y + b$, irrespective of the

---

[18] *Ibid.*, p. 31.

division of L between **A** and **B**. Finally, a special case of constant-sum games is the "zero-sum" game, perhaps best illustrated by the game of matching pennies. Briefly, in a zero-sum game the winnings of one player are matched exactly by the losses of another. The constant to which the winnings sum, in other words, is zero.

With these preliminaries out of the way let us turn to a constant-sum, strictly adversary, "strictly determined" game. In this case the Von Neumann–Morgenstern "minimax" solution is most readily explicable. Assume that player **A** can choose among three strategies (a, b, c), while player **B** has four possible strategies (a', b', c', d'). Any two-person, constant-sum game of this nature can be completely described by a "payoff" matrix, as represented in Table 11.2.1.

TABLE 11.2.1

Payoff Matrix for a Two-person, Constant-Sum Game

A's Strategies	*B's Strategies*				
	a'	b'	c'	d'	Row Min.
a...................	10	9	14	13	9
b...................	11	8	4	15	4
c...................	6	7	15	17	6
Col. Max...............	11	9	15	17	$9 = 9$

A's alternative strategies are listed in the column stub and **B**'s in the row stub. **A**'s payoff for each possible combination of strategies is given by an element in the matrix. For example, if **A** chooses strategy c and **B** chooses strategy d', **A** wins six. **B** wins the constant value of the game minus **A**'s winnings. If the constant value is 20, **B** wins 14. In summary, each element e_{ij} in the matrix represents the amount obtained by **A** if he chooses the strategy corresponding to the i-th row and **B** chooses the strategy corresponding to the j-th column.

Initially, assume **A** is allowed to select his strategy first and he chooses c. **B**, who selects next, would immediately choose d' to maximize his winnings, given the strategy adopted by **A**. On the other hand, suppose **B** chooses first and selects c'. **A** would choose strategy c to obtain maximum winnings for **B**'s chosen strategy. In actuality, with full knowledge assumed (each player knows the precise entries in the payoff matrix), the choices indicated above would never be made.

A realizes that for any strategy (row) he selects, **B** will select the strategy (column) which minimizes **A**'s winnings (or maximizes **B**'s return). Thus **A** is really interested in the row minima, shown in the last column of Table 11.2.1. He chooses strategy a because it guarantees him the largest return. In all cases, **A** adopts the strategy that corresponds to the maximum of the row minima. He "maximins." Similarly, **B** is only interested in the column maxima, or more precisely, in the constant sum minus the column maxima. He knows, for example, if he selects strategy *a′*, **A** will choose strategy *b*. Hence **B**'s return would be 20 — 11, or 9. Consequently, to assure his maximum payoff **B** selects the strategy corresponding to the minimum of the column maxima; he "minimaxes."

The strategy pair *a, b′* is determined; **A** wins 9 and **B** wins 20 — 9, or 11. This game is strictly determined because each player selects and pursues a unique, pure strategy; when these two strategies are adopted, the maximum of the row minima equals the minimum of the column maxima. Neither player could possibly accomplish more.

The case of unique or "pure" strategies is an interesting one from the standpoint of economic theory. The more sophisticated treatments of duopoly using the older tools of analysis stress the importance of recognizing mutual interdependence. But in a strictly determined game this is irrelevant so long as each participant behaves rationally. So long as one of the rivals pursues a minimax strategy the other cannot improve upon a minimax strategy himself. Furthermore, advanced knowledge of the opponent's strategy does not aid one in determining his own plan of action. Thus the Hotelling duopolist locates at the midpoint and the Chamberlin duopolist sets monopoly price.

Unfortunately, both the more common games of chance and game theoretic models of economic behavior are not strictly determined. In essence this means that if pure strategies are selected by the participants, the maximum value of the row minima is less than the minimum value of the column maxima. Such a game is illustrated by Figure 11.2.6 and Table 11.2.2.[19]

The diagram in Figure 11.2.6 represents a market in which demand is completely inelastic, as in the Hotelling model. Twelve customers are located in the circular portion of the market and are numbered like hours on a clock. At 5, 9, and 12 o'clock there are branch markets containing 5, 9, and 12 buyers each. Each buyer purchases one unit of commodity per unit of time. There are two sellers, **A** and **B**, of a homogeneous commodity; they can choose among three different locations: 3, 8, and 11 o'clock. Both may situate at the same location. Since the commodities are identical and we now assume zero transportation cost, price must be the same for each seller. Buyers purchase from the nearer seller.

---

[19] This example is due to William Vickrey, "Theoretical Economics," Part III-A (mimeograph manuscript).

FIGURE 11.2.6

A Nonstrictly Determined Game

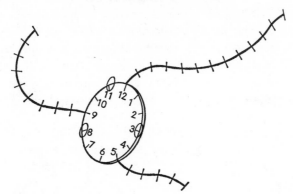

This market game is represented by the payoff matrix in Table 11.2.2. The entries show **A**'s sales per unit of time as a function of the locations (strategies) selected by **A** and **B**. The game has a constant value of 38. **B**'s sale for any pair of strategies is found by subtracting **A**'s sales from the constant value of the game.

Let us suppose **A** must locate first. Assume that he selects 11 o'clock. **B** will then locate at 8 o'clock so as to maximize his sales (or minimize **A**'s). With **B** established at 8 o'clock, **A** can increase his sales from 18 to 23 by relocating at 3 o'clock. But when he does so, **B** moves to 11 o'clock, captures the two larger branch markets, and **A**'s sales decline to 11 units. But with **B** at 11 o'clock, **A** moves to 8 o'clock, expanding his sales to 20 units. Then **B** moves to 3 o'clock, **A** moves to 11 o'clock, and we are right back where we started. The process of continuous relocation goes on because there is no unique minimax: the minimum of the column maxima exceeds the maximum of the row minima. As this game is constructed there is no unique stable solution.

TABLE 11.2.2

Payoff Matrix for a Nonstrictly Determined Game

A's Location	B's Location			
	3	8	11	Row. Min.
3	19	23	11	11
8	15	19	20	15
11	27	18	19	18
Col. Max.	27	23	20	20 ≠ 18

There is a way out of the impasse in many games, however. To illustrate, consider the game of matching pennies, represented by the payoff matrix in Table 11.2.3. A tries to match **B**; if so, he wins 1 cent, losing 1 cent otherwise. As in the market game, the minimum of the column maxima exceeds the maximum of the row minima. To this stage there is no formal equilibrium solution. Von Neumann and Morgenstern provided a solution, however, by introducing the concept of mixed strategies, defined as ". . . an assignment of probabilities to the

TABLE 11.2.3

A Nonstrictly Determined Game: Matching Pennies

A's Strategy	B's Strategy Heads	Tails	Row. Min.
Heads......................	1	−1	−1
Tails.......................	−1	1	−1
Col. max..................	1	1	$1 \neq -1$

feasible pure strategies in such manner that the sum of the probabilities is unity for each participant."[20]

Since probability elements are now present in the analysis of a game, the object of each participant can no longer be stated as the maximization or minimization of a particular value. One must look to the *expected value* of the game, which is determined by performing two simple operations on the payoff matrix: (*a*) multiply each element in the matrix by the compound probability that it is selected and (*b*) sum these products for all elements in the payoff matrix.

To illustrate further, let p_i be the probability that **A** selects the strategy corresponding to the *i*-th row. Similarly, q_j is the probability that **B** chooses the strategy corresponding to the *j*-th column. Thus $p_i q_j$ is the compound probability that the strategy pair *i, j* is selected. If a_{ij} is the associated element in the payoff matrix, step (*a*) above involves computing $p_i q_j a_{ij}$ for all *i* and *j*. Step (*b*) simply requires summing, so the expected value of the game ($\bar{v}$) is

$$\bar{v} = \sum_i \sum_j p_i q_j a_{ij},$$

where, by requirement,

---

[20] Von Neumann and Morgenstern, *op. cit.*, p. 145.

$$p_i \geq 0, q_j \geq 0, \quad \sum_i p_i = 1, \quad \text{and} \quad \sum_j q_j = 1.$$

In the game of matching pennies suppose each player chooses heads with probability one half. Thus each must also choose tails with probability one half. Consequently, the expected value of the game is

$$\bar{v} = (\tfrac{1}{2})(\tfrac{1}{2})(1) + (\tfrac{1}{2})(\tfrac{1}{2})(-1) + (\tfrac{1}{2})(\tfrac{1}{2})(-1) + (\tfrac{1}{2})(\tfrac{1}{2})(1) = 0.$$

Von Neumann and Morgenstern showed that if mixed strategies are allowed every constant-sum game has a unique minimax solution. That such a minimax strategy actually exists for the game of matching pennies can easily be shown. Compute the expected value of the game from A's standpoint for all possible probability assignments by A, assuming B always selects the probability combination most advantageous to himself, given A's selection. As an example, try the following probabilities for A: one-third heads, two-thirds tails. Then B can set probabilities as nine-tenths heads, one-tenth tails. The expected value of the game is minus four-fifteenths to A.[21] Assuming B always selects his best strategy, given A's selection, the maximum expected value of the game for A is zero, obtained when he sets probabilities one-half heads, one-half tails. Thus the *optimal mixed strategy* for A is $p_H = p_T = \tfrac{1}{2}$. When A plays this strategy, the best B can do is set $q_H = q_T = \tfrac{1}{2}$; the expected value of the game to B is also zero.

In contrast to strictly determined games, advanced knowledge of the opponent's plans is very important in games requiring mixed strategies for a minimax solution. As Von Neumann and Morgenstern wrote

. . . It constitutes a definite disadvantage for each player to have his intentions found out by his opponent. Thus one important consideration for a player in such a game is to protect himself against having his intentions found out by his opponent. Playing several different strategies at random, so that only their probabilities are determined, is a very effective way to achieve a degree of such protection: By this device, the opponent cannot possibly find out what the player's strategy is going to be, since the player does not

---

[21] The probabilities for B were limited to small numbers. B can gain more the closer he sets the probability of heads to unity. In the limit, given A's choice of one-third heads, two-thirds tails, B can gain one third (that is, the expected value of the game to A is minus one third). More generally, if A sets probability $p_H < p_T$, B always wins by setting probabilities $q_H = 1$, $q_T = 0$. If A sets probabilities $p_H > p_T$, B always wins by setting $q_H = 0$, $q_T = 1$.

know it himself. Ignorance is obviously a very good safeguard against disclosing information directly or indirectly.

In other words, the best way of deciding whether to show heads or tails is to flip a coin and let the toss decide.

Having sketched the outlines of game theory, we can now turn to some more general considerations. The heart of game theory is the minimax principle; and there are numerous criticisms of applying this principle to decision making in economics and business. Essentially, the minimax principle requires the player to maximize his payoff (or minimize his rival's) under the assumption that his rival always takes the least desirable course of action from the former's standpoint. Slightly less precisely, the minimax principle requires the player (or entrepreneur) to adopt the plan of action that will make the best of the worst possible situation. But this plan of action will not be the best if the worst possible situation does not arise. It does not allow the entrepreneur to exploit favorable changes in the market or, in any sense, to be "dynamic."

Many economists believe the minimax principle is an unnecessarily conservative standard. Furthermore, it is frequently asserted that minimax strategy is not compatible with the dominant entrepreneurial psychology. The object of most entrepreneurs is not to make the best of a bad situation. Indeed, it appears that many entrepreneurs attempt to maximize their objective under the assumption that very favorable conditions will prevail. And, of course, they generally expend considerable effort to influence the market so as to make the assumption correct.

If mixed strategies are required, the minimax principle is subject to another criticism. Specifically, random choice among strategies introduces uncertainty, which many entrepreneurs—perhaps almost all—go to great lengths to avoid. Thus entrepreneurs may not adopt a minimax strategy even if it is available.

On a more theoretical level, game theory requires more information than is likely to be available. Also, game theoretic models are absolutely static, seldom permitting even comparative static analysis. Furthermore, and of particular relevance to oligopoly markets, collusion cannot be introduced in a constant-sum game.

A final conclusion as to the value of game theory in economics is not possible at this time. On the technical or engineering side, the contributions of mathematical programming are unquestionable. But in theoretical economics it seems that success must await further refinements, if, indeed, it is achieved at all.

11.3 SOME "MARKET" SOLUTIONS TO THE DUOPOLY PROBLEM

The classical treatments of duopoly, with the possible exception of Chamberlin's, are based upon the assumption that entrepreneurs act independently of one another even though they are interdependent in the market. We turn now to some theories based upon explicit or implicit collusion among firms.

11.3.a Cartels and Profit Maximization

A *cartel* is a combination of firms whose object is to limit the scope of competitive forces within a market. It may take the form of open collusion, the member firms entering into an enforceable contract pertaining to price and possibly other market variables. This is perhaps best illustrated by the German *Kartelle;* but the NRA codes of our Great Depression years fall into this category as well. On the other hand, a cartel may be formed by secret collusion among sellers; many examples of this exist in American economic history. Most tend to date to the early years of the 20th century; but at the time of this writing the Antitrust Division of the Department of Justice has pending an action against a group of paperboard manufacturers, charging them with collusive price fixing—that is, with forming an illegal cartel.[22]

The cases of open and secret collusion offer the best examples of cartels. However, in a broad sense trade associations, professional organizations, and the like perform many functions usually associated with a cartel.

Of the wide variety of services a cartel may perform for its mem-

---

[22] I here give only one example. As a matter of fact, government prosecution of collusive price-fixing activities in violation of Section 1 of the Sherman Act are filed regularly.

In fiscal 1970, the Antitrust Division filed 19 price-fixing cases and 23 in the preceding fiscal year. It should be noted that vertical price-fixing agreements, that is, those agreements not exempt from prosecution under Fair Trade exemptions, constituted about 75 percent of those cases filed in 1970 and roughly 40 percent of those filed in 1969.

The Federal Trade Commission, under Section 5 of the Federal Trade Commission Act, may file civil suits against price-fixing conspirators. However, this would be rare since under present liaison arrangements with the Antitrust Division all hard-core price-fixing cases, of the type discussed in "Cartels and Profit Maximization," are prosecuted by the Antitrust Division.

I am indebted to Mr. William J. Curran for helpful advice regarding this point.

bers, two are of central importance: price fixing and market sharing. In this section, we will examine price fixing in an "ideal" cartel.

Suppose a group of firms producing a homogeneous commodity forms a cartel. A central management body is appointed, its function being to determine the uniform cartel price. The task, in theory, is relatively simple, as illustrated by Figure 11.3.1. Market demand for the homogeneous commodity is given by DD', so marginal revenue is

FIGURE 11.3.1

Cartel Profit Maximization

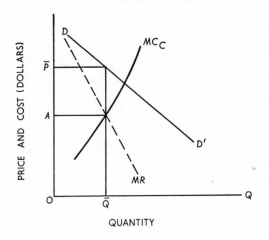

given by the dashed line MR. The cartel marginal cost curve must be determined by the management body. If all firms in the cartel purchase all inputs in perfectly competitive markets, the cartel marginal cost curve (MC_c) is simply the horizontal sum of the component marginal cost curves of the member firms. Otherwise, allowance must be made for the increase in input price accompanying an increase in input usage; MC_c will stand further to the left than it would if all input markets were perfectly competitive.

In either case the management group determines cartel marginal cost, MC_c. The problem is the simple one of determining the price that maximizes cartel profit—the monopoly price. From Figure 11.3.1, marginal cost and marginal revenue intersect at the level OA; thus the market price $O\overline{P}$ is the one the cartel management will establish. Given the demand curve DD', buyers will purchase $O\overline{Q}$ units from the members of the cartel. The second important problem confronting the cartel management is *how* to distribute the total sales of $O\overline{Q}$ units among the member firms.

11.3.b Cartels and Market Sharing

Fundamentally there are two methods of sales allocation: non-price competition and quotas. The former is usually associated with "loose" cartels. A uniform price is fixed, and each firm is allowed to sell all it can at that price. The only requirement is that firms do not reduce price below the cartel price. There are many examples of this type of cartel organization in the United States today. For instance, in most localities both medical doctors and lawyers have associations whose Code of Ethics is frequently the basis of price agreement. All doctors, for example, will charge the same rate for office and house calls. The patient market is divided among the various doctors by nonprice competition: each patient selects the doctor of his choice. Similarly, the generally uniform prices of haircuts, major brands of gasoline, and movie tickets does not result from perfect competition within the market. Rather, they result from tacit, and sometimes open, agreement upon a price; the sellers compete with one another but *not* by price variations.

The so-called fair-trade laws of many states establish loose, but very legal, cartels. Under these laws the manufacturer of a commodity may set its retail price. The retail sellers of the commodity (the sometimes reluctant members of the cartel) are forbidden by law to charge a lower price. The various retailers compete for sales by advertising, customer credit policies, repair and maintenance services, delivery, and such. But price is not a variable in the market.

The second method of market sharing is the *quota* system, of which there are several variants. Indeed, there is no uniform principle by which quotas can be determined. In practice, the bargaining ability of a firm's representative and the importance of the firm to the cartel are likely to be the most important elements in determining a quota. Beyond this there are two popular methods. The first of these has a statistical base, either the relative sales of the firm in some precartel base period or the "productive capacity" of the firm. As a practical matter, the choice of base period or of the measure of capacity is a matter of bargaining among the members. Thus, as said above, the most skillful bargainer is likely to come out best.

The second popular basis for the quota system is geographical division of the market. Some of the more dramatic illustrations involve international markets. For example, an agreement between Du Pont and Imperial Chemicals divided the market for certain products so that the former had exclusive sales rights in North and Central America (except for British possessions) and the latter had exclusive rights in the British Empire and Egypt. Another example is an agreement between the American company Rohm and Haas and its German counterpart Roehm und Haas. The former was given exclusive rights in North, Central and South America, and in Australia, New Zealand, and Japan; the latter was given Europe and Asia, except for Japan. The illustrations can be multiplied many times over, but these should serve to indicate the quota by geographical division.

While quota agreement is quite difficult in practice, in theory some guidelines can be laid down. Consider the "ideal" cartel represented by Figure 11.3.1. A reasonable criterion for the management group would be "minimize total cartel cost." This is identical to the short-run problem of allocating monopoly output among plants in a multiplant monopoly (see Figure 9.4.7). Minimum cartel cost is achieved when each firm produces the rate of output for which its marginal cost equals the common value of cartel marginal cost and marginal revenue. Thus each firm would produce the amount for which its marginal cost equals OA (Figure 11.3.1); by the summing process to obtain MC_c, total cartel output will be $O\overline{Q}$. The difficulty involved with this method is that the lower cost firms obtain the bulk of the market and the bulk of profits. To make this method of allocation acceptable to all members, a profit-sharing system more or less independent of sales quota must be devised.

In certain cases the member firms may be able to agree upon the share of the market each is to have. This is illustrated in Figure 11.3.2 for an "ideal" situation. Suppose only two firms are in the market and they decide to divide the market evenly. The market demand curve is DD', so the half-share curve for each firm is Dd. The curve marginal to Dd is the dashed line MR, the half-share marginal revenue for each firm. Suppose each firm has identical costs, represented by SAC and SMC. Each will decide to produce $O\overline{Q}$ units with price $O\overline{P}$, corresponding to the intersection of marginal revenue and marginal cost. A uniform price of $O\overline{P}$ is established and $OQ_c = 2 O\overline{Q}$ units are supplied. This happens, in our special case, to be a tenable solution because the market demand curve is consistent with the sale of OQ_c units at the price $O\overline{P}$.

To see this, let us go the other way around. Suppose a cartel management group is formed and given the task of maximizing cartel profit. With the demand curve DD', the management group views Dd as marginal revenue. Next, summing the identical SMC curves it obtains cartel marginal cost MC_c.[23] The intersection of cartel marginal cost and cartel marginal revenue occurs at the level OF, corresponding to output OQ_c and price $O\overline{P}$. The same is true for the individual firms, so the firms' decision to share the market equally is consistent with the objective market conditions. But this is a rare condition; cost differences between the firms would have created a situation inconsistent with market conditions and the voluntary market-sharing agreement would have collapsed. That, as we shall see, is what is most likely to happen to cartels anyhow.

FIGURE 11.3.2   **Ideal Market-sharing in a Cartel**

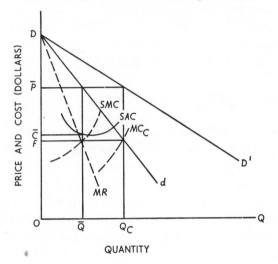

11.3.c   Short and Turbulent Life of Cartels

Unless backed by strong legal provisions, cartels are very likely to collapse from internal pressure (before being found out by the Antitrust Division of the Department of Justice). A few large, geographically concentrated firms producing a homogeneous commodity may form a very successful cartel and maintain it, at least during periods of prosperity. But the greater the number of firms, the greater the scope for product differentiation, and the greater the geographical dispersion of firms the easier is it to "cheat" on the cartel's policy. In times of marked prosperity profit may be so great that there is little incentive to cheat. But when profits are low or negative there is a marked incentive; and when the incentive exists enterprising entrepreneurs will discover what they believe to be ingenious methods of cheating.

---

[23] The problem, of course, will be more complicated if input prices vary with input usage. In this case, the cartel marginal cost cannot be directly obtained by summing the members' marginal cost curves.

The typical cartel as a functioning organization is characterized by high (perhaps monopoly) price, relatively low output, and a distribution of sales among firms such that each firm operates at less than minimum unit cost. In this situation any one firm can profit greatly from secret price concessions. Indeed, with homogeneous products, a firm offering price concessions can capture as much of the market as it desires, providing the other members adhere to the cartel's price policy. Thus secret price concessions do not have to be extensive before the obedient members experience a marked decline in sales. Recognizing that one or more members are cheating, the formerly obedient members must themselves reduce price in order to remain viable. The cartel accordingly collapses. Without effective *legal* sanctions, the life of a cartel is likely to be brief, ending whenever a business recession occurs.

11.3.d Price Leadership in Oligopoly

Another type of market solution of the oligopoly problem is *price leadership* by one or a few firms. This solution does not require open collusion but the firms must tacitly agree to the solution. Price leadership has in fact been quite common in certain industries. For example, Clair Wilcox lists, among others, the following industries as characterized by price leadership: nonferrous alloys, steel, agricultural implements, and newsprint.[24] Similarly, in their interview study Kaplan, Dirlam, and Lanzillotti found that Goodyear Tire and Rubber, National Steel, Gulf Oil, and Kroger Grocery follow the price leadership of other firms in the market.[25]

To introduce the price-leadership model, consider the simple illustration in Figure 11.3.3, an extension of the market-sharing cartel model of Figure 11.3.2. Two firms produce a homogeneous commodity whose market demand is given by DD'. By either explicit collusion or tacit agreement the firms decide to split the market evenly. Thus each views dd' as his demand curve and MR as his marginal revenue curve. In this case, however, the costs of the two producers are different; firm 1 has substantially higher costs than firm 2, as shown by $SAC_1 - SMC_1$ and $SAC_2 - SMC_2$, respectively.

Other things equal, firm 1 would like to charge OP_1 per unit, selling OQ_1 units. This price-output constellation would lead to maximum

[24] Clair Wilcox, *Competition and Monopoly in American Industry,* Temporary National Economic Committee, Monograph No. 21 (Washington, D.C.: U.S. Government Printing Office, 1940), pp. 121–32.

[25] A. D. H. Kaplan, Joel B. Dirlam, and Robert F. Lanzillotti, *Pricing in Big Business* (Washington, D.C.: The Brookings Institution, 1958), pp. 201–7.

profit for firm 1; but firm 2 can do much better since its marginal cost is substantially below its marginal revenue at this point. In this situation, firm 2 has an effective control. Being a lower cost producer, entrepreneur 2 can set the lower price OP_2 that maximizes his profit. Entrepreneur 1 has no choice but to follow; if he tries to retain OP_1, his sales will be zero. Hence the higher cost firm must be content to accept the price decision of the lower cost firm.

FIGURE 11.3.3

Price Leadership by the Lower Cost Firm

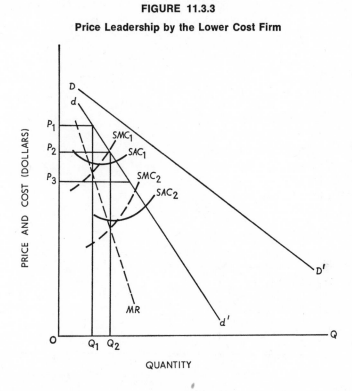

The particular solution shown here is not a very likely one. If this situation existed in a market, entrepreneur 2 would hardly agree, tacitly or otherwise, to split the market evenly. But given the antitrust laws in the United States he would not drive entrepreneur 1 out of the market. He has the power to do so. By setting a price such as OP_3, he can earn a pure profit and ultimately drive firm 1 out of the market. But then he would face the legal problems of monopoly. A better solution, from the viewpoint of the lower cost firm, is to tolerate a "competitor." Thus while not sharing the market equally, as in this illustration, entrepreneur 2 would nevertheless set a price high enough for entrepreneur 1 to remain in the market.

A much more typical example of price leadership is illustrated by Figure 11.3.4. The model is a somewhat exaggerated representation of a situation which, some say, exists in several American industries. There is one (or a small number of) dominant firm(s) and numerous small ones. As shown by the marginal cost curves in Figure 11.3.4, the dominant firm is almost as large as all the small firms combined.

FIGURE 11.3.4

Price Leadership by the Dominant Firm

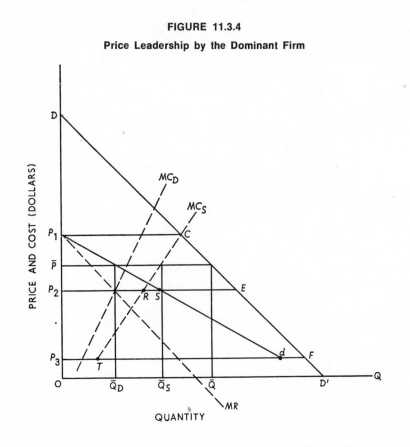

The dominant firm could possibly eliminate all its rivals by a price war. But this would establish a monopoly with its attendant legal problems. A more desirable course of action for the dominant firm is to establish the market price and let the small firms sell all they wish at that price. The small firms, recognizing their position, will behave just as perfectly competitive firms. That is, they will regard their demand curve as a horizontal line at the prevailing price and sell that amount for which marginal cost equals price. Notice this does not entail the long-run zero profit solution because price may be set far above (minimum) unit cost.

The problem confronting the dominant firm is to determine the price that will maximize its profit while allowing the small firms to sell all they wish at that price. To do this it is necessary to find the demand curve for the dominant firm. Suppose DD' is the market demand curve and MC_S is the horizontal summation of the marginal cost curves of the small firms. Since the small firms equate marginal cost and price, MC_S is also the collective supply curve of the small firms.[26]

First, suppose the dominant firm sets the price OP_1. The small firms would sell P_1C units, exactly the market quantity demanded. Hence sales by the dominant firm would be zero, and P_1 would be a point on its demand curve. If price OP_2 were set by the dominant firm, the small firms would sell P_2R units, and the dominant firm would sell $RE = P_2S$ units; thus S is also a point on its demand curve. Finally, suppose the price were set at OP_3. The small firms would sell P_3T units and the dominant firm $TF = P_3d$ units. For a price below OP_3, only the dominant firm would sell. Hence its demand curve is P_1dFD', and its marginal revenue is given by the dashed line MR.

Equating marginal revenue and marginal cost (MC_D), the dominant firm sets the price $O\overline{P}$ and sells $O\overline{Q}_D$ units. At this price the small firms sell $O\overline{Q}_S$ units; and by construction of the demand curve P_1dFD', $O\overline{Q}_D + O\overline{Q}_S$ must equal $O\overline{Q}$, the total quantity sold at price $O\overline{P}$.

Many variations of this basic price-leadership model can be constructed by changing the assumptions. One may allow for two or more dominant firms, for product differentiation, for geographically separated sellers and transportation cost, and so on. Nonetheless, the basic results are much the same; and they may help to explain price-output policies in a variety of oligopoly markets.

11.4 COMPETITION IN OLIGOPOLY MARKETS

Practically speaking, active price competition is seldom if ever observed in oligopolistic markets. To be sure, price wars occasionally erupt; but this really does not indicate price competition. A price war

---

[26] Again, for simplicity, we ignore the problem created by rising input prices. In principle, the solution is determinate if input prices rise as input usage increases; however, this case cannot be analyzed graphically.

indicates that the (probably implicit) communication channels among firms in the market are temporarily out of repair. In the normal course of events, the pre–price-war situation is quickly restored.

Absence of price competition, as we have said, is what one typically observes in the real world. It is also the inference to be drawn from almost every model of oligopoly behavior analyzed so far. With the exception of the Edgeworth model, the normal prediction is stable price with competition for market sales taking some form other than active price competition. The alternative forms of nonprice competition are as diverse as the minds of inventive entrepreneurs can make them. Yet there is one central feature: an entrepreneur attempts to attract customers to himself (and, therefore, away from rivals) by some means other than a price differential. Nonprice competition accordingly involves the differentiation of a product fundamentally more or less homogeneous among producers. The ways of differentiating are diverse, but three principal methods deserve mention.

Perhaps the most important technique of nonprice competition is advertising. In the United States, and increasingly in European countries, advertising is the uniformly most accepted and acceptable method of attracting customers, at least to businessmen if not to economists. The "pros and cons" of advertising expenditure have been argued at length; the argument is likely to continue because the question at stake is a moot one. But for good or not, advertising is an established practice that is presumably considered worthwhile, for otherwise businessmen would not continue to spend billions of dollars annually on this type of nonprice competition.

Another important type of nonprice competition consists in creating bona fide (and sometimes spurious) quality differentials among products. The general effect of quality differentiation is to divide a broad market into a group of submarkets among which there is usually a relatively large price differential. The automobile market offers a good example. There are definite, physically specifiable differences between a Ford Falcon and the Ford Motor Company's Continental. There is also a substantial price difference; no one buyer is likely to be a potential customer in both markets, except perhaps for automobiles to perform two fundamentally different services (family car and business runabout).

Ford is not alone in creating quality differentials, however. General Motors and Chrysler do the same; and they engage in active nonprice competition within each of the submarkets. Further, the automobile market example brings to light a social criticism of quality competition. Too many quality differentials may be created so that items supposedly in one class overlap with items in another. Falcons and Fairlanes overlap, for example, as do Pontiac, Oldsmobile, and Buick. Thus within the broad market not only is there competition to create new quality classes and gain the competitive edge of being the first in the market; there is also competition within quality classes.

Finally, a third major technique of nonprice competition is design differences. This type could also be illustrated by the automobile market; but the market for golf clubs serves just as well. MacGregor, Wilson, Spaulding, and other producers now "change models" annually, just as do the automobile manufacturers. They also create (possibly spurious) quality differentials as between sporting-goods stores and pro shops. But within, say, the pro-shop market, the competition among companies is strictly a matter of club design.

These three types of nonprice competition far from exhaust the possible methods but they do illustrate the ways in which entrepreneurs can spend resources in an effort to attract customers to their particular "brands."

11.5 WELFARE EFFECTS OF OLIGOPOLY

Since there are many models of oligopoly behavior, each predicting somewhat different results, it is impossible to be precise about the welfare effects of oligopolistic market organization. Furthermore, any set of static welfare criteria one applies to the situation may be relatively insignificant in a dynamic context. Nonetheless, a few things may be said.

First, whatever the model, two characteristics common to all oligopoly markets can be isolated. Firms in an oligopoly presumably produce their output at the minimum attainable unit cost. But there is no reason to believe their output uniquely corresponds to minimum long-run unit cost. Hence oligopoly organization requires more units of resources per unit of commodity produced than absolutely necessary. Furthermore, since pure economic profit normally accompanies oligopolistic market organization, price is higher than both unit and marginal cost. In whatever equilibrium is reached the marginal valuation of buyers is greater than the marginal cost of output. If the commodity were priced at either marginal or average cost, buyers would like to purchase more than producers would be willing to sell.

A second consideration is also important. Vast amounts of resources are devoted to advertising and to creating quality and design differentials. The allocation of some resources for these purposes is doubtless justifiable. For example, to the extent that advertising merely reports price and seller location, it helps keep buyers better informed. Similarly, certain quality and design differentials may be socially desirable. Nonetheless, there is a strong presumption (based upon purely empirical grounds) that oligopolists push all forms of nonprice competition beyond the socially desirable limits. In absence of evidence to the contrary, it is reasonable to conclude that buyers in oligopoly markets would be better off if there were more active price competition and less nonprice competition.

As noted, the welfare criteria imposed so far are *static;* and from the standpoint of these criteria oligopoly fares rather badly. However, dynamic considerations should not be entirely ignored. Industrial research and development, the now-famous R. & D., was essential to the evolution of our modern industrial society and is now essential to its continued viability and growth. Many argue, with considerable persuasiveness, that R. & D. usually thrives only in oligopolistic markets. Neither perfect competitors nor pure monopolists have the incentive to undertake industrial research; and perfect competitors are usually not large enough to support research departments. Oligopolistic firms, on the other hand, always have the incentive: improve the product or reduce its cost so as to increase profit. Furthermore, such firms are typically large enough to absorb the short-run cost of R. & D. in order to reap its long-run payoff. In short, all sorts of static welfare criteria may be violated more or less with impunity if the dynamic rate of growth is sufficiently rapid. Some economists, and all oligopolists, hold that oligopolistic market organization is essential for the dynamic growth of the economy.

QUESTIONS

1. Assume that the skilled laborers in a competitive industry are represented by a strong union that is able to fix the wage at its monopoly level. Also assume that the firms are effectively prevented from colluding by strong antitrust laws, but unions are free to collude.

   a) Is it in the interest of the firms to have the union enforce an output restriction on behalf of the employers, assuming that the union would not change the wage rate for skilled labor or otherwise make new demands on the firms?

b) Would the above output restriction be in the union's interest?

c) If your answer to (*a*) is *yes* and (*b*) is *no*, could the firms make the output restriction attractive both to themselves and the union by offering a higher wage?

d) If your answer to (*c*) is *no,* is there any arrangement that would make output restriction mutually beneficial?

2. Explain the nature of the harm, if any, done to the efficiency of the economy when the firms in an industry:

a) Organize to prevent other firms from entering the industry;

b) Agree to charge a uniform price;

c) Restrict the output of the firms so as to increase the total profit earned by all of the firms together;

d) Sell all their output through a cooperative selling agency;

e) Establish different selling prices for two different markets.

3. Discuss the following statement: "In oligopoly there is a tendency toward the maximization of aggregate industry profits. . . . But this tendency is counteracted by other forces." (Fellner, *Competition among the Few,* p. 142.)

4. "The problem of bilateral monopoly is obviously one of negotiating and bargaining in order to reach an agreement between certain limits of feasibility. . . . [it] is useful to consider the oligopoly problem as being 'essentially' of this character" (Fellner, *Competition among the Few,* p. 23).

a) What are the aspects of oligopoly behavior that Fellner views as equivalent to "negotiating and bargaining"?

b) Why is such behavior to be expected in an oligopoly situation?

5. In discussing the American automobile industry, in which four firms accounted for about 99 percent of total output in 1963, the late Senator Kefauver wrote: ". . . nonprice forms of competition yield very different results from those flowing out of price competition. These results involve great economic waste and are often positively harmful to the economy" (*In a Few Hands,* 1965).
Discuss this statement, including

a) Why nonprice competition is likely in an industry with this kind of market structure;

b) The probable effect of this kind of market structure on resource allocation and economic efficiency;

c) Possible limitations of economic theory in analyzing this kind of problem.

6. Assume that the bituminous coal industry is a competitive industry and

that it is in long-run equilibrium. Now assume that the firms in the industry form a cartel.

a) What will happen to the equilibrium output and price of coal and why?

b) How should the output be distributed among the individual firms?

c) After the cartel is operating, are there incentives for the individual firms to cheat, and why or why not?

d) Does the possibility of entry by other firms make a difference in the behavior of the cartel?

SUGGESTED READINGS

Chamberlin, E. H. *The Theory of Monopolistic Competition,* pp. 30–55, pp. 221–29. Cambridge, Mass.: Harvard University Press, 1933 (8th ed., 1962). [Elementary math required.]

Fellner, William. *Competition among the Few: Oligopoly and Similar Market Structures.* New York: Alfred A. Knopf, Inc., 1949.

Hicks, J. R. "Annual Survey of Economic Theory: The Theory of Monopoly," *Econometrica,* Vol. III (1935), pp. 1–20. [Elementary math required.]

Hotelling, Harold. "Stability in Competition," *Economic Journal,* Vol. XXXIX (1929), pp. 41–57. [Elementary math required.]

Machlup, Fritz. *The Economics of Sellers' Competition,* pp. 347–514, esp. pp. 368–413. Baltimore: Johns Hopkins Press, 1952.

Rothchild, K. W. "Price Theory and Oligopoly," *Economic Journal,* Vol. LVII (1947), pp. 299–320.

Shubik, Martin. *Strategy and Market Structure,* esp. pp. 1–18 and pp. 59–78. New York: John Wiley & Sons, Inc., 1959. [Advanced math required.]

Stigler, George J. "The Kinked Oligopoly Demand Curve and Rigid Prices," *Journal of Political Economy,* Vol. LV (1947), pp. 432–49.

———. "Notes on a Theory of Duopoly," *Journal of Political Economy,* Vol. XLVIII (1940), pp. 521–41.

Sweezy, Paul. "Demand under Conditions of Oligopoly," *Journal of Political Economy,* Vol. XLVII (1939), pp. 568–73.

LINEAR PROGRAMMING: AN APPROACH TO DECISION MAKING IN GOVERNMENT AND BUSINESS

12.1 INTRODUCTION

To this point in Part III, our analysis has been concentrated upon the *economic theory* of business behavior. The object has been *qualitative analyses* of business decision making (e.g., produce that quantity for which $MC = MR$) that permit *qualitative inferences* concerning the behavior of markets and the overall performance of the market system.

There is a reason for this. The object of the economist is to develop general models of business behavior that cover a wide variety of specific cases. Thus the economist must deal with general functional and behavioral relations that are only constrained to have economically or technologically meaningful properties. For example, we assume that quantity demanded is inversely related to price; but we do not assume that the two are linearly related. Of course, linear demand functions have been used for illustrative simplicity; but they have not been used in cases where the linearity assumption would have a qualitative impact upon the analytical results. In like manner, we have assumed that production functions have a region over which marginal and average products decline and cost functions have a region over which marginal and average costs rise.

But that is *all* we have assumed. In our general analysis we have never assumed, for example, that $q = 1,000 - 4p$ is the demand function or that $q = 100x^{1/4}\, y^{3/4}$ is the production function. Had we used explicit functions such as these, we could in many cases have obtained quantitative or numerical answers to the problems posed. But the gain in precision would have entailed a tremendous loss in generality. We could say that *if* all functions had the precise form assumed, *then* the results would be what we found them to be. But that is all we could say; no generalizations would be possible.

As indicated above, theory (i.e., generality) is the job of the theorist; and as theorists, we have devoted most of our time and effort to it. As a result, we can furnish businessmen and government officials with qualitative analysis of specific problems; we cannot, on the other hand, furnish them the precise, numerical solutions that are often required in specific decision-making situations. Now, to be sure, any real world decision-making situation is likely to be so complex that one cannot be both precise and specific. That is, if the complex functional relations are given precise formulation, the resulting problem is too difficult to solve for specific answers, even by means of the most advanced millisecond computers.

To be told that his problem is too difficult for precise solution is no help to the businessman or government official. These groups of people must make decisions; they have no alternative. The only alternative they have is to make decisions in total ignorance or to make them in light of the best information that is *practicably obtainable.* To this end it is sometimes desirable to sacrifice generality and precision in favor of pragmatism; to use simple but imprecise relations to obtain approximate but inexact answers. Linear programming is a mathematical technique, often simply rules of thumb, whose object is to provide inexact answers to be used in actual decision-making situations.

12.2 LINEAR PROGRAMMING PROBLEMS

We have so far been very imprecise in describing the imprecise technique known as linear programming. To some extent this imprecision will remain throughout the chapter. That is, the mathematical techniques used to solve linear programming problems—the chief one is called the "simplex tableau"—will not be discussed. They are essentially cookbook methods that are easy but laborious to learn and quickly forgotten. Instead, we shall focus upon the types of problems that are suitable for analysis by linear programming, some of the limitations of this technique, and a graphical overview of linear programming.

Our first object is to give an intuitive feeling for linear programming by discussing some of the problems that historically gave rise to its development. It should be emphasized that linear programming is "new." It was developed during World War II,[1] first as an *ad hoc*

---

[1] Assigning priority is a risky business. However, I think it is fair to say that linear programming was developed by a group of scientists under the direction of Marshall K. Wood. This group worked for the U.S. Air Force during World War II. Their chief task involved using generalized Leontief models to determine resource

method of solving actual problems, only later as a theoretically established mathematical technique. Next, we should stress that it is essentially *mathematical*—or at least arithmetical and algebraic. An exposition of the technique must necessarily use symbols; and we shall use them. But that is as far as we shall go. Neither the arithmetical methods of solution nor their mathematical foundations are discussed.

12.2.a The Diet Problem[2]

Suppose you are the warden of a prison. One of your jobs is to supply the inmates with a diet that meets established minimum nutritional requirements at the least possible cost. The problem you confront is a classic in linear programming.

Suppose there are n foods from which to choose. These foods are consumed in quantities $x_1, x_2, \ldots, x_n$ and are bought at fixed market prices $p_1, p_2, \ldots, p_n$. The "minimum diet" must contain m nutritional elements (calories, all sorts of vitamins, minerals, etc.). Let a_{ij} denote the number of units of nutritional element i contained in one unit of food j. The minimum diet is specified by listing the *least amount*

---

allocations that would maximize or minimize some *linear objective function* (see below for definition). One member of this group was George B. Dantzig, who formulated the general linear programming problem and devised the "simplex tableau" solution in 1947.

The bit of history in the paragraph above is very specific. There were, of course, intellectual antecedents. Linear programming, in one view, is a systematic method for determining resource allocation. It is little wonder, therefore, that the intellectual antecedents are chiefly attributable to economists. During the 1930's there was a remarkable group of mathematical economists concentrated in Vienna, using Menger's mathematical colloquium and *Zeitschrift für Nationalökonomie* as sounding boards for their studies of general equilibrium models (see Chapter 15). Among this group were many then-young economists who were subsequently to become famous—Neisser, Schlesinger, and Abraham Wald. But most important among this group were Oskar Morgenstern (then editor of *Zeitschrift*) and John von Neumann. Von Neumann's linear model of an expanding economy is generally regarded as containing the mathematical antecedents of linear programming. [The original paper appeared in 1936; the English translation appeared as "A Model of General Economic Equilibrium," *Review of Economic Studies,* Vol. XIII (1945), pp. 1–9.]

Subsequently, a more practical approach was developed by Leontief in his input-output models, which appeared just at the start of World War II. After Dantzig's work, important theoretical contributions were made by Gale, Kuhn, Tucker, and Charnes. Professor W. W. Cooper of Carnegie-Mellon University certainly took the lead in encouraging industrial applications of linear programming.

[2] This problem was first posed and solved—not by linear programming methods—by George Stigler. See G. J. Stigler, "The Cost of Subsistence," *Journal of Farm Economics,* Vol. XXVII (1945), pp. 303–314.

of each nutritional element that must be consumed each day. Denote these minima by $c_1, c_2, \ldots, c_m$.

Using the notation just introduced, the problem may be given a precise formulation. There are, for example, $a_{12}x_2$ units of nutritional element 1 contained in the daily consumption of food 2 and, more generally, $a_{ij}x_j$ units of element i in the daily consumption of food j. To satisfy the minimum requirement for nutritional element 1, we must have

$$a_{11}x_1 + a_{12}x_2 + \cdots + a_{1n}x_n \geq c_1 .$$

A similar expression must hold for each nutritional element. Hence we may express our minimum requirements more compactly as

$$\sum_{j=1}^{n} a_{ij}x_j \geq c_i \quad \text{for} \quad i = 1, 2, \ldots, m . \tag{12.2.1}$$

Expressions (12.2.1) impose m constraints upon the warden. Subject to these constraints, he must select the foods to be contained in the diet so as to minimize the cost of feeding each inmate. The cost of purchasing x_j units of food j is $p_j x_j$, and the cost of all foods consumed is

$$Z = \sum_{j=1}^{n} p_j x_j . \tag{12.2.2}$$

Finally, there is an obvious but sometimes ignored restraint. It is impossible to consume a *negative* quantity of any commodity. Thus we must list some additional restraints:

$$x_j \geq 0 \quad \text{for} \quad j = 1, 2, \ldots, n . \tag{12.2.3}$$

Now we can bring all the conditions together and state our linear programming problem:

$$\text{minimize } Z = \sum_{j=1}^{n} p_j x_j , \tag{12.2.2}$$

$$\text{subject to } \sum_{j=1}^{n} a_{ij}x_j \geq c_i \quad (i = 1, 2, \ldots, m) , \tag{12.2.1}$$

$$x_j \geq 0 \quad (j = 1, 2, \ldots, n) . \tag{12.2.3}$$

When this problem is solved, the warden will know the diet—probably a very unpalatable one—that provides each inmate with the minimum health requirements at the least possible cost.

The "diet problem" has many variants, one of which was among the first industrial applications of linear programming. A leading producer of cattle feed brought the following problem to Professor W. W. Cooper. The U.S. Department of Agriculture stipulates the minimum amounts of about a dozen nutritional elements that must be contained in every 100 pound bag of food. There are seven or eight types of grain that can be used in cattle food. These grains have different nutritional content and different prices. What is the minimum-cost combination of grains that will satisfy the USDA minima? Professor Cooper solved the problem, and in doing so he established linear programming as a valuable tool for solving a certain class of problems faced by businessmen.

12.2.b Terminology

It is now time to introduce some standard terminology to use in the remainder of the chapter. Equation (12.2.2) is called the *objective function,* and the x_j's are called the *decision variables.* Expressions (12.2.1) are called the *constraints,* and expressions (12.2.3) the *nonnegativity restraints.* Any set of values of the decision variables that satisfies the constraints and nonnegativity restraints is called a *feasible solution.* The particular set (or sets) of values that satisfies the objective function is called the *optimal feasible solution.*

The general linear programming problem can be described as follows:

Definition: Given *m* linear inequalities in *n* decision variables, find the optimal feasible solution of the objective function, i.e., find a set of nonnegative values of the decision variables that will satisfy the constraints and maximize or minimize some linear function of these variables.

We now turn to another example of a linear programming problem.

12.2.c The Transportation Problem[3]

The transportation problem has a number of variants, some of which will be mentioned below. But to show how government officials, especially military, can use linear programming, we will examine the

---

[3] This problem was first posed and solved in 1941. See F. L. Hitchcock, "The Distribution of a Product from Several Sources to Numerous Localities," *Journal of Mathematics and Physics,* Vol. XX (1941), pp. 224–30. The problem was also posed independently in 1942 by a Russian, L. Kantorovitch. An English translation of his paper appears as "On the Translocation of Masses," *Management Science,* Vol. V (1958), pp. 1–4.

following problem. The U.S. Army Ordnance Corps maintains central arsenals (warehouses) in a number of locations throughout the United States. The arsenals today function as warehouses for spare parts, for example, replacement gaskets for jeep vehicles. Every Army post or outpost may be regarded as a retail outlet. That is, each Army installation has jeeps and one or more motor pools that serve as repair and maintenance agencies. The motor pools stock gaskets, among other things, to be used in repairing jeeps. The stocks must come from an arsenal, the latter being the direct recipient from the manufacturer.

Now we may state the problem and formulate its linear programming equivalent. There are given amounts of a uniform spare part (say jeep gaskets) available at a number of arsenals situated in different parts of the country. It is necessary to send specified amounts of the spare part to each of a number of Army installations scattered throughout the country. The cost of shipping a unit amount from each arsenal to every installation is known. The problem is to determine the minimum-cost routing from arsenals to installations.

Suppose there are m arsenals and n installations. Let x_{ij} denote the number of units of the spare part to be shipped from arsenal i to installation j. Since spare parts are *not* shipped from installations to arsenals, $x_{ij} \geq 0$ (nonnegativity restraints on the decision variables). Next, let a_i be the number of units of the spare part available at arsenal i and b_j be the number of units required at installation j.

Obviously, it is not possible to ship more spare parts from any arsenal than are available there. Since a_1 is the amount available at arsenal 1, we have

$$x_{11} + x_{12} + \cdots + x_{1n} \leq a_1 .$$

More generally, a similar constraint applies to all arsenals. Hence we may write

$$\sum_{j=1}^{n} x_{ij} \leq a_i \quad \text{for} \quad i = 1, 2, \ldots, m . \tag{12.2.4}$$

There are m of these constraints, one for each arsenal.

Next, the needs of each installation must be met. Since b_2 units of the spare part are required at installation 2, we have

$$x_{12} + x_{22} + \cdots + x_{m2} = b_2 ,$$

or more generally,

$$\sum_{i=1}^{m} x_{ij} = b_j \quad \text{for} \quad j = 1, 2, \ldots, n . \tag{12.2.5}$$

There are n of these constraints, one of them for each installation.[4]

Let the cost of shipping one unit of the spare part from arsenal i to installation j be c_{ij}. The cost of shipping parts from arsenal 1 to all installations is

$$c_{11}x_{11} + c_{12}x_{12} + \cdots + c_{1n}x_{1n} = \sum_{j=1}^{n} c_{1j}x_{1j} ,$$

that is, the *unit* cost of shipping *multiplied* by the number of units shipped and *summed* over all destinations. Thus the cost of shipping from all arsenals to all installations is

$$Z = \sum_{i=1}^{m} \sum_{j=1}^{n} c_{ij}x_{ij} . \qquad (12.2.6)$$

The linear programming problem follows immediately:

$$\text{minimize } Z = \sum_{i=1}^{m} \sum_{j=1}^{n} c_{ij}x_{ij} , \qquad (12.2.6)$$

$$\text{subject to } \sum_{j=1}^{n} x_{ij} \leqq a_i \qquad (i = 1, 2, \ldots , m) , \qquad (12.2.4)$$

$$\sum_{i=1}^{m} x_{ij} = b_j \qquad (j = 1, 2, \ldots n) , \qquad (12.2.5)$$

$$x_{ij} \geqq 0 \qquad (i = 1, 2, \ldots , m; j = 1, 2, \ldots , n) . \qquad (12.2.7)$$

The *general* transportation problem may be obtained by making the following substitution of words in the example above: "product" for "spare part," "origin" for "arsenal," and "destination" for "installation." Another example, which is not formulated algebraically, is the following.

12.2.d The Traveling Salesman

A textbook salesman representing Richard D. Irwin, Inc., lives in Homewood, Illinois. Periodically, he must make trips to 50 college and university campuses in an attempt to sell *Microeconomic Theory* and other texts in the Irwin Series. On each trip he visits all 50 campuses.

---

[4] Obviously, the problem has no solution unless the number of units available is at least as great as the number of units required. We assume this to be so, that is

$$\sum_{i=1}^{m} a_i \geqq \sum_{j=1}^{n} b_j .$$

Each campus is located in a different city, and he may begin his trip by going from Homewood to any one of the 50 cities. From there, he goes on city-by-city until he has visited each campus.

The salesman has two alternative modes of transportation: he may fly on a regularly scheduled commercial airline or he may rent a car. He may either fly or drive between every pair of cities. Further, for each pair of cities, the cost of flying and of driving is known. The problem is to select the route and the modes of transportation that minimize the cost of traveling.

12.2.e Numerical Example

So far our attention has focused upon a general formulation of linear programming problems. To make it more concrete, we turn to a numerical example. A certain cigarette factory has three types of machines —cutting machines (which reduce the tobacco leaf to cigarette tobacco), rolling machines (which produce the cigarette), and packaging machines. Four different types of cigarettes are produced: standard 70 millimeter, standard 85 millimeter, filter 85 millimeter, and filter 100 millimeter.

The various types of cigarettes require different amounts of machine time and have different amounts of profit per unit (say, per 1,000 cartons). Further, the total amount of machine time available per week is fixed and cannot be changed in the short run. Assuming that whatever is produced can be sold, the problem is to find the combination of outputs that maximizes weekly profit.

Now let's add some figures, as shown in Table 12.2.1. The entries in the body of the table show the amount of time of each machine required to produce one unit of each type of cigarette. The right-hand stub shows the maximum number of machine-hours available per week for each machine, and the last row shows the profit (revenue minus cost) per unit for each type of cigarette. For example, a unit of Standard 70's requires two hours of cutting machine time, one-half hour of rolling time, and a bit over one-half hour of packaging time; the unit so produced yields a profit of 56 cents.

Denote the number of units of each type produced by x_1 for Standard 70's, x_2 for Standard 85's, x_3 for Filter 85's, and x_4 for Filter 100's. First consider the cutting machines. No more than 4,000 machine hours can be used per week. Therefore, whatever the quantities of the various types of cigarettes produced, the total cutting machine time re-

TABLE 12.2.1

Data for Hypothetical Cigarette Factory

Machine Type	Product				Machine Time Available per Week
	Standard 70	Standard 85	Filter 85	Filter 100	
Cutting..........	2. hrs.	2.5 hrs.	2 hrs.	2.5 hrs.	4,000 hrs.
Rolling..........	0.5	1.5	2	2.5	1,800
Packaging.......	0.55	0.50	1	1.55	1,000
Unit profit.....	$0.56	$1.00	$1.50	$2.00	

quired cannot exceed the time available. Algebraically, this may be stated as

$$2x_1 + 2.5x_2 + 2x_3 + 2.5x_4 \leq 4,000 . \qquad (12.2.8)$$

Note that we cannot use a straight equality in this expression because there may be no feasible set of outputs that precisely require 4,000 hours of cutting machine time.

Similar expressions hold for the other machines. Thus we have

$$0.5x_1 + 1.5x_2 + 2x_3 + 2.5x_4 \leq 1,800 \text{ (rolling machines)} \quad (12.2.9)$$

and

$$0.55x_1 + 0.5x_2 + x_3 + 1.55x_4 \leq 1,000 \text{ (packing machines)} . \quad (12.2.10)$$

The objective function is the expression for total profit, which is simply unit profit *multiplied* by the number of units produced and summed over all types produced. From the last row of Table 12.2.1, this equation is

$$Z = 0.56x_1 + x_2 + 1.50x_3 + 2.00x_4 . \qquad (12.2.11)$$

Finally, our nonnegativity restrictions require that the output of each type of cigarette be positive or zero:

$$x_1 \geq 0, \quad x_2 \geq 0, \quad x_3 \geq 0, \quad x_4 \geq 0 . \qquad (12.2.12)$$

Putting together all the elements, the linear programming problem that confronts the cigarette manufacturer is as follows:

$$\text{maximize } Z = 0.56x_1 + x_2 + 1.50x_3 + 2.00x_4 , \qquad (12.2.11)$$
$$\text{subject to } 2x_1 + 2.5x_2 + 2x_3 + 2.5x_4 \leq 4,000 , \qquad (12.2.8)$$
$$0.5x_1 + 1.5x_2 + 2x_3 + 2.5x_4 \leq 1,800 , \qquad (12.2.9)$$
$$0.55x_1 + 0.5x_2 + x_3 + 1.55x_4 \leq 1,000 , \qquad (12.2.10)$$
$$x_1 \geq 0, \quad x_2 \geq 0, \quad x_3 \geq 0, \quad x_4 \geq 0 . \qquad (12.2.12)$$

When this problem is solved, and it is easily solvable, the cigarette manufacturer will know which types to produce and the profit-maximizing volumes of output of each type.

12.3   LINEAR PROGRAMMING: A GRAPHICAL ANALYSIS

In section 12.2 no limitation was placed upon the number of decision variables or the number of constraints. This freedom enabled us to consider some very general linear programming problems; but we could not solve the problems without going into the messy arithmetic of the simplex tableau. But if we are willing to restrict the number of decision variables to two, we can easily obtain a graphical solution. We now turn to this. Admittedly, it is a great oversimplification, but the graphical solutions will accomplish two objectives. First, graphical methods highlight some essential features of linear programming. Second, they enable us to make some comparisons between marginal analysis and linear programming.

12.3.a   The Graphical Technique

Without regard to contriving an application, consider the following linear programming problem:

$$\text{maximize } Z = 2x + 5y, \tag{12.3.1}$$
$$\text{subject to } x \leq 4, \tag{12.3.2}$$
$$y \leq 6, \tag{12.3.3}$$
$$x + y \leq 8, \tag{12.3.4}$$
$$x \geq 0, \quad y \geq 0. \tag{12.3.5}$$

This problem contains all the essential ingredients: the linear objective function [equation (12.3.1)], the linear inequality constraints [expressions (12.3.2)–(12.3.4)], and the nonnegativity requirements [expressions (12.3.5)]. The problem is illustrated graphically by Figure 12.3.1.

First consider the nonnegativity requirements. These two requirements are shown in panel a. Since both x and y must equal or exceed zero, the arrows illustrate that the final solution must lie on the axes or properly within the positive quadrant. Next, panel b depicts the constraints graphically. A vertical line has been constructed to represent $x = 4$. As the arrows indicate, any feasible solution (i.e., $x \leq 4$) must lie *on* or *to the left of* the line $x = 4$. Similarly, the restraint $y \leq 6$ is represented by the horizontal line $y = 6$ and the arrows pointing down-

FIGURE 12.3.1

Graphical Analysis of Linear Programming Problem

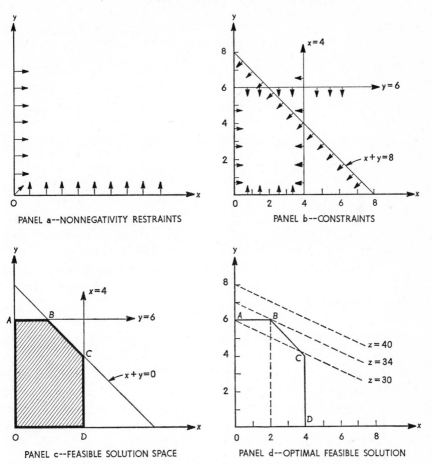

PANEL a--NONNEGATIVITY RESTRAINTS

PANEL b--CONSTRAINTS

PANEL c--FEASIBLE SOLUTION SPACE

PANEL d--OPTIMAL FEASIBLE SOLUTION

ward. That is, any feasible solution must lie *on* or *below* the line $y = 6$. Finally, the straight line labeled $x + y = 8$ and the arrows show that any feasible solution must lie *on or to the left of* this line.

The restraints and constraints are combined in panel c to determine the *feasible solution space.* The nonnegativity restraints require that feasible solutions lie on or above the axes. The constraints impose outward boundaries. Hence taking account of all restrictions, the feasible solution space is the *convex polyhedron OABCD* in panel c.

Definition: A polyhedron is a geometrical construction all of whose sides (facets) are straight hyperplanes.

Definition: A set of points is said to be convex if every pair of points in the set can be connected by a straight line that lies within or on the boundary of the set.[5]

Proposition: If a linear programming problem is to be solvable, the constraints and nonnegativity restraints must define a convex polyhedron.

Finally, the linear programming problem is solved in panel d. Write the objective function as

$$y = \frac{1}{5} Z - \frac{2}{5} x. \qquad (12.3.6)$$

Expression (12.3.6) is the equation of a straight line in the $x - y$ plane. Substituting various numerical values of Z permits one to construct a set of "iso-Z" curves, some of which are shown by the dashed lines in panel d. Consider the line $Z = 30$. All points on this line and inside the convex polyhedron $OABCD$ are feasible solutions. However, as is apparent, none of these points is the optimal feasible solution. A higher Z-value can be obtained. Next, try $Z = 40$. This is a higher, and therefore more desirable, value of Z. But it is immediately seen that no point on $Z = 40$ is a feasible solution. By experimentally trying different values of Z, one finally arrives at the highest attainable value, $Z = 34$, where the "iso-Z" curve is tangent to the convex polyhedron.

The optimal feasible solution is $x = 2$, $y = 6$. The nonnegativity restraints are satisfied; the constraints (12.3.3) and (12.3.4) are satisfied by an equality sign, while the constraint (12.3.2) is satisfied by the inequality.

One feature of the solution in panel d is that it is unique. That is, there is one, and only one, optimal feasible solution. This need not be the case. Indeed, there may be an infinite number of optimal feasible solutions, as we now illustrate. Consider the following linear programming problem:

maximize $Z = 2.5x + y$,   (12.3.7)
subject to $3x + 5y \leq 15$,   (12.3.8)
$5x + 2y \leq 10$,   (12.3.9)
$x = 0$, $y \geq 0$.   (12.3.10)

---

[5] Thus, for example, the following set is *not* convex:

The set is the space $ABCDE$. The points a and b are within the set, but a portion of the straight line joining a and b lies properly outside of the set.

The problem is illustrated by Figure 12.3.2. The nonnegativity restraints and the constraints establish the feasible solution space as the convex polyhedron $OABC$. "Iso-Z" lines have also been constructed. But the point of tangency is not unique. The maximum attainable value of Z is unique, namely max $Z = 5$. But the combinations of x and y are not unique. One optimal feasible solution is point B, where $x = 1$, $y =$

FIGURE 12.3.2

**Linear Programming Problem
with an Infinite Number of Feasible Solutions**

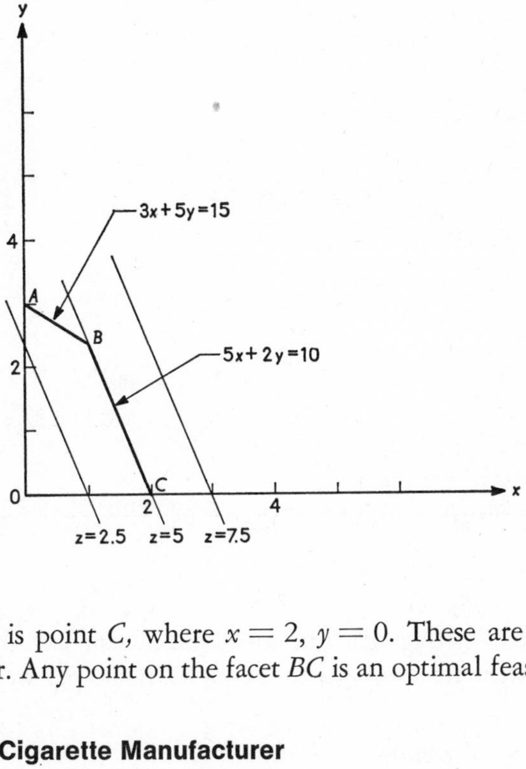

2.5; another is point C, where $x = 2$, $y = 0$. These are not the only two, however. Any point on the facet BC is an optimal feasible solution.

12.3.b The Cigarette Manufacturer

Let us now return to our example of the cigarette manufacturer in section 12.2.e. To make graphical analysis possible, suppose only Standard 70's and Standard 85's are made; the data in Table 12.2.1 have otherwise been retained. Therefore, the linear programming problem may be written as:

$$\text{maximize } Z = 0.56x_1 + x_2, \tag{12.3.11}$$
$$\text{subject to } 2x_1 + 2.5x_2 \leq 4{,}000 \text{ (cutting)}, \tag{12.3.12}$$
$$0.5x_1 + 1.5x_2 \leq 1{,}800 \text{ (rolling)}, \tag{12.3.13}$$
$$0.55x_1 + 0.5x_2 \leq 1{,}000 \text{ (packaging)}. \tag{12.3.14}$$

The nonnegativity restraints and the constraints establish the feasible solution space represented by the convex polyhedron $OABCD$ in Figure 12.3.3. Only one Z-line has been plotted, that which is tangent to the polyhedron. Given the profit function and the constraints, the maximum attainable profit is $1,394 per week. This profit is associated with the optimal feasible solution, point B. This is a unique solution: 857 units of Standard 70's and 914 units of Standard 85's are produced.

FIGURE 12.3.3

Optimal Feasible Solution for Cigarette Manufacturer

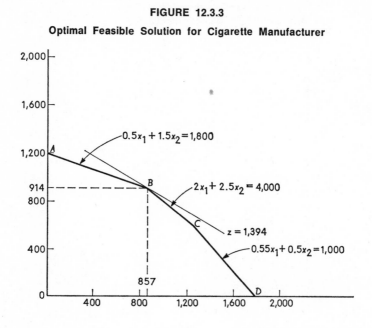

The cutting and rolling machine availabilities are exactly exhausted; the packaging machines are idle for about 82 hours per week.

12.3.c The Diet Problem

The diet problem in subsection 12.2.a may be solved graphically if we restrict the number of decision variables (i.e., foods) to two. Denote the quantities of the two foods by x_1 and x_2. Table 12.3.1 contains the relevant information. There are, we suppose, only three nutritional requirements: each day, a person must consume *at least* 600 units of vitamins, 500 units of minerals, and 700 calories. The two foods cost 2 cents and 3 cents per unit; the nutritional contents per unit of the foods are shown in the table.

Given this information, the problem is to determine the minimum

TABLE 12.3.1

The Diet Problem

Nutrient	Food 1	Food 2	Minimum Requirement
Vitamins.............	2	1	600
Minerals.............	1	1	500
Calories.............	1	2	700
Price............	$0.02	$0.03	

cost diet that satisfies the minimum nutrition requirement. The linear programming problem is formulated as follows:

$$\text{minimize } Z = 2x_1 + 3x_2, \tag{12.3.15}$$
$$\text{subject to } 2x_1 + x_2 \geqq 600, \tag{12.3.16}$$
$$x_1 + x_2 \geqq 500, \tag{12.3.17}$$
$$x_1 + 2x_2 \geqq 700, \tag{12.3.18}$$
$$x_1 \geqq 0, \quad x_2 \geqq 0. \tag{12.3.19}$$

The constraints are plotted in Figure 12.3.4. The convex polyhedron formed by the constraints is somewhat different from the polyhedron

FIGURE 12.3.4

Feasible Solution Space for Diet Problem

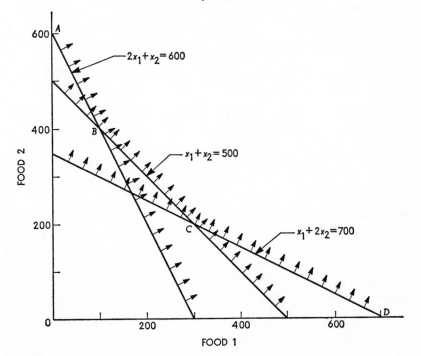

associated with a maximization problem. In this case, a feasible solution must lie on *or above* the constraining lines. Hence the outermost facets comprise the *effective* constraints and generate the convex polyhedron *ABCD*. This convex polyhedron is plotted in Figure 12.3.5 together with the minimum attainable "iso-Z" line, the one for which

FIGURE 12.3.5

Optimal Feasible Solution for Diet Problem

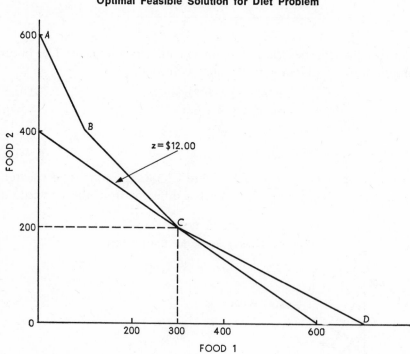

$Z = \$12$. The optimum feasible solution is attained at point C, with the daily consumption of 300 units of food 1 and 200 units of food 2.

12.4 CONCLUSION

The object of this chapter has been to convey a notion of the type of problems that can be submitted to linear programming analysis, to give a heuristic notion of solution techniques by means of graphical analysis, and to point up some of the limitations inherent in linear programming. The limitations have not yet been discussed explicitly, although the examples used above should infer some of these.

Before turning to the limitations, however, let us restate the nature of linear programming. Linear programming is a technique for specifying how to use limited resources or capacities, which have alternative uses, so as to attain a given objective. Stated somewhat differently, linear programming systematizes the process of selecting the most desirable course of action when thare are a number of courses of action available. To the extent it is applicable, linear programming gives information that is relevant and therefore aids in making more effective decisions about the allocation of resources.

The crucial phrase in the sentence above is "to the extent it is applicable." Linear programming, because of the *linearity* involved, is often not applicable. At the outset we stressed that linear programming is a technique using "simple but imprecise relations to obtain approximate but inexact answers." It is now time to explain this statement in some detail.

The *linearity* of linear programming is the feature that limits its applicability. Linearity is characterized by two central properties. Consider the following linear equation:

$$ax_1 + bx_2 = c,$$

where $a, b,$ and c are constants.

The first property concerns *additivity:* ax_1 can be independently added to or mixed with bx_2. In certain cases additivity does hold. The number of calories in each food consumed can be added together to obtain the total number of calories consumed in a meal; the profit made on two unrelated products may be added together to obtain total profit. But in other cases additivity poses a problem. For example, if one blends several liquids of different chemical composition, it is in general *not* true that the volume of the mixture is the sum of the volumes of the individual compounds. Or consider our cigarette manufacturing example. We assumed that it takes 0.5 hours of rolling machine time to produce a unit of Standard 70's and 1.5 hours for Standard 85's. Our linear programming analysis is correct if, and only if, one unit of Standard 70's and one unit of Standard 85's together require $0.5 + 1.5 = 2$ hours of rolling machine time. In fact, to produce a unit of each requires more than two hours because of the time involved in converting the machine to its different usages. Thus one should be aware that even in simple situations, the necessary additive property may not hold. That is, the assumption of additivity may cause the approximation to be intolerably poor.

The second property concerns a *multiplicative* relation: x_1 can be multiplied by the same constant a (or x_2 by b) irrespective of the value of x_1. This often holds. If it takes 1 hour to make 1 unit of a good on a given machine, it takes 10 hours to make 10 units. Or in our diet problem, if 1 unit of food 1 costs 2 cents, 300 units cost \$6. These examples of the necessary multiplicative property are plausible. But it is not a pervasive relation. In the typical case, for example, quantity demanded varies inversely with price and marginal cost varies directly with output. Yet for a profit-maximizing linear programming problem, we have to be able to write

$$\text{PROFIT} = pq - Cq \,,$$

where p and C are constants. Obviously, this requires that the firm be a perfect competitor in the output market; and it also requires that marginal and average cost be constant over the relevant range of output.

In summary, if a real world problem gives rise to conditions that are suitably approximated by the additive and multiplicative properties, linear programming is a powerful tool. But one must be circumspect; the real world may not be as linear as some think.

PROBLEMS

Solve the following linear programming problems by graphical techniques.

1. maximize $Z = x_1 + 1.5\,x_2$,
   subject to $2x_1 + 3x_2 \leq 6$,
   $\quad\quad\quad\quad x_1 + 4x_2 \leq 4$,
   $\quad\quad\quad\quad x_1 \geq 0,\ x_2 \geq 0$.

2. minimize $Z = 6x_1 + 4x_2$,
   subject to $2x_1 + x_2 \geq 1$,
   $\quad\quad\quad\quad 3x_1 + 4x_2 \geq 1.5$,
   $\quad\quad\quad\quad x_1 \geq 0,\ x_2 \geq 0$.

3. maximize $Z = 5x_1 + 3x_2$,
   subject to $3x_1 + 5x_2 \leq 15$,
   $\quad\quad\quad\quad 5x_1 + 2x_2 \leq 10$,
   $\quad\quad\quad\quad x_1 \geq 0,\ x_2 \geq 0$,

4. maximize $Z = 2.5x_1 + x_2$,
   subject to $3x_1 + 5x_2 \leq 15$,
   $\quad\quad\quad\quad 5x_1 + 2x_2 \leq 10$,
   $\quad\quad\quad\quad x_1 \geq 0,\ x_2 \geq 0$.

SUGGESTED READING

Baumol, William J. *Economic Theory and Operations Analysis* (Englewood Cliffs, N.J.: Prentice-Hall, Inc., 1961), pp. 64–97.

Charnes, A., and Cooper, W. W. *Management Models and Industrial Applications of Linear Programming,* Vol. I (New York: John Wiley & Sons, Inc., 1961), pp. 1–40.

Dorfman, Robert. "Mathematical or 'Linear' Programming: A Nonmathematical Exposition," *American Economic Review,* Vol. XLIII (1953), pp. 805–06.

————; Samuelson, Paul A.; and Solow, Robert M. *Linear Programming and Economic Analysis* (New York: McGraw-Hill Book Co., Inc., 1958), pp. 8–38.

Advanced Reading, Part III

I. ALTERNATIVE VIEWS OF THE THEORY OF THE FIRM

Baumol, William J. *Business Behavior, Value and Growth,* pp. 45–82. New York: The Macmillan Co., 1959.

Boulding, Kenneth E. "The Theory of the Firm in the Last Ten Years," *American Economic Review,* Vol. XXXII (1942), pp. 791–802.

Cooper, W. W. "Theory of the Firm: Some Suggestions for Revision," *American Economic Review,* Vol. XXXIX (1949), pp. 1204–22.

Dorfman, Robert. *Application of Linear Programming to the Theory of the Firm.* Berkeley, Calif.: University of California Press, 1951.

Edwards, Edgar O. "An Indifference Approach to the Theory of the Firm," *Southern Economic Journal,* Vol. XXVIII (1961), pp. 123–29.

Encarnacion, Jose. "Constraints and the Firm's Utility Function," *Review of Economic Studies,* Vol. XXXI (1964), pp. 113–20.

Ferguson, C. E. "Static Models of Average-Cost Pricing," *Southern Economic Journal,* Vol. XXIII (1957), pp. 272–84.

————. "The Theory of Multidimensional Utility Analysis in Relation to Multiple-Goal Business Behavior: A Synthesis," *Southern Economic Journal,* Vol. XXXII (1965), pp. 169–75.

Kaphan, A. D. H.; Dirlam, Joel B.; and Lanzillotti, Robert F. *Pricing in Big Business.* Washington, D.C.: The Brookings Institution, 1958.

Makower, Helen, and Baumol, W. J. "The Analogy between Producer and Consumer Equilibrium Analysis," *Economica,* N.S. Vol. XVII (1950), pp. 63–80.

Scitovsky, Tibor. "A Note on Profit Maximization and Its Implications," *Review of Economic Studies,* Vol. XI (1943–44), pp. 57–60.

388

Simon, Herbert A. "New Developments in the Theory of the Firm," *American Economic Review, Papers and Proceedings,* Vol. LII (1962), pp. 1–15.

II. TOPICS IN THE THEORY OF MONOPOLY

Clemens, E. W. "Price Discrimination and the Multi-Product Firm," *Review of Economic Studies,* Vol. XIX (1951–52), pp. 1–11.

Coase, R. H. "Some Notes on Monopoly Price," *Review of Economic Studies,* Vol. V (1937–38), pp. 17–31.

Dhrymes, Phoebus J. "On the Theory of the Monopolistic Multiproduct Firm under Uncertainty," *International Economic Review,* Vol. V (1964), pp. 239–57.

Hicks, John R. "Annual Survey of Economic Theory: The Theory of Monopoly," *Econometrica,* Vol. III (1935), pp. 1–20.

Pfouts, Ralph W. "The Theory of Cost and Production in the Multi-Product Firm," *Econometrica,* Vol. XXIX (1961), pp. 650–58.

Simkin, C. G. F. "Some Aspects and Generalizations of the Theory of Discrimination," *Review of Economic Studies,* Vol. XV (1948–49), pp. 1–13.

Weldon, J. C. "The Multi-Product Firm," *Canadian Journal of Economics and Political Science,* Vol. XIV (1948), pp. 176–90.

III. TOPICS IN THE THEORY OF MONOPOLISTIC COMPETITION

Brems, Hans. *Product Equilibrium under Monopolistic Competition.* Cambridge, Mass.: Harvard University Press, 1951.

Cassels, John M. "Excess Capacity and Monopolistic Competition," *Quarterly Journal of Economics,* Vol. LI (1936–37), pp. 426–43.

Demsetz, Harold. "The Nature of Equilibrium in Monopolistic Competition," *Journal of Political Economy,* Vol. LXVII (1959), pp. 21–30.

————. "The Welfare and Empirical Implications of Monopolistic Competition," *Economic Journal,* Vol. LXXIV (1964), pp. 623–41.

Dorfman, Robert, and Steiner, P. O. "Optimal Advertising and Optimal Quality," *American Economic Review,* Vol. XLIV (1954), pp. 826–36.

Ferguson, C. E. "A Social Concept of Excess Capacity," *Metroeconomica,* Vol. VIII (1956), pp. 84–93.

Harrod, R. F. "Doctrines of Imperfect Competition," *Quarterly Journal of Economics,* Vol. XLIX (1933–34), pp. 442–70.

————. "Theory of Imperfect Competition Revised," *Economic Essays,* pp. 139–87. New York: Harcourt, Brace, 1952.

Hicks, J. R. "The Process of Imperfect Competition," *Oxford Economic Papers,* N.S. Vol. VI (1954), pp. 41–54.

Kaldor, Nicholas. "Market Imperfection and Excess Capacity," *Economica,* N.S. Vol. II (1935), pp. 33–50.

Paul, M. E. "Notes on Excess Capacity," *Oxford Economic Papers,* N.S. Vol. VI (1954), pp. 33–40.

Triffin, Robert. *Monopolistic Competition and General Equilibrium Theory.* Cambridge, Mass.: Harvard University Press, 1949.

IV. TOPICS IN THE THEORY OF OLIGOPOLY

Bishop, Robert L. "Duopoly: Collusion or Warfare?" *American Economic Review,* Vol. L (1960), pp. 933–61.

Cournot, A. A. *Researches into the Mathematical Principles of the Theory of Wealth* (trans. by Nathaniel T. Bacon), esp. pp. 78–89. New York: The Macmillan Co., 1897.

Edgeworth, Francis Y. "The Pure Theory of Monopoly," *Papers Relating to Political Economy,* I, pp. 111–42. London: Macmillan & Co., Ltd., 1925.

Fellner, William. *Competition among the Few: Oligopoly and Similar Market Structures.* New York: Knopf, 1949.

Ferguson, C. E. and Pfouts, Ralph W. "Learning and Expectations in Dynamic Duopoly Behavior," *Behavioral Science,* Vol. VII (1962), pp. 223–37.

Frisch, Ragnar. "Monopoly-Polypoly—The Concept of Force in the Economy," *International Economic Papers,* No. 1 (1951), pp. 23–36.

Hicks, John R. "Annual Survey of Economic Theory: The Theory of Monopoly," *Econometrica,* Vol. III (1935), pp. 1–20.

Hotelling, Harold. "Stability in Competition," *Economic Journal,* Vol. XXXIX (1929), pp. 41–57.

Mayberry, J. P.; Nash, J. E.; and Shubik, Martin. "A Comparison of Treatments of a Duopoly Situation," *Econometrica,* Vol. XXI (1953), pp. 141–54.

Modigliani, Franco. "New Developments on the Oligopoly Front," *Journal of Political Economy,* Vol. LXVI (1958), pp. 215–32.

Shubik, Martin. "A Comparison of Treatments of a Duopoly Problem, II," *Econometrica,* Vol. XXIII (1955), pp. 417–31.

———. *Strategy and Market Structure.* New York: John Wiley & Sons, Inc., 1959.

Smithies, Arthur, and Savage, L. J. "A Dynamic Problem in Duopoly," *Econometrica,* Vol. VIII (1940), pp. 130–43.

Stigler, George J. "Notes on the Theory of Duopoly," *Journal of Political Economy,* Vol. XLVIII (1940), pp. 521–41.

PART IV

Theory of Distribution

Parts I and III, together with the tools developed in Part II, present the modern or neoclassical theory of *value*—a theory explaining the origin of demand, supply, and market price. Hopefully, the market price so determined represents the marginal social valuation of the commodity. If so, some theoretical statements concerning economic welfare can be made (Part V).

A central part of this theory of value is the marginal cost of production and its possible reflection in the supply curve. Costs and supply, in turn, depend upon the technological conditions of production and the cost of productive services. So far we have assumed that both are given; and we will continue to assume that the physical conditions of production are technologically given and do not change over the time period relevant to our analysis. But now we must determine the prices of productive services, the *distribution* half of "Value and Distribution," or modern microeconomic theory. The theories of value and distribution are then brought together in Part V, first to discuss the general economic equilibrium and second to analyze economic welfare in a competitive society.

Broadly speaking, the theory of input pricing does not differ from the theory of pricing goods. Both are fundamentally based upon the interaction of demand and supply. In the present case, demand arises from business firms (rather than consumers) and supply, at least the supply of labor services, arises from individuals who are not only sellers of labor time but also consumers. Furthermore, for the more interesting cases of capital and labor, one determines the price of using the resource for a stipulated period of time, not the price of purchasing the resource. In other respects, however, the theory of distribution is the theory of value of productive services.

The previous level of abstraction is maintained throughout Part IV. This is certainly to be expected in Chapter 13, which presents the marginal productivity theory of distribution in perfectly competitive input and output markets. When imperfections appear in either market, however, the situation changes appreciably. This is especially true when large employers bargain directly with representatives of powerful labor organizations. When market imperfections arise, labor unions tend to arise as well. The theoretical discussion in Chapter 14 may seem far removed from the dramatic world of *GM* v. *UAW*. Indeed it is, in a certain sense. Yet the theoretical results obtained do set limits within which collective bargaining agreements are likely to occur.

Our point of view is that collective bargaining between management and union representatives constitutes bilateral monopoly, an indeterminate economic situation. Our analysis sets broad limits within which the solution lies. To push further requires one or more *courses,* not chapters. For example, there is a substantial body of theory concerning the collective bargaining process,[1] but an understanding of labor markets also requires an extensive knowledge of the institutional framework within which labor unions and business management operate.[2] This type of knowledge must be acquired in "applied" courses or contexts, just as "applied" courses supplement the other portions of microeconomic theory.

---

[1] For a taste of this body of theory, see Allan M. Cartter, *Theory of Wages and Employment* (Homewood, Ill.: Richard D. Irwin, Inc., 1959), pp. 77–133.

[2] For institutional setting, see John T. Dunlop and James J. Healy, *Collective Bargaining: Principles and Cases* (rev. ed.; Homewood, Ill.: Richard D. Irwin, Inc., 1953).

Chapter	MARGINAL PRODUCTIVITY
13	THEORY OF DISTRIBUTION
	IN PERFECTLY
	COMPETITIVE MARKETS

13.1 INTRODUCTION

As indicated in the introduction to Part IV, this section is not intended to be a practical man's guide to wage determination. Yet the marginal productivity theory constitutes a framework in which practical problems can be analyzed; thus it is a useful analytical tool for economic theorists.

The origin of marginal productivity theory is more or less dim.[1] Perhaps John Bates Clark is most widely associated with its development;[2] however, earlier hints appeared in Von Thünen's *Der isolierte Staat* (1826), Longfield's *Lectures on Political Economy,* and Henry George's *Progress and Poverty* (1879). Indeed, George presented a "universal law of wages" that clearly indicates marginal productivity analysis:

Wages depend upon the margin of production, or upon the produce which labor can obtain at the highest point of natural productiveness open to it without the payment of rent. . . . Thus the wages which an employer must pay will be measured by the lowest point of natural productiveness to which production extends, and wages will rise or fall as the point rises or falls.[3]

In the preface to his important work, Clark acknowledged his indebtedness to George and summarized his theory simultaneously:

It was the claim advanced by Mr. Henry George, that wages are fixed by the product which a man can create by tilling rentless land, that just led me to seek a method by which the product of labor everywhere may be dis-

---

[1] For a survey of its development, see Allan M. Cartter, *Theory of Wages and Employment* (Homewood, Ill.: Richard D. Irwin, Inc., 1959), pp. 11–32.

[2] John Bates Clark, *The Distribution of Wealth* (New York: The Macmillan Co., 1902).

[3] Henry George, *Progress and Poverty* (1879), p. 213.

entangled from the product of cooperating agents and separately identified; and it was this quest which led to the attainment of the law that is here presented, according to which the wages of all labor tend, under perfectly free competition, to equal the product that is separately attributable to labor.[4]

But in the 1880's and 1890's, Clark was not alone in developing the marginal productivity concept. Jevons, Wicksteed, Marshall, Wood, Walras, Barone, and others made important contributions.[5] Indeed, during this period an important distinction between views of marginal productivity theory arose.

First, to state the *marginal productivity principle* (developed in subsection 13.2.a): there is a direct functional relation between wages and the level of employment; each profit-maximizing entrepreneur will attempt to adjust employment so that the marginal product of labor equals the wage rate.

From Clark's point of view, this principle, slightly embellished, constituted the theory of wages. Marshall strongly disagreed:

> This doctrine [the marginal productivity principle] has sometimes been put forward as a theory of wages. But there is no valid ground for any such pretension. . . . Demand and supply exert equally important influences on wages; neither has a claim to predominance; any more than has either blade of a scissors, or either pier of an arch . . . [but] the doctrine throws into clear light the action of one of the causes that govern wages.[6]

According to Clark, the marginal productivity principle determines wages. Marshall, and later Hicks, and most other theorists, regard the principle as determining only the *demand* for labor. The supply of labor, or any other productive service, must enter before a full theory of wage determination is developed. This modern, or neoclassical, view is adopted here.

13.2 DEMAND FOR A PRODUCTIVE SERVICE[7]

Following the Marshall-Hicks approach, one must pay heed both to the demand for and supply of a productive service. In this section the

---

[4] Clark, *op. cit.,* p. viii.

[5] W. Stanley Jevons, *The Theory of Political Economy;* Philip Wicksteed, *An Essay on the Coordination of the Theory of Distribution;* Alfred Marshall, *Principles of Economics;* Stuart Wood, "The Theory of Wages," AEA Publications, IV (1889); Leon Walras, *Elements d'économie politique pure;* Enrico Barone, "Studi sulla distribuzione," *Giornale degli economisti,* Vol. XII (1896).

[6] Marshall, *op. cit.,* pp. 518, 538.

[7] The analysis of sections 13.2 and 13.4 relies heavily upon the tools developed in Chapters 5 and 6. The student should review these chapters unless he is thoroughly familiar with them.

theory of input demand, based upon the marginal productivity principle, is developed. The theory is applicable to any productive service although the most natural application, and the bulk of literary treatments, refers to the demand for labor. Thus we shall usually speak of "the demand for labor," but "the demand for a productive service of any sort" is implied.

13.2.a   Demand of a Firm for One Variable Productive Service

Before embarking on a formal analysis it may be useful to point out the direct analogy between the behavior of the firm in determining its profit-maximizing output and its profit-maximizing combination of resources. In the former study, we assumed that market demand and supply determine market equilibrium price, without first explaining the origin of market supply. Next, since each firm is too small to affect price by changes in its output, the demand curve confronting each producer is a perfectly elastic horizontal line at the level of market price. Our problem in this case was to determine marginal cost, and thus supply, given the state of technology and input prices. The analysis was completed by obtaining market supply from the individual supply curves.

The procedure in the present case is completely analogous, but reversed. First, we assume that the market demand for and supply of labor determine the market equilibrium wage rate, without initially explaining the origin of the demand for labor curve.[8] Next, since each firm is too small to affect the wage rate by changes in its labor input, the supply of labor curve confronting each producer is a perfectly elastic horizontal line at the level of the market wage rate. Our problem now is to determine the individual demand for labor curve, given the state of technology and the market price of the output produced. The analysis is then completed by obtaining market demand from the individual demand curves.

---

[8] The supply curve, in this instance, has not been explained either. It is analyzed in section 13.3.

Let us begin with an example, given in Table 13.2.1 and graphically illustrated in panels a and b, Figure 13.2.1. We consider a production process involving fixed inputs, and thus fixed costs, but only *one* variable input, labor. Thus total labor cost equals total variable cost. The product sells for $5 per unit and labor costs $20 per unit. The production function is specified by the first three columns. Column 5 shows total revenue (total product multiplied by commodity price), and column 8 lists total variable cost (units of labor input multiplied by the price per unit). Finally, the last column shows total revenue minus total variable cost, a proxy for profit inasmuch as it (profit) differs from column 9 only by the constant fixed cost.[9] The difference between total revenue and total variable cost is greatest when seven units of labor are used; this solution accordingly corresponds to the profit-maximizing organization of production. The total revenue–total variable cost approach is illustrated in panel a, Figure 13.2.1. The maximum distance between the two curves occurs when their slopes are equal, or when marginal revenue per unit of labor equals marginal cost per unit of labor.

TABLE 13.2.1

Value of the Marginal Product and Individual Demand for Labor

Units of Labor Input	Total Product	Marginal Product	Product Price	Total Revenue	Value of Marginal Product	Wage per Unit of Labor	Total Variable Cost	TR Minus TVC
0......	0	—	$5.00	$ 0	—	$20	$ 0	$ 0
1......	10	10	5.00	50	$50	20	20	30
2......	19	9	5.00	95	45	20	40	55
3......	27	8	5.00	135	40	20	60	75
4......	34	7	5.00	170	35	20	80	90
5......	40	6	5.00	200	30	20	100	100
6......	45	5	5.00	225	25	20	120	105
7......	49	4	5.00	245	20	20	140	105
8......	52	3	5.00	260	15	20	160	100
9......	54	2	5.00	270	10	20	180	90
10......	55	1	5.00	275	5	20	200	75

From the standpoint of input analysis it is more useful to approach the profit-maximization problem in a different way. First, note that the

---

[9] For example, if total fixed cost is $50, profit is column 9 minus $50. Thus maximum profit corresponds to the maximum entry in column 9.

supply of labor curve (panel b) is given by the entries in column 7, Table 13.2.1. It is a horizontal line at the $20 level, indicating the addition to total cost attributable to the addition of one unit of labor. The marginal product of successive additional units of labor is shown in column 3. Multiplying these entries by commodity price, one obtains the value of the marginal product, shown in column 6.

Definition: The value of the marginal product of a variable productive service is equal to its marginal product multiplied by the market price of the commodity in question.

From panel b, Figure 13.2.1, it is easily seen that the value of the marginal product curve intersects the supply of labor curve at a point corresponding to seven units of labor input. As we have previously seen, this is precisely the profit-maximizing labor input.

To get more directly to the proposition we seek, consider the generalization of panel b shown in Figure 13.2.2. Suppose the value of the marginal product is given by the curve labeled *VMP* in Figure

FIGURE 13.2.1

Graphical Illustration of Profit Maximization by Two Approaches

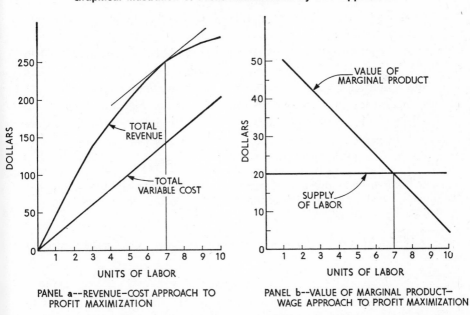

PANEL a--REVENUE–COST APPROACH TO PROFIT MAXIMIZATION

PANEL b--VALUE OF MARGINAL PRODUCT– WAGE APPROACH TO PROFIT MAXIMIZATION

13.2.2. The market wage rate is $O\bar{w}$, so the supply of labor to the firm is the horizontal line S_L. First, suppose the firm employed only OL_1 units of labor. At that rate of employment, the value of the marginal product is $L_1C = Ow_1 > O\bar{w}$, the wage rate. At this point of operation an additional unit of labor adds more to total revenue than to total cost (inasmuch as it adds the value of its marginal product to total revenue and its unit wage rate to cost). Hence a profit-maximizing entrepreneur would add additional units of labor; and indeed, he would continue to add units so long as the value of the marginal product exceeds the wage rate.

Next, suppose OL_2 units of labor were employed. At this point the value of the marginal product $L_2F = Ow_2$ is less than the wage rate. Each unit of labor adds more to total cost than to total revenue. Hence a profit-maximizing entrepreneur would not employ OL_2 units, or any number for which the wage rate exceeds the value of the marginal product. These arguments show that neither more nor fewer than $O\overline{L}$ units of labor would be employed and that to employ $O\overline{L}$ units leads to profit maximization. The statements are summarized as follows:

Proposition: A profit-maximizing entrepreneur will employ units of a variable productive service until the point is reached at which the value of the marginal product of the input is exactly equal to the input price.

In other words, given the market wage rate or the supply of labor curve to the firm, a perfectly competitive producer determines the quantity of labor to hire by equating the value of the marginal product to the wage rate. If the wage rate were Ow_1 (Figure 13.2.2), the firm would employ OL_1 units of labor to equate the value of the marginal product to the given wage rate. Similarly, if the wage rate were Ow_2, the firm would employ OL_2 units of labor. By definition of a demand curve, therefore, the value of the marginal product curve is established as the individual demand for labor curve.[10]

Definition: The individual demand curve for a single variable productive service is given by the value of the marginal product curve of the productive service in question.

---

[10] The results of this section can be developed mathematically. Let the production function be

$$q = f(x),\qquad(13.10.1)$$

where x is the single variable productive service. Marginal product is accordingly given by $f'(x)$. Under the assumptions of this chapter, the producer is a perfect competitor in both commodity and factor markets. Hence the market price of the commodity (p) and the market price of the input (w) are given.

The profit function is

$$\pi = pq - wx - F = pf(x) - wx - F,\qquad(13.10.2)$$

FIGURE 13.2.2

Proof of $VMP = \bar{w}$ Theorem

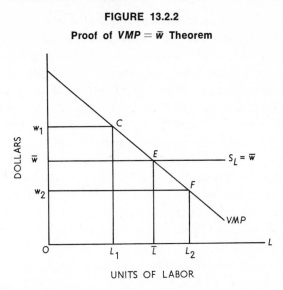

UNITS OF LABOR

13.2.b. Individual Demand Curves When Several Variable Inputs Are Used

When a production process involves more than one variable productive service, the value of the marginal product curve of an input is not its demand curve. The reason lies in the fact that the various inputs are interdependent in the production process, so that a change in the price of one input leads to changes in the rates of utilization of the others. The latter, in turn, shifts the marginal product curve of the input whose price initially changed.[11]

Consider Figure 13.2.3. Suppose an equilibrium initially exists at point A. The market wage rate is Ow_1, the value of the marginal product curve for labor is VMP_1 when labor is the only input varied, and OL_1 units of labor are employed. Now let the equilibrium wage rate fall to

---

where F represents fixed cost and wx is the variable cost. The entrepreneur adjusts his input usage so as to maximize profit. Mathematically, this is represented by

$$\frac{d\pi}{dx} = pf'(x) - w = 0,$$ (13.10.3)

or

$$pf'(x) = w,$$ (13.10.4)

the theorem stated in the text.

[11] For a review, see Chapter 5, subsection 5.2.d, especially Figures 5.2.3 and 5.2.4.

Ow_2, so that the perfectly elastic supply curve of labor to the firm is S_{L2}.

The change in the wage rate *in general* has three effects that are admittedly difficult to explain because they do not lend themselves conveniently to graphical analysis. Two effects—the substitution effect and the output effect—were explained in Chapter 6. These two effects are reexamined here by means of Figure 13.2.4. For convenience, assume that there are only two variable inputs, capital (K) and labor (L). Q_1 and Q_2 are production isoquants, and the initial input price ratio (when the wage rate is Ow_1 in Figure 13.2.3) is given by the slope of EF. As explained in Chapter 6, equilibrium is attained at point A, with inputs of OL_1 units of labor and OK_1 units of capital. Now let the wage rate fall to Ow_2, the cost of capital remaining constant. The new input price ratio is represented by the slope of the new isocost curve EF'. Equilibrium is ultimately attained at point C on the higher isoquant Q_2, with OL_2 units of labor and OK_2 units of capital employed.

The movement from A to C can be decomposed into two separate "effects." The first is a *substitution effect,* represented by the movement along the original isoquant from A to B. To understand this movement, construct the fictional isocost curve GG' with the following characteristics: (a) it is parallel to EF', thus representing the new input price ratio, but (b) it is tangent to Q_1, thus restricting output to the initial level. The movement from A to B is a pure substitution of labor for capital as a result of the decrease in the relative price of labor. The movement *would* occur if the entrepreneur were restricted to his original level of output at the new input price ratio.

The movement from B to C represents the *output effect.* First, recall

FIGURE 13.2.3

Individual Input Demand When Several Variable Inputs Are Used

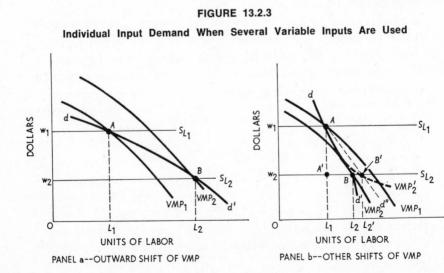

PANEL a--OUTWARD SHIFT OF VMP

PANEL b--OTHER SHIFTS OF VMP

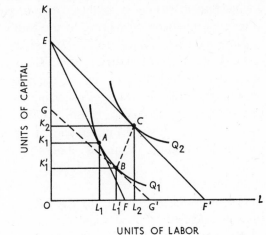

FIGURE 13.2.4

Substitution and Output Effects of a Change in Input Price

that Figure 13.2.4 depicts the maximization of output for a *given* expenditure on resources. When the price of labor falls, more labor, more capital, or more of both may be bought at the given, constant expenditure. The movement from B to C represents this, and position C indicates the ratio in which the inputs will be combined if expenditure on resources remains unchanged.[12]

In summary, the substitution effect resulting from a reduction in the wage rate causes a substitution of labor for capital. This effect alone, therefore, shifts labor's marginal product curve to the left because there is less of the cooperating factor (capital) with which to work. The output effect generally[13] results in an increased usage of both inputs. Thus the output effect alone tends to shift labor's marginal product curve to the right because there is usually more of the cooperating factor with which to work.

Let us now reemphasize that point C, Figure 13.2.4, indicates the optimal input *ratio* for the given expenditure on resources; but it does not show the profit-maximizing *amounts* of the inputs. When the wage rate falls, the marginal cost of production is reduced for every level of output unless labor is an inferior factor. The marginal cost curve shifts to the right, and the profit-maximizing output of the perfectly competitive firm increases. This is a separate effect that may be called the *profit maximizing effect*. In terms of Figure 13.2.4, the isocost curve EF' shifts outward and to the right, remaining parallel to itself, as it were. The profit maximizing effect normally leads, via an expansion of output, to

---

[12] The analysis is not affected if either of the inputs is "inferior" (see Chapter 6).

[13] There can be exceptions, but they are unusual. See the references in footnote 14.

an increase in the usage of both inputs. Hence this effect also shifts labor's marginal product curve to the right.

Now return to Figure 13.2.3. When the wage rate falls from Ow_1 to Ow_2, the usage of labor expands. However, the expansion does not take place along VMP_1. When the quantity of labor used and the level of output change, the usage of other inputs changes as well. The substitution effect of the change causes a leftward shift of labor's marginal product curve. But the output and profit maximizing effects cause a reverse shift to the right unless labor is an inferior factor.

Panels a and b, Figure 13.2.3, illustrate the ways in which the VMP curve may shift. In panel a, the value of the marginal product curve shifts uniformly outward to the right, from VMP_1 to VMP_2. The equilibrium usage of labor at wage rates Ow_1 and Ow_2 correspond to the points A and B respectively. Generating a series of points such as A and B by varying the wage rate also generates the labor demand curve dd'. Panel b illustrates that the value of the marginal product curve may shift uniformly inward to the left (VMP_2) or that it may "twist" (VMP_2'). In either case, connecting points such as A and B or A and B' generates factor demand functions such as dd' or dd'' respectively. The only requirement is that the new VMP curve intersect S_{L_2} at a point to the right of A in panel b. The factor demand curve, that is, *must* be negatively sloped.[14]

Thus the input demand curve, while more difficult to derive, is just as determinate in the multiple-input case as in the single-input situation. The results of this section may be summarized in the following important

Proposition: An entrepreneur's demand curve for a variable productive agent can be derived when more than one variable input is used. The demand curve must be negatively sloped because, on balance, the three effects of an input price change *must* cause quantity demanded to vary inversely with price.

---

[14] Unfortunately this assertion, which is essential for the results of this section, cannot be proved graphically and the mathematical proof is long and tedious. For detailed treatments of the general case, see C. E. Ferguson, "Production, Prices, and the Theory of Jointly Derived Input Demand Functions," *Economica*, N.S. Vol. XXXIII (1966), pp. 454–61; C. E. Ferguson, " 'Inferior Factors' and the Theories of Production and Input Demand," *Economica*, N.S. Vol. XXXV (1968), pp. 140–50; C. E. Ferguson, *The Neoclassical Theory of Production and Distribution* (London and New York: Cambridge University Press, 1969), chaps. 6 and 9; and C. E. Ferguson and Thomas R. Saving, "Long-Run Scale Adjustments of a Perfectly Competitive Firm and Industry," *American Economic Review*, Vol. LIX (1969), pp. 774–83.

13.2.c Determinants of the Demand for a Productive Service

The determinants of the demand for a variable productive service by an individual firm, while embodied in our derivation of the demand curve, have not been stated explicitly. It may serve well to enumerate them now.

First, the greater the quantity of cooperating services employed, the greater the demand for a given quantity of the variable service in question. This proposition follows immediately from the facts that (a) the product price is fixed for our analysis and (b) the greater the quantity of cooperating inputs the greater the marginal product of the input in question.

Second, the demand price for a variable productive service will be greater the higher the selling price of the commodity it is used to produce. Fixing marginal product, the greater the commodity price the greater the value of the marginal product.

Third, the demand price for a variable productive service will be lower the greater the quantity of the service currently in use. For a given commodity price, this proposition follows immediately from the law of diminishing marginal physical returns.

Finally, the demand for a variable productive service depends upon "the state of the art," or technology. Given the production function, marginal product and the value of the marginal product for each commodity price are known and do not change except for the first point above. However, technology does change; and it should be apparent that technological progress changes the marginal productivity of all inputs. Thus a technological change that makes a variable input more productive also makes the demand for any given quantity of it greater, and vice versa.[15]

13.2.d Market Demand for a Variable Productive Service

The market demand for a variable productive service, just as the market demand for a commodity, is the horizontal sum of the constituent individual demands. However, in the case of productive services the process of addition is considerably more complicated because when all firms expand or contract simultaneously, the market price of the com-

---

[15] For more explanation, see Alfred Marshall, *Principles of Economics* (8th ed.; New York: The Macmillan Co., 1920), pp. 381–93.

modity changes.[16] Nonetheless, the market demand curve can be obtained, as illustrated in Figure 13.2.5.

A typical employing firm is depicted in panel a. For the going market price of the commodity produced, d_1d_1' is the firm's demand curve for the variable productive service, as derived in Figure 13.2.3. If the market price of the resource is Ow_1, the firm uses Ov_1 units. Aggregating over all employing firms, OV_1 units of the service are used. Thus point A in panel b is one point on the market demand curve for the variable productive service.

FIGURE 13.2.5

Derivation of the Market Demand for a Variable Productive Service

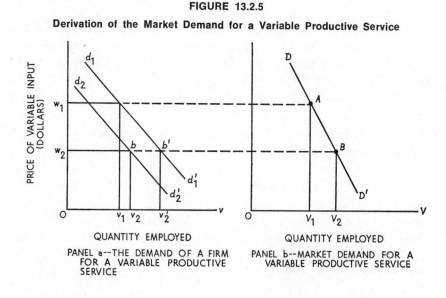

QUANTITY EMPLOYED

QUANTITY EMPLOYED

PANEL a--THE DEMAND OF A FIRM
FOR A VARIABLE PRODUCTIVE
SERVICE

PANEL b--MARKET DEMAND FOR A
VARIABLE PRODUCTIVE SERVICE

Next, suppose the price of the service declines to Ow_2 (because, for example, the supply curve of the variable service shifts to the right). Other things being equal, the firm would move along d_1d_1' to point b', employing Ov_2' units of the service. But other things are not equal.[17] When all firms expand their usage of the input, total output expands. Or stated differently, the market supply curve for the commodity produced shifts to the right because of the decline in the input's price. For a given commodity demand, commodity price must fall; and when it does

---

[16] An algebraic analysis of the derivation of market demand is simple but lengthy. For one version, see George J. Stigler, *The Theory of Price* (New York: The Macmillan Co., 1949), pp. 184–86.

[17] Compare the following to the derivation of market commodity supply by summing individual supply curves.

the individual demand curves for the variable productive service also fall.[18]

In panel a, the decline in individual input demand attributable to the decline in commodity price is represented by the shift leftward from d_1d_1' to d_2d_2'. At input price Ow_2, b is the equilibrium point, with Ov_2 units employed. Aggregating for all employers, OV_2 units of the productive service are used and point B is obtained in panel b. Any number of points such as A and B can be generated by varying the market price of the productive service. Connecting these points by a line, one obtains DD', the market demand for the variable productive service.

13.3 SUPPLY OF A VARIABLE PRODUCTIVE SERVICE

All variable productive services may be broadly classified into three groups: natural resources, intermediate goods, and labor. Intermediate goods are those produced by one entrepreneur and sold to another who, in turn, utilizes them in his productive process. For example, cotton is produced by a farmer and (after middlemen) sold as an intermediate good to a manufacturer of damask; the damask, in turn, becomes an intermediate good in the manufacture of upholstered furniture. The supply curves of intermediate goods are positively sloped because they are the *commodity outputs* of manufacturers, even if they are variable inputs to others; and, as shown in Part III, commodity supply curves are positively sloped.

Natural resources may be regarded as the commodity outputs of (usually) mining operations. As such, they also have positively sloped supply curves.[19] Thus our attention can be restricted to the final, and most important, category: labor.

13.3.a General Considerations

As population increases and its age composition changes, as people migrate from one area to another, and as education and reeducation enable people to shift occupations, rather dramatic changes can occur in the supply curves of various types of labor at various locations through-

---

[18] Let p_1 and p_2 be the original and the new commodity prices respectively. Thus $VMP_1 = p_1MP$, $VMP_2 = p_2MP$, and $VMP_1 > VMP_2$ since $p_1 > p_2$.

[19] There is some difficulty involving the optimal time for marketing natural resources; but this generally does not affect the slope of their supply curves. For an elegant treatment, see Harold Hotelling, "The Economics of Exhaustible Resources," *Journal of Political Economy*, Vol. XXXIX (1931), pp. 137–75.

out the nation. These changes represent *shifts* in the supply curve and are quite independent of its slope. To get at the supply curve for a well-defined market, assume that the following are constants (they are temporarily impounded in *ceteris paribus*): the size of the population, the labor-force participation rate, and the occupational and geographic distribution of the labor force. Thus one first asks, what induces a person to forego leisure for work?

13.3.b Indifference Curve Analysis of Labor Supply

The supply of labor offered by one individual can, in principle, be determined by indifference curve analysis, as shown in Figure 13.3.1. Hours of leisure are measured along the horizontal axis, OM represent-

FIGURE 13.3.1

Indifference Curve Analysis of Labor Supply

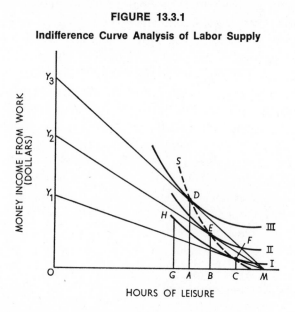

ing the maximum, or the total number of potential work hours in the week. The total money income from work is measured along the vertical axis. The slope of a line connecting M and any point on the vertical axis represents a wage per hour. For example, if OY_1 is the money income that would be received for OM hours of work, the hourly wage rate is OY_1/OM, or the slope of MY_1. Finally, curves *I, II,* and *III* represent indifference curves between income and leisure. For example, along the lowest shown level of indifference *I,* an individual is indifferent between OC hours of leisure (he works CM hours) and income CF, and OG hours of leisure (GM hours of work) and income GH.

When the wage rate is given by the slope of MY_1, the tangency condition for maximization[20] establishes equilibrium at point F on curve *I*. The individual works CM hours for income CF. His leisure, therefore, is OC. Let the wage rate increase, as given by the slope of MY_2. The new equilibrium is E on curve *II*. Hours of work expand from CM to BM as a result of the increase in the wage rate; they would further expand to AM if the wage line changed to MY_3. The equilibrium points $F, E, D, \ldots$ can be connected by the dashed line S, showing the supply of labor offered by one individual. In this case the supply curve is positively sloped since an increase in the wage rate results in an increase in the number of hours worked.

Figure 13.3.2 illustrates the opposite case. Individual labor supply curves can behave in a variety of ways; the crucial question is how their *sum* behaves—what is the shape of the market supply curve of any specified type of labor?

FIGURE 13.3.2

**Indifference Curve Analysis of Labor Supply,
Negatively Sloped Curve**

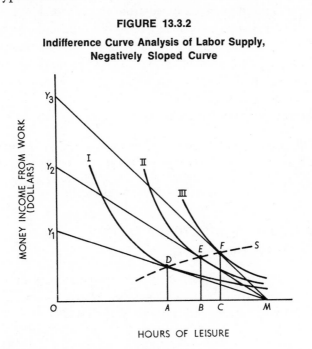

13.3.c The Market Supply of Labor

In fact, considerably more can be said about the *sum* than about the constituent parts. First, consider the situation in which one industry uses

---

[20] Utility is regarded as a function of income and leisure. The problem is to maximize utility for a given hourly wage rate.

exclusively a specialized type of labor (obviously, technically skilled). In the short run nothing can be said about the slope or shape of the labor supply curve. It may be positive, it may be negative, or it may have segments of positive and negative slope. But now let us relax our assumption concerning occupational immobility; and in the long run, one must. The master baker can become an apprentice candlestick maker if the financial inducement is sufficient. But more to the point, young people planning their education and career must surely be affected by current returns in various professions. Thus in the long run the supply of specialized labor is likely to have a positive slope.

The other case, in which labor is not specialized to one particular industry, is even more clear. In particular, if more than one industry uses a particular type of labor, the labor supply curve to any one industry must be positively sloped. Suppose any one industry increases its employment; the wage rate must rise for two reasons. First, to expand employment workers must be obtained from the other industries, thereby increasing the demand price of labor. Second, the industries that lose labor must reduce output; hence commodity prices in these industries will tend to rise, causing an additional upward pressure on the demand price of labor. Thus the industry attempting to expand employment must face a positively sloped supply of labor curve.[21]

In summary, we have the following

Relation: The supply curves of raw materials and intermediate goods are positively sloped, as are the supply curves of nonspecialized types of labor. In the very short run the supply of specialized labor may take any shape or slope; but in the long run it too tends to be positively sloped.

13.4 MARGINAL PRODUCTIVITY THEORY OF INPUT RETURNS

The currently accepted version of marginal productivity theory follows immediately from the tools developed above. Indeed, it is merely another application of demand and supply analysis.

---

[21] There are two possible exceptions, each of which leads to a horizontal industry supply of labor curve. First, if the industry is exceedingly small or if it uses only very small quantities of labor, its effect upon the market may be negligible. That is, the industry may stand to the market as a perfectly competitive firm does to the industry. Second, if there is unemployment of the particular type of labor under consideration, the supply of labor to all industries may be perfectly elastic up to the point of full employment. Thereafter the supply curve would rise. The latter is a disequilibrium situation that is actually not encompassed in the analysis here.

13.4.a   Market Equilibrium and the Returns to Variable Productive Services

The demand for and supply of a variable productive service jointly determine its market equilibrium price; this is precisely marginal productivity theory. In Figure 13.4.1, DD' and SS' are the demand and supply curves. Their intersection at point E determines the stable[22] market equilibrium price $O\overline{W}$ and quantity demanded and supplied $O\overline{V}$. The

FIGURE 13.4.1

Market Equilibrium Determination of the Price of a Variable Productive Service

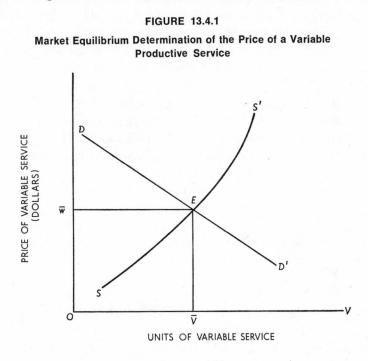

UNITS OF VARIABLE SERVICE

only features unique to this analysis are the methods of determining the demand for variable productive services and the supply of labor services. The fact that input demand is based upon the value of the marginal product of the input gives rise to the label "marginal productivity theory."

13.4.b   Short Run and Quasi Rents

Up to this point we have not been very specific about the short run and the long. Indeed it has not been necessary, because marginal pro-

---

[22] *Exercise:* Prove graphically that this is a stable equilibrium. Next, let the *SS'* curve bend back upon itself. Can you generate an unstable case?

ductivity theory is concerned with the price of *variable* productive services. In the long run all inputs are variable; so marginal productivity theory covers all resources in the long run. However, in the short run certain inputs are *fixed;* they cannot be varied and hence a "marginal product" cannot readily be generated. The return to short-run fixed inputs therefore requires another explanation. Following Marshall, this return is denoted "quasi rent."[23]

The explanation of quasi rents requires the customary cost curve graph, illustrated in Figure 13.4.2. In that figure, ATC, AVC, and MC denote average total cost, average variable cost, and marginal cost respectively. Suppose market price is $O\overline{P}$. The profit-maximizing firm produces $O\overline{Q}$ units of output and incurs variable costs which, on average, amount to $OA = \overline{Q}D$ dollars per unit of output. Thus the total expenditure required to sustain the necessary employment of variable productive services is represented by $OAD\overline{Q}$. Total revenue is $O\overline{P}E\overline{Q}$; thus the difference between total revenue and total variable cost is $A\overline{P}ED$. Similarly, if market price were OA per unit, the difference between total revenue and total variable cost would be $HAFG$.

This difference *is* quasi rent, which must always be nonnegative (if price fell to OJ, total revenue and total variable cost would be equal; if price fell below OJ, production would cease and total revenue and total variable cost would both equal zero). Notice that quasi rent is the total return ascribable to the fixed inputs. If price is $O\overline{P}$, quasi rent can be divided into two components: the amount $ABCD$, representing their opportunity cost; and the amount $B\overline{P}EC$, representing the pure economic profit attributable to their use in this industry rather than in their best alternative use. Similarly, if market price is OA, quasi rent ($HAFG$) has two components: the amount $HLKG$, the opportunity cost of using the fixed inputs in this industry; and the (negative) amount $ALKF$, representing the pure economic loss incurred as a penalty for using the resources in their current employment.

---

[23] In classical usage, "rent" is the return to a resource whose supply is absolutely fixed and nonaugmentable (that is, whose supply curve is a line perpendicular to the quantity axis). The return to short-run fixed inputs is called quasi rent because their quantities are variable in the long run.

The definition of quasi rent used in the text, which is the customary modern definition, differs slightly from Marshall's original definition (see his *Principles of Economics* [8th ed.; London: Macmillan & Co., Ltd., 1920], footnote on pp. 426–27). Marshall defined quasi rent as the return to a temporarily fixed input *minus* the cost of maintenance and replacement. Quasi rent as defined by Marshall cannot be illustrated by means of conventional cost diagrams. In particular, Marshall's definition is *not* equivalent to the text definition minus the area $ABCD$ in Figure 13.4.2.

FIGURE 13.4.2

Determination of Quasi Rent

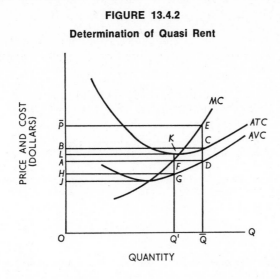

Finally, a rather obvious point should be noted: the sum of (total) variable cost and quasi rent as imputed above precisely equals the dollar value of the total product. This is simply a matter of definition and arithmetic; but it has a logical foundation, as we shall now see.

13.4.c Clark-Wicksteed Product Exhaustion Theorem

In short-run equilibrium the sum of total variable cost and quasi rent definitionally equals the dollar value of output. As has been said, this is a simple and obvious matter of arithmetic. It is not obvious, however, that in long-run competitive equilibrium the total physical product will be exactly sufficient to pay each input its marginal product. This is an important theorem attributable to Clark, Wicksteed, and other pioneers of marginal productivity theory.[24]

---

[24] A mathematical treatment can be given at the outset. First, it is useful to distinguish between the Clark-Wicksteed theorem (product exhaustion in long-run competitive equilibrium) and Euler's (mathematical) theorem concerning homogeneous functions. Let the production function be

$$q = f(x_1, x_2, \ldots, x_n),   \text{(13.24.1)}$$

where q is physical output and x_i is the input of the i-th productive service. Denote $\partial f / \partial x_i$ by f_i. Product exhaustion implies that

$$q = \sum_{i=1}^{n} f_i x_i .   \text{(13.24.2)}$$

Now according to Euler's theorem, if expression (13.24.1) is homogeneous of degree one, expression (13.24.2) is not an equation but an *identity* holding for

To repeat:

Proposition: In long-run competitive equilibrium, rewarding each input according to its marginal physical product precisely exhausts the total physical product.

A mathematical proof of the Clark-Wicksteed theorem is contained in footnote 24; in this section a graphical proof attributable to Chapman is presented.[25]

---

all values of the variables. The importance of the Clark-Wicksteed theorem is that it holds irrespective of the form of expression (13.24.1). To show this, we use a proof attributable to Erich Schneider in his *Theorie der Produktion* (Vienna: Springer Verlag, 1935), pp. 19–21.

From expression (13.24.1) we have

$$dq = \sum_i f_i dx_i .$$ (13.24.3)

Increase all inputs proportionately and denote the constant proportion by λ. Thus

$$\lambda = \frac{dx_1}{x_1} = \frac{dx_2}{x_2} = \cdots = \frac{dx_n}{x_n} .$$ (13.24.4)

Substitute expression (13.24.4) in (13.24.3) and divide the result by λq, thereby obtaining

$$q\frac{dq}{\lambda q} = \sum f_i x_i .$$ (13.24.5)

Consider the term $dq/\lambda q$, which shows the relative change in output attributable to the same relative change in all inputs. This term may be called the *function coefficient* or the *elasticity of the production function*. (Schneider's term [*op. cit.*, p. 10] is "ergiebigkeitsgrad." The term "elasticity of production" is attributable to W. E. Johnson, "The Pure Theory of Utility Curves," *Economic Journal*, Vol. XXIII [1913], p. 507. The term "function coefficient" is used by Sune Carlson, *A Study on the Pure Theory of Production*, Stockholm Economic Studies, No. 9, 1939, p. 17.)

Denote the function coefficient by ϵ. Thus from expression (13.24.5) we have

$$q\epsilon = \sum_i f_i x_i .$$ (13.24.6)

Thus competitive imputations (paying each input its marginal product) precisely exhaust the total product if, and only if, $\epsilon = 1$. If there are constant returns to scale, $\epsilon = 1$; in this case, average cost is also constant. But this is precisely the condition for long-run competitive equilibrium, in which output is expanded or contracted by the entry or exit of firms each producing at the point of minimum long-run average cost. Thus the Clark-Wicksteed theorem holds at the point of long-run competitive equilibrium—that is, expression (13.24.2) is an equation holding only for the precise set of equilibrium inputs, not an identity holding for any set of values of the variables.

[25] S. J. Chapman, "The Remuneration of Employers," *Economic Journal*, Vol. XVI (1906), pp. 523–28. This is a problem in long-run analysis. In terms of Figure 13.4.3, in the short run there is an excess rent or profit equal to the area of triangle CDE. In the long run the number of farms must adjust so that area CDE approaches zero.

Consider an economy composed of n identical farms, each worked by an identical number of laborers. In Figure 13.4.3 the horizontal axis

FIGURE 13.4.3

Product-Exhaustion Theorem

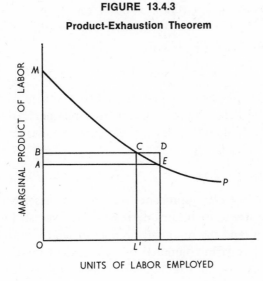

UNITS OF LABOR EMPLOYED

represents the number of workers per farm and the curve *MP* is the marginal product of labor. Suppose *OL* workers are employed per farm and that each is paid his marginal physical product. The real wage is *OA = LE,* and total wages are *OAEL.* The total physical product per farm is *OMEL,* so rent per farm is *AME.* Rent so computed is merely a residual; our problem is to prove that *AME* is also the marginal product of land.

First, observe that the total product of the economy is $n \times OMEL$. Next, suppose another farm is added to the economy, the number of workers remaining unchanged. If we can determine total output with $n + 1$ farms, the difference in total output when there are $n + 1$ and n farms is the marginal product of land.

When the $(n + 1)$-st farm is added, each existing farm must supply its proportional share of workers to the new farm. There are $n \times OL$ workers available; each farm now employs a number of workers, say *OL',* such that $(n + 1) \times OL' = n \times OL$. When each farm employs *OL'* workers, output per farm is *OMCL'* and the total output of the economy is

$$(n + 1) \times OMCL' = n \times OMCL' + OMCL'.$$

The total product with n farms is

$$n \times OMEL = n \times OMCL' + n \times L'CEL .$$

The marginal product of land, therefore, is the difference, or

$$n \times OMCL' + OMCL' - n \times OMCL' - n \times L'CEL$$
$$= OMCL' - n \times L'CEL = BMC + OBCL' - n \times L'CEL .$$

Now consider the last term above:

$$n \times L'CEL = n \times L'CDL - n \times CDE .$$

Since $n \times L'L = OL'$ by the equal division of workers, it follows that $n \times L'CDL = OBCL'$, the total return to labor per farm when OL' workers are employed on each farm. Therefore, the marginal product of the $(n + 1)$-st farm is

$$BMC + OBCL' - OBCL' + n \times CDE = BMC + n \times CDE .$$

The last term, $n \times CDE$, approaches zero as n increases without bound —that is, as the size of each farm decreases. Thus for an infinitesimally small increase in land the marginal product of land is BMC. But BMC is also the rent per farm computed by the residual method when OL' workers are on each farm. Consequently, the marginal product of land is the same as the residual, proving the Clark-Wicksteed theorem.

13.5 DISTRIBUTION AND RELATIVE FACTOR SHARES

The basic elements of marginal productivity theory have been known since the time of Marshall, Clark, and Wicksteed. However a fully systematic exposition, together with a theory of relative factor shares, was not presented until Hicks published his important *Theory of Wages*.[26] This may be regarded as the foundation of the modern neo-classical theory of distribution and relative factor shares. Before we get into concepts, however, a bit of review is in order.

13.5.a Least-Cost Combination of Inputs and Linearly Homogeneous Production Functions

The present section is a brief review of the topics developed in Chapter 6, especially subsections 6.3.c and 6.4.c. First recall that the least-cost combination of inputs is obtained when the marginal rate of technical substitution equals the input-price ratio. This proposition is illustrated in Figure 13.5.1, in which Q_0 is an isoquant and the slope of

---

[26] John R. Hicks, *The Theory of Wages* (2d ed.; London: Macmillan & Co., Ltd., 1932, 1963).

AB represents the wage-rent ratio. The slope of the isoquant at any point is the ratio of the marginal product of labor to that of capital. Least-cost input proportions are attained only when the ratio of marginal products (the marginal rate of technical substitution) equals the input-price ratio. This occurs at point *E,* and the slope of the ray *OE* defines the optimal input (capital-labor) ratio.

The capital-labor ratio is important in any circumstance; but when the production function is homogeneous of degree one it plays an even more vital role. To say a production function is linearly homogeneous implies that the marginal product of each input, and hence the marginal rate of technical substitution, is a function of the input ratio exclusively. Or, in terms of Figure 13.5.2, the marginal rate of technical substitution

FIGURE 13.5.1

Least-Cost Combination of Inputs

FIGURE 13.5.2

Isoquant Map for Homogeneous Production Function

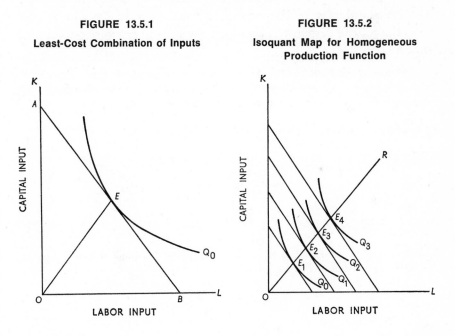

of capital for labor is a function of the capital-labor ratio only. In particular, the marginal rate of technical substitution is *not* a function of the scale of output.[27]

---

[27] Let the production function be

$$Q = F(K, L),$$ (13.27.1)

where $F(K, L)$ is homogeneous of degree one in K and L. By its homogeneity property, equation (13.27.1) may be written

An isoquant map for a linearly homogeneous production function is shown in Figure 13.5.2. Consider any ray from the origin, say *OR*, which specifies a capital-labor ratio. This ray intersects all isoquants in points (such as $E_1, \ldots, E_4$) such that the slopes of the isoquants are identical; in other words, the marginal rate of technical substitution is the same at E_1, E_2, E_3, and E_4. This is true not only of the ray *OR* but of *any* other ray as well. Hence a single isoquant fully describes the isoquant map when the production function is homogeneous of degree one.

13.5.b The Elasticity of Substitution

At the heart of neoclassical theory is the *elasticity of substitution*, a concept introduced by Hicks in 1932.[28] Just as every elasticity, it measures the relative responsiveness of one variable to proportional changes in another.

Definition: The elasticity of substitution measures the relative responsiveness of the capital-labor ratio to given proportional changes in the marginal rate of technical substitution of capital for labor.

Thus by formula, the elasticity of substitution (σ) is

$$\sigma = \frac{\Delta\left(\frac{K}{L}\right)}{\left(\frac{K}{L}\right)} \div \frac{\Delta(MRTS)}{MRTS} = \frac{\Delta\left(\frac{K}{L}\right)}{\Delta(MRTS)} \cdot \frac{MRTS}{\left(\frac{K}{L}\right)}. \text{[29]} \tag{13.5.1}$$

$$q = f(k), \tag{13.27.2}$$

where $q = Q/L$ and $k = K/L$. It is a simple matter to show that the marginal products $\partial Q/\partial K$ and $\partial Q/\partial L$ are given by

$$\frac{\partial Q}{\partial K} = f'(k) \tag{13.27.3}$$

and

$$\frac{\partial Q}{\partial L} = f(k) - kf'(k). \tag{13.27.4}$$

These last two equations show that the marginal products are functions of the capital-labor ratio only.

[28] Hicks, *op. cit.*, p. 117.

[29] Let the production function be

$$Q = F(K, L), \tag{13.29.1}$$

where *F* is homogeneous of degree one in *K* and *L*. In light of its homogeneity property, (13.29.1) may be written

The formula expressed above, however, can be made more meaningful. Recall that the marginal rate of technical substitution of capital for labor is the ratio of the marginal product of labor to that of capital.

$$Q = LF\left(\frac{K}{L}, 1\right) \tag{13.29.2}$$

or

$$y = f(k), \tag{13.29.3}$$

where $y = Q/L$ is the average product of labor and $k = K/L$ is the capital-labor ratio.

Let s denote the marginal rate of technical substitution of capital for labor. Then by definition,

$$\sigma = \frac{dk}{ds}\frac{s}{k}. \tag{13.29.4}$$

Using (13.29.2) and (13.29.3), the marginal product of labor is

$$\frac{\partial Q}{\partial L} = \frac{\partial(Ly)}{\partial L} = \frac{\partial[Lf(k)]}{\partial L} = f(k) + Lf'(k)\frac{\partial k}{\partial L} \tag{13.29.5}$$

$$= f(k) + Lf'(k)\left(-\frac{K}{L^2}\right) = f(k) - \frac{K}{L}f'(k)$$

$$= f(k) - kf'(k).$$

Similarly, the marginal product of capital is

$$\frac{\partial Q}{\partial K} = \frac{\partial[Lf(k)]}{\partial K} = Lf'(k)\frac{\partial k}{\partial K} = Lf'(k)\cdot\frac{1}{L} = f'(k). \tag{13.29.6}$$

From (13.29.5) and (13.29.6) the marginal rate of technical substitution of capital for labor is

$$s = \frac{MP_L}{MP_K} = \frac{f(k) - kf'(k)}{f'(k)}. \tag{13.29.7}$$

Now take the derivative of s with respect to k:

$$\frac{ds}{dk} = \frac{f'(k)[f'(k) - f'(k) - kf''(k)] - [f(k) - kf'(k)]f''(k)}{[f'(k)]^2} \tag{13.29.8}$$

$$= -\frac{f(k)f''(k)}{[f'(k)]^2}.$$

Inverting (13.29.8) and multiplying by the s/k ratio gives the desired expression for the elasticity of substitution:

$$\sigma = \frac{dk}{ds}\frac{s}{k} = -\frac{[f'(k)]^2}{f(k)f''(k)}\cdot\frac{f(k) - kf'(k)}{kf'(k)} \tag{13.29.9}$$

$$= -\frac{f'(k)[f(k) - kf'(k)]}{kf(k)f''(k)}.$$

To be more specific, suppose the production function takes the Cobb-Douglas form:

Let w, r, and p denote the prices of labor, capital, and output respectively. Rearranging the "VMP rule," we have

$$MRTS = \frac{MP_L}{MP_K} = \frac{(w/p)}{(r/p)} = \frac{w}{r}.$$

Hence in equilibrium, the elasticity of substitution may be written as

$$\sigma = \frac{\Delta\left(\frac{K}{L}\right) \cdot \left(\frac{w}{r}\right)}{\Delta\left(\frac{w}{r}\right)\left(\frac{K}{L}\right)} = \frac{\Delta\left(\frac{K}{L}\right)}{\left(\frac{K}{L}\right)} \div \frac{\Delta\left(\frac{w}{r}\right)}{\left(\frac{w}{r}\right)} \qquad (13.5.2)$$

In this form, the elasticity of substitution shows the proportional change in the capital-labor ratio induced by a given proportional change in the factor-price ratio.

$$Q = AK^\alpha L^{1-\alpha}. \qquad (13.29.10)$$

Then

$$s = \left(\frac{1-\alpha}{\alpha}\right)\left(\frac{K}{L}\right) = \left(\frac{1-\alpha}{\alpha}\right)k, \qquad (13.29.11)$$

and

$$\frac{ds}{dk} = \frac{1-\alpha}{\alpha}. \qquad (13.29.12)$$

Finally,

$$\sigma = \frac{dk}{ds}\frac{s}{k} = \left(\frac{\alpha}{1-\alpha}\right)\left(\frac{1-\alpha}{\alpha}\right)(k)\left(\frac{1}{k}\right) = 1. \qquad (13.29.13)$$

In the Cobb-Douglas case, the elasticity of substitution is precisely unity. Since fixed proportions production does not permit factor substitution, the elasticity of substitution is zero in that case.

Exercise: Suppose the production function has the CES form:

$$Q = \gamma[\delta K^{-\rho} + (1-\delta)L^{-\rho}]^{-\frac{1}{\rho}}.$$

Show that

$$\sigma = \frac{1}{1+\rho}.$$

For derivations, illustrations, and a more detailed discussion, see C. E. Ferguson, *The Neoclassical Theory of Production and Distribution* (London and New York: Cambridge University Press, 1969), chap. 5.

13.5.c Elasticity of Substitution and Changes in Relative Factor Shares

In the notation introduced just above, the relative share of labor in output—that is, the total payment to labor divided by the total value of output—is

$$\frac{wL}{pQ}.$$

Similarly, the relative share of capital is

$$\frac{rK}{pQ};$$

thus the ratio of relative shares is

$$\frac{wL}{rK}.\;^{30}$$

Now consider the right-most expression in (13.5.2). Suppose the wage-rent ratio increases by 10 percent. An increase in the relative price of labor will, of course, lead to a substitution of capital for labor and, thereby, to an increase in the capital-labor ratio. Suppose it increases by 5 percent. Then the elasticity of substitution is less than one. Knowing this allows us to infer the behavior of relative factor shares. In the case above, w/r increases by 10 percent and K/L increases by only 5 percent. It therefore follows that wL/rK increases.

Let us look briefly at the cause. By assumption, the wage-rent ratio increases—because, perhaps, the supply of capital increases proportionately more than the supply of labor. As labor becomes relatively more expensive, entrepreneurs substitute capital for labor to the extent permitted by the production function. Now if the production function is characterized by inelastic substitutability, entrepreneurs cannot substitute capital for labor in the same proportion as the wage rate has risen relative to capital rent. Thus the relative share of labor must rise.

The same sort of reasoning applies when the elasticity of substitution

---

[30] Consider the expression for labor's relative share. The real marginal product of labor is w/p, and L/Q is the reciprocal of labor's average product. Hence

$$\text{labor's relative share} = \frac{MP_L}{AP_L} = \epsilon_L,$$

the output elasticity of labor (see Chapter 5). This is always true when the production function is homogeneous of degree one. Thus we may state the following

Relation: The relative share of an input is equal to its output elasticity.

is equal to or greater than unity. Hence we may summarize the relation between the elasticity of substitution and the behavior of relative factor shares in the following

Proposition: Consider a two-factor model in which the absolute return to one factor increases relative to the absolute return to the other; the relative share of the former will increase, remain unchanged, or decrease according as the elasticity of substitution is less than, equal to, or greater than unity.[31]

Whether the elasticity of substitution is greater than, less than, or equal to unity is an empirical question; but it is one of great importance to various socioeconomic groups. For the American economy and for the manufacturing sector as a whole, there is strong evidence that the elasticity of substitution is substantially less than unity.[32] This is in keeping with the increases in the relative wage rate and in the relative share of labor. On the other hand, however, many specific industries and product groups apparently have production functions whose elasticities of substitution exceed unity.[33] In such industries the share of capital increases even though its relative return diminishes.

13.5.d   Classification of Technological Progress

So far we have operated under the tacit assumption that a production function is both given and unchanging over the period of analysis; our case has been strictly static. Technological progress does occur; and it is of some interest to classify the nature of technological change.

Many years ago Hicks defined technological progress as capital-using, neutral, or labor-using according as the marginal rate of technical substitution of capital for labor diminishes, remains unchanged, or increases at the originally prevailing capital-labor ratio. In other words, if technological change increases the marginal product of capital more

---

[31] *Exercise:* Explain this same proposition as stated by Hicks (*Theory of Wages,* p. 117): "An increase in the supply of any factor will increase its relative share if its 'elasticity of substitution' is greater than unity."

[32] As only one example, see J. W. Kendrick and Ryuzo Sato, "Factor Prices, Productivity, and Growth," *American Economic Review,* Vol. LIII (1963), pp. 974–1003.

[33] See C. E. Ferguson, "Cross-Section Production Functions and the Elasticity of Substitution in American Manufacturing Industry," *Review of Economics and Statistics,* Vol. XLV (1963), pp. 305–13; and "Time-Series Production Functions and Technological Progress in American Manufacturing Industry," *Journal of Political Economy,* Vol. LXXIII (1965), pp. 135–47.

than the marginal product of labor (at a given capital-labor ratio), progress is capital-using because a producer now has an incentive to use more capital relative to labor because its (capital's) marginal product has increased relative to that of labor. The same type of statement holds, *mutatis mutandis,* for neutral and for labor-using technological progress.

Basically, technological progress consists of any change (graphically, shift) of the production function that either permits the same level of output to be produced with less input or enables the former level of inputs to produce a greater output.

Technological progress is shown graphically in Figures 13.5.3 and 13.5.4. The figures are constructed with uniform notation. The level of output is *I*, and the various isoquants (*I*, *I'*, and *I''*) show the combinations of inputs capable of producing this given level of output. *OR* is the ray whose slope gives a constant capital-labor ratio. The points *A*, *B*, and *C* show the points of production at the given capital-labor ratio as technological progress occurs.

FIGURE 13.5.3

Neutral Technological Progress

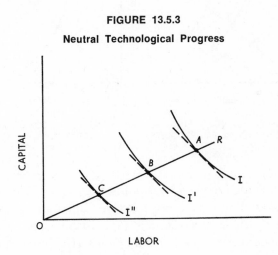

Technological progress is shown graphically by a shift of an isoquant in the direction of the origin. In Figure 13.5.3, the three isoquants— *I*, *I'*, and *I''*—all represent the same level of output. As technological progress takes place *I'* shows that the given level of output can be produced by smaller quantities of inputs than at *I*. Similarly, as technological progress continues *I''* shows that still smaller input combinations can produce the same level of output.

Figure 13.5.3 illustrates neutral technological progress. Recalling the definition, technological progress is neutral if at a constant capital-labor ratio the marginal rate of technical substitution of capital for labor is unchanged. The constant capital-labor ratio ray *OR* intersects the three isoquants at points *A, B,* and *C* respectively. At these points, the slope of the isoquant—or the marginal rate of technical substitution of capital for labor—is the same. Hence it represents a shifting production function characterized by neutral technological progress.

FIGURE 13.5.4

Biased Technological Progress

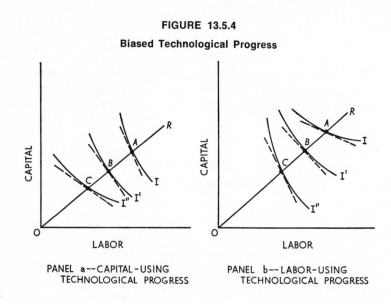

PANEL a--CAPITAL-USING
TECHNOLOGICAL PROGRESS

PANEL b--LABOR-USING
TECHNOLOGICAL PROGRESS

Panels a and b, Figure 13.5.4, illustrate capital-using and labor-using technological progress respectively. Capital-using technological progress occurs when at a constant capital-labor ratio, the marginal product of capital increases relative to the marginal product of labor. In other words, since the marginal rate of technical substitution of capital for labor is the ratio of the marginal product of labor to that of capital, capital-using technological progress occurs when the marginal rate of technical substitution declines along a constant capital-labor ray. As one moves from *A* to *B* to *C* in panel a, the slope of the isoquant diminishes, representing a decline in the marginal rate of technical substitution. Hence this panel depicts a shifting production function characterized by capital-using technological progress.

By the same line of reasoning, panel b illustrates labor-using technological progress because the marginal rate of technical substitution increases as one moves from *A* to *B* to *C.*

13.5.e Biased Technological Progress and Relative Factor Shares

Observed changes in relative shares depend upon changes in relative input prices and in the responsiveness of input proportions to these changes. Over time, changes in relative shares depend upon the nature of technological progress as well. Indeed, this is evident from the definition of biased technological progress introduced in the subsection above.[34]

First consider neutral technological progress. By definition, the capital-labor ratio and the marginal rate of technical substitution of capital for labor remain unchanged. Next, recall that in equilibrium, the marginal rate of technical substitution of capital for labor must equal the input-price ratio. Therefore the wage-rent ratio also remains unchanged. That is, both (K/L) and (w/r) are unchanged by neutral technological progress. Consequently, relative shares are not affected by technological progress when the latter is neutral.

Now suppose technological progress is capital-using. This implies that at a constant capital-labor ratio the marginal rate of technical substitution, and hence the wage-rent ratio, declines. This is tantamount to saying that r increases relative to w while K/L is constant. The relative share of capital accordingly increases and that of labor declines.

By a similar line of reasoning, one may show that labor-using technological progress causes a decrease in the relative share of capital with a corresponding increase in the relative share of labor. Summarizing, we have the following

Relations: The relative share of labor increases, remains unchanged, or decreases according as technological progress is labor-using, neutral, or capital-using; the opposite relation holds for the relative share of capital.

As a final empirical note, there is some evidence that the American economy has been characterized by labor-using technological progress over the postwar years.[35]

---

[34] The relations among relative shares, changes in relative factor supplies, the elasticity of substitution, and the nature of technological progress can readily be developed mathematically. However, a mathematical treatment requires more space than is here available. For details, see C. E. Ferguson, "Neoclassical Theory of Technical Progress and Relative Factor Shares," *Southern Economic Journal,* Vol. XXXIV (1968), pp. 490–504; and Ferguson, *The Neoclassical Theory of Production and Distribution,* chaps. 11 and 12.

[35] See Murray Brown and John S. de Cani, "Technological Changes in the United States, 1950–1960," *Productivity Measurement Review,* No. 29 (May, 1962), pp. 26–39; and C. E. Ferguson, "Substitution, Technical Progress, and Returns to Scale," *American Economic Review, Papers and Proceedings,* Vol. LV (1965), pp. 296–305.

QUESTIONS

1. The United States has a law that requires equal pay for women who perform the same job as men in a given plant. What is the effect of this law on the wage and employment of men and women?

2. "An increase in the income tax rate will induce laborers to work more since their net incomes will decline." Discuss.

3. "The completion of the marginal productivity theory of distribution was achieved only with the development of the proof that if all productive agents are rewarded in accord with their marginal products, then the total product will be exhausted." Explain.

4. Consider a model that rationalizes a person's choice between income and leisure. If leisure is a normal good, the resulting supply of labor curve may be negatively sloped. Derive such a labor-supply function. How would the analysis be affected if we were to introduce a progressive income tax? If the wage rate for overtime work is 150 percent of the basic wage rate?

5. How do the elasticity of substitution and the change in relative factor supply relate to changes in relative factor shares?

6. "If the production function in a particular industry exhibits constant returns to scale, a tax imposed on the employment of one factor will in the short run increase that factor's marginal product and in the long run will have no effect." Discuss.

7. "Inputs *A* and *B* are used in the production of the same product. An increase in the price of *A* (due to a shift in *A*'s supply curve) will result in a decline in the price of *B*." Discuss.

8. "*A* is a product used in the production of *B*. Price control is imposed on the production of *A* but not *B*. The ceiling price imposed on *A* is less than the equilibrium price. This will result in a fall in the price of *B*." Discuss.

9. "Increasing the minimum wage to $1.75 per hour would have no effect outside the South if all workers earning less than $1.75 are located in the South." Discuss.

10. Part of the following statement follows directly from price theory, part not. Separate into the components: "Southern wages are lower than wages in the North (even in the same industry) because Southern workers have less education and the Southern climate causes everybody to work at a slower pace. Southern plants typically employ less capital per man. So, all in all, Southern workers are less efficient. They get paid less because they deserve less."

SUGGESTED READINGS

Cartter, Allan M. *Theory of Wages and Employment,* pp. 11–74. Homewood, Ill.: Richard D. Irwin, Inc., 1959.

Douglas, Paul H. *The Theory of Wages.* New York: The Macmillan Co., 1934.

Ferguson, C. E. " 'Inferior Factors' and the Theories of Production and Input Demand," *Economica,* N.S. Vol. XXXV (1968), pp. 140–50. [Advanced math necessary.]

————. *The Neoclassical Theory of Production and Distribution,* chaps. 6 and 9. London and New York: Cambridge University Press, 1969. [Advanced math necessary.]

————. "Production, Prices, and the Theory of Jointly-Derived Input Demand Functions," *Economica,* N.S. Vol. XXXIII (1966), pp. 454–61. [Advanced math necessary.]

————, and Saving, Thomas R. "Long-Run Scale Adjustments of a Perfectly Competitive Firm and Industry," *American Economic Review,* Vol. LIX (1969), pp. 774–83. [Advanced math necessary.]

Hicks, John R. *The Theory of Wages.* London: Macmillan & Co., Ltd., 1932.

————. *Value and Capital,* pp. 78–111. 2d ed. Oxford: Clarendon Press, 1946.

Samuelson, Paul A. *Foundations of Economic Analysis,* pp. 57–89. Cambridge, Mass.: Harvard University Press, 1947. [Advanced math necessary.]

Stigler, George J. *Production and Distribution Theories,* pp. 296–387. New York: The Macmillan Co., 1941. [Elementary math necessary.]

THEORY OF EMPLOYMENT
IN IMPERFECTLY
COMPETITIVE MARKETS

14.1 INTRODUCTION

The analytical principles underlying the theory of resource price and employment are the same for perfectly and imperfectly competitive markets. Demand and supply determine market equilibrium resource price and employment; and marginal productivity considerations are the fundamental determinants of demand. To be sure, some adjustments must be made to allow for the fact that commodity price and marginal revenue are different in imperfectly competitive markets. Thus the value of the marginal product of a variable service is not the relevant guide. Furthermore, imperfect competition in the resource buying market must be introduced. Hence two additions to marginal productivity theory are presented in this chapter.

14.2 MONOPOLY IN THE COMMODITY MARKET

The first situation is that of a monopolist in the commodity market, or more generally an oligopolist or a monopolistic competitor, purchasing variable productive services in perfectly competitive input markets. Since the principle is precisely the same for all types of imperfect competition in the selling market, our attention is restricted to monopoly, except for subsection 14.2.d.

14.2.a Marginal Revenue Product

When a perfectly competitive seller employs an additional unit of, say, labor, his output is augmented by the marginal product of that unit. In like manner, his total revenue is augmented by the value of its marginal product inasmuch as market (selling) price remains unchanged. When a monopolist employs an additional unit of labor, his output is also increased by the marginal product of the worker. However, to sell his larger output, market price must be reduced; hence total revenue is not augmented by the value of the marginal product of the additional worker. A numerical example is given in Table 14.2.1.

The first three columns of the table give the production function. Column 4 shows the price at which the total product can be sold; hence columns 2 and 4 give the demand function. Columns 5 and 6 contain the figures for total and marginal revenue respectively. Finally, column 7 shows marginal revenue product, whose meaning and derivation must be explained.

Suppose the monopolist is producing and selling 27 units of the

TABLE 14.2.1

Marginal Revenue Product for a Monopolistic Seller

Units of Variable Service	Total Product	Marginal Product	Selling Price per Unit	Total Revenue*	Marginal Revenue	Marginal Revenue Product
0...........	0	—	—	—	—	—
1...........	10	10	$10.00	$100	$10	$100
2...........	19	9	9.05	172	8	72
3...........	27	8	8.45	228	7	56
4...........	34	7	7.94	270	6	42
5...........	40	6	7.50	300	5	30
6...........	45	5	7.11	320	4	20
7...........	49	4	6.78	332	3	12
8...........	52	3	6.44	335	1	3
9...........	54	2	6.20	335	0	0
10...........	55	1	6.05	333	−2	−2

* Rounded to nearest even dollar.

commodity at $8.45 per unit. This rate of output and sales requires three units of the variable productive service. Now consider what happens if a fourth unit of the variable service is used. Output increases to 34, or the marginal physical product of the fourth unit is 7. To sell 34 units per period of time, the monopolist must decrease his price to $7.94 per unit. His total revenue expands, but *not* by 7 × $8.45 or 7 × $7.94. Total revenue expands by only $42; so on average, marginal revenue is $6. The addition of a unit of the variable service expands revenue, therefore, by the product of marginal revenue and marginal product, or by the increase in total revenue attributable to the addition of the marginal product (not one unit) to output and sales. This magnitude is called the *marginal revenue product* of the variable service.

An alternative arithmetic derivation of marginal revenue product may be helpful. When labor input expands from 3 to 4 units, output and sales expand by 7 units (from 27 to 34). Consequently, one might say that the *gross* increase in revenue attributable to the fourth unit of labor is $7 \times \$7.94$ which, rounded, equals \$56. That is, the gross increase equals the increase in output multiplied by the new market price per unit of output. However, when output expands, market price falls by 51 cents, from \$8.45 to \$7.94. Therefore, the 27 units that had been selling at \$8.45 must now be sold at \$7.94; thus 27×51 cents, or, rounded, \$14 must be deducted from the gross increase in revenue. As a result the *net* increase in revenue, or the marginal revenue product of the fourth unit of labor, is $\$56 - \$14$, or $\$42.$[1]

---

[1] A simple algebraic demonstration that marginal revenue product equals marginal revenue multiplied by marginal physical product is also revealing. Let *MRP, TR, TP, MPP,* and *L* denote marginal revenue product, total revenue, total product, marginal physical product, and labor input respectively. Also, as customary, let Δ denote "the change in."

By definition (in the text)

$$MRP = \frac{\Delta TR}{\Delta L}. \qquad (14.1.1)$$

From the definition of marginal revenue $(MR = \Delta TR/\Delta TP)$, one may write

$$\Delta TR = MR \times \Delta TP. \qquad (14.1.2)$$

Similarly, from the definition of marginal physical product $(MPP = \Delta TP/\Delta L)$, the change in labor input may be expressed as

$$\Delta L = \frac{\Delta TP}{MPP}. \qquad (14.1.3)$$

Substituting expressions (14.1.2) and (14.1.3) in (14.1.1), the definition of marginal revenue product is obtained:

$$MRP = \frac{MR \times \Delta TP}{\dfrac{\Delta TP}{MPP}} = MR \times MPP. \qquad (14.1.4)$$

A more directly mathematical derivation may be given. Let the demand function in inverse form be

$$p = h(q), \qquad h' < 0. \qquad (14.1.5)$$

Definition: Marginal revenue product equals marginal revenue multiplied by the marginal physical product of the variable productive service; or, marginal revenue product is the net addition to total revenue attributable to the addition of one unit of the variable productive service.

Before utilizing marginal revenue product to determine the monopolist's demand for a variable productive service, it may be well to show a graphical derivation of marginal revenue product. Panel a, Figure

Thus total revenue is

$$TR = qb(q),\tag{14.1.6}$$

and marginal revenue is

$$MR = b(q) + qb'(q).\tag{14.1.7}$$

The production function, assuming only one variable input x, is

$$q = f(x),\qquad f' > 0.\tag{14.1.8}$$

By definition, marginal revenue product is the change in total revenue attributable to a small (say, unit) change in input. Thus

$$MRP = \frac{d(TR)}{dx}.\tag{14.1.9}$$

From (14.1.6), we find

$$MRP = b(q)\frac{dq}{dx} + qb'(q)\frac{dq}{dx}.\tag{14.1.10}$$

From (14.1.8), $\frac{dq}{dx} = f'(x)$. Hence we have

$$MRP = [b(q) + qb'(q)]f'(x).\tag{14.1.11}$$

By (14.1.7) and (14.1.8),

$$MRP = MR \cdot MP.\tag{14.1.12}$$

If there is a multi-input production function, $f'(x)$ is replaced by $\partial f/\partial x_i$ for the i-th input. Equation (14.1.10) becomes

$$MRP_i = [b(q) + qb'(q)]\frac{\partial f}{\partial x_i},\tag{14.1.13}$$

or

$$MRP_i = MR \cdot MP_i.\tag{14.1.14}$$

FIGURE 14.2.1

**Derivation of the Marginal Revenue Product Curve
for a Single Productive Service**

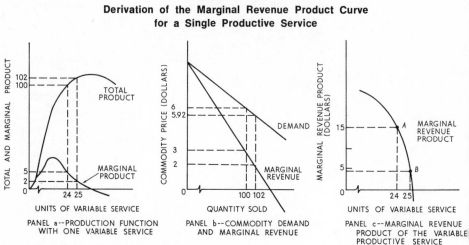

PANEL a--PRODUCTION FUNCTION
WITH ONE VARIABLE SERVICE

PANEL b--COMMODITY DEMAND
AND MARGINAL REVENUE

PANEL c--MARGINAL REVENUE
PRODUCT OF THE VARIABLE
PRODUCTIVE SERVICE

14.2.1, shows a smooth production function for a certain commodity whose production requires the input of only one variable service. Suppose the monopolistic seller initially uses 24 units of the variable service, thereby producing 100 units of output. At that point, marginal product is five units.

Panel b shows the demand and marginal revenue curves that confront the monopolist. When 100 units are sold, price is $6 per unit and marginal revenue is $3. Hence marginal revenue product of the 24th unit of the variable service is 5 × $3 or $15, plotted as point *A* in panel c. Now let the monopolist add an additional unit of the variable service. Output increases to 102 units per period, and the marginal physical product of the 25th unit of variable service is 2. When output expands to 102 units per period, the monopolist must reduce his selling price to $5.92 per unit to clear the market. Hence marginal revenue declines to $2 per unit. As a consequence, when 25 units of the variable service are employed, marginal revenue product becomes 2 × $2, or $4, plotted as point *B* in panel c.

Performing this operation for all feasible levels of employment generates the marginal revenue product curve. It must quite obviously slope downward to the right because two forces are working to cause marginal revenue product to diminish as the level of employment increases: (*a*) the marginal physical product declines (over the relevant range of production) as additional units of the variable service are added, and (*b*) marginal revenue declines as output expands and market price falls.

14.2.b   Monopoly Demand for a Single Variable Service

Under the present assumption the monopolist purchases the variable service in a perfectly competitive input market. Hence, just as a perfectly competitive producer, he views his supply (of variable service) curve as a horizontal line at the level of the prevailing market price. Such a supply curve is illustrated by S_v in Figure 14.2.2, where the market price of the input is $O\bar{w}$.

The marginal revenue product curve is also shown in the figure; our task is to prove the following

Proposition: An imperfectly competitive producer who purchases a variable productive service in a perfectly competitive input market will employ that amount of the service for which marginal revenue product equals market price. Consequently, the marginal revenue product curve is the monopolist's demand curve for the variable service when only one variable input is used.

Given the market price $O\bar{w}$, our task is to prove that equilibrium employment is $O\bar{v}$. Suppose the contrary, in particular, that Ov_1 units of the variable service are used. At the Ov_1 level of utilization the last unit adds Ow_1 to total revenue but only $O\bar{w}$ to total cost. Since $Ow_1 > O\bar{w}$, profit is augmented by employing that unit. Furthermore, profit increases when additional units are employed so long as marginal revenue product exceeds the market equilibrium price of the input. Thus a profit-maximizing monopolist would never employ fewer than $O\bar{v}$ units of the variable service. The opposite argument holds when more than $O\bar{v}$ units

FIGURE 14.2.2

Monopoly Demand for a Single Variable Service

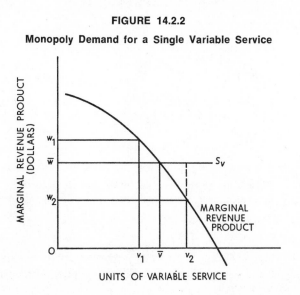

are employed, for then an additional unit of the variable service adds more to total cost than to total revenue. Therefore, a profit-maximizing monopolist will adjust employment so that marginal revenue product equals market equilibrium input price. If only one variable productive service is used, the marginal revenue product curve is the monopolist's demand curve for the variable service in question.[2]

14.2.c Monopoly Demand for a Variable Productive Service When Several Variable Inputs Are Used

When more than one variable input is used in the production process, the marginal revenue product curve is not the demand curve for the reasons discussed in Chapter 13. However, the demand curve can be derived just as it was derived in that chapter.

Suppose, as in Figure 14.2.3, that at a given moment the market in-

---

[2] In the notation of footnote 1, let the demand and production functions be given, respectively, by

$$p = h(q), \qquad h' < 0; \qquad q = f(x), \qquad f' > 0. \qquad (14.2.1)$$

Let the competitively given price of the input be w. Thus total profit (π) may be written

$$\pi = pq - wx - F, \qquad (14.2.2)$$

where F is fixed cost. Using (14.2.1), we may rewrite (14.2.2) as

$$\pi = h[f(x)]f(x) - wx - F. \qquad (14.2.3)$$

Maximizing profit, one obtains

$$\frac{d\pi}{dx} = f(x)\frac{dp}{dq}\frac{dq}{dx} + p\frac{dq}{dx} - w = 0, \qquad (14.2.4)$$

or

$$\left(q\frac{dp}{dq} + p\right)\frac{dq}{dx} - w = 0. \qquad (14.2.5)$$

This may be written as

$$[h(q) + qh'(q)]f'(x) = w. \qquad (14.2.6)$$

This establishes the relation in the text, i.e., $MRP = w$. It is further interesting to note that using the expression for marginal revenue developed in Part III, we may write

$$p\left(1 - \frac{1}{\eta}\right)f'(x) = w, \qquad (14.2.7)$$

showing the relations among commodity price, factor price, elasticity of demand, and the production function.

FIGURE 14.2.3

Monopoly Demand for a Variable Productive Service
When Several Variable Services Are Used

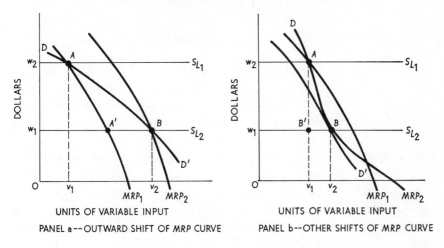

PANEL a--OUTWARD SHIFT OF MRP CURVE   PANEL b--OTHER SHIFTS OF MRP CURVE

put price of a particular variable service is Ow_2 and that its marginal revenue product is given by MRP_1. The monopolist attains equilibrium employment at point A, using Ov_1 units of the variable service. Next, let the price of the service fall to Ow_1 (because, for example, the market supply curve for the input shifts to the right). Other things being equal, the monopolist would expand along MRP_1 to A' in panel a. But other things are not equal.

Substitution, output, and profit maximizing effects exist, as explained in Chapter 13. Exactly the same analysis applies to a monopolist or set of oligopolists as applies to a set of perfectly competitive producers. The substitution, output, and profit maximizing effects, on balance, cause a shift of the marginal revenue product curve, which may be outward, inward, or twisted. Panel a, Figure 14.2.3, illustrates the first mentioned; panel b illustrates the last mentioned. In any event, as in Chapter 13, the fall in marginal revenue cannot completely offset the expansive forces. The factor demand function must be negatively sloped.[3]

---

[3] For proofs, see C. E. Ferguson, "Production, Prices, and the Theory of Jointly-Derived Input Demand Functions," *Economica,* N.S. Vol XXXIII (1966), pp. 454–61; C. E. Ferguson, " 'Inferior Factors' and the Theories of Production and Input Demand," *Economica,* N.S. Vol. XXXV (1968), pp. 140–50; C. E. Ferguson and Thomas R. Saving, "Long-Run Scale Adjustments of a Perfectly Competitive Firm and Industry," *American Economic Review,* Vol. LIX (1969), pp. 774–83. The mathematical analysis contained in these papers is presented in greater detail in C. E. Ferguson, *The Neoclassical Theory of Production and Distribution* (London and New York: Cambridge University Press, 1969), chaps. 6 and 9.

The results of this section may be summarized in the following

Proposition: Input demand curves are negatively sloped regardless of the market organization in the product market.

14.2.d Market Demand for a Variable Productive Service

If a group of monopolists uses a variable productive service, the market demand for the service is simply the sum of the individual demands of the various monopolists. There are no *external* effects of expanded output on price; the effect of expansion is internal to each monopolist and has already been considered in obtaining his individual demand curve. Similarly, if all sorts of producers use the variable service, the market demand curve is the sum of the various component *industry* demand curves, where the industries may be composed of any number of firms. However, a minor qualification is required in cases of oligopoly and monopolistic competition. Since the situation is the same in both cases, only monopolistic competition is considered.

The demand curve for a variable service on the part of any one monopolistically competitive producer is derived in the same way as a monopolist's demand curve. But when all sellers in the product group expand output, market price diminishes (along Chamberlin's *DD'* curve), just as in a perfectly competitive industry. Thus to obtain the market demand from individual demand curves one must allow for the decrease in market price and marginal revenue. Graphically, the derivation is exactly like that in Figure 13.2.5, except that the individual demand curves are based upon marginal revenue product rather than the value of the marginal product.

14.2.e Equilibrium Price and Employment

The analysis of market equilibrium price and employment of a variable agent is no different whether the employers are monopolists or perfectly competitive producers. The determination of quasi rents is also the same; thus the discussion of Chapter 13, subsections 13.4.a and 13.4.b, applies equally well in the present context.

While the *analysis* does not change, there is one important difference to bear in mind: in cases of monopoly the demand curve is based upon the marginal revenue product of the variable productive service rather than upon the value of its marginal product. This gives rise to what is sometimes called monopolistic exploitation.[4]

---

[4] This term is apparently attributable to Joan Robinson. See her *Economics of Imperfect Competition* (London: Macmillan & Co., Ltd., 1933), pp. 281–91.

14.2.f Monopolistic Exploitation

According to Mrs. Robinson's definition, a productive service is exploited if it is employed at a price that is less than the value of its marginal product.[5] As we have seen in Chapter 13 and in the foregoing portion of this chapter, it is to the advantage of any individual producer (whether monopolist or competitor) to hire a variable service until the point is reached at which an additional unit adds precisely the same amount to total cost and total revenue. This is simply the input market implication of profit maximization.

When a perfectly competitive producer follows this rule a variable service receives the value of its marginal product because price and marginal revenue are the same. This is not true, however, when the commodity market is imperfect. Marginal revenue is less than price and marginal revenue product is correspondingly less than the value of the marginal product. Profit-maximizing behavior of imperfectly competitive producers causes the market price of a productive service to be less than the value of its marginal product.

If the market price of the commodity reflects its social value, the productive service receives less than its contribution to social value. Raising the input price is not a remedy, however, because producers would merely reduce the level of employment until marginal revenue product equaled the higher input price. The trouble initially lies in the fact that imperfectly competitive producers do not use as much of the resource as is socially desirable and do not attain the correspondingly desirable level of output. The fundamental difficulty rests in the difference between price (marginal social valuation) and marginal (social) cost at the profit-maximizing output. Thus so long as imperfectly competitive producers exist there must be some "monopolistic exploitation" of productive agents.

The significance of this "exploitation" can easily be exaggerated. Following Chamberlin, product differentiation is desired per se; and whenever there is differentiation, price and marginal revenue diverge so that "exploitation" is inevitable. Furthermore, the alternatives to "exploitation" are not attractive. Either there must be state ownership and operation of all nonperfectly competitive industries or else there must be rigid price control by the state. For a variety of reasons, either alternative is likely to raise more problems than it solves.[6]

---

[5] *Ibid.*, p. 281.

[6] Cf. C. E. Ferguson, *A Macroeconomic Theory of Workable Competition* (Durham, N.C.: Duke University Press, 1964).

14.3 MONOPSONY: MONOPOLY IN THE INPUT MARKET

The analysis of pricing and employment of productive services has so far rested upon the assumption that each producer (buyer of the service in question) cannot affect the market price of the service by changes in his utilization of it. This assumption obviously does not hold in all situations. There are sometimes only a few, and in the limit one, purchasers of a productive service. Where there is a single buyer of an input a *monopsony* is said to exist; if there are several buyers *oligopsony* is the proper designation.

A wide variety of categories can be classified. Broadly speaking, commodity markets may be perfectly competitive, monopolistically competitive, oligopolistic, or monopolistic. For each of these four types of commodity market organizations the input market can be either a monopsony or an oligopsony. However, the analytical principle is the same irrespective of the organization of the commodity and input markets (so long as there is not perfect competition in the input market). Thus we restrict our attention to the case in which there is monopoly in the commodity market combined with monopsony in the input market.

14.3.a Marginal Expense of Input

The supply curve for most productive services or production agents is positively sloped. A buyer in a perfectly competitive input market views the supply of input curve as a horizontal line because his purchases are so small, relative to the market, that changes on his part do not perceptibly affect market price. A monopsonist, however, being the only buyer in the market, faces a positively sloped market supply of input curve. As a result, changes in his volume of purchases do affect input price; as he expands input usage, input price increases. The monopsonist, therefore, must consider the *marginal expense* of purchasing an additional unit of a variable productive agent.

Computation of the marginal expense of input is shown in Table 14.3.1, and the supply and marginal expense of input curves are illustrated in Figure 14.3.1. Columns 1 and 2 show the supply curve, plotted as the right-most curve in Figure 14.3.1. When only one unit of the variable agent is employed its cost is $2; thus the total cost of the input, and total variable cost when only one agent is used, is also $2. If two units are used the supply price per unit is $2.50; total cost of the input is $5, an increase of $3 over the previous total cost, even though the price per unit increased by only 50 cents. In other words, hiring an additional unit of input increases total cost by more than the price of the unit because all units employed receive the new, higher price.

TABLE 14.3.1

Monopsony and the Marginal Expense of Input

Units of Variable Input	Price per Unit	Total Cost of Input	Marginal Expense of Input
1.	$2.00	$ 2.00	—
2.	2.50	5.00	$ 3.00
3.	3.00	9.00	4.00
4.	3.50	14.00	5.00
5.	4.00	20.00	6.00
6.	4.50	27.00	7.00
7.	5.00	35.00	8.00
8.	5.50	44.00	9.00
9.	6.00	54.00	10.00
10.	6.50	65.00	11.00

FIGURE 14.3.1

Marginal Expense of Input

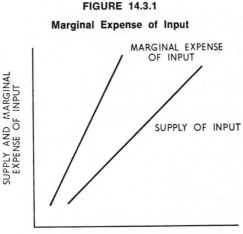

The marginal expense of input, the left-most curve in Figure 14.3.1, is calculated by successive subtraction in the "total cost of input" column. Since the price per unit rises as employment increases, the marginal expense of input exceeds its price at all employment levels; and the marginal expense of input curve is positively sloped, lies to the left of the supply of input curve, and typically rises more rapidly than the latter.[7]

Definition: The marginal expense of input is the increase in total cost (and in total variable cost and in total cost of input) attributable to the addition of one unit of the variable productive agent.

14.3.b Price and Employment under Monopsony When One Variable Input Is Used

The market demand curve for a productive service is the demand curve of the single buyer under monopsony conditions. Furthermore, if only one variable input is used in the production process, the demand curve is the monopsonist's marginal revenue product curve. Confronting the monopsonist is the positively sloped supply of input curve and the higher marginal expense of input curve. The situation is illustrated in Figure 14.3.2. Using this graph we will prove the following

Proposition: A profit-maximizing monopsonist will employ a variable productive service until the point is reached at which the marginal expense of input equals its marginal revenue product. The price of the input is determined by the corresponding point on its supply curve.

The proof of this proposition follows immediately from the definitions of marginal revenue product and marginal expense of input. Marginal revenue product is the addition to total revenue attributable to the addition of one unit of the variable input; the marginal expense of input is the addition to total cost resulting from the employment of an additional unit. Therefore, so long as marginal revenue product exceeds the marginal expense of input, profit can be augmented by expanding input usage. On the other hand, if the marginal expense of input exceeds its marginal revenue product, profit is less or loss greater than if fewer units of the input were employed. Consequently, profit is maximized by employing that quantity of the variable service for which marginal expense of input equals marginal revenue product.

---

[7] These statements can easily be proven. Let the input supply function in inverse form be

$$w = g(x), \tag{14.7.1}$$

where w is input price, x is the quantity of the input supplied, and $g'(x) = dw/dx > 0$ by assumption (i.e., the input supply curve is positively sloped). Total variable cost is

$$C(x) = wx = xg(x). \tag{14.7.2}$$

FIGURE 14.3.2

Price and Employment under Monopsony

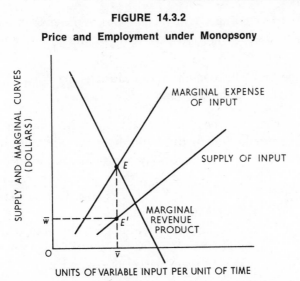

This equality occurs at point E in Figure 14.3.2; $O\bar{v}$ units of the service are accordingly employed. At this point the supply of input curve becomes particularly relevant. $O\bar{v}$ units of the variable productive agent are associated with point E' on the supply of input curve. Thus $O\bar{v}$ units

---

By definition, the marginal expense of input is

$$MEI = \frac{dC(x)}{dx} = g(x) + xg'(x) = w + x\frac{dw}{dx}. \tag{14.7.3}$$

Since $g'(x) > 0$ by assumption, a comparison of (14.7.1) and (14.7.3) shows that the marginal expense of input curve must lie above the input supply curve for each quantity supplied. Further, $g'(x) > 0$ also implies that the MEI-curve is positively sloped. Finally, the MEI-curve usually rises more rapidly than the input supply curve. The slope of the latter is $g'(x)$, while the slope of the former is given by

$$\frac{dMEI}{dx} = 2g'(x) + xg''(x). \tag{14.7.4}$$

Thus MEI must have the steeper slope unless the input supply curve is *very* concave from below (i.e., $g'' < 0$ and large in absolute value).

Finally, we may relate the MEI to input price and input supply elasticity in the same way that marginal revenue is related to commodity price and the elasticity of commodity demand. By definition, the elasticity of input supply is

$$\theta = \frac{dx}{dw}\frac{w}{x}. \tag{14.7.5}$$

Now write (14.7.3) as

$$MEI = w + x\frac{dw}{dx} = w\left(1 + \frac{x}{w}\frac{dw}{dx}\right). \tag{14.7.6}$$

will be offered at $O\bar{w}$ per unit. Hence $O\bar{w}$ is the market equilibrium input price corresponding to market equilibrium employment $O\bar{v}$.[8]

14.3.c Price and Employment under Monopsony When Several Variable Inputs Are Used

To secure the least-cost combination of variable inputs an entrepreneur must employ productive services in such proportion that the marginal rate of technical substitution equals the input-price ratio. But this proposition holds if, and only if, the inputs are purchased in perfectly competitive markets. Otherwise a change in input composition entails a change in relative input prices.

Let us illustrate this algebraically. Suppose there are two variable inputs, capital (K) and labor (L). Denote the marginal physical products by MP_K and MP_L and their market prices by r and w respectively. If the input markets are perfectly competitive, the least-cost combination rule requires that

$$\frac{MP_K}{MP_L} = \frac{r}{w}.\tag{14.3.1}$$

Stated alternatively,

$$\frac{MP_K}{r} = \frac{MP_L}{w}.\tag{14.3.2}$$

Using (14.7.5) in (14.7.6), one obtains

$$MEI = w\left(1 + \frac{1}{\theta}\right).\tag{14.7.7}$$

When the input supply curve is perfectly elastic, $\theta \to \infty$ and $MEI = w$, i.e., monopsony does not exist.

Exercise: State and explain all of the relations between $MR = p\left(1 - \frac{1}{\eta}\right)$ and $MEI = w\left(1 + \frac{1}{\theta}\right)$.

[8] This proposition may easily be proved by using footnotes 1 and 7. Summarizing,

$$p = h(q), \qquad q = f(x), \qquad \text{and} \qquad w = g(x)\tag{14.8.1}$$

are the commodity demand function, the production function, and the input supply function respectively. Ignoring fixed cost, the profit function is

$$\pi = pq - wx = qh(q) - xg(x) = f(x)h[f(x)] - xg(x).\tag{14.8.2}$$

The entrepreneur determines the amount of the variable input so as to maximize profit:

Equation (14.3.2) implies that the marginal product per dollar spent on each input must be the same. The *reason* for this rule is that marginal physical product represents the additional revenue, and input price the additional cost, attributable to the input. This holds for both competitive and monopolistic commodity markets; price changes as output changes in monopoly markets, but the price change is the same whether output is expanded by increasing the employment of capital, the employment of labor, or both.

The proposition stated in equation (14.3.2) is fairly obvious, but it might be well to discuss it some more. Suppose

$$\frac{MP_K}{r} > \frac{MP_L}{w}. \tag{14.3.3}$$

By inequality (14.3.3), a dollar's worth of capital contributes more to output than a dollar's worth of labor, at the *present* capital-labor ratio. If the input markets are perfectly competitive, rates of employment can be changed without affecting input prices. Therefore the entrepreneur would substitute capital for labor because he can obtain the same output for less cost. As he makes this substitution, the marginal product of capital declines and the marginal product of labor increases. With market determined r and w, the entrepreneur will continue the substitution until equality (14.3.2) is established.

If the input markets are monopsonistic, changes in the volume of employment cause corresponding changes in input prices. In particular, the entrepreneur must look to the marginal expense of input (*MEI*) rather than its market price when making employment decisions. Consider labor only, for the moment. An additional unit adds its marginal

---

$$\frac{d\pi}{dx} = h[f(x)]f'(x) + \frac{dh(q)}{dq} f'(x)f(x) - g(x) - xg'(x) = 0, \tag{14.8.3}$$

or

$$\left[h(q) + q\frac{dh}{dq} \right] f'(x) = [g(x) + xg'(x)]. \tag{14.8.4}$$

By footnote 1, the left-hand side of (14.8.4) is marginal revenue product. By footnote 7, the right-hand side is the marginal expense of input. Thus the theorem is proved.

Also using footnotes 1 and 7, we may write this relation as

$$p\left(1 - \frac{1}{\eta}\right)f'(x) = w\left(1 + \frac{1}{\theta}\right). \tag{14.8.5}$$

Exercise: State and explain the interesting relations implicit in equation (14.8.5).

product to output, but it does not add w to total cost; instead, with a positively sloped input supply curve it adds its marginal expense MEI_L.

Suppose the capital-labor ratio in production at a given moment is such that

$$\frac{MP_K}{MEI_K} > \frac{MP_L}{MEI_L}. \tag{14.3.4}$$

Inequality (14.3.4) has the following meaning: at the prevailing input combination an entrepreneur can obtain a greater increase in output per additional dollar of cost by employing capital rather than labor. Consequently, he can maintain the same output but reduce cost by substituting capital for labor. As he does so, two forces work to bring about an equality: as the employment of capital expands and that of labor declines (a) the marginal product of capital declines and that of labor increases and (b) the marginal expense of input of capital rises and that of labor declines. Since the entrepreneur can reduce cost so long as the inequality in expression (14.3.4) prevails, he will substitute capital for labor until

$$\frac{MP_K}{MEI_K} = \frac{MP_L}{MEI_L}. \tag{14.3.5}$$

When equality (14.3.5) obtains, no change in input composition will reduce cost. Consequently, we have proved that:[9]

Proposition: A monopsonist who uses several variable productive inputs will adjust input composition until the ratio of marginal product to marginal expense of input is the same for all variable inputs used. The least-cost combination is accordingly obtained when the marginal rate of technical substitution equals the marginal expense of input ratio.

In the two-input situation, we have

$$\frac{MP_L}{MP_K} = \frac{MEI_L}{MEI_K}. \tag{14.3.6}$$

Thus one sees that rule (14.3.1) for perfectly competitive input markets is a special case of rule (14.3.6); rule (14.3.1) is valid because in per-

---

[9] The proof of this proposition is accomplished by an easy extension of footnote 8. Let

$$p = b(q), \qquad q = f(K, L), \qquad r = g(K), \qquad w = m(L) \tag{14.9.1}$$

be the commodity demand function, the production function, the supply of capital function, and the labor supply function respectively. The profit function is, accordingly,

$$\pi = qb(q) - Kg(K) - Lm(L). \tag{14.9.2}$$

fectly competitive input markets, the marginal expense of input is precisely equal to its market price.[10]

14.3.d Monopsonistic Exploitation

In subsection 14.2.f it was shown that monopoly in the commodity market leads to "monopolistic exploitation" in the input market. Mo-

---

The entrepreneur adjusts both inputs so as to maximize profit:

$$\frac{\partial \pi}{\partial K} = q \frac{dh}{dq} \frac{\partial f}{\partial K} + h(q) \frac{\partial f}{\partial K} - g(K) - Kg'(K) = 0, \tag{14.9.3}$$

$$\frac{\partial \pi}{\partial L} = q \frac{dh}{dq} \frac{\partial f}{\partial L} + h(q) \frac{\partial f}{\partial L} - m(L) - Lm'(L) = 0, \tag{14.9.4}$$

or

$$[qh'(q) + h(q)] \frac{\partial f}{\partial K} = g(K) + Kg'(K), \tag{14.9.5}$$

$$[qh'(q) + h(q)] \frac{\partial f}{\partial L} = m(L) + Lm'(L). \tag{14.9.6}$$

The two equations just above state that the marginal revenue product of each input must equal its marginal expense of input. Taking the ratio of the two equations and canceling the marginal revenue term yields

$$\frac{MP_K}{MP_L} = \frac{MEI_K}{MEI_L}. \tag{14.9.7}$$

Transforming (14.9.7) yields the relation stated in the text.

[10] An important matter is here relegated to a footnote because even a graphical exposition requires some mathematics. *But note:* the student, whether mathematically trained or not, should read this footnote.

The relation in equation (14.3.6) in the text states that the marginal rate of technical substitution of capital for labor equals the ratio of their marginal expenses of input. This is the "rule" for optimum input proportions. As explained in the text and in footnote 9, the "rule" is based upon profit maximization. It can, of course, be so based. But the important point is that this rule can be established upon the much weaker assumption that entrepreneurs minimize the cost of producing a given output or maximize the output obtainable from a given expenditure upon resources.

Just as in Chapter 6, this may be shown graphically by use of isoquants and isocost curves. The mathematics enters in showing that the isocost curve is not a straight line. Everything else follows from the definitions introduced above.

Exercise: For mathematically trained students only. Suppose $\bar{C}$ is spent on resources. Thus the isocost curve is $Kg(K) + Lm(L) = \bar{C}$. Show the following relations: (a) the isocost curve is "usually" concave from below, but may be concave from above if an input supply function is negatively sloped; (b) the "rule" stated in equation (14.3.6) mathematically; (c) if an input supply function is negatively sloped, *economically* efficient operation may require the entrepreneur to produce in the *technologically* inefficient region (i.e., the region in which one marginal product is negative).

nopolistic exploitation exists in the sense that each productive service is paid its marginal revenue product which, because of the negatively sloped commodity demand curve, is less than the value of its marginal product. Each unit of resource receives the amount which, on average, it contributes to the firm's total receipts; but the units of resources do not receive the values of their marginal products.

Monopsonistic exploitation is something in addition to this, as illustrated by Figure 14.3.3. The figure is constructed to cover a variety of cases; the curves would doubtlessly change as the type of market organization changes. However, allowing for this, Figure 14.3.3 is a schematic device for illustrating monopolistic and monopsonistic exploitation.

First, suppose both the commodity and input markets are perfectly competitive. The value of the marginal product curve is the industry demand for input curve.[11] As you will recall, it is not the *direct* sum of

FIGURE 14.3.3

Monopsonistic Exploitation

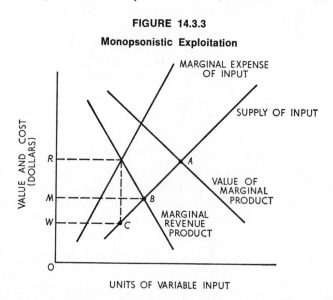

UNITS OF VARIABLE INPUT

Exercise: Give an economically rational explanation of (c) above.

Reference for exercises: Ferguson, *The Neoclassical Theory of Production and Distribution,* chaps. 7 and 8.

[11] The concept of a *VMP* curve for an industry is somewhat ambiguous. For a firm it is clear: it is the input's marginal product multiplied by the *constant* (to the firm) commodity price. For an industry it is somewhat different. For each level of employment and output, industry *VMP* is the marginal product of the input (efficient operation of firms assures equality among firms) multiplied by the market price associated with that level of output. Of course, market price decreases as output increases; and the various marginal products are multiplied by the relevant, *but changing,* market price.

the individual curves; however, it does represent the value of the input's marginal product to the industry as a whole. Demand and supply intersect at point *A,* each unit of input receiving the market value of its marginal product.

Next, let the commodity market be monopolistic, while the input market is perfectly competitive. The marginal revenue product curve represents the collection of monopoly demand curves (just as the value of the marginal product curve represents the collection of individual demand curves). Equilibrium is attained at point *B.* The difference between the wage rates corresponding to points *A* and *B* ($OR - OM = RM$) is the "monopolistic exploitation" of the input. Because of monopolistic exploitation, fewer units of the input are employed and the unit price of each is less. Nonetheless, each unit of input receives an amount equal to what its employment adds to total receipts.

Finally, suppose there is monopoly in the commodity market and monopsony in the input market. Equilibrium is attained at *C,* at a still lower price and employment level. Monopsonistic exploitation is represented by the difference between points *A* and *C,* or by the difference in input prices between the competitive and monopsonistic equilibria ($OR - OW = RW$). The portion *RM* is attributable to monopoly in the commodity market; it is not unique to monopsony. The additional portion *MW,* however, is uniquely attributable to monopsony (or more generally, to oligopsony). The existence of the differential *MW* is caused by the fact that each unit of input contributes *OM* to total receipts but receives only *OW* in return. Thus the chief feature of monopsonistic exploitation is that each unit of input does not receive in pay an amount equal to its contribution to total receipts.

In subsection 14.2.f it was indicated that while monopolistic exploitation could be removed, the "cure" might be worse than the "disease." Indeed, within a free enterprise economic system monopolistic exploitation is bound to arise. Even bona fide product differentiation causes this type of "exploitation." The same is not true of monopsonistic exploitation. Countermeasures exist, and they are not fundamentally destructive to a free-enterprise system.

14.3.e Monopsony and the Economic Effects of Labor Unions

A study of labor unions and of the collective-bargaining process even on a purely theoretical level, is beyond the scope of this work.[12] How-

---

[12] For an excellent theoretical treatment, see Allan M. Cartter, *Theory of Wages and Employment* (Homewood, Ill.: Richard D. Irwin, Inc., 1959), pp. 77–133.

ever, the issue of monopsonistic exploitation allows one briefly to indicate the economic effects of labor unions. Consider any typical labor market with some kind of supply of labor curve; for simplicity, assume that it is positively sloped. If the workers in this market are unionized, the union bargaining representative fundamentally has one power to exert: he can make the effective supply of labor curve a horizontal line at any wage level he wishes, at least until the horizontal line reaches the existing supply curve. Thus the marginal expense of input is the same as the supply price of labor over the horizontal stretch of the union supply curve. That is to say, the union representative can name a wage rate and guarantee the availability of workers at this price.[13]

To introduce this topic, let us suppose the labor market in question is perfectly competitive (large number of purchasers of this type of labor) and unorganized. The situation is depicted in panel a, Figure 14.3.4, where D_L and S_L are the demand for and supply of labor respectively. The market equilibrium wage rate is $O\overline{W}$ and $O\overline{Q}$ units of labor are employed. Each individual firm (panel b) accordingly employs $O\overline{q}$ units. Next, suppose the labor market is unionized. If the union does not attempt to raise wages the situation might remain as it is. However, scoring wage increases is the *raison d'être* of unions. Thus suppose the bargaining agency sets $O\overline{W}_u$ as the wage rate; in other words, the union supply of labor curve $W_u S_u S_L$ is established. OQ_u units of labor are employed, each firm taking Oq_u units. The result is a rise in wages and a decline in employment. In perfectly competitive input markets this is *all* unions can do.

This does not necessarily mean a union cannot benefit its members. If the demand for labor is inelastic, an increase in the wage rate will result in an increase in total wages paid to the workers, even though the number of workers employed is less. If the union can somehow equitably divide the proceeds of OQ_u employed workers among the $O\overline{Q}$ po-

---

[13] This is, of course, an heroic oversimplification, but it is a useful one for analytical purposes.

tential workers, all will benefit. Such a division is easy to achieve. Suppose $OQ_u = \frac{1}{2} O\overline{Q}$ and that a 40-hour week characterizes the market. Then OQ_u units of labor can be furnished by having $O\overline{Q}$ units work a 20-hour week.

FIGURE 14.3.4

Effects of a Labor Union in a Perfectly Competitive Labor Market

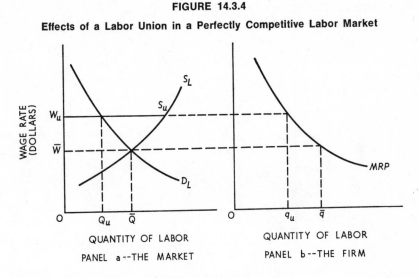

QUANTITY OF LABOR

PANEL a--THE MARKET

QUANTITY OF LABOR

PANEL b--THE FIRM

The other side of the coin is worth noting, however. If the demand for labor is elastic, total wage receipts will decline and the union cannot compensate the $Q_u\overline{Q}$ workers who are unemployed because of the increase in wage rates. Thus in perfectly competitive labor markets labor unions are not an unmitigated blessing.[14]

In monopsonistic or oligopsonistic markets, however, unions *must* benefit their members if they employ rational policies. Consider the

---

[14] *Exercise:* Suppose panel a, Figure 14.3.4, represents the market for unskilled labor in absence of a minimum-wage law. What are the market effects of the establishment of a minimum wage by some government agency? Is there any empirical evidence that the analytical result you obtain is descriptive of the real world?

FIGURE 14.3.5

**Economic Effects of a Labor Union
in a Monopsonistic Labor Market**

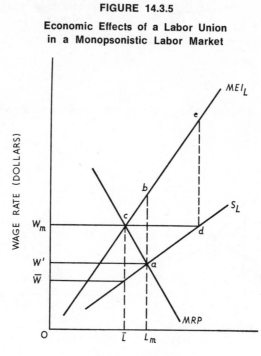

QUANTITY OF LABOR

monopsony labor market represented by Figure 14.3.5. If the labor force is not organized, equilibrium is attained at point c, where marginal revenue product equals the marginal expense of input (based upon the positively sloped supply of input curve S_L). The equilibrium wage is $O\bar{W}$, and equilibrium employment is $O\bar{L}$. Now suppose the workers establish a union that bargains collectively with the monopsonist.

At one extreme the union may attempt to achieve maximum employment for its members. To this end, it establishes the supply of labor curve $W'aS_L$. The associated marginal expense of input curve accordingly becomes $W'abMEI_L$. Marginal revenue product equals the marginal expense of input at point a; OL_m units of labor are therefore employed at the wage OW'. Consequently, as one alternative, the union can achieve a small increase in wages accompanied by an increase in the number of workers employed. Each unit of labor receives its contribution to the firm's total receipts; the exploitation uniquely attributable to monopsony is eliminated.

At another extreme, suppose the union decides to maintain the initial level of employment $O\bar{L}$. It accordingly establishes the supply curve $W_m dS_L$. The corresponding marginal expense of input curve is $W_m deMEI_L$. Marginal revenue product equals the marginal expense of input at point c; hence equilibrium employment is $O\overline{L}$ and the associated equilibrium wage is OW_m. This wage rate is the maximum attainable without a reduction in employment below the pre-union level. At the wage OW_m, however, the union can achieve a substantial wage increase without affecting employment. Again, the unique portion of monopsonistic exploitation is removed.

We have considered only two extremes. The union can, in fact, select intermediate policies, scoring increases in both employment and the wage rate. The union can harm its members only if the demand for labor is elastic, and it sets the supply of labor curve so that the equilibrium wage exceeds OW_m. But even then the unique portion of monopsonistic exploitation would be eliminated. Thus we have a general principle that broadly describes the economic effects of labor unions: labor unions can eliminate the portion of total monopsonistic exploitation that is uniquely attributable to monopsony in the labor market; however, the portion attributable to monopoly can in no way be eliminated by trade union activity.

QUESTIONS

1. Since monopolists do not pay factors of production the value of their marginal products, how do monopolists retain factors when perfect competitors use the same kind of resources in producing their output?
2. Provide an economic analysis of the U.S. minimum wage law. Do the same thing for a *state* (or county, or city) minimum wage law.
3. The government imposes a ceiling price on commodity A but not on the competing commodity B. C, D, and E are factors used in producing A, while D, E, and F are factors used in producing B. C is used in the production of A only and not in the production of any other commodity in the economy. Discuss the effects of this ceiling price on the product and factor markets.
4. "Without collective bargaining, the workers' market disadvantage would enable the owners of other productive agents to appropriate income that would otherwise go to labor." Discuss.
5. Assume that an industrial union's primary purpose is to raise the wages of its members above the competitive level. (a) Explain on a theoretical level how this increase might be accomplished; (b) what conditions would make the union's job easier?
6. Consider a trade union that is strong enough to prevent nonmembers

from working at the trade in question. For simplicity, assume that membership is not affected by the level of returns to members. Finally, assume that there is immigration into the country of unskilled workers. What will be the effect of the immigration on the incomes of the union members? What factors tend to increase income, what factors tend to cause it to decline? Is there a clear balance in favor of either increase or decline?

7. "If a union succeeds in raising wages, it will cause the ratio of the cost of union labor to total cost to rise." Discuss.

SUGGESTED READINGS

Cartter, Allan M. *Theory of Wages and Employment,* pp. 77–133. Homewood, Ill.: Richard D. Irwin, Inc., 1959.

Hicks, John R. *The Theory of Wages.* London: Macmillan & Co., Ltd., 1932.

Robinson, Joan. *The Economics of Imperfect Competition,* pp. 218–28, 281–304. London: Macmillan & Co., Ltd., 1933.

Advanced Reading, Part IV

I. MARGINAL PRODUCTIVITY AND INPUT DEMAND

Chamberlin, E. H. "Monopolistic Competition and the Productivity Theory of Distribution," *Explorations in Economics,* pp. 237–49. New York: McGraw-Hill Book Co., Inc., 1936.

Douglas, P. H. *The Theory of Wages.* New York: The Macmillan Co., 1934.

Ferguson, C. E. " 'Inferior Factors' and the Theories of Production and Input Demand," *Economica,* May, 1968.

———. *The Neoclassical Theory of Production and Distribution,* chaps. 6 and 7. London and New York: Cambridge University Press, 1969.

———. "Production, Prices, and the Theory of Jointly Derived Input Demand Functions," *Economica,* November, 1966.

———, and **Saving, Thomas R.** "Long-Run Scale Adjustments of a Perfectly Competitive Firm and Industy," *American Economic Review,* Vol. LIX (1969), pp. 774–83.

Hicks, John R. *The Theory of Wages.* London: Macmillan & Co., Ltd., 1932.

Mosak, Jacob L. "Interrelations of Production, Price and Derived Demand," *Journal of Political Economy,* Vol. XLVI (1938), pp. 761–87.

Pfouts, R. W. "Distribution Theory in a Certain Case of Oligopoly and Oligopsony," *Metroeconomica,* Vol. VII (1955), pp. 137–46.

Schultz, Henry. "Marginal Productivity and the General Pricing Process," *Journal of Political Economy,* Vol. XXXVII (1929), pp. 505–51.

Stigler, George J. "Production and Distribution in the Short Run," *Journal of Political Economy,* Vol. XLVII (1939), pp. 305–27.

II. DISTRIBUTION AND RELATIVE SHARES

Ferguson, C. E. "Neoclassical Theory of Technical Progress and Relative Factor Shares," *Southern Economic Journal,* Vol. XXXIV (1968), pp. 490–504.

————. *The Neoclassical Theory of Production and Distribution,* chaps. 11 and 12. London and New York: Cambridge University Press, 1969.

Robinson, Joan. "Euler's Theorem and the Problem of Distribution," *Economic Journal,* Vol. XLIV (1934), pp. 398–414.

Stigler, George J. *Production and Distribution Theories.* New York: The Macmillan Co., 1941.

PART V
Theory of General Equilibrium
and Economic Welfare

Well over 100 years ago Frederic Bastiat, a noted French economist, wrote about the Paris of his day. Hundreds of thousands of people then lived in Paris, each consuming a wide variety of commodities, especially food products not produced in the city. The survival of the city required the constant influx of goods and services. No single agency planned the daily inflow of commodities; but each day goods did arrive in approximately correct quantities: Paris survived. "Imagination is baffled when it tries to appreciate the vast multiplicity of commodities which must enter tomorrow in order to preserve the inhabitants from falling prey to the convulsions of famine, rebellion, and pillage," Bastiat wrote. "Yet all sleep, and their slumbers are not disturbed for a single minute by the prospect of such a frightful catastrophe."

Paris survived because of the unplanned cooperation of many people, most of whom competed against each other. Not for altruistic motives, to be sure, but for the profit to be gained from selling in the Paris market. Even before the days of Bastiat, Adam Smith had observed the effects of cooperation in production. Smith visited a small pin factory, one doubtless primitive by modern standards. Yet Smith was so struck by the gain in productivity resulting from cooperation and the specialization of labor that he wrote an account now classic in economic literature:

One man draws out the wire, another straights it, a third cuts it, a fourth points it, a fifth grinds it at the top for receiving the head; to make the head

requires two or three distinct operations; to put it on is a peculiar business;
to whiten it is another; it is even a trade by itself to put them into paper.
. . . I have seen a small factory of this kind where ten men only were employed and where some of them consequently performed two or three distinct operations. But though they were very poor and therefore but indiffer-
ently accommodated with the necessary machinery, they could, when they
exerted themselves, make among them about twelve pounds of pins in a
day. There are in a pound upwards of 4,000 pins of middling size. Those
ten persons, therefore, could make among them upwards of 48,000 pins a
day. . . . But if they had all wrought separately and independently . . .
they could certainly not each of them make twenty, perhaps not one pin in
a day. . . .

Specialization and division of labor make possible a larger output
than if each person worked alone and were self-sufficient. But self-
sufficiency does guarantee that the consumer gets what he wants, or what
he wants most and what is within his ability to achieve. When each
person is not self-sufficient, the economy either must be *planned* by
some central agency or there must be some mechanism that accom-
plishes the same goal. Adam Smith chose to call this mechanism the
"invisible hand"; in the terminology of today it might better be called
a "great IBM machine in the sky." But whatever the terminology, a
free enterprise price system generally functions so as to achieve the
goals of state planning, usually much more efficiently than planned
economies achieve them. Economic welfare under a free enterprise system is the topic of Chapter 16, after we analyze general economic equilibrium in Chapter 15.

To this point our discussion has focused only upon the economic behavior of single economic agents or of single industries or product
groups. But there are millions of economic agents in the economy, and
we have not yet seen how the behavior of each is coordinated to achieve
a general equilibrium.

Looked at differently, the familiar graph in Figure V.1 illustrates
the problem. On the one hand, households function both as consumers
and resource suppliers. On the other hand, business firms use the resources, organize production, and sell the products of the process. There
is a flow of *real* productive services from households to businesses and
a return flow of *real* goods and services from business firms to households. If a barter system were feasible in an advanced industrial nation,
we should have to go no further. But it is not; money must be introduced.

Rather than trade output for input, business firms pay households

FIGURE V.1

Circular Flow of Economic Activity

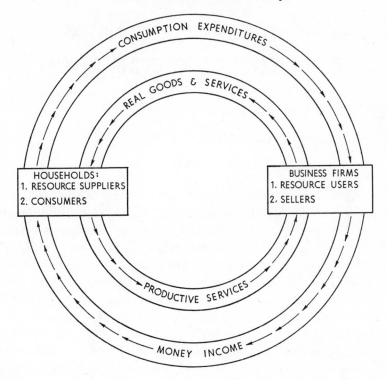

money income for the productive services supplied. In their roles as consumers, households create a counterflow of consumption expenditures to business firms, exchanging their money income for the real goods and services supplied to them. Thus there is a monetary flow in one direction to offset each real flow in the opposite direction. The problem of general equilibrium analysis is to determine the process by which the various flows balance.

Chapter 15

THEORY OF GENERAL ECONOMIC EQUILIBRIUM

15.1 INTRODUCTION

According to the principle of maximization adhered to throughout the book, each economic agent attains an equilibrium position when *something* is maximized. A consumer maximizes satisfaction subject to a budget constraint; an entrepreneur maximizes profit, possibly subject to the constraint imposed by a production function; workers may determine their labor supply curves by maximizing satisfaction derived from leisure, subject to given wage rates. In terms of an old cliché, we have studied the trees fairly intensely but we have not yet seen the forest.

The problem of forests arises, however. Millions of economic agents pursue their own goals and strive for their own equilibrium without particular regard for others. The problem is to determine whether the more-or-less independent behavior of economic agents is consistent with each agent's attaining equilibrium. All economic agents, whether consumer, producer, or resource supplier, are *interdependent;* will *independent* action by each lead to a position in which equilibrium is achieved by all? This is the problem of general (static or stationary) economic equilibrium.

15.1.a Quesnay's "Tableau Economique"

At this point a digression to history may be useful. Perhaps the earliest notion of stationary general equilibrium is in the work of a group of French economists called the "physiocrats." Foremost among them was an economist named Quesnay who, as early as 1758, presented a picture of general equilibrium by means of his "Tableau économique."[1] Quesnay divided the economic agents of a society into three

---

[1] F. Quesnay, *Tableau économique et maximes générales du gouvernement économique* (Paris, 1758). For a later contribution, see J. Turgot, *Reflections sur la formation et la distribution des richesses* (Paris, 1776).

classes: the productive or agricultural class, the proprietary class, and the nonproductive class. He then suggested that the riches of a nation must be distributed among the three classes so as to attain a stationary (or flowing) equilibrium.

Quesnay's concept may be explained by an example taken from his book. Suppose there is a country with 130 million acres of land and 30 million people. The land properly tilled will produce 4 million units of food and 1 million units of raw material. Quesnay suggested that the "riches" must be distributed in the following manner. The productive class will retain 2 million units of food, which comprise the "avances annuelles" to sustain it during the next year. The productive class will pay 2 million units of food to the proprietary class as rent for the land, and trade the 1 million units of raw material to the nonproductive class (manufacturers) for 2 million units of manufactured goods. The proprietary class will retain 1 million units of food for subsistence and trade 1 million units to the nonproductive class for manufactured goods. Finally, the nonproductive class receives 1 million units of raw material from the productive class, transforms it into 3 million units of manufactured products, and exchanges 2 million units for 1 million units of raw materials from the productive class and 1 million units of food from the proprietary class.

Now we are back where we started; the system can continue to function in the same way year after year. It is very simple model; perhaps it may seem trivial. Yet it represents a beginning point for general equilibrium theory. To quote Fossati:

> It is against a background like this, which in essence is the idea of the stationary state, that the concept of the equilibrium of the economic system has been defined. . . . The stationary state is one in which every year the same processes are repeated, and the same distribution of goods takes place through the same channels. The stationary state of the "Tableau economique" is a model showing the conditions required for certain processes to function steadily and maintain each other in being on an unchanging scale indefinitely, like fountain-jets ever in movement yet always rising to the same height. It may not seem to offer a great contribution to the analysis of equilibrium, yet in view of the time of its formulation, it is a landmark in our science.[2]

15.1.b Walras, Pareto, and Leontief

The theory of general equilibrium was developed much more thoroughly by the "Lausanne School," especially by Leon Walras and

---

[2] Eraldo Fossati, *The Theory of General Static Equilibrium* (Oxford: Basil Blackwell, 1957), pp. 37–38.

Vilfredo Pareto.[3] Concerned as it is with the individual equilibrium of millions of economic agents and the overall equilibrium of the system, the theory of general economic equilibrium has always been essentially mathematical in nature. Yet it has been given an operationally usable form by Leontief, resulting in his justly famous "input-output" analysis.[4]

15.1.c Algebraic Statement of the Problem

In sections 15.2 and 15.3, a graphical treatment of general equilibrium is presented. However, to supplement this simple treatment of a simple economy, it seems desirable to set out an algebraic formulation of the general equilibrium model. It enables one to see that a solution of this complicated problem might exist; and it points forcefully to the general interdependence of all economic agents. Furthermore, the algebraic formulation shows that several important theoretical inferences may be drawn from the model, even though empirical implementation or verification of general or special (input-output) models of general equilibrium presents gigantic computation problems. (*Note:* Readers may go directly to section 15.2.)

15.1.d Equilibrium of Exchange

Let us begin with an extremely artificial case. Suppose there is a small, isolated country containing n individuals, each of whom possesses a well-defined parcel of land. These individuals truly resemble the lily of the valley, for they neither toil nor do they reap. They merely gather and exchange manna which, providentially enough, falls nightly upon their land. Indeed, m different types of manna fall in different concentrations on the various parcels of land. Every morning each individual gathers the various types of manna that fell upon his own ground.

For convenience, let us represent each individual by the subscript i. Thus with n individuals in the society, i takes the values 1, 2 . . . , n. In like manner, denote the different types of manna by the subscript j; this subscript accordingly has the values 1, 2, . . . , m. With this convention, let $\bar{x}_{ji}$ represent the quantity of type j manna gathered by

---

[3] Leon Walras, *Elements d'économie politique pure* (Lausanne: F. Rouge, 1874); for translation, see suggested readings at end of chapter. Vilfredo Pareto, *Cours d'économie politique* (Lausanne: F. Rouge, 1897).

[4] W. W. Leontief, *The Structure of the American Economy, 1919–1939* (New York: Oxford University Press, 1951).

individual i on a given morning; thus $\bar{x}_{1i}, \bar{x}_{2i}, \ldots, \bar{x}_{mi}$ is a complete list of individual i's initial manna holdings.

Our mythical society would be ideal except for the fact that the composition of the manna fall on each plot of land is not the composition desired by the individual who possesses the plot in question. That is, individual i wishes to have x_{ji} units of type j manna; but in fact he gathers $\bar{x}_{ji}$ units, and typically $\bar{x}_{ji} \neq x_{ji}$. Indeed, if $x_{ji} > \bar{x}_{ji}$, the individual must somehow obtain $x_{ji} - \bar{x}_{ji}$ units of type j manna from someone else if his consumption plan is to be realized. On the other hand, if $\bar{x}_{ji} > x_{ji}$, the individual may dispose of the surplus, $\bar{x}_{ji} - x_{ji}$, in the market. Of course, his consumption plan must be realistically constructed; he must plan to trade enough of some types of manna to finance his acquisition of other types.

For expository purposes it is convenient to play the exchange game in a way slightly different from that indicated above. In particular, suppose that each morning individual i first trades his entire stocks of manna of types $1, 2, \ldots, m - 1$ for type m manna. After the initial exchanges, his entire manna holding is concentrated in type m manna; and the physical quantity of this manna stock represents his daily *real income*. Next, since it is difficult for us to deal with real income and for our imaginary citizens to engage in unrestricted barter, it is convenient to introduce "money" as a *unit of account* (but *not* as a medium of exchange or as a store of value).

To this end, let p_j represent the nominal market price of type j manna in terms of the unit of account. As it happens, the model of general equilibrium does not bring in the monetary side of the economy; as a consequence there is neither datum nor equation, such as the supply of money or the equation of exchange, to determine the *absolute* price level. Only *relative prices* are determind by the model—prices relative to the unit of account. Therefore, one must arbitrarily select some type of manna whose price is to be the unit of account or the numeraire for the system of relative prices. Since one may select the numeraire good and its unit price, let us specify type m manna as the numeraire and set its unit price at unity: $p_m = 1$. Using the notation just introduced, the monetary value of individual i's real income after the initial exchange is $M = p_1\bar{x}_{1i} + p_2\bar{x}_{2i} + \ldots + x_{mi}$ or, more compactly,

$$M = \sum_{j=1}^{m} p_j\bar{x}_{ji} .$$

Next, suppose individual i allocates the money value of his real income by trading for the various types of manna he desires. Since x_{ji}

represents his barter purchases of type j manna, allocating his entire money income means that $M = p_1 x_{1i} + p_2 x_{2i} + \ldots + x_{mi}$ or, more simply,

$$M = \sum_{j=1}^{m} p_j x_{ji} .$$

Since the two M's are equal, or the monetary value of his income is equal to the monetary value of the things he wishes and is able to command, the *budget constraint* for individual i may be written as

$$\sum_{j=1}^{m} p_j(x_{ji} - \bar{x}_{ji}) = 0 . \tag{15.1.1}$$

As in Part I of the text, we assume that the level of satisfaction attained by any consumer depends upon the quantities of the various types of manna he consumes. In particular, suppose the level of satisfaction attained by individual i may be represented by the ordinal preference function

$$u_i = u_i(x_{1i}, x_{2i}, \ldots , x_{mi}) . \tag{15.1.2}$$

Still following the development of the theory of consumer behavior in Part I, assume that individual i ($i = 1, 2, \ldots , n$) attempts to maximize his satisfaction [expression (15.1.2)] subject to his budget constraint [expression (15.1.1)]. As you already know, maximization requires a condition that may be expressed in either of two ways: (*a*) the marginal rate of substitution in consumption between any two types of manna must be equal to the ratio of their prices; or (*b*) the marginal utility of a dollar's worth of one type of manna must equal the marginal utility of a dollar's worth of every other type.

Let u_{ji} denote the marginal utility of type j manna to individual i. The consumer-maximization requirement stated in (*b*) above may be expressed as

$$\frac{u_{1i}}{p_1} = \frac{u_{2i}}{p_2} = \cdots = u_{mi},$$

since $p_m = 1$. Furthermore, this same relation must hold for each individual in the economy. Utilizing this knowledge, we may write out a set of equations that formally describes the *exchange equilibrium* in a system of general equilibrium:

$$\frac{u_{ji}}{p_j} = u_{mi} \qquad \begin{array}{l} (j = 1, 2, \ldots, m-1) \\ (i = 1, 2, \ldots, n), \end{array} \qquad (15.1.3)$$

$$\sum_{j=1}^{m} p_j(x_{ji} - \bar{x}_{ji}) = 0 \qquad (i = 1, 2, \ldots, n).$$

To reiterate: equations (15.1.3) imply that each individual in the economy exchanges manna with other individuals until all individuals as consumers are in a satisfaction-maximizing equilibrium. The first subset of equations states that for general equilibrium to obtain, *each individual* ($i = 1, 2, \ldots, n$) must finally hold manna in such proportions that the marginal utility of a dollar's worth of one type of manna is the same as the marginal utility of a dollar's worth of every other type of manna. The second subset of equations stipulates that each individual must abide by his budget constraint.

15.1.e Equilibrium of Production

As fanciful as the manna-exchange model might seem to be, it actually applies to an ever-expanding segment of the American economy. More specifically, the problem confronting welfare recipients is precisely the same as that confronting manna gatherers: a consumer in either group must allocate his *given* money income so as to maximize satisfaction. Nonetheless, to present a formal model of the entire economy the exchange model must be supplemented by a model of production. Let us therefore turn to the production side of the model of general economic equilibrium.

Let there be q business firms in the economy, and denote them by the subscript s; thus s takes the values $1, 2, \ldots, q$. Our x symbols must now represent both commodities and resources. Firm s uses various resources and commodities to produce one or more commodities. As in Part II, we assume that there is a production function showing the output possibilities for each commodity. For example, firm s might produce commodity two by using resources five, six, and seven. We may thus write the production function for firm s as

$$x_{2s} = f_s(x_{5s}, x_{6s}, x_{7s}).$$

However, to allow for the production of several commodities by means of commodities and resources, it is more convenient to write a *transformation function* for each firm. The transformation function is based upon the underlying production functions for each commodity;

it merely shows that one set of commodities and resources can be transformed into another set by the production process. The transformation function for firm s is written as

$$f_s(x_{1s}, x_{2s}, \ldots, x_{ms}) = 0 . \tag{15.1.4}$$

In equation (15.1.4) the x symbols represent both outputs and inputs. Thus we must adopt another convention: (a) if x_{js} represents the output of commodity j by firm s, it is a *positive* quantity; and (b) if x_{ks} represents the input of commodity or resource k into the production process of firm s, it is a *negative* quantity.

Let us now return briefly to the example of the firm that produces commodity two by using inputs five, six, and seven. The total revenue of the firm (say, firm s) is $p_2 x_{2s}$; its total cost is $p_5 x_{5s} + p_6 x_{6s} + p_7 x_{7s}$. Accordingly, the profit of firm s, denoted r_s, is $r_s = p_2 x_{2s} + p_5 x_{5s} + p_6 x_{6s} + p_7 x_{7s}$, since x_{5s}, x_{6s}, and x_{7s} are all negative. That is, since each of these is itself negative, a *plus* sign must be used in the profit equation in order to subtract cost from revenue. Generalizing to the transformation function (15.1.4), the profit accruing to firm s may be expressed as

$$r_s = \sum_{j=1}^{m} p_j x_{js} . \tag{15.1.5}$$

As in Part III, we assume that each firm attempts to maximize profit [expression (15.1.5)] subject to the constraint imposed by its transformation function (15.1.4). The maximization process leads to the following set of equations, which formally describes the production side of the economy:

$$\frac{f_{js}}{p_j} = f_{ms} \quad \begin{array}{l} (j = 1, 2, \ldots, m - 1) \\ (s = 1, 2, \ldots, q) , \end{array} \tag{15.1.6}$$
$$f_s(x_{1s}, x_{2s}, \ldots, x_{ms}) = 0 \quad (s = 1, 2, \ldots, q) .$$

You already know the meaning of the equations in the first subset of (15.1.6), even though it may take quite a bit of explanation before the conditions become familiar. If both j and m represent inputs, f_{js} and f_{ms} are the total marginal products of input j and input m respectively (for example, f_{js} shows the increase in all outputs of firm s attributable to the addition of one unit of input j in the production process). In this case, the first subset of equations states the conditions for economically efficient operation. In particular, the marginal product of a dollar's worth of any one input must equal the marginal product of a dollar's worth of every other input. Expressed alternatively, the marginal rate of technical substitution between any two inputs must be equal to the ratio of their prices.

To explain the meaning of the first subset of equations when j and m are outputs, and when j is an output and m an input, requires somewhat more discussion. To begin, suppose both j and m are outputs of firm s. A typical equation of the first subset may then be written $f_{js}/f_{ms} = p_j/p_m = p_j$, since $p_m = 1$ by hypothesis. The expression f_{js}/f_{ms} is called the marginal rate of transformation of output j into output m. It shows the amount by which the output of commodity m may be expanded if the output of commodity j is reduced by one unit, given the volume of inputs available and used.

A little reflection will convince the reader that the marginal rate of transformation equals the ratio of the marginal cost of j to the marginal cost of m. First, the value of the inputs saved when the output of j is reduced by one unit is, by definition, the marginal cost of commodity j. Next, the same inputs are used to produce additional units of m. If the output of m increases by two units (the marginal rate of transformation is $2:1$), then on average the marginal cost of producing m at the current rate of output must be one half the marginal cost of producing j. If we let the marginal cost of commodity j be, say, 10, the marginal cost of m must be 5. Therefore, f_{js} is proportional to 10, f_{ms} is proportional to 5, and the ratio of marginal costs is 2, which is precisely the same as the marginal rate of transformation.

In this light, the maximization conditions simply state that if the marginal cost of producing commodity j is twice as great as the marginal cost of producing commodity m, the price of commodity j must also be twice as great as the price of commodity m. More generally, when both j and m represent outputs, the first subset of equations imposes requirements that may be stated in three alternative ways: (a) the marginal rate of transformation must equal the price ratio; (b) the ratio of marginal costs must equal the price ratio; and (c) the ratio of marginal cost to price must be the same for each commodity produced. The last alternative ties in closely with perfect competition, for under that form of market organization price equals marginal cost for each commodity.

The reason behind this requirement may easily be explained. Suppose price equals marginal cost in the production of commodity m but the price of j exceeds its marginal cost. Clearly, the entrepreneur can increase his profit by shifting resources from the production of m into the production of j. Since the output of m declines, its marginal cost declines also; and the marginal cost of j rises as its output expands. The entrepreneur can increase his profit by shifting resources from m to j until the point is reached at which the marginal cost-price ratio is the same for both commodities.

Finally, consider the case in which j is an output and m is an input. The maximizing conditions in the first subset of equations may then be written

$$p_m = p_j \frac{f_{ms}}{f_{js}}.$$

As you will recall, f_{ms} is the addition to the outputs of all commodities produced by firm s attributable to the addition of one unit of input m into the production process. The ratio f_{ms}/f_{js} is the marginal product of input m in the production of output j alone. The condition thus states that the price of the input must be equal to the value of its marginal product.

Now return to equations (15.1.6). The first subset of equations has been explained from the standpoint of one business firm. The entire subset requires that the described conditions holds for all firms and for all pairs of outputs, for all pairs of inputs, and for all combinations of an output and an input. The second subset stipulates that each firm must operate subject to the limitations imposed by the technical conditions of production.

15.1.f Perfect Competition

The model of general equilibrium may be expanded so as to include some aspects of imperfect competition. However, the present treatment is restricted to the perfectly competitive model as originally developed by Walras. If we further restrict our analysis to long-run equilibrium under perfect competition, entrance into and exit from industries by business firms reduces pure profit to zero. Hence r_s in equation (15.1.5) is zero, and the budget constraints in equations (15.1.1) do not have to be modified to allow for the existence of profit.

15.1.g Market Equilibrium

Equations (15.1.3) and (15.1.6) impose certain equilibrium conditions upon each individual and each business firm operating in the economy. However, to ensure that a *general* equilibrium is in fact attained, a set of market conditions must also be imposed. More specifically, we must require that quantity demanded equals quantity supplied for each resource and each commodity.

The net amount of commodity j demanded (if positive) or supplied (if negative) by individuals is

$$\sum_{i=1}^{n} (x_{ji} - \bar{x}_{ji}).$$

Similarly, the net amount of commodity j supplied (if positive) or demanded (if negative) by business firms is

$$\sum_{s=1}^{q} x_{js}.$$

Thus the market condition that quantity demanded equals quantity supplied for all items traded is represented by[5]

$$\sum_{s=1}^{q} x_{js} = \sum_{i=1}^{n} (x_{ji} - \bar{x}_{ji}) \qquad (j = 1, 2, \ldots, m - 1). \quad (15.1.7)$$

15.1.h General Economic Equilibrium

Now let us take stock. Equations (15.1.3) show the conditions that must hold if each consumer is to maximize satisfaction subject to his budget constraint. Similarly, equations (15.1.6) show the profit-maximizing conditions for each firm. Finally, equations (15.1.7) give the market equilibrium conditions on quantities demanded and supplied. We now have all the trees; do they constitute a forest?

The algebraic formulation of the general equilibrium model is obtained by combining these three sets of equations, repeated below:

$$\frac{u_{ji}}{p_j} = u_{mi} \qquad \begin{matrix} (j = 1, 2, \ldots, m - 1) \\ (i = 1, 2, \ldots, n), \end{matrix} \qquad \text{(i)}$$

$$\sum_{j=1}^{m} p_j(x_{ji} - \bar{x}_{ji}) = 0 \qquad (i = 1, 2, \ldots, n), \qquad \text{(ii)}$$

$$\frac{f_{js}}{p_j} = f_{ms} \qquad \begin{matrix} (j = 1, 2, \ldots, m - 1) \\ (s = 1, 2, \ldots, q), \end{matrix} \qquad \text{(iii)}$$

$$f_s(x_{1s}, x_{2s}, \ldots, x_{ms}) = 0 \qquad (s = 1, 2, \ldots, q), \qquad \text{(iv)}$$

---

[5] In equation (15.1.7), j varies over all commodities and there are actually m equations. However, it can be shown that one equation is not independent. Hence j is shown varying from one to $m - 1$.

$$\sum_{s=1}^{q} x_{js} = \sum_{i=1}^{n} (x_{ji} - \bar{x}_{ji}) \qquad (j = 1, 2, \ldots, m - 1). \qquad \text{(v)}$$

If a general equilibrium exists, the equations above may be solved for all of the economic variables. In particular, equations (i) and (ii) give *individual demands* x_{ji} in terms of the prices; thus they give aggregate demand for each commodity as well. Furthermore, equations (iii) and (iv) give *production by firms* x_{js} in terms of the prices, so the aggregate supply of each commodity is also given. Finally, equations (v) guarantee that quantity demanded equals quantity supplied in each market.

But none of this tells us whether a general economic equilibrium exists. At this level of analysis, the best we can do is to count variables and equations and thereby determine whether the model is consistent with the existence of a general economic equilibrium.

The variables in the system (i)–(v) are: (*a*) the mn quantities demanded x_{ji} of the m goods by the n individuals; (*b*) the mq quantities supplied x_{js} of the m commodities by the q firms; and (*c*) the $m - 1$ prices p_j (remembering that $p_m = 1$ by definition). The general equilibrium model, therefore, contains $mn + mq + (m - 1)$ variables. Now count equations: set (i) provides $n(m - 1)$; set (ii) contains n; set (iii) has $q(m - 1)$; set (iv) provides q; and set (v) gives an additional $m - 1$. Thus there are $n(m - 1) + n + q(m - 1) + q + (m - 1)$ equations, or more simply, $mn + mq + (m - 1)$. The number of unknowns precisely equals the number of equations; thus a consistent and determinate solution may exist.

In other words, a general economic equilibrium may exist; the independent behavior of interdependent economic agents may provide a consistent equilibrium. On a formal level, quite a number of behavioral relations were deduced and the process of economic interaction illustrated. To be sure, the discussion was restricted to a highly simplified economy, more especially because monetary problems were removed by the assumption that "money" exists only as a unit of account and not a medium of exchange. Yet even in this simplified setting the theory of general equilibrium is complex; small wonder we concentrate primarily on the partial economic equilibrium of individual economic agents rather than on the general economic equilibrium of interdependent agents.

15.2 GENERAL EQUILIBRIUM OF EXCHANGE

The algebraic formulation of subsections 15.1.c–15.1.h may cast general equilibrium theory in somewhat the wrong light. Thus the basic general equilibrium model is now given a graphical treatment. In the simplest models a good bit of insight into the economic process can be obtained. To be sure, the model used is simple, perhaps naïvely so; nonetheless it depicts the fundamental essentials of a multiperson economy in which individual behavior is not coordinated by a central planning agency.

At the outset we consider an economy in which exchange but not production takes place. There are only two people and only two goods. Each person has an *initial endowment* of each good, but he does not necessarily have the goods in the proportion that yields him greatest satisfaction. If not, some exchange of commodities between individuals will arise. To analyze exchange, and other problems as well, we need to develop a graphical device known as the Edgeworth box diagram.

15.2.a Edgeworth Box Diagram

The Edgeworth box diagram is a graphical technique for illustrating the interaction between two economic activities when their inputs are fixed in quantity. It is thus an ideal instrument for analyzing general equilibrium and economic welfare.

Two basic Edgeworth box diagrams are illustrated in Figure 15.2.2. Panel a shows the construction for a consumption problem whose inputs are types of, say, food; panel b refers to production activities whose inputs are factors of production.

First consider Figure 15.2.1. There are two consumption goods, X and Y; these goods are available in absolutely fixed amounts. In addition, there are only two individuals in the society, A and B; they initially possess an endowment of X and Y, but the endowment ratio is not the one either would choose if he were allowed to specify it. This general equilibrium problem is graphically illustrated by constructing an *origin* for A, labeled O_A, and plotting quantities of the two goods along the abscissa and ordinate. Thus from the origin O_A, the quantity of X held by $A(X_A)$ is plotted on the abscissa and the quantity of $Y(Y_A)$ on the ordinate. A similar graph for B, with origin O_B, may be constructed beside the graph for A. These two basic graphs are illustrated in panel a, Figure 15.2.1.

Next, rotate the B-graph $180°$ to the left, so that it is actually "upside down" when viewed normally, as shown in panel b. The Edgeworth box diagram is formed by bringing the two graphs together. There could conceivably be a problem involving the lengths of the axes; if the X axes meshed, the Y axes might not. The problem does not in fact exist, however, because of our assumption concerning fixed

FIGURE 15.2.1

Constructing the Edgeworth Box Diagram for a Consumption Problem

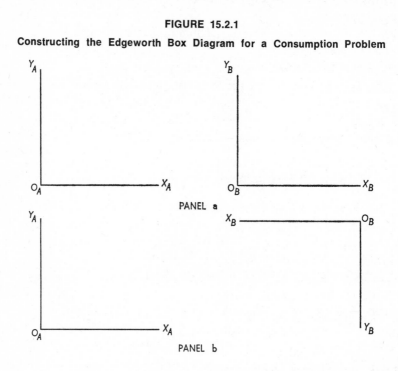

PANEL a

PANEL b

availabilities of X and Y. $X_A + X_B$ must equal X, and $Y_A + Y_B$ must equal Y. The length of each axis measures the fixed quantity of the good it represents; when the two "halves" in panel b are brought together both axes mesh. One thus obtains panel a, Figure 15.2.2.

The point D in panel a indicates the initial endowment of X and Y possessed by A and B. A begins with $O_A x_A$ units of X and $O_A y_A$ units of Y. Since the aggregates are fixed, B must originally hold $O_B x_B = X - O_A x_A$ units of X and $O_B y_B = Y - O_A y_A$ units of Y.

In a similar fashion, not illustrated in detail, one may construct an Edgeworth diagram for a production problem. The finished product is shown in panel b, Figure 15.2.2. Two goods, X and Y, are produced by means of two inputs, K and L. The two inputs are fixed in aggregate quantity. The origin of coordinates for good X is O_X, for good Y is O_Y. The inputs of K and L used in producing X and Y are plotted along the axes. Accordingly, any point in the box represents a particular allocation of the two inputs between the two production processes. At point E, for example, $O_x k_x$ units of K and $O_x l_x$ units of L are used in producing X. As a consequence, $O_Y k_Y = K - O_x k_x$ units of K, and $O_Y l_Y = L - O_x l_x$ units of L, are allocated to the production of Y.

FIGURE 15.2.2

Edgeworth Box Diagram

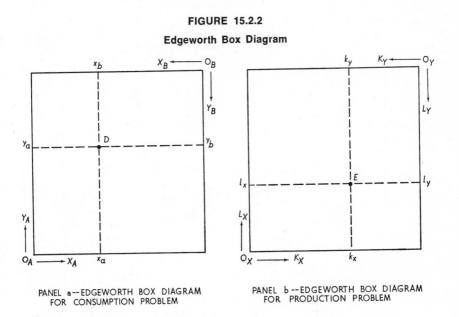

PANEL a--EDGEWORTH BOX DIAGRAM
FOR CONSUMPTION PROBLEM

PANEL b--EDGEWORTH BOX DIAGRAM
FOR PRODUCTION PROBLEM

15.2.b Equilibrium of Exchange

As a first step toward general equilibrium analysis, consider an economy in which exchange of initial endowments takes place. For the moment, production is ignored. If you like, you may think of the problem in the following context. There exists a small country with two inhabitants, A and B, each of whom owns one half the land area. As in our other manna example, A and B neither sow nor reap; they merely gather manna of types X and Y that fall nightly. Each gathers the manna that falls on his land; but the two types do not fall uniformly. There is a relatively heavy concentration of Y-manna on A's property and, consequently, a relatively heavy concentration of X-manna on B's land.

The problem of exchange is analyzed by means of the Edgeworth box diagram in Figure 15.2.3. To the basic box diagram, whose dimensions represent the nightly precipitation of manna, we add indifference curves for A and B. For example, the curve I_A shows combinations of X and Y that yield A the same level of satisfaction. In ordinary fashion, II_A represents a greater level of satisfaction than I_A; III_A than II_A; and so on. Quite generally, A's well being is enhanced by moving toward the B origin; B, in turn, enjoys greater satisfaction the closer he moves toward the A origin.

Suppose the initial endowment (the nightly fall of manna) is point

FIGURE 15.2.3

General Equilibrium of Exchange

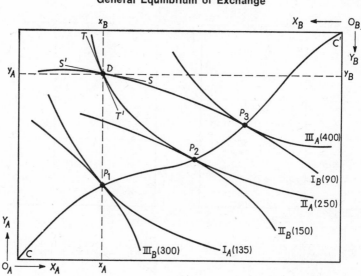

D; A has $O_A x_A$ units of X and $O_A y_A$ units of Y. Similarly, B has $O_B x_B$ and $O_B y_B$ units of X and Y respectively. The initial endowment places A on his indifference curve II_A and B on his curve I_B. At point D, A's marginal rate of substitution of X for Y, given by the slope of TT', is relatively high; A would be willing to sacrifice, say, three units of Y in order to obtain one additional unit of X. At the same point, B has a relatively low marginal rate of substitution, as shown by the slope of SS'. Or turning it around, B has a relatively high marginal rate of substitution of Y for X. He may, for example, be willing to forego four units of X to obtain one unit of Y.

A situation such as this will always lead to exchange if the parties concerned are free to trade. From the point D, A will trade some Y to B, receiving X in exchange. The exact bargain reached by the two traders cannot be determined. If B is the more skillful negotiator, he may induce A to move along II_A to the point P_2. All the benefit of trade goes to B, who jumps from I_B to II_B. Just oppositely, A might steer the bargain to point P_3, thereby increasing his level of satisfaction from II_A to III_A, B's real income remaining I_B. Starting from point D, the ultimate exchange is very likely to lead to some point between P_2 and P_3; but the skill of the bargainers and their initial endowments determine the exact location.

One important thing can be said, however. Exchange will take place until the marginal rate of substitution of X for Y is the same for both traders. If the two marginal rates are different, one or both parties can benefit from exchange; neither party need lose. In other words, the exchange equilibrium can occur only at points such as P_1, P_2, and P_3 in Figure 15.2.3. The locus CC', called the *contract* or *conflict curve*, is a curve joining all points of tangency between one of A's indifference curves and one of B's. It is thus the locus along which the marginal rates of substitution are equal for both traders. We accordingly have the following

Proposition: The general equilibrium of exchange occurs at a point where the marginal rate of substitution between every pair of goods is the same for all parties consuming both goods. The exchange equilibrium is not unique; it may occur at any point along the contract curve (for multiple traders, it is more properly called the contract hypersurface).

The contract curve is an optimal locus in the sense that if the trading parties are located at some point not on the curve, one or both can benefit, and neither suffer a loss, by exchanging goods so as to move to a point on the curve. To be sure, some points not on the curve are preferable to some points on the curve. But for any point not on the curve, one or more attainable points on the curve are preferable.

The chief characteristic of each point on the contract curve is that a movement away from the point must benefit one party and harm the other. More generally, suppose there are n people in a society. This society has attained exchange equilibrium (i.e., a point on the contract curve) if, and only if, there is *no reorganization* that will benefit some of the n members without harming at least one. Turning the statement around, an organization does not represent a point on the curve if there is any change that will make some people better off and will not make anyone worse off. Every organization that leads to a point on the contract curve is said to be a *Pareto-optimal organization.*

Definition: A Pareto-optimal organization is one such that any change which makes some people better off makes some others worse off. That is, an organization is Pareto-optimal if, and only if, there is no change that will make one or more better off without making anyone worse off. Thus every point on the contract curve is Pareto optimal, and the contract curve is a locus of Pareto optimality.

15.2.c Deriving the Utility-Possibility Frontier

The contract curve is a Pareto-optimal locus in *commodity space;* it shows all pairs of allocations of X and Y to A and B such that the marginal rate of substitution is equal for both parties. This exchange equilibrium locus can be transformed from commodity space to utility space, obtaining what is called the *utility-possibility frontier* relative to the particular endowment aggregate in Figure 15.2.3. The process of derivation is illustrated in Figure 15.2.4.

First consider the point P_1 in Figure 15.2.3. In A's scale of utility measurement, all points on I_A are valued at 135; thus P_1 is associated with a utility value of 135. Similarly, in B's utility scale, all points

FIGURE 15.2.4

Deriving the Utility-Possibility Frontier from the Contract Curve

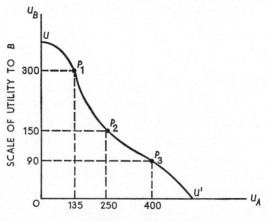

along III_B have the value 300. Now construct a graph, as in Figure 15.2.4, whose coordinate axes are A's and B's utility scales. The point P_1, with coordinates 135 and 300, can be plotted on this graph. Similarly, all other points along the contract curve in commodity space can be plotted in utility space by noting the pair of utility values associated with each point of tangency. Connect all such points by a curve, labeled UU' in Figure 15.2.4. This curve is the utility-possibility frontier.

Definition: The utility-possibility frontier is the locus showing the maximum level of satisfaction attainable by one trading party for every given level of satisfaction of the other. The curve so generated depends upon the absolute endowment of each commodity and upon the aggregate commodity endowment ratio—that is, upon X, Y, and Y/X.[6]

15.3 GENERAL EQUILIBRIUM OF PRODUCTION AND EXCHANGE

The topic of general equilibrium has been introduced by discussing a model in which production does not occur; consumers simply exchange existing stocks or endowments of commodities. We shall now expand by adding a production side to the basic model. There are still only two consuming units in the society, A and $B;$ there are also only two *producible* commodities, X and Y. But now they must be produced by means of two inputs, K and L. The production functions for X and Y are assumed to be given, and there are fixed, nonaugmentable quantities of the inputs K and L. In other words, the initial endowments in the present model are the fixed input supplies rather than fixed quantities of the two consumption goods.

15.3.a General Equilibrium of Production

The analysis of the general equilibrium of production is precisely the same as that of the general equilibrium of exchange. The only difference is terminology (economic jargon). The fixed endowments of inputs K and L determine the dimensions of the Edgeworth box diagram

---

[6] The student should remember that the utility numbers are purely arbitrary so far as interpersonal utility comparisons are concerned. In particular, 300 for B is not necessarily greater than 135 for A, although to A, 136 is greater than 135.

in Figure 15.3.1. Next, the given and unchanging production functions for goods X and Y enable us to construct the isoquant maps for each, illustrated by curves such as II_x and III_Y.

Suppose inputs are originally allocated between production of X and Y so that $O_x k_x$ units of K and $O_x l_x$ units of L are used in making X; the remainder, $O_Y k_Y$ and $O_Y l_Y$ units of K and L respectively, is used to produce Y. This allocation is represented by point D in the Edgeworth box—the point at which II_x intersects II_Y. At the allocation D, the marginal rate of technical substitution of K for L in producing X, given by the slope of SS', is relatively low. The marginal product of K in producing X is high relative to the marginal product of L. The II_x level of production can be maintained by substituting a relatively small amount of K for a relatively larger amount of L. The opposite situation prevails in Y production, as shown by the slope of TT'. The marginal rate of technical substitution of K for L in producing Y is relatively high; thus a comparatively large amount of K can be released by substituting a relatively small amount of L while maintaining the II_Y level of output.

If the producer of X at point D substitutes one unit of K he can, let us suppose, release two units of L. The producer of Y, by employing the two units of L released from X production, can maintain output and release, let us suppose, four units of K. Thus from a point such as D input substitution by producers will enable the society to move to

FIGURE 15.3.1

General Equilibrium of Production

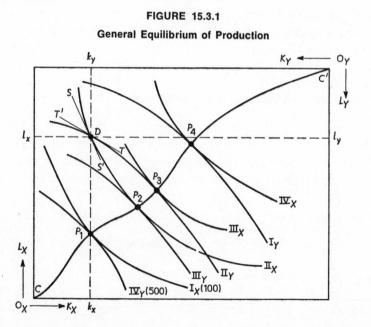

P_2, P_3, or any point in between, At P_2, the output of X is the same as at D but the output of Y has been increased to the III_Y level. If the movement is to P_3, the output of X increases with no change in the volume of Y production.

The foregoing discussion establishes a pervasive principle. Whenever the marginal rate of technical substitution between two inputs is different for two producers, one or both outputs may be increased, and neither decreased, by making the appropriate input substitutions. In the example in Figure 15.3.1, the X producer would substitute K for L, decreasing the marginal product of K, increasing that of L, and thereby raising the marginal rate of technical substitution. The producer of Y, on the other hand, should substitute L for K, with the opposite results. Production of one or both goods can always be increased without an aggregate increase in inputs unless the marginal rates of technical substitution between the inputs are the same for both producers.

The locus CC', again called the *contract* or *conflict curve*, is a curve showing all input allocations that equalize the marginal rates of technical substitution—that is, the locus of tangencies between an X isoquant and a Y isoquant. We can accordingly state the following

Proposition: The general equilibrium of production occurs at a point where the marginal rate of technical substitution between every pair of inputs is the same for all producers who use both inputs. The production equilibrium is not unique; it may occur at any point along the contract curve; but each point represents a Pareto-optimal equilibrium organization.

The contract curve is an optimal locus in the sense that if the producers are located at a point not on the curve, the output of one or both commodities can be increased, and the output of neither decreased, by making input substitutions so as to move to a point on the curve. To be sure, some points not on the curve correspond to a greater aggregate output than some points on the curve. But for any point not on the curve there are one or more attainable points on the curve associated with a greater aggregate output.

15.3.b General Equilibrium of Production and Exchange

For any input endowment there are an infinite number of potential production equilibria that are Pareto optimal, i.e., any point on the contract curve in Figure 15.3.1. Each point represents a particular volume of output of X and of Y, and thereby dictates the dimensions of an Edgeworth box diagram for exchange (such as Figure 15.2.3). Furthermore, each consumption-exchange box leads to an infinite number of potential exchange equilibria that are Pareto optimal, i.e., any point on the contract curve associated with the box in question. Accordingly, there are a multiple infinity of potential general equilibria of production and exchange.

The object of any society is to attain that particular general equilibrium which maximizes the economic welfare of its inhabitants. As we shall see in Chapter 16, there are ways by which either a free enterprise system or a decentralized socialist state may attain the optimum.

15.3.c Deriving the Production-Possibility Frontier or Transformation Curve

The contract curve associated with the general equilibrium of production is a locus of points in *input space;* the curve shows the optimal output of each commodity corresponding to every possible allocation of K and L between X and Y. With the allocation of inputs indicated by point P_1 in Figure 15.3.1, 500 units of Y and 100 units of X are the maximum attainable production. By constructing a graph whose coordinate axes show the quantities of X and Y produced, and plotting the output pairs corresponding to each isoquant tangency in Figure 15.3.1, one may generate the curve labeled TT' in Figure 15.3.2. The curve so obtained is called the *production-possibility frontier* or the *transformation curve.*

FIGURE 15.3.2

Deriving Production-Possibility Frontier from the Contract Curve

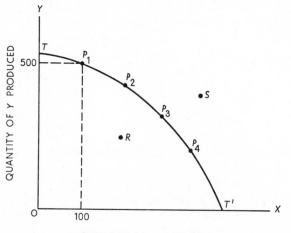

QUANTITY OF X PRODUCED

The transformation curve is obtained by mapping the contract curve from input space into output space. Fundamentally, this locus depicts the choices a society can make. It shows, in other words, the various (maximum) combinations of X and Y that are attainable from the given resource base (input endowment). No output combination represented by a point lying outside the production-possibility frontier (such as S) can be attained; such a level of output would require a greater resource base. On the other hand, a point lying inside the locus (such as R) is neither necessary nor desirable; it would entail a needless sacrifice of goods attributable to unemployment of available resources. Thus one object of a society is to attain an equilibrium position *on,* not below, its production-possibility frontier.

Definition: The production-possibility frontier or transformation curve is a locus showing the maximum attainable output of one commodity for every possible volume of output of the other commodity, given the fixed resource base. The curve so generated depends upon the absolute endowment of each resource, upon the aggregate input endowment ratio, and upon the "state of the art" (the production functions for both goods).[7]

SUGGESTED READINGS

Fossati, Eraldo. *The Theory of General Static Equilibrium,* pp. 79–183. Oxford: Basil Blackwell, 1957.

Henderson, James M., and Quandt, Richard E. *Microeconomic Theory,* pp. 126–40. New York: McGraw-Hill Book Co., Inc., 1958. [Elementary math required.]

Kuenne, Robert E. *The Theory of General Economic Equilibrium.* Princeton N.J.: Princeton University Press, 1963. Chapter 1 (pp. 3–39) is an excellent statement concerning methodology; here little, if any, mathematics is required of the reader. Otherwise, the level of mathematics is as indicated. Especially relevant are pp. 43–195. [Advanced math required.]

Leontief, Wassily. *The Structure of the American Economy, 1919–1939.* New York: Oxford University Press, 1951. [Advanced math required.]

Walras, Leon. *Elements of Pure Economics* (Jaffe trans.). London: George Allen & Unwin, 1954. [Advanced math required.]

---

[7] For a numerical example of the derivation of the transformation curve, and a simple mathematical formulation, see C. E. Ferguson, "Transformation Curve in Production Theory: A Pedagogical Note," *Southern Economic Journal,* Vol. XXIX (1962), pp. 96–102.

Chapter 16 THEORY OF WELFARE ECONOMICS

16.1 INTRODUCTION

The general equilibrium conditions of production and exchange, analyzed in Chapter 15, can be used to develop the "marginal" conditions for maximum social welfare and to assess the efficiency of a perfectly competitive economy. It might also help explain why there is only one unique general equilibrium of relevance among the multiple infinity of possible general equilibria that are Pareto optimal.

16.1.a Marginal Conditions for Social Welfare

First return to Figure 15.2.3, which illustrates the general equilibrium of exchange. As you will recall, we proved that a position of equilibrium must occur on the contract curve because if some other distribution momentarily existed one or both trading parties could benefit, and neither be harmed, by moving to a point on the contract curve. Any point on the contract curve satisfies the *optimum conditions of exchange* and gives rise to the first marginal condition for a Pareto-welfare maximum.

Marginal Condition for Exchange: To attain a Pareto maximum, the marginal rate of substitution between any pair of consumer goods must be the same for all individuals who consume both goods.

If this does not hold, one or more individuals would benefit from exchange (without injuring others), as shown by Figure 15.2.3.

The second marginal condition is based upon Figure 15.3.1, which illustrates the general equilibrium of production. With the aid of that figure we proved that equilibrium must be attained on the contract curve because if a different allocation of inputs momentarily prevailed the output of one or both commodities could be increased, and the output

478

of neither decreased, by moving to a point on the curve. All points on the production contract curve satisfy the *optimum conditions of factor substitution* and lead to the second marginal condition for a Pareto-welfare maximum:

Marginal Condition for Factor Substitution: To attain a Pareto maximum, the marginal rate of technical substitution between any pair of inputs must be the same for all producers who use both inputs.

Otherwise, a reallocation of resources would result in a greater aggregate output, without a reduction in the output of any commodity.

The final marginal condition for a welfare maximum is based upon the *optimum conditions of product substitution.* It is actually a combination of the two previous sets of conditions and may be stated as

Marginal Condition for Product Substitution: To attain a Pareto maximum, the marginal rate of transformation in production must equal the marginal rate of substitution in consumption for every pair of commodities and for every individual who consumes both.

This final proposition is established with the aid of Figure 16.1.1.

The curve labeled TT' is the production-possibility frontier or transformation curve, as derived in Figure 15.3.2. Given full resource utilization, it shows the maximum producible amount of either commodity for every given level of output of the other. The slope of the transformation curve at any point shows the number of units of good Y that must be sacrificed in order to free enough resources to produce one additional unit of good X. With full employment of all resources, more of one good necessarily entails less of another.

Definition: The slope of the transformation curve is called the marginal rate of transformation of X into Y. It shows the number of units by which the production of Y must be decreased in order to expand the output of X by one unit.

Now suppose a pair of consumers has attained an exchange equilibrium, which means that their marginal rates of substitution in consumption are equal. Further, suppose the common marginal rate of substitution is such that both consumers are willing to exchange two units of Y for three units of X. Next, suppose a producer (or producers) has attained an equilibrium of production, in which the marginal rate of technical substitution between each pair of inputs is the same in the production of X as in the production of Y. Finally, suppose this organization of production leads to the point P on the transformation curve TT' in Figure 16.1.1, at which the marginal rate of transformation is 4:2—that is,

FIGURE 16.1.1

Marginal Condition for Product Substitution

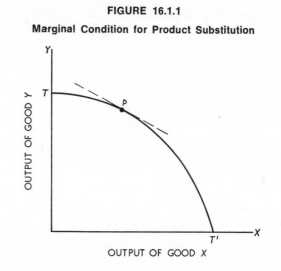

OUTPUT OF GOOD X

by curtailing the output of Y by two units, four additional units of X may be produced.

Clearly a general equilibrium has not been obtained. By reducing the output of Y, the output of X can be expanded *by more than enough* to keep each consumer on his original indifference curve. Thus if producers shift some resources from Y-production to X-production, both consumers may be made better off. Consequently, the initial position could not have been one of Pareto optimality.

In the two paragraphs above, it has been shown that if the marginal rate of transformation exceeds the common marginal rate of substitution in consumption, a point of Pareto optimality cannot exist. A similar line of reasoning will show that if the marginal rate of transformation is less than the common marginal rate of substitution in consumption, producers should shift some resources from X production to Y production. Therefore, since an organization cannot be Pareto optimal if the marginal rate of transformation is not equal to the common marginal rate of substitution in consumption, the marginal condition for product substitution is established: a Pareto-optimal organization is achieved only if the marginal rate of transformation is equal to the common marginal rate of substitution in consumption for all pairs of consumer goods.

16.1.b Welfare Maximization and Perfect Competition

The three sets of marginal conditions developed above state the necessary conditions for welfare maximization in any type of society, i.e.

for the attainment of a Pareto-optimal equilibrium. We now wish to show, subject to the reservations in section 16.3, that a perfectly competitive, free enterprise system guarantees the attainment of maximum social welfare. The proof rests upon the *maximizing* behavior of producers and consumers. To recall the dictum of Adam Smith, each individual, in pursuing his own self-interest, is led as if by an "invisible hand" to a course of action that promotes the general welfare of all.

Look just at the marginal condition for exchange, which requires equality of the marginal rates of substitution between every pair of goods for all consumers. As shown in Chapter 2, to maximize satisfaction subject to limited income each consumer must arrange his purchases so that the marginal rate of substitution is equal to the price ratio for every pair of goods. Under perfect competition prices, and therefore price ratios, are uniform for all buyers. Hence each consumer purchases goods in such quantity that *his* marginal rate of substitution equals the *common* price ratio faced by all consumers. Therefore, the marginal rate of substitution between every pair of goods must be the same for all consumers; the marginal conditions for exchange are a consequence of the price system under perfect competition.

Next consider the marginal condition for factor substitution: the marginal rate of technical substitution between every pair of inputs must be the same for all producers who utilize them. As shown in Chapter 13, each perfectly competitive producer employs inputs in such proportions that the marginal rate of technical substitution (the ratio of marginal products) equals the input-price ratio. He must do this to maximize profit (obtain the least cost combination of inputs). In a perfectly competitive market input prices are the same to all producers; hence each equates the marginal rate of technical substitution relevant to him to a common input-price ratio. The marginal rates of technical substitution are accordingly equal; and the marginal condition of factor substitution is also a consequence of the price system under perfect competition.

Finally, we come to the marginal condition for product substitution: the marginal rate of transformation in production must equal the marginal rate of substitution in consumption for each pair of goods. The proof in this case requires a slight digression.

As previously said, the marginal rate of transformation shows the number of units by which the production of Y must be curtailed in order to free enough resources to produce an additional unit of X. If the output of X is increased by one unit, the marginal cost of producing X shows how much each additional unit of X costs. But if the output of X is increased, the output of Y must be diminished; hence the marginal cost of producing Y shows how much is saved by reducing Y output one unit. Hence dividing the marginal cost of producing X by the marginal cost of producing Y, one finds the number of units of Y that must be sacrificed to obtain an additional unit of X.[1] Accordingly, the marginal rate of transformation of X into Y equals the ratio of the marginal cost of X to the marginal cost of Y.

Under perfect competition profit maximization is achieved by producing that volume of output for which marginal cost equals price. Thus under perfect competition the marginal rate of transformation of X into Y must equal the ratio of the price of X to that of Y (because both must equal the marginal cost ratio). By previous argument, the marginal rate of substitution of X for Y must equal the ratio of the price of X to the price of Y. As in the two previous cases, the marginal condition for product substitution is a consequence of the price system under perfect competition.

The results of this section may be summarized by the following

Proposition: If the political organization of a society is such as to accord paramount importance to its individual members, social welfare, or the economic well-being of the society, will be maximized if every consumer, every firm, every industry, and every input market is perfectly competitive.

An interesting extension of this proposition applies to a decentralized socialist society. In the introduction to Part V it was said that the "invisible hand" might more appropriately be called the invisible IBM machine. Neither designation gives much hint to the underlying principle: each individual maximizes in light of *market-determined* (parametric) prices. The functioning of the price system in perfectly competitive markets leads to the social welfare maximum; stated alternatively, when each individual implicitly solves his constrained maximization problem, the result is a set of prices that, given the individual behavior, leads to maximum social welfare. Speaking mathematically, these prices are nothing more than Lagrange multipliers, perhaps ground out by the "invisible IBM machine" in the process of solving the welfare maximization problem.

This invisible IBM machine is not available to a planned socialist society; however a visible, tangible one (or its equivalent) is. The state planning agency (given knowledge of individual preference patterns

---

[1] Consider point P in Figure 16.1.1. With the output of Y great relative to the output of X, the marginal cost of Y will be large relative to that of X. Suppose the marginal cost of Y is \$10, and the marginal cost of X is \$2. Their ratio is \$2/\$10 or 1/5. Thus one fifth of a unit of Y must be sacrificed to produce one additional unit of X.

and production functions) could use the visible machine to solve the now explicit constrained maximization problem. The resulting Lagrange multipliers are "shadow" prices, the equivalent of market-determined prices under perfect competition. Maximum social welfare in this type of society can be attained by following the so-called Lange-Lerner rule:

Proposition (Lange-Lerner Rule): To attain maximum social welfare in a decentralized socialist society, the state planning agency should solve the constrained maximization problem and obtain the shadow prices of all inputs and outputs. Publish this price list and distribute it to all members of the society. Instruct all consumers and all plant managers to behave as though they were satisfaction or profit maximizers operating in perfectly competitive markets.

16.2 INPUT, OUTPUT, AND DISTRIBUTION

One approach to the problem of welfare maximization has been analyzed in section 16.1. We now turn to a somewhat different and more thorough analysis.[2]

16.2.a General Assumptions

The model employed here is identical to that used in the general equilibrium analysis of production and exchange, except that one additional assumption (*iv* below) is required. Our original assumptions are now recounted and the additional one supplied.

(*i*) There exist fixed, nonaugmentable endowments of two homogeneous and perfectly divisible inputs, labor (L) and capital (K). Alternatively, one may assume that these inputs are inelastically supplied and the period of analysis is not sufficiently long to permit a change in the given supplies.

(*ii*) Only two homogeneous goods are produced in the economy, fish (F) and cabbage (C). The production function for each is given and does not change during the analysis. Each production function is smooth (continuous), and each exhibits constant returns to scale and diminishing marginal rates of technical substitution along any isoquant.

(*iii*) There are two individuals in the society, A and B. Each has a well-defined ordinal preference function yielding indifference curves of normal shape. For convenience, an arbitrary numerical index is adopted for each function, denoted U_A and U_B.

(*iv*) There exists a *social welfare function* that depends exclusively on the positions of A and B in their own preference scales [for example,

---

[2] This section is based upon Francis M. Bator, "The Simple Analytics of Welfare Maximization," *American Economic Review*, Vol. XLVII (1957), pp. 22–59, esp. pp. 23–31.

$W = W(U_A, U_B)$]. The social welfare function permits a unique preference ordering of all possible situations (hereafter called *states*).[3]

With these assumptions, our problem is to determine the welfare maximizing value of the following variables: the input of labor into fish and cabbage production (L_F, L_C); the input of capital into fish and cabbage production (K_F, K_C); the total amount of fish (F) and cabbage (C) produced; and the distribution of F and C between A and B (F_A, F_B, C_A, C_B).

16.2.b Retracing Some Steps: From Production Functions to the Production-Possibility Frontier

By assumption (i), there are fixed endowments of two homogeneous inputs; suppose the amounts are $\bar{K}$ and $\bar{L}$ of capital and labor respectively. The magnitudes of these endowments determine the dimensions of the Edgeworth box diagram shown in Figure 16.2.1. Next, by assumption (ii), the production function for each commodity is given

FIGURE 16.2.1

**Production Map in Input Space:
Optimum Conditions of Factor Substitution**

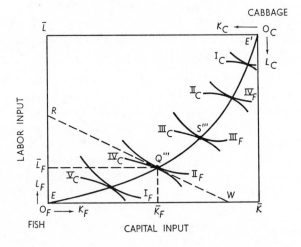

---

[3] Assumption (iv) is heroic and involves some controversy. Clearly, it includes some ethical valuations concerning the relative positions of A and B. On this thorny problem, see Kenneth J. Arrow, *Social Choice and Individual Values* (New York: John Wiley & Sons, Inc., 1951); Paul A. Samuelson, *Foundations of Economic Analysis* (Cambridge, Mass.: Harvard University Press, 1947), pp. 203–53; and Paul A. Samuelson, "Social Indifference Curves," *Quarterly Journal of Economics*, Vol. LXX (1956), pp. 1–22.

and characterized by smooth isoquants that exhibit constant returns to scale and diminishing marginal rates of technical substitution. These isoquants are plotted as $I_F, \ldots, IV_F$ and $I_C, \ldots, V_C$ in Figure 16.2.1. Satisfying the optimum conditions of factor substitution (equal marginal rates of technical substitution) leads to the contract curve in input space, labeled EE'. As we have already shown in Chapter 15, subsection 15.3.c, the contract curve may be mapped from input space into output space, thereby becoming the production-possibility frontier or transformation curve.

The particular transformation curve associated with the contract curve EE', and therefore directly associated with the fixed input endowments, is plotted as TT' in Figure 16.2.2. As you will recall, the slope

FIGURE 16.2.2

Production-Possibility Frontier in Output Space: Optimum Conditions of Exchange

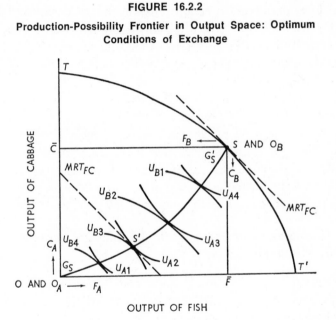

OUTPUT OF FISH

of this curve indicates the marginal rate of transformation of fish into cabbage. It indicates exactly how many cabbages can be produced by a marginal transfer of capital and labor from fish production to cabbage production, under the assumption that inputs are optimally reallocated in each production process after the transfer (so as to maintain the optimal conditions of factor substitution). Consequently, the marginal rate of transformation is the marginal cabbage cost of an additional fish, or the inverse of the marginal fish cost of an additional cabbage.

16.2.c Production Possibilities and the Optimum Conditions of Exchange

Select any point on the transformation curve TT' in Figure 16.2.2. Let the point be S, so that the total outputs of fish and cabbage are $\overline{OF}$ and $\overline{OC}$ respectively. The corresponding point in input space (and the associated allocation of K and L to F and C production) is labeled S''' in Figure 16.2.1.

The outputs $\overline{OF}$ and $\overline{OC}$ determine a particular volume of goods available to A and B; these outputs accordingly determine the dimensions of an Edgeworth box diagram for exchange. This diagram is constructed in Figure 16.2.2 by dropping perpendiculars to the axes from the point S. The original origin O becomes the origin for A, O_A, and the point S becomes B's origin, O_B. By assumption (*iii*) each individual has a well-defined preference function. Thus in the usual way, indifference curves for A and B are constructed in the exchange box. Curves U_{A1}, . . . , U_{A4} illustrate A's preference field and U_{B1}, . . . , U_{B4} show B's. The locus of tangencies, or the *feasible* points of exchange, is the contract curve $G_S G_S'$. The points on this contract curve are feasible because (*a*) an increase in the level of satisfaction of one trading party can be achieved only at the expense of the other, and (*b*) consumption at any point on the curve precisely exhausts the entire output of fish and cabbage. Thus the contract curve is labeled $G_S G_S'$ to denote it is the curve relative to the point S on the transformation curve; and, as you will recall, it is the locus of exchange possibilities satisfying the optimum conditions of exchange (i.e., it is a locus of Pareto-optimal points).

16.2.d Retracing Some Steps: From the Contract Curve to the Utility-Possibility Frontier

By observing the utility levels for A and B at each point along the contract curve in Figure 16.2.2, one may generate the utility-possibility curve relative to the output point S, as shown in Chapter 15, subsection 15.2.c. The utility-possibility curve relative to S is plotted as $G_S G_S'$ in Figure 16.2.3. This curve alone does not help us much because it shows an infinite number of Pareto-optimal utility pairs corresponding to each of an infinite number of Pareto-optimal production pairs. We are just where we were at the end of Chapter 15; a multiple infinity of possible equilibria exist. Using a principle developed in section 16.1, however, we can remove one "infinity" dimension.

The optimum conditions of product substitution require equality between the marginal rate of transformation in production and the marginal rate of substitution in consumption for all pairs of goods and for all individuals consuming these goods. For our particular model, the conditions require equality between the marginal rate of transformation of fish into cabbage and both A's and B's marginal rate of substitution of fish for cabbage.

At the production point S in Figure 16.2.2, the marginal rate of transformation is indicated by the slope of the dashed line tangent to TT' at S, labeled MRT_{FC}. To satisfy the optimum conditions of product

FIGURE 16.2.3

Utility-Possibility Frontier: From Output to Utility Space

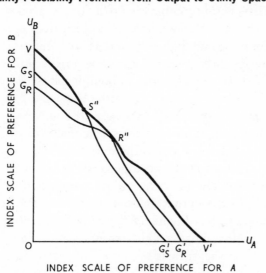

substitution, the marginal rate of substitution of both A and B must equal this particular value of the marginal rate of transformation. As indicated graphically, this condition is satisfied at the unique point S' in Figure 16.2.2. Consequently, while the locus G_SG_S' in Figure 16.2.3 is the utility-possibility frontier relative to S, only the single point S'', corresponding to S' in Figure 16.2.2, is relevant. Relative to the output combination S, S''' in Figure 16.2.1 is the only allocation of inputs that satisfies the optimum conditions of factor substitution. Furthermore, relative to the same output combination S, S'' is the only allocation of fish and cabbage between A and B that satisfies both the optimum conditions of exchange and the optimum conditions of substitution. As a consequence, S'' is the only relevant point on G_SG_S'. One dimension of "infinity" is removed: S'' is the only efficient output allocation relative to S; but S can be anywhere on TT'. One dimension of 'infinity" remains.

16.2.e From a Utility-Possibility Point to the Grand Utility-Possibility Frontier

Still using Figures 16.2.2 and 16.2.3, we can generate the "grand" utility-possibility frontier, or the utility-possibility frontier relative to *any* point on the production-possibility frontier. Imagine S moving to a point further down TT'. At the new point there would be more fish and fewer cabbages; a new Edgeworth exchange diagram would be constructed and a new contract curve generated. When mapped into utility space, the new contract curve might look like $G_R G_R'$ in Figure 16.2.3.

Yet at the new output combination point on the production-possibility frontier TT', there would be a unique marginal rate of transformation. Again, the optimum conditions of product substitution would dictate a single relevant point on the contract curve or the utility curve $G_R G_R'$ in Figure 16.2.3. This single relevant point is indicated by R'' in Figure 16.2.3.

As the output combination varies over all points on TT', new Edgeworth exchange boxes and new contract curves are generated. But at each output combination point there is a unique marginal rate of transformation. This unique rate, together with the optimum conditions of product substitution, dictates a unique output allocation between A and B relative to the output combination; and each of these unique points can be plotted in Figure 16.2.3 as a unique utility combination point. The overall utility-possibility frontier is obtained by connecting all these points (points such as S'' and R'' in Figure 16.2.3). This frontier is shown by the heavily shaded line VV'. Each point on this line shows: (*a*) a unique utility combination for A and B associated with (*b*) a unique output allocation between A and B corresponding to (*c*) equality between the marginal rate of transformation and marginal rate of substitution of F for C (*d*) at a particular F—C output combination on the production-possibility frontier; furthermore, each F—C output combination dictates (*e*) a unique allocation of the K—L input endowments between the production of fish and cabbage. Quite a bit is embodied in VV'; but there is still a single infinity of possible solutions (any point on VV').[4]

---

[4] The mathematically inclined student will realize that VV' may be derived as the envelope of the utility-possibility curves associated with each point on the production-possibility frontier.

16.2.f From the Utility-Possibility Frontier to the Point of "Constrained Bliss"

Up to this point the analysis of social welfare has required only assumptions $(i)-(iii)$ in subsection 16.2.a. To reduce the single infinity of possible solutions to a unique solution requires the fourth assumption: there exists a *social welfare function* that depends exclusively on the positions of A and B in their own preference scales.

As previously indicated, this is a heroic assumption. It definitely requires ethical valuations regarding the "deservingness" of A and $B;$ in this respect it is unquestionably an ascientific concept. Furthermore, even the construction of a theoretical social welfare function is a difficult conceptual task, unless the society is ruled by a dictator. In that case the social welfare function is the dictator's individual preference function.

In the absence of a dictator (ironclad adherence to tradition, customs, mores, and such can be a "dictator" for social welfare purposes), how is a welfare function developed? "By direct vote" or "by representative vote through a legislature" would seem logical answers. But either method is likely to fail because of the famous "voting paradox."[5]

The matter may be viewed somewhat differently. Suppose you are A. Your principle interest is $U_A;$ and with given and fully employed resources, the greater U_A the lower U_B. You wish to push as far down and to the right on VV' as possible. You probably want a social welfare function that dictates a position very close to V' (and distant from V). But not necessarily. You are interested in U_A as a *consumer;* you are interested in the social welfare function as a *citizen.* In the latter capacity, you may prefer somewhat less U_A in order for some U_B to exist. This is more or less the situation when a property owner whose son attends a private school votes for a bond issue (and increased property tax) to improve the public school system. Similarly, any contribution to charity is an act that reduces one's satisfaction as a consumer but increases his satisfaction as a citizen.

Nonetheless, a social welfare function is difficult to construct. We merely assume that one exists. Its existence enables us to represent it by a family of social indifference curves, just as an individual's preference function can be represented by a family of consumption indifference

---

[5] The "voting paradox" cannot be explained here. Basically, it involves the fact that ordering states by voting is likely to cause inconsistent (intransitive) orderings. For somewhat more explanation and bibliography, see C. E. Ferguson, *Macroeconomic Theory of Workable Competition* (Durham, N.C.: Duke University Press, 1964), pp. 10–11.

curves. A portion of this family of curves is shown by the set $W_1 W_1'$, . . . , $W_4 W_4'$ in Figure 16.2.4.

The utility-posibility frontier VV' is also plotted in this figure. It shows all possible combinations of utilities to A and B, given the existing resource base, the production functions, and the individual preference orderings. In other words, it shows the utility combinations that are physically achievable. The social indifference curves show utility combinations that result in equal levels of social welfare. The higher the curve, the greater is aggregate social welfare.

For reasons that should now be thoroughly familiar, maximum social welfare is attained at Q, where a social indifference curve is just tangent to the utility-possibility frontier. The infinity of possible equilibria has been reduced to a unique equilibrium point by considering the welfare of the society as a whole. This unique equilibrium Q is called the point of "constrained bliss" because it represents the unique organization of production, exchange, and distribution that leads to the maximum *attainable* social welfare. The society, of course, would be more "blissful" on $W_4 W_4'$. But a state on this higher curve is not attainable. The resource endowment and the state of the arts "constrains" the society to a point on VV'. In view of the constraint, society reaches its point of "constrained bliss" at Q.

FIGURE 16.2.4

Maximization of Social Welfare: From Utility Possibilities to "Constrained Bliss"

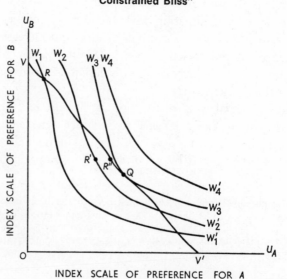

16.2.g Constrained Bliss and Efficiency

This section begins with a digression to recount the meaning of Pareto optimality or efficiency.

Definition: Any organization (point) is said to be Pareto optimal or Pareto efficient when every reorganization that augments the value of one variable necessarily reduces the value of another.

Some examples should make this definition clear.

The contract curve for exchange is a Pareto-optimal locus. In deriving the locus in Chapter 15, Figure 15.2.3, the following argument was made.

Suppose the original distribution of the initial commodity endowment placed A and B at point D (not on the contract curve). At this point, A is willing to trade a relatively large amount of Y for a unit of X, and B is willing to trade a relatively large amount of X for a unit of Y. Both parties generally benefit from exchange; in the limit, B receives all the benefit, but A is no worse off, if trading moves the distribution to P_2. Similarly, A receives all the benefit, but B does not suffer, if the move is from D to P_3. At any point on CC' between P_2 and P_3, both parties benefit from exchange.

Clearly the point D is not Pareto optimal or efficient. A reorganization from D can benefit both traders (can augment the value of both utility variables). But *all* points on the contract curve are Pareto optimal. For example, a reorganization from P_2 to P_3 benefits A; but it simultaneously places B on a lower indifference curve.

The very same line of reasoning shows that the contract curve for production is a Pareto-optimal locus. If the allocation of inputs initially leads to a point not on the curve, the output of one or both goods can be increased, and the output of neither reduced, by moving to a point on the curve. But once on the curve, a reorganization that increases the output of one good must cause a reduction in the output of another. For example, in Figure 16.2.1, a reorganization from Q''' to S''' increases the output of fish but reduces cabbage production.

This then is the concept of Pareto optimality or efficiency: an organization such that a change that "helps" one must "hurt" another. As we have repeatedly seen, an infinite number of Pareto-optimal points (or organizations) are associated with each problem. One example is the utility-possibility frontier VV' in Figure 16.2.4. An infinite number of points such as R and Q are on this curve. A reorganization from, say, R to Q definitely benefits A because U_A is greater; but B suffers a loss because U_B declines. Thus each point on VV' is Pareto efficient and the entire curve is a Pareto-optimal locus.

Let us now examine a unique characteristic of the "constrained bliss" point Q in Figure 16.2.4. It is the only point of the infinitely many on the utility-possibility frontier that has unequivocal prescriptive significance. It is not only Pareto optimal, it is uniquely associated with maximum social welfare. Pareto optimality or efficiency is a *necessary*, but not *sufficient*, condition for a welfare maximum. The marginal conditions developed in section 16.1 only give the Pareto efficiency requirements; alone they do not guarantee a welfare maximum. For this an explicit welfare function is required.

Furthermore, once a social welfare function is defined the limited importance of "efficiency" becomes clear. The point of "constrained bliss" is, to be sure, Pareto optimal. But compare points R and R'. The former is Pareto efficient inasmuch as it lies on VV'. Yet a reorganization from R to R', a point that is Pareto inefficient, is clearly desirable because a higher level of social welfare is attained. Of course, starting from an "inefficient" point such as R', one or more points on VV' (such as R'' and Q) are socially preferable. But with the single exception of the "constrained-bliss" point Q, for any efficient point on VV' one or more inefficient points are socially more desirable.

Exercise: The validity of the last statement depends upon the social welfare function having the general properties illustrated in Figure 16.2.4. What are the ethical valuations underlying a social welfare function with this configuration? What might be the configuration if the social welfare function were constructed by individual *A* alone if he were a masochist? An extreme Calvinist?

16.2.h Inputs, Outputs, Distribution, and Welfare

Using assumptions (i)–(iv) in subsection 16.2.a, a unique constrained-bliss point has been determined by means of Figures 16.2.1–16.2.4. The process may now be reversed to find the *optimizing* values of the 10 variables listed in subsection 16.2.a: the inputs of labor and capital into the production of fish and cabbage (L_F, L_C, K_F, and K_C); the total outputs of fish and cabbage (F and C); and the distribution of fish and cabbage to A and B (F_A, F_B, C_A, and C_B).

The constrained-bliss point Q in Figure 16.2.4 is a unique point on VV'. As shown in subsection 16.2.e, each point on VV' is associated with a unique point on the production-possibility frontier because the marginal conditions for product substitution must be satisfied. Let the point on the production-possibility frontier corresponding to the constrained-bliss point Q be Q' in Figure 16.2.5, where TT' is the transformation curve. Locating the point Q' immediately determines two variables: the

general equilibrium and maximum welfare outputs of fish and cabbage
are $O\overline{F}$ and $O\overline{C}$ respectively.

Next, return to Figure 16.2.1. The total outputs $O\overline{F}$ and $O\overline{C}$ associated with Q' can be produced efficiently in only one way, by producing
at the point on the contract curve EE' corresponding to Q' on TT'. Let
this point be Q'''. The organization of production is determined by this
point, as are the values of four more variables. The input of capital into
fish production (K_F) is $O\overline{K}_F$; labor input (L_F) is $O\overline{L}_F$. Thus the input

FIGURE 16.2.5

**General Equilibrium: From "Constrained Bliss" to Inputs, Outputs,
and Distribution**

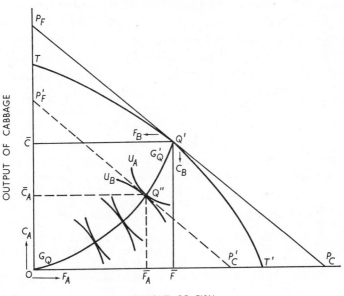

OUTPUT OF FISH

of capital into cabbage production (K_C) is $\overline{K} - O\overline{K}_F$, and labor input (L_C) is $\overline{L} - O\overline{L}_F$.

The final four variables are determined by constructing the Edgeworth exchange diagram whose dimensions represent the optimizing
values of fish and cabbage output. Dropping perpendiculars from Q' in
Figure 16.2.5, the box is given by $O\overline{C}Q'\overline{F}$. The contract curve relative to
Q', labeled $G_Q G_Q'$, is constructed in the usual way. Finally, imposing the
condition that the marginal rate of transformation (given by the slope of
$P_F P_C$) must equal the common marginal rate of substitution (given by
the slope of $P_F'P_C'$), one determines the unique point Q'' associated with
Q'. Thus A gets $O\overline{F}_A$ units of fish and $O\overline{C}_A$ units of cabbage. B gets the
rest: $\overline{F} - O\overline{F}_A$ units of fish and $\overline{C} - O\overline{C}_A$ units of cabbage.

In summary, a unique general equilibrium has been attained and this equilibrium point is uniquely associated with the maximum social welfare attainable by the society from the given resource base.

16.2.i   From "Constrained Bliss" to Prices, Wages, and Rent

Subsection 16.1.b contained an informal suggestion of the way the price system under perfect competition leads to the point of maximum social welfare. Our final step is to determine these prices for the two inputs and the two outputs,[6] denoted as p_F (price of fish), p_C (price of cabbage), w (wage rate), and r (capital rent).

Let us first concentrate our attention upon wages and rent (see Figure 16.2.1). To attain the least cost combination of resources, each producer must employ inputs in such proportions that their marginal rate of technical substitution equals the input-price ratio. Furthermore, the optimum conditions of factor substitution require equality of the marginal rate of technical substitution among all producers using the two inputs in question. This principle establishes the point Q''' in Figure 16.2.1. The common marginal rate of technical substitution is indicated by the slope of the dashed line RW. Since this common marginal rate must equal the input price ratio, we know that the rent-wage ratio (r/w) must be indicated by the slope of RW.

Next consider Figure 16.2.5. At the maximizing point Q', the marginal rate of transformation of fish into cabbage is given by the slope of $P_F P_C$. The optimum condition for product substitution requires that

---

[6] The social welfare maximum has been called the point of constrained bliss because constraints are imposed by input limitations and the production function. Let $K = \bar{K}$ and $L = \bar{L}$ represent the input endowments; and $K_F + K_C = \bar{K}$ and $L_F + L_C = \bar{L}$. Further, suppose the production functions for fish and cabbage are $F = F(K_F, L_F)$ and $C = C(K_C, L_C)$ respectively. Finally, let the social welfare function be given by $W = W(U_A, U_B)$ where $U_A = U_A(F_A, C_A)$ and $U_B = U_B(F_B, C_B)$, and where $F_A + F_B = F$ and $C_A + C_B = C$.

The constrained maximization problem is represented by the following equations: maximize $W = W(U_A, U_B)$, subject to $K - \bar{K} = 0$, $L - \bar{L} = 0$, $F(K_F, L_F) - \bar{F} = 0$, $C(K_C, L_C) - \bar{C} = 0$. The corresponding Lagrange expression may be written

$$\Lambda = W(U_A, U_B) - r(K - \bar{K}) - w(L - \bar{L}) - p_F(F(K_F, L_F) - \bar{F})$$
$$- p_C(C(K_C, L_C) - \bar{C}),$$

where r, w, p_F, and p_C are Lagrange multipliers. As already indicated, these multipliers are actually prices, so that the solution to the Lagrange problem gives (scale) solutions for the prices of fish and cabbage (p_F and p_C), the wage rate (w), and the rental on capital (r). The solution prices are the maximizing ones whether the economic system is a free enterprise system with perfect competition or a decentralized socialist economy following the Lange-Lerner rule. Smith's "invisible hand" is the market mechanism which, if perfectly competitive, happens to establish w, r, p_F, and p_C. An IBM machine (conceptually) can solve the Lagrange problem to obtain the "shadow prices" w, r, p_F, and p_C.

the marginal rate of transformation in production equal the common marginal rate of substitution in consumption. This principle determines the point Q'' and the marginal rate of substitution given by the slope of the dashed line $P_F'P_C'$. Finally, the optimum condition for exchange requires equality between the common marginal rate of substitution of fish for cabbage and the fish-cabbage price ratio. Hence p_F/p_C is given by the slope of $P_F'P_C'$ (which equals the slope of P_FP_C).

Graphical analysis enables us to determine the optimizing input- and output-price *ratios;* absolute values, however, are so far unknown. Given the production functions and input allocation, one principle enables us to relate input prices to output prices: each profit-maximizing entrepreneur must employ units of each resource until the point is reached at which the value of its marginal product equals its (input) price. Denoting the marginal product of input i in producing output j by MP_{ij}, we have

$$r = p_F MP_{KF} = p_C MP_{KC} , \qquad (16.2.1)$$

and

$$w = p_F MP_{LF} = p_C MP_{LC} . \qquad (16.2.2)$$

Now let us take stock. Denote the marginal rate of technical substitution by $MRTS$ and the marginal rate of substitution by MRS. Equality of the marginal rate of technical substitution and the input-price ratio may be represented by

$$r = w(MRTS) . \qquad (16.2.3)$$

Similarly, equality between the marginal rate of substitution and the output-price ratio implies

$$p_F = p_C(MRS) . \qquad (16.2.4)$$

Substitute expression (16.2.4) in, say, the first part of expression (16.2.2), obtaining

$$w = p_C(MRS)(MP_{LF}) . \qquad (16.2.5)$$

Next, substituting expression (16.2.5) into (16.2.3) yields

$$r = p_C(MRS)(MP_{LF})(MRTS) . \qquad (16.2.6)$$

All terms in parentheses in equation (16.2.6) represent *known* values—values determined by the welfare maximizing equilibrium solution. Hence r can be determined once p_C is known. If r is known, equation (16.2.3) can be solved for w. Finally, equation (16.2.4) will give the optimum value of p_F if p_C is known.[7] But there is no equation

---

[7] The entire manipulation can be turned around to express r, w, and p_C as a function of p_F.

to determine p_C. Prices, wages, and rents are not unique (although the general equilibrium is). They are determined only as to scale or ratio. One of the prices must be designated as the numéraire of the system; then all other prices will be known. For example, one might specify that the price of one unit of cabbage is unity, $p_C = 1$. Then values of r, w, and p_F, corresponding to $p_C = 1$, can be found.

The reason the price side of the system is determinate only as to scale lies in the fact that our discussion has involved only *real* (non-monetary) variables. The general equilibrium system can be completed by adding one monetary equation. Then unique (not scale) values can be determined for all input and output prices. For example, Fisher's "equation of exchange" could be added to the system, the familiar $MV = PT$. M is determined by the banking system and is a parameter. V, by assumption, is a psychologically determined parameter; and T is given by the (known) real output of goods. Hence the price level P is determined, thereby determining p_C and thus p_F, r, and w. But unless a monetary equation is explicitly introduced, the price side of the model depends upon an endogenous numéraire. Fortunately, ratios are all that are needed for the process of welfare maximization.

16.3 EXTERNAL ECONOMIES AND WELFARE ECONOMICS: A FINAL WORD ON FREE ENTERPRISE

Sections 16.1 and 16.2 contain two different approaches to the problem of social welfare; but the conclusion of each is the same. Perfect competition in all markets will lead to a position of maximum social welfare, *given* the assumptions that underlie the analysis. If these assumptions are not valid, however, perfect competition may not be so "perfect" after all. The perfectly competitive prices (or the Lange-Lerner Lagrange multipliers) may not be the right ones; or at the set of prices that would properly ration the constrained-bliss outputs, profit-maximizing entrepreneurs will not in fact produce the bliss configuration. If this happens maximum welfare is not achieved, despite the existence of perfect competition in all markets.

To explain this market failure a third approach to welfare maximization is necessary.

16.3.a Social Benefits and Costs

In several instances it has been stated that demand represents the marginal social valuation or the marginal social benefit derived from an additional unit of the commodity in question. The demand for each commodity, in other words, shows the price or marginal resource cost consumers are *willing* to pay for an additional unit. In perfect competition price equals marginal cost; hopefully, marginal cost is the marginal resource cost society *must* incur to have an additional unit produced. Thus by the customary "marginal" argument social welfare is a maximum when marginal social cost equals marginal social benefit, or when the resource sacrifice consumers are willing to make exactly equals the resource sacrifice society must make to secure an additional unit of output.

In certain cases, however, the marginal cost that governs the behavior of profit-maximizing entrepreneurs is not the same as the marginal cost to society as a whole. With obvious definitions, marginal *private* cost does not equal marginal *social* cost. In perfect competition, profit maximization implies that price equals marginal private cost. Maximum social welfare is only attained, however, if marginal private cost also equals marginal social cost, for it is only then that marginal social benefit and marginal social cost are equal.

Definition: An external economy (diseconomy) is said to exist when marginal social cost is less than (is greater than) marginal social benefit.

In this terminology perfect competition does not lead to maximum social welfare if external economies or diseconomies are present.

16.3.b Ownership Externalities[8]

There are three sources of external economies and diseconomies, or three reasons for a divergence between marginal social cost and marginal social benefit. The first is called "ownership externality." An explanation of this source of divergence may make the notion of "externality" somewhat clearer.

The classic example of an external diseconomy involves the poor widow who supports herself by hand laundry, and the factory next door whose smoke blackens the laundry. A more recent and relevant example is smog. The private cost of smoke disposal is the cost incurred in building smokestacks, automobile exhausts, and the like; and the *marginal* private cost to which price is equated is virtually zero. However the social cost is definitely positive when smoke disposal by many factories and automobiles causes smog. Marginal social cost exceeds (the zero) marginal private cost and hence price; social welfare is not maximized.

[8] The remainder of this chapter is based upon Francis M. Bator, "The Anatomy of Market Failure," *Quarterly Journal of Economics,* Vol. LXXII (1958), pp. 351–79.

The externality concept should become even clearer from the following example of an external economy (due to Meade). A beekeeper and an apple orchardist are situated side by side. The production of apples, we may assume, requires only labor; thus the apple production function may be written $A = A(L)$. Now in the course of growing, apple blossoms first appear upon the trees; the apples come later. The bees feed upon the essential apple nectar from the blossoms and subsequently produce honey. The labor of the beekeeper is naturally involved; but so is the availability of apple blossoms and, accordingly, the level of apple production. As a consequence, the honey production function is $H = H(L, A)$.[9]

The marginal private cost of increased apple production depends only upon the (perfectly competitive) wage rate. If one additional unit of labor can produce one additional unit of apples, the marginal private cost of apples is the wage rate. But producing an additional unit of apples entails more apple blossoms and apple nectar; more bees can be fed and more honey produced. The marginal social cost of apples equals marginal private cost *minus* the value of the increment in honey production; the perfectly competitive output of apples is not as great as it "should" be for welfare maximization.

Where is the difficulty? Apple blossoms clearly enter into honey production; they have a positive marginal product and should, therefore, have a positive market price. But the orchardist cannot protect his equity in apple nectar; this scarce factor of production is divorced from his effective ownership. Apple nectar has a zero market price; even a perfectly competitive market fails to impute the correct value to apple nectar. Profit-maximizing decisions therefore fail properly to allocate resources at the margin because scarcity is divorced from ownership. In this situation market failure is attributable to an ownership externality.

16.3.c Technical Externalities

A more important source of externalities may be attributable to technology. If production functions exhibit indivisibilities (for instance, can you add one tenth of an IBM machine or of a blast furnace?) or smoothly *increasing* returns to scale, a technical externality exists. The market can fail to achieve the welfare maximum for two reasons. With increasing returns to scale, and perfectly competitive

---

[9] We abstract from the bee service of cross-pollenization.

input markets, average cost declines over the relevant range. This is likely to lead, via economic warfare, to monopoly and monopoly price, violating the marginal benefit–marginal cost requirement.

If the situation does not lead to monopoly it nonetheless leads to market failure. So long as average cost declines, marginal cost is less than average cost. Equality of marginal social benefit and marginal social cost requires equality of price and marginal cost. But at a price equal to marginal cost a pure loss would be sustained by each producer. Thus the socially correct price would not induce profit-maximizing enterpreneurs to produce the socially correct output.

In summary, a technical externality causes market failure either because it leads to monopoly, in which case price does not equal marginal cost; or because free competitive enterprise is not viable at a marginal-cost price.

16.3.d Public Good Externalities

Let us return to the two-person, two-good model: A and B consume X and Y. Let X be available in amount $\overline{X}$. Then X is said to be a public good if both A *and* B can each consume $\overline{X}$ units of X (rather than having $X_A + X_B = \overline{X}$). For example, one person viewing a pyrotechnic display does not preclude another from viewing it as well; concerts may be attended by more than one person; and, to a point, so too may public schools.

Perfect competition establishes equality between the marginal rate of transformation of X into Y and A's and B's common marginal rate of substitution of X for Y. But in the public good case, since A's consumption of X does not restrict B's, the marginal rate of transformation should equal the *sum* of the two marginal rates of substitution. Perfect competition, and perfectly competitive prices, lead to underproduction and underconsumption of public goods.

16.3.e Externalities and Free Enterprise

The existence of externalities places a definite limit on the scope of free competitive enterprise if a (static) social welfare maximum is to be attained. As obviously implied in subsections 16.3.b–16.3.d, public ownership or public control is sometimes necessary. This type of analysis provides the rationale for government ownership and operation of public schools (public good) and postal services (technical externality), and for government control of monopoly price (railway tariffs, telephone tolls). But in a final evaluation one should remember that this analysis is *static;* dynamic considerations are not included, especially considerations of economic growth.

The static theory of welfare economics has been placed on a very rigorous basis and the static criteria for a welfare maximum deduced. But these criteria may not be applicable to a growth economy. One reason is uncertainty of the future. Another, and more important, is that growth itself tends to offset errors of judgment and of management. Doubtless some rate of growth, if sustained in an economy, would allow that economy to violate every static optimality condition with impunity. Therefore, the conclusions of static welfare economics may not afford suitable standards by which to appraise a truly dynamic economy. If free enterprise tends to establish a higher rate of growth than socialized industry, then dynamic arguments are in its favor, even though the free enterprise system may be shot through with oligopoly and monopoly elements. Innovation and growth are more important in the long run.

QUESTIONS

1. In 1965, the first hurricane in many years struck New Orleans, causing severe property damage. The government, in the guise of aid to distressed areas, paid property owners for part, and sometimes all, of their losses. What considerations would be uppermost in your mind if you were asked to write a lengthy essay on the impact of these payments upon the allocation of resources and the distribution of income?

2. Excise taxes are said harmfully to distort the allocation of resources in favor of untaxed commodities. Why?

3. Modern welfare economics frequently makes use of the concept of Pareto optimality. Define the concept and explain its role in the theory of welfare economics. Demonstrate the application of the above welfare criterion to a typical welfare problem (e.g., the distribution of income, resource allocation, etc.), and be sure to include in your discussion the problem of evaluating alternative positions from which society may choose.

4. If completely free trade implies maximum economic welfare, does it necessarily follow that any movement toward free trade would *improve* welfare?

5. Show the conditions that ensure efficient distribution of a given combination of products between two consumers. Would the same conditions ensure maximum *equity?*

6. "Resources are misallocated in the television industry since the cost is borne by advertisers rather than by viewers directly." Discuss.

7. It is often asserted that a monopolist generally operates inefficiently, i.e., at some point on his average cost curve other than its minimum point, while competitive firms operate at their minimum average cost, and hence operate efficiently. Critically analyze this definition of economic efficiency, and if you find it unsatisfactory, suggest an alternative.

8. How might a community attempt to control a monopoly in the public interest? Does it make any difference whether or not this is the only monopoly in existence?

9. "A society or firm that is capable of imputing appropriate prices to the factors of production has, in those prices, a tool that can be used to provide efficient direction to its productive activities." Explain.

10. Assume that we now have a socially optimal distribution of factors of production among industries. The imposition of an income tax will not affect this distribution. True or false, and explain.

11. "The government's policies toward agriculture over the last 30 years or so have been basically defective because the policies fail to separate the 'economic' problem of resource allocation from the 'ethical' problem of income distribution." Discuss.

12. "Increasing returns to scale make the achievement of Pareto optimality easier for a society." Discuss.

13. Assume that resources are now allocated optimally within a community. How will the following affect this allocation: (a) the imposition of a progressive income tax, (b) the imposition of a proportional income tax, (c) an industry in the economy becomes monopolized, and (d) a new method of producing some product is introduced that has an undesirable by-product (e.g., water pollution)?

SUGGESTED READINGS

Bator, Francis M. "The Anatomy of Market Failure," *Quarterly Journal of Economics,* Vol. LXXII (1958), pp. 351–79. [Elementary math required.]

———. "The Simple Analytics of Welfare Maximization," *American Economic Review,* Vol. XLVII (1957), pp. 22–59.

Ferguson, C. E. "Transformation Curve in Production Theory: A Pedagogical Note," *Southern Economic Journal,* Vol. XXIX (1962), pp. 96–102. [Elementary math required.]

Henderson, James M., and Quandt, Richard E. *Microeconomic Theory,* pp. 201–23. New York: McGraw-Hill Book Co., Inc., 1958. [Elementary math required.]

Kenen, Peter B. "On the Geometry of Welfare Economics," *Quarterly Journal of Economics,* Vol. LXXI (1957), pp. 426–47.

Reder, Melvin W. *Studies in the Theory of Welfare Economics.* New York: Columbia University Press, 1947.

Samuelson, Paul A. *Foundations of Economic Analysis,* pp. 203–53. Cambridge, Mass.: Harvard University Press, 1947. [Advanced math required.]

Scitovsky, Tibor. *Welfare and Competition.* Homewood, Ill.: Richard D. Irwin, Inc., 1971. [Elementary math required.]

Advanced Reading, Part V

I. GENERAL EQUILIBRIUM

Kuenne, Robert E. *The Theory of General Economic Equilibrium.* Princeton, N.J.: Princeton University Press, 1963. This work is so thorough that no other citations are required.

II. WELFARE ECONOMICS: GENERAL AND EXPOSITORY

Bator, F. M. "The Simple Analytics of Welfare Maximization," *American Economic Review,* Vol. XLVII (1957), pp. 22–59.

Baumol, William J. *Welfare Economics and the Theory of the State.* Cambridge, Mass.: Harvard University Press, 1952.

Hicks, J. R. "The Foundations of Welfare Economics," *Economic Journal,* Vol. XLIX (1939), pp. 696–712.

Kenan, Peter B. "On the Geometry of Welfare Economics," *Quarterly Journal of Economics,* Vol. LXXI (1957), pp. 426–47.

Lange, Oscar. "The Foundations of Welfare Economics," *Econometrica,* Vol. X (1942), pp. 215–28.

Lerner, A. P. *The Economics of Control: Principles of Welfare Economics.* New York: The Macmillan Co., 1944.

Little, I. M. D. *Welfare Economics.* 2d ed. Oxford: Clarendon Press, 1957.

Mishan, E. J. "A Survey of Welfare Economics, 1939–1959," *Economic Journal,* Vol. LXX (1960), pp. 197–265, with extensive bibliography.

Reder, M. W. *Studies in the Theory of Welfare Economics.* New York: Columbia University Press, 1947.

Rothenberg, Jerome. *The Measurement of Social Welfare.* Englewood Cliffs, N.J.: Prentice-Hall, Inc., 1961.

Samuelson, Paul A. *Foundations of Economic Analysis,* pp. 203–53. Cambridge, Mass.: Harvard University Press, 1947.

III. WELFARE PROPOSITIONS AND THE SOCIAL WELFARE FUNCTION

Arrow, Kenneth J. *Social Choice and Individual Values.* New York: John Wiley & Sons, Inc., 1951.

Burk (Bergson), Abram. "A Reformulation of Certain Aspects of Welfare Economics," *Quarterly Journal of Economics,* Vol. LII (1937–38), pp. 310–34.

Goodman, Leo A., and Markowitz, Harry. "Social Welfare Functions Based on Individual Rankings," *American Journal of Sociology,* Vol. LVIII (1952–53), pp. 257–62.

Kaldor Nicholas. "Welfare Propositions in Economics and Interpersonal Comparisons of Utility," *Economic Journal,* Vol. XLIX (1939), pp. 549–52.

Majumdar, Tapas. *The Measurement of Utility.* London: Macmillan & Co., Ltd., 1958.

Samuelson, Paul A. "Social Indifference Curves," *Quarterly Journal of Economics,* Vol. LXX (1956), pp. 1–22.

Scitovsky, Tibor. "A Note on Welfare Propositions in Economics," *Review of Economic Studies,* Vol. IX (1941–42), pp. 77–88.

IV. CONSUMER'S SURPLUS

Henderson, A. "Consumer's Surplus and the Compensating Variation," *Review of Economic Studies,* Vol. VIII (1940–41), pp. 117–21.

Hicks, J. R. "The Rehabilitation of Consumer's Surplus," *Review of Economic Studies,* Vol. VIII (1940–41), pp. 108–16.

———. *A Revision of Demand Theory.* Oxford: Clarendon Press, 1956.

Hotelling, Harold. "The General Welfare in Relation to Problems of Taxation and of Railway and Utility Rates," *Econometrica,* Vol. VI (1938), pp. 242–69.

Pfouts, R. W. "A Critique of Some Recent Contributions to the Theory of Consumers' Surplus," *Southern Economic Journal,* Vol. XIX (1953), pp. 315–33.

V. MARGINAL-COST PRICING

Barone, E. "The Ministry of Production in the Collectivist State," in *Collectivist Economic Planning* (ed. F. A. Hayek), pp. 245–90. London: Routledge & Son, 1935.

Coase, R. H. "The Marginal Cost Controversy," *Economica,* N.S. Vol. XIII (1946), pp. 169–82.

Hotelling, Harold. "The General Welfare in Relation to Problems of Taxation and of Railway and Utility Rates," *Econometrica,* Vol. VI (1938), pp. 242–69.

Lerner, A. P. "Statics and Dynamics in Socialist Economics," *Economic Journal,* Vol. XLVII (1937), pp. 253–70.

Ruggles, Nancy. "Recent Developments in the Theory of Marginal Cost Pricing," *Review of Economic Studies,* Vol. XVII (1949–50), pp. 107–26.

————. "The Welfare Basis of the Marginal Cost Pricing Principle," *Review of Economic Studies,* Vol. XVII (1949–50), pp. 29–46.

Vickrey, William. "Some Objections to Marginal-Cost Pricing," *Journal of Political Economy,* Vol. LVI (1948), pp. 218–38.

VI. IDEAL OUTPUT

Kahn, R. F. "Some Notes on Ideal Output," *Economic Journal,* Vol. XLV (1935), pp. 1–35.

Lipsey, R. G., and Lancaster, Kelvin. "The General Theory of Second Best," *Review of Economic Studies,* Vol. XXIV (1956–57), pp. 11–32.

McKenzie, Lionel. "Ideal Output and the Interdependence of Firms," *Economic Journal,* Vol. LXI (1951), pp. 785–803.

VII. EXTERNAL ECONOMIES

Bator, F. M. "The Anatomy of Market Failure," *Quarterly Journal of Economics,* Vol. LXXII (1958), pp. 351–79.

Baumol, W. J. "External Economies and Second-Order Conditions," *American Economic Review,* Vol. LIV (1964), pp. 358–72.

Buchanan, James M., and Kafoglis, Milton Z. "A Note on Public Goods Supply," *American Economic Review,* Vol. LIII (1963), pp. 403–14.

————, and Stubblebine, W. Craig. "Externality," *Economica,* N.S. Vol. XXIX (1962), pp. 371–84.

Davis, Otto A., and Whinston, Andrew. "Externalities, Welfare, and the Theory of Games," *Journal of Political Economy,* Vol. LXX (1962), pp. 241–62.

APPENDIX

A Comprehensive Examination in

Microeconomic Theory for

Graduate Students

The following questions, furnished the author by Professor Fritz Machlup of Princeton University, constitute a comprehensive and rather exhaustive examination in microeconomic theory for graduate students. The reader will note that some topics covered in the examination are not treated in this text and that welfare economics is not covered explicitly in the questions.

I. QUESTIONS ON THE THEORY OF RELATIVE PRICES

A. The Equilibrium of the Household

1. "Valuation is a subjective process. We cannot *observe* valuation. It is therefore out of place in a scientific explanation." Discuss.

2. Discuss briefly the claims made concerning the methodological superiority of indifference curve theory over marginal utility theory.

3. Present a short outline or organization, in brief sentences or merely in headings for chapters and sections, but not exceeding the space of one page, of a lengthy essay on the question: "Cardinal or Ordinal Utility?"

4. Under what conditions (concerning prices or products) would it be possible for a consumer to be in "equilibrium":
   a) While the marginal utilities of some goods he consumes are zero?
   b) While the marginal utilities of some goods he refuses to purchase are greater than the marginal utilities of some goods he does puchase?

c) While the marginal utilities of all the goods he purchases are exactly proportional to their prices?

d) While the marginal utilities of all the goods he purchases are exactly equal?

5. What does it mean if an indifference curve between goods X and Y (*a*) becomes parallel to the Y axis, (*b*) is positively sloped and has higher indifference curves to its right, (*c*) is positively sloped and has higher indifference curves to its left, (*d*) is negatively sloped and has higher indifference curves to its left?

6. Draw a family of indifference curves between money and commodity X; construct the price-consumption curve; calculate from the graph the corresponding demand schedule and draw the demand curve.

7. Explain the income effect of a price change and connect it with the income elasticity of demand.

8. The slope of income-consumption curves in an indifference map for goods X and Y has definite implications concerning the income elasticities of demand for X and Y, either absolutely or relative to each other; and the slope of price-consumption curves in an indifference map for good X and money (along the Y axis) has definite implications concerning the price elasticity of demand for X. State what these implications are, first, if the income-consumption curve and, then, if the price-consumption curve runs (*a*) to the northwest, (*b*) straight to the north, (*c*) to the north-northeast, (*d*) to the east-northeast, (*e*) straight to the east, (*f*) to the southeast.

9. Explain the concepts of substitutability and complementarity (*a*) in terms of marginal utility theory and (*b*) in terms of indifference curve theory.

10. Pareto thought that the shape of an indifference curve would reflect whether the two goods under consideration were complementary or substitutable. Hicks denied this was the case except under extreme circumstances. J. M. Clark found that the shapes of a family of indifference curves would reflect complementarity or substitutability between the two goods in question.

Present in a few words, with or without the aid of graphical demonstration, the essentials of (*a*) Pareto's opinion, (*b*) Hicks' criticism, and (*c*) Clark's resolution. Then, (*d*) discuss the possibility of expressing or measuring complementarity and substitutability by means of cross-elasticities of demand.

Finally, (*e*) explain what a cross-elasticity of zero may imply concerning the complementarity or substitutability between the two goods if it is known that neither of the goods is inferior, and (*f*) what it may imply if one of them is markedly inferior.

11. If a price reduction of commodity *A* results in increased consumption of commodity *B* and in reduced consumption of commodity *C*, we cannot

know offhand whether this is to be attributed to substitution effects or to income effects.

a) State the possible relations (substitutability, complementarity) among the three commodities that may explain the described changes, assuming that income effects are negligible.

b) Assuming that the three commodities are almost unrelated with one another, how could income effects explain the described changes?

c) How could you in actual fact attempt to ascertain which of the possible explanations is most likely valid?

12. The "diamond case," the "case of speculative demand," and the "Giffen case" are regarded as the most important exceptions to the law of demand. The first two are sometimes ruled out because not all premises of the law are fulfilled; the last is conceded as a real exception.

a) State the law of demand in one sentence.

b) State, in one short sentence each, the three cases mentioned above.

c) State on what ground the first two cases are considered "exclusions" rather than "exceptions" of the law.

d) Give Professor Hicks' explanation of the Giffen case.

13. Hicks, after stating the "reversibility of complementarity" between goods X and Y, warns: "Observe that it is only the substitution effects that are reversible. If a fall in the price of X increases the demand for Y, it does not necessarily follow that a fall in the price of Y will increase the demand for X." Explain.

14. During World War II many consumer goods were rationed; one of the techniques used in rationing was the issuance of books of coupons, in different colors for different commodity groups, and the fixing of "ration-point values" for each commodity. For example, each person had each week a fixed number of "brown ration points," which were good for the purchase of meats and fats. Each person had, so to speak, a fixed weekly "income" of ration points—apart from any money income—and each rationed commodity had a "price" fixed in terms of ration points—apart from its price in terms of money.

In December, 1943, the ration-point values of meats were reduced. This "price reduction" was intended to cause an increase in purchases of meat. Yet it probably caused also an increased demand for butter, although the ration-point values of butter were left unchanged.

a) Would you regard this as a symptom of complementarity between meat and butter? Why or why not?

b) Would you think that butter and meat are more likely substitutes or complements of each other? Why?

c) How can you explain the increased demand for butter in terms of substitution effect and income effect? (Note: These effects refer here to ration points, not money.)

d) Assuming, for the sake of simplicity, that beef and butter are the only things available for brown ration points, draw an indifference map for the two commodities, show the price relation and its change, exhibit the income and substitution effects, and mark the combinations chosen by the consumer before and after the price change. (A rough sketch is sufficient.)

15. Certain "peculiarities of indifference maps involving money" are presented by Hart, particularly (*a*) that all indifference curves will intercept the *Y* axis measuring "money," but not the axis measuring quantities of the good *X* except if the latter were "leisure;" (*b*) that all indifference curves will have lowest points, (*c*) that these lowest points will lie further to the left on higher indifference curves, (*d*) that for given quantities of *X*, if this is not an inferior good, higher indifference curves will be steeper. Explain and comment on all these points.

16. Frank H. Knight states "that we know in general only three facts" about the shape of indifference curves involving money: "They always have a negative slope (within the significant range), they do not intersect (or meet), and they cannot have a uniform slope and vertical spacing for different values of *X*. This third feature would involve zero income elasticity of demand for *X;* and this . . . is conceivable only for a good with a complex utility so arranged that displacement of other goods would exactly offset the diminishing utility of the various component types of satisfaction which it yields." Explain and comment on all these points.

17. Robert L. Bishop discussed seven different concepts of consumer's surplus, and J. R. Hicks presented four concepts (which he interpreted as compensating or equivalent variations). Choose any four of these concepts for a brief exposition, emphasizing the differences between them.

18. Present some of the uses made of consumer-surplus arguments in favor of particular methods of taxation.

B. Production Functions and the Cost of Production

1. Assume that a curve is drawn showing along the abscissa the amounts of a factor *A* employed in combination with a fixed amount of a group of factors called *B*, and along the ordinate the amount of physical product obtainable from these combinations of factors.

a) How can you find (geometrically) the amount of *A* for which the average physical product per unit of *A* is a maximum?

b) How can you find (geometrically) the amount of *A* for which the marginal physical product of *A* is a maximum?

c) Between the two points defined in questions (*a*) and (*b*), will the marginal physical product of *A* increase or decrease as more of *A* is used?

d) Between these two points, will the average physical product per unit of *A* increase or decrease as more of *A* is used?

e) At the point defined (*a*), will the marginal physical product of *A* be higher or lower than the average physical product per unit of A? Give reasons.

f) At the point defined in (*b*), will the marginal physical product of A be higher or lower than the average physical product per unit of A? Give reasons.

g) How can you find (geometrically) the amount of A for which the marginal physical product of A is zero?

h) At which point will the average physical product per unit of B (the fixed factor group) be a maximum, assuming linear homogeneity?

i) It is more efficient to work in a phase of increasing returns or decreasing returns? Give reasons.

j) What will determine the proportion between factors A and B that a producer will choose?

k) Under what condition would he choose the proportion between factors A and B at which the average physical product per unit of B is a maximum?

l) Under what conditions would he choose any of the proportions between factors A and B in the range between the points defined in (*a*) and (*b*)?

2. Assuming linear homogeneity, prove that, according to the laws of return to factors of production combined in varying proportions, (*a*) average product per unit of factor B will increase when additional amounts of factor A are employed with increasing returns; (*b*) average product per unit of factor B will also increase when additional amounts of factor A are employed with diminishing returns; (*c*) marginal product per unit of factor B will be negative when factor A is employed in a proportion that lies within the phase of increasing returns.

3. If engineers prepare a table giving the amounts of product that can be obtained from combining all the necessary factors of production in all possible proportions, can one find a point of "maximum efficiency" or "optimum proportion of factors?" Give reasons for your answer.

4. The law of diminishing returns (or nonproportional output) has been empirically tested and verified for several different factors of production. However, it is said that if "factors of production" are defined in a certain way the "law of diminishing returns" can be logically deduced from that definition and, thus, is an a priori statement. Explain.

5. "That people do not grow all the crops they want in just a few little flower pots is sufficient proof for the existence of diminishing returns." Explain.

6. If the application of auxiliary factors to a fixed factor has been pushed beyond the point where "diminishing returns" set in, does this indicate an inefficient (or uneconomical) proportion of the factors? Give reasons.

7. Under what conditions, if any, might a producer find it preferable to produce within a range of increasing returns?

8. Distinguish the "indivisibility" that may cause a monopolist to employ a variable factor under increasing returns from the "indivisibility" that may be responsible for his monopoly position.

9. While producers may undertake to create or aggravate indivisibilities that might protect their monopoly position, they may at the same time undertake to remove or reduce indivisibilities that force them to produce sometimes under increasing returns. Explain and illustrate.

10. What may be the reason for the fact that early economists believed agricultural production was governed by the law of diminishing returns while increasing returns would prevail in industry?

11. Discuss the essential difference between the laws of proportions and the laws of returns to scale.

12. The same economies of production have sometimes been explained in terms of increasing returns to scale and sometimes in terms of factor substitution. Likewise, the same diseconomies that have been regarded as instances of diminishing returns to scale have alternatively been interpreted as cases of varying proportions among factors. Explain.

13. Draw—on graph paper—a total product curve for combinations of varying amounts of factor *A* with a fixed amount, say four units, of factor *B*. Then draw, on the same graph, the total product curves for combinations of varying amounts of *A* with two units of *B* and with eight units of *B*, on the assumption that up to four units of *B* increasing returns to scale prevail, whereas from this scale upward the returns to scale are constant. It is essential that the three curves reflect the mentioned assumptions.

14. Calculate, on the basis of the productivity curves drawn as directed in the preceding question, the schedules of total cost, average total cost, average variable cost, and marginal cost of production, if factor *A* costs $1 per unit and is the only variable cost of production, while factor *B* stands for the equipment of the firm and costs $6.25 per day for each unit installed, whether or not it is used.

a) Assume first that the firm is equipped with four units of *B*, which are coupled in such a way as to make it impossible to work with less than the entire equipment. (Thus, only one of the three product curves will be relevant for the input-output relations in question.)

b) Now, altering the preceding assumption, assume that the firm is equipped with two sets of four units of *B*—that is, with eight *B* units—and that the operation of only two units becomes possible, so that the firm can operate two, four, six, or eight units of *B*. (Mention for each output volume listed on your cost schedule how many units of *B* will be operated for its production.)

15. What is the logical relation between increasing returns and decreasing costs?

16. Write a short essay on the concept of "decreasing costs."

17. Fixed costs are often very substantial and real. Is it incomprehensible how the economic theorist can say we should neglect them in the short run and that they don't exist in the long run? Explain.

18. Show the similarities and differences between (*a*) spreading of overhead, (*b*) increasing returns of fuller use of inflexible plant, (*c*) internal economies of large-scale production, and (*d*) external economies of large-scale industry.

19. Considering only elements of internal cost calculations of a firm, explain the situations making for a coincidence of (*a*) decreasing short-run cost and increasing long-run cost; (*b*) increasing short-run cost and decreasing long-run cost; (*c*) increasing short-run cost and increasing long-run cost; (*d*) decreasing short-run cost and decreasing long-run cost; (*e*) constant short-run cost and decreasing long-run cost; (*f*) increasing short-run cost and constant long-run cost.

20. How can the existence of constant short-run marginal cost be reconciled with the law of variable proportions and the *U*-shaped cost curves that are customarily derived from it?

21. The short-run marginal cost curve of an individual manufacturing establishment is often drawn with a *U*-shape, steeply falling to a minimum point and steeply rising thereafter. The long-run marginal cost curve of the same firm may be drawn much flatter—perhaps falling not less steeply but often moving horizontally over a substantial range and certainly rising much more gradually—than the short-run curve. Sometimes, however, even the short-run marginal cost curve of the firm is drawn horizontally over a considerable range.

Explain the most plausible technological reasons for the conditions pictured in these curves, that is, for (*a*) the steeply *U*-shaped short-run curve, (*b*) the flat bottom and gentler rise of the long-run curve, and (*c*) the flat bottom of the short-run curve in some instances.

22. "The depreciation of machinery is usually in the short run a fixed cost and in the long run a variable cost; but it may also in the short run be partly a fixed and partly a variable cost." Explain (*a*) depreciation as a short-run fixed cost; (*b*) depreciation as a long-run variable cost; (*c*) depreciation as a short-run variable cost.

23. A student once was asked to show a cost schedule for a firm where "increasing returns" prevail. He gave the following schedule of average total cost:

Output	*ATC*
60 units	$15
70 units	12
80 units	8

What would you say to the student?

24. Confusion may easily arise in discussing comparisons and variations of cost, even when we deal with only one firm and specify the kind of cost we mean. Contrast, with the aid of graphs, the meaning of the cost variations referred to in the following sentences:

a) "After a certain point diseconomies of large scale may outweigh the economies, and *marginal costs may rise.*" (Joan Robinson, *The Economics of Imperfect Competition,* p. 49.)

b) "The tax . . . may be taken to stand for a *rise in marginal costs* brought about by a rise in wages." (*Ibid.,* p. 82.)

c) "The rise in price due to the imposition of the tax is equal to half the *increase in marginal cost* [which may be equal or more or less than the tax]." (*Ibid.,* p. 77. All italics supplied.)

25. Discuss the comparative difficulties of calculating the total cost, average cost, and marginal cost for a product produced by a multiproduct firm.

26. "When, in a problem of output and price determination, a cost curve is drawn, all problems of factor input and of the technological substitution between factors of production are considered as solved beforehand." Discuss.

27. Explain the differences—regarding the underlying causes—between (*a*) constant costs in the individual firm; (*b*) constant costs in the industry with increasing costs in every single firm; and (*c*) constant supply prices in the industry owing to external economies offsetting the conditions of increasing costs.

28. What are the methodological differences between (*a*) external economies, (*b*) economies due to economic development, and (*c*) economies due to new inventions?

C. The Equilibrium of the Firm

1. Multiproduct firms are more frequently observed in reality; single-product firms are more frequently treated by theory. Give reasons for both these facts.

2. Without revealing your own position, present the strongest possible arguments for and against the view that the principle of profit maximization is merely an empty tautology and useless for any explanatory or predictive purposes.

3. Discuss the alleged dichotomy between maximum profit and security as goals of business conduct in an uncertain world, and the contention that

profit maximization is meaningless as a guide to action where there is uncertainty.

4. Demand curves, in the theory of the equilibrium of the firm, are supposed to describe subjective expectations of future sales possibilities. How does theory allow for the facts (*a*) that such expectations are always uncertain (and usually the more uncertain the more distant the future to which they pertain) and (*b*) that the revenues which can be expected from alternative policies may refer to different points of time?

5. "An entrepreneur will, so we assume, always produce any given output in such a way that the cost to him of that given output is at a minimum. But it is not to his interest to choose from all possible outputs that output whose average cost is least." Explain.

6. State the relation between marginal revenue and elasticity of demand, deriving it by geometrical and algebraic analysis.

7. Can marginal cost and marginal revenue be equal at a volume of output where the average cost curve is intersected by the demand curve? Why or why not?

8. Draw a neat and precise graph according to the following instructions:

a) Draw an average fixed cost curve and mark it *AFC*.

b) Draw a *U*-shaped average variable cost curve and mark it *AVC*.

c) Construct the average total cost curve and mark it *ATC*.

d) Construct the marginal cost curve and mark it *MC*.

e) Draw a not steeply sloping, straight-line demand curve, cutting the *ATC* curve in its increasing range, and mark it D_1.

f) Construct the corresponding marginal revenue curve and mark it MR_1.

g) Mark the point *K* on the *X* axis to show the chosen output.

h) Mark the point *P* to show the chosen price.

i) Mark and indicate points needed to show quasi rent (the excess of total revenue over total variable cost).

j) Mark and indicate points needed to show net profit (the excess of total revenue over all cost).

k) Draw now another demand curve which, presumably under the influence of newcomers' competition, is so much further downward and to the left that it is a tangent to the *ATC* curve; mark it D_2.

l) Construct the corresponding marginal revenue curve and mark it MR_2.

m) Mark the point *L* on the *X* axis to show the chosen output.

n) Mark the point *T* to show the chosen price.

o) Mark and indicate all points needed to show quasi rent.

p) Mark and indicate points needed to show net profit.

9. Draw a smooth demand curve with some concavity from above and then the corresponding marginal revenue curve, constructing at least three points of the latter with ruler and compass and the rest freehand.

10. "Average cost may be the most important datum for the estimate of long-run demand elasticity." Explain how this can be so and what significance it may have for the explanation of so-called full-cost pricing.

11. Explain how the existence of interventions against "selling below cost" and "profiteering" may be referred to as arguments against the average-cost theory of pricing.

12. "The analysis of the size of the firm in the theory of relative prices relates to problems very different from those with which the theory of growth is concerned." Explain.

13. How is it possible, as is asserted by the theory of monopolistic competition, that firms may possess much "excess capacity" and yet be "undersized?"

14. Prove that, for a monopolist faced with a straight-line demand curve and forced to charge a uniform price to all takers, *total revenue* will be maximized if the quantity sold is exactly half the quantity which buyers would take at a price of zero.

15. "It is often said that a monopolist will restrict output by less the greater the elasticity of demand for his product and the more rapid the rate of decreasing cost, or that he will restrict output more the less the elasticity of demand and the more rapid the rate of increasing cost." Mrs. Robinson calls this a "common confusion" and "fallacy" but admits that it "turns out to be correct" in special cases. Explain why the "common view" is incorrect "in general" but correct in special cases, and discuss whether these special cases are very exceptional.

16. "The difference between marginal cost and average variable cost is average rent per unit of output." Prove this proposition for cases of pure competition and show that it does not hold otherwise.

17. An increase in demand for the product of an individual firm may be accompanied by (1) an increase in elasticity; (2) a decrease in elasticity; or (3) no change in elasticity.

State for *each* of the three cases:

a) What may be the actual conditions responsible for the change, or absence of change, in elasticity?

b) What would be the geometric properties of the new demand curve in comparison with the old?

c) What would be the effect upon the selling price of the product if it is produced under constant marginal cost?

d) What would be the effect upon the selling price of the product if it is produced under increasing marginal cost?

e) What would be the effect upon the selling price of the product if it is produced under decreasing marginal cost?

18. An increase in the demand for the product of an individual firm not

in an oligopoly position may leave selling price unchanged although marginal cost is not constant.

a) State what condition would account for the unchanged selling price if marginal cost was increasing.

b) State what condition would account for the unchanged selling price if marginal cost was decreasing.

c) Draw a graph picturing the condition under (*b*)—that is, showing the decreasing marginal cost curve, the "previous" (curvilinear) demand curve, and the "new" demand curve that would call for no change of price.

19. Firms are occasionally found to raise prices when trade is bad and the demand for their goods has fallen. The businessmen's explanation usually is that as output has fallen off each unit has to bear a higher share of the overhead cost than before. (*a*) Discuss this explanation. (*b*) Provide another explanation if you reject the first.

20. Can a decrease in the demand for the product of a monopolistic seller induce him to increase his output? If so, under what conditions?

21. Solve the following problem by means of geometrical devices: given are a stretch of a sloping demand curve and a long stretch of a decreasing marginal cost curve, so that you can construct the chosen output volume and selling price. Now demand increases so much that, under the given cost conditions and new demand conditions, output will be increased to exactly three times the former volume and price will be maintained at the former level. (a) How must the elasticity of demand have changed to bring forth this result? (*b*) Construct the relevant stretch of the new demand curve.

22. "A disappearance of rival firms may just as well increase as decrease the elasticity of demand for the products of the remaining firms." State the conditions that are apt to cause either result.

23. If a firm through efficient advertising succeeds in increasing the demand for its product, will the elasticity of this demand be higher or lower than before? Why?

24. Demand is often conveniently expressed in terms of net prices (average net revenue) received by the seller rather than gross prices paid by the consumer. Different kinds of deductions from the prices paid by the consumers may result in significant differences in the elasticities of the demand curves in terms of average net receipts.

Compare the elasticities of the "previous" and various "new" demand curves (average revenue curves) at (*a*) given net prices and (*b*) given quantities of output, under the following three assumptions: a specific excise tax is introduced (a tax per unit of physical sales); an *ad valorem* excise tax is introduced (a tax as a percentage of price); and a progressive *ad valorem* excise tax is introduced with tax rates increasing with price (with higher percentages of higher prices and lower percentages of lower prices).

[*Note:* For the sake of simplicity assume first that the "previous" demand curve is a straight line. But afterwards examine whether conclusions drawn from straight-line reasoning have to be qualified if the demand curve is concave from above.]

25. Discuss and compare the effects a subsidy given to a monopolist is likely to have upon prices paid by the consumer and upon quantities sold: (*a*) when the subsidy is a fixed sum irrespective of output; (*b*) when the subsidy is a fixed amount on each unit of output produced; (*c*) when the subsidy is a fixed percentage of the price of each unit produced; and (*d*) when the subsidy is progressive (when it increases per unit as the output increases).

26. Draw a graph picturing the situation where the imposition of an excise tax upon a product which a monopolist produces under increasing marginal cost will raise the selling price by more than half the tax. State briefly the essential properties of the curves that account for the result.

27. An individual producer is compelled to raise the hourly wage rates of all his workers by 20 percent. He has been operating under increasing marginal cost.

a) If you expect his marginal cost curve to shift upward in consequence of the wage increase, have you reasons to believe that it will have the same slope, be steeper, or less steep? Why?

b) If wages had been 50 percent of the total variable cost of the output the firm had been producing, would you expect the marginal cost of that same output to rise by 50 percent, 20 percent, 10 percent, something between 10 and 20 percent, or less than 10 percent? Why?

c) If the firm is not in an oligopolistic position and anticipates no change in the demand for its products, will it be apt to raise or lower its output, or leave it unchanged, in consequence of the higher wages? Why?

d) If the demand curve as seen by the firm is a sloping straight line, can you make a statement about the magnitude of the change in the price the firm will charge relative to: the difference between the old marginal cost of the original output and the new marginal cost of any changed output; the absolute change in the marginal cost of the original output; and the percentage change in wage rates?

e) If the demand curve were concave from above, rather than a straight line, how would the answers to the questions in *d* have to be altered?

28. "The problem of the optimal selling effort can be solved independently of production costs, just as the problem of the optimal production technique is ordinarily solved independently of demand and revenue considerations. This solution overcomes the apparent interdependence of cost and demand curves for a producer whose selling efforts as well as selling prices are variable." Explain.

29. Demonstrate geometrically that recognition of rent as cost will re-

move "monopoly profit" but increase "monopolistic underutilization of capacity."

30. Product differentiation has "indivisibility" as a logical prerequisite according to Kaldor but not according to Chamberlin. How can there be an unresolved argument about a purely logical inference? Explain the disagreement.

31. Assume that it were possible to achieve standardization of the now differentiated products offered by an industry of many sellers. Discuss the probable effects of such standardization upon prices paid by consumers. Take account of elasticities of demand as seen by the sellers, costs of standardization to sellers and buyers, consumers' reactions to standardization, and sellers' opportunities for collusive arrangements.

32. Discuss the possibility of empirical verifications of propositions asserting that oligopoly or monopoly prevails in a specific situation.

33. "The smaller a seller's share in the market the greater the temptation for him to cut prices in slack times." Discuss.

34. (*a*) Draw a kinked oligopoly demand curve; (*b*) construct the marginal revenue curve; (*c*) show by drawing two marginal cost curves at different levels that price and output need not be affected by a change in the cost of the firm; (*d*) explain in a sentence or two the seller's reasoning pictured by the kinked curve; (*e*) explain why the exhibited insensitiveness of price to the change in cost holds only in cases in which the competitors of the firm are not faced with similar changes in cost.

35. If an oligopolist knows that a given change in production cost will affect not only him but also his rivals, he may assume that the demand for his particular product will be changed. But in which direction and why? Distinguish between several cases: (*a*) he is one of an uncoordinated group of oligopolists; (*b*) he is a price leader; (*c*) he is a price follower, though not a small producer; (*d*) he is an insignificantly small producer; (*e*) he is a member of a quota cartel.

36. "While the 'theory of the firm' can be helpful in analyzing the conduct of a cartel member, it is less helpful in explaining the determination of price in a price cartel." Discuss.

37. State in a very few sentences and without a graph the essential points in Edgeworth's theory of duopoly.

38. What are the essential differences between Cournot's and Edgeworth's theories of duopoly?

39. What is meant by "symmetry" and "asymmetry" in the duopolists' attitudes, and what is the significance of such attitudes in duopoly theory?

40. Is competition among three or four sellers more "competitive" than among only two? Present arguments on both sides of the question.

41. According to Stigler, "Potential competition does not in general exert any influence on duopoly (or monopoly) price." Discuss.

42. Passenger transportation and freight transportation are jointly produced services; eastbound and westbound transportation are also jointly produced services. Does the first or the second of these pairs of joint products more nearly correspond to what some writers call "true" joint products? Give reasons.

43. Whether "joint products" are true products (complementary in their production) or alternative products (substitutes in production) depends often on the degree of utilization of plant capacity. Sometimes they are substitute products in the short run and complementary products in the long run. Explain.

44. Present a graphical demonstration of a monopolist's pricing of a pair of strictly joint products. Assume that demands are not interrelated; that the two markets cannot be subdivided; that the disposal of unsold output is not without cost (make it a constant cost).

45. Assume a case of inseparably joint production in a firm selling under monopolistic conditions. The two joint products, A and B, need some separate processing before they can be marketed. State what effects upon the prices of the two products you would expect in the short run (a) if a processing tax is imposed on A; (b) if the real property tax of the firm is increased; (c) if the demand for A rises; (d) if the demand for B is found to be less elastic than has previously been assumed; (e) if a rival develops and offers a close substitute for A. Consider each of the five cases separately, giving reasons for all answers.

46. State under what conditions price discrimination is (a) possible, and (b) profitable.

47. State the circumstances under which, according to Mrs. Robinson, price discrimination will result in a higher output than nondiscriminating monopoly, and the reasons she believes these circumstances are more likely to exist than are conditions making for a smaller output under discrimination.

48. Present graphically, with precise construction of all relevant points and curves, a case in which a profit-maximizing monopolist who sells in two separate markets with unrelated demand will increase his production when he is prohibited from practicing price discrimination.

49. Assume that a monopolist is able to divide his market into two separate markets independent of each other; thus, he has the power to engage in price discrimination of the third degree.

a) What may be the properties of the relevant curves accounting for the following situations: (i) He finds it most profitable to charge the same price in both markets. (ii) He finds it most profitable to charge different prices, but not to change his output. (*iii*) He finds it most profitable to charge different prices and to increase his total output.

b) Concerning the second situation, state which of the markets will be charged increased or reduced prices and will receive reduced or increased deliveries.

c) Concerning the third situation, state whether and why it is possible or impossible that: both markets are charged increased prices; both markets are charged reduced prices; or one market is charged an increased price, the other a reduced price, but both markets receive increased deliveries.

50. Milk cooperatives usually charge a higher price for milk in the "fluid" market (for direct consumption) than in the industrial market (for butter and cheese). Why? What assumptions does this imply about the demand in these two markets? Can you give reasons why those assumptions prevail in fact?

51. Marshall discusses four conditions determining the elasticity of derived demand. State the rules (in any order you like) and tell which of these rules, if any, help explain the following instances of price discrimination:

a) Railroads usually charge higher freight rates for materials that have a higher value per ton than for materials of lower value.

b) Utility companies often charge higher rates to consumers of electricity for lighting than to consumers of electricity for heating.

c) A producer of plastics sells the same material at high prices to dentists and dental technicians for use as dentures and at lower prices to other industrial users.

d) A producer sells aluminum ingots at higher prices than aluminum made into cable.

e) A producer sells plate glass in large sheets at higher prices than glass cut into small pieces.

52. Pigou stated that under price discrimination of the "first degree . . . no consumers' surplus was left to the buyer."

a) What is price discrimination of the first degree?

b) What is consumers' surplus, broadly speaking, without distinguishing between the dozens of different definitions?

c) Is one particular definition or measurement of consumers' surplus implied in Pigou's quoted statement; if so, which one?

d) What is Knight's opinion on this particular definition or measurement?

D. The Equilibrium of the Industry

1. Discuss purposes and definitions of the concept of the "industry."

2. "If the world were such that perfect competition were possible, it would be such that the demarcation of commodities would present no diffi-

culty." Explain. (In order to specify the meaning of "perfect competition" it is necessary to reveal that the statement is by Mrs. Robinson.)

3. Explain why the notion of a supply curve is not very meaningful except for a perfectly polypolistic industry.

4. Discuss Chamberlin's statement of "group equilibrium" where a large number of producers offers, with different selling efforts, products of different quality to buyers with different preferences. Place major emphasis on the various effects of advertising upon sellers outside the group as well as on those within, upon the scale of production, and upon the prices paid by consumers.

5. "The supply curve of a commodity produced under perfect competition is the curve of average costs including rent." Is this proposition based on empirical evidence or is it a tautology? Show how and from which facts, assumptions, or definitions the proposition is derived.

6. "If we include the economic rents in our average total cost we can show that the minimum average total cost of *all* firms, not merely of the marginal firm, will be equal to the price of the product when an industry is in equilibrium." Explain and prove this proposition.

7. Discuss, connect, and compare the following three statements by Mrs. Robinson:

"Normal profits is that level of profit at which there is no tendency for new firms to enter the trade, or for old firms to disappear out of it." (P. 92.)

"The level of normal profits must be defined in respect to the particular industry. . . . The level of normal profits in trades which are easy to enter . . . are likely to be low relatively to the normal profits of industries requiring a very large initial investment or peculiar efficiency or peculiar facilities of various kinds. . . ." (P. 93.)

"Indeed it is when profits are abnormally high (because new firms are failing to enter the industry to a sufficient extent to keep profits at the normal level) that the firms are of more than optimum size." (P. 97.)

8. Discuss the nature and significance of divergent profit calculations by insiders, outsiders, and disinterested economists.

9. Explain briefly the theory of "equilibrium with excess capacity."

10. It is stated that with perfectly easy entry into the industry the demand curves will be tangent to average cost curves of all individual firms. What is meant? What would absence of the "tangency condition" imply? What forces are supposed to bring about the tangency?

11. How could it be said that "competition" could result in production at the lowest possible cost?

12. Prove that firms under monopolistic competition, in an industry into which entry is easy, will be of less than optimum size.

13. Newcomers' competition may increase cost by forcing individual producers to operate with more excess capacity, to reduce specialization, to pay higher factor prices, and probably in some other ways. May one conclude that newcomers' competition is wasteful? Argue both sides of the case without revealing your own opinion.

14. Explain the distinction and relation between "cost at the margin" and "intensive marginal cost."

15. "The fact that when entrepreneurship is a scarce factor intramarginal firms are larger than what . . . would be called their optimum size merely shows that the differential advantages of entrepreneurs whose efficiency cost is relatively low are being fully exploited, so that the marginal cost of their output is not less than the marginal cost of the outputs of more expensive entrepreneurs." Explain and discuss.

16. "If the statisticians assure Mr. Sraffa that he is right, and that almost every industry works under conditions of constant costs, the task of the monopoly analysis will be much simplified. But it will lose none of its validity and will gain considerably in charm." Explain and discuss every part of this statement by Mrs. Robinson, including the reasons for Sraffa's view that constant costs prevail in almost every industry.

17. According to Mrs. Robinson, "A rising supply curve of the factor to an industry is not a sufficient condition, although it is a necessary condition, for the existence of rent from the point of view of that industry." (a) Explain why it is a necessary condition. (b) Explain why it is not a sufficient condition.

18. Explain the difference between rent from the point of view of an industry and rent from other points of view.

19. Whether a factor of production earns rent in an industry will depend, among other things, on the extension of the group of firms that one chooses to regard as a separate industry. Explain and discuss.

20. Boulding states: "There is no rule which will tell us *a priori* whether the rent in a firm will rise or fall when the price of the variable input rises. . . . Probably rents will tend to rise in low-cost firms and fall in high-cost firms." Boulding's statement refers to firms in an industry where competition is pure and perfect; and it takes account of "industry effects" as well as "firm effects." Explain the statement.

21. When Marshall in Book V of his *Principles of Economics* resorts to the highly fictitious assumption "that a meteoric shower of a few thousand large stones harder than diamonds" fell on the earth, what principles does he try to illustrate?

22. If the supply of factors of production is fixed and there are no economies of a large-scale industry, one may say that "for any commodity con-

sidered separately there is rising supply price, because an increase in the output of any commodity turns the relative factor prices against itself." Explain both the proposition and its presuppositions; then comment on the significance of the statement within the theory of relative prices and output as contrasted with the theory of aggregate output.

23. What is the significance of the distinction between external economies depending on reductions in the prices of products furnished by other industries, and external economies depending on improvements in services rendered by factors of production?

24. Discuss the similarities and differences between increasing transfer costs of productive factors, seen as external diseconomies of an industry, and decreasing costs due to external economies of large-scale industry.

25. "When economies [of large-scale industry] are present it is no longer true that marginal cost of the industry, excluding rent, is equal to the cost of the additional factors employed when output increases. The cost of the additional factors employed, or cost at the margin, must necessarily be equal to supply price, but marginal cost to the industry, excluding rent, is now less than the supply price by the amount of the induced economies." Elucidate.

26. Under conditions of constant cost due to absence of economies of large-scale production and absence of any scarce factors to the industry, monopoly output is smaller than competitive output. By how much (a) if the demand curve is a sloping straight line; (b) if it is concave from above; (c) if it convex from above?

27. Making the four general assumptions on p. 98 in Mrs. Robinson's *Economics of Imperfect Competition,* that (1) cost conditions are not a function of time but only of volume of output and size of establishment, (2) all firms adjust immediately to changes and reach equilibrium positions without delay, (3) cost curves of individual firms are independent of changes in the number of firms in the industry, and (4) all firms—old as well as newly entering—have identical cost and selling conditions; and further assuming that (5) all sellers in the industry are in positions of monopolistic competition, but (6) there is perfect newcomers' competition, and that (7) an increase in the number of firms by reducing average transportation costs will increase the elasticity of all demand curves; how will an increase in total demand affect (a) the selling price, (b) the volume of output of each firm, (c) the number of firms, and (d) the relative change in the number of firms compared with the relative change in the output of the whole industry?

28. Demonstrate Mrs. Robinson's contention that "when there is a scarce factor for which the full rent is not paid, and at the same time there are economies of large-scale industry . . . it is possible that monopoly output may be greater than competitive output."

29. According to Mrs. Robinson, "An increase in the total demand for the

commodity, when the market is imperfect, is far more likely to lower the average cost curves of the firms than when the market is perfect." Her reason for this statement is the "reservoir of potential economies of large-scale industry" likely to exist under imperfect competition because of a retarded process of specialization. Explain.

30. The theory of derived demand was formulated as a part of the analysis of the equilibrium of the industry; with minor adaptations it is used also in the analysis of the firm. Besides these uses in the theory of relative prices it is also employed in the theory of relative incomes. Discuss the adaptations, the changes in emphasis, and the differences in purposes.

31. Marshall distinguishes four conditions "under which a check to the supply of a thing that is wanted not for direct use, but as a factor of production of some commodity, may cause a very great rise in its price." These four conditions resulting in inelasticity of derived demand relate to the technological substitutability of the factor of production, the demand for the product, the portion of the total expenses of production that consists of the cost of this factor, and the supply of other factors of production. Discuss the ways in which these conditions are related to the elasticity of the derived demand.

32. Graphs of the sort of Marshall's knifeblade-handle diagram must necessarily oversimplify one of the conditions that is often the most essential for the elasticity of derived demand. Which condition? Why can more realistic assumptions about this condition not be dealt with in the diagrammatical representation?

33. A product, X, is made from three "ingredients" or factors of production, A, B, and C, all of which are necessary and can be used only in a fixed proportion. Total output of X is 1,000 units per unit of time; the product sells at a price of $100 per unit. The factor costs per unit of product are $60 for A, $30 for B, and $10 for C. The supplies of A and B are perfectly elastic to the industry. The demand for X has an elasticity of minus two. The industry is competitive both in its buying and in its selling.

Assume that the quantity of C available to the industry is reduced by 20 percent. Calculate the elasticity of the industry's derived demand for C. Show your reasoning step by step.

34. Change the assumptions of problem 33 in that the elasticities of supply of A and B to the industry are plus four and plus two, respectively. Then make the calculation again.

35. Change the assumptions of problem 33 in that the supplies of B and C to the industry are perfectly elastic and that it is the quantity of A which is reduced by 20 percent. You are now asked to calculate the elasticity of the industry's demand for A.

36. If a commodity is jointly demanded with others, the elasticity of the market demand for its tends to be low. Why?

37. "When charcoal was generally used in making iron, the price of leather depended in some measure on that of iron; and the tanners petitioned for the exclusion of foreign iron in order that the demand on the part of English iron smelters for oak charcoal might cause the production of English oak to be kept up, and thus prevent oak bark from becoming dear."

Explain first the economic relations between (*a*) oak charcoal and English iron, (*b*) oak bark and English leather, (*c*) oak charcoal and oak bark, (*d*) foreign iron and English iron; and then (*e*) explain how the price of leather was affected by the price of iron and therefore by the importation of iron.

38. Discuss and compare the usefulness of alternative "measurements" of the degree of monopoly, including the indexes of concentration, profitability, price flexibility, and price-marginal-cost discrepancy.

E. Equilibrium of the Market

1. Discuss the concept and definition of the "perfect market" as distinguished from the various concepts of pure or perfect competition.

2. To what extent is the existence of reservation prices compatible with a "perfect market"?

3. "The cobweb theorem as an illustration of an unstable equilibrium rests on the assumption that the adjustment of supply lags behind the movement of market price." Explain.

4. Assuming that adjustments of supply lag behind the movements of market price, draw three sets of supply and demand curves, the first such that an accidental disturbance of equilibrium will result in dampening oscillations of market price with a gradual return to the initial equilibrium position; the second such that an accidental disturbance of equilibrium will result in perpetual and constant oscillations of market price around the initial equilibrium position; and the third such that an accidental disturbance of equilibrium will result in oscillations of ever-increasing amplitude.

5. It is conceivable that demand and supply curves may both have negative slopes and intersect each other several times. Some of the intersections are regarded as defining positions of "stable equilibrium," and others of "unstable equilibrium." According to Marshall, "It will be found to be a characteristic of stable equilibria that in them the demand price is greater than the supply price for amounts just less than the equilibrium amount, and vice versa." Other writers—for example, J. R. Hicks—took exception to this statement. Discuss.

6. Prove geometrically that Hicks' "excess-demand curve" must have the same properties as Wicksteed's demand curve, differing from it only by a constant.

7. "The only possible case of instability [of exchange between X and Y] is when . . . the sellers of X will . . . be much more anxious to consume more X when they become better off than the buyers of X are." Explain.

8. Explain Hicks' concepts of perfectly stable and imperfectly stable market systems.

9. For the equilibrium price to be attained in a market certain types of reaction to disequilibrium positions must occur. What kinds of reactions?

II. QUESTIONS IN THE THEORY OF INCOME DISTRIBUTION AND GENERAL EQUILIBRIUM

A. General Equilibrium Theory

1. Describe in words, without using any symbols, Walras's system of general equilibrium, stating the essential assumptions, the variables assumed to be given, and the unknown variables to be derived.

2. How does the Walras system of general equilibrium, as first presented by him and usually reproduced by his expositors, deal—explicitly or implicitly—with the following: (a) the law of diminishing returns (or of nonproportional output); (b) the law of returns to scale; (c) the optimum size of the firm; (d) the degree of competition; (e) the homogeneity or heterogeneity of productive resources; (f) the mobility of productive resources; (g) the profits of entrepreneurs; (h) the elasticity of supply of labor; (i) the liquidity preference; (j) the supply of money; (k) the time structure of the production process; (l) the accumulation of capital?

3. In any general equilibrium model certain restrictive assumptions are made. Some of them simplify the system only slightly and can be dropped without difficulty while others simplify the system so much that dropping them would unduly complicate the analysis; others are indispensable and could not be dropped without wrecking the model. Put each of the assumptions below into one of these three categories and explain why. State also whether the particular assumption was in fact made by Walras or any other model builder of whom you know.

Assumptions: (1) There are only three or four factors of production. (2) All labor is perfectly homogeneous. (3) Labor is perfectly mobile. (4) Labor responds only to pecuniary rewards. (5) The supply of factors of production is fixed and perfectly inelastic. (6) The coefficients of production are fixed. (7) The production functions are homogeneous of the first degree. (8) All sellers and buyers operate under pure competition (as perfect polypolists and perfect polypsonists, respectively). (9) Entry into all trades is easy (there is perfect pliopoly and perfect pliopsony). (10) All available factors of production are fully employed. (11) The elasticity of price expectations is equal to unity. (12) Receipts and outlays balance for every firm and household.

B. Derived Demand

1. After formulating his "law of derived demand" Marshall set forth four conditions determining the elasticity of derived demand. State each of these conditions, alternatively (*a*) expressing the independent variation as "a check to the supply" of the factor of production in question and the dependent variation as "a rise in its price," and expressing the "conditions" likewise without using the term "elasticity"; (*b*) expressing the independent variation as "a reduction in the price" of the factor of production in question and the dependent variation as "a rise in its employment," and expressing the "conditions" likewise without using the term "elasticity"; and (*c*) expressing the "conditions" as well as the general relation between independent and dependent variations in terms of "elasticities."

2. Marshall's "third condition" determining the elasticity of derived demand—sometimes referred to as "the importance of being unimportant"—has been found by Mrs. Robinson to hold only under certain circumstances.

a) State the condition without Mrs. Robinson's qualification.

b) Give an example of its practical significance in economic life.

c) State Mrs. Robinson's qualification. [You need not reproduce the proof.]

3. If the elasticity of demand for the product is infinitely elastic, the elasticity of derived demand for a factor of production, say labor, will be $\dfrac{\sigma + ke}{1 - k}$ where σ is the elasticity of substitution between labor and non-labor, e is the elasticity of supply of nonlabor, and k is the proportionate share of labor in the value of the product. Prove that, when the quantity of nonlabor is fixed, a certain relation between σ and k will guarantee that the absolute share of labor will increase as the quantity of labor increases, even if its relative share is reduced.

C. Marginal Productivity and Substitution

1. If a product X is made out of factors A and B, both of which are perfectly divisible, the chosen proportion between the amounts of factors employed will ordinarily be such that diminishing returns will prevail with regard to both factors. Yet increased employment of A would permit an increased average product per unit of B. Is this not inconsistent with diminishing returns? Explain your answer.

2. "If the proportion between the amounts of factors A and B employed were such that the employment of A could be increased with increasing returns—that is, increasing average product—the average product per unit of

B would also be increased when the employment of *A* is increased. The marginal product of *B*, however, would be negative." Assuming linear homogeneity of the production function, is the first sentence of the statement correct? Why or why not? Is the second sentence correct and consistent with the first? Why or why not?

3. Given is the total product curve for combinations of varying amounts of *A* with four units of *B*. If you want to construct a total product curve for combinations of varying amounts of *B* with eight units of *A*, you will be able to compute the needed values provided constant returns to scale prevail and both factors are perfectly divisible. Show how you would compute the product of (*a*) 1*B* and 8*A;* (*b*) 3*B* and 8*A;* (*c*) 6*B* and 8*A;* (*d*) 8*B* and 8*A;* (*e*) 16*B* and 8*A*.

4. The phases of increasing and diminishing returns within the law of variable proportions are often defined in terms of average product but sometimes in terms of marginal product. Discuss the differences in demarcations between the two phases under the two definitions, indicating the geometrical techniques of finding the exact locations of the phases, their relative lengths, and so on.

5. Assume a production surface that depicts total physical output of a certain product (*P*) as a function of two factors of production (*A* and *B*).

a) What geometrical operations with this surface will best aid in a demonstration of the laws of variable proportions? The laws of scale? The elasticity of substitution?

b) What factual conditions determine whether the surface will have a peak or extend upwards without limits?

c) What factual conditions determine whether there will be any increasing returns to scale?

6. "It is possible that both marginal physical product and the marginal gross revenue product are zero and, nevertheless, the marginal net revenue product is positive."

a) Under what conditions will the marginal physical product be zero?

b) Under what conditions will the marginal gross revenue product be zero while the marginal physical product is positive?

c) Under what conditions will the marginal net revenue product be positive although the marginal gross revenue product is zero?

7. Define or explain the concept of elasticity of substitution as it is used by Mrs. Robinson. Is "technical" substitution or "total" substitution involved in Mrs. Robinson's concept? What is the difference between the two?

D. Wages of Labor

1. "The marginal productivity theory of wages is of a naïve unrealism. How can one say that wages are determined by the marginal productivity of

labor when it is obvious to all but the blind and deaf that in our society wage rates are the result of bargaining; and that the employer, where he need not bargain but can dictate his terms, will surely fix wage rates well below the marginal productivity of labor?"

a) List the parts of the above statement that you would select for criticism and indicate (in one brief sentence each) your line of attack.

b) Explain briefly the relation between wage bargaining, contractual wage rates, and marginal productivity.

c) Explain briefly the relation between employer-dictated wage rates and marginal productivity.

2. "The marginal productivity theory of wages is unsatisfactory for several reasons: first, the separation of a certain physical product attributable to the 'marginal laborer' is impossible; second, employers try to pay less than the marginal product, however it be computed, unless they are pressed by powerful labor organizations; third, in times of large unemployment employers can easily succeed in reducing wage rates below the marginal product, even if there is collective bargaining." Explain and discuss point by point.

3. "The wage rate is determined by the marginal productivity of labor." If someone offers this statement as a formulation of the "marginal productivity theory of wages," what corrections or amendments will you offer?

4. Theorists hold that in any trade or industry the wage rate, or marginal factor cost, tends to be equal to the marginal productivity of labor. How can this be reconciled with the fact that wage rates of several kinds of workers have increased over the decades while their output per hour has hardly changed at all? Think of the "productivity" of house painters who use, by and large, the same techniques they used half a century ago but receive wage rates that have increased as much, if not more, than those of workers whose output per hour has doubled several times. Explain the apparent paradox.

5. To what extent will wage differentials prevailing between different occupations, different geographic areas, and different industries reflect differences in the qualifications or efficiencies of the various types of workers?

6. How, if at all, does the marginal productivity curve (marginal net revenue product curve) of a factor employed in a given firm reflect: (*a*) the operation of diminishing returns? (*b*) the possibility of technical substitution? (*c*) the elasticity of demand for the product? (*d*) the elasticity of supply of the factor? (*e*) the elasticity of supply of other factors?

7. Mrs. Robinson states that "for full equilibrium it is necessary that the marginal cost of labor (the wage) should be equal to average net productivity." Explain.

8. Mrs. Robinson states, "When the supply of labor to the individual unit is perfectly elastic . . . the double condition of equilibrium can only

be fulfilled when the wage is equal to the value at which the marginal and average net productivity curves cut."

a) Under what conditions is the supply of labor to the firm perfectly elastic?

b) Under these conditions what will the marginal cost of labor be in comparison with the average cost of labor?

c) What is meant by "the double condition of equilibrium?" Answer first in terms of general principles and then in terms of net productivity and cost of labor.

d) At what value of the average net productivity curve will this curve be cut by the marginal net productivity curve? Does this depend on perfect competition? On profit maximization? Or on what else?

e) Why, under the conditions cited in the statement, must the wage be equal to the value of net productivity at which the marginal and average curves intersect?

f) Give a graphical presentation of the situation to which the statement refers.

9. Assume that men and women are equally efficient in a certain occupation but the conditions of supply of men and women workers are different. It is possible for the employer to pay different wage rates to men and women; there are no trade unions. With the marginal net productivity curve and the two labor supply curves given, show in a graph the wage rates the employer will pay and the number of men and women he will employ. (Exact geometric construction is essential.)

10. "Professor Pigou once defined exploitation of laborers as the compensation of labor at a rate below the marginal product. If marginal product stands here for the value of the marginal physical product, then, indeed, exploitation is almost generally practiced in industry, though perhaps the relative 'underpayment' is not substantial in the majority of cases. If, however, marginal product stands for marginal value product, then exploitation seems to be less frequent. Labor scarcity, on the one hand, and oligopolistic peculiarities in selling the product, on the other hand, appear to be the most important reasons for such exploitation." Explain all parts of this statement.

11. The gap between the value of the marginal physical product and the wage rate has been attributed for one part to monopolistic exploitation and for another to monopsonistic exploitation; in some cases a third part is attributed to imperfect divisibility. Show these three parts of the "gap" on a graph and point out the facts behind each.

12. What can a trade union do to prevent (*a*) monopolistic exploitation, and (*b*) monopsonistic exploitation?

13. Explain and discuss the "shock theory" of wage-rate boosts, according to which increased productivity will be induced by successful wage pressures by unions.

14. What theoretical arguments or empirical evidence can be adduced to support or refute the contention that trade unions have succeeded in increasing the share of labor in the national income at the expense of profit?

15. Discuss the case for and against wage increases in proportion to the increase in productivity in those industries which, because of lower production cost, can afford to pay higher wages without charging higher prices.

16. It may be possible for a trade union to raise the wage rate and yet increase employment in an industry faced with unchanged demand for its products and unchanged supply of all factors of production. How, why, and under what conditions?

17. "From the point of view of a whole industry, the supply of a certain type of skilled labor may be scarce and, at the same time, of infinite elasticity from the point of view of each single firm within the industry." Explain.

18. Discuss the probability of a negative elasticity of the supply of labor (*a*) to the individual firm, (*b*) to the industry, and (*c*) in the economy as a whole.

19. Explain the possibility of a backward-rising supply curve of labor (*a*) in terms of the income elasticity of demand for leisure, (*b*) in terms of the elasticity of demand for income in terms of effort, and (*c*) in terms of the substitution effects and income effects of changes in the price of labor.

20. Dennis H. Robertson divides the effects that "an artificial raising of the wages" is apt to have upon employment into two analytically separable reactions—first, "a movement along the existing [marginal productivity] curve," and second, "a cumulative lowering of the curve." Explain the two reactions and indicate what assumptions concerning other factors of production, especially capital, are involved.

21. Assuming that workers have the possibility of varying by small amounts the total of labor or effort they supply, and that the elasticity of their demand for income in terms of effort is smaller than unity, what effect will the imposition or increase of an income tax have upon the amount of labor supplied? Show how your answer can be deduced from the definitions of the term employed and show how the assumption concerning the "elasticity of demand for income in terms of effort" can be translated into "price elasticity of supply of labor."

E. Rent of Land and Scarce Resources

1. In his discussion of "differential rents versus scarcity rents" Marshall makes the following statement (*Principles of Economics,* p. 424): "The opinion that the existence of inferior land, or other agents of production, tends to raise the rents of the better agents is not merely untrue. It is the

reverse of the truth." Explain and discuss. Distinguish between rent from the point of view of the industry and rent from the point of view of the economy.

2. Develop a statement on "sufficient and necessary conditions" for the existence of a positive land rent by discussing imaginary situations in which all existing land is (*a*) of equal fertility and equal locational advantage, (*b*) of equal fertility but different locational advantage, (*c*) of different fertility and locational advantage but not subject to diminishing returns.

3. "Rent is equal to the difference between marginal cost and average cost, multiplied by output." (*a*) Prove this proposition with the aid of a graph. (*b*) Is the proposition true also if competition is not pure? Why, or why not? Explain with a graph. (*c*) If a tenant-farmer pays full rent to the landowner and considers this rent a fixed cost, what will be the relation between average total cost and marginal cost? Explain.

4. Ricardo says, in "On Rent," *Principles of Political Economy and Taxation:* "If the high price of corn were the effect and not the cause of rent, price would be proportionately influenced as rents were high or low, and rent would be a component part of price. But that corn which is produced by the greatest quantity of labor is the regulator of the price of corn; and rent does not and cannot enter in the least degree as a component part of its price." Discuss.

5. Explain the relation between scarcity, the law of diminishing returns, and rent.

6. What will you expect to be the effect on the rent of land: (*a*) if a new type of fertilizer is developed, capable of increasing the productivity of land of all qualities by 10 percent? (*b*) if a flood makes all low-grade land uncultivatable, spoiling all "marginal" and "submarginal" land and leaving only the land that had been called "superior" available for cultivation?
Note: Distinguish also (*a*) rent per unit of output, (*b*) rent per acre of land under cultivation (perhaps divided between land of different quality), and (*c*) total rent.

7. Give the meaning of all terms listed below and indicate their place in the general theory of rent: (*a*) explicit and implicit rent; (*b*) intensive and extensive margin; (*c*) differential and scarcity rent; (*d*) inelastic factor supply; (*e*) imperfect homogeneity of the factor supply; (*f*) quasi rent.

8. Decide the following argument between Mr. A and Mr. B:
A: The rent of an office in these high houses and skyscrapers is much higher than the rent of equal space in smaller uptown houses.
B: Of course, that's why the skyscrapers were built.
A: But it is surely the high building cost and high land value that makes for high rent in high houses.
B: No, high land values are not the cause but the effect of high rents.

A: But, anyway, the high rents are due to the high houses, and, in particular, to the cost of building high houses.

B: No, people have built high houses because of the high land values, so as to economize on the scarce land.

A: You have it all twisted. If the cost of building these skyscrapers were lower, rents would be lower, wouldn't they?

B: I stick to my position that rents are the result of demand, not of costs.

A: You are being dogmatic. If building costs fall, rents will fall. Likewise, if site values fall, rents will fall.

B: Well, let's ask the student who has just completed his course in economic theory. He will explain just what the relation is between height of houses, height of rents, height of building costs, and height of site values.

9. "Rent is not the income of some particular factor of production, but merely an aspect of the income of any factor of production." Explain.

10. Take that old phrase about rent not entering into cost and (*a*) explain what it means; (*b*) state to what extent it is true (or under what conditions it aids in explaining observed facts); and (*c*) discuss the advantage or disadvantage of making it true by definition.

11. Classical "pessimism" generally expected that the increase in population and the increase in the supply of capital would result in ever-increasing land rents. State the conditions under which this expectation would or would not come true; refer also to the history of the last 150 years.

12. "Rent, like all prices, is a test, even though an imperfect one, of social need: its payment roughly ensures the most economical distribution of land between different uses; and its remission, by a land-owning state, to those in a position to pay it, whether private persons or public enterprises, would in general promote waste." Explain every part of this statement.

F. Interest on Capital

1. If you expect a certain piece of land to yield a yearly net rent of $1,500, what will its present value be (*a*) at a current rate of interest of 3 percent, (*b*) at a current rate of interest of 6 percent?

2. Explain how and why individuals and business firms might react to an increase in the market rates of interest. Divide your answer into these parts: (*a*) consumption, (*b*) production, (*c*) securities, and (*d*) cash.

3. "The schedule of marginal rates of time preference may be represented either as a consumption function or as a saving function with the interest rate as a variable and income as parameter."

a) Sketch such functions, labeling the axes precisely, and explain their meaning and significance.

b) Contrast these functions for low and high incomes.

c) What would be the meaning of a negative rate of time preference?

d) Could the marginal rate of time preference be negative if the same individual's marginal rate of liquidity preference is positive? Why or why not?

4. Explain the relation between expected future changes in interest rates and present liquidity preference.

5. Explain the relation between the interest rate and the demand for durable goods.

6. *a*) State how a change in liquidity preference affects the rate of interest and how a change in the rate of interest affects the rate of liquidity preference. Explain how it works.

b) State how a change in time preference affects the rate of interest and how a change in the rate of interest affects the rate of time preference. Explain how it works.

c) State how a change in the marginal efficiency of investment affects the rate of interest and how a change in the rate of interest affects the marginal efficiency of investment. Explain how it works.

7. How are "hoarding" and "dishoarding" accounted for (*a*) in the loanable-funds theory of interest and (*b*) in the liquidity-preference theory of interest?

8. A certain government bond carries a stated rate of interest of 3 percent per year.

a) If the market rate of interest is 3½ percent, will the bond sell above or below par value? Why?

b) If the market rate of interest rises to 4 percent, will the price of the bond rise or fall? Why?

c) Would this rise or fall be smaller or greater for a bond that matures in 10 years or for one that matures in 15 years?

d) What can you learn from the above relations that might be relevant to the explanation of demand conditions for durable equipment, houses, and such?

e) Bond yields are usually affected by people's expectations concerning future changes in the interest rate. How and why?

9. "If depreciation allowances are included among the sources of supply of investment funds, the marginal efficiency of capital will have to refer to gross-investment rather than net-investment." Explain.

10. (*a*) How are capital values affected by changes in the rate of interest? Explain your answer. (*b*) How and why does the reaction of present values of future income series to given changes in interest rates depend on the length of these future income series?

11. The following quotation is taken from Marshall (*Principles of Economics,* p. 412): "That which is rightly regarded as interest on 'free' or

'floating' capital, or on new investments of capital, is more properly treated as a sort of rent—a quasi rent—on old investments of capital. And there is no sharp line of division between floating capital and that which has been 'sunk' for a special branch of production, nor between new and old investments of capital; each group shades into the other gradually." Explain.

12. Accountants are often bewildered by the economic theorist's treatment of interest as cost. The theorist dealing with short-run output neglects interest on investment as a cost even if interest is actually paid out to creditors. The theorist dealing with long-run output includes interest in cost even if there are no debts and no interest is paid out to anybody. Explain all three ways of treating interest: (*a*) in accounting, (*b*) in short-run theory, and (*c*) in long-run theory.

13. Explain why the long-term interest rate (*a*) can never fluctuate as widely as the short rate; (*b*) may move temporarily contrariwise to the short rate; and (*c*) will usually be higher than the short rate, but may sometimes be lower.

14. Explain what is meant by the "marginal efficiency of money measured in terms of ittself" and contrast it with the "marginal efficiency of capital."

15. What are the essential differences between the "supply of money," the supply of "loanable funds," the "supply of liquidity," and the "supply of finance," as conceived by the economists making use of these concepts?

16. "Thus the rate of interest is what it is because it is expected to become other than it is; if it is not expected to become other than it is, there is nothing left to tell us why it is what it is. . . ." Explain this statement by first stating concisely the theory it criticizes and then discussing the main point of the criticism.

17. What is the difference, if any, between Keynes' "marginal efficiency of capital" and Lerner's "marginal efficiency of investment"?

18. State the three grounds on which Böhm-Bawerk bases his explanation of the existence of interest and discuss whether each or any of them constitutes a necessary and/or sufficient condition for the existence of interest. (You may avoid committing yourself to the arguments expressed by attributing them to "some writers.")

19. Reasoning along the lines of Böhm-Bawerk's capital theory, assume that land is abundant and that there are two, and only two, alternative ways of using labor in the production of consumers' goods: one without any roundabout ways and the other with an average investment period of one year. With the latter method labor is 20 percent more productive than with the former.

From these assumptions one might conclude: (*a*) that the rate of interest will be 20 percent; (*b*) that the interest rate will be zero and wages will be determined by the productivity of labor used in the more productive way;

(*c*) that the rate of interest might be anything between zero and 20 percent; (*d*) that the rate of interest might be well above 20 percent. Discuss each of these alleged possibilities and state any additional assumptions needed for it to be realized.

20. Without indicating your own opinions or inclinations, present both sides in the controversy between Frank H. Knight and the "Austrians" with respect to the following points: (*a*) that all capital is conceptually perpetual or conceptually nonpermanent; (*b*) that economic progress may result in a "shortening" of the investment period; (*c*) that an increase in the supply of capital need not change the production period of any single product; and (*d*) that it is not possible to identify the contributions of the original factors of the remote past.

21. State the reasons for which certain theorists prefer not to regard capital as a factor of production in models constructed for the analysis of the economy as a whole and examine whether these reasons would hold for models constructed for industry and firm analysis.

22. "The quantity of capital as a value magnitude, no less than the different investment periods, are not data but are among the unknowns which have to be determined." Explain.

23. Give a brief exposition of Hayek's explanation of the causes of the productivity of investment.

24. What are the chief differences between the capital theories of Böhm-Bawerk and Hayek?

25. Explain Hayek's concept of an "intertemporal equilibrium" and the use to which it is put.

26. In a sense capital theory is inherently dynamic; yet Knut Wicksell presents what he calls a "static theory of capital" (*Lectures on Political Economy,* Vol. I, p. 165). Discuss briefly the "static" features in Wicksell's theory and then reconcile their use with the "inherently dynamic" character of capital theory.

27. Knut Wicksell wrote (*Lectures on Political Economy,* Vol. I, p. 164): "The capitalist saver is thus, fundamentally, the friend of labor, though the technical inventor is not infrequently its enemy. The great inventions by which industry has from time to time been revolutionized at first reduced a number of workers to beggary, as experience shows, whilst causing the profits of the capitalists to soar. There is no need to explain away this circumstance by invoking 'economic friction,' and so on, for it is in full accord with a rational and consistent theory. But it is really not capital which should bear the blame; in proportion as accumulation continues, these evils must disappear, interest on capital will fall and wages will rise—unless the laborers on their part simultaneously counteract this result by a large increase in their numbers." Explain Wicksell's reasoning.

28. In a footnote (*Lectures,* Vol. I, p. 164), Wicksell observed that "capital investment undoubtedly tends to disturb the conditions under which labor and land are able to replace each other at the margin of production. It may therefore happen in exceptional cases that wages alone reap the benefit of a growth of capital, whilst rents fall; or vice versa." Explain and discuss.

29. Explain how Wicksell related the rate of interest to the marginal productivities of labor and land.

30. On p. 208 of his *Lectures,* Vol. I, Wicksell quotes the following statement by Gustav Cassel: "A man who attaches the same importance to future needs as to present ones, if he expects to be able to provide for his needs in the future just as easily as he does now, has no reason for setting aside anything of his present income." According to Wicksell, "Cassel is not quite correct," inasmuch as his "argument actually presupposes the absence of any rate of interest." Explain.

31. Theorists distinguish two basic concepts of fixed capital: the *net* depreciated value of the stock of productive plant and equipment—that is, its value taking account of its remaining service life—and the *gross* value of that stock, without regard to depreciation, constituting productive capacity available for complementary use with current inputs of other productive factors. Discuss the rationale of the distinction; indicate the problems for which either concept proves useful; and comment on the bearing obsolescence may have on either or both of the concepts.

G. Profit of Enterprise

1. Discuss the difference between "economic profit" and profit in the business or accounting sense.

2. Define profit, interest, and rent; and explain the essential differences between these concepts.

3. Discuss the problems that arise if profit is defined as the income of "entrepreneurship" or "enterprise."

4. Discuss the arguments for and against regarding "enterprise" as a factor of production.

5. Contrast various profit theories with some of the empirical studies of business profits and discuss the mutual relevancies.

6. "A positive aggregate net profit above all losses means a bias on the side of caution, while a preponderance of the spirit of adventure will entail net loss on the whole." Explain this statement and give the essentials of the profit theory on which it is based.

7. Evaluate whatever role in the explanation of profit can be assigned to

the following factors: (*a*) differential ability or talent, (*b*) innovating drive of entrepreneurs, (*c*) immobility of resources, (*d*) indivisibility, (*e*) economic change, (*f*) impediments of entry, (*g*) insurable risk, (*h*) uncertainty.

8. Discuss the possibility of long-run profit (in an industry or firm) that cannot be characterized as a rent.

9. Compare the usefulness of considering profit as an *ex ante* or as an *ex post* concept.

10. What place may windfall profits arising from an increase in inventory valuations have in the theory of profits?

11. Explain the concept of normal profit, show its role in value theory, and discuss its place in the theory of income distribution.

12. Discuss the lack of parallelism in the profit rates and the profit margins of various industries.

13. Discuss the relativity of profit from the points of view of the insider, the outsider, and the economist; then comment on the relevance of these notions for the theory of income distribution.

H. Relative Shares, Total-Product Distribution

1. Economists dealing with the theory of distribution often refer to a theorem by the mathematician Euler. (*a*) State the theorem without any reference to economics. (*b*) Explain its connection with the theory of distribution. (*c*) Reasoning in terms of the theorem, show what significance the phenomenon of "increasing returns to scale" has for the distribution of income. (*d*) Indicate how Mrs. Robinson attempts to solve the "contradiction" involved.

2. State and discuss Kalecki's theory of income distribution, giving special emphasis to his method of defining the "degree of monopoly" as the "ratio of sales going to gross profit" and of explaining the distributive share going to nonlabor as determined by the "average degree of monopoly."

3. According to Kaldor, "no hypothesis as regards the forces determining distributive shares could be intellectually satisfying unless it succeeds in accounting for the relative stability of these shares in the advanced capitalist economies over the last 100 years or so, despite the phenomenal changes in the techniques of production, in the accumulation of capital relative to labor and in real income per head." Discuss (*a*) the facts in question, (*b*) the claim that a hypothesis is needed to account for the facts, and (*c*) the hypothesis or hypotheses proposed by Kaldor.

4. Discuss the meaning of "relative stability of relative shares," especially the reference of the first of the two "relativities."

5. "It would be nice to have a single aggregative bulldozer principle with which to crash through the hedge of microeconomic interconnections and analogies." Explain (*a*) the general idea expressed in this sentence, (*b*) the meaning of the "single aggregative bulldozer principle," and (*c*) the meaning of "the hedge of microeconomic interconnections and analogies."

6. Assuming an aggregate production function for two factors, labor and capital, and constant returns to scale, "how different from unity need the elasticity of substitution be in order that it convert a strong trend· in the capital/labor ratio into a strong trend in relative shares"? Before you attempt an answer, explain (*a*) the issue to which this question refers, (*b*) the implied causal connections between the three variables mentioned in the quotation, and (*c*) the significance of the question for the problem under discussion.

7. "If it were possible to separate out the part of nominal wages and salaries which is really a return on investment, the share of property income in the total might be found to be steadily increasing." Explain all parts of this comment by Solow.

Indexes

AUTHOR INDEX

SUBJECT INDEX

A

Absolute price, 459
Acreage controls, 248
Advertising as nonprice competition technique, 364
Agricultural industry, production in, 132
Agricultural markets, government regulation of, 248
Agricultural output, 133 ff., 167 ff.
Allocation of resources; *see* Resource allocation
Alternative cost defined, 208
Aluminum Company of America (Alcoa), 286
American Tobacco Company, 318–19
Antitrust Division of Department of Justice, 355, 359
Antitrust regulations, 248
Arc elasticity, 101
  formula for, 102
Assigning priority, 370 n
Assumptions in consumer behavior analysis, 17–19
  maximization of satisfaction, 35
Assumptions in welfare economics analytical model, 483–84
Average cost curves, 216–20
  long-run, 223–24
Average costs, 211–15
  long-run
    changes in factor price, effect of, 238–39
    diseconomies of scale, 237–38
    economies of scale, 235–37
    shape of, 235–38
    relation between short-run and long-run, 228–30
    short-run, shape of, 235
Average fixed costs defined, 212
Average product, 147–50; *see also* Production function
  defined, 139
  geometry of curves of, 144–46

Average product—*Cont.*
  maximum value of, 145–46
  total product in relation to, 138–41
Average total cost defined, 215
Average variable cost; *see also* Cost curves
  average product and, 215
  competitive supply and, 262–64
  defined, 213

B

Barter system, 454
Bases of monopoly, 286–88
Bilateral monopoly, 313–15
Box diagram, 467–69, 493
Budget constraint, 460, 465
Budget equation, 93 n
Budget line
  comparative statistics, 38
  defined, 37
  shifting of, 38–40
Budget map, information from use of, 80–81
Budget space
  defined, 38
  diagram, 38
  indifference map and, 41

C

Camel cigarettes, 319
Capital equipment, production requirements of, 131–32
Cardinal measure
  output levels, 203
  utility, 21–22, 27
Carnegie-Mellon University, 371 n
Cartels
  collapse of, 359–60
  collusion, 355
  defined, 355
  fair trade laws, 357
  geographical quotas, 357–58
  life of, 359–60
  loose, 357
  market-sharing services, 356–59